EMPIRE'S ALLY
CANADA AND THE WAR IN AFGHANISTAN

The war in Afghanistan has been a major policy commitment and central undertaking of the Canadian state since 2001: Canada has been a leading force in the war and has spent hundreds of millions of dollars on aid and reconstruction. After a decade of conflict, however, there is considerable debate about the efficacy of the mission, as well as calls to reassess Canada's role in the conflict. An authoritative and strongly analytical work, *Empire's Ally* provides a much-needed critical investigation into one of the most polarizing events of our time.

This collection draws on new primary evidence – including government documents, think-tank and NGO reports, international media files, and interviews in Afghanistan – to provide context for Canadian foreign policy, to offer critical perspectives on the war itself, and to link the conflict to broader issues of political economy, international relations, and Canada's role on the world stage. Spanning academic and public debates, *Empire's Ally* opens a new line of argument on why the mission has entered a stage of crisis.

JEROME KLASSEN is a SSHRC Postdoctoral Fellow in the MIT Center for International Studies at the Massachusetts Institute of Technology.

GREG ALBO is an associate professor in the Department of Political Science at York University.

Empire's Ally

Canada and the War in Afghanistan

Edited by
JEROME KLASSEN AND GREG ALBO

UNIVERSITY OF TORONTO PRESS
Toronto Buffalo London

ISBN 978-1-4426-4515-8 (cloth)
ISBN 978-1-4426-1304-1 (paper)

Printed on acid-free, 100% post-consumer recycled paper with
vegetable-based inks.

Library and Archives Canada Cataloguing in Publication

Empire's ally: Canada and the war in Afghanistan/edited by
Jerome Klassen and Greg Albo.

Includes bibliographical references and index.
ISBN 978-1-4426-4515-8 (bound). – ISBN 978-1-4426-1304-1 (pbk.)

1. Afghan War, 2001–. 2. Afghan War, 2001– – Participation, Canadian.
3. Canada – Foreign relations – 21st century. 4. War on Terrorism, 2001–2009.
5. Imperialism. 6. Capitalism. I. Klassen, Jerome, 1977– II. Albo, Gregory

DS371.412.E47 2013   958.104'7   C2012-904802-X

This book has been published with the help of a grant from the Canadian
Federation for the Humanities and Social Sciences, through the Awards to
Scholarly Publications Program, using funds provided by the Social Sciences
and Humanities Research Council of Canada.

University of Toronto Press acknowledges the financial assistance to its publishing program of the Canada Council for the Arts and the Ontario Arts Council.

University of Toronto Press acknowledges the financial support of the Government of Canada through the Canada Book Fund for its publishing activities.

Contents

Preface

This book addresses a critical gap in the social science literature on Canadian foreign policy and Canadian political economy – namely, the absence to date of a systematic study of Canada's role in Afghanistan over the past decade. For ten years successive Canadian governments have been deeply involved in the Afghan war and military occupation. In the process they have radically transformed the strategies and tactics of Canadian foreign policy as well as the institutional structure of the state. The war has been a central means by which Canadian governments have engineered a new military agenda of fighting terrorism, weapons of mass destruction, and 'failed states' in the Third World. The war has also been a means by which Canada has increased defence spending and established new forms of 'interoperability' with US and NATO forces. In Afghanistan, this multitrack agenda was tested through Canada's war in Kandahar province – a war fought in the name of peace, development, women's rights, and international security.

After ten years of fighting, however, Canada has yet to achieve these objectives. On the contrary, violence, corruption, and narcotics still permeate the Afghan political economy and in fact were fostered in several ways by the US-NATO intervention. In Kandahar, where Canada has spent billions of dollars on a '3D' strategy of defence, diplomacy, and development, approximately 150 soldiers have been killed and 2,000 wounded. Aid and development programs have failed to make a qualitative difference in the standard of living in the province, and diplomacy has been shunted in favour of military action against the Taliban.[1] Civilian casualties have increased dramatically in Kandahar, and Canadian soldiers have been guilty of transferring prisoners to torture by Afghan security forces. In summer 2011, the Canadian military withdrew from Kandahar without having achieved the stated goals of the mission.

In this context there is an urgent need to assess the problematic course of Canada's war. It is a striking fact that researchers in Canada have yet to produce a systematic study that evaluates the mission as it evolved towards the current state of crisis. Although a majority of the Canadian public has opposed the mission in Kandahar for several years, this opposition has not been reflected in academic debates, which typically accept the parameters, goals, and methods of the mission. As a result the academic literature is quite distant from the public discussion on both the failures of the war and the direction of Canadian policy abroad.

This book is a necessary redress to this imbalance. It consists of new essays on global politics, Canadian foreign policy, and Afghan history, all of which critically analyse the way in which Canada joined the war as an *ally to empire*. The book is framed by the theoretical insights of critical international relations theory and Marxist political economy, both of which offer a new approach to understanding the war and its movement towards crisis over the past decade.[2] To synthesize this perspective the book draws on the expertise of established and emerging scholars in international relations and Canadian political economy, and from key voices in the social movement sector.

The book advances two core arguments. The first is that the war in Afghanistan must be theorized in the context of recent transformations in the world market and nation-state system. In the aftermath of the Cold War a new system of *empire* emerged through the globalization of capital and the political dominance of the United States. With the demise of communism and Third World nationalism, the United States achieved the fundamental goal of all post-war strategy: an integrated world economy in which US capital and US foreign policy were globally dominant (see Kolko and Kolko 1972; Chomsky 1996; Bacevich 2002; Harvey 2003; Layne 2006).

US hegemony was attained in two particular ways. First, the world economy was anchored by what the late Peter Gowan (1999) dubbed the 'Dollar-Wall Street Regime.' The structural interface between the US Federal Reserve and Wall Street established the US economy as the financial hub of global capitalism. With the US dollar serving as world money, Wall Street attracted the global savings necessary to finance US trade and budget deficits as well as domestic consumption and technological innovation. These mechanisms also pooled capital for US global investments, and gave the US government new means to finance external military engagements. The 'interactive embeddedness' between Wall Street and the US Federal Reserve thus established a new financial architecture through which US capital gained international leverage (see Seabrooke 2001; Panitch and Gindin 2005).

In this context the United States emerged as the undisputed global hegemon. Through the Dollar-Wall Street Regime, the US government gained the financial, political, and military wherewithal to manage and police the capitalist world system. Across the 1990s US foreign policy promoted the globalization of capital through a nested hierarchy of institutions, including the North American Free Trade Agreement and the World Trade Organization. Although such agreements were constituted by formally sovereign nation-states, they in fact embodied the de facto inequalities and hierarchies of the capitalist world market and thus consolidated the economic and political leverage of the American state. The political outcome was that US primacy was advanced through the mechanisms of formal sovereignty and equality in the world market and nation-state system.

The global expansion of US military might was another sign of the 'unipolar moment.' Indeed, US military power became more entrenched at a structural level. American primacy was achieved not simply through the conflicts in the Balkans, Iraq, Somalia, Haiti, Colombia, Panama, and Afghanistan, but also through what Barry Posen (2003) has called 'command of the commons': the military dominance of space, the sea, and the air. Organized across six regional command structures (in addition to US Strategic Command), the US military managed the global system through which commodities, labour, and digital information flowed. Not only did the US military contain the 'rogue' and 'failed' states that threatened the American vision of world order; it also supervised the global system of trade and transportation through which the world market functions. In the process, other states became even more dependent on US hegemony.

A new US empire thus emerged in the aftermath of the Cold War. This new structure of empire was dictated by a double logic: on the one hand, by the internationalization of capital across the world market and the corresponding *internationalization of the state* and, on the other, by the political oversight and hegemonic strategies of the US government (see Panitch 1994; Layne 2006). These two features were interlaced *within* the political economy of US capitalism, and produced the financial, diplomatic, and military means for an external strategy of global primacy.

But the new American empire was ripé with contradiction (see Gill 2005). For the purpose of this book, the contradictions of US policy in the Middle East and Central Asia were most salient. After the first Gulf War, the United States maintained military bases on the Arabian Peninsula, enhanced support for the monarchies and dictatorships of the region, backed the Oslo Accords through which the occupation of Palestine was entrenched, and imposed sanctions on Iraq as a segue to war. These policies were guided by three principal objectives: (1) to liberalize the economic space of the Middle East through the Gulf Co-operation Council and the 'normalization' of Israel; (2) to access and regulate the distribution of oil supplies in the face of increased competition with Europe and Asia; and (3) to implant US military bases for the purpose of regional stabilization under US hegemony (see Achcar 2004, 2006; Hanieh 2011).

The consequence of this strategy was that popular grievances were bottled up or repressed by governments of the region, prompting non-state groups such as al-Qaeda to launch armed attacks against the United States and its allies. The events of 9/11, then, were not just blowback from the Afghan *jihad* of the 1980s, but a *political symptom* of the structure of empire imposed on the Middle East in the 1990s (see Johnson 2004; Mohamedou 2006; Saull 2006; AbuKhalil 2011). Against this backdrop the war in Afghanistan was launched to stamp out any opposition to US primacy objectives in Central Asia and the Middle East and to pave the way for 'regime change' in Iraq, Iran, and other states outside the sphere of western influence. For these reasons we argue that the war in Afghanistan must be analysed in relation to the structural tendencies of the capitalist world market and to the primacy goals of US foreign policy.

The second argument of this book is that the interests of empire have dictated Canada's role in Afghanistan. As a secondary power in the US-led system of empire, Canada joined the war in 2001 for a host of geopolitical and geo-economic reasons. At the scale of global politics, the war was a key opportunity for the Canadian state to entrench itself as a secondary power in the western or NATO alliance. It was also a means by which Canada could develop a military infrastructure for confronting the emerging set of 'security threats' to what Ellen Meiksins Wood (2005) calls the 'Empire of Capital.' Related to this, the war was an opening for the Canadian state to develop a set of military and security doctrines that would match and support the internationalization of Canadian corporate investment. On a regional scale the war helped fortify the 'special relationship' with Washington as well as the continental system of trade through which Canada has earned a balance-of-payments surplus. Finally, at a national level, the war served as a catalyst for ramping up defence spending and for reorganizing the foreign policy apparatus around a strategy of global neoliberalism, continental integration, and counterinsurgency warfare. In the pages of this book this multiscale strategy is conceptualized as one of *stratified multilateralism* with US imperialism, and *disciplinary militarism* towards the Third World.

The argument offered here is that Canada's war in Afghanistan has embodied and reproduced the logic of empire described above. Successive Canadian governments have rationalized the war in terms of building peace, security, democracy, and development. Yet these objectives have been compromised by the real activities of the mission. For instance, development aid has been closely tied to the military project of fighting the Ṭaliban, while diplomacy has been linked to the Karzai government and its legacy of corruption. Furthermore Canada has worked, both directly and indirectly, with warlords and drug traffickers, and has violated international law by transferring prisoners to torture. More broadly Canada's escalation in 2003–4 was linked to the US project of 'regime change' in Iraq and to new plans for 'deep integration' of the North American bloc.[3]

In these and other ways Canada's war has represented the *imperial policy of a secondary state in the US-led Empire of Capital*. More than this, it has been linked to a *capitalist class strategy within the Canadian state to build and advance a policy of global militarism in line with the deep integration of the North American bloc and the internationalization of Canadian capital*.[4] As such the war demands an explanation that goes beyond both the positivist methods of realist theory and the idealist methods of liberal theory (see Cox 1981; Ashley 1984; Burnham 1994). In using the concepts of critical political economy – in particular the notions of capital, class, and empire – this book addresses the real trajectory of the conflict in Afghanistan and the wider set of economic, political, and military calculations of the Canadian state and the NATO alliance.

Although the book provides a broad critique of Canada's war, it does not pretend to offer a final word on the subject. In the years and decades to come, more information and data will appear, and new research questions will emerge. The project of assessing the war will be enhanced only when more students of Canadian foreign policy specialize in Afghan history and learn the major languages of that country. The study of the war will also be improved when soldiers, diplomats, and government officials have had time to reflect on their own experiences and to publish the requisite memoirs and histories. It goes without saying that the war will be much better understood when Afghans themselves are given greater space to voice their own opinions and perspectives (see, for example, Joya 2009). The true nature of the war will be further appreciated when it is removed from the political debates of the present – debates that have too often been sabotaged by red-herring arguments, authoritarian secrecy, and accusations of treason. Thus, while this book tries to offer a comprehensive view of the war so far, we think of it as the first stage of a long-term research program, involving other scholars and commentators in Canada and around the world.

Unfortunately the volume leaves several issues unexamined. War, masculinity, and gender is one such issue. From the start the war was justified in the simple terms of 'liberating Afghan women.' However, there is an emerging consensus among researchers and non-governmental organizations that, despite several gains, the western intervention has compounded and exacerbated many of the oppressions facing Afghan women and girls (see Drumbl 2004; Jones 2006; Kolhatkar and Ingalls 2006; Womankind Worldwide 2006). Indeed, '[o]ngoing conflict, NATO airstrikes and cultural practices combined' leave Afghanistan the world's 'most dangerous country for women,' according to a 2011 study by TrustLaw Women (see also Bowcott 2011). The negative impact of war on women's rights and freedoms in Afghanistan – and the masculine discourse of politicians, media pundits, and military personnel in Canada in favour of war – should be deconstructed and linked analytically in future research.

Other scholars might also explore Canada's links to warlords in Kabul and Kandahar, as well as Canada's role in NATO. The final say on Canada's role in the torture of Afghan prisoners must also be addressed when – and if – the full collection of primary documents is released. Lastly, it would be worthwhile to consider the militarization of Canadian political culture that has attended the war – and to examine how public and private advocates of the mission have inculcated this culture. Related to this, further research must address how racism towards Muslims has been a key ingredient of the new Canadian foreign policy agenda, especially in terms of building a political and ideological rationale for occupation, militarism, and torture (see, for example, Razack 2008; and Boswell 2012).

Finally, while this book offers the most comprehensive review to date of Canada's role in Afghanistan, we are fully aware that other perspectives will emerge in the future. We welcome these alongside our own commitment to broadening the debate on Afghanistan beyond the discussions of the present.

For their principled opposition to the war in Afghanistan, the activists of the Canadian peace movement, including many Afghan-Canadians, earn the dedication of this book. As they have shown in theory and practice, international solidarity flows not through the violence of military occupation, but through social movements against the logic of empire in Canadian foreign policy and the capitalist world system.

Jerome Klassen
Greg Albo
May 2012

NOTES

1 For example, according to the Canadian Press (2011), '[s]chools in Kandahar that were built or renovated on the Canadian government's dime have far fewer students than official enrolment numbers suggest . . . The findings call into question the efficacy of one of the Conservative government's legacy projects in southern Afghanistan." See Canadian Press (2011).

2 For seminal texts in 'critical international relations theory,' see Gill (1993) and Cox (1996). The Marxist theory of imperialism is developed, in different ways, by Bukharin ([1915]); Lenin ([1917]); Poulantzas (1978); Harvey (2003); Magdoff (2003); Panitch and Gindin (2004); and Wood (2005).

3 In the lead-up to the war in Iraq, the Liberal government made a secret deal with the United States: Canada would beef up troops in Kabul in exchange for not joining the 'coalition of the willing' in Iraq; see Stein and Lang (2007, 48–50). On 'deep integration,' see Grinspun and Shamsie (2007); and Clarkson (2008).

4 On the internationalization of the Canadian capitalist class, see Klassen (2009); and Klassen and Carroll (2011). A 'class theory' of Canadian foreign policy was first developed by Pratt (1983). See also Neufeld (1995).

References

AbuKhalil, As'ad. 2011. 'The Phenomenon of Bin Laden: Terrorism of the Right and the Cold War.' *Al-Akhbar*, 28 May. http://www.al-akhbar.com/node/13438.

Achcar, Gilbert. 2004. *Eastern Cauldron: Islam, Afghanistan, Palestine and Iraq in a Marxist Mirror.* New York: Monthly Review Press.

–. 2006. *The Clash of Barbarisms: The Making of a New World Disorder.* Boulder, CO: Paradigm.

Ashley, Richard K. 1984. 'The Poverty of Neorealism.' *International Organization* 38, no. 2: 225–86.

Bacevich, Andrew. 2002. *American Empire: The Realities and Consequences of U.S. Diplomacy.* Cambridge, MA: Harvard University Press.

Boswell, Randy. 2012. 'More than half of Canadians mistrust Muslims, poll says.' *Postmedia News*, 20 March.

Bowcott, Owen. 2011. 'Afghanistan worst place in the world for women, but India in top five.' *Guardian*, 15 July. http://www.guardian.co.uk/world/2011/jun/15/worst-place-women-afghanistan-india.

Bukharin, Nikolai. [1915]. *Imperialism and World Economy.* London: Martin Lawrence.

Burnham, Peter. 1994. 'Open Marxism and Vulgar International Political Economy.' *Review of International Political Economy* 1, no. 2: 221–31.

Canadian Press. 2011. 'Afghan enrollment claims fail to make grade.' 10 February.

Chomsky, Noam. 1996. *World Orders, Old and New.* New York: Columbia University Press.

Clarkson, Stephen. 2008. *Does North America Exist? Governing the Continent after NATO and 9/11.* Toronto: University of Toronto Press.

Cox, Robert. 1981. 'Social Forces, States and World Orders: Beyond International Relations Theory.' *Journal of International Studies, Millennium* 10, no. 2: 126–55.

–. 1996. *Production, Power and World Order: Social Forces in the Making of History.* New York: Columbia University Press.

Drumbl, Mark A. 2004. 'Rights, Culture, and Crime: The Role of Rule of Law for the Women of Afghanistan.' *Columbia Journal of Transnational Law* 42, no. 2: 349–90.

Gill, Stephen, ed. 1993. *Gramsci, Historical Materialism, and International Relations.* Cambridge: Cambridge University Press.

–. 2005. 'The Contradictions of US Supremacy.' In *The Socialist Register 2005: The Empire Reloaded*, ed. Leo Panitch and Colin Leys. London: Merlin.

Gowan, Peter. 1999. *The Global Gamble: Washington's Faustian Bid for Global Dominance*. London: Verso.

Grinspun, Ricardo, and Yasmine Shamsie, eds. 2007. *Whose Canada? Continental Integration, Fortress North America and the Corporate Agenda*. Montreal; Kingston, ON: McGill-Queen's University Press.

Hanieh, Adam. 2011. *Capitalism and Class in the Gulf Arab States*. New York: Palgrave-Macmillan.

Harvey, David. 2003. *The New Imperialism*. Oxford: Oxford University Press.

Johnson, Chalmers A. 2004. *Blowback: The Costs and Consequences of American Empire*. New York: Macmillan.

Jones, Ann. 2006. *Kabul in Winter*. New York: Henry Holt.

Joya, Malalai. 2009. *A Woman among Warlords: The Extraordinary Story of an Afghan Who Dared to Raise Her Voice*. New York: Scribner.

Klassen, Jerome. 2009. 'Canada and the New Imperialism: The Economics of a Secondary Power.' *Studies in Political Economy* 83 (Spring): 163–90.

Klassen, Jerome, and William K. Carroll. 2011. 'Transnational Class Formation? Globalization and the Canadian Corporate Network.' *Journal of World-Systems Research* 17, no. 2: 379–402.

Kolhatkar, Sonali, and James Ingalls. 2006. *Bleeding Afghanistan: Washington, Warlords and the Propaganda of Silence*. New York: Seven Stories Press.

Kolko, Joyce, and Gabriel Kolko. 1972. *The Limits to Power: The World and United States Foreign Policy, 1945–54*. New York: Harper and Row.

Layne, Christopher. 2006. *The Peace of Illusions: American Grand Strategy from 1940 to the Present*. Ithaca, NY: Cornell University Press

Lenin, V.I. [1917]. *Imperialism, the Highest Stage of Capitalism*. Moscow: Progress Publishers.

Magdoff, Harry. 2003. *Imperialism without Colonies*. New York: Monthly Review Press.

Mohamedou, Mohammad Mahmoud. 2006. *Understanding Al Qaeda: The Transformation of War*. Ann Arbor: University of Michigan Press

Neufeld, Mark. 1995. 'Hegemony and Foreign Policy Analysis: The Case of Canada as a Middle Power.' *Studies in Political Economy* 48 (Autumn): 7–29.

Panitch, Leo. 1994. 'Globalisation and the State.' In *The Socialist Register 1994: Between Globalism and Nationalism*, ed. Ralph Miliband and Leo Panitch. London: Merlin Press.

Panitch, Leo, and Sam Gindin. 2004. 'Global Capitalism and American Empire.' In *The Socialist Register: The New Imperial Challenge*, ed. Leo Panitch and Colin Leys. London: Merlin Press.

–. 2005. 'Finance and American Empire.' In *The Socialist Register 2005: The Empire Reloaded*, ed. Leo Panitch and Colin Leys. London: Merlin Press.

Posen, Barry. 2003. 'Command of the Commons: The Military Foundation of
    U.S. Hegemony.' *International Security* 28, no. 1: 5–46.
Poulantzas, Nicos. 1978. *Classes in Contemporary Capitalism.* London: Verso.
Pratt, Cranford. 1983. 'Dominant Class Theory and Canadian Foreign Policy:
    The Case of the Counter-Consensus.' *International Journal* 39, no. 1: 99–135.
Razack, Sherene H. 2008. *Casting Out: The Eviction of Muslims for Western Law
    and Politics.* Toronto: University of Toronto Press.
Saull, Richard. 2006. 'Reactionary Blowback: The Uneven Ends of the Cold
    War and the Origins of Contemporary Conflict in World Politics.' In *The War
    on Terrorism and the American 'Empire' after the Cold War*, ed. Alejandro Colas
    and Richard Saull. London: Routledge.
Seabrooke, Leonard. 2001. *US Power in International Finance.* New York:
    Palgrave.
Stein, Janice Gross, and Eugene Lang. 2007. *Unexpected War: Canada in Kanda-
    har.* Toronto: Viking Canada.
TrustLaw. 2011. *The World's Most Dangerous Countries for Women*, 15 June.
    http://www.trust.org/trustlaw/news/special-coverage-the-worlds-
    most-dangerous-countries-for-women.
Womankind Worldwide. 2006. *Taking Stock: Afghan Women and Girls Five Years
    On.* London: Womankind Worldwide.
Wood, Ellen Meiksins. 2005. *Empire of Capital.* London: Verso.

EMPIRE'S ALLY
CANADA AND THE WAR IN AFGHANISTAN

1

Introduction: Empire, Afghanistan, and Canadian Foreign Policy

JEROME KLASSEN

There is a growing consensus among international relations experts that the war in Afghanistan has reached an impasse or possibly a terminal point of crisis (Afghanistan Study Group 2010; Dorronsoro 2010; Ruttig 2010a). More than a decade of war has resulted in a very different outcome than that predicted in 2001, after the US-led Operation Enduring Freedom (OEF) invaded Afghanistan in the first battle of the 'global war on terror.' The western intervention, which followed the terrorist attacks on New York and Washington on 11 September 2001, was immediately successful at forcing the Taliban from power and destroying al-Qaeda bases. With the support of the Afghan Northern Alliance,[1] the western intervention quickly conquered all major cities and provinces, forcing the Taliban leadership and al-Qaeda 'remnants' to surrender or flee to Pakistan. In December 2001, the victors signed the Bonn Agreement, a political pact on security, development, and nation building. After the Soviet occupation of the 1980s, the civil war of the 1990s, and the Taliban years before 9/11, there was much hope and enthusiasm for Afghanistan's escaping the cycle of conflict in which it had been stuck for decades. Under the aegis of the United States, the United Nations, the North Atlantic Treaty Organization (NATO), and the major international financial institutions, Afghanistan was promised a future of democracy, development, peace, and prosperity. As an ally of the United States and a member of NATO, Canada joined the war in 2001 and made similar commitments in terms of nation building and development.

Ten years later, however, such commitments have not been fulfilled. Across a wide spectrum of metrics, Afghanistan is reeling in crisis. On the political front, the government of Hamid Karzai has lost much legitimacy both inside and outside of Afghanistan. While Karzai came to power with much optimism in 2001 and was elected by a majority in 2004, his authority has been eroded by persistent allegations of corruption, as well as by political relations with warlords and religious fundamentalists. The major turning point for Karzai's government was the presidential election in July 2009, when Karzai and his supporters engaged in systematic fraud, including vote buying, forgery, and ballot stuffing. So extreme was the cheating that Karzai's main contender, Abdullah Abdullah, withdrew in protest from the runoff demanded by the United States. The election was further undermined by mass abstention and Taliban violence, both of which diminished the credibility of the political process and the resulting executive authority. For the US government of Barack Obama, the results of the Afghan presidential election troubled the strategy of military escalation, which occurred in two stages in 2009. Without a credible partner in Afghanistan, the US-led mission faces an uncertain future in which military objectives are disconnected from political accomplishments – a recipe for endless war without direction or purpose beyond international credibility and domestic politicking.

The same conundrum appears in the development and reconstruction agenda. As part of the Bonn Process, the international community pledged billions of dollars of aid and humanitarian assistance. Non-governmental organizations (NGOs) established thousands of small-scale projects across Afghanistan. NATO deployed Provincial Reconstruction Teams (PRTs) to provide security for an array of development works. Yet major problems afflicted the reconstruction agenda from the start. Donors failed to meet pledges. Drug money linked to opium and heroin production emerged as a primary lubricant of the economy. NGOs and foreign consultants monopolized the distribution of funds and thus eroded the nascent capacities of the Afghan state. More controversially, the delivery of aid was instrumentalized as a weapon of war, especially after 2005 when the Taliban insurgency gained traction. In this context, the insurgency targeted aid workers, and many, if not most, NGOs abandoned rural areas and the provinces in which the war currently rages (United Nations 2011). Despite billions of dollars spent on aid and development projects over the past decade, 70 per cent of the Afghan population lives in extreme poverty and health vulnerability, and thirty thousand Afghan children die annually from malnutrition and related diseases (World Health Organization 2011; Deutsche Presse-Agentur 2012). The marked weakening, or failure, of the development agenda represents, then, a second moment of crisis for the US-led mission in Afghanistan.

The growing power of the Taliban insurgency represents a third such moment. According to Anand Gopal (2010), the Taliban leadership and rank and file initially surrendered to, and wished to work with, the new Karzai government. However, as issues of warlordism, corruption, sectarianism, mal-development, and military occupation became more contentious in Afghanistan, the Taliban re-emerged as a powerful insurgency, operating a parallel system of governance and law and order. Since 2005 the Taliban have inflicted major losses on coalition forces and claimed ever more territory and power vis-à-vis the Karzai government. The Taliban insurgency was at first a political movement and guerrilla force of certain Pashtun tribes in southern Afghanistan. As Gopal (2010) and Ruttig (2010b) argue, however, the Taliban have successfully transformed themselves into a quasi-national liberation movement, anchored by an Islamic political identity. This transformation from a tribal to a political-national-religious movement has allowed the Taliban to form alliances with insurgent factions based among non-Pashtun ethnic groups and thereby to expand operations across the country. Indeed, for this reason, the Taliban now lead a fighting force of 35,000 insurgents in four-fifths of Afghanistan, and are setting the pace and conditions of negotiations with the Karzai government (Deutsche Presse-Agentur 2011). The growing influence of the Taliban, mixed with the counterinsurgency of US and NATO forces, has had a catastrophic impact on Afghan civilians, who are increasingly caught in the crossfire and displaced from their homes and villages.[2] Although no firm numbers exist on Afghan civilian casualties, the UN Assistance Mission to Afghanistan estimates that more than 10,000 civilians died between 2006 and 2010.[3] Likewise, the UN High Commissioner for Refugees estimates that, in January 2011, 400,000 people were 'internally displaced' by fighting (UN High Commissioner for Refugees 2011).

Not surprisingly coalition spokespeople rarely acknowledge the true extent of the political, social, and military crisis in Afghanistan. In the same week in July 2010 when US and NATO officials claimed progress in 'cornering' and 'squeezing' the insurgency (Taylor 2010), the Afghanistan Rights Monitor offered a more objective mid-year report, concluding that, '[i]n terms of insecurity, 2010 has been the worst year since the demise of the Taliban regime in late 2001. Not only have the number of security incidents increased, the space and depth of the insurgency and counter-insurgency-related violence have maximized dramatically. Up to 1,200 security incidents were recorded in June, the highest number . . . compared to any month since 2002' (2010, 4). Over subsequent months, the level of violence only increased. According to the US Department of Defense, insurgent violence in the third quarter of 2010 increased by 55 per cent over the second quarter and by 65 per cent over the same quarter of the previous year. As a result, '[e]fforts to reduce insurgent capacity, such as safe havens and logistic support . . . have not produced measurable results;' on the contrary, 'the insurgency has proven resilient with sustained logistics capacity and command and control' (United States 2010, 53, 41–2, 44). For this reason, the humanitarian and security situation in Afghanistan has 'never been as poor,' according to the International Committee of the Red Cross (Burch 2010).

Although the US 'surge' of 2009–11 achieved a modicum of military success in terms of reclaiming territory and killing or arresting Taliban commanders, it did so by using scorched-earth tactics, including the razing of villages, and did not reverse the trend of escalating Taliban attacks or achieve any notable political victories (ICSD 2011). As a case in point, Taliban-led attacks in the province of Kandahar during the first quarter of 2011 *increased* by 9 per cent over the same quarter of the previous year (Afghanistan NGO Safety Office 2011, 9). Likewise, in May 2011, the total number of insurgent attacks across the country reached a record high. By the end of August, insurgent attacks were trending 39 per cent higher than for the previous year (Associated Press 2011) – a clear sign that the surge failed to accomplish the military goal of weakening the Taliban insurgency.[4]

One reason for this is that the surge employed a counterproductive set of tactics and strategies. In Kandahar, the surge financed and trained local defence militias, which were empowered to 'beat, rob and kill with impunity' in the areas cleared of Taliban fighters (Farmer 2011; see also Human Rights Watch 2011). As a result, political power in Kandahar remained concentrated in the hands of local warlords and strongmen (Smith 2011). According to one study of 'politics and power' in Kandahar, '[t]he local population sees the government as an exclusive oligarchy devoted to its own enrichment and closely tied to the international coalition' (Forsberg 2010, 7). In this context, 'the end result [of the surge] appears to be a *perpetually escalating stalemate* which could sustain itself indefinitely' (Afghanistan NGO Safety Office 2011, 8).

The augmented power of the Taliban-led insurgency, combined with the political weakness of the Afghan state and the limitations of the development agenda, have therefore triggered a new crisis in Afghanistan. The failure of western states to effect democratization and political reconstruction, economic and social development, and peace and security for the Afghan people is a major reason for the Taliban redux and a challenge to those who argued for 'regime change' as a primary tool of the 'American empire' in the 'global war on terror' (Mallaby 2002; Ignatieff 2003).

In one respect this book is dedicated to explaining what Pakistani journalist Ahmed Rashid (2008) calls the 'descent into chaos' in Afghanistan. It considers the way in which the crisis emerged from the very logic of nation building under military occupation since 2001. More specifically it examines the crisis as an outcome of the pro-warlord military strategy and neoliberal economic strategy of the western occupation. It also highlights the geopolitical strategy of the United States and NATO in Central Asia and the Middle East – in particular, the effort to outflank China and Russia in the competition for hydrocarbon and mineral resources. In developing these lines of analysis, this book critiques the common theories of the Afghan crisis as one resulting from tactical errors, western state apathy, policy imbalances, or hostile interventions by non-NATO actors.

The second goal of this book is to explain and assess Canada's role in Afghanistan and the regional system of geopolitics. As Canadians are aware, this role has been considerable. In 2001, Canada provided direct military support to the US-led OEF against the Taliban regime and the al-Qaeda network. In 2004 Canada took command of the NATO-led International Security Assistance Force (ISAF) in Kabul. Since 2005 Canada has led the counterinsurgency in Kandahar province and played a critical role in shaping the Afghan political process and the military involvement of NATO.[5] The Canadian mission has used what the Paul Martin government termed a '3D' approach to stabilization and reconstruction – a political intervention combining defence, developmental, and diplomatic responsibilities. The same strategy has been advanced, but relabelled a 'whole-of-government' approach, by the current government of Stephen Harper.

As part of this strategy, the Department of National Defence (DND), the Canadian International Development Agency (CIDA), the Department of Foreign Affairs and International Trade, and the Royal Canadian Mounted Police (RCMP) have jointly operated a combat mission and a PRT in Kandahar, as well as a Strategic Advisory Team within the Presidential Office of Hamid Karzai. CIDA has allocated hundreds of millions of dollars in reconstruction and development funds, while the RCMP has worked closely with DND on a police training and security sector reform project. By July 2011 Canada will have spent more than $18 billion in Afghanistan, the vast majority of which has been dedicated to military operations as opposed to aid or nation-building endeavours. As Alexander Moens (2008) emphasizes, this ten-year involvement in Afghanistan has ushered in a qualitative shift in the form and function of the Canadian military, in the patterns and requirements of defence spending, in the organizational hierarchy of the Canadian foreign policy apparatus, and in US-Canadian relations. These structural changes, according to Moens, constitute nothing less than a 'revolution in Canadian foreign policy' and are the direct result of Canada's leading role in the counterinsurgency in Afghanistan.

This type of foreign policy and military engagement, however, has been highly contentious in the Canadian Parliament and among the Canadian public. As violence spread across Afghanistan and as casualties mounted on all sides, the Canadian public turned strongly against the war (EKOS 2009; Angus Reid 2010b). For a majority or plurality of the public, it became increasingly clear that Canada's mission had failed to achieve the stated goals of democratization, development, and political reconstruction. On the contrary, it became widely understood that Canadian forces in Kandahar were working closely with many militia leaders and provincial governors who stood accused of war crimes, corruption, drug dealing, torture, and political repression.[6] Furthermore the Taliban seemed to operate a de facto state in the province, and most aid organizations cancelled projects and commitments. Moreover, Canada had lost more than one hundred and fifty soldiers, and more than two thousand had been wounded (Berthiaume 2012b). Although Prime Minister Harper claimed in 2006 that Canada would never 'cut and run' from Kandahar, he was forced under popular pressure to withdraw combat troops in July 2011 without having achieved the stated goals of the mission.[7]

Until 2014 Canadian forces will operate instead 'behind the wire' on a training program for the Afghan National Army and the Afghan National Police. Although the Conservative government has defended this tactical shift (with Liberal Party support) as a 'non-combat' mission, it is in reality inextricable from the broader counterinsurgency war and, in fact, was designed to release US soldiers for combat against the Taliban (Berthiaume 2012a). Over the same timeframe, Canada will contribute $100 million for aid and reconstruction, although none of these funds

Introduction 9

will be dispensed through the Afghan state. In such ways the new mission replicates past methods of Canada's involvement – methods that have already proven unable to bring democracy, development, peace, and security to Afghanistan (Byers and Webb 2011).

Opinion polls in Kandahar province provide additional cause for concern. According to a 2010 survey in Kandahar for NATO, 94 per cent of the population wants the Afghan government to negotiate with the Taliban, 54 per cent 'strongly support' the Taliban, and 37 per cent 'somewhat support' the Taliban (Glevum Associates 2010, 53). According to another survey, by Anthony Cordesman (2009, 32) for the Center for Strategic and International Studies, a majority in Kandahar opposes the presence of foreign troops. In still another poll, by the International Council on Security and Development (ICSD 2010), 70 per cent of respondents in Kandahar and Helmand opposed military actions by coalition forces. In the same poll, 75 per cent believed that foreign forces disrespect local traditions and religion, 74 per cent opposed working with foreign forces, and 55 per cent believed 'the international community is in Afghanistan for its own benefit, to destroy or occupy the country.' In a May 2011 ICSD survey (2011, 25), 76 per cent of respondents in northern Afghanistan and 87 per cent in southern Afghanistan believed that US-NATO military operations are 'bad for the Afghan people.'

These polls should be highly troubling for the Canadian military and foreign policy establishment. Canadian generals justified the war in the tough language of killing 'detestable murderers and scumbags' who are 'insidious by their very nature,' 'detest our freedoms,' and want to 'break our society' (CBC News 2005, 2008). Yet Canada has been implicated in civilian casualties, the torture of prisoners by Afghan authorities, aggressive military tactics, and the aforementioned failures of aid delivery. In this context a number of 'Death to Canada' protests occurred in Kandahar, and Canadian forces on patrol were often pelted with rocks (CBC News 2007, 2009; Canadian Press 2008). The systemic crisis in Afghanistan, then, also appears as a *crisis of Canadian foreign policy*. Given the time and resources committed to this major undertaking, and the role of Afghanistan in recasting the foreign policy orientation of the state, it is vital to assess the mission and the reasons Canada allied itself to such a project.

Why did the Canadian government go to war in Afghanistan in 2001? What geopolitical and geo-economic interests did this mission serve? What role did continental concerns play in shaping and determining the mission? What has Canada actually done in Afghanistan?

What are the successes and failures of the mission? What responsibility does Canada hold for the current crisis in Afghanistan? How has the war recalibrated the institutions of the foreign policy apparatus? And how should the mission be understood in relation to the changing political economy of Canada and the wider world system? This anthology will attempt to answer these questions.

Making Sense of the Mission

The war in Afghanistan has been a major if not central policy commitment of the Canadian state since 2001. However, little academic analysis has been offered to make sense of this commitment and the implications it holds for Canadian politics and Canadian foreign policy. As mentioned, Moens (2008) has examined the 'revolutionary' impact of the war on defence spending patterns, foreign policy strategies, state restructuring, and continental relations with the United States. His study lays out key terms for analysing the meaning of the war for the foreign policy apparatus, but does not situate the conflict in terms of broader transformations in the Canadian or global political economy. Nor does it review the course of events in Afghanistan that have contradicted the military thrust of Canadian policy. In short, it lacks a critical assessment of the mission and its movement towards crisis. It largely accepts the stated goals of the mission, while overlooking its problematic features.

Canadian military historian Sean Maloney provides a more audacious line of argument for the mission. For instance, when the Taliban insurgency was heating up in 2004, he opined that '[m]edia pronouncements . . . that a new Taliban-led jihad is in the offing, are greatly exaggerated' (2004, 9). Furthermore, 'there will be no more large-scale military operations by enemy forces' (10) and to 'suggest that American policy has failed in Afghanistan . . . is reaching too far and requires substantial amounts of intellectual dishonesty' (12). As a result the 'Vietnam analogy remains . . . the wishful thinking of a small group of misinformed or misleading pundits' (15). Although Maloney recognizes the obstacles to political reconstruction and nation building in Afghanistan (12–13), his 'realist' approach places a higher value on winning the military mission. To this end he argues that '[t]he so-called "warlords" and their violent operating methods are a reality. It is critical that the more zealous members of international legal institutions recognize that antagonizing them or calling them to account under

Western legal structures is completely counterproductive to the recon-
stitution of Afghanistan. We must resist the inclination to be judgmen-
tal. *We need to work with them*' (13, emphasis added).

Janice Stein and Eugene Lang (2007) offer a more critical, if still sympathetic, account of Canada's 'unexpected war' in Kandahar. Their
study makes two important contributions. First, it reveals the deliberations through which Prime Ministers Jean Chrétien and Paul Martin
committed troops to Afghanistan in the first years of the mission. As the
authors discover through interviews with key cabinet ministers, the primary considerations were fighting terrorism, supporting a NATO ally,
and appeasing Canada's largest trading partner. According to these interviews, Canadian politicians hoped to gain favour with the Bush administration through a series of 'early in, early out' deployments.

Second, Stein and Lang reveal how bureaucratic torpor in Ottawa
left Canada with no choice but to deploy to Kandahar in 2005 as part of
NATO efforts to establish PRTs in all 34 provinces in Afghanistan. The
contradictory nature of Canada's 3D strategy, which tried to combine
development, diplomacy, and defence in a single setting, created serious problems for the mission, which was dominated by the military
under the leadership of General Rick Hillier. The mission was further
weakened by the emerging story of torture and detainee abuse. Despite
these setbacks and problems, Stein and Lang endorse the 3D strategy.
In a striking example of methodological idealism, the authors compare
the Canadian military mission in Afghanistan to the antislavery movement in nineteenth-century Britain (2007, 302). They posit a 'common
destiny' between Canadian military personnel and the people of Afghanistan and cite former Liberal cabinet minister John Manley, who
was told by an Afghan named Farid that 'Afghanistan is your child. If
you do not support a child, teaching it how to walk, it cannot stand on
its own two feet' (304). To empower this act of neocolonial paternalism,
the authors advocate new techniques through which the 'military and
[Canada's] development assistance program . . . work together outside
Canada.' In addition, government officials must 'speak clearly to the
public' and describe why 'we are there for a generation' (297).

Stein and Lang's *Unexpected War* has been reviewed in detail elsewhere (Hubble 2008; Klassen 2009b). One limitation of the book is
the liberal method through which it conceptualizes state activity and
foreign policy decision-making. This method makes sense of the mission largely in terms of the individual thoughts and actions of those
in positions of political power. This method of inquiry abstracts the

individuals in question from the social relations of capitalism in which they are embedded as political agents with a class agenda for governing. In other words, missing from the analysis is a political-economic understanding of Canadian foreign policy as a particular expression of 'dominant class interests' (Pratt 1983). The upshot of this methodological approach is an inability to theorize the war as a reflection and catalyst of wider changes in the Canadian political economy. The war represents a definite strategy of corporate, state, and military elites (Staples 2007), but this strategy is clouded by the individualist and normative method described above.

Stein and Lang's notion of 'unexpected war' raises further questions. While the war is certainly a new mode of operation for Canadian foreign policy, it fits within a larger pattern and longer history of Canadian military and diplomatic intervention in the Third World (Carty and Smith 1981; Clarke and Swift 1982; Pratt 1984; Swift and Tomlinson 1997; Engler 2009). As an advanced capitalist country with economic interests across the world market, including extensive investments in the Third World, it is unsurprising that Canada has developed diplomatic and military strategies to advance and secure the economic and political interests of transnational capital. If the capitalist world system is constituted by an *imperialist* structure of power through which economic surpluses are distributed unevenly through the competing strategies of nation-states and their respective capitalist classes, then Canada must be located near the top of this hierarchical system, and the question of Canadian imperialism must be explored. If Canadian foreign policy is understood as a 'secondary' component of the 'new imperialism' (Harvey 2003; Klassen 2009a), then the war in Afghanistan, though unique and transformative, cannot be interpreted as unexpected or unusual.

Stein and Lang's focus on bureaucratic competition within the Canadian foreign policy apparatus is a common theme in the literature (Cornish 2007; Brown 2008; Manley 2008). For example, Nipa Banerjee (2009) highlights institutional imbalances between departments as a primary source of Canada's failures in Afghanistan. Her assessment of Canada's development policy emphasizes the lack of clear objectives in 2001, the absence of evidence-based programming, and poor coordination among donors and between CIDA and DND. These problems were evident in Canada's 3D strategy in Kandahar: 'No unitary objective was established and no division of functions between the 3-Ds to achieve the objective was envisaged. The result was confusion, with the limited resources of the 3-Ds not complimenting each other and the defence and development wings overlapping and sometimes duplicating activities' (67–8). Despite these problems Banerjee endorses the military occupation and the war against the 'jihadist Taliban movement, based on terrorism,' and offers strategies by which a 'human security' agenda can be included as a more central component of the mission (71). However, by accepting the paradigm of the 'war on terror' and the military objective of 'repressing' the Taliban, Banerjee is unable to critique the use of aid as a means of counterinsurgency warfare. Her position also discounts the military occupation and the 'warlord strategy' of the United States and NATO as primary sources of instability (Rashid 2008, 129, 133). Furthermore, she does not situate the conflict in terms of geopolitical and geo-economic rivalries in Central Asia between the United States and NATO on the one side and emerging powers in the region on the other.

Unfortunately the one study of Canada's role in Afghanistan that does take seriously the question of geopolitics, geo-economics, and the changing political economy of global capitalism (Warnock 2008), dedicates only one chapter to Canada and focuses primarily on US grand strategy and the general course of events in Afghanistan since 2001. Thus the need is evident for a new study of Canada's war – one that highlights the geopolitical context of the mission, the problematic course of events in Afghanistan since 2001, and the way in which Canadian foreign policy has been grafted onto the new strategies of Washington and NATO. At the most abstract level, this study seeks to locate the impetus to war in the political economy of global capitalism and the social and class agencies through which it operates. To this end it draws upon the new theories of 'imperialism' and 'American empire' developed by researchers over the past decade (Gowan 1999; Bacevich 2002; Harvey 2003; Panitch and Gindin 2004; Wood 2005). Through such theories the war in Afghanistan can be understood in relation to wider transformations in the world economy and nation-state system.

On the domestic front any new study of the war must also connect the transformation of Canadian foreign policy to the restructuring of the state apparatus as part of neoliberal globalization and the recomposition of class relations in Canada. In other words it must offer a *political economy of Canadian foreign policy*. This type of analysis, first, maps the economic relations through which Canada has secured a secondary position in the hierarchy of states; and, second, isolates and identifies the social logic by which the state apparatus has been reorganized around the institutions most connected to the world economy as well as those involving military, security, and defence.

Finally, this study analyses the course of events in Afghanistan itself that culminated in the current crisis. In particular it considers the way in which the military occupation used a neoliberal development strategy and a pro-warlord military strategy to construct a state apparatus that could only be afflicted by corruption, fundamentalism, patriarchy, and violence.

In presenting this three-tiered analysis, the book's authors argue that the goal of the conflict in Afghanistan is to *impose occupation, assert western power, and globalize neoliberal economics*. More specifically for Canada, we argue that the war is a *deliberate and self-conscious strategy of the state and corporate elite to fashion a military infrastructure for managing the Third World in conjunction with US imperialism*. By staking out these arguments in comprehensive form, the volume contributes to the field of critical international relations theory and Marxist political economy, both of which are well established in the Canadian social sciences (see, for example, Panitch 1977; Carroll 1986; Neufeld 1995; Clement 1997; Judson 2003; Grinspun and Shamsie 2007; and Beier and Wylie 2009). Beyond this the purpose of the book is to engage and enrich the current debates in Canada on the war – a war that has sparked much controversy and loss for both Canadians and Afghans. After ten years of conflict, it is time to assess the mission in a new light.

Theory, Method, and Organization

This book brings together a new collection of essays on the war in Afghanistan and Canadian foreign policy. Although each chapter develops a unique perspective on the conflict, a critical mode of analysis ties them into a unified or coherent whole. In the classic formulation of Robert Cox (1981, 129), a 'critical' theory stands opposed to 'problem-solving' theory:

> It is critical in the sense that it stands apart from the prevailing order of the world and asks how that order came about. Critical theory, unlike problem-solving theory, does not take institutions and social and power relations for granted but calls them into question by concerning itself with their origins and how and whether they might be in the process of changing. It is directed towards an appraisal of the very framework for action, problematic, which problem-solving theory accepts as its parameters. Critical theory is directed to the social and political complex as a whole rather than to the separate parts. As a matter of practice, critical theory,

like problem-solving theory, takes as its starting point some aspect or particular sphere of human activity. But whereas the problem-solving approach leads to further analytical sub-division and limitation of the issue to be dealt with, the critical approach leads towards the construction of a larger picture of the whole of which the initially contemplated part is just one component, and seeks to understand the process of change in which both parts and whole are involved . . . Problem-solving theories can be represented, in the broader perspective of critical theory, as serving particular national, sectional, or class interests, which are comfortable within the given order.

If the scholarship to date on Canada's role in Afghanistan represents 'problem-solving' theory – in other words, if it is geared towards fixing 'some aspect or particular sphere' of the mission and serves 'particular national, sectional, or class interests' – then this book stakes out a 'critical' approach – one that 'stands apart from the prevailing [mission] and asks how that [mission] came about' in relation to the 'social and political complex' of Canadian capitalism and the wider world system. In short the book seeks to comprehend Canada's war without recourse to nationalistic bias, government propaganda, and positivist or idealist understandings of state power and international relations. To this end it is open to multiple, comparative, and global sources of information and data and to critical theories of empire, capital, ideology, and class (see Ashley 1984; Burnham 1994; Gowan 1999; Harvey 2003; Panitch and Gindin 2004; Wood 2005; and Beier and Wylie 2009). Certain chapters are based on personal experiences and fieldwork in Afghanistan, while others are based on an analytic expertise in global politics and Canadian foreign policy. Still others are based on 'participant-observer' work in the anti-war movements in Quebec and English Canada.

The structure of the book corresponds to these theoretical insights and methodological objectives. In conceptual terms the book proceeds from the 'abstract' to the 'concrete,' and from the 'universal' to the 'particular' (Mandel 1975, chap. 1; Ilyenkov 1982; Ollman 1993). In this way it develops or unfolds across four parts, each of which considers the war at a greater level of historical and conjunctural specificity, or as a 'progressive concretization' of abstract tendencies and determinations in the capitalist world system. The presentation of chapters thus begins with the history of Afghanistan before turning to the political economy of global capitalism and the structural transformation of Canadian foreign policy in the context of recent wars in Afghanistan and beyond.

Afghanistan, Empire, and the 'War on Terror'

Part I, entitled 'Afghanistan, Empire, and the "War on Terror",' covers the history of Afghanistan, the nature of capitalist imperialism, and the logic of western policy in the Middle East and Central Asia in the current period of neoliberal globalization. In the process, the chapters in this part offer a framework for understanding the war as a particular flashpoint in the evolution of global capitalism over the past three decades.

Chapter 2, 'Afghanistan and Empire,' by John Warnock, examines the history of Afghanistan with a particular focus on the internal dialectic of modernization and reaction and the external role of imperial powers. As the chapter reveals, Afghanistan's history cannot be understood outside this matrix of contradictory forces. For example, the popular characterization of Afghanistan as a 'failed state' makes little sense in abstraction from the legacy of colonialism, the impact of the Cold War, the trajectory of class struggle in the 1970s and 1980s, and the role of US imperialism in funding and supporting the *mujahideen*. In presenting this argument, Warnock provides a useful counterpoint to the many studies that identify 'state failure' in Afghanistan solely in relation to the Soviet occupation and the Taliban regime of the 1990s. His argument, which is much broader and more historical, is that state formation in Afghanistan is the outcome of complex processes of outside intervention and domestic social conflict, and that such a dialectic is still operative in Afghanistan today.

These themes are given greater context in Chapter 3, 'A "Single" War: The Political Economy of Intervention in the Middle East and Central Asia,' by Adam Hanieh, who theorizes the war in relation to the contradictory logic of capitalist imperialism. For Hanieh new forms of *inter-imperialist rivalry* motivate the conflict. The internationalization of capital has generated new centres of production and accumulation in the world market, especially in China and India. In this context, the energy resources of Central Asia and the Middle East have been imbued with new significance, as advanced capitalist countries vie for access with newly emerging superpowers. For Hanieh it is this structural context that frames the war in Afghanistan and ties together the conflicts of the entire region, from Iraq and Palestine to Iran, into a 'single war' between western imperialism on the one hand and resistance movements and bourgeois-nationalist state projects on the other. As such, Hanieh's argument is that the war in Afghanistan, when properly theorized, is a *war of global capitalism*.

The geopolitical and geo-economic calculations of western powers are the focus of Chapter 4, 'The Empire of Capital and the Latest Inning of the Great Game,' by Michael Skinner. This chapter reviews the new literature in the social sciences on 'empire' and 'imperialism,' and theorizes the war in terms of securing the United States' 'global primacy' and the free flow of trade and investment. Skinner examines the 'Silk Road Strategy' of US foreign policy and the way in which the war in Afghanistan is being used to counter Chinese expansion, privatize Afghan resources, and generally expand the space of global capitalism and the American empire. In the process he confirms the critical theories of the war and occupation that many Afghans articulated in the course of field interviews in 2007.

The final chapter in Part I is my 'Methods of Empire: State Building, Development, and War in Afghanistan,' which reviews the history of the occupation since 2001. The chapter describes the way in which the western intervention used a pro-warlord military strategy and a free market development strategy to build a state in the service of western governments and transnational capital. The movement towards crisis over the past ten years, then, occurred not because of bureaucratic, technical, or policy failures but largely because of the occupation itself. To make this argument, I review the ways in which the Bonn Process, the development agenda, and the counterinsurgency war have been subordinated to the interests of empire.

With these four chapters, Part I sets the context for understanding Canada's role in Afghanistan.

The Political Economy of Canadian Foreign Policy

Part II starts from the premise that Canadian foreign policy is best understood through a political economy perspective. From a theoretical standpoint, Canadian foreign policy must be linked to the patterns of accumulation through which the state is reproduced as an institutional configuration of capitalist class power. In this conceptualization, the state is structurally connected to the relations of exploitation that constitute the capitalist mode of production. The state guarantees private property, issues the money form, regulates class relations, mediates all cross-border transactions, and taxes various points of exchange. With this in mind, the 'autonomy' of the state is rooted in the particular institutionalization of capitalist social relations.

How does this work? As Ellen Meiksins Wood (1995) demonstrates, the unique relation of capitalism between the buyers and sellers of labour power creates the material foundation for an institutional bifurcation of class power – for a distinct separation of the *expropriation of economic surpluses* and the *exercise of political coercion*. The extraction of surplus value or profit from the production process is privatized under the rights of capital, while the task of regulating the macroeconomy and its class relations is mandated to the state. The state is both structurally dependent upon this mandate and a terrain of conflict upon which this mandate is negotiated. As such, it is constituted by a 'relative autonomy' from capital, though such autonomy is directly grounded in the social relations of exploitation. In this context public policies and the governments that devise them are inextricably connected to the accumulation process and its class relationships. The state is institutionally separate from the concrete processes of value production and exchange, yet simultaneously operates as the guarantor and ultimate manager of these processes. The task of a critical social science, then, is to highlight the ways in which government agents and policies express the economic and political interests of social classes within domestic 'power blocs' (Poulantzas 1978a,b).

With these concepts and propositions in mind, Part II delineates what Cranford Pratt (1983) calls a 'class theory' of Canadian foreign policy. In Chapter 6, 'From the Avro Arrow to Afghanistan: The Political Economy of Canadian Militarism,' Paul Kellogg examines the economic foundation of Canadian foreign policy in the post-war period. During the Cold War Canada took advantage of the US security umbrella to avoid the burden of military spending. In practising this form of 'military parasitism,' Canada was able to specialize in peacekeeping and to direct economic surpluses into the accumulation process and state sector instead of into the arms industry. Over the past two decades, however, as US power began to decline, there emerged a new imperative for defence spending in Canada (and in other NATO countries). For Kellogg the war in Afghanistan is a reflection of this changing political economy, whereby military parasitism in the Cold War laid the foundation for rearmament in the present.

In Chapter 7, 'Canada in the Third World: The Political Economy of Intervention,' Todd Gordon lays out a political-economic framework for understanding Canada's role in the periphery of the global capitalist system. In particular he draws a connection between the new military policies of the state and the foreign direct investments of Canadian firms in developing countries. He highlights the matrix of tools by which Canadian governments relate to Third World nations, and then examines the deployment of these tools in Latin America, the Caribbean, and Afghanistan.

In the final chapter of Part II, 'Fewer Illusions: Canadian Foreign Policy since 2001,' Greg Albo analyses the new security doctrines and institutions of the Canadian state. Albo argues that Canada's position as a secondary power in the North American bloc explains the new foreign policies of 'stratified multilateralism' with US imperialism, and 'disciplinary militarism' towards 'security threats' in developing countries. He shows, in particular, how the war in Afghanistan has been a catalyst for a radical remaking of the state around national security agencies.

With these papers, Part II develops a materialist understanding of Canada's external statecraft, one that is grounded in the political economy of capitalism and class.

Canada's War

Part III focuses directly on Canada's role in Afghanistan. In Chapter 9, 'Failed States and Canada's 3D Policy in Afghanistan,' Angela Joya interrogates the framing of the war in terms of rebuilding a failed state. She demonstrates that this framework tends to ignore the external conditions of state formation and the history of western intervention in developing countries. She describes how Canada implemented a 3D strategy, which in effect reproduced a situation of state failure in Afghanistan. Her fundamental argument is that peace and democracy cannot be achieved under military occupation.

Anthony Fenton and Jon Elmer then examine Canada's attempt at 'democracy promotion' in Afghanistan. Their chapter, 'Building an Expeditionary Force for Democracy Promotion,' analyses the new political infrastructure through which Canada exports a particular version of democracy – an elitist 'polyarchy' – to developing countries. To this end the authors dissect the recent history of state building in Afghanistan, and argue that Canada's practice of exporting democracy is linked to making the world safe for capitalism.

In Chapter 11, 'Incompatible Objectives: Counterinsurgency and Development in Afghanistan,' Justin Podur argues that the western intervention has exacerbated local 'blockages' to development, that Canada's mission has reproduced conditions of external dependence and economic backwardness, and that political sovereignty is a requisite of peace and 'human development' in the country.

In Chapter 12, 'From the Somalia Affair to Canada's Afghan Detainee Torture Scandal: How Stories of Torture Define the Nation,' Sherene Razack addresses the most controversial aspect of Canada's mission. Razack offers a timeline of events and then reviews the parliamentary testimony of diplomat Richard Colvin, who first raised concerns of torture in 2006. Drawing upon other case studies, including Canada's practice of torture in Somalia in 1994, Razack theorizes torture as a manifestation of racism towards Muslims and those occupied by foreign armies. The torture of Afghan prisoners is not an isolated or accidental outcome but a social mechanism by which occupation forces establish a sense of racial and national superiority, both of which are ideological prerequisites of the new imperialism.

The Anti-war Movement

Part IV gives focus to the anti-war movement in English Canada and Quebec, in order to highlight the opposition that emerged to both the war in Kandahar and the broader shift in Canadian foreign policy. While the combat mission in Kandahar finally ended in summer 2011, a plurality or majority of the public had opposed the mission for several years (Angus Reid 2010b).[8] In this context the anti-war movement tried to mobilize the public around a number of campaigns to end the conflict and Canada's role within it.

To examine these efforts the two chapters in Part IV consider the peace movement in Canada and the strategies and tactics through which it has operated. In particular, they draw from the expertise of several movement organizers in Quebec and English Canada. In Chapter 13, Benoit Renaud and Jessica Squires examine the peace movement in Quebec and the critical role played by new parties of the left, including Québec solidaire. They identify Islamophobia as a major obstacle to building the anti-war movement, and review the way in which Québec solidaire has grappled with the link between racism and imperialism. In the process, they offer a unique perspective on social movement advocacy in Quebec today.

The anthology is completed with Derrick O'Keefe's chapter on the anti-war movement in English Canada, in which he reviews the debates on how Canada should proceed in Afghanistan after the combat mission ends in Kandahar. He argues that Canada has supported a 'narco-state' in Afghanistan, and outlines a strategy by which the anti-war movement can revive itself and challenge the new consensus in

Ottawa on training Afghan security forces. His argument is that, for the anti-war movement to succeed, it must build direct ties of solidarity with progressive Afghan organizations, confront and challenge the growing culture of militarism in Canada, rediscover the lost art of civil disobedience, and make connections to the panoply of social movements in Canada and around the world against neoliberalism, climate change, and militarism.

In these ways the anthology offers a new understanding of the war in Afghanistan, one that combines a critical theory of international relations and global capitalism, a political-economic analysis of Canadian foreign policy trends, and a detailed assessment of the western intervention since 2001. To expound the logic of the war and occupation, this Introduction closes with a summary of the principal findings of this anthology. It synthesizes a framework through which to understand the conflict in Afghanistan, and proposes methods by which peace, democracy, and development might be achieved. It argues that western forces should withdraw from Afghanistan, allowing for domestic and regional settlements to emerge alongside a reconciliation and reconstruction agenda.

Conclusion: Afghanistan, the 'War on Terror,' and Canada's New Imperialism

In the aftermath of 9/11, the Bush administration launched the war in Afghanistan as the first salvo in a 'global war on terror.' Across a few weeks of fighting in October and November 2001, US and NATO forces quickly disposed of the Taliban government and al-Qaeda bases in the country. In December of that year, the United States and NATO helped establish a new government in Afghanistan, run predominantly by the warlords of the United Islamic Front or 'Northern Alliance.' In the wake of this perceived success, the Bush administration began to threaten the governments of Iran, Syria, Iraq, and North Korea, all of which stood accused of exporting weapons of mass destruction or terrorism. In March 2003 Iraq was invaded and occupied illegally by a US-led 'coalition of the willing.' As in Afghanistan, the government in Iraq fell quickly amidst the Pentagon's 'shock and awe' campaign. However, at the same time that President Bush proclaimed 'mission accomplished' in Iraq, sectarian violence and guerrilla warfare were emerging as lethal forces. The occupation government of Paul Bremer imposed a radical package of neoliberal economic reforms (Klein 2007), and was quickly targeted by an armed insurgency, which inflicted major losses on US forces between 2004 and 2007. If the war in Iraq had not become a quagmire for the US military, it is possible that Iran, Syria, and other countries in the 'axis of evil' would have faced 'regime change' by the same western powers that invaded Afghanistan.[9]

As the international peace movement argued at the time, the basic premise of the 'global war on terror' – that western states faced an onslaught of violence by Islamic fundamentalists who 'hate our free-doms' – was highly dubious if not intentionally spurious. Leaders of the peace movement – as well as many scholars of international rela-tions – pointed out that 9/11 occurred for widely known *political rea-sons* – namely, the history of US foreign policy in Afghanistan and the Middle East, the positioning of US military bases in the Gulf, and US support for Israeli occupations and Arab dictatorships (Ali 2003; Pape 2005). These political issues were in fact the dominant themes of al-Qaeda's and Osama bin Laden's many communiqués before and after 9/11 (Mohamedou 2006). The paradox that '[d]irect American interven-tion in the Muslim world has . . . elevated the stature of and support for radical Islamists' was clearly recognized by the US Department of Defense (United States 2004, 40): 'Muslims do not "hate our freedom," but rather, they hate our policies. The overwhelming majority voice their objections to what they see as one-sided support in favor of Israel and against Palestinian rights, and the longstanding, even increasing support for what Muslims collectively see as tyrannies, most notably Egypt, Saudi Arabia, Jordan, Pakistan, and the Gulf states . . . Thus when American public diplomacy talks about bringing democracy to Islamic societies, this is seen as no more than self-serving hypocrisy.' With precisely this understanding of US foreign policy and its connec-tion to 9/11, the international peace movement argued for legal, diplo-matic, and multilateral means of apprehending al-Qaeda suspects and for a change in US policy in the Middle East and Central Asia.[10] This kind of approach, however, was anathema to the United States and its western allies, whose economic and political powers are reproduced through an imperial structure of world order. For reasons of empire, not justice or peace, they responded to 9/11 with violence and warfare.

As a result it soon became clear that the 'war on terror' had less to do with terrorism itself and more to do imposing US dominance in Cen-tral Asia and the Middle East, as a first step towards reasserting US primacy *globally* (Brzezinski 1997a,b; Mearsheimer 2010). This geopo-litical endeavour, which neoconservatives labelled a 'Project for a New

American Century,' was made transparent with the invasion of Iraq and with the manoeuvres against Iran, Lebanon, Syria, Somalia, China, and other developing countries over the past ten years. Simply put, the war in Afghanistan was always linked to the aspirations of empire on a much broader scale. In particular, it was a means by which the United States could gain leverage over hydrocarbon resources in the Middle East and Central Asia; a conflict through which the United States and NATO could implant military bases near the borders of China, Pakistan, Russia, and Iran; a platform on which the United States could initiate 'regime change' across the wider region; and a war through which NATO could reinvent itself as an 'out of theatre' alliance.

NATO leaders and analysts have been forthright about these objectives. In June 2007, at the Euro-Atlantic Security Partnership Forum, the secretary general of NATO, Jaap de Hoop Scheffer (2007), warned about the 'security of [global energy] supply,' and argued that NATO should 'consider providing support to Allies and Partners in situations of increased risk to critical energy infrastructure.' In addition NATO should command 'maritime domain awareness' over critical sea lanes for transporting energy. His arguments around energy security must be situated in the context of broader NATO strategies towards a changing global capitalism. According to one NATO planner (Lindley-French 2005), alliance policy is to 're-establish the West at the centre of global security' and to 'project systemic stability beyond its borders.' In this context, 'Chinese military modernization must be of concern to Western planners.' Furthermore, '[t]here can be no systemic security without Asian security and there will be no Asian security without a strong role for the West therein.' Related to this, Zbigniew Brzezinski (2009) argues that NATO must function as an 'effective global security mechanism' to police 'the dispersal of global power,' 'intensifying popular unrest,' and 'humanity's recent political awakening.'

Driven by such concerns of empire, the 'global war on terror' was bound to operate in ways that trumped or disregarded the norms, regulations, and laws of the UN system. The wars in Afghanistan and Iraq were violations of international law, undertaken without sanction of the UN Security Council (Cohn 2005; Duffy 2005; Williamson 2009).[11] As a result these wars can be viewed as 'supreme international crimes of aggression,' if judged by the legal standards of the Nuremburg Tribunal (Mandel 2004). The US-led 'war on terror' also used rendition, detention, and torture on a systematic basis, as reported at Camp X-Ray (Guantánamo Bay, Cuba), Abu Ghraib (Iraq), Bagram air base (Afghanistan), and countless 'black sites' operated by the Central Intelligence Agency around the world (Andersson 2010; UNAMA 2011b). Western forces in Afghanistan and Iraq have committed other war crimes, including deliberate attacks on civilians. In one example from Afghanistan, US soldiers based in Kandahar formed a secret 'kill team,' which shot Afghan civilians at random, posed for pictures with their victims' corpses, and collected fingers as trophies (Associated Press 2010; McGreal 2010). This case is only one example of how the 'global war on terror' has spawned racialized acts of violence. The torture regime of Abu Ghraib, the killing of tens of thousands in Iraq and Afghanistan, and the growing racism towards Muslims in North America and western Europe – all of these are interrelated, logical, and functional outcomes, if not material prerequisites, of the new imperial project (Razack 2008).

As a consequence there were many reasons to doubt that the United States and NATO could ever support nation building and development in the occupied zones of empire. In Afghanistan, for instance, the US-NATO occupation allied itself with the warlords of the Northern Alliance – that is, with the same actors who destroyed the country during the civil war of the mid-1990s. The US-NATO occupation also imposed a neoliberal, free market development plan, which has been administered by the international financial institutions as well as by NGOs, corporations, militaries, and aid agencies from western countries. With few exceptions, the development agenda has focused on integrating Afghanistan into the world market and limiting the state as a meaningful guide of economic growth and social progress. From the start the anti-war movement opposed this combination of warlord politics and neoliberalism, and predicted a reproduction of 'state failure' and the re-emergence of armed conflict (Warnock 2008).

Given the way in which real events in Afghanistan have met these predictions, the anti-war movement argues – with the support of many Afghans and Afghan analysts – for a redeployment of foreign troops as part of peace negotiations with the Taliban, the Afghan government, and democratic, secular parties (Ali 2008; Joya 2009; Lieven 2011). Finding peace and security in Afghanistan requires an *end to the military occupation*, without which Afghans will be unable to achieve the political compromises for peace building and reconstruction to occur. Ending the occupation is necessary for Afghans to establish sovereignty over their own territory and to negotiate the determinants of state power and economic development apart from outside intervention and division.

In his book on reconciliation in Afghanistan, Michael Semple (2009, 91) notes that 'Afghanistan has a rich heritage of traditions and institutions related to conflict avoidance and resolution upon which actors in the current conflict have drawn and that can provide authentic local content for any reconciliation program.'[12] However, 'the large-scale commitment of international military forces to a counterinsurgency war substantially changes the context of attempts at reconciliation' (11). The war aggravates and compounds the cycle of violence in Afghanistan and must be countered by 'an unambiguous strategy . . . of reconciliation as the preferred way out of the current conflict' (92).

Three further considerations must be included as part of any program to end the war. First, the Taliban will have to accept, as many Afghans and their interlocutors point out (Johnson and Leslie 2004, 178), that 'a state in which the interests of other [that is, non-Pashtun] ethnic groups are not fully taken on board' will be 'impossible to envisage,' just as an 'American puppet state or a [Northern Alliance] state . . . would provoke resistance.' From this recognition, a *federal* state may be necessary for power sharing among all ethnic groups in Afghanistan. The Afghan state should therefore be reconfigured to balance against the problems of centralization in the current constitution. In the aftermath of a reconciliation process, many Afghans argue that central authorities might focus on national services and infrastructure, while key forms of governance and administration might be decentralized to provincial, district, or tribal levels, reflecting the wishes and needs of Afghans themselves. The disarming of warlords by a new central government would be highly popular, as would be ending the corruption of the current regime (Johnson and Leslie 2004, 178–81).

Second, as several chapters in this volume argue, the path to peace and development requires a *regional agreement* among the states of Afghanistan, Pakistan, India, Iran, and Russia (Ali 2008; Rashid 2008; Semple 2009, 92–3; Thier 2010, 133–4). In combination with the western intervention, these states have turned Afghanistan into a geopolitical minefield, backing political or sectional allies in a de facto civil war. Such a settlement would have to include a peace agreement or rapprochement between India and Pakistan, a redeployment of western forces from Central Asia, a plan for regional economic development, and security for Iran against western belligerence. As part of this plan, Afghanistan must be granted sovereignty to pursue an internal settlement and an external balance free of outside domination.

Third, as part of ending the occupation, the United States and NATO must offer *reparations and grants* for reconstruction and development to occur after the violence and loss of the past ten years (Canadian Peace Alliance 2007). These funds must not be tied to the economic or political ends of western states, but self-administered by a new Afghan government with a genuine program for 'human development' (see Podur, in this volume).

It is important to underline that such a program to end the occupation, disarm the warlords, counter the Taliban, and build a democratic state with a 'human development' agenda is articulated clearly by many Afghans themselves, especially those on the political left (Joya 2009). In the words of the late Afghan journalist Dad Noorani:

> For the people of Afghanistan, one way remains, and this is to think about the establishment of a *third force* [opposed to both the western occupation and the warlords and the Taliban]. This force can arise from the freedom-loving intellectuals inside and outside the country, the tribal elders who have not disgraced themselves with partiality and pettiness, democratic people who have not succumbed to those two forces, and political movements that have not welcomed any violence. [They should] form a united front, [and] fight with different means for the expulsion of the foreigners and the prevention of the interference of the neighbours and their servants . . . and strive for independence, freedom and neutrality in order to save the people from the current blood stained situation. (Quoted by Ruttig 2011b; emphasis added)

There remain, unfortunately, many obstacles to ending the war and occupation and to proceeding with a reconciliation and reconstruction plan. Beyond the truculence of the Taliban-led insurgency and the corruption of the Karzai government, the very logic of the western mission runs against that of reconciliation and peace building. This is true in two respects.

First, the US strategy of counterinsurgency has 'undermined rather than improved the chances of negotiations,' as 'the Taliban leadership – along with large parts of the Afghan population, including the political class – does not really believe that the United States is really committed to "reconciliation"' (Ruttig 2011b, 4). As a case in point, there was no mention of reconciliation with the Taliban in the final statement of the NATO Lisbon Summit of November 2010. Although the United States began secret negotiations with the Taliban in summer 2011, these meetings have been lacking in democratic accountability and structured continuity, and have failed to involve a neutral third party such as the United Nations. According to the International Crisis Group (2012):

> Instead of a sequenced roadmap that would prioritise domestic reconciliation and include basic political reforms, accompanied by a multilateral meditation effort, the Afghan government and its international backers have adopted a market-bazaar approach to negotiations. Bargains are being cut with any and all comers, regardless of their political relevance or ability to influence outcomes. Far from being Afghan-led, the negotiating agenda has been dominated by Washington's desire to obtain a decent interval between the planned U.S. troop drawdown and the possibility of another bloody chapter in the conflict. The material effect of international support for negotiations so far has been to increase the incentives for spoilers, who include insurgents, government officials and war profiteers of all backgrounds.

As a result, '[a] lasting peace accord will ultimately require far more structured negotiations, under the imprimatur of the UN, than are presently being pursued' (ibid.).

Second, the geopolitical interests of the United States and NATO in Afghanistan and the wider region contradict more general interests of peace and stability, and will not allow any perception of defeat or failure to appear (see Woodward 2010, 127). With China emerging as a regional power, with Iran leading an 'axis of resistance' in the Middle East, with the 'Arab Spring' threatening several regimes in the Gulf, and with the war in Afghanistan spilling into Pakistan, the United States and NATO will not abandon the region any time soon, even if their military strategies generate the very threats they claim to oppose (Lieven 2011). In fact, even if the United States and NATO attempt to wind down their direct participation in the Afghanistan war, they are unlikely to abandon the military bases or the economic contracts won through the occupation to date. Indeed, they will not quit Afghanistan even if security details are wholly transferred to the Afghan National Army and the Afghan National Police by 2014, as the current plan entails. For example, the White House plan to withdraw 33,000 troops by summer 2012 will still leave nearly 70,000 US soldiers in Afghanistan, twice the amount as when President Obama assumed office. As US Secretary of State Hillary Clinton has explained the White House strategy, '[w]e need to underscore that we are transitioning, not leaving' (see Tandon 2011).

For this reason, in spring 2011, Marc Grossman, the US special envoy to Afghanistan and Pakistan, began negotiations with the Karzai government on a deal to maintain a long-term political and military presence in Afghanistan beyond 2014 (Nordland 2011). On 2 May 2012 Presidents Karzai and Obama inked the Enduring Strategic Partnership Agreement, outlining the conditions under which the United States will remain in Afghanistan through 2024. Under the guise of 'defeating al-Qaeda and its affiliates,' the governments of the United States and Afghanistan will sign a future bilateral security agreement, addressing issues such as troop levels, special operations, military bases, aid and development funding, police and army training, prisons, detainees, air strikes, and drone deployments. According to White House officials, the Enduring Strategic Partnership Agreement is also designed to secure 'a regional equilibrium that serves our national security interest – and that's ultimately why we went there in the first place' (see Landler 2012). As a result, instead of ending the war, the Agreement will remodulate the occupation of Afghanistan, extend the conflict with the Taliban under the pretext of fighting 'al-Qaeda,' and reposition the United States and NATO for other confrontations in the region. In the process, the interests of peace, reconciliation, and self-determination for Afghans will be trumped or neglected.

It is against this backdrop that the 'revolution in Canadian foreign policy' must be theorized and assessed. As the chapters in this book make clear, the new direction of Canadian foreign policy cannot be explained simply by policy mistakes, US demands, military adventurism, security threats, or abstract notions of liberal idealism. More accurately, it is best explained by structural tendencies in the Canadian political economy – in particular, by the internationalization of Canadian capital and the realignment of the state as a secondary power in the US-led system of empire. The new patterns of economic internationalization – both within and beyond the North American bloc – have created a material interest in new forms of 'international security' for the Canadian state and capitalist class. These new flows of value have positioned the state as a secondary power, whose economic and political interests are achieved through new forms of 'cooperative specialization' with US foreign policy objectives. For this reason, the Canadian state has increasingly internalized the security doctrines and military guidelines of Washington (Lennox 2007; Sloan 2010). Since 9/11 in particular, the Canadian state has reorganized the foreign policy apparatus around a strategy of 'disciplinary militarism.' This strategy combines the military objectives of the US empire with the neoliberal agenda of Canadian capital, and has been codified across the foreign policy and national security doctrines of both Liberal and Conservative governments. This dual-track strategy of 'cooperative specialization' with US imperialism and 'disciplinary militarism' towards the Third World has been shaped and guided by a new domestic power structure, or 'historic bloc,' which includes the most internationalized fractions of Canadian capital, as well as the defence lobby, the private media, and the dominant parties in Ottawa.[13] This new bloc exerts a hegemonic influence over Canadian foreign policy, and is broadly unified around a strategy of domestic neoliberalism, continental integration, and global military force projection against any perceived threats to capital.

Viewed in this light Canada's war in Afghanistan assumes new meaning. The war is not simply an intervention in a foreign country called forth by external issues of 'global security,' as liberal and realist frameworks tend to view the conflict. More important, the war is linked to the structural dynamics of capital accumulation and class formation through which the Canadian state and corporate elite gain leverage in the world market and nation-state system. The war has been a central strategy of these actors to position the Canadian state as a leading force in the new imperialism. More specifically it has been a catalyst for deepening the modes of 'cooperation specialization' with US foreign policy objectives and for rearming the military for counterinsurgency and 'shock and awe' deployments. The war has also been a vital testing ground for Canada's new technologies of warfare and for the '3D' or 'whole-of-government' strategy by which economic, military, and diplomatic objectives are fused on the battlefield. In addition, the war has supported the military-industrial complex at home and opened up new avenues for direct investment in Central Asia and the Middle East by Canadian multinational corporations. As a catalyst for all of these changes, the war has brought to the fore a new power bloc in charge of Canadian foreign policy – a new network of corporate, state, military, intellectual, and civil society actors who profit from or direct Canada's new international policies (Staples 2007; Klassen and Carroll 2011).

In developing such arguments this book presents a critical theory of Canadian foreign policy in Afghanistan. While each chapter offers a unique perspective on the conflict, the anthology as a whole attempts to theorize the war in relation to the political economy of Canadian capitalism and the class agency of those who command the higher reaches of the market and state. Understood as a ruling class strategy, the war is linked directly to the US-NATO project of reasserting primacy across the world system and to the class-conscious efforts of the Canadian state to align itself as a secondary ally to empire.

With this theory of the conflict it becomes transparent why Canada's war has not achieved the stated goals of democratization, peace, and development. In fact it is precisely because of the calculations outlined above that Canada's war has been associated with the corruption and sectarianism of the Bonn Process, with the warlords and drug traffickers of Kandahar, with the militarization of aid and development funds, with the detention and torture of political prisoners, and with the building of a national security state at home, linked to global, continental, and national forms of capital accumulation. These interlocking features of the mission have little to do with 'mistakes' or 'errors' in the tactical balance of operations and everything to do with the *bona fide* imperialism of the war and occupation. In the words of Canada's Senate Standing Committee on National Security and Defence (Canada 2007, 9), '[t]hings may be improving in some parts of [Afghanistan], but where Canada is trying to have its biggest impact – in Kandahar – life is clearly *more perilous because we are there.*'

One conclusion of this study, then, is that there is little correspondence between the discourse and the practice of Canadian foreign policy in Afghanistan. For strategic calculations, Canada is supporting a structure of political, economic, military, and tribal power in Afghanistan that runs against the discourse of democracy, development, and self-determination. More precisely Canada is waging war to expand western hegemony across Eurasia and the wider world system, to elevate Canada's political, economic, and military rank within that system, and to expand the interests of Canadian capital on national, regional, and global scales. Because the war is motivated by such concerns of empire, the Canadian public has reason to question the official rationales for extending and remodulating the mission, whether through (top-down) aid and development projects or training Afghan security forces. As a direct contributor to the Afghan crisis, Canada should withdraw its military and foreign policy agencies, and dedicate any future efforts to peacemaking, reparations, and reconstruction through the UN system and global civil society. Only in these ways will Canada's discourse for Afghanistan find a practice in reality. It is the hope of this book that Canadians will act upon such findings to reverse course in Afghanistan and to build a new foreign policy, one that offers peace, justice, and equality instead of war, empire, and occupation.

NOTES

1 In Afghanistan, the 'Northern Alliance' is known as the United Islamic Front for the Salvation of Afghanistan.

2 According to the *New York Times*, the US 'surge' campaign in Kandahar (in fall 2010) deliberately destroyed hundreds of homes and farms (Shah and Norland 2010). According to the Red Cross, the US surge in August and September 2010 contributed to record civilian casualties and war-wounded patients (*Reuters* 2010).

3 See UNAMA (2011a); see also *Guardian* (2010). The UN statistics on civilian casualties surely underestimate the overall numbers and the responsibility of coalition forces. For example, the 'war logs' published by Wikileaks in July 2010 revealed nearly 150 incidents between January 2004 and December 2009 in which coalition forces killed or injured Afghan civilians, most of which were never reported.

4 Although the US Department of Defense claims that overall insurgent attacks in 2011 were slightly lower than in the previous year, the US Senate and House Intelligence Committees assessed the Taliban as stronger in spring 2012 than before the Obama surge (see Reuters 2012).

5 In 2003–4, Canada played an important role in mobilizing NATO for expansion across Afghanistan (Odell 2003, 2). In 2004, Canadian forces constituted approximately 40 per cent of ISAF troops in Afghanistan; hence the effort to achieve greater commitments from NATO members. In the process, Canada tried to boost its waning influence in NATO (Nunez 2004, 92, fn 47).

6 See Zia-Zarifi (2004, 7); Blanchfield and Mayeda (2007); *CTV* (2007); Taylor (2007); Johnson and Leslie (2008, 68); Saunders (2008); Smith (2008, 2011); Engler (2009, 145–6); Hutchinson (2009); and Rennie (2009).

7 See, for example, Ormiston (2011). Before the US 'surge,' Kandahar province was largely under Taliban control, and Canadian forces had been forced to withdraw from several key outposts, concentrating instead on a few 'model villages' and districts. By spring 2011, the scorched-earth tactics of the US surge seemed to have disrupted Taliban command and control networks and weakened their hold on certain areas such as Arghandab. Several Taliban commanders were killed and many foot soldiers were forced to flee to Pakistan. However, the surge has not achieved any significant political gains, and the Taliban still operates in the Panjwayi-Zheray-Maiwand region. With the escalation of violence across the country, and a massive prison break in April 2011, a summer 'countersurge' by the Taliban occurred. As part of the US surge, Canada largely ceased operations in Kandahar City, Arghandab, and Zheray, and confined itself to small

areas in Dand and Panjwayi. Perkel (2011a,b) estimates that one lasting accomplishment of the Canadian mission may be a fifteen-kilometre road built in Panjwayi – for which Canada paid roughly $1 million to farmers in compensation for the destruction of their fields. The Canadian mission in Kandahar is also leaving in charge a drug-trafficking warlord, Brigadier General Abdul Razick (see Aikens 2009; Smith 2011). See my Chapter 5, in this volume, for a critical review of the violence of the American surge.

 8 A December 2010 Angus Reid poll (2010a) shows that a strong majority (56%) opposes the current mission in Kandahar and that a strong plurality (45%) believes that Canada made a mistake in sending troops to Afghanistan in the first place. Although a plurality (48%) supports the planned redeployment to Kabul in 2011, 44 per cent disagree with this course of action. For this reason, the Afghan policy of the Conservative government and Liberal opposition will continue to lack legitimacy among the majority of Canadians.

 9 Retired US Army general Wesley Clark (2003, 130) has revealed that, within a few weeks of 9/11, the Pentagon and the Bush administration had drawn up plans for regime change in eight countries: Afghanistan, Iraq, Syria, Iran, Sudan, Somalia, Lebanon, and Libya.

10 The neoconservative and liberal defence of the war in 2001 rested, in part, on an assertion that there was no recourse to diplomacy or international law at the time. However, the United States refused three offers of negotiation from the Taliban: on 19 September and again on 30 September to extradite bin Laden if evidence of guilt was offered, and on 5 October to present bin Laden for trial in a neutral country if evidence was forthcoming (Mandel 2004, chap. 2; Warnock 2008, 18–19). The Bush administration rejected or ignored these offers and planned the war in Afghanistan as a trial run for regime change in Iraq, Syria, and Iran, and to reassert US power globally (Woodward 2002).

11 It is often claimed that the UN sanctioned the war by way of UN Security Council Resolutions 1368 (12 September 2001) and 1373 (28 September 2001). However, the first recognized the inherent right of states to self-defence but did not authorize a war against Afghanistan, let alone regime change, while the second called upon the international community to act against states, organizations, and institutions that support terrorism, but did not authorize any specific act of war against Afghanistan. As such, the war violated the UN Charter and standard international law, and thus stands as a war crime of 'supreme' magnitude (Mandel 2004, 5–6, chap. 2).

12 At the same time, Semple (2009) lacks any analysis of the political economy of western imperialism, is entirely apologetic of the US-NATO

war and occupation, and is especially uncritical of the Northern Alliance commanders, who were brought to power by the war he supported, against the wishes of the vast majority of Afghans (see Smith 2011). *Contra* Semple, the international peace movement argued that impunity for warlords in Afghanistan would lead only to escalating human rights abuses.

13 The concept of 'historic bloc' is derived from the Gramscian tradition of international relations theory or international political economy. According to Stephen Gill (2002, 58), '[a]n historical bloc refers to an historical congruence between material forces, institutions and ideologies, or broadly, an alliance of different class forces politically organized around a set of hegemonic ideas that gave strategic direction and coherence to its constituent elements. Moreover, for a new historical bloc to emerge, its leaders must engage in conscious planned struggle. Any new historical bloc must have not only power within the civil society and economy, it also needs persuasive ideas, arguments and initiatives that build on, catalyze and develop its political networks and organization.'

References

Afghanistan NGO Safety Office. 2011. *ANSO Quarterly Data Report: January 1–March 31*. Kabul: Afghanistan NGO Safety Office.

Afghanistan Rights Monitor. 2010. *ARM Mid-Year Report: Civilian Casualties of Conflict, January–June 2010*. Kabul: Afghanistan Rights Monitor.

Afghanistan Study Group. 2010. *A New Way Forward: Rethinking U.S. Strategy in Afghanistan*. http://www.afghanistanstudygroup.org/.

Aikens, Matthieu. 2009. 'The Master of Spin Boldak: Undercover with Afghanistan's Drug-Trafficking Border Police.' *Harper's Magazine* (December).

Ali, Tariq. 2003. *The Clash of Fundamentalisms: Crusades, Jihads and Modernity*. London: Verso.

–. 2008. 'Afghanistan: Mirage of the Good War.' *New Left Review* 50 (March-April): 5–22.

Andersson, Hilary. 2010. 'Afghans "abused at secret prison" at Bagram airbase.' *BBC News*, 15 April. http://news.bbc.co.uk/2/hi/8621973.stm.

Angus Reid. 2010a. 'Canadians divided on assuming non-combat role in Afghanistan.' 13 December.

–. 2010b. 'Three-in-Five Canadians oppose Afghan mission.' 20 June.

Ashley, Richard K. 1984. 'The Poverty of Neorealism.' *International Organization* 38, no. 2: 225–86.

Associated Press. 2010. 'Army: US soldiers plotted to kill Afghan civilians.'
    27 August.

–. 2011. 'Violent incidents up 39 percent in Afghanistan.' 28 September.

Bacevich, Andrew J. 2002. *American Empire: The Realities and Consequences of
    U.S. Diplomacy.* Cambridge, MA: Harvard University Press.

Banerjee, Nipa. 2009. 'Afghanistan: No Security, No Development.' *Policy Op-
    tions / Options Politiques* (November): 66–71.

Beier, J. Marshall, and Lana Wylie, eds. 2009. *Canadian Foreign Policy in Critical
    Perspective.* Oxford: Oxford University Press.

Berthiaume, Lee. 2012a. 'Canadian training mission meant to free up U.S. sol-
    diers for Afghan combat: documents.' *Postmedia News*, 14 March.

–. 2012b. 'Final tally says 2,000 Canadians wounded in Afghanistan.' *Postmedia
    News*, 2 February.

Blanchfield, Mike, and Andrew Mayeda. 2007. '1.1 million dollar contract of
    Canadian military with a company of infamous warlord.' *Ottawa Citizen*,
    19 November.

Brown, Stephen. 2008. 'CIDA under the Gun.' In *Canada Among Nations: What
    Room for Manoeuvre?*, ed. Jean Daudelin and Daniel Schwanen. Montreal;
    Kingston, ON: McGill-Queen's University Press.

Brzezinski, Zbigniew. 1997a. 'A Geostrategy for Eurasia.' *Foreign Affairs* 76,
    no. 5: 50–64.

–. 1997b. *The Grand Chessboard: American Primacy and its Geostrategic Impera-
    tives.* New York: Basic Books.

–. 2009. 'An Agenda for NATO: Toward a Global Security Web.' *Foreign
    Affairs* 88, no. 5: 2–20. http://www.foreignaffairs.com/articles/65240/
    zbigniew-brzezinski/an-agenda-for-nato.

Burch, Jonathan. 2010. 'Red Cross says Afghan conditions worst in 30 years.'
    Reuters, 15 December.

Burnham, Peter. 1994. 'Open Marxism and Vulgar International Political Econ-
    omy.' *Review of International Political Economy* 1, no. 2: 221–31.

Byers, Michael, and Stewart Webb. 2011. 'Training Can Be Dangerous:
    A Realistic Assessment of the Proposed Canadian Mission to Train
    Afghan National Security Forces.' Ottawa: Canadian Centre for Policy
    Alternatives.

Canada. 2007. Parliament. Senate. Standing Committee on National Security
    and Defence. *Canadian Troops in Afghanistan: Taking a Hard Look at a Hard
    Mission (An Interim Report).* Ottawa.

Canadian Peace Alliance. 2007. 'Bring the Troops Home Now: Why a Military
    Mission Will Not Bring Peace to Afghanistan.' Toronto: Canadian Peace
    Alliance.

Canadian Press. 2008. 'Assessing Afghan security no easy task for troops.'
26 October.

Carroll, William K. 1986. *Corporate Power and Canadian Capitalism.* Vancouver:
University of British Columbia Press.

Carty, Robert, and Virginia Smith. 1981. *Perpetuating Poverty: The Political Economy of Canadian Foreign Aid.* Toronto: Between the Lines.

CBC News. 2005. 'Helping Afghanistan will protect Canada, says top soldier.'
15 July.

–. 2007. ' "Death to Canada," some protestors chant.' 26 September.

–. 2008. 'Sophistication of deadly Taliban attack concerning: Natynczyck.'
4 September.

–. 2009. 'Crowds blame Canadians for deaths of 2 children in Afghanistan.'
23 February.

Clark, Wesley. 2003. *Winning Modern Wars: Iraq, Terrorism and the American Empire.* New York: Public Affairs.

Clarke, Robert, and Richard Swift, eds. *Ties that Bind: Canada and the Third
World.* Toronto: Between the Lines. 1982.

Clement, Wallace, ed. 1997. *Understanding Canada: Building on the New Canadian Political Economy.* Montreal; Kingston, ON: McGill-Queen's University
Press.

Cohn, Marjorie. 2005. 'United States Violations of International Law in Yugoslavia, Afghanistan, and Iraq.' In *Challenges of Multi-Level Constitutionalism,*
ed. J. Nergelius, P. Policastro, and K. Urata. Chicago: Polpress.

Cordesman, Anthony. 2009. 'Afghan Public Opinion and the Afghan War:
Shifts by Region and Province.' Washington, DC: Center for Strategic &
International Studies, 10 April.

Cornish, Stephen. 2007. 'No Room for Humanitarianism in 3D Policies: Have
Forcible Humanitarian Interventions and Integrated Approaches Lost Their
Way?' *Journal of Military and Strategic Studies* 10, no. 1.

Cox, Robert W. 1981. 'Social Forces, States and World Orders: Beyond International Relations Theory.' *Journal of International Studies, Millennium* 10, no. 2:
126–55.

CTV. 2007. 'Taliban preparing for attack on Afghan warlord.' 16 September.

de Hoop Scheffer, Jaap. 2007. Keynote Address to the Euro-Atlantic Security
Forum, Ohrid, Macedonia, 29 June.

Deutsche Presse-Agentur. 2011. 'Afghan officials estimate up to 35,000 insurgents active.' 9 February.

–. 2012. 'Drought hits Afghanistan's malnourished children.' 16 February.

Dorronsoro, Gilles. 2010. *Afghanistan at the Breaking Point.* Washington, DC:
Carnegie Endowment for International Peace.

Duffy, Helen. 2005. *The 'War on Terror' and the Framework of International Law.*
    Cambridge: Cambridge University Press.

EKOS Research Associates. 2009. 'Decisive opposition to Canada's Afghan
    mission.' 16 July.

Engler, Yves. 2009. *The Black Book of Canadian Foreign Policy.* Halifax, NS:
    Fernwood.

Farmer, Ben. 2011. 'US-funded Afghan militias "beat, rob and kill with impu-
    nity."' *Telegraph* (UK), 13 July.

Forsberg, Carl. 2010. *Politics and Power in Kandahar.* Washington, DC: Institute
    for the Study of War.

Gill, Stephen. 2002. *Power and Resistance in the New World Order.* New York:
    Palgrave-Macmillan.

Glevum Associates. 2010. *Kandahar Province Survey Report: March 2010.* Burl-
    ington, MA.

Gopal, Anand. 2010. *The Battle for Afghanistan: Militancy and Conflict in Kanda-
    har.* Washington, DC: New America Foundation.

Gowan, Peter. 1999. *The Global Gamble: Washington's Faustian Bid for Global
    Dominance.* London: Verso.

Grinspun, Ricardo, and Yasmine Shamsie, eds. 2007. *Whose Canada? Continen-
    tal Integration, Fortress North America, and the Corporate Agenda.* Montreal;
    Kingston, ON: McGill-Queen's University Press.

Guardian. 2010. 'Afghanistan civilian casualties: year by year, month by
    month.' 10 August. http://www.guardian.co.uk/news/datablog/2010/
    aug/10/afghanistan-civilian-casualties-statistics#data.

Harvey, David. 2003. *The New Imperialism.* Oxford: Oxford University
    Press.

Hubble, Jonathan. 2008. 'The Unexpected War: Canada in Kandahar.' Book
    review. *Canadian Army Journal* 11, no. 1: 135–7.

Human Rights Watch. 2011. ' "Just Don't Call It a Militia": Impunity, Militias,
    and the "Afghan Local Police." ' New York: Human Rights Watch.

Hutchinson, Brian. 2009. 'Afghanistan's election gets rough, and it hasn't even
    started.' *CanWest News Service,* 26 May.

ICSD (International Council on Security and Development). 2010. *Afghanistan:
    The Relationship Gap.* Kabul: ICSD.

–. 2011. *Afghanistan Transition: The Death of Bin Laden and Local Dynamics.*
    Kabul: ICSD.

Ignatieff, Michael. 2003. *Empire Lite: Nation-Building in Bosnia, Kosovo and Af-
    ghanistan.* Toronto: Penguin.

Ilyenkov, Evald. 1982 [1960]. *Dialectics of the Abstract and the Concrete in Marx's
    Capital.* Moscow: Progress Publishers.

International Crisis Group. 2012. 'Talking about Talks: Toward a Political Settlement in Afghanistan.' Asia Report 221. Kabul; Brussels. 26 March. Executive Summary. http://www.crisisgroup.org/en/regions/asia/south-asia/afghanistan/221-talking-about-talks-toward-a-political-settlement-in-afghanistan.aspx.

Johnson, Chris, and Jolyon Leslie. 2008. *Afghanistan: The Mirage of Peace.* London: Zed Books.

Joya, Malalai. 2009. *A Woman Among Warlords: The Extraordinary Story of an Afghan Who Dared to Raise her Voice.* New York: Simon & Schuster.

Judson, Fred. 2003. 'For an Eclectic and Critical Political Economy Perspective on Canadian Foreign Economic Policy.' *Studies in Political Economy* 71/72 (Autumn-Winter): 109–32.

Klassen, Jerome. 2009a. 'Canada and the New Imperialism: The Economics of a Secondary Power.' *Studies in Political Economy* 83 (Spring): 163–90.

–. 2009b. 'Social Science and the Afghan War: Canadian Perspectives.' *Socialist Studies* 5, no. 2: 123–32.

Klassen, Jerome, and William K. Carroll. 2011. 'Transnational Class Formation? Globalization and the Canadian Corporate Network.' *Journal of World-Systems Research* 17, no. 2: 379–402.

Klein, Naomi. 2007. *The Shock Doctrine: The Rise of Disaster Capitalism.* New York: Henry Holt.

Landler, Mark. 2012. 'On surprise trip to Kabul, Obama signs Afghan pact.' *New York Times*, 1 May.

Lennox, Patrick. 2007. 'From Golden Straitjacket to Kevlar Vest: Canada's Transformation to a Security State.' *Canadian Journal of Political Science* 40, no. 4: 1017–38.

Lieven, Anatol. 2011. 'A Mutiny Grows in Punjab.' *National Interest* 112: 15–23.

Lindley-French, Julian. 2005. 'Big World, Big Future, Big NATO.' *NATO Review* 4 (Spring). http://www.nato.int/docu/review/2005/issue4/english/opinion.html.

Mallaby, Sebastian. 2002. 'The Reluctant Imperialist: Terrorism, Failed States and the Case for American Empire.' *Foreign Affairs* 81, no. 2: 2–7.

Maloney, Sean M. 2004. 'Afghanistan: From Here to Eternity?' *Parameters* 34, no. 1: 4–15.

Mandel, Ernest. 1975. *Late Capitalism.* London: Verso.

Mandel, Michael. 2004. *How America Gets Away with Murder: Illegal Wars, Collateral Damage and Crimes against Humanity.* London: Pluto Press.

Manley, John, et al. 2008. *Independent Panel on Canada's Future Role in Afghanistan.* Ottawa: Government of Canada.

McGreal, Chris. 2010. 'US soldiers "killed Afghan civilians for sport and collected fingers as trophies."' *Guardian*, 9 September.

Mearsheimer, John J. 2010. 'Imperial by Design.' *National Interest* 111: 16–34.

Moens, Alexander. 2008. 'Afghanistan and the Revolution in Canadian Foreign Policy.' *International Journal* 63, no. 3: 569–86.

Mohamedou, Mohammad Mahmoud. 2006. *Understanding Al Qaeda: The Transformation of War*. Ann Arbor: University of Michigan Press.

Neufeld, Mark. 1995. 'Hegemony and Foreign Policy Analysis: The Case of Canada as a Middle Power.' *Studies in Political Economy* 48 (Autumn): 7–29.

Nordland, Rod. 2011. 'Talks on U.S. presence in Afghanistan after pullout unnerve region.' *New York Times*, 18 April.

Nunez, Joseph R. 2004. 'Canada's Global Role: A Strategic Assessment of its Military Power.' *Parameters* 34, no. 3: 75–93.

Mark Odell. 2003. 'Canada calls for greater commitment from NATO countries to mission in Afghanistan.' *Financial Times*, 4 December, 2.

Ollman, Bertell. 1993. *Dialectical Investigations*. New York: Routledge.

Ormiston, Susan. 2011. 'End of mission: Canada leaves much unchanged in Kandahar.' *CBC News*, 17 May.

Panitch, Leo, ed. 1977. *The Canadian State: Political Economy and Political Power*. Toronto: University of Toronto Press.

Panitch, Leo, and Sam Gindin. 2004. *Global Capitalism and American Empire*. London: Merlin Press.

Pape, Robert A. 2005. *Dying the Win: The Strategic Logic of Suicide Terrorism*. New York: Random House.

Perkel, Colin. 2011a. 'Panjwaii road dubbed "dagger" in insurgency heart: A lasting Canadian legacy?' *Canadian Press*, 1 May.

–. 2011b. 'Pride and regret for Canadian troops leaving Afghanistan as mission winds up.' *Canadian Press*, 15 May.

Poulantzas, Nicos. 1978a. *Classes in Contemporary Capitalism*. London: Verso.

–. 1978b. *Political Power and Social Classes*. London: Verso.

Pratt, Cranford. 1983. 'Dominant Class Theory and Canadian Foreign Policy: The Case of the Counter-Consensus.' *International Journal* 39, no. 1: 99–135.

–. 1984. 'Canadian Policy towards the Third World: Basis for an Explanation.' *Studies in Political Economy* 13 (Spring): 27–55.

Rashid, Ahmed. 2008. *Descent into Chaos: The United States and the Failure of Nation Building in Pakistan, Afghanistan, and Central Asia*. London: Penguin.

Razack, Sherene H. 2008. *Casting Out: The Eviction of Muslims from Western Law and Politics*. Toronto: University of Toronto Press.

Rennie, Steve. 2009. 'Afghan Canadian to be new Governor of Kandahar.' *Canadian Press*, 29 April.

Reuters. 2010. 'War casualties soar in south Afghanistan – Red Cross.'
    12 October.

–. 2012. 'Taliban stronger than before U.S. troop surge: lawmakers.' 6 May.

Ruttig, Thomas. 2010a. 'The General in his Labyrinth.' Afghanistan Analysts
    Network, 23 June. http://aan-afghanistan.com/index.asp?id=845.

–. 2010b. 'How tribal are the Taleban? Afghanistan's largest insurgent move-
    ment between its tribal roots and Islamist ideology.' Afghanistan Analysts
    Network, June.

–. 2011a. 'Dad Noorani, critic of warlordism, passed away.' Afghanistan Ana-
    lysts Network. http://aan-afghanistan.com/index.asp?id=1930.

–. 2011b. Negotiations with the Taliban: History and Prospects for the Future. Wash-
    ington, DC: New America Foundation.

Saunders, Doug. 2008. 'Corruption eats away at Afghan government.' Globe
    and Mail, 3 May.

Semple, Michael. 2009. Reconciliation in Afghanistan. Washington, DC: United
    States Institute of Peace Press.

Shah, Taimoor, and Rod Norland. 2010. 'NATO is razing booby-trapped Af-
    ghan homes.' New York Times, 16 November.

Sloan, Elinor. 2010. Security and Defence in the Terrorist Era: Canada and the
    United States Homeland. Montreal; Kingston, ON: McGill-Queen's University
    Press.

Smith, Graeme. 2008. 'Troops' goals appear more distant.' Global and Mail,
    5 December.

–. 2011. 'Wedded to the warlords: NATO's unholy Afghan alliance.' Globe and
    Mail, 4 June.

Staples, Steven. 2007. 'Fortress North America: The Drive towards Military
    and Security Integration and Its Impact on Canadian Democratic Sover-
    eignty.' In Whose Canada? Continental Integration, Fortress North America, and
    the Corporate Agenda, ed. Ricardo Grinspun and Yasmin Shamsie. Montreal;
    Kingston, ON: McGill-Queen's University Press.

Stein, Janice Gross, and Eugene Lang. 2007. Unexpected War: Canada in Kanda-
    har. Toronto: Viking Canada.

Swift, Jamie, and Brian Tomlinson, eds. 1997. Conflicts of Interest: Canada and
    the Third World. Toronto: Between the Lines.

Tandon, Shaun. 2011. 'Clinton warns against hasty Afghan withdrawal.'
    Agence France-Presse, 14 April.

Taylor, Rob. 2010. 'NATO denies Taliban ascendant as Afghan toll mounts.'
    Reuters, 11 June.

Taylor, Scott. 2007. 'The warlords return to Kandahar.' Esprit de Corps,
    8 February.

Thier, J. Alexander. 2010. 'Afghanistan's Rocky Path to Peace.' *Current History* (April): 131–7.

UNAMA (United Nations Assistance Mission in Afghanistan). 2011a. *Afghanistan: Annual Report 2010, Protection of Civilians in Armed Conflict.* Kabul: UNAMA.

–. 2011b. *Treatment of Conflict Related Detainees in Afghan Custody.* Kabul: United Nations Office of the High Commissioner for Human Rights.

United Nations. 2011. *To Stay and Deliver: Good Practice for Humanitarians in Complex Security Environments.* New York: United Nations Office for the Coordination of Humanitarian Affairs.

United Nations High Commissioner for Refugees. 2011. *2011 UNHCR Country Operations Profile – Afghanistan.* http://www.unhcr.org/cgi-bin/texis/vtx/page?page=49e486eb6.

United States. 2004. Department of Defense. *Report of the Defense Science Board Task Force on Strategic Communication.* Washington, DC: Department of Defense.

–. 2010. Department of Defense. *Report on Progress toward Security and Stability in Afghanistan.* November. Washington, DC: Department of Defense.

Warnock, John W. 2008. *Creating a Failed State: The US and Canada in Afghanistan.* Halifax, NS: Fernwood.

Williamson, Myra. 2009. *Terrorism, War, and International Law: The Legality of the Use of Force against Afghanistan in 2001.* Burlington, VT: Ashgate.

Wood, Ellen Meiksins. 1995. *Democracy against Capitalism: Renewing Historical Materialism.* Princeton, NJ: Princeton University Press.

–. 2005. *Empire of Capital.* London: Verso.

Woodward, Bob. 2002. *Bush at War.* New York: Simon & Schuster.

–. 2010. *Obama's Wars.* New York: Simon & Schuster.

World Health Organization. 2011. *Country Cooperation Strategy at a Glance: The Islamic Republic of Afghanistan.* Geneva. May.

Zia-Zarifi, Sam. 2004. *Losing the Peace in Afghanistan.* New York: Human Rights Watch.

PART I

Afghanistan, Empire, and the 'War on Terror'

2

Afghanistan and Empire

JOHN W. WARNOCK

Afghanistan is an unlikely country. A stretch of land that sits between the Middle East, Central Asia, South Asia, and China, it has been invaded by imperial powers for more than two thousand years and incorporated into empires based in Persia, India, and, to the north of the Hindu Kush, by Uzbeks. The term 'Afghan' was originally another name for the Pashtun people. There are two branches of Pashtun, the Durrani confederation and the Ghilzai confederation, which have always been in competition for political leadership and influence.

Historians cite 1747 as the beginning of the Afghan territorial state. In that year, Ahmad Shah and his army broke with the Persian emperor Nadir Shah Afshar. Back in Kandahar, tribal leaders called a *loya jirga* (grand council), which declared independence from Persia, chose Ahmad Shah as their new king, and proclaimed the Durrani confederation. Ahmed Shah was an aggressive military commander and leader, first seizing Kabul and Ghazni, then moving south and taking much of India. After seizing Herat from Persia, he moved north of the Hindu Kush and occupied the territory up to the Amu Darya (Oxus) River. At this time, an agreement with the Uzbek Emir of Bukhara established the Amu Darya as the northern territorial border.

But Afghanistan at this time was hardly anything approaching a modern territorial state; it was, at best, a loose confederation of Pashtun tribes whose primary activities were expansion, conquest, and the extraction of tribute. Ahmed Shah died in 1772 and was replaced by his son Timur. The capital was moved from Kandahar to Kabul. With many sons competing for power and influence, the Afghan empire entered a period known as the 'time of trouble,' and the outlying districts – north of the Hindu Kush and much of the south – broke away to become part of what is now India. The dust settled in 1826 when Dost Mohammed Khan, a Barakzai Durrani, became king.

Empire and Social Structure

Like those of almost all of today's less-developed countries, Afghanistan's territorial boundaries were set by European imperial powers. Competition between the expanding Russian Empire to the north and the British Empire, which controlled India to the south – the 'Great Game' of the nineteenth century – led to the creation of Afghanistan as a buffer state. Beginning in 1873 a series of Joint Boundary Commissions set the country's territorial limits: in 1885 the Amu Darya was confirmed once again as the northern boundary, in 1893 the British established the Durand Line between Afghanistan and British India, and in 1896 the two imperial powers created the Wakhan Corridor, in the Pamir Mountains in the northeast up to the border of China. The result of the Great Game was a territorial state consisting of Hazaras, Turkmen, Uzbeks, Tajiks, Aymacs, Baluchi, Nuristani, and Pashai peoples. To all of this boundary setting King Abdur Rahman Khan and the Afghan people were mere bystanders. Thereafter, political leaders in Afghanistan did their best to play off the Russians against the British, seeking to create an independent, non-aligned country. It was not until after World War One that Afghanistan won full independence and was admitted to the League of Nations.

Between 45 and 50 per cent of Afghanistan's population is Pashtun, but half of all the Pashtun people actually live on the other side of the Durand Line, in present-day Pakistan. There are two major languages: Pashto, spoken by the Durrani tribes, and Dari, a variation of Persian spoken by most of the population in the northern part of the country. By 870 AD Islam had been imposed on Afghanistan; currently, 90 per cent of Afghans are Sunni and the remainder are Shia (Dupree 1980; Rasanayagam 2003; Meyer 2004; Saikal 2004). The large majority of the population is engaged in agriculture and herding. At the local level, the historic tribal system is deeply entrenched, with kinship and family ties paramount. The social structure is strongly patriarchal, with patrilocal residency and property ownership by patrilineal descent, and is reenforced by Sharia law (Tapper 1991; Emadi 2005; Khan 2006; AIHRC 2008). Throughout the country, the system of patrimony is linked to family honour, or *namus*. Part of this tradition is *purdah*, the isolation of women, and *chadri*, the veiling of women. Thus, even today, it is normal in Afghanistan that women are secluded in the household and can be seen only by the males in the family. When women go out of the household, they are expected be veiled and to do so only when accompanied by a male member of their own family. This practice, known as *maharam*, was included in the moral code drafted by the Afghan legislature in 2008. Marriages normally are arranged, and the *haq mehr*, or bride price – the sum that a man is required to pay in order to obtain permission to marry a woman – is usually a part of the marriage arrangement. Child marriages are common; even today, 60 per cent of marriages involve girls under the age of sixteen. Wealthy men normally have more than one wife and may also have concubines.

Constructing a Modern State

Once the territorial boundaries had been set and Afghanistan had been recognized as an independent state, its kings began a drive for modernization. Abdur Rahman Khan, who ruled from 1880 until 1901, used military force to try to establish a central authority above the feudal and tribal system. He appointed a national *loya jirga* as an advisory group, and emphasized building a national army and central administration. Like many rulers who followed, he used state repression to deal with his political enemies, and did not hesitate to use force against the conservative religious leaders who opposed his political course.

After the First World War Afghan kings and political leaders were most impressed with the modernization program that Mustafa Kemal Ataturk was undertaking in Turkey. They were also greatly influenced by Mahmud Beg Tarzi, who, after a period of exile in Syria, returned to Afghanistan in 1901 and became the chief adviser to King Habibullah. A strong opponent of European imperialism and a supporter of Ataturk's modernization, Tarzi also was very critical of the conservative Muslim religious leadership.

King Amanullah (ruled 1919 to 1929) pushed for a range of political, economic, and religious reforms, all based on the Turkish experiment, and began to establish a modern representative government, a constitutional monarchy, and a national army. Foreign advisers were used to begin a system of public education. A treaty of non-aggression and neutrality was signed with the Soviet Union. Following the Turkish model, the constitution of 1923 was based on constitutional law, secular laws, and the separation of religion and state. The modernization process included a change in the feudal system of land ownership; in the

1920s, only 20 per cent of agricultural land was owned by peasants. To encourage the development of the private ownership of land, Amanullah sold off crown land to peasants at a very low price and introduced a system of monetized land taxes, thus undermining tribal and religious ownership of large land tracts.

After a trip to Turkey and Europe, Amanullah returned determined to break the system of subjugation of women. A secular system of education was promoted, co-education was introduced, and, for the first time, education was also extended to nomads. As well, women were no longer required to wear the veil, and laws were promulgated giving women free choice in marriage and an equal right to family property. Conservative religious forces, however, opposed these modernization policies, and in this they were supported by the British government. In 1924 a revolt, led by mullahs, broke out in Khost, and in 1928 a major revolt began in Jalalabad, which was joined by an uprising of Tajiks in the North, forcing Amanullah into exile in Italy (Dupree 1980, 449–50; Saikal 2004, 58–84).

In 1929 Mohammad Nadir Shah became king and abolished the reforms that had been designed to begin the liberation of women. A relatively weak army and central government meant that power shifted back to conservative religious and tribal leaders. In 1931 a new constitution established a National Council and Parliament, but it also declared Afghanistan to be an Islamic country and proclaimed Hanafi Sharia law.

Nadir Shah was assassinated in 1933, and his son, Mohammad Zahir Shah, reigned as king until 1973 (Dupree 1980, 417–76; Rasanayagam 2003, 22–5; Saikal 2004, 17–92).

The Road to Liberal Democracy

When Zahir Shah assumed the throne in 1933, he was nineteen. Thus, for many years, the Afghan government was dominated by his father's brothers. A strategy of independence and non-alignment was developed, and economic aid was sought from Germany, Japan, and Italy, but not from the Soviet Union or Britain. In 1940 Afghanistan proclaimed its neutrality; the country thus remained out of the Second World War.

A major issue for Afghans has always been their relationship with the Pashtuns who had been alienated from their nation by the British-imposed Durand Line. In 1901, on the Indian side of the line, the British had created the Northwest Frontier Province and five Tribal Agencies

(Malakand, Khyber, Kurram, North Waziristan, and South Waziristan). These areas maintained considerable independence from British rule in Delhi, but the British also denied these Pashtuns the right to develop a constitutional form of government, which was granted to the rest of India.

After the end of the Second World War, when the British government decided it had to give India independence, the issue of the relationship between Pashtuns on both sides of the border became paramount. In the elections in India in 1946 and the referendum on the partition of the colony into India and Pakistan, the Pashtun peoples were refused the option of joining Afghanistan, and most boycotted the referendum. The British then called a *loya jirga* of the five Tribal Agencies, but again presented them only with the option of joining India or Pakistan. These tribal leaders opted for Pakistan, the Muslim state. As a political concession, the new government of Pakistan granted virtual autonomy to the tribal areas. Conflict over the Pashtun areas, however, has remained a key issue for both Afghanistan and Pakistan. Since the latter, which received increased aid and political support from the United States, strongly opposed the reunification of the Pashtun nation, Afghan governments turned increasingly to aid and trade with the Soviet Union (Dupree 1980, 485–94).

In 1949 Zahir Shah encouraged the development of a new 'liberal parliament,' including elections. It was a step towards responsible government. Reform-minded parliamentarians passed laws supporting freedom of the press and, as Louis Dupree notes, newspapers emerged overnight, all opposing the authoritarian nature of the monarchical regime: 'Conservative religious leaders and their supporters in government received the brunt of the attacks in the free press' (1980, 496). The educated classes, however, viewed religious fanaticism as the major barrier to Afghan progress, and political struggle led to the creation of the National Democratic Party and the Kabul University student union (Dupree 1980, 494–8; Rasanayagam 2003, 27–37).

The Impact of Daoud Khan

In September 1953 General Sardar Mohammad Daoud Khan, commander of the Central Forces, seized power with the consent of the king and the royal family and became prime minister. The Cold War was on the rise, and the US government pressed Afghanistan to join the Bagdad Pact and become a political and military ally of Pakistan.

Daoud rejected this pressure and confirmed Afghanistan to remain non-aligned. When the United States responded by cutting off foreign aid, Daoud turned to the Soviet Union for assistance. The USSR and other members of the Soviet bloc offered economic and technical aid, which greatly helped the five-year plans that were introduced by the minister of finance, General Abdul Malik, who had studied in Turkey and was very impressed with its planned economy. The United States, alarmed by this growth of Soviet influence, restored its economic assistance program, focusing particularly on education.

On the cultural front Daoud, influenced by the progress of women's rights in Turkey, became convinced that *purdah* and *chadri* (confining and veiling) were not required by Sharia law. Accordingly, when Afghan government officials went abroad, the women who accompanied them were not veiled. At the 1959 celebration of independence, the wives and daughters of the prime minister, his cabinet, and members of the royal family appeared on the viewing stand without veils. When a group of mullahs objected and began preaching against the government, Daoud had them arrested, jailed, and charged with treason and heresy. As Dupree (1980, 533) notes, '[n]ot all religious leaders accepted the voluntary abolition of the veil and other reforms, however, because each intrusion into their customary power erodes their secular influence. They oppose secular education for in the past they have controlled the educational institution; they call land reform anti-Islamic, for they own large tracts of land in the name of *waqf* (religious endowments); they oppose a constitutionally-separated Church and state, for such a move diminishes their temporal power.' The voluntary abolition of *purdah* at this time opened the opportunity of employment for Afghan women, who began to enter government and educational service.

Developing a Constitutional Democracy

In March 1963 Daoud Khan resigned. The new prime minister, Dr. Mohammad Yousuf, and the cabinet were committed to the development of modern liberal democracy, and the king announced the appointment of a commission to draft a new constitution. A national *loya jirga* was selected; some of its members were appointed but most were elected at the provincial level. There was serious debate throughout the country, and at the *loya jirga* itself there was vigorous discussion, amendments, and decisions by consensus.

The resulting new constitution, approved by the king in 1964, was a model of liberal democracy. There was to be an elected parliament of two houses. Individual rights would take precedence over tribal rights, and women were to have equal rights with men. There would be an independent, secular judiciary and, most important, secular law was to have precedence over Sharia law (Dupree 1980, 561–87; Saikal 2004, 140–9).

An election was held in 1965, but political parties, though recognized under the constitution, had not yet been legally established. Voter turnout was very low, and later the election was widely denounced as having been rigged. As Amin Saikal notes, without political parties, 'people voted according to ethnic or kinship ties and at the behest of powerful individuals, propelling the true power elite, the rural khans, begs, boyars, maliks, and mullahs, to parliamentary seats in Kabul' (2004, 149; see also Halliday 1978, 24–5). In fact, the Political Parties Bill, following the provisions of the constitution, had been passed by the parliament but the king refused to sign it into law – the royal family and the political elite were afraid that it would result immediately in the formation of left-wing and radical democratic parties.

In 1965 the legislature passed a Press Law, and many new publications appeared. The secular system of public education was expanded, and the number of students at the University of Kabul increased. Politics came to the forefront. Afghanistan was a member of the Bandung Conference of non-aligned states, which took a strong anti-imperialist and anti-colonial stance. Opposition was growing to the US war in Vietnam. Muslims around the world rallied to the cause of the Palestinians in their struggle with Israel and the United States. Throughout the Muslim world, movements were growing in support of Third World nationalism, anti-imperialism, socialism, and Marxism.

Thus it came as no surprise that the political left grew in Afghanistan, and students at the university marched in protest against the government and in support of striking workers. In October 1965 troops fired on a student demonstration, killing three and wounding many. In November and December, students at the university held general strikes demanding reforms. When the left organized a major student-led demonstration in Kabul, Yusuf resigned as prime minister and was replaced by Mohammad Hashim Maiwandwal (Dupree 1980, 648–58; Saikal 2004, 133–60).

The Formation of the People's Democratic Party of Afghanistan

While Afghan nationalists generally looked to Turkey as a model, the political left was impressed by developments in the Central Asian republics of the Soviet Union. There, women had been liberated from conservative Islamic traditions: they had been given equal rights, and polygamy, levirate, child marriage, bride price, and the seclusion of women were banned. Secular laws and courts had been established.

But educated Afghans were most impressed by the economic development that occurred after the success of the Soviet revolution. The feudal land system had been abolished. There were literacy campaigns and universal education and medicare. Furthermore, there was significant industrialization and the development of a working class. By the 1960s, there was a dramatic difference in the standard of living between Afghanistan and the Soviet republics to the north.

In January 1965 a group of young people met to form the People's Democratic Party of Afghanistan (PDPA). In April 1966 the party's publication *Khalq* (The People) reported the party's platform. It called for the development of a united national front government – an alliance of progressive forces, workers, farmers, intellectuals, and nationalists – in order to build an industrial country and an organized working class. In the 1965 elections the PDPA fielded eight candidates, though running without party affiliation, and four were elected, one of whom was Dr. Anahita Ratebzad, a prominent Marxist from Kabul.

The party, however, had its factions. One, known as *Khalq*, like the party's paper, was led by Nur Mohammed Taraki and Hafizullah Amin. They wanted to use the army and the political vanguard to seize power and implement a socialist state. This was the model Ataturk had used in Turkey. In 1970 it was estimated that this faction had around 2,500 members, which made it the largest party in Afghanistan. Its members were more likely to have a rural background and most spoke Pashto. The other faction, known as *Parcham* (The Banner), was led by Babrak Karmal. Its members were more likely to speak Dari and to include non-Pushtuns, and it was strongest in Kabul. This group was more committed to the united democratic front road to power, which put it closer to the official position of the Communist Party of the Soviet Union. It had around 1,500 members in 1970. The PDPA, moreover, had a very strong presence in the officer class of the armed forces, hundreds of whom had been trained in the Central Asian republics of the Soviet Union.

The father of the Afghan Marxists, Dr. Abdul Rahman Mahmoodi, the first editor of *Khalq*, was arrested and jailed by Daoud. His followers formed *Shula-ye Jawid* (Burning Flame), a Maoist party with a serious presence in both the small, organized working class and the Hazara community; it denounced the revisionism of the mainstream Marxists. A second Maoist faction, *Setam-e Melli* (National Oppression), headed by Taher Badakhshi, was formed in 1966. Its base of support was mainly among the Tajik peasants in northern Afghanistan and the Panjsher Valley, as well as from China. After launching a series of attacks from Pakistan, many of its members were captured and sent to Kabul, where they were murdered by Daoud (Halliday 1978, 26).

Both Louis Dupree and Amin Saikal emphasize that the development of the PDPA in Afghanistan was a local, indigenous movement – there was no link to the Comintern, and party members were not invited to events in Moscow. Indeed, the official position of the USSR was that 'Afghanistan is not ready for a socialist revolution.' The Afghan tradition of nationalism and non-alignment was a major part of their basic program (Halliday 1978, 19–26; Dupree 1980, 769–76; Rubin 2002, 90–105; Rasanayagam 2003, 47–9; Saikal 2004, 160–5).

The Rise of the Islamists

The Islamist movement began in Afghanistan around 1958 under the leadership of Dr. Gholam Mohammad Niyazi, who would become the dean of the Faculty of Theology at Kabul University. A number of professors at the faculty had studied at Al-Azhar University in Cairo, where they were close to the Muslim Brotherhood. Two of the leading professors were Burhannuddin Rabbani and Abdul Rasul Sayyaf, founding members of the Islamic Society of Afghanistan. Another prominent professor, Gulbuddin Hekmatyar of the Faculty of Engineering, founded the Islamic Party.

It is now well known that the US government, through the Central Intelligence Agency (CIA), gave assistance to the Islamists in Pakistan and Afghanistan as early as the 1950s. This was part of a world strategy of supporting 'Muslim fundamentalism' in an attempt to undermine the secular nationalist, anti-imperialist, socialist, and Marxist movements. In Afghanistan this was done through the Asia Foundation, a CIA front organization, which financed the Faculty of Theology at Kabul University and worked with student groups to oppose the Marxist student organizations. Funding increased after Daoud seized power in 1973. The Central Teachers Training School, where Hafizullah Amin was principal, received extensive economic assistance from American Friends of the Middle East, another CIA front organization (Cordovez and Harrison 1995, 17–9; Gerges 1999, 68; Prados 2002, 466–72; Dreyfuss 2005, 256–63).

Between 1965 and 1970, a group at the University of Kabul called the Organization of Muslim Youth grew in strength and engaged in physical confrontations with the modernists, particularly the Maoists. They were strongly opposed to the liberation of women, and two of the prominent Islamist professors, Rabbani and Hekmatyar, threw acid on women who were wearing western clothes. Hekmatyar also violently attacked women who exposed their face, arms, or legs. Eventually he was imprisoned for killing a Maoist student activist, but was released after serving only two years. The Islamists won the 1970s student elections, replacing the various communist organizations and sparking demonstrations by women in Kabul who opposed their violent attacks, including the shooting in the legs of women who wore stockings. As well, the All-Afghanistan Women's Council stepped up its demands for women's literacy campaigns and women's rights in general (Dupree 1980, 665; Roy 1985, 69–74; Hartman 2002, 478–80; Saikal 2004, 164–6; Jones 2006, 18–21).

Daoud and the Republican Alternative

On 17 July 1973 Muhammad Daoud seized control of the government and abolished the monarchy. The coup had the support of a large section of the *Parcham* faction of the PDPA, particularly those in the military. He proclaimed a republic, shut down the parliament, and suspended the constitution. Arguing that the parliamentary government under the king, Zahir Shah, had produced anarchy, he banned political parties, newspapers, and magazines. Members of *Parcham* were included in his cabinet, and many also joined the lower levels of the government bureaucracy, a move *Parcham* argued was fully consistent with the strategy of the united national front. Daoud, a secular nationalist, arrested and jailed many of the more radical Islamists, and repressed the Maoist organizations, arresting, imprisoning, and killing many. He also organized KHAD, the Afghan secret police, and built the infamous Pul-e-Charkhi prison.

The Islamists split at this time, with the more radical group following Hekmatyar, who wanted to begin a general uprising. Rabbani argued, in contrast, that the people were not ready for an Islamist revolt; he preferred to infiltrate the armed forces. Hekmatyar and many of the Islamists moved across the border to Peshawar, in Pakistan, where they were trained by the Pakistan army and carried out raids into Afghanistan. They also had the support of the CIA and the shah of Iran's secret police, SAVAK. In Afghanistan itself, they were in alliance with Ahmad Shah Massoud from the Polytechnic Institute and the Panjshir Valley. In July 1975 the Islamists attempted a general uprising, but found no support from the population. Daoud's subsequent repression was severe: disappearances, executions, and imprisonment. The Islamists retreated once more to Peshawar, where they were supported by Pakistan's president Zulfikar Ali Bhutto (Dupree 1980, 761–2; Roy 1985, 69–83).

Daoud, who ruled by decree, introduced a number of progressive changes. Men, women, and national minorities were given equal rights, and education and welfare were expanded. The centrepiece of his administration was an attempt at land reform. He also instituted modern penal and civil codes. While maintaining a strong commitment to nonalignment, Daoud sought and received additional economic assistance from the USSR. But he failed to get Soviet support in his dispute with Pakistan over his dream of a united Pashtunistan, and moved to the political right, seeking assistance from the United States, Saudi Arabia, Kuwait, and Iraq. Iran under the shah, closely tied to the US government, doubled its aid to Afghanistan, while US secretary of state Henry Kissinger visited Afghanistan and gave strong support to Daoud's government.

Beginning in 1975 Daoud started to remove *Parcham* members from his government and purged the armed forces. The Afghan secret police worked with Iran's SAVAK to identify Marxists in the government. In January 1977 a new constitution was proclaimed, central to which was a strong presidency, with only one legal party, the National Revolutionary Party, to be headed by Daoud. Meanwhile, Soviet premier Leonid Brezhnev, using the mediation of the Communist Party of India, convinced the two factions of the PDPA to reunite, and together they denounced the anti-democratic nature of the new constitution and government. Daoud responded with a major repression of the left (Halliday 1978, 28–30; Dupree 1980, 761–8; Rasanayagam 2003, 59–66; Saikal 2004: 169–186).

On 17 April 1978 Mir Akbar Khaibar, a prominent leader of the PDPA, was murdered, apparently by Daoud's secret police. Two days later, at his funeral, there was a major rally and protest march against the government by an estimated 15,000 people. Daoud moved quickly against the PDPA by arresting seven members of the Politburo. Hafizullah Amin, the only prominent leader to escape arrest, alerted the armed forces, which engineered a hastily planned PDPA coup. The Soviet Union was not involved (Halliday 1978, 28–30; Dupree 1980, 770–7; Saikal 2004, 182–6).

Geopolitics: The New Great Game

In the period after the Second World War, the US government had two basic strategic goals. The first was to contain and reverse the development of communist and left-wing governments. The second was to guarantee access to the oil resources of the Persian Gulf area. A key aspect of this policy was to support the reactionary and feudal regimes of Saudi Arabia, the Persian Gulf mini-states, and other anti-democratic governments in the Middle East. When a popular leftist government was elected in Iran in 1953, for example, the US and British governments intervened to overthrow the government and restore Shah Mohammed Reza Pahlevi as the absolute ruler and US proconsul.

Accordingly, when the PDPA seized power in Afghanistan, US president Jimmy Carter faced a challenge. Many in the US government saw the coup as an expansion of the Soviet sphere of influence and a threat to US interests. Then, in January 1979, the shah of Iran was overthrown by a revolution led by Ayatollah Ruholla Khomeini, a radical Islamist who not only attacked the communists but was also critical of US policy in the Middle East – the Persian Gulf, in particular.

In July 1978 Carter accepted the advice of his national security advisor, Zbigniew Brzezinski, and agreed to provide major military and financial assistance to the Islamists in Afghanistan who were beginning an armed resistance to the PDPA government. As the rebellion spread and the government weakened, the Marxist leaders convinced the USSR to go beyond its financial and technical support and provide military forces. Soviet troops began to arrive in December 1979.

In his State of the Union address on 23 January 1980, President Carter issued what is now known as the Carter Doctrine. He declared that the movement of Soviet troops into Afghanistan represented 'a grave threat to the free movement of Middle East oil.' If the US government had not responded, it 'would have resulted in the temptation to move again until they reached warm water ports or until they acquired control over a major portion of the world's oil supplies.' The move into

Afghanistan 'places the Soviets within aircraft striking range of vital oil resources of the Persian Gulf.' Carter then set forth US policy for Central Asia and the Middle East: 'Let our position be absolutely clear. An attempt by any outside force to gain control of the Persian Gulf region will be regarded as an assault on the vital interests of the United States of America, and such an assault will be repelled by any means necessary, including military force' (quoted in Emadi 1990, 113–14).

Carter then established the Rapid Deployment Force, expanded to become CENTCOM during the Ronald Reagan administration, whereby the United States would station aircraft carrier strike groups and develop new permanent military bases in the region. In expanding the Carter Doctrine, Reagan proclaimed that the US government would guarantee the 'internal stability' of the royalist regime of Saudi Arabia, the protectors of the key strategic foreign source of US oil and indirectly the US voice in the Organization of Petroleum Exporting Countries (OPEC). The Carter Doctrine has been the cornerstone of US policy in the Middle East and Central Asia since that time. As Brzezinski argued, giving assistance to the Islamist radicals in Afghanistan would lure the USSR into a trap where it would bleed away in its own Vietnam War (Cordovez and Harrison 1995, 25–32; Klare 2002, 29–40; Johnson 2004, 217–53; Warnock 2008, 62–86).

The PDPA in Government

In a broad sense the rise in strength of the Marxist parties was due to the stagnation of the economy, the lack of real social change, and the resistance of the ruling elite to real democracy. In 1978 Afghanistan was listed as the poorest country in the world, with annual per capita income of only US$157. Around 85 per cent of the people were still occupied in agriculture. Three-quarters of all children received no education, and illiteracy was overwhelming. More than 80 per cent of all doctors were in Kabul. The rural areas remained feudal, with the economy under the control of the large landowners, khans, tribal chiefs, and mullahs – indeed, tribal khans were even extending their ownership of the herds. More than 40 per cent of the rural population was landless farm labourers. Of those with some land, 40 per cent owned less than one hectare and another 40 per cent had less than 4 hectares; for most, this was not enough land to provide subsistence. As well, a drought that lasted from 1969 to 1972 produced famine and dependence on food aid (Halliday 1978, 30; Male 1982, 68–86).

In the beginning, the PDPA government was representative of both factions, with Mohammad Taraki as president and prime minister and two other prominent leaders, Babrak Karmal and Hafizullah Amin, as deputy prime ministers. But the *Khalq* faction gained control, and the *Parcham* leaders were pushed out of office; many of them, including Karmal, were sent abroad as ambassadors. Taraki quickly revealed the Stalinist nature of his faction as thousands of political opponents were rounded up, sent to prison, and tortured. Many – estimates range between 1,000 and 12,000 – were killed (Dupree 1980, 769–74; Male 1982, 15–17; Rasanayagam 2003, 67–74; Dorronsoro 2005, 85–7).

A few months after taking power the Revolutionary Council proclaimed major social and economic reforms. The key was the agrarian reform. The old feudal mortgage system and usury were abolished, ownership of mortgaged lands was to be allocated to those who farmed them, a development bank was to replace the landlord-peasant system of mortgages and loans, land was to be redistributed so that no family would own more than six hectares, with landless peasants and agricultural labourers the recipients of the redistribution, and the government would assist farmers in forming cooperatives (Male 1982, 109–13; Giustozzi 2000, 24–32). However, the PDPA government did not have the financial base or the government structure to carry out these reforms, which were designed to undermine the feudal system and create a petit-bourgeois class of farmers. The best farmland was irrigated, but the state did not have the finances or expertise to take over the historic communal and feudal system of water management. As Oliver Roy points out, the peasants were originally in favour of the changes, but the state could not provide an alternative to the local system of entrenched rural power. The mullahs strongly opposed the reforms, claiming that they were contrary to the teachings of the Qur'an, which supports the sanctity of private property, the class system, and inequality (Roy 1985, 86–92).

The second major reform was to move towards greater equality for women, to 'end oppressive patriarchal and feudal conditions.' Decree Number 7 guaranteed equal rights for women and put a very low ceiling on the amount of the bride price. Child marriages were banned, with the minimum age for marriage set at eighteen for boys and sixteen for girls. No marriage was to take place without mutual consent. These proclamations were widely supported in the urban centres – as Selig Harrison notes, '[f]eminist leaders in Kabul hailed the reforms' (Cordovez and Harrison 1995, 31) – but in the rural areas they were seen as an attack on the historic patriarchal family and male property rights. Marriage contracts traditionally had been arranged by families, based on property considerations. Now, for the first time in Afghan history, women were to be allowed to choose their own marriage partner (Giustozzi 2000, 20–2).

The third major reform provoked the most opposition. There was to be a major literacy campaign, carried out across the country, for all sexes and ages. This campaign had the support of the United Nations Educational, Scientific and Cultural Organization (UNESCO) in Kabul. The expansion of education introduced by previous governments had not been opposed, but it had been very ineffective, covered boys almost exclusively, and did not include adults. Now, however, the strongest opposition was directed at educational schools and classes that included both boys and girls. Furthermore, the communists had sent male teachers out from the urban centres to teach girls. There were also objections to the secular and socialist school texts that were used. Opposition to the literacy campaign was so strong that it was abandoned in the winter of 1979–80 (Roy 1985, 82–3, 93–5; Male 1982, 113–16; Giustozzi 2000, 22–4; Rasanayagam 2003, 76–8).

The United States Backs the Islamist Resistance

Resistance to the PDPA government's programs began in the summer of 1978. At first it took a relatively unorganized form, starting with the local murder of teachers and the burning of schools. The mullahs, however, led a broader revolt. The first large rebellion was in Herat in March 1979, again led by a group of mullahs who opposed education for women and changes in the marriage laws. The Herat revolt included the defection of most of the army's 17th Division, led by Ismael Khan, later to emerge as a major warlord. As Pakistan's Mohammad Yousaf recounts, officials from the PDPA government and Soviet advisers, as well as their families, were 'rounded up, tortured, cut to pieces, and their heads stuck on poles for parading around the city' (Yousaf and Adkin 1992, 57–8). Selig Harrison recalls that Vadim Zagladin, a high official with the Central Committee of the Communist Party, told him that the Herat massacre was a turning point in the decision to enter Afghanistan: 'The ferocity of the opposition came as a very great shock to us. We became genuinely alarmed about Afghanistan for the first time. You can imagine how we felt when they paraded the bodies of our advisers through the street, when even some of our women and children were killed' (Cordovez and Harrison 1995, 35–6). The *New York Times* reported that a favourite tactic of the *mujahideen* rebels was 'to torture victims by first cutting off their noses, ears, and genitals, then removing one slice of skin after another, producing a slow, very painful death.' John Fullerton noted that 'one Soviet group was killed, skinned and hung up in a butcher's shop' (1983). In 1980 Mullah Nassim Akhundzada, who dominated Helmand province and was a favourite of the CIA, entered Musa Qala and killed everyone and their families who had any connection with the Afghan government, the PDPA, Soviet technicians, and their supporters – around two thousand people (Blum 1998; Giustozzi 2000, 96).

In July 1978 President Carter signed a National Security Council directive to give substantial aid to the Islamist rebellion. This operation was to be covert, run by the CIA. The general public was not to know that the United States was directly involved in the operation, so the arms that were delivered were not to be US arms; instead, Soviet-manufactured arms were bought from China, Egypt, and Israel, and shipped through Pakistan, whose government turned the operation over to the Directorate of Inter-Services Intelligence (ISI), part of the Pakistan Armed Forces. Saudi Arabia agreed to match US financial contributions, and Saudi assistance was put under the control of Prince Turki al-Faisal, head of the General Intelligence Department (GID). The exact amount of US assistance has not been made public, but estimates range between US$3 and US$7 billion. At the same time, over the 1980s, the US government also gave US$7.2 billion to Pakistan. (See Lohbeck 1993; Rubin 2002, 179–83; Crile 2003; Coll 2004, 62–8; Dorronsoro 2005, 142–7.)

The Islamist Parties

The bulk of the financial, economic, and military assistance provided by the US and Saudi governments was directed to seven *mujahideen* parties based in Peshawar and Quetta, a condition imposed by the Pakistani government. Around 85 per cent of this aid went to four radical Islamist parties:

- the Islamic Party of Afghanistan, headed by Gulbuddin Hekmatyar, seen as the most radical of Islamists, received around 50 per cent of all the aid from the United States and Saudi Arabia, had the strongest support from Pakistani generals and the operations branch of the CIA and the strongest presence in the large refugee camps in

Pakistan, controlled around 250 *madrassa* (religious) schools in Pakistan, and had a staff of 1,500;

- the Islamic Society of Afghanistan (*Jamiat*), led by Burhanuddin Rabbani of the School of Theology at Kabul University, it included commanders/warlords Ahmad Shah Massoud, Ismail Khan, and Abdul Basir Khalid;
- the Islamic Party of Afghanistan (*Hizb-Khalis*), headed by Mawlawi Khalis, primarily representing the charismatic Islamists from the eastern Ghilzai Pashtuns; and
- the Islamic Union for the Freedom of Afghanistan (*Ittihad*), led by Abd al-Rabb al-Rasul Sayyaf from the Kabul University Faculty of Theology, who had very close ties to Saudi Arabia, Wahhabi Islam, and the bin Laden family.

These four parties had a weak political presence in 1978, but after the massive external aid program and support from the western countries, they came to dominate Afghan politics. Today they have a major role in the government of Hamid Karzai and dominate the Afghanistan parliament. The other three parties were:

- the National Islamic Front of Afghanistan (*Mahaz*), led by Pir Sayyid Ahman Gailani, closely allied with the royal family, the old ruling order, the US Committee for a Free Afghanistan, and the Heritage Foundation;
- the Afghanistan National Liberation Front (*Jabhi-yi*), led by Sibghatullah Mojaddedi and representing the tribal aristocracy of Ghilzai Pashtun families; members of the Karzai family were key leaders in this party and, in the 1980s, Hamid Karzai headed its office and distributed humanitarian assistance from the US government; and
- the Movement of the Islamic Revolution (*Harakat*), led by Mawlawi Muhammad Nabi Muhammadi and based in the Ghilzai Ahmadzai tribe (Rubin 2002, 196–225; Dorronsoro 2005, 137–72).

In addition, there were fifty-five bases where *mujahideen* were trained in all sorts of black arts. They were financed and sometimes overseen by officials from the CIA and the British MI6. At least 100,000 volunteers from Afghanistan and around the world went through these training programs (Yousaf and Adkins 1992, 113–27; Hartman 2002, 480; Scott 2007, 122–3).

Support for the Afghan Arabs

Most histories of the Afghan proxy war play down the role of Osama bin Laden and the support his organization received from the US government. Bin Laden was twenty-three when he finished his studies at Jeddah University. His family had a close friendship with Prince Turki, head of the Saudi GID. In December 1979, following the Soviet invasion, Turki sent bin Laden to Peshawar to assess the possibility of raising a volunteer army of Arabs to support the Islamist rebellion.

In Pakistan bin Laden met with Abdullah Azzam, a former teacher and friend, as well as the generals running Pakistan's ISI. Back in Saudi Arabia, bin Laden pledged his family's construction company to the *mujahideen* cause and began to solicit funds across the Middle East. He had the full support of the CIA and the government of Pakistan. Assam established the central service centre, *Makhab al-Khidmar* (MAK), in Peshawar to provide support for the Islamists, and bin Laden became his partner.

By 1982 bin Laden had raised enough funds to begin importing construction machinery. Between 1984 and 1985 the family construction team built infrastructure, tunnels, hospitals, and training camps for the Afghan and Arab insurgents. He also raised funds and used family money to bring Arab volunteers to Peshawar. Bin Laden's Islamic Salvation Foundation established a network of recruitment centres in Egypt, Saudi Arabia, and Pakistan. The CIA was well aware of his activities. In 1984 bin Laden moved to Peshawar to direct his family's construction operation and the Wahhabi *madrassas*. In 1986 Azzam and bin Laden were joined by Ayman al-Zawahari, an Egyptian who had been active in the Muslim Brotherhood, later to become bin Laden's right-hand man. That year bin Laden broke with Azzam and set up his own organization, building his own base at Jaji, Afghanistan, and his first guerrilla training base. It is estimated that 30,000 Arab volunteers from thirty-five countries went through the jihadist training camps set up by bin Laden and his organization, which became known as al-Qaeda (Cooley 2002, 96–8, 202–3; Reeve 2002, 162–9; Lance 2003, 40–6; Coll 2004, 153–8).

In 1981 President Reagan chose William Casey to head the CIA. Reagan was determined that the US government would do everything it could to support the *mujahideen* and expand the Islamist rebellion into the Soviet Central Asian republics. Under Carter the US military had established bases in Egypt, where the US special forces trained Egyptians, who in turn trained the volunteers who went to Afghanistan. Casey would expand on this. Training the trainers was undertaken by Green Beret Special Forces at Fort Bragg, NC, the home of the John F. Kennedy Special Warfare Center. Other training took place at Camp Peary – 'The Farm,' as the CIA calls it – which specializes in covert operations, and at Harvey Point, NC, home of the US Army Special Forces. Pakistani military officers and special operators from the Afghan *mujahideen* were trained at Fort Hill and Camp Pickett, VA, run by the US Navy Seals and the Green Berets. At these sessions, the trainers were taught the full range of actions, weapons use, building bombs, murder and assassination, and strategic sabotage. Some instruction included how to hijack aircraft (Lohbeck 1993; Cooley 2002, 21–3, 69–80; Mather 2003, 91–116; Dreyfuss 2005, 274–81; Scott 2007, 122–4).

The Soviet Occupation and Military Stalemate

The Soviet Union had limited goals in Afghanistan: it wanted the country to remain a non-aligned friendly neighbour. While it did not believe that Afghanistan was ready for a communist revolution or a soviet form of government, it felt an obligation to support a fraternal Marxist regime that was under attack from 'foreign imperialists aided by a local counterrevolution.' Their official goals included resistance to the creation of a 'US sphere of influence on the Soviet border.' There is no evidence that the Soviets were interested in pushing south to the Arabian Sea and threatening US control of the oil industry in the Middle East. A policy statement of December 1979 declared that the Soviet Union would be willing to withdraw all its forces as long as 'all forms of outside interference are fully terminated,' They supported the efforts by UN mediator Diego Cordovez to bring the war to an end (Gupta 1986, 131–7; Gibbs 2006, 250–63).

The Soviet armed forces in Afghanistan peaked at around one hundred thousand. As in the Vietnam template, they had an enormous advantage in firepower over the *mujahideen* guerrillas. They used bombers, attack aircraft, and helicopters extensively and armoured forces to try to keep the roads open. Later in the war they also engaged in carpet bombing in an attempt to drive the people living near the border across into Pakistan.

As in Vietnam, the government and its Soviet supporters controlled the main cities and tried to clear the roads of guerrilla activity. But in the rural areas the *mujahideen* forces dominated, and representatives of

the central government were killed and driven out as a matter of practice. For example, education expanded in the cities under government
control but virtually disappeared in areas under the control of the Islamists. The government reported that '2,000 teachers had been killed
and 2,000 schools destroyed, while 9,000 teachers had been "physically assaulted" before the end of 1983' (Giustozzi 2000, 23). The *mujahideen* engaged in guerrilla warfare against the national and Soviet
armed forces, including large-scale ambushes. But, as Giustozzi points
out, they 'were never able to seize any garrison with more than a few
hundred defenders, and that was even exceptional.' For example, in
summer 1988 around seven thousand *mujahideen* attacked the seven-
hundred-strong garrison of Qalat, but failed to take it (2000, 114).

Beginning in 1986, the UN hosted negotiations between the Soviet
Union and the United States to plan the withdrawal of Soviet forces
and end the war. An agreement was finally reached in April 1988, and
the Soviet withdrawal was completed on 15 February 1989. The consensus of western Cold War observers was that the Afghan regime would
fall within a month. In March 1989 the *mujahideen* gathered their forces
to launch an attack on the city of Jalalabad, one of the government's
strongholds, but suffered a major defeat, with ten thousand fighters
killed. As Giustozzi reports, 'with the Soviet withdrawal and the *mujahideen* defeat at Jalalabad, fighting subsided throughout the country.
Government sources in autumn 1989 claimed that 70–80% of the *mujahideen* commanders were not fighting anymore' (2000, 185, 187).

The war had a high cost. It is said that more than one million Afghans
were killed and another six million went into exile in Pakistan or Iran.
The educated and wealthy elite fled to the west. The Soviet Union reported 14,263 killed and 49,985 wounded. The US government admits
that it spent over US$10 billion on the war, with Saudi Arabia match-
ing that total. Over the nine-year period of the occupation, the Soviets
reported that the war cost them between US$2 billion and US$3 billion
per year (Griffiths 2001, 181–3).

The Collapse of the PDPA Government

Najibullah's government stayed in power for three years after the withdrawal of the Soviet armed forces. This was only possible because of
the financial and military aid that continued to come from the USSR.
When the Soviet Union came to an end, this aid was cut off and the
PDPA's collapse was inevitable. Indeed, since the time of Daoud's

republic, Afghan governments have been able to survive only because of extensive foreign aid. If the United States and its allies in the North Atlantic Treaty Organization (NATO) were to pull out of Afghanistan and cut off their enormous contribution to the Afghan budget, it is unlikely that the Karzai government would last a month. That is the reality of Afghanistan: it is a 'failed state' by any definition because of the many years of foreign imperial intervention and domination.

The PDPA government is remembered by women for the progress made towards equality with men. The constitution of 1964 granted women equal rights, and by the 1970s Kabul had become a modern city where women could be educated and employed, seek their own professions, and choose their own clothes. Gilles Dorronsoro argues that, on the question of women's issues, '[t]he continuity between the communist regime in Kabul and previous projects of modernization was marked.' Women strongly supported the literacy campaign and the expansion of the enrolment of girls in schools. Under the PDPA regime 50 per cent of the teachers in schools were women and 55 per cent of the students were girls. Half of the students at Kabul University were women. Kabul was a beacon of light for women and a refuge for those wishing to escape rural patriarchal culture (Dorronsoro 2005, 296–8).

Malise Ruthven (2004, 109–10) notes that the PDPA government included women at the highest levels of administration and that women did not play a role in the Islamist resistance. Women were supporters of the government and very active in the militias, where four of the seven commanders were women. For the first time in Afghan history, women were employed extensively in the government administration, the professions, as police officers, and even as workers and managers in the factories. In 1986, 270,000 women were employed, compared with only 5,000 in 1978 (Giustozzi 2000, 20–2). Kathy Gannon, who covered Afghanistan for the Associated Press between 1986 and 2005, has written that '[t]he only time girls really prospered in Afghanistan was during the Communist regime, the regime that the West sought to overthrow by using Islamic fervor of militant Muslims' (2005, 49). A similar view was expressed by Ann Jones, commenting on her experience of working in Afghanistan after 2001: 'Many Kabulis – men and women – say the very best years were the 1980s, during the Soviet occupation, when the communist government guaranteed equal access to education and work, and massive Soviet aid brought the capital a period of relative plenty' (2006, 151).

The *Mujahideen* Seize Power

The UN tried to get the Islamic parties to work together and agree to a transition from the PDPA regime to an interim government, to be followed by general elections. But the various *mujahideen* warlords and commanders were jockeying for power. Finally, in April 1992, the Pakistan government was able to broker the Peshawar Agreement, under which Sibghatullah Mujaddidi would be interim president for two months, followed by a four-month presidency by Burhanuddin Rabbani, head of *Jamiat*; Ahmad Shah Massoud would be minister of defence and Abdul Rasul Sayyaf minister of the interior. But Gulbuddin Hekmatyar, who was to become prime minister, refused to sign. In the meantime, General Dostum, no longer being paid by the PDPA government, formed a new organization, the National Islamic Movement, and joined forces with Massoud and *Jamiat*. This new northern alliance moved south to the edge of Kabul, and on 25 April entered the city to take de facto control of the government. Hekmatyar, now in alliance with a few *Khalq* ministers and their armed forces, set up his headquarters just south of Kabul. Some non-Pashtun Parchamis armed the Shia factions in their section of Kabul.

From May through August, Kabul was the site of a major confrontation between the different *mujahideen* groups. Hekmatyar and his forces regularly bombarded the city with artillery and rockets. Battles also raged between the various ethnic groups that had divided up the city. Tens of thousands of armed men roamed Kabul, killing, looting, and raping women. Sayyaf's men attacked the Hazara neighbourhood, raped the women, killed them, and then scalped them. When the armed struggle ended in February 1995, an estimated 50,000 people had been killed and around 80 per cent of the city had been destroyed. Hundreds of thousands had been injured, and the population had fallen from two million to 500,000.

The winning faction, the National Islamic Movement headed by Massoud and Rabbani, was quick to implement its own version of Sharia law and culture. It established the Ministry for the Promotion of Virtue and Prevention of Vice and created the religious police. The Rabbani government issued edicts requiring women to wear traditional Muslim dress and to cover their heads in public. It also proclaimed that women were 'not to leave their homes at all, unless absolutely necessary, in which case they are to cover themselves completely.' Students at the University of Kabul went back to wearing the old chador (Cogan 1993,

73–82; Rubin 2002, 265–71; Dorronsoro 2005, 299; Kolhatkar and Ingalls 2006, 18–22).

The Revised Carter Doctrine

The collapse of the Soviet Union was a great victory for the United States in its worldwide battle against socialism and communism. It also opened the door for a more aggressive political and military expansion into the former Soviet sphere of influence. New US policy goals included the establishment of capitalist regimes in the states of the former Soviet Union and eastern Europe. Many of these countries would then be invited to join NATO and accept the presence of US military bases. In Central Asia the US government moved to create close political ties to the new regimes in the independent republics.

In addition, the Carter Doctrine was amended to include the goal of the development of Caspian Sea oil and gas by private western oil corporations. The American Petroleum Institute, worried about peak oil and the disappearance of new sources of oil, had urged the US government to focus on the newly discovered oil and gas resources in the Caspian Basin, 'the area of greatest resource potential outside of the Middle East' (Klare 2002, 82–92). By the early 1990s US oil corporations, including Chevron, Amoco (BP), Exxon, and Conoco-Phillips, were becoming active in Turkmenistan, Azerbaijan, and Kazakhstan. Many prominent Americans were involved in the negotiations between the oil corporations and the new governments, including Richard Armitage, James Baker, Dick Cheney, Alexander Haig, Henry Kissinger, Condoleezza Rice, and Brent Snowcroft. Sheila Heslin, of the National Security Council, and Laila Helms, chief consultant for the Taliban, became the key promoters of the development of Caspian Sea oil.

The Carter Doctrine was also extended to cover the export of the Caspian Sea resources by pipelines that did not traverse either Russia or Iran. In 1993 the governments of Pakistan and Turkmenistan negotiated an agreement to support the building of oil and gas pipelines running from the Caspian Sea to the Arabian Sea. These pipelines would have to traverse Afghanistan. The instrument was the Union Oil Corporation of California (UNOCAL) and its junior partners in the Central Asia Gas and Pipeline Consortium (CentGas). The key to this geopolitical strategy, strongly supported by the administration of Bill Clinton, was the creation of a stable government in Afghanistan (Forsythe 1996; United States 1997; Johnson 2004, 168–77; Klare 2008, 115–45; Warnock 2008, 81–7).

Supporting the Taliban

The main problem for the US government and its oil corporations was the chronic conflict in Afghanistan between the various Islamic factions. There was no peace or order where the pipeline was to run. The government of Pakistan had given full support to Hekmatyar, but he had proven to be completely unstable and unreliable. Both governments were looking for an alternative.

Ahmed Rashid (2001) recounts the rise of the Taliban and the support they received from UNOCAL, Pakistan's prime minister Benazir Bhutto, and the US administration of Bill Clinton. Afghans were tired of the constant conflict, the lack of government, and the abuse of women and others by the Islamist warlords and commanders. They were ready for change.

In 1994 Amir Mullah Mohammed Omar rallied a small group of people to free two teenage girls in Kandahar who had been kidnapped by a local commander, taken to a military base, and repeatedly raped. They hanged the commander from a water tank. A short while later two other commanders in Kandahar were in a dispute over a young boy whom both wanted to sodomize. Omar and his group freed the boy. The new movement of the *madrassa* students (the Talibs) was emerging. When they began to clear the Islamist commanders from the roads and eliminate piracy, popular support for the Taliban blossomed (Rashid 2001, 21–8).

In November 1994 the Taliban captured Kandahar and began to move north against the Islamist government. In September 1995 they captured Herat. In July 1996 the Taliban received the endorsement and support of Prince Turki and the Saudi government. Shortly thereafter they moved on Jalalabad and took control of eastern Afghanistan. On 26 September 1996 the Taliban captured Kabul and became the de facto government. They seized Najibullah from the UN headquarters, tortured and killed him, and hanged his body in the public square. They then issued public morality decrees that went beyond those of the Islamists, with the western press focusing on those that further controlled women and their activities (Rubin 1997, 286–90; Mackenzie 1998, 96–100).

UNOCAL immediately announced that the pipeline project would now go ahead, and within hours a US State Department official said the United States would quickly establish diplomatic relations with the new Afghan government, noting that the United States found 'nothing objectionable' about the Taliban's version of Islam, and describing it as 'anti-modern' and not 'anti-western.' Members of the US Congress also gave their support. In Pakistan, the new government of Nawaz Sharif, the army, and the ISI backed UNOCAL and the new Taliban regime (Rashid 2001, 165–9). As Ahmed Rashid reminds us, 'the strategy over pipelines had become the driving force behind Washington's interest in the Taliban . . . The policy was not being driven by politicians and diplomats, but by the secretive oil companies and intelligence services of the regional states' (163). In October 1995 the government of Turkmenistan signed an agreement with UNOCAL and its partner, Delta Oil Corporation of Saudi Arabia, to build the pipelines across Afghanistan. Chalmers Johnson notes that UNOCAL was aided by two well-connected Afghans, Zalmay Khalilzad and Hamid Karzi, to help influence the Taliban in its favour. Both men were 'pro-Taliban, thinking of the new government as UNOCAL's best hope for stability' (2004, 178–9).

The following March the Clinton administration threw its weight behind the UNOCAL pipeline project. As Sheila Heslin of the National Security Council put it, US policy was 'to break Russia's monopoly control over the transportation of oil from that region, and frankly, to promote Western energy security through diversification of supply.' In November 1997 Taliban officials travelled to Houston, Texas, to meet with UNOCAL and US government officials; Khalilzad played a key role (Rashid 2001, 173–5).

US Regime Change in Afghanistan

In February 1996 the Rabbani government had announced that it had signed an agreement to allow the building of oil and gas pipelines from Turkmenistan to the Arabian Sea, but by September the Taliban controlled the proposed route. Accordingly, that month, UNOCAL began negotiations with the Taliban, announcing that 'they have been very supportive of the project.' The Centgas consortium was established, funding was arranged, and construction was to begin in 1998, but UNOCAL decided it would not start the project until the Taliban government received international recognition.

By then, bin Laden had moved from Sudan to Jalalabad, welcomed by Jalaluddin Haqqani, Younis Khalis, and Abdul Sayyaf, three of the Islamist commanders bankrolled by the US government during the war against the PDPA government; only later did he meet Mullah Omar and the Taliban. Bin Laden established bases at Khost, where an estimated 10,000 jihadists were trained; these men fought in Bosnia, Chechnya, Kosovo, Macedonia, and elsewhere (Rashid 2001, 133–4; Wright 2007, 254–5, 339–42). Then came the bombings of the US embassies in East Africa, attributed to al-Qaeda, by men trained by bin Laden in Afghanistan. President Clinton responded by launching cruise missiles at bin Laden's camp, and UNOCAL put the pipeline project on hold (Griffin 2003, 92–104, 147–55).

The US government, however, was strongly behind the pipeline project and, realizing how unpopular the Taliban regime had become, due primarily to its extreme interpretation of Sharia law and its gross discrimination against women, another option was begun. Already, in fall 1997, the United States and Russia had founded the Six-Plus-Two group – the six countries bordering on Afghanistan plus the United States and Russia – under the authority and organization of the UN Security Council. The mediator was Lakhdar Brahimi, an Algerian special UN diplomat. The goal was to convince the Taliban to form a broad coalition government that would include other ethnic and political groups, including the Northern Alliance. In return, the pipeline would be built, Afghanistan would receive royalties from the pipeline, and the UN and the United States would provide Afghanistan with significant economic assistance.

Negotiations went on through 1999 with no results. In October the Pakistan government announced that the Taliban government was willing to cooperate. But later that month the UN Security Council passed a resolution, introduced by the US government, ordering Afghanistan to extradite Osama bin Laden to New York for trial for the African bombings. Nevertheless, in January 2000, the Clinton administration once again took up the pipeline negotiations. UN secretary-general Kofi Annan named Spanish diplomat Francesc Vendrell to facilitate the Six-Plus-Two negotiations, and formal meetings took place in Washington that summer. The negotiations collapsed, however, as a result of disagreements among the parties, the US presidential election, and strong opposition from some members of the US Congress (Brisard and Dasquie 2002, 29–36).

In February 2001 Laili Helms, public relations agent for the Taliban, again pushed for negotiations. Many of the key people in the new administration of George W. Bush had close ties with the Caspian Sea oil project. Vice-President Dick Cheney's Energy Policy Task Force urged new partnerships in Central Asia and gave support to the pipeline policy, particularly as the Russians were opening pipelines to take Caspian oil to Europe. In April the Six-Plus-Two negotiations resumed, and a 'sub-group' met in Berlin in July 2001. (At a separate meeting in England that same month, the Afghan opposition, representatives of the Northern Alliance, and representatives of twenty-one other countries agreed to a plan for a coalition government, with the return of the Afghan king as head of state.) The agenda of these meetings, as reported by Niaz Naik, the participant for the government of Pakistan and former foreign minister, included the signing of an armistice between the Taliban and the Northern Alliance, the extradition of bin Laden, and the promise of billions of dollars in aid if a national unity government were formed. Abdullah Abdullah was there to represent the Northern Alliance, but the representative of the Taliban did not arrive. At these meetings, the US government began to express openly its dissatisfaction with the Taliban. One US official present stated, '[e]ither you accept our offer of a carpet of gold, or we bury you under a carpet of bombs.' The US delegation also stated that the United States would use 'a military option' if the Taliban did not change their position, that it would launch an attack on the Taliban government from US bases in Tajikistan, and that it had the support of Russia and Uzbekistan. On 17 July the Six-Plus-Two talks ended (Brisard and Dasquie 2002, 37–46; Griffin 2003, 240–1; Ahmed 2002, 54–61).

Early in 2001 the US military had been asked to prepare a battle plan for the invasion of Afghanistan. In April the US National Security Council recommended arming the Northern Alliance and forming a confederation of anti-Taliban warlords and tribes, and in July it approved a plan to 'destabilize the Taliban.' National Security Advisor Condoleezza Rice approved a National Security Council Directive to be forwarded to President Bush on 10 September, and on 12 September CIA director George Tenant reported that an expanded plan had been prepared that would cost around US$1 billion (Woodward 2002, 35–40). Meanwhile, Secretary of State Colin Powell had been arguing that the general public would not approve an invasion of Afghanistan for the purpose of finding bin Laden and imposing a new government, but this all changed with the attacks of 11 September.

President Bush declared immediately that there would be no further negotiations with the Taliban government. Plans were revised for a new invasion strategy, using the Northern Alliance exclusively as the ground forces and limiting US participation to the aerial war. On 12 September the UN Security Council and the General Assembly passed resolutions condemning the attacks on the United States and called on all states 'to work together urgently to bring to justice the perpetrators, organizers and sponsors of these terrorist attacks.' The Taliban government pledged support. But two days later Congress gave the Bush administration a blank cheque to use 'all necessary and appropriate force' against those who were responsible for the attacks. On 20 September, President Bush addressed a joint session of Congress, declaring that we now faced a choice between two ways of life, 'the civilized world' and 'the forces of evil.' Freedom was under attack. We must respond with a war on terrorism. 'You are either with us or you are with the terrorists.'

On 7 October 2001 the United States launched a massive aerial attack on Afghanistan. The Northern Alliance began to move south against the Taliban, with close support from US air forces. By the middle of November most of the major cities in Afghanistan had surrendered to the Northern Alliance, and on 12 November the Taliban forces and government fled Kabul. By early December Kandahar had fallen. The remains of the Taliban government and Afghan Arabs with Osama bin Laden fled into the mountains and then into Pakistan (Lambeth 2005).

Conclusion

Like those of most developing countries, the territorial boundaries of Afghanistan were established by imperial powers. Russia and Britain wanted to create a buffer state between their two empires, and they were not concerned that the Afghanistan they created was a conglomeration of different ethnic and linguistic peoples, had no access to the sea or any railways, and its rugged terrain was a major obstacle to modern economic development. The Afghans were never consulted.

Nevertheless, the people of the territorial state tried to create a national identity and a modern industrial state, following the examples of Turkey and the Central Asian republics of the USSR. Indeed, Afghanistan became a formally independent state well before most colonized areas of the Third World. As a member of the League of Nations and then of the UN, Afghanistan insisted on remaining non-aligned and not a part of any military bloc, and received economic and technical assistance from a wide range of countries. Beginning in the reign of King Amanullah, there was a steady push towards not only modernization but modernity. The more educated population, and urban residents, were committed to expanded education, equal rights for women, and the development of a liberal democracy with a constitution and civil rights. The 1964 constitution, developed through a democratic process, declared Afghanistan to be a secular Muslim country.

The process of development was halted and reversed, however, with the onset of the proxy war between the United States and the Soviet Union. The devastation was horrific. The enormous military and economic aid that the US government and its allies gave to the radical Islamists greatly disrupted the process of development and modernization, and in 1992 the Islamists took power in Kabul. Their horrendous government sparked a popular rising, but it came in the form of the Taliban. Today, after the United States' 'humanitarian intervention,' the Islamists are in full control of the Afghan parliament and hold prominent positions in President Hamid Karzai's government. Once again, the people of Afghanistan have been victimized by imperial powers.

References

AIHRC (Afghanistan Independent Human Rights Commission). 2008. *Economic and Social Rights in Afghanistan – III*. Kabul. December.

Ahmed, Nafeez Mosaddeq. 2002. *The War on Freedom: How and Why America Was Attacked September 11, 2001*. Joshua Tree, CA: Media Messenger Books.

Blum, William. 1998. *Killing Hope: US Military and CIA Intervention since World War II*. Montreal: Black Rose Books.

Brisard, Jean-Charles, and Guillaume Dasquie. 2002. *Forbidden Truth: US-Taliban Secret Oil Diplomacy and the Failed Hunt for Bin Laden*. New York: Nation Books.

Cogan, Charles G. 1993. 'Partners in Time: The CIA and Afghanistan since 1979.' *World Policy Journal* 10, no. 2: 73–82.

Coll, Steve. 2004. *Ghost Wars: The Secret History of the CIA, Afghanistan, and Bin Laden, from the Soviet Invasion to September 10, 2001*. New York: Penguin Books.

Cooley, John. 2002. *Unholy Wars: Afghanistan, America and International Terrorism*. London: Pluto Press.

Cordovez, Diego, and Selig S. Harrison. 1995. *Out of Afghanistan: The Inside Story of the Soviet Withdrawal*. Oxford: Oxford University Press.

Crile, George. 2003. *Charlie Wilson's War: The Extraordinary Story of the Largest Covert Operation in History*. New York: Atlantic Monthly Press.

Dorronsoro, Gilles. 2005. *Revolution Unending: Afghanistan, 1979 to the Present*. New York: Columbia University Press.

Dreyfuss, Robert. 2005. *The Devil's Game: How the United States Helped Unleash Fundamentalist Islam*. New York: Henry Holt.

Dupree, Louis. 1980. *Afghanistan*. Oxford: Oxford University Press.

Emadi, Hafizullah. 1990. *State, Revolution, and Superpowers in Afghanistan*. New York: Praeger.

–. 2005. *Culture and Customs of Afghanistan*. Westport, CT: Greenwood Press.

Forsythe, Rosemarie. 1996. *The Politics of Oil in the Caucasus and Central Asia*. Oxford: Oxford University Press.

Fullerton, John. 1983. *The Soviet Occupation of Afghanistan*. Hong Kong: Far East Economic Review.

Gannon, Kathy. 2005. *I Is for Infidel: From Holy War to Holy Terror, 18 Years Inside Afghanistan*. New York: Public Affairs.

Gerges. Fawaz. 1999. *America and Political Islam*. Cambridge: Cambridge University Press.

Gibbs, David N. 2006. 'Reassessing Soviet Motives for Invading Afghanistan: A Declassified History.' *Critical Asian Studies* 38, no. 2: 239–63.

Giustozzi, Antonio. 2000. *War, Politics and Society in Afghanistan, 1978–1992*. Washington, DC: Georgetown University Press.

Griffin, Michael. 2003. *Reaping the Whirlwind: Afghanistan, Al Qa'ida and the Holy War*. London: Pluto Press.

Griffiths, John C. 2001. *Afghanistan: A History of Conflict*. London: Carlton Books.

Gupta, Bhabani Sen. 1986. *Afghanistan: Politics, Economics and Society*. London: Frances Printer.

Halliday, Fred. 1978. 'Revolution in Afghanistan.' *New Left Review* I/112: 3–44.

Hartman, Andrew. 2002. '"The Red Template": US Policy in Soviet-Occupied Afghanistan.' *Third World Quarterly* 23, no. 3: 467–89.

Johnson, Chalmers. 2004. *The Sorrows of Empire: Militarism, Secrecy, and the End of the Republic*. New York: Henry Holt.

Jones, Ann. 2006. *Kabul in Winter: Life without Peace in Afghanistan*. New York: Henry Holt.

Khan, Tahira S. 2006. *Beyond Honour: A Historical Materialist Explanation of Honour Related Violence*. Oxford: Oxford University Press.

Klare, Michael T. 2002. *Resource Wars: The New Landscape of Global Conflict*. New York: Henry Holt.

–. 2008. *Rising Powers, Shrinking Planet: The New Geopolitics of Energy*. New York: Henry Holt.

Kolhatkar, Sonali, and James Ingalls. 2006. *Bleeding Afghanistan: Washington, Warlords, and the Propaganda of Silence*. New York: Seven Stories Press.

Lambeth, Benjamin S. 2005. *Air Power against Terror: America's Conduct of Operation Enduring Freedom*. Santa Monica, CA: RAND Defense Research Institute.

Lance, Peter. 2003. *1000 Years for Revenge: International Terrorism and the FBI, the Untold Story*. New York: HarperCollins.

Lohbeck, Kurt. 1993. *Holy War, Unholy Victory; Eyewitness to the CIA's Secret War in Afghanistan*. Washington, DC: Regnery Gateway.

Mackenzie, Richard. 1998. 'The United States and the Taliban.' In *Fundamentalism Reborn? Afghanistan and the Taliban*, ed. William Maley. London: Hurst.

Male, Beverly. 1982. *Revolutionary Afghanistan: An Appraisal*. London: Croom Helm.

Mather, Dave. 2003. 'Afghanistan: Foreign Intervention and Social Transformation.' *Critique: Journal of Socialist Theory* 34 (May): 91–116.

Meyer, Karl E. 2004. *The Dust of Empire*. New York: Public Affairs.

Prados, John. 2002. 'Notes on the CIA's Secret War in Afghanistan.' *Journal of American History* 89, no. 2: 466–72.

Rasanayagam, Angelo. 2003. *Afghanistan: A Modern History*. London: I.B. Tauris.

Rashid, Ahmed. 2001. *Taliban: Militant Islam, Oil, and Fundamentalism in Central Asia*. New Haven: Yale University Press.

Reeve, Simon. 2002. *The New Jackals: Ramzi Yousef, Osama bin Laden, and the Future of Terrorism*. Boston: Northeastern University Press.

Roy, Oliver. 1985. *Islam and Resistance in Afghanistan*. Cambridge: Cambridge University Press.

Rubin, Barnett R. 1997. 'Women and Pipelines: Afghanistan's Proxy Wars.' *International Affairs* 73, no. 2: 283–96.

–. 2002. *The Fragmentation of Afghanistan*. New Haven, CT: Yale University Press.

Ruthven, Malise. 2004. *Fundamentalism: The Search for Meaning*. Oxford: Oxford University Press.

Saikal, Amin. 2004. *Modern Afghanistan: A History of Struggle and Survival*. London: I.B. Tauris.

Scott, Peter Dale. 2007. *The Road to 9/11: Wealth, Empire, and the Future of America*. Berkeley: University of California Press.

Tapper, Nancy. 1991. *Battered Brides: Politics, Gender and Marriage in an Afghan Tribal Society*. Cambridge: Cambridge University Press.

United States. 1997. Congress. Senate. Committee on Foreign Relations. *US Economic and Strategic Interests in the Caspian Sea Region*. Washington, DC.

Warnock, John W. 2008. *Creating a Failed State: The US and Canada in Afghanistan*. Halifax, NS: Fernwood.

Woodward, Bob. 2002. *Bush at War*. New York: Simon & Schuster.

Wright, Lawrence. 2007. *The Looming Tower: Al-Qaeda and the Road to 9/11*. New York: Random House.

Yousaf, Mohammad, and Mark Adkin. 1992. *Afghanistan – The Bear Trap: The Defeat of a Superpower*. Havertown, PA: Casemate.

3

A 'Single War': The Political Economy of Intervention in the Middle East and Central Asia

ADAM HANIEH

It is a striking fact that the 2001 bombing campaign and subsequent occupation of Afghanistan by US and NATO (North Atlantic Treaty Organization) forces only really began to engender widespread debate among Canadians in early 2008. In January of that year, the findings of the Manley Panel – an investigative commission established by Prime Minister Stephen Harper to review Canada's role in Afghanistan – were released.[1] Its report called for an indefinite extension of Canadian military presence backed up by increased troops and equipment, and was promptly accepted by the Conservative government and Liberal opposition. Despite this bipartisan agreement, however, the seemingly intractable nature of the war – coupled with the growing number of troop deaths – began to precipitate growing doubts from the wider Canadian public about the country's presence in Afghanistan for the first time.

The lengthy period that it took for a public debate to emerge around Afghanistan is one reflection of how the war has been framed ideologically within Canadian political discourse. Intervention in Afghanistan is seen as the 'good war' – a just and morally necessary step to protect human rights and ensure peace in the region. Even those on the social democratic left, such as the New Democratic Party (NDP), equivocate over immediate withdrawal and – reaching back to the mythology of Canadian 'peacebuilding' – prefer to debate the character of the Canadian presence rather than the actual intervention itself.

This assessment stands in stark contrast to the 'bad war' – the 2003 invasion of Iraq by US and British forces. In this case, large demonstrations occurred in every major Canadian city and public opinion was firmly opposed to any Canadian troop deployment. Unions and prominent public figures came out strongly against the war, which was widely interpreted as a predatory grab at Iraqi oil. Even Stephen Harper was to admit in a leader's debate during the 2008 election that the war in Iraq 'was absolutely an error' – conveniently overlooking his strong support for such an intervention in 2002–3 (Canadian Press 2008).

What explains these divergent popular conceptions of the wars in Iraq and Afghanistan? There clearly has been a significant difference in their ideological framing; governments could 'sell' Afghanistan easier than they could Iraq. In much of the public mind, Afghanistan was seen as the operational and planning centre for the 11 September attacks. The images of Afghanistan that filled the western media – burqa-clad women, TVs hanging from trees, acres of poppy farms, destroyed Buddha statues, and so forth – helped to construct the view that this was a bizarre and strangely reactionary society deeply in need of outside intervention. Iraq, on the other hand, with no evident connection to the 11 September attacks, had endured ten years of devastating sanctions. US secretary of state Colin Powell's flimsy attempt to build a case for war in front of the United Nations was unconvincing and easily debunked, and Iraq's oil supplies provided a clear ulterior motive. But beyond these obvious comparisons, the contrasting beliefs of the Canadian public about these wars reflect something much more significant about the way the region is conceived in popular consciousness. For most Canadians, the wars in Afghanistan and Iraq *could* be seen as entirely different missions. There was no logical inconsistency in opposing one of these wars and supporting the other – the question of intervention in each case was completely separate and unrelated.

A core argument of this chapter is that this view of two distinct wars is deeply problematic: they form part of a *single war.* Understanding events in Central Asia, including Afghanistan, means seeing the region as incontrovertibly linked to the broader Middle East. The US-led strategy connects not only Iraq and Afghanistan, but also events in Palestine, Lebanon, and elsewhere across the Middle East. This intervention did not begin in 2001 or 2003, but is decades old. Without this wider, inclusive understanding, it is easy to be convinced of the 'good' war – and ideologically disarmed in the ability to oppose these military interventions effectively.

This chapter sets out to explain the underlying unity of military intervention in the Middle East and Central Asia. An overarching feature of this intervention is the attempt by the world's leading states to carve up and control the most energy-rich area on the planet. These resources are a potentially enormous source of profits and also confer a profound geopolitical power to those states that dominate the region. But a full understanding of these conflicts needs to go beyond the simple description of geopolitical competition and ask more systemic questions. Why is there competition between states? How can we understand the relationship between economic competition and the geopolitical considerations of states? And, importantly, why is the global system structured in such an uneven and hierarchical fashion, constantly marked by war and conflict? Much analysis simply takes these systemic features as given – the world market, typically, is assumed *a priori* to be competitive, conflictual, and hierarchical. But to understand why states act as they do, there is a need to go further and develop a theory that can explain competition, war, and hierarchy as arising from the nature of capitalism itself.

A principal theme of this chapter is thus the distinction between the policies adopted by states and the systemic factors that shape, determine, and generate these policies. The manner in which the United States, Canada, and other leading states act towards and relate to the Middle East and Central Asia – what is henceforth described as *imperialism* – cannot be explained as solely a set of foreign policy decisions. These policies arise as a result of the way the world market operates as a system, not simply because governments adopt certain ideological perspectives. In short, imperialism and competition between states needs to be explained – not simply assumed – if the foreign policies of the United States, Canada, and other leading powers are to be understood fully.

The chapter begins by tackling these theoretical questions concerning the nature of imperialism and the competition between states. I argue that the roots of imperialism lie in the very nature of capitalism – a system characterized by the production of commodities and driven by the pursuit of private profit. Competition between owners of capital means that the system has an immanent tendency to expand and seek accumulation opportunities at a global level. Since the end of the Second World War, this expansionary tendency – called the internationalization of capital – has underpinned the development of capitalism and the world market. Most important, the critical significance of oil and gas to contemporary capitalism is tied to this process of internationalization. Within this context, the second part of this chapter looks in more detail at US strategy in the Middle East and its location in the broader global political economy. The final section tracks the changes within capitalism and the world market since the 1990s, and links these to the rise of Central Asia as a vital area of geopolitics. The shifting structure of the world market has raised the prominence of the Middle East and Central Asia within geostrategic calculations – particularly in the context of a sharpening rivalry between the United States and the emerging powers of Russia and China. Seen through the rivalry and cooperation that intertwines the leading capitalist states, the unity of the Middle East and Central Asia is essential to understanding the wars across this region.

Imperialism, Capitalism, and Nation-State Rivalry

Writing in the September 2009 issue of *Foreign Policy*, former US deputy secretary of defense Paul Wolfowitz declared his fears of a 'realist' turn in the US government following the election of Barack Obama. Wolfowitz, one of the key architects of the 2003 US invasion of Iraq, believed the 'realists' who were now driving US policy looked towards 'manag[ing] relations between states' rather than 'alter[ing] the nature of states.' In place of realism, Wolfowitz maintained, the United States should seek wherever possible to change the internal structure of other states in the name of the 'US national interest' – a policy he euphemistically described as the 'promotion of democratic reform' (2009, 67).

Ignoring for a moment the content of his argument, Wolfowitz provides an illuminating illustration of what is wrong methodologically with much conventional international relations theory. His starting point for explaining what the US state does at the international scale is an understanding of the *ideas* that the US president and his coterie of closest advisors hold. US foreign policy is said to revolve around competing assessments of how to promote the 'national interest.' Do they believe in pragmatic negotiations with, in Wolfowitz's terms, 'extremists' and 'populist dictatorships' or the 'promotion of democratic reform' and the desire to change the way states operate? Once the dominant ideas are identified, the logic goes, then US foreign policy can be understood and recommendations made to change it.

The problem with such an approach is that it turns reality on its head. Instead of identifying what it is about the world that generates a particular set of dominant ideas, ideas themselves are held to create reality. This view of history, therefore, tends to reduce to a battle of ideas or competing policy perspectives. Imperialism – although foreign policy analysts rarely use the word – is simply one policy choice among many.

An alternative approach to understanding US imperialism is offered by Marxian political economy. Marxists argue that an explanation of why governments, states, and their representatives act as they do cannot simply be found in the ideas they purport to hold or champion. Rather, an understanding of 'foreign policy' and 'international relations' must begin with an explanation of how capitalism itself functions. There is a need to penetrate beneath the decisions and desires of people and institutions to trace how these reflect and represent the nature of the system through which human beings reproduce their material existence. In other words, the challenge becomes one of framing imperialism through the nature of capitalism itself.

Capitalism and Imperialism

Capitalism as a system of social organization differs from any other in human history. Its distinguishing characteristic is generalized commodity production – the channelling of all human activity into the production of commodities for sale in the marketplace. Unlike earlier historical periods in which a large part of production was organized through non-market spheres such as the tribe, extended family, or kinship group, the market becomes the primary venue for supplying goods. But the aim of production under capitalism is not human happiness or satisfaction of needs. Instead, under the constant whip of competition, capitalists are forced relentlessly to pursue the accumulation of profit or face being swallowed by a more successful rival.

Competition creates inequalities between different capitalists and is internal to the nature of capitalism itself (Arthur 2002, 140). Those capitalists able to engage in large-scale investments generally outperform smaller capitalists because of economies of scale – they have better ability to produce cheaper commodities, and can swamp markets and engage in price wars. Over time the cost of engaging in business tends to increase and, in periods of crisis, smaller capitalists tend to get captured by larger firms (Marx [1867] 1992: 775), and increasing amounts of capital are amassed in fewer and fewer hands. Karl Marx called this feature of capitalism its *concentration and centralization*, and it is powerfully confirmed in the development of very large conglomerates that dominate all sectors of today's world market (Shaikh 1983).

This structure has crucial implications for how the world market develops. In its drive to accumulate, capitalism pushes to expand the boundaries in which it operates while simultaneously attempting to reduce the time taken for the movement of capital and commodities between places (Harvey 1999, 416–17). Due to the increasingly large scale of production, national markets become too small for the largest capitalists to operate profitably within. Marx noted the powerful tendency of capital to 'tear down every spatial barrier to intercourse, i.e. to exchange, and conquer the whole earth for its market . . . [as capital develops] the more does it strive simultaneously for an even greater extension of the market' (1973, 539). This tendency springs immanent from the nature of the system itself and is known as *the internationalization of capital*.

Internationalization describes capitalism's drive to swallow the globe in the search for new markets and to bring ever-larger swathes of human activity into its orbit. It means that the production and sale of commodities is 'conceptualized, produced, and realized at the level of the world market,' rather than within the borders of a single nation-state (Palloix 1977, 20). There is a very close connection between the internationalization of capital and its concentration and centralization, a fact emphasized by early theorists of imperialism such as V.I. Lenin, Nikolai Bukharin, and Rosa Luxemburg. Bukharin pointed out in the early 1900s that the internationalization of capital could actually be understood as its concentration and centralization across national borders ([1929] 1972, 41). As markets grow geographically, the production and sale of commodities is interlocked across different national spaces, with ownership concentrated in the hands of the world's largest corporations.

The internationalization of capital is also intimately tied to the growing importance of finance within capitalist accumulation. Finance initially developed alongside capitalist trade and early industry as a means of ameliorating potential barriers to profit making, such as insufficient capital to engage in production or the need to cover the costs of expensive trading expeditions before goods could be brought to market (Rosdolsky 1977). It developed through different institutional forms – banks, joint-stock companies, trusts, cartels, and monopolies – that brought together idle capital held in a variety of hands and different groups of people so that it could be used for accumulation (Marois 2012). In more recent times finance has played a very particular role in enabling the internationalization of capital. As the geographical scale of accumulation grows, the costs of doing business rise exponentially, generating the need for global financial markets and international banking systems (McNally 2009). The development of highly complex global production and marketing chains means dealing with potentially disastrous fluctuations in currencies, interest rates, and other variables. This is the origin of financial instruments such as derivatives, which enable capitalists to manage the risk associated with fluctuations in value that occur across time and space (Panitch and Gindin 2004, 64; Bryan and Rafferty 2006). The role that finance has played in internationalization is reflected through the rapid increases in portfolio and foreign direct investment flows across borders, as well as the global expansion of stock markets and private firms dealing in financial instruments.[2]

Internationalization – and its associated tendencies of concentration, centralization, and financialization – is the key link between capitalism and imperialism. *As capitalism develops, it is driven inexorably towards the domination of space.* This is the core difference between Marxist political economy and other theories of international relations: imperialism is not a result of the policy choices of governments or the dominance of a particular ideological trend; it is, instead, inherently bound up in the development of capitalism itself. This does not mean that the specific form of imperialism at any point in time can be read directly from 'economics' – as many critics like to claim that the Marxist approach implies (Callinicos 2010, 19). The concrete form of the world market and relations between states is mediated by policy debates among ruling elites, the actions that governments choose to undertake, and – often overlooked – the struggles of ordinary people to influence these factors. What the Marxist approach emphasizes, however, is that all of these factors – while helping us understand the particular expression of international politics at any point in time – do not explain the systemic and underlying drive to dominate space that is wrapped up in the very nature of capitalist accumulation (Harvey 1999, 439–45).

Nation-State Rivalry and Cooperation

Although a certain strand of thinking about 'globalization' interprets the deep interconnectedness of the world market as implying 'the end of the nation-state' (Ohmae 1995), the continuing saliency of national conflict shows this claim to be highly exaggerated. The production and consumption of commodities is always territorialized – there must be 'a certain 'coherence' and 'materialization' in time and space' for accumulation to take place (Albo 2004, 91; Wood 2005). Precisely because of this territorialization of accumulation, a number of theorists have argued that the nation-state takes on even greater importance in the context of internationalization (Callinicos 2010, 17). The disciplining of labour, protection of private property rights, maintenance of financial conditions and laws, and so forth requires regulation, and thus encourages the strengthening of state institutions (Panitch and Gindin 2003); thus, internationalization does not undermine but actually reinforces the process of state formation. Each national space is brought into line with the nature of accumulation at the global scale, and thereby helps to sustain the conditions that enable internationalization itself to deepen.

This produces a contradictory relationship between nation-states. On the one hand, the internationalization of capital heightens the competition between the large corporations that dominate the global scale. The struggle of different capitals to obtain control over markets, sources of raw material, and cheap labour is refracted through increased interstate competition. At the same time, the very nature of internationalization demands greater coordination and cooperation between states in order to maintain the necessary conditions for capitalist accumulation as a whole (particularly in the context of increased financial instability). International relations are characterized, therefore, by dual tendencies of cooperation and rivalry between imperialist powers.[3]

These dual tendencies can be illustrated by the specific relationship that existed between the leading capitalist powers after the Second World War. There were three aspects to this relationship. First, particularly from the 1960s onwards, there was increasing rivalry and competition between the United States, Japan, and West Germany as the industries of the latter two states underwent reconstruction after the war (Brenner 2000). Large capitalist firms in these countries competed for ownership and control over markets. This inter-capitalist rivalry materialized, however, in the context of the second element of the post-war state system: the growing weight of the USSR, China, and other state-socialist countries. Although these countries were non-capitalist (their economies were not driven by the pursuit of private profit), their foreign policies nevertheless aimed at obtaining influence across the globe. This inevitably generated rivalry with the advanced capitalist countries as a whole, and thus reinforced a deep unity of interest among the major capitalist powers. Finally, the third aspect of the post-war international state system was the growing strength of anticolonial and anti-imperialist struggles following the end of the war. These movements unfolded within the context of a world system that was defined by the two features described previously – inter-imperialist rivalry and struggle with the non-capitalist countries – and, as a result, the anticolonial movements often allied with the USSR or China as a means to strengthen their struggle for independence. While this support did enable some countries to carve out greater independence from the leading capitalist states it usually came with a political price and, consequently, the struggle for national liberation was frequently subordinated to the foreign policy goals of the USSR and China. Within the Middle East, these dynamics were particularly important given the role that hydrocarbons played within the development of capitalism as a whole.

These three interrelated features of the post-war state system demonstrate the simultaneous trends of both rivalry and unity between the leading capitalist states. These states held a strong common interest in confronting the rivalry of the non-capitalist bloc as well as any potential challenge to their dominance from anticolonial and left-wing movements. As internationalization deepened, they also required the development of laws, regulations, and institutions that governed financial markets and other aspects of accumulation. At the same time, the leading capitalist states remained in stiff competition over access to resources, markets, and influence. The principal mediating force in this relationship of unity and rivalry was the United States, which both promoted the interests of US-based capital on the world stage while attempting to manage capitalism in its totality (Bromley 1991; Altvater 1993; Panitch and Gindin 2003; Stokes 2007).

This framework provides a window into Canada's particular location in the world market. Canadian corporations, like those in all leading capitalist states, have been propelled by the deepening tendencies of internationalization since the end of the Second World War. As a result, the Canadian state has looked to ways of extending the global reach of Canadian capital, which, for particular historical reasons, is concentrated in the mining, energy, and banking sectors and seeks 'a worldwide base of accumulation from which to generate surplus value and . . . an independent interest in the new imperialism' (Klassen 2009, 184). Much as in Australia and Britain, this imperialist role has been articulated through a strategy of building a 'special relationship' with the United States, through which Canadian capital hopes to gain a share of the overall benefits accruing to imperialism from overseas control. This particular relationship is located within the ever-present rivalry that exists between the advanced capitalist states – Canadian capital is still in competition with that of the United States and other capitalist states, but this competition takes place within a framework of shared interests.

Imperialism and the Middle East in the Post-war Era

Up until the mid-twentieth century, internationalization mostly took the form of seeking out potential markets for commodities produced in the advanced capitalist countries or finding and controlling cheap sources of raw materials in the colonies (Palloix 1977). Many countries were integrated into the world market on the basis of exports of single commodities to the advanced capitalist countries; examples include the extraction of rubber in Malaysia, tea in Sri Lanka, sodium nitrate in Chile, sugar in Cuba, tin in Bolivia, and cotton in Egypt. The Second World War and the subsequent decades saw a shift in the form of these internationalization tendencies. Entire industrial sectors began to be organized on an international scale. Large companies began to locate production facilities across the globe, sourcing raw materials and labour from a variety of different geographical spaces and selling their goods to markets worldwide. This meant that ownership itself began to be internationalized, as a variety of different 'national' capitals were often integrated in joint management and share-holding structures.

A major factor enabling this post-war leap in the internationalization of capital was the shift to an oil-centred global economy. The development of truly global production chains marked a considerable expansion in the scale of output. The rebuilding of Europe and much of Asia after the war, the rearmament of the main capitalist powers, the industrialization of many areas of the world that previously had been marked by pre-capitalist social relations – all inaugurated an expansion of production unseen in human history. New industrial sectors emerged at this time, notably the petrochemical industry, which substituted for naturally occurring materials manufactured commodities such as plastics, synthetic fibres, pesticides, fertilizers, and detergents.[4] As the increasingly global nature of accumulation took shape, the transportation sector also grew in prominence – with large-scale commercial land and air transit complementing the ubiquitous spread of automobile markets throughout Europe and the United States.

All of these developments rested upon a growing demand for inputs of energy and raw materials. Oil and natural gas were the fundamental components of the new internationalized production regime, displacing relatively energy-inefficient coal (Bromley 1991; Mitchell 2009), supplying the necessary energy for industrial production, and forming the basic feedstock for new industries such as petrochemicals. This shift in the global energy regime brought the importance of the Middle East into sharp focus. It had become evident, following a wave of discoveries during the 1920s and 1930s, that Saudi Arabia, Kuwait, Iraq, Iran, and the smaller Gulf states held the world's largest supplies of cheap and easily accessible oil and gas. This meant that, as the United States increasingly took upon itself the role of 'hegemonic guarantor' (Altvater 1993, 114), the projection of US power throughout the Middle East became an essential element to its broader geopolitical control.

The Transition to US Power in the Middle East, 1950–70

The end of World War Two inaugurated a shift in the politics of the Middle East that had begun in the first few decades of the twentieth century but was fully consolidated only following the collapse of the region's former colonial powers, Britain and France. Shortly after the war, US president Harry Truman gave a speech to Congress in which he promised that the United States would intervene actively around the world in support of US interests and those of the 'free world.' The Truman Doctrine, as it became known, did not directly reference the Middle East, although an earlier draft had apparently noted the importance of the region's 'great natural resources' (Stork 1980, 14). Despite this absence, the explicit linkage been the oil supplies of the Middle East and US power had been a frequent refrain of US strategic documents – well illustrated in a 1945 State Department memo that had described Saudi Arabia's oil supplies as 'a stupendous source of strategic power, and one of the greatest material prizes in world history' (United States 1945, 45). In recognition of this 'stupendous source of strategic power,' the United States moved assiduously to assert its control over the region as British and French influence underwent a slow decline.

From the perspective of the United States and other leading capitalist states, this projection of power became increasingly urgent during the 1950s with the emergence of powerful challenges to the old colonial order. In key countries across the region, left-wing organizations worked alongside (and in competition with) more conservative nationalist movements in an attempt to break free from colonial dominance. Of particular note were developments in Iran, Egypt, and Iraq, where – in large part due to the greater weight of their working classes – long histories of militant trade unionism helped to nurture radical and nationalist sentiments through wide layers of the population. Most important in this respect was the growth of nationalist agitation in the military, where underground societies and other political organizations brought together officers and lower-ranked soldiers. Despite the contradictory nature of these movements – ranging from communist forces to those backed by cautious nationalist bourgeoisies – they presented an existential threat to the region's established order.

The reality of this threat was confirmed in 1951 with the nationalization of the British-owned and operated Anglo-Iranian Oil Company (AIOC) in Iran. The country's newly appointed prime minister, Mohammed Mossadegh, had been emboldened by mass mobilizations across the country to expel AIOC and place Iran's oil in state hands (Abrahamian 2001). The nationalization of AIOC was followed a year later by a dramatic turn of events in Egypt, whose monarch and a principal ally of colonialism in the region, King Farouk, was ousted in a military coup led by the popular military officer Gamal Abdel Nasser. In July 1956, in an action that was celebrated by millions of people across the entire Middle East, Nasser's government demonstrated its nationalist credentials by nationalizing the British- and French-controlled Suez Canal.

In response to events such as these, the United States moved to assert its control over changes in the region. Initially, it drew upon the continued presence of British troops – most notably along the Trucial Coast – a network of small sheikhdoms in the Gulf that had been under British control since the early 1800s and that eventually became the United Arab Emirates (UAE), Bahrain, and Qatar (Zahlan 1998). British bases were located in Bahrain and Sharjah, and much of the region's military forces, including those of Abu Dhabi, Kuwait, and Oman, were commanded by British officers. In 1968, however, Prime Minister Harold Wilson announced the withdrawal of British troops from the Gulf by 1971 as a consequence of the spiralling cost of maintaining overseas bases. In response to the British withdrawal, the US government developed the 'Nixon Doctrine' as a new strategic framework aimed at managing its interests. The essential thrust of this new strategy was to incorporate economic and political elites of principal US allies more directly into the maintenance of US power. In the Middle East, Nixon's strategy was based on three countries in particular: Israel, Iran, and Saudi Arabia.

The embrace of Israel arguably ended up being the most important element of US policy in the Middle East. Israel, founded upon the expulsion of around 80 per cent of the Palestinian people in 1947–8, had been from its inception a fundamental feature of imperialist policy – linked initially to Britain and France (Chomsky 1999). In neighbouring countries, colonial strategy had long relied upon fostering a tiny

layer of the population as a base of support. But the coming to power
of anticolonial governments in Iran (1951), Egypt (1952), Iraq (1958),
and North Yemen (1962) showed that this strategy always remained exposed to the threat of popular revolt. Even in those Arab countries that
remained loyal allies of the United States, Britain, and France during
the 1960s – Jordan and Lebanon, for example – the ruling regimes were
forced to accommodate themselves to mass pressure in certain ways
(if only in rhetoric). Israel, however, was a settler-colonial state based
upon ethno-religious exclusivity (maintained through the continued
denial of Palestinian refugees the right to return to their homes and
lands). Organically tied to external support for its continued viability
in a hostile environment, it could be counted upon as a much more reliable ally than any Arab client state.

The 1967 war between Israel and its neighbouring Arab states marked
the full confirmation of this role. In just six days, Israel destroyed the
Egyptian and Syrian air forces and occupied the West Bank, Gaza Strip,
(Egyptian) Sinai Peninsula, and (Syrian) Golan Heights. The ideas of
Arab unity and resistance that had been growing throughout the region
received a devastating blow from which it never recovered. The United
States moved quickly to cement itself as Israel's primary patron, sup-
plying the country with billions of dollars worth of military hardware
and financial support. In return, Israel was to operate as an extension of
US power in the region (Chomsky 1999).

While Israel was located on the western flank of the Middle East,
its ultimate role was tied to US (and broader imperialist) interests in
the Gulf region. Within the Gulf itself, US power relied centrally upon
Iran, at that time dominated by the US-backed shah following a CIA-
supported coup against Mossadegh in 1953 (Abrahamian 2001). The
United States massively increased its military funding to Iran, reaching
US$1.7 billion under the first Nixon administration (1968–72), nearly
three times the limit set by Nixon's predecessor Lyndon Johnson (Stork
1975, 19). The influential US think-tank, the RAND Corporation, noted
in a 1969 report that Iran could 'help [the United States] achieve many
of the goals we find desirable without the need to intervene in the region' (cited in Stork 1975, 19). This role was confirmed in the early part
of the 1970s as US military aid grew rapidly, reaching more than US$6
billion annually by 1973. As the United States extended military support to Iran, it also helped the shah build a domestic security apparatus
(SAVAK) that became renowned for its vicious repression of any internal dissent. Iran was also Israel's main ally in the Middle East.

Alongside Israel and Iran, Saudi Arabia formed the third main pillar of US strategy in the region during the 1960s and 1970s (Achcar 2004, 228–30). The Saudi monarch, King Saud, had long been reliant on US aid and military support following the arrival of US oil companies to the country in the 1920s. But Saud's anachronistic regime – and close relationship with the United States – was threatened by the rise of revolutionary and nationalist movements during the 1950s and 1960s. During the earlier 1960s, Saudis working for the US oil companies had engaged in a series of militant strikes and demonstrations, often raising political demands that reflected the nationalist sentiments spreading through neighbouring countries such as Egypt, Iraq, and Yemen (Vitalis 2007). New political organizations formed alongside these strikes that openly expressed a desire to remove US influence in the region and overthrow the Saudi monarchy.

For all these reasons, Saudi Arabia and the United States developed an extremely close relationship based on mutual opposition to revolutionary movements in the region (Achcar 2004). Domestic political movements in Saudi Arabia were severely repressed with the open support of US and British advisors (Vitalis 2007). Further afield, Saudi Arabia's ideological innovation was its use of Islam as a counterweight to nationalist and left-wing organizations. During the 1960s, in an attempt to undermine various pan-Arab summits that drew together the nationalist regimes in the region, Saudi Arabia organized 'Islamic summits' that asserted Saudi influence and challenged Egypt's role as the leading Arab state. The Saudi monarchy also began to extend financial support to Islamist movements across all countries. Both the United States and Britain helped Saudi Arabia devise this strategy of using religion as a means of holding back potential challenges to their dominance of the Middle East (Vassiliev 1998, 386).

Imperialism in the Middle East: 1970s–90s

The decade of the 1970s was a vital turning point for imperialist policy in the region. Changes were driven by the way that capitalism itself developed at the international scale, as well as by internal shifts precipitated by the continuing struggle against foreign domination. Both these factors need to be appreciated to comprehend fully the nature of imperialist policy as it has developed into the contemporary period.

At the level of the world market, the 1970s marked a further leap in the internationalization and financialization of capital. The continuing development of 'multinational' companies – based largely in North America, Europe, and Japan – helped to consolidate the growing significance of finance to the global economy. Large companies, requiring huge loans to engage in the increasingly expensive business of globally oriented production, borrowed from offshore financial markets where banks could evade capital controls put in place in their national markets (Gowan 1999, 23). The United States' break with the dollar-gold standard, announced by President Nixon in 1971, coupled with the increasing liberalization of capital controls, meant that financial flows rose dramatically through the decade (Eichengreen 2008, 135). Moreover, the end of the economic growth that had characterized the first two decades of the post-war period forced capitalist governments to switch to deficit spending and a reliance on debt to support demand (Mandel 1983). This further reinforced the importance of finance at the global scale.

This deepening of internationalization and financialization had very significant implications for the oil-producing Gulf countries and hence for the nature of imperialism in the Middle East.[5] As the oil-producing states gained greater control over the upstream production of oil during the 1960s and 1970s, they obtained large revenues of 'petrodollars' through the sale of their oil exports. The magnitude of these funds increased rapidly following a rise in the price of oil in 1973 and, as a result, Gulf petrodollars played an important role in the development of the global financial architecture from the 1970s onwards (Gibson 1989; Spiro 1999). Most significantly, as newly industrializing countries in the South were faced with the increased cost of energy imports, petrodollars were 'recycled' as loans through US and other financial institutions located in the leading capitalist states. This was a principal step in the consolidation of neoliberalism through the 1980s – as countries became increasingly indebted, they were forced (through so-called conditionality agreements) to open up their economies to foreign investment and liberalize ownership laws in order to continue to receive financial support (Woods 2006).

The tight linkage between the United States and the Gulf states, particularly Saudi Arabia, was a critical factor in this process. The US government made a special effort to ensure that the oil trade would be denominated in US dollars, thus guaranteeing that the world's most important commodity was tied to the world's most important currency (Spiro 1999; Gowan 1999). Saudi Arabia gladly acquiesced to this in return for extensive military and political support from the United States.[6] The Saudis then used their influence as the world's largest producer to prevent the cartel of oil-producing nations, OPEC, from pricing oil in a diversified basket of currencies (Spiro 1999, 105–26). Moreover, in 1974, an agreement was reached between the Saudi government and the US Treasury that saw Saudi Arabia deposit billions of dollars in the US Federal Reserve through a secret arrangement to buy US treasuries outside the normal auction for such securities (Spiro 1999, 109). David Spiro points out that, '[h]aving agreed to invest so much in dollars, the Saudis now shared a stake in maintaining the dollar as an international reserve currency . . . dollars constituted 90 percent of Saudi government revenues in 1979, and . . . Saudi investments were, roughly at the same time, 83 percent dollar denominated' (1999, 122–3). At the level of OPEC as a whole, reserves held in US dollars increased from 57 per cent of total reserves in 1973 to 93 per cent in 1978 (United States 1981, 35).

The 1979 Iranian Revolution

In the late 1970s, however, US strategy in the Gulf was shaken by two pivotal events. First, in early 1979, a mass movement in Iran overthrew the US-backed shah and abruptly terminated the close alliance between the US and Iranian governments. The revolution echoed throughout the rest of the Gulf, finding sympathy among the large Shia populations in Iraq, Bahrain, Kuwait, Saudi Arabia, and the UAE. As the Iranian revolution unfolded, events in neighbouring Afghanistan also appeared to pose a threat to US hegemony over the region. The Soviet-aligned People's Democratic Party of Afghanistan (PDPA) had come to power in 1978. In late 1979 the Soviet Union entered Afghanistan in support of the new government, viewing this as an opportunity to strengthen its influence in the strategic zone surrounding the Gulf states.

Both the Soviet intervention in Afghanistan and the Iranian revolution fuelled US concerns over the future stability of the Gulf monarchies. In response, the United States adopted a two-pronged strategy. First, in order to undercut the Iranian threat, it encouraged a long-brewing conflict between Iraq and Iran, both of which had the potential to assert themselves in the Gulf due to their relative wealth and strong military power. The devastating eight-year war between them effectively prevented either country from emerging as a challenger to US power in the Gulf during the 1980s.[7]

The second element of US strategy in the Gulf was to draw even closer to the Gulf monarchies. On 4 February 1981, shortly after the Iran-Iraq war began, the United States supported Bahrain, Saudi Arabia, Kuwait,

Oman, Qatar, and the UAE in establishing the Gulf Cooperation Council (GCC), a regional integration project that had both economic and security implications. The GCC quickly became a foremost ally of US power in the Gulf region. The United States also began moving expensive weapons systems to the GCC states and, in 1983, established a regional unified command known as US Central Command (CENTCOM), which was based initially on US navy ships permanently stationed at Bahraini ports that liaised with US embassies and nations across the Middle East (Stork 1985, 5). CENTCOM is now one of the most important of US military institutions, responsible for all military engagement, planning, and operations in twenty-seven countries spanning the Horn of Africa through the Gulf and into Central Asia. Its forward command headquarters was moved to Qatar in 2003.

The US alliance with the GCC states was built on the continuing close relationship with Saudi Arabia, a linkage the United States was to draw upon as a means of undercutting the Soviet presence in Afghanistan. Invoking the notion of 'leadership of the Islamic world' that had been cultivated in the 1960s as a counterweight to the left and Arab nationalist movements, the United States encouraged Saudi Arabia to develop an ideological pole that was solidly anticommunist and thereby would act in conjunction with US policy objectives. A major outcome of this strategy was the ideological and material aid provided by Saudi Arabia to volunteers ready to fight against the Soviet army in Afghanistan. In close cooperation with the United States and Pakistan's Inter-Services Intelligence, Saudi Arabia encouraged Muslims from across the Arab world (and elsewhere) to move to Afghanistan and Pakistan for training. The US-Saudi support of these *mujahideen* was a key element in the birth of al-Qaeda and the modern-day Taliban (Achcar 2002, 2004).

While the GCC-US relationship tightened in the Gulf and a bloody war raged between Iran and Iraq, Israel continued to play a key role on the region's western flank. By then, Israel had become the largest recipient of US military and financial aid in the world. During the 1980s, it launched successive invasions of Lebanon aimed at strengthening the pro-US government and destroying the Palestinian Liberation Organization (PLO), the most radical sections of which had formed an alliance with the Lebanese left. The Palestinian struggle, which had emerged as the locus of anti-imperialist sentiment in the region following the demise of Arab nationalism, presented a potential threat to all the US client regimes in the region. Although Israel was unsuccessful in physically liquidating the Palestinian movement, it did force the PLO to relocate to faraway Tunisia, where it began to be undermined by political rivalries and the corrupting influence of money from the Gulf region.

US Power and the Middle East and Central Asia in the Post–Cold War Era

By the early 1990s, US power appeared triumphant. The collapse of the Soviet Union and its satellites between 1989 and 1992 made it much more difficult for those states and political movements that had relied upon Soviet support to pursue independent policies. The United States used the opportunity to further extend its influence in the Middle East. The target chosen in this respect was Iraq, which possessed oil reserves estimated to be second only to those of Saudi Arabia. Iraq's president, Saddam Hussein, had worked closely with the United States for many decades, but he was considered an unreliable ally. Hussein's leadership rested partly on a claim to Arab nationalism and, in 1972, US and British oil companies had been expelled from the country after the nationalization of oil. Control of this resource would give the United States a powerful lever over any potential rivals. Most important, however, US policy was driven by the recurring theme of its decades-long history in the Middle East: the attempt to deny the people of the Middle East direct control of the region's resources. Iraq, unlike its GCC neighbours, which relied on easily deportable migrant labour, had a militant and active workers' movement with a rich history of struggle. Iraq was thus always a potential threat regardless of the government in power.

The first stage in what was to be a two-decade-long attempt by the United States to gain control over Iraq began with the invasion and aerial bombardment of the country in 1991. The United States used an Iraqi invasion of Kuwait – Iraq claimed that Kuwait was drilling for oil underneath its border – as pretence to attack the country. Although the Iraqi government was not ousted, its military was severely weakened and the country was cut in three by 'no-fly zones' imposed by the United States and Britain after the war. The 1991 war was followed by a decade-long sanctions regime that devastated the country's industrial and social infrastructure.[8] US president George H. Bush used the occasion of the war to announce what he described as the 'New World Order': untrammelled US supremacy across the globe. US troops levels in the Gulf region remained high throughout the 1990s, with GCC states providing extensive basing, training, and port facilities for the US military (Katzman 2006, 7).

Concurrent with military action against Iraq, the United States moved to establish an economic framework throughout the Middle East based upon the free flow of capital and commodities.[9] This economic zone would be dominated by US capital and anchored by its two key allies, Israel on the western flank and the GCC on the east. Vital to the success of this project was the political integration of Israel into the Middle East. The first step towards achieving this goal was the 1993 Oslo Accords between Israel and the PLO, which aimed to neutralize the Palestinian movement by providing limited self-rule to the Palestinian population in the West Bank and Gaza Strip in return for normalization of relations between the Arab states and Israel. Over the 1990s, for Palestinians the Oslo Accords developed into a situation akin to the bantustans of apartheid-era South Africa, with Israel retaining full control of Palestinian movement, the entry and exit of goods, and economic development in isolated patchworks of territory while a small layer of Palestinians mediated the occupation on behalf of the occupying power (Hanieh 2008). At the same time, because this process occurred under the rubric of 'peaceful negotiations' and the blessing of the advanced capitalist states, the Oslo Accords and subsequent agreements were used to deepen Israel's normalization in the broader Middle East – Jordan and Egypt, in particular, moved quickly to sign economic agreements with Israel.

Despite the rhetoric of 'peace,' the United States continued its attempt to subdue Iraq and gain access to the country's huge oil resources. In October 1998 President Bill Clinton signed the Iraq Liberation Act, which called for 'regime change.' In December he launched Operation Desert Fox – a four-day bombing campaign against the country. In an indication of British and Canadian alignment with US imperialism, both countries participated in the attack and the further bombing campaigns that occurred during 1999. US moves against Iraq accelerated with the election of George W. Bush in 2000. According to the memoirs of former Bush treasury secretary Paul O'Neill, the first meeting of the National Security Council after Bush's election was headlined by a discussion of Iraq.[10] An energy task force chaired by Vice President Dick Cheney in early 2001 reviewed detailed maps of Iraqi oil reserves, pipelines, and refineries, as well as contracts of foreign companies for Iraqi oilfields.[11] The events of 11 September 2001 were to provide the official justification for bringing these plans to fruition.

A New Wave of Internationalization

Chalmers Johnson has described the 2001 attacks on the Pentagon and World Trade Center as 'blowback' – retaliation for US foreign policy decisions that were often kept secret from the American public (Johnson 2004). In this case, US support (through Saudi Arabia and Pakistan) of anticommunist Islamic movements in Afghanistan helped to cultivate and strengthen a militant anti-US fundamentalism (Achcar 2002). The US government came to use the 11 September attacks as ideological legitimacy for the projection of US military power throughout the Middle East and Central Asia. This process, however, was not simply ideological. Once again, it was deeply linked to changes in the nature of the capitalist world market in the new millennium.

Most important, the collapse of the Soviet Union and a series of economic policy changes in China enabled a further massive leap in the internationalization of capital. An expansion in the capitalist world market facilitated the relocation of much of the manufacturing that had taken place in the advanced capitalist countries to low-wage and poorly regulated zones in China and elsewhere in the global South; similarly, capital in western Europe moved much of its low-wage production to eastern Europe. This caused a dramatic cheapening of the cost of production and a large increase in the quantity of commodities entering the world market. At the other end of the world market was the sale of commodities, with consumption increasingly structured around the US market – and, to a lesser extent, Europe and Japan – in this sharply hierarchical world market. The World Bank noted that one-tenth of the world's population was responsible for nearly six-tenths of global consumption in 2005, with private consumption accounting for 70 per cent of US gross domestic product (GDP) compared with a world average of 59.2 per cent and a figure of 38 per cent for China (World Bank 2008, 4). With the United States representing just under 30 per cent of global GDP, the US consumer was thus the largest single source of demand in the global economy. Control of this global chain of production and consumption continued to rest firmly in the hands of large US, European, and Japanese conglomerates.

As with earlier phases of internationalization, these shifts had important implications for the Middle East. First, Middle East oil and gas exports began to shift eastwards, underpinning the rise of Chinese production. From 2000 to 2006, world energy consumption increased by close to 20 per cent, with China alone responsible for 45 per cent of the increase during this period (IEA 2007, 54). By 2007 nearly 50 per cent of China's crude oil imports came from the Middle East (ibid., 325), and by 2025 Chinese imports of Gulf oil are expected to be three times more than US imports from the region (Blanche 2009, 14). Already, half of Saudi Arabia's oil output now goes to China.

Second, the price of oil rose dramatically on the back of this spectacular increase in demand for energy, bringing with it further implications for the Middle East because of the enormous surge in petrodollar flows. From January 1999 to November 2007, the world price of oil rose from US$9.76 per barrel to US$90.32 per barrel, a nearly tenfold increase.[12] A second phase occurred in the first half of 2008, with the price of oil peaking at US$145 in July of that year. As oil and gas flowed eastwards, most of the petrodollars flowed westwards into US financial markets where they were recycled as credit for US consumers and businesses (Hanieh 2011, 94–8). For the Gulf alone, more than US$510 billion of extra liquidity over and above the level received in the 1990s was generated in the 2002–6 period (IMF 2007, 29). Along with similar capital flows from Asian countries, these petrodollars enabled the United States to continue running a growing current account deficit and to absorb the ever-increasing mass of commodities produced in China and other low-wage zones across the globe.

In short, the Middle East's location at the nexus of internationalization, financialization, and global hierarchies once again consolidated the region as a key strategic zone for the advanced capitalist states. The sharply hierarchical character of the world market – low-wage production based in Asia with consumption centred in the advanced capitalist countries, principally the United States – was structured around the Gulf's location in flows of commodities and finance. Precisely because of these trends there was a simultaneous sharpening of the dual tendencies noted throughout this chapter – rivalry and the commonality of interests – between the leading capitalist states.

It is important, however, to differentiate somewhat the rivalries that emerged in this new phase of internationalization. Although sharp competitive rivalries between Europe and the United States were ever present, the EU-US relationship continued to be characterized by a deep synchronicity of views towards the running of global capitalism and the strategic significance that this implies for the Middle East region. In contrast, as Gilbert Achcar (1998) has emphasized, the relationship between the United States and emerging rivals such as Russia and

China took a different form. Russia and China each possessed redoubt-able military strength as a legacy of the earlier period of conflict with the United States. China's economic power in the global economy, sig-nified by its holding of US debt, and Russia's control of large reserves of oil and gas generated a sharper antagonism towards the United States than that between the United States and Europe.

This differentiation of global rivalries and US interests helps to ex-plain the character of recent US military doctrine and its focus on being able to wage two 'Major Theater Wars' (Achcar 1998, 93). China and Russia are not advanced capitalist states in the sense of the United States or the European countries, but they were the 'only two declared opponents of American hegemony whose behaviour [was] unpredict-able in the middle and long term and whose physical scale places them on comparable footing with the US' (ibid., 102). Although this chal-lenge has not led to any direct military conflict, it is a central element in understanding the recalibration of US interests and their articula-tion in the most recent period. Specifically, these rivalries (and the ever-present commonality of interests) underpin the decisive feature of this latest phase of internationalization: the rise of Central Asia and its link-ages with the fortunes of the Middle East.

The Rise of Central Asia

Following the collapse of the USSR, a number of newly independent states in the Caucasus and Central Asia emerged at the meeting point of Russia, Europe, Asia, and the Middle East. These states – notably Uz-bekistan, Kyrgyzstan, Tajikistan, Kazakhstan, Turkmenistan, Georgia, and Azerbaijan – presented a critical test of the United States' ability to project its power at a global scale. Strategically located between the leading capitalist powers and their emerging rivals, these states consti-tute a zone at the centre of what former Carter administration national security advisor Zbigniew Brzezinski described as 'Eurasia.' More than a decade ago, Brzezinski, the prime architect of Saudi support for the mujahideen in Afghanistan during the 1980s (and later an advisor to Obama), portrayed the region's significance as follows: 'For America, the chief geopolitical prize is Eurasia . . . Now a non-Eurasian power is preeminent in Eurasia – and America's global primacy is directly dependent on how long and how effectively its preponderance on the Eurasian continent is sustained' (1998, 30). Brzezinski's thesis came to encapsulate the views of all leading capitalist states and the emerging

rivals China and Russia; control over this region will be a prime determinant of the form the capitalist world market takes – and hence its
specific balance of rivalry and unity – into the foreseeable future.

Sharply reinforcing the strategic location of the region, each of the
Central Asian states also possesses large quantities of oil, gas, and
other mineral resources. With the restoration of capitalism in Russia
and China and the massive increase in demand for energy in China
that has accompanied deepening internationalization, control of these
resources has become an important element in global power. Of signal
importance is the Caspian Sea, bordered by Russia, Iran, Kazakhstan,
Turkmenistan, and Azerbaijan – the latter three countries gaining their
independence following the collapse of the Soviet Union. According
to estimates by international oil companies, in 2005 the Caspian Sea
region held proven oil reserves equivalent to about 4 per cent of total
world reserves (48 billion barrels) – far exceeding that of the United
States (29 billion barrels). Likewise, proven gas reserves constituted
4 per cent of world reserves (Gelb 2006, 2–3). Most significant, many
areas of the Caspian Sea basin remain unexplored. It is estimated that additional crude oil reserves in the region approach the amount now held
by Saudi Arabia (reaching about 15 per cent of total world reserves) and
that natural gas reserves potentially exceed Saudi deposits (ibid., 3).

The Caspian Sea is landlocked, and neighbouring countries are therefore reliant upon a complex network of pipelines to deliver oil and gas
to consumer markets.[13] For this reason, pipeline geography is highly
significant to dominating the region – both because of the potentially
massive profits and as a means of controlling supplies to erstwhile rivals. Predictably, four major protagonists have emerged in the struggle
over these resources – the United States, the European Union, Russia,
and China. While these four powers attempt to assert their influence
over Central Asia (remembering the careful distinction between the
US-EU and the US-Russia/China relationships noted above), they also
have a common interest in making sure that the region remains 'secure'
for capitalism as a whole. Moreover, corporate profits intersect with –
and sometimes contradict – these geostrategic concerns. All these factors are evident in the range of alternative pipeline projects that have
been built, proposed, or are currently under construction to bring Caspian oil and gas to market.

Reflecting the historical relationship with the Soviet Union, most
of the Caspian oil and gas currently depends upon the Russian pipeline system. Russian control is particularly pertinent to the European

Union, which receives about a third of its gas through Russian pipelines; indeed, some European countries are 100 per cent dependent on that source (Friefeld 2009, 122). This gives Russia significant pressure to determine the price (by increasing transit fees) and potentially even the actual supply of these energy resources, as demonstrated in January 2009 when Russia cut off gas to the Ukraine and thereby severely impacted the supply to several EU countries. European dependency will increase drastically over the next decade – it is estimated that, by 2020, 90 per cent of EU oil needs and 70 per cent of its gas needs will be supplied by imports (European Commission 2008, 18). In this context, Caspian reserves are a vital potential supply source for the European market.

Within the European Union, some forces are pushing for an alignment with Russia over these potential supplies while others seek to reduce the reliance on Russian-controlled pipelines by rerouting supplies through an alternative path. These different approaches are well illustrated by disputes within Germany, where former chancellor Gerhard Schröder has emerged as a primary advocate of Russian supply routes and in 2005 became a consultant with Gazprom, the chief Russian oil and gas company. Symbolizing opposition to the Russian approach is the former foreign minister in Schroder's government, Joschka Fischer, who in 2009 became an advisor to the rival Nabucco project, which aims to ship gas from Azerbaijan to Europe via Turkey, thereby bypassing Russia altogether. This alternative is strongly supported by the US government (Freifeld 2009, 126–7).

Propelled by its growing demand for energy, China is also attempting to project its influence into the region. Chinese control over oil and natural gas is the cornerstone of the country's foreign policy objectives. In 2009, China completed the first stage of a 1,800-kilometre pipeline that will transport gas from Turkmenistan to China's Xinjiang province via Kazakhstan; this, incidentally, is the context of the unrest of the Uyghur people in Xinjiang that received extensive media attention in mid-2009. Noticeably, one of the elements of the deal with Turkmenistan is a proviso to keep 'third parties' – a thinly veiled reference to NATO bases – out of the country. China has also completed a massive 2,228-kilometre oil pipeline from Kazakhstan, and is pursuing a strategy of building oil pipelines through Burma, thereby bypassing the transport of Gulf oil through the narrow Strait of Malacca. China's ability to source oil and gas from Central Asia, linked to pipeline connections with Russia and Iran, has led some to speak of a 'Pan Asian global energy bridge' by which China will act as the main transit point for Central Asian and Middle East energy to the East Asian economies (Troush 1999).

The Unity of the Wars in Central Asia and the Middle East

These geopolitical rivalries and the post-9/11 interventions in Afghanistan and Iraq signal the essential unity of Central Asia and the Middle East. The zone of territory encompassing the GCC countries, Iraq, Iran, Afghanistan, Pakistan, and the new Central Asian states is a single arc constituting one of the most important geographical spaces on the planet. This location symbolizes both the shared interests of the various capitalist powers – the systemic need to protect the Gulf and Central Asia from any challengers to the existing order – as well as the 'Great Power' rivalry that simultaneously exists between them over access to the region's resources. This singular conception of Central Asia and the Middle East is the framework through which to understand all of the conflicts in the region, and is fully shared, as the earlier quote of Brzezinski illustrates, by the leading architects of US policy. A confirmation of this geopolitical unity occurred in 1999, when CENTCOM was extended to include five Central Asian countries: Turkmenistan, Uzbekistan, Kazakhstan, Kyrgyzstan, and Tajikistan.

The US-NATO invasion of Afghanistan in 2001 was the first attempt in the post-9/11 environment to assert control over this area. The Afghanistan-Pakistan region, located at the intersection of the Gulf and Central Asia, is of extreme strategic significance. Not only does it form the crossroads of these two energy-rich areas, but (through Pakistan) it also adjoins the Indian Ocean, which remains the primary shipping route for Gulf oil. China and India are building ports in Gwadar, Pakistan, and Chah Bahar, Iran respectively, through which gas might be shipped one day from Central Asia (transited through Afghanistan) to China and the Pacific (Kaplan 2009, 18).

While Afghanistan's position in these rivalries is largely related to its strategic location, the war in Iraq was more directly related to the promise of oil and gas wealth. Despite later admissions that the evidence linking Iraq with the 9/11 attacks and weapons of mass destruction was fabricated, the United States used the opportunity to launch an invasion in 2003 to finish the war it had begun in January 1991. The US-led forces established a dependent government – destroying the country's political and social fabric in the process – and passed a series of laws that opened the economy to foreign ownership. Passage of a new Iraqi oil law that would reverse the 1972 nationalization has been protracted and widely opposed by Iraqi unions and political forces, yet indications are that such a law will be passed in the coming period. Access to this oil (and significant amounts of natural gas) will be a prime determinant of power in the global economy over the next decade.

This notion of a single region stretching from Central Asia through the Middle East is also the context in which to understand the decades-long threats against Iran. The country is extremely energy rich, holding the third-largest proven oil reserves in the world and the second-largest proven gas reserves. It also has high strategic significance – sandwiched between Iraq, Afghanistan, and the Caspian Sea, and therefore an important potential conduit for oil and gas. A Turkmenistan-Iran gas pipeline was opened January 2010, and Iran has announced plans to build a pipeline that will take oil from the Caspian Sea to the Gulf of Oman. As noted above, the United States is opposed to these schemes, and is attempting to have Caspian oil and gas transported through Turkey, rather than through Iran or Russia. For their part, Russia, India, and China are all keen on establishing energy links with Iran as a means of undercutting US dominance. Indeed, Iran is China's largest supplier of oil.

Canada, the 'Single War,' and Imperialism

It is through this lens of a 'single war' that Canadian military intervention in Afghanistan should be understood. In the post–Second World War period, Canadian capitalism moved away from its historical relationship with Britain to forge a close alliance with the United States as the leading power on the world stage. Canadian capitalism has always been an imperialist force – as seen in the investments and political actions of Canadian mining companies in Latin America, Africa, and the Asia Pacific region and the dominant role of Canadian banks in global financial markets. Canada has pursued its overseas expansion, however, as a junior partner of the United States – often using the rhetoric of 'humanitarian intervention' to enter markets that were closed to its neighbour.

The war in Afghanistan is a major test for Canadian capitalism, as it marks a shift towards a more overtly aggressive posture alongside the extension of US power in the Middle East and Central Asia. Through this intervention, Canadian capital hopes to assert its position at the table, thereby gaining a share of the potential wealth arising from control of the region's resources as well as the less tangible – but no less real – benefits that come from sitting alongside the dominant global power. Canadian mining, engineering, and financial companies have an extensive network of interests in the Gulf, and are well poised to take advantage of the region's possible riches. It should also be noted that, while popular opposition and mobilization prevented a large Canadian troop deployment to Iraq, Canada has conducted a quiet and very close participation with the United States in the occupation of that country. Canada is closely involved through troop exchanges with the US military, engineering work, private security, and – most pointedly – the exploitation of Iraqi oil resources. At least fifteen Canadian-based companies have signed some form of exploration, production, or production-sharing contract in Iraq since 2004 (Fenton 2009).

Despite these very material interests, however, it is important to emphasize once again that oil and gas supplies are not the *source* of imperialist intervention in the Middle East and Central Asia. Marx warned of 'commodity fetishism,' a tendency to use commodities to explain the character of social development rather than understanding the significance given to those commodities by the social relations in which they are embedded. It is the successive deepening of capitalist internationalization – distinguished by the stages of the immediate post-war era, the 1970s, and the period following the opening of Russia and China to capitalism – that have imbued the oil commodity with a central significance in the reproduction of capital and hence power on the global scale. Energy resources are the proximate cause – but the fundamental reasons for intervention in the region are found in the immanent tendencies driving capitalist accumulation.

An understanding that capitalism's tendencies to expand and control space are inherent to the process of accumulation thus highlights a careful distinction between imperialist *policy* – the historically concrete strategies of states to dominate certain geographical areas – and imperialism as a *systemic feature* – with its origins in the political economy of capitalism. Canadian intervention in Afghanistan does not arise from a faulty political platform or the right-wing ambush of decision-making (as many believe of the Harper government). Rather, it stems from the deep interests of Canadian capitalism. Today, a golden thread ties the interventions in Iraq and Afghanistan, the sabre-rattling against Iran and Syria, and US support of Israel and the Arab client regimes.[14] A failure to appreciate fully this unity fragments any popular response and weakens the ability of solidarity movements to build meaningful alliances in places such as Canada. The foreign policy architects of the United States, Canada, and all the leading states share this perspective of a single war. It behooves those opposed to their policies to do the same.

NOTES

1 The Manley Panel findings are available at http://publications.gc.ca/ pub?id=324639&sl=0.

2 There is a rich debate on the concept of 'financialization,' which revolves around the reasons for the rise of finance as well as the associated changes in the forms of accumulation, and the nature of banking and the capitalist firm. It is beyond the scope of this chapter to examine this debate in any detail, but see Marois (2012) for a summation.

3 The relationship between the territorialization of capital and geopolitical rivalry between states is one that is heavily contested within Marxist debates on imperialism and cannot be adequately treated here. For an excellent survey of these debates, see Anievas (2010).

4 The petrochemical industry depended upon petroleum and natural gas as the primary feedstock, in contrast to pre-war production that had used coal; see Spitz (1988) and Chapman (1991) for detailed histories.

5 For a full discussion of this theme and its impact on class and state formation in the GCC states, see Hanieh (2011).

6 In March 1978, US treasury secretary Michael Blumenthal secretly flew to Saudi Arabia to negotiate a deal with the Saudis to sell their oil solely in US dollars, according to an internal US Treasury memo to Blumenthal from Assistant Treasury Secretary C. Fred Bergsten entitled 'Briefing for Your Meeting with Ambassador to Saudi Arabia, John C. West,' 10 March 1978 (cited in Clark 2005, 2).

7 The United States did this through actively supporting Iraq with weapons and intelligence (typically supplied and financed through the Gulf states) and, as later came to light in the Iran-Contra scandal, simultaneously supplying Iran with weapons.

8 A UNICEF study noted, 'if the substantial reduction in child mortality throughout Iraq during the 1980s had continued through the 1990s, there would have been half a million fewer deaths of children under-five in the country as a whole during the eight year period 1991 to 1998' (UNICEF 1999).

9 See Hanieh (2008) for further discussion of these changes in the regional political economy.

10 At the 30 January meeting, Defense Secretary Donald Rumsfeld was reported to have said, 'Imagine what the region would look like without

Saddam and with a regime that's aligned with U.S. interests . . . It would
change everything in the region and beyond. It would demonstrate what
U.S. policy is all about' (Suskind 2004, 85).

11 According to documents obtained by Judicial Watch under the Freedom of
Information Act in 2003.

12 United States, Energy Information Administration. http://www.eia.gov.

13 Over the past decade, Brazilian journalist Pepe Escobar has carefully expli-
cated the significance of this pipeline geography; see Escobar (2002) for an
early example of his work.

14 This chapter was written prior to the tremendous changes in the Middle
East and North Africa that unfolded with the uprisings of 2011. The uprisings have confirmed, however, the general unity of the Middle East and
Central Asia and the overall trajectory of imperialist foreign policy towards the region.

References

Abrahamian, Ervand. 2001. 'The 1953 Coup in Iran.' *Science and Society* 65,
no. 2: 182–215.

Achcar, Gilbert. 1998. 'The Strategic Triad: The United States, Russia, and
China.' *New Left Review* I/228 (March–April): 91–126.

–. 2002. *Clash of Barbarisms: September 11 and the Making of the New World Disorder*. New York: Monthly Review Press.

–. 2004. *Eastern Cauldron: Islam, Afghanistan and Palestine in a Marxist Mirror*.
London: Pluto Press.

Albo, Gregory. 2004. 'The Old and New Economics of Imperialism.' In *Socialist Register 2004: The New Imperial Challenge*, ed. Colin Leys and Leo Panitch.
London: Merlin Press.

Altvater, Elmar. 1993. *The Future of the Market: An Essay on the Regulation of
Money and Nature after the Collapse of 'Actually Existing Socialism.'* London:
Verso.

Anievas, Alex, ed. 2010. *Marxism and World Politics: Contesting Global Capitalism*. London; New York: Routledge.

Arthur, Chris. 2002. 'Capital, Competition and Many Capitals.' In *The Culmination of Capital: Essays on Volume III of Marx's 'Capital'*, ed. Martha Campbell
and Geert Reuten. Basingstoke, UK: Palgrave.

Blanche, Ed. 2009. 'Weaving a New Silk Road.' *Middle East* (May).

Brenner, Robert. 2000. *The Boom and the Bubble: The US in the World Economy*.
London: Verso.

Bromley, Simon. 1991. *American Hegemony and World Oil*. Cambridge, UK: Polity Press.

Bryan, Dick, and Michael Rafferty. 2006. *Capitalism with Derivatives: A Political Economy of Financial Derivatives, Capital and Class*. Basingstoke, UK; New York: Palgrave-Macmillan.

Brzezinski, Zbigniew. 1998. *The Grand Chessboard: American Primacy and Its Geostrategic Imperatives*. New York: Basic Books.

Bukharin, Nikolai. [1929] 1972. *Imperialism and World Economy*. London: Merlin Press.

Callinicos, Alex. 2010. 'Does Capitalism Need the State System.' In *Marxism and World Politics: Contesting Global Capitalism*, ed. Alex Anievas. London and New York: Routledge.

Canadian Press. 2008. 'Iraq war a mistake, Harper admits.' 3 October.

Chapman, Keith. 1991. *The International Petrochemical Industry: Evolution and Location*. Oxford: Blackwell.

Chomsky, Noam. 1999. *Fateful Triangle: The United States, Israel, and the Palestinians*, 2nd ed. Cambridge, MA: South End Press.

Clark, William. 2005. *Petrodollar Warfare: Oil, Iraq and the Future of the Dollar*. Gabriola Island, BC: New Society Publishers.

Eichengreen, Barry. 2008. *Globalizing Capital*, 2nd ed. Princeton, NJ: Princeton University Press.

Escobar, Pepe. 2002. 'Pipelineistan, Part 1: The rules of the game.' *Asia Times*, 25 January.

European Commission. 2008. 'Second Strategic Energy Review, an EU Energy Security and Solidarity Action Plan.' Brussels.

Fenton, Anthony. 2009. 'Hostile Takeover: Canada's Outsourced War for Iraq's Oil Riches.' *THIS Magazine*, 1 September.

Freifeld, Daniel. 2009. 'The Great Pipeline Opera.' *Foreign Policy* (September–October): 122–7.

Gelb, Bernard. 2006. 'Caspian Oil and Gas: Production and Prospects.' Washington, DC: Congressional Research Services.

Gibson, Heather. 1989. *The Eurocurrency Markets, Domestic Financial Policy and International Instability*. London: Macmillan.

Gowan, Peter. 1999. *The Global Gamble: Washington's Faustian Bid for World Dominance*. London: Verso.

Hanieh, Adam. 2008. 'Palestine in the Middle East: Opposing Neoliberalism and US Power.' *MRzine*, 19 July. http://www.monthlyreview.org/mrzine/hanieh190708a.html.

–. 2011. *Capitalism and Class in the Gulf Arab States*. New York: Palgrave Macmillan.

Harvey, David. 1999. *The Limits to Capital*. London: Verso.

IEA (International Energy Agency). 2007. *World Energy Outlook 2007: China and India Insights*. Paris: IEA.

IMF (International Monetary Fund). 2007. *World Economic Outlook October 2007*. Washington, DC: IMF.

Johnson, Chalmers. 2004. *Blowback: The Costs and Consequences of American Empire*. New York: Owl Books.

Kaplan, Robert. 2009. 'Center Stage for the Twenty-First Century.' *Foreign Affairs* 88, no. 2: 16–32.

Katzman, Kenneth. 2006. 'The Persian Gulf States: Issues for U.S. Policy.' Washington, DC: Congressional Research Service.

Klassen, Jerome. 2009. 'Canada and the New Imperialism: The Economics of a Secondary Power.' *Studies in Political Economy* 83 (Spring): 163–90.

Mandel, Ernest. 1983. *Late Capitalism*. London: Verso.

Marois, Thomas. 2012. 'Finance, Finance Capital, and Financialisation.' In *The Elgar Companion to Marxist Economics*, ed. Ben Fine and Alfredo Saad Filho. Cheltenham, UK: Edward Elgar Publishing.

Marx, Karl. 1973. *Grundrisse*. Harmondsworth, UK: Penguin Books.

–. [1867] 1992. *Capital: Volume One*. London: Penguin Classics.

McNally, David. 2009. 'From Financial Crisis to World Slump: Accumulation, Financialisation, and the Global Slowdown.' *Historical Materialism* 17, no. 1: 35–8.

Mitchell, Timothy. 2009. 'Carbon Democracy.' *Economy and Society* 38, no. 3: 399–432.

Ohmae, Kenichi. 1995. *The End of the Nation State: The Rise of Regional Economies.* New York: Free Press.

Palloix, Christian. 1977. 'Conceptualizing the Internationalization of Capital.' *Review of Radical Political Economics* 9, no. 2: 17–28.

Panitch, Leo, and Sam Gindin. 2003. 'Global Capitalism and American Empire.' In *Socialist Register 2004: The New Imperial Challenge*, ed. Colin Leys and Leo Panitch. London: Merlin Press.

–. 2004. 'Finance and American Empire.' In *Socialist Register 2005: The Empire Reloaded*, ed. Colin Leys and Leo Panitch. London: Merlin Press.

Rosdolsky, Roman. 1977. *The Making of Marx's Capital*. London: Pluto Press.

Shaikh, Anwar. 1983. 'The Concentration and Centralization of Capital.' In *A Dictionary of Marxist Thought*, ed. T. Bottomore. Cambridge, MA: Harvard University Press.

Spiro, David. 1999. *The Hidden Hand of American Hegemony: Petrodollar Recycling and International Markets*. Ithaca, NY: Cornell University Press.

Spitz, Peter. 1988. *Petrochemicals: The Rise of an Industry*. New York: John Wiley.

Stokes, Doug. 2007. 'Blood for Oil? Global Capital, Counter-Insurgency and the Dual Logic of American Energy Security.' *Review of International Studies* 33, no. 2: 245–64.

Stork, Joe. 1975. 'US Strategy in the Gulf.' *MERIP Reports* 36 (April): 17–28.

–. 1980. 'The Carter Doctrine and US Bases in the Middle East.' *MERIP Reports* 90 (September): 3–14, 32.

Suskind, Ron. 2004. *The Price of Loyalty*. New York: Simon & Schuster.

Troush, Sergei. 1999. 'China's Changing Oil Strategy and Its Foreign Policy Implications.' Washington, DC: Brookings Institution, Center for Northeast Asian Policy Studies.

UNICEF (United Nations Children's Fund). 1999. 'Iraq Surveys Show "Humanitarian Emergency."' *Information Newsline*, 12 August. http://www.unicef.org/newsline/99pr29.htm.

United States. 1945. Department of State. *Foreign Relations of the United States: Diplomatic Papers 1945*, vol. 8, *The Near East and Africa*. Washington, DC: US Government Printing Office.

–. 1981. Congressional Budget Office. 'The Effect of OPEC Oil Pricing on Output, Prices, and Exchange Rates in the United States and Other Industrialized Countries.' Washington, DC.

Vassiliev, Alexei. 1998. *The History of Saudi Arabia*. London: Saqi Books.

Vitalis, Robert. 2007. *America's Kingdom: Mythmaking on the Saudi Oil Frontier*. Palo Alto, CA: Stanford University Press.

Wolfowitz, Paul. 2009. 'Realism.' *Foreign Policy* (September–October): 67–72.

Wood, Ellen Meiksins. 2005. *Empire of Capital*. London: Verso.

Woods, Ngaire. 2006. *The Globalizers: The IMF, the World Bank, and Their Borrowers*. Ithaca, NY: Cornell University Press.

World Bank. 2008. *World Development Indicators*. Washington, DC: World Bank.

Zahlan, Rosemary. 1998. *The Making of the Modern Gulf States*. London: Ithaca Press.

4

The Empire of Capital and the Latest Inning of the Great Game

MICHAEL SKINNER

What happens with the distribution of power on the Eurasian landmass will be of decisive importance to America's global primacy and historical legacy.
– Zbigniew Brzezinski, 1997

The concept of 'free trade' arose as a moral principle even before it became a pillar of economics . . . This is real freedom.
– US National Security Strategy, 2002

In fact, America's entire war on terror is an exercise in imperialism. This may come as a shock to Americans, who don't like to think of their country as an empire. But what else can you call America's legions of soldiers, spooks and Special Forces straddling the globe?
– Michael Ignatieff, 2003

I will not hesitate to use force to protect the American people or our vital interests.
– Barack Obama, 2009

Since 2001 the public debate among Canadians about whether to support Canada's role in Afghanistan as part of the 'global war on terror' has been dominated largely by red-herring arguments: 'patriots' support the war, while 'traitors' or 'Taliban sympathizers' oppose it. This polarizing debate culminated in the anti-democratic prorogation of Parliament in December 2009. The initial debate that provoked Prime Minister Stephen Harper to shut down Parliament – a question about whether Canadian Forces personnel were complicit in war crimes regarding the mistreatment of Afghan detainees – is of grave importance.

But further exploration of this moral and legal question, as crucial as it is, does not answer the fundamental question: why is Canada fighting in Afghanistan and beyond?

Political and military leaders have repeatedly asked the public to support the war for defensive and humanitarian purposes. Yet, after a decade of conflict, these rationales seem ever distant from the real course of the mission. The intervention has been characterized by an endless occupation and counterinsurgency war through which Afghans have been made less secure in terms of physical safety, social progress, and economic development. The fact is, the war is being fought for other reasons. Afghanistan is one of many battlefronts in a global war with far-flung overt and covert operations not only in Pakistan, Iraq, and the Horn of Africa, but also in the Philippines, South Asia, Latin America, and the Caribbean (Bush 2007; United States 2009). In early 2009 the Obama administration rebranded the 'global war on terror,' calling it Overseas Contingency Operations and rebranded the battlefront in Afghanistan and Pakistan simply as AfPak. But rebranding this global war does not change the vital interests at stake.[1] Canadian leaders may claim that fighting in this war provides security at home and liberates Afghans from tyranny; nonetheless the paramount objectives are to secure what Zbigniew Brzezinski (1997a,b) has called 'America's global primacy' and to liberalize trade and investment on a global scale. This is the 'real freedom' – freedom for capital – that Canadian Forces fight for in Afghanistan and beyond (United States 2002b). As this chapter demonstrates, the big winners in this latest inning of the Great Game[2] will likely be investors secured by what Ellen Wood (2005) describes as a US-led 'Empire of Capital,'[3] while working-class Canadians and especially most Afghans have a great deal more to lose.

Listening to Afghans

In 2007 I travelled throughout Afghanistan with an Afghan-Canadian research partner, Hamayon Rastgar.[4] We asked more than one hundred Afghans: 'What do you think about the international intervention in Afghanistan'?[5] We listened to people generally not heard in the West. Some were Afghanistan's leading intellectuals whose works have not been translated into English or published outside the country. Others were opposition political leaders, some of whom must remain underground because, in the politically oppressive Islamic Republic, socialists and atheists face imprisonment and the death penalty – a fact confirmed by US State Department reports (United States 2004, 2007). We also listened to aid workers and representatives of human rights organizations, but most people we heard were bricklayers, cabdrivers, farmers, miners, university students, shopkeepers, schoolteachers, and other working-class Afghans. Many elaborated at length about why they thought the Operation Enduring Freedom (OEF) coalition led by the United States and the International Security and Assistance Force (ISAF) led by the North Atlantic Treaty Organization (NATO) continue to occupy Afghanistan. Many argued that OEF and ISAF forces are motivated by geopolitical and economic interests that trump ideas of liberating Afghans.

We went to Afghanistan because we had not heard a complete explanation of why the United States and the United Kingdom unilaterally invaded Afghanistan on 7 October 2001, without United Nations sanction.[6] The combat units of the OEF coalition were composed of regular and covert forces from those two countries and from Canada, Australia, New Zealand, Germany, and France (United Kingdom 2001a; United States 2002a). OEF Special Forces, including Canada's JTF-2, led militia members of the United Islamic and National Front for the Salvation of Afghanistan (UIF). The UIF was a loose coalition of *mujahideen* militias led by Islamic fundamentalists, entrepreneurial war profiteers, and alleged war criminals, better known in the West by the sanitized label, the Northern Alliance. Both Germany and France soon withdrew from OEF combat operations due to domestic political pressures, leaving an exclusive Anglo-Saxon coalition fighting under the OEF banner. The occupation began when the signatories of the Bonn Agreement awarded Afghanistan to leaders of the UIF and sanctioned the ISAF force in December 2001 (Warnock 2008).

We wondered why so many Afghans oppose the occupation. We found that many Afghans are sceptical of the coalition of powerful states composing OEF that claims to uphold world order but violated international law to invade Afghanistan and relied on the services of accused war criminals and human rights violators to do much of the fighting. Afghans became more sceptical when both OEF and ISAF forces conducted artillery, tank, and aerial bombardments; fired weapons into crowds of civilians; destroyed homes, farms, businesses, vehicles, and other property; raided homes to abduct people; tortured and abused prisoners; and generally humiliated the population. Afghans quickly realized that promised human development projects were not materializing. Meanwhile, they observed that the OEF-ISAF occupation facili-

tated multi-billion-dollar development projects, which are potentially
profitable for investors and of strategic value to the Empire of Capital,
but also potentially socially disruptive and environmentally destructive for Afghans. We listened to Afghans with a wide range of political and religious ideas, who are motivated to defend their homeland
through a diversity of tactics from non-violent resistance to warfare.

Afghans recognize the geopolitical position of their country, which is
both rich in resources and of strategic value because it lies at the crossroads of Eurasia between powerful neighbours. This geopolitical reality is why the territory now called Afghanistan has suffered repeated
invasions for millennia. It is why the British and Russians, and later
the Americans and Soviets, fought successive innings of a Great Game
of imperial rivalry. It remains the reason why this Great Game has not
concluded; instead, a larger number of players has begun a new inning
on a global scale. Some Canadians might believe that Afghanistan is a
remote, barren corner of the world – a place full of supposedly ignorant
or violent people who must be saved from backwardness, defeated, or
even eliminated. Afghans, however, recognize their central position in
the Great Game of geopolitical strategy played on their land with few
interruptions since the nineteenth century, and in their region since
Elizabeth I granted a royal charter to the founders of the East India
Company, in 1600.

The primary objective of successive British and US-led empires in
the Great Game has been to expand capitalist social relations; both the
British and US states have dedicated significant resources to this venture, while the Russian Tsarists and then the Soviets opposed any expansion of political, economic, and military power on their southern
border. There is a crucial difference in the Great Game today, however.
Whereas, throughout the nineteenth and twentieth centuries, imperial
powers used Afghanistan as a barrier to separate their rival empires
(Rubin 1995), Afghanistan is now being used by the US-led Empire of
Capital as a bridgehead to open all Eurasia to global free trade while
simultaneously containing the aspirations of its potential challengers
(Brzezinski 1997a,b; United States 2008). The vital interest of globalizing capitalist social relations while securing US primacy has motivated
every US president, even the supposed isolationists, since the nineteenth century (Bacevich 2002). What is unique in this conjuncture is
the overwhelming military power possessed by the United States and
its allies in an emerging Empire of Capital and, for the moment, the
relative weakness of any potential state-based challengers.

Below I examine a select few of the many geopolitical and economic interests of the US-led Empire of Capital in Afghanistan. Some are the 'vital interests' to which President Barack Obama (2009) has referred as justification for what he claims is a necessary war. Other interests are independently insufficient to rationalize war, but add to the complex calculus of rational-choice-based decision-making employed by US strategists. Since returning from Afghanistan, I have evaluated these interests by researching government and media documents, the pronouncements of state leaders, and the theories of influential North American intellectuals. This research challenges the common-sense understanding of the 'global war on terror' as a just war of retaliation, self-defence, and liberation. Since 9/11, many in the West have participated in a 'retreat from evidence-based thinking' towards placing faith in powerful leaders who communicate information via propaganda (Keen 2006, 115–30). Many well-intentioned Canadian Forces and government personnel undoubtedly believe they are fighting in Afghanistan for the cause of goodness versus evil. Nonetheless, as Michael Ignatieff (2003: 6) has observed, '[t]here might be reason, even though the awakening has been brutal, to be thankful to the barbarians. After all, they are, as the poet Celan said, a kind of solution. They have offered the empire a new *raison d'être* and a long-term strategic objective: the global eradication of terror.' This new imperial *raison d'être*, which George W. Bush called the 'global war on terror,' is an opportunity to justify the latest inning of the Great Game in which the US-led Empire of Capital is using Afghanistan as a bridgehead to forcefully insert capitalist social relations deeper into Eurasia and to maintain US global primacy.

Rationalizing the 'Global War on Terror'

On 20 September 2001 President Bush declared that OEF would achieve 'far more than instant retaliation' (Bush 2001). In fact, for almost a decade, retaliation has disproportionately affected millions of Afghans who bore no responsibility for the 9/11 terrorist attacks. An astounding 96 per cent of Afghans have been personally affected by death, injury, disability, and the destruction of their homes, assets, and livelihoods (United Nations 2010, 2–8). Retaliation might have been a sufficient reason to satisfy a critical mass of Bush's constituency. Retaliation is also useful strategically to demonstrate that the United States and its closest allies possess the political will and military capacity to punish any challengers, regardless of the human, material, and political costs.

Retaliation, however, does not satisfy the criteria of international law: only *self-defence* and *last resort* meet these criteria (Mandel 2004; Duffy 2005). Neither criterion was argued within the United Nations, and it is unlikely that either could have been proven. International law expert Helen Duffy (2005, 162) argues that, to justify self-defence, 'there must be imminent *threat* of force or a continuing attack . . . and any response must be *necessary* to avert that threat.' The threat must be 'instant, overwhelming, and leaving no choice of means, and no moment for deliberation.' Moreover, '[i]f measures against those responsible for an attack will increase the threat then they can hardly be said to be necessary to avert it.' Finally, '[p]roportionality and necessity are intertwined, with proportionality requiring that the force used be *no more* than necessary to meet the threat presented.' The United States and the United Kingdom unilaterally launched OEF, thus avoiding debate in the UN Security Council on these and other legal points.

Instead of legitimizing the invasion based on the criteria of international law, President Bush justified the war on broader philosophical terms, stating, '[t]his is civilization's fight. This is the fight of all who believe in progress and pluralism, tolerance and freedom . . . Freedom and fear are at war. The advance of human freedom, the great achievement of our time and the great hope of every time, now depends on us' (Bush 2001). After OEF began Laura Bush added that the 'fight against terrorism is also a fight for the rights and dignity of women' and because 'in Afghanistan we see the world the terrorists would like to impose on the rest of us' (2001). Thus a claimed right to retaliation and self-defence and abstract concepts of securing freedom and the rights of women were officially stated as goals of this war.

It was not until publication of the US National Security Strategy (United States 2002b), popularly referred to as the Bush Doctrine, that the Bush administration defined what it really meant by 'freedom.' In a chapter titled 'Ignite a New Era of Global Economic Growth through Free Markets and Free Trade,' the Bush Doctrine defines 'real freedom' as free trade (17–20). Pre-emptive warfare, which most analysts identify as the radical innovation of the Bush Doctrine, is merely the means to liberate capital. Neither pre-emptive warfare nor wars fought to expand free trade are departures from US practice (Bacevich 2002). The only radical action of the Bush administration was to articulate this objective and the means to pursue it so clearly. Neither the Obama administration nor any Canadian government has repudiated the means and objectives identified by the Bush Doctrine; instead, the Obama administration has intensified the 'global war on terror,' now referred to as Overseas Contingency Operations, in Afghanistan, Pakistan, Yemen, Somalia, and beyond.

According to then-prime minister Jean Chrétien (2001) and defence minister Art Eggleton (2001), Canada joined the OEF invasion of Afghanistan to demonstrate support for the United States. Major-General Jonathan Vance of the Canadian Forces has argued (2005, 286–7) that Canadian foreign policy is 'more concerned with the political advantages of being seen to participate' in US-led missions, and that Canadian strategy is centred around 'protecting Canadian interests rather than pursuing them.' Nonetheless the interests of investors, whether Canadian or US, tend to be synonymous when it comes to integrating contested regions into the globalizing system of liberal capitalism. Rather than merely kowtowing as a subordinate state to US dominance, the leaders of the Canadian state took a proactive stance to secure Canada's position as a subdominant ally in the US-led Empire of Capital.

Stein and Lang (2008, 10) claim that Canada was 'legally committed and obligated' to join OEF to defend the United States after Article 5 of the NATO treaty was invoked on 4 October 2001. Curiously, however, only two other NATO states – the United Kingdom and Germany – provided combat support for OEF; evidently, most NATO states did not feel obliged to fight as part of OEF or to act more aggressively in later ISAF operations. Perhaps their leaders feared the limits of their own military capacities or the costs associated with war. Perhaps they recognized the fact that international law and the UN Charter supersede treaty obligations. They certainly knew that popular opinion was against joining OEF or acting more aggressively during the ensuing OEF-ISAF occupation.

Before the war began, massive protests around the world in September and October 2001 demonstrated popular opposition to the invasion of Afghanistan and President Bush's declaration of the 'global war on terror' (Becker 2001; *Democracy Now* 2001; Featherstone 2001; *Guardian* 2001; *National Catholic Reporter* 2001). With the exception of Americans, Israelis, and Indians, most people in the world opposed the 'global war on terror' and, instead, supported legal means of investigating, apprehending, and prosecuting the 9/11 perpetrators, according to a Gallup poll conducted in thirty-seven countries in late September 2001 (Gallup International 2001; Miller 2002). Yet the leaders of OEF claimed to be supported by a global consensus to invade and occupy Afghanistan. As if Afghan history began in 2004, Canadian government documents typically state that Canadian Forces 'are in Afghanistan at the request of the democratically elected government of President Hamid Karzai to help the Afghan people rebuild their nation' as part of the UN-sanctioned ISAF mission (Canada 2010). However, this narrative ignores Canada's role in the *unsanctioned* OEF invasion in 2001 and ongoing OEF counterinsurgency operations in both Afghanistan and Pakistan. It also ignores the mission creep of the ISAF operations, which began as a UN-sanctioned complex peace operation, but metamorphosed into an aggressive counterinsurgency operation under NATO command beginning in 2003. In 2009 President Obama appointed General Stanley McChrystal as joint commander of both OEF and ISAF operations.

Since 2001 worldwide opposition to the 'global war on terror' and the escalating warfare in Afghanistan and Pakistan has grown. The resignation and protests of highly ranked US military officers, such as Major General Antonio Taguba (2008) and Colonel Ann Wright (2009), and civilian military personnel, such as General Counsel Alberto Mora (2006) of the US Navy, indicate serious problems with the means used during the 'global war on terror,' which include torture and other illegal acts. A Canadian senior diplomat, Richard Colvin, reported evidence of Canadian Forces complicity with the torture of detainees in 2006, although his allegations were not widely publicized until 2009, after a House of Commons committee called Colvin as a witness (CBC News 2009). While these and other high-ranking military and diplomatic officials have critiqued the legality of the means used to wage war, a diverse range of social activists has critiqued the legitimacy of the objectives sought by the leaders of the 'global war on terror.' In 2008 the Canadian Labour Congress, in solidarity with the Canadian Peace Alliance and numerous social justice movements, demanded the withdrawal of Canadian Forces from Afghanistan (Canadian Labour Congress 2008; Skinner 2008a). On 1 May 2008 thousands of unionized dockworkers shut down twenty-nine North American ports to protest the 'global war on terror' (Serjeant and Woodall 2008; Yardley 2008).

These protesters recognized that the 'global war on terror' cannot ensure security, because it exacerbates and multiplies rather than settles grievances. According to UK House of Commons Library researchers (United Kingdom 2001b), the 9/11 attacks were motivated by a desire to support Palestinians and to remove US military bases from Saudi Arabia. Their research contradicts Ignatieff's suggestion that al-Qaeda 'made no political demands at all, and it seems clear that they were not pursuing properly political goals, so much as seeking to bring down a

mighty religious malediction on their adversary' (2003, 7). Until politicians negotiate settlement of the *bona fide* grievances that motivate
groups like al-Qaeda, conflicts will fester and multiply. The violent
means al-Qaeda used to publicize such grievances were illegal and ultimately ineffective, but neither terrorist acts nor the propaganda used to
hide the terrorists' motivations make the grievances any less legitimate.
Rather than negotiate political settlements, the 'global war on terror'
has multiplied popular grievances around the world. Consequently,
since the 'global war on terror' began, US and international security
has deteriorated, according to the US Congressional Research Service
(Katzman 2010).

Nor has the war liberated Afghans in any meaningful way. Not
only are 96 per cent of Afghans negatively affected by the war, but
poverty reduction and economic development policies are based on
'a simplistic and apolitical understanding of poverty as an individual
material condition' and the assumption that economic development
benefits everyone, which will lead to stability (Kantor 2010, 21). In
2010 36 per cent of Afghans remained in 'absolute poverty' and another 37 per cent lived only slightly above the poverty line (United
Nations 2010, 2–8).

The many failures of the mission to secure Afghanistan for humanitarian reconstruction are often attributed to gross ineptitude or to
overly optimistic expectations, but OEF-ISAF forces may have failed
to meet these objectives *because of other priorities*. Since 2001 any well-
intended efforts to address human development in Afghanistan have
been trumped by the interests of a US-led Empire of Capital. The
Bush administration used the issues of retaliation, self-defence, and
humanitarian intervention to rationalize the war in Afghanistan. Many
Afghans recognize a far more complex set of motivations based on the
pursuit of geopolitical and economic objectives. Through the course of
our interviews, Afghans articulated *geopolitical interests* as motivating
the 'global war on terror':

- to assert US *global primacy* and dominant position as global arbiter;
- to establish NATO as a US-led forum of global governance with the
  capacity and legitimacy to bypass the United Nations' authority, ab-
  rogate existing international laws, and create new international laws;
- to demonstrate US/NATO resolve for war;
- to test the capacity of military equipment and interoperability of
  national military systems and to train personnel;

- to establish forces in Afghanistan, because it is strategically located between the emerging empires of Russia, China, and India, the politically volatile Central Asian republics, a potentially 'failing' yet militarily powerful Pakistan, and a 'rogue' state, Iran;
- to initiate a strategy of *creative destruction* in Greater Central Asia to allow the subsequent *stabilization and reconstruction* necessary for the further globalization of liberal world order; and *economic interests*
- to generate profits by further opening Greater Central Asia to global free trade;
- to generate profits by reconnecting Eurasia along the underused transportation, communications, and energy transmission corridors that crisscross the Greater Central Asia region in which Afghanistan is a central node;
- to generate profits by transferring public resources of allied states to corporations in the military, security, and development sectors;
- to generate profits by selling weapons developed to meet the contingencies of the current war and proven on the 'sales floor' of the battlefield; and
- to generate profits by privatizing Afghan industries and abundant natural resources.

Of course, none of these explanations stands alone as *the* reason for invading and occupying Afghanistan. Instead, all these rationales, in addition to those more often stated by politicians, work together synergistically. Recognition of this complexly interacting set of principles and interests helps explain the depth and breadth of the non-violent resistance and armed insurgency in Afghanistan, which cannot be explained by religious radicalism alone. We observed that the perception of threats to religious and traditional values and practices, which consequently have motivated many Muslims to defend their religious beliefs, is certainly a social binder that provides a mutual point of reference for many Afghans. Nevertheless religion is not the primary cause of resistance. The violent and non-violent resistance movements opposing occupation are motivated by previously existing grievances, by new grievances generated by personal and collective losses during the war, and by rational perceptions of the interests that motivate the states engaged in military intervention. In short, Afghans perceive there are more reasons than ostensibly liberating Afghans and prosecuting terrorists for occupying Afghanistan.

Indeed, as Allan English (2005, 2) notes, 'war has been more or less a functional institution in human society because it provided benefits for societies that were good at it, although the cost of the benefits could be high.' One of the things the principal states of the Empire of Capital have proven good at is propagandizing the moral principles for going to war, while obscuring the material state and corporate interests that underlie these principles. As Ignatieff (2003, 111) argues, '[e]mpires that are successful learn to ration their service to moral principle to the few strategic zones where the defence of principle is simultaneously the defence of a vital interest and where the risks do not outweigh the benefits. This is why modern imperial ethics can only be hypocritical.' For this reason, we must look at the geopolitical and economic interests of those waging the 'global war on terror.' In the space remaining I examine the concept of US 'global primacy' and then analyse western efforts to reconnect Eurasia economically and to privatize Afghan resources.

The Geopolitics of the 'Global War on Terror': Asserting US Global Primacy

In the immediate wake of the Cold War 'victory' over the USSR, influential US grand strategists began to rethink how to consolidate and expand US power on a global scale. Zalmay Khalilzad (1995a,b), Samuel Huntington (1996), and Zbigniew Brzezinski (1997a,b) all recognized that US dominance would be brief unless US power was expanded in Eurasia to pre-empt the emergence of rival empires – especially China, but also Russia and India.

Brzezinski foresaw expansion in Eurasia occurring primarily on diplomatic and economic fronts, but Khalilzad raised the spectre of warfare on the Eurasian supercontinent, which Huntington predicted would be a violent 'clash of civilizations.' However, rather than a war between the West and the rest, as his argument is often portrayed, Huntington predicted a *class war* between what he called the 'Davos Culture' of the World Economic Forum and the world's poor and marginalized. Huntington described this 'Davos Culture' as a transnational but nonetheless US-led bourgeoisie that derives wealth and power through the exploitation of labour and resources in world markets. Khalilzad (1995b, 95) advocated US leadership of an alliance of states sharing 'common values, most important among them democracy and a commitment to free markets' forcefully expanding a 'zone of peace' across the globe. Like Khalilzad and Huntington, Brzezinski suggested that the maintenance of this leadership role or 'global primacy' should be the main objective of US foreign policy. He argued that 'the immediate task [regarding Eurasia] is to ensure that no state or combination of states gains the ability to expel the United States or even diminish its decisive role' (1997a, 52). The long-term objective should be to perpetuate US global primacy, which is based on its 'decisive role as Eurasia's arbitrator' (64). In sum, the policies to expand the global primacy of the United States that these and other like-minded grand strategists have prescribed are integral to understanding the implementation of US and, consequently, Canadian foreign policy in reaction to 9/11 and throughout the 'global war on terror.'

More specifically Brzezinski (2009) claimed that US global primacy is threatened today not only because the 'global center of political and economic gravity is shifting away from the North Atlantic toward Asia and the Pacific,' but also because of 'intensifying popular unrest.' The 'global war on terror' forcefully contains both of these perceived threats by strengthening the powers of state and private security forces to suppress popular resistance while aggressively thrusting a US-led military coalition deep into Central Asia. In the best scenario this bold manoeuvre provides opportunities to *engage* potential challengers – China, Russia, and India – in a range of mutual political and economic interests. In the worst scenario of unending war, the military coalition is in a forward position to *contain* these potential state challengers, as well as potential spoilers – Iran, Pakistan, and the Central Asian republics. The demonstration effect of invading and occupying states such as Afghanistan, Iraq, and Haiti, as well as forcefully suppressing popular unrest in these countries, while expensive in personnel and material costs, may be cost effective in the long term if US-led allied forces demonstrate the futility of resistance to US primacy and economic liberalization. One objective served by initiating unilateral warfare, whether the US fights alone or by assembling a multinational coalition (as opposed to a United Nations multilaterally sanctioned coalition), is to maintain the credibility of deterrence as a threat to any potential challenger.[7] Regardless of the spectrum of possible outcomes of warfare, investors in the military, security, and development industries in North America and Europe profit.

US power is projected through a matrix of alliances and organizations that sets the agenda for subordinate states. Subdominant powerful states, including Canada, support a dominant United States in this hierarchical global system. This structure of power is relatively consensual among the dominant and subdominant states, corporate substate/transnational actors, and the many non-governmental organizations that are dependent on states and corporations, but generally coercive towards subordinate states and many substate/transnational actors.[8] Indeed, according to Ignatieff, a 'globalized economy cannot function without this structure of authority and coercive power' (2003, 124). In his view, 'this is not a new *American* empire, since other Western powers have formidable stakes in the success of the enterprise . . . but it is American in its leadership, and without its leadership the new imperium will founder' (112).

The US-led project to create an Empire of Capital through military, political, and economic coercion is clearly intended to expand and intensify capital accumulation on a global scale. In this way, the social relations of capitalism are being universalized across the states of the world economy and forcefully maintained and managed by the military infrastructure of NATO and the Pentagon. The Empire of Capital thus is a fusion of the economic interests of transnational capital with the political and military interests of the United States and other NATO states. Its fundamental objective is to globalize and secure the capitalist mode of production and the liberal state forms that best facilitate capitalism under the political and military aegis of Washington and a close-knit community of allies.

It is important to recognize how the political advocacy for empire by Ignatieff, Huntington, Khalilzad, and Brzezinski rests upon a conceptual dichotomy of liberal and antiliberal actors. This discourse ignores or conceals the critics we heard in Afghanistan. Many Afghans support various concepts of social and political rights congruent with many if not all concepts of liberal human rights, but perceive privatization of Afghan resources as theft of common public property and observe the quasi-theocratic government imposed upon them as a puppet dictatorship. Such critics speak from a diverse range of national, traditional, religious, liberal humanist, and socialist perspectives. However, the hegemonic discourse can interpret such critics only as antiliberal deviants, 'mouthpieces of the Taliban,' or, in Ignatieff's racist rhetoric, 'barbarians.' Many Afghans observe that the *mujahideen* of the UIF are as antiliberal regarding most political and social issues as are the Taliban. The *mujahideen*, nonetheless, embrace economic liberalization, even if only for personal reward, as opposed to the Taliban, who reject all aspects of liberalization. Afghans who recognize a greater plurality of economic, political, and social ideas than the liberal/antiliberal dichotomy allows, remain oppressively trapped between the Islamic Republic of the *mujahideen* and the Islamic Republic of the Taliban. In this way, the advocates of empire give a 'monopoly of anti-imperialism' to the Taliban, despite the existence in Afghanistan of armed insurgencies and non-violent resistance movements based on diverse ideologies.[9] In this context state-sanctioned violence aids economic liberalization at the expense of political and social liberalization by effectively suppressing those who might otherwise challenge both economic liberalization and regressive Talibanization.

The hegemonic discourse also legitimates US primacy by juxtaposing the globalizing regime of liberalism, which is uncritically assumed to be benign, against all state and non-state challengers that are assumed to be both antiliberal and malign. If, on occasion, the US-led Empire of Capital must act in a malign way, so the discourse goes, it does so only in self-defence against antiliberal actors and in ways that are temporary and proportional. The legitimacy of this discourse, however, has unravelled during the 'global war on terror,' as the war demonstrates time and again the violence inherent to empire. The Empire of Capital needs violence to destroy the normative foundations of precapitalist systems, particularly systems of collective welfare and reciprocity. Some of our Afghan interlocutors would agree with Harvey's (2003) understanding of the new imperialism as a form of 'accumulation by dispossession' – a rational deployment of violence to clear the land of peasants, artisanal miners, and traditional craftspeople whose presence would otherwise constrain large-scale economic development. To this end, the empire deploys violence to overcome resistance that flares up in reaction to the destruction of traditional norms and livelihoods. More broadly, '[w]hat is required is a compliant population accepting of the benefits of global capitalism and cowed by threats of physical punishment. Governments unwilling or unable to police within their borders cannot, according to the new line of thinking, be left to their own devices. The United States must supply the training, equipment and oversight to ensure that local forces are up to the job. And, if governments refuse, Washington will see to the job' (Lipschutz 2002, 230).

As Ignatieff observes, the 'American empire that since defeat in Vietnam had been cautious in its designs has been roused by barbarian attack to go on the offensive' (2003, 6). The 9/11 attacks provided an opportunity to project US-led military power deep into Eurasia. As the next section demonstrates, this geopolitical campaign for global primacy is intertwined with economic interests in Afghanistan and

Greater Central Asia. As such, it represents a new stage of development for the Empire of Capital.

The Geo-economics of the 'Global War on Terror'

Invaders throughout history have sought to control Afghanistan's real estate, which is both rich in natural resources and of immense geopolitical and economic value. While western leaders describe retaliation, liberation, and security as motivations for the 'global war on terror.' Afghans are sceptical of claims that leaders of the Empire of Capital have no interest in exploiting the resources and geographic centrality of their country.

The Silk Road Strategy

The transition of Afghanistan from a barrier separating rival empires to a bridgehead from which to further advance economic liberalization is key to maintaining US global primacy. As Brzezinski indicated, 'the distribution of power on the Eurasian landmass will be of decisive importance to America's global primacy' (1997a, 51). This distribution of power will favour those who dominate trade on the supercontinent. Striving to achieve US dominance over the process of reconnecting Eurasia through Afghanistan and the Greater Central Asia region is a central component of this quest for power. The material reality is that the shortest routes between China and Europe, as well as between India and Russia, are via Afghanistan. As in previous imperial ages, the empire that achieves primacy is the one that, among other aspects of power, establishes itself as arbiter, builder, and protector of trade routes. But the long-delayed reconstruction of the ancient Silk Road trade network into a modern transportation, energy transmission, and communications infrastructure, which will be a determining factor of how wealth and power are distributed in Eurasia, will occur with or without the United States. The United States and its closest allies have few political or economic advantages in Greater Central Asia; military power is their only clear advantage. By employing *creative destruction* leading to *stabilization and reconstruction*, the United States and its allies might, however, establish advantages in financing, designing, constructing, and servicing the infrastructure to expand free trade. Whatever the outcome, investors in the military-industrial complex and its sibling, the development-industrial complex, profit from war.

The Silk Road Strategy Act of 1997, introduced by Representative Benjamin Gilman (1997) in the US Congress, did not pass into law but nonetheless reflected the strategic thinking of Brzezinski and other grand strategists who advocate empire. Gilman aimed 'to focus American diplomatic and commercial attention, as well as American foreign assistance, on the important regions of the Caucasus and Central Asia' in order to rebuild 'links to Europe and Asia.' While the bill focused on facilitating oil and gas exports to the West, it also aimed more broadly to establish 'economic interdependence' and to develop 'open market economies and open democratic systems' in the region. Gilman designed the bill to: (1) 'help promote market-oriented principles and practices'; (2) 'assist in the development of the infrastructure necessary for communications, transportation, and energy and trade'; and (3) 'support United States business interests and investments in the region' (1997, 2–3). According to Doug Bereuter, who chaired the subcommittee meetings on the bill, 'the collapse of the Soviet Union has unleashed a new great game, where the interests of the East India Trading Company have been replaced by those of the Union Oil Corporation of California (UNOCAL) and Total, and many other organizations and firms' (United States 1998, 6). As Gilman indicated in the bill, the US objective has been to secure investors and liberate capital in general, of which the oil and gas sectors are vital commercial interests but by no means the only ones – in Afghanistan, mineral mining is of even greater concern. Nonetheless all economic development requires constructing a comprehensive transportation, energy transmission, and communications network.

Since the invasion of Afghanistan, some analysts of the Silk Road Strategy Act have focused on UNOCAL's attempts to negotiate a pipeline contract with the *mujahideen* factions and the Taliban in the 1990s (United States 1998, 37); John Foster's (2008) analysis of the Turkmenistan-Afghanistan-Pakistan-India (TAPI) natural gas pipeline plan is an excellent contribution to the debate. Nonetheless, TAPI and other oil and gas pipeline proposals are only one aspect of the infrastructure needed to accomplish the trans-Eurasian strategy Brzezinski envisaged. The Silk Road Strategy indicates a broader range of US interests in Afghanistan and Greater Central Asia, necessitating a comprehensive strategy to establish a transportation, energy transmission, and communications infrastructure for the benefit of US and allied investors. On 29 September 2011, the US State Department publicly announced its 'New Silk Road' strategy (United States 2011).

Today massive infrastructure construction remains essential to complete the project to open Afghanistan for business. Due to the

British-Russian and later US-Soviet uses of Afghanistan as a buffer state
(Rubin 1995) and the security concerns of Afghan leaders (Shroder 1981),
no railways and few roads penetrate the country from neighbouring
states. Soviet engineers began to build modern highway access and a
short railway spur into Afghanistan in the 1970s, but except for the ring
road that circles Afghanistan, there is virtually no infrastructure to fulfill the country's exceptional potential as a vital node in a trans-Eurasian
network. Nonetheless, as the Afghanistan Investment Support Agency
(2010) advertises, 'Afghanistan is ideally situated to again function as
a strategic gateway,' offering 'a point of access to an extended regional
market of more than 2 billion people.' In other words Afghanistan is a
new frontier for capital development. Building and operating the necessary infrastructure to exploit this potential will be a capital-intensive
but highly profitable venture.

The Trans-Eurasian Railway

One key infrastructure project is railway building. The Asian Development Bank (2009, 1) has recognized the 'great potential of Afghanistan
to serve as a transit route for traffic and trade' and that Afghanistan's
'significant mineral, industrial, and agricultural potential' requires rail
transport. To date, however, the OEF-ISAF occupation has a poor record
of facilitating railway construction, perhaps due to strict adherence to
neoliberal principles and the fact that insurgents can easily sabotage
railways. The only railway project to materialize from the OEF-ISAF
occupation is a sixty-seven-kilometre extension to a twenty-five-
kilometre track constructed during the Soviet occupation. The track,
which runs south from Termez, Uzbekistan, supplied the Soviet military and now serves the same purpose for German ISAF forces based
near Mazar-e-Sharif (Reuters 2008). In 2009 the Asian Development
Bank announced it would finance the project 'in a bid to improve trade
and aid and undermine highway bandits helping to fund insurgents,
including the Taliban' (McCombs 2009).

Meanwhile Iranian and Chinese state enterprises are well on their
way to extending their railway networks across Afghanistan to create a
trans-Eurasian railway. The Iranian state-owned RAI Railway Corporation, which 'sees itself as a natural hub' in Eurasia, is rapidly expanding
its railway network into both Iraq and Afghanistan (Brice 2008). Perhaps
one of the many Chinese and Iranian sources of 'coercive pressure' that
could 'challenge or reduce U.S. influence' implied by the US National

Defense Strategy (United States 2008) is the high priority these countries place on expanding international rail links (Brice 2008; Hughes 2008). Planning for a 1,250-kilometre railway to connect the Afghan cities of Herat and Mazar-e-Sharif with Tehran began in June 2002, and construction began in July 2006 (Hughes 2008; Reuters 2008; Fars News Agency 2009). The Afghan rail line will link to the recently completed 6,500-kilometre Islamabad-Tehran-Istanbul railway that connects Pakistan via Iran to Turkey and onwards to Europe. This was a project of the Economic Cooperation Organization (ECO), which consists of Afghanistan, Azerbaijan, Iran, Kazakhstan, Kyrgyzstan, Pakistan, Tajikistan, Turkey, Turkmenistan, and Uzbekistan (Fars News Agency 2009). The Iran-Afghanistan line will provide the shortest route to Iranian ports from the five Central Asian states, which have a combined 'Malaysia-sized' gross domestic product of US$187 billion (Najafizada and Rupert 2010a). In early 2010 the ECO (2010) announced that completing a railway from China via Tajikistan to connect to the Afghan-Iranian line is also 'being considered' to create the shortest, fastest, and cheapest railway linking China to Europe.

It is significant that the supposed 'rogue' state, Iran, is instrumental among other regional states in constructing the transportation infrastructure needed to reconstruct Afghanistan, stimulate economic development in the region, and provide the best land route between China and Europe. Afghanistan's potential economic independence based on the economic independence of Iran, its regional partners, and China is vexing for US strategists, considering both the perceived need to demonstrate US primacy in the region and the real material need to demonstrate a comparative advantage if western corporations are to finance, construct, and service the regional infrastructure for trade. In the case of constructing a trans-Eurasian rail network, North American and European companies do not have a competitive advantage in financing, engineering, constructing, and maintaining railway infrastructure or manufacturing equipment, all of which are performed by companies throughout the immediate region. Iran and Afghanistan stand to profit and gain geopolitical advantages when the railways now under construction begin operating. These benefits will exponentially multiply when the Iranian-Afghan project connects to China's railways. The ability of an Iranian-Afghan partnership to launch a massive transportation infrastructure project based on regional finance and technology is problematic for US strategists trying to both isolate Iran and establish profitable enterprises in the region. An escalation of the 'global war on terror' along the Afghan-Iranian border or even into Iran might solve this problem for US strategists, but it would open a host of other problems. For this reason, among many, governments in the region are wary of the escalation of the 'global war on terror' and US threats towards Iran.[10]

Privatizing Afghan Industries and Natural Resources

The US Department of State reports that Afghanistan 'has taken significant steps toward fostering a business-friendly environment for both foreign and domestic investment' (United States 2010). Afghanistan's new investment law allows 100 per cent foreign ownership and provides generous tax allowances to foreign investors, but without providing any protection for Afghan workers or the environment (Noorzoy 2006). As part of Afghanistan's economic liberalization and privatization strategy, a subdepartment of the United States Agency for International Development (USAID), the Land Titling and Economic Restructuring Activity (LTERA), is directing the sale of every Afghan state enterprise in transportation, communications, manufacturing, commerce, and resource extraction. Afghanistan's immense wealth of minerals, hydrocarbons, and gems tops the list of resources with high probability for profit. Moreover, these resources are of strategic interest to the players of the Great Game. However, the liberal concept of private ownership is a radical departure from previously entrenched conceptions of traditional or socialist property, and is one cause of Afghan resistance.

On 31 January 2010 Afghan president Hamid Karzai told reporters that, according to an 'almost-finished' US Geological Survey (USGS) report, Afghanistan's mineral resources are worth a trillion US dollars (Najafizada and Rupert 2010b), but the story of Afghanistan's vast mineral wealth reached the front page of the *New York Times* only in June of that year (Risen 2010). The *New York Times* framed the story as if US geologists had suddenly discovered these resources following the US-led invasion. But, while recent work by the USGS, assisted by the Canadian Forces' Mapping and Charting Establishment, might have quantified these resources more accurately, Afghanistan's geological wealth was well known and exploited for millennia and extensively surveyed, beginning with British surveys in the late eighteenth century (Shroder 1981).

In the early 1930s the Afghan government granted American Inland Oil Company a twenty-five-year exclusive concession to oil and mineral exploration rights, but the company soon backed out of the deal, upsetting the Afghans in 'their first real experience with voluntary foreign penetration' (Shroder 1981, 44). After the Second World War the Afghan government initiated geological exploration, seeking technical and financial assistance from US, western European, Czech, and Soviet sources, often pitting First and Second World prospectors against one another on overlapping but secretive exploration projects. By the 1970s more than seven hundred geological reports indicated that a wealth of resources awaited exploitation. The Ministry of Mines and Resources and the UN in Kabul concealed additional reports containing 'information on resources perceived to be world-strategic and therefore a threat to Afghan independence should too much notice be attracted' (Shroder 1981, 45). Despite holding some of the world's largest deposits of resources and minerals, only limited development of oil, gas, salt, coal, building materials, and lapis lazuli began after the Second World War, primarily by Soviet-trained engineers. From the early 1970s through the early 1990s, Afghans did, however, derive much of their foreign exchange from natural gas sales to the USSR, even if the Soviets underpaid for the resource (Noorzoy 1985, 2006). Greater resource exploitation was limited in part because of the lack of road and railway access as well as political instability, but most foreign investors stayed out of Afghanistan primarily because 'minerals were traditionally considered to be state property' (Shroder 1981, 49). The OEF invasion secured the freedom for investors finally to access Afghanistan's wealth.

In 2002 the USGS published its first of several post-invasion reports. This early report listed more than a thousand deposits, mines, and occurrences in Afghanistan. Among the minerals found in abundance are gold, copper, iron, mercury, lead, uranium, and rare metals such as chromium, cesium, lithium, niobium, and tantalum. Tantalum, also known as coltan, is essential in the manufacture of cell phones, computers, and digital cameras. Lithium is necessary for high-tech batteries, specialty glasses and ceramics, and for some high-performance metal alloys. Niobium is used in steel alloys. Chromium is also used in high-grade steel, including most steel for military uses, but North America and Europe lack supplies. Oil and natural gas reserves identified by the USGS in 2002 far surpass earlier Soviet estimates (Klett et al. 2006; *Oil & Gas Journal* 2006; Shroder 2007).

Leaders of the OEF coalition downplay the profit motives of their own corporations in Afghanistan. However, Afghan geological resources are of greater interest than just accumulating wealth. After the Second World War, the United States and the USSR had strategic interests in an array of radioactive and rare minerals found in Afghanistan, while in recent years China has begun to corner the markets in many of these strategic resources – a fact perceived as a potential threat by western strategists (Eunjang Cha 2009; Reuters 2009; Vulcan 2009). More common minerals, such as copper and iron, as well as hydrocarbon fuels, all of which Afghanistan has in abundance, are desperately sought today by China and India. Exploiting these resources is an economic imperative, but tactical strategizing to control or deny access, even at the expense of perpetuating chaos in the region, could override the profit imperative if US strategists deemed this necessary for national security.

The geopolitical struggle for control of resources exacerbates conflict at the local level. In 2007 we visited geologists at the University of Bamiyan, who warned of the impending confrontations over mining development in their province (Skinner 2008b). The Afghanistan Ministry of Mines claims that the Hajigak iron deposit in Bamiyan is one of the richest in the world (Afghanistan Geological Survey 2008). Abundant coal nearby, which is necessary for the coking process and to generate electricity, makes this a world-class site for mine development. The potential for large-scale industrial mining here is astounding; all that is missing is the infrastructure to support it and the security forces to protect it from popular resistance.

On 24 November 2011 the government of Afghanistan awarded the rights to mine the Hajigak deposit to an Indian consortium of seven steel and mining companies led by the state enterprises Steel Authority of India and NMDC, which will develop three of four blocks, and to Canada's Kilo Goldmines, a company which built its fortune mining in the troubled Democratic Republic of Congo and which will develop the fourth block. Two Iranian companies, Gol-e-Gohar and Behin Sanata Diba, as well as a US-Afghan firm, Arcato, lost the race for Hajigak's wealth (Seth 2011).

Western journalists claim that privatizing Afghan mineral resources will create tens of thousands of jobs and generate taxes to build infrastructure such as roads, hospitals, schools, mosques, and water sources (Synovitz 2008; Landay 2009). One journalist claims that China's investment in the Aynak mining project, analysed below, 'dovetails with the

[Obama] administration's emerging strategy for ending the war in part by delivering on unfulfilled vows to better the lives of the poor Afghans who constitute the vast majority of the Taliban's foot soldiers' (Landay 2009, 15). Following the Afghan government's awarding of mining rights at Hajigak to Kilo Goldmines, Ed Fast, minister for International Trade and for the Asia-Pacific Gateway, stated: 'Canada is strongly committed to helping Afghans rebuild their county, and this investment by Kilo Goldmines will create jobs for Afghans and Canadians alike' (Canada 2011). However, according to a study commissioned by the Canadian mining industry, 'Canadian mining companies are far and away the worst offenders in environmental, human rights and other abuses around the world' (Whittington 2010). Canadian mining companies have shown consistently that they can maximize profits for investors at the expense of the local people who are negatively affected by mining development. It is likely that the bulk of taxes and royalties generated by mining inevitably will finance the immense security apparatus that Canada and other states are constructing in Afghanistan, which is ostensibly designed to contain the complex insurgency, but which can just as well contain popular resistance to unfavourable development projects.

Based on their understanding of the well-known 'resource curse' that people throughout the developing world suffer, Afghans fear they will be condemned to even greater suffering when their collectively owned wealth of resources is privatized and sold to transnational companies. In the Bamiyan Valley, for example, every available niche of land is filled with productive, sustainable agriculture in a delicate balance of nature. This is an extremely fragile environment, similar to the arid US southwest, but intensively cultivated. Building the infrastructure to support mining and spewing toxic waste into the atmosphere and watershed will have a destructive impact on the ecological balance that local farmers have maintained for millennia. Prior to 1978 Afghanistan was a net exporter of food and other agricultural products, including craft-manufactured textiles, with more than 87 per cent of the population living in 22,750 rural villages (Noorzoy 1990, 83–5). War has since displaced many Afghans, but many still live on traditional land claims. Afghans know that the indigenous peoples of the Americas suffered five centuries of displacement and genocidal slaughter to make way for economic development and that ecological destruction results from resource extraction. Afghans fear for their future, because they understand extractive industries can destroy social and environmental systems. As in many places in the world, including Canada, conflicts exist between those who live on the land and those who want to exploit what lies beneath it.

Privatization of Afghanistan's geological resources began in earnest in 2006 with auctions of the Jawzjan gas field, the Karkar-e Dodkash coal mine in Baghlan, a fluoride mine in Uruzagan, a gold mine in Herat, a precious stones mine in Nuristan, and cement factories in Ghori and Parwan. The largest asset auctioned since is the huge Aynak copper deposit, which is estimated to contain more than 11 million metric tons of recoverable copper (Shroder 2007). While the LTERA office of USAID oversees the privatization program, the ultimate decision to accept a winning auction bid rests with the Afghan government. Many Afghans question, however, whether the Karzai government has the power to make autonomous decisions, noting that US, UK, and Canadian diplomatic and military advisors have acted as Karzai's shadow cabinet. Moreover, Karzai's personal survival and his government depend on the OEF-ISAF occupation, although, by 2010, it was evident that friction was increasing between the Karzai administration and the OEF-ISAF forces. The privatization program is one of many sources of this friction.

The privatization process also exhibits inter-imperial competition among NATO allies, and with China and Russia. For example, Vancouver-based Hunter-Dickinson was the frontrunner to win the bidding process on the massive Aynak copper deposit, with an offer in the neighbourhood of US$2 billion. Other bidders were Phoenix-based Phelps Dodge, London-based Kazakhmys Consortium, and a subsidiary of Russia's Basic Element Group. Ironically, Aynak, like the later sale of Hajigak, which was split between Indian state enterprises and a Canadian enterprise, was not privatized in accordance with liberalization doctrine – it was sold to Jiangxi Copper Company Inc., a subsidiary of the Chinese state enterprise, China Metallurgical Group (CMCC). Journalists originally estimated the sale at an astounding US$3.0–3.5 billion (Page 2008; Synovitz 2008), but the sale agreement posted by the Stock Exchange of Hong Kong (2008) indicates a total investment of US$4.39 billion. The Aynak bidding process was suspect from the start, with a critic of the process, James Yeager, alleging he was the target of an assassination plot (Dalton 2007). Nonetheless the winning bid came under closer scrutiny only in late 2009, when the Karzai government removed the minister of mines, Muhammad Ibrahim Adel, from his post for allegedly accepting a US$30 million bribe from CMCC (Partlow 2009).

Bidding on the Hajigak iron deposit in Bamiyan was consequently halted for a short time in early 2010 (Najafizada and Rupert 2010b).

Robert Kaplan (2009) and Michael Wines (2009) question why OEF-ISAF soldiers should protect a Chinese state investment, but awarding the Aynak mine to CMCC could be a shrewd move on the part of US, NATO, and Chinese strategists (Skinner 2008b). The Chinese will construct a four-hundred-megawatt power plant to feed the mine and its smelters, develop a nearby coal mine to feed the power plant, and construct a railway that will stretch from western China through Tajikistan to the Aynak mine and on to Pakistan. This railway will also link to the Iranian-Afghan rail project discussed above. It is unlikely that any private company would undertake such a large infrastructure project, considering the high capital cost, compounded by the political and commercial risks of investing in Afghanistan. The US, Canadian, and UK governments operate state-financed insurance schemes to protect investors from political risk in foreign investments, but they will not insure investments of this scale (Skinner 2008b).

Considering the high degree of influence of US, Canadian, and UK diplomats and military advisors inside the Afghan government, it is conceivable that the deal with CMCC is a deliberate strategy designed to shift the burden of infrastructure development to China. Whether deliberate or not, private western companies will benefit from the surplus capacity of the Chinese coal mine, power plant, and railway to service the Hajigak mine and the many other mines and development sites yet to be sold. Facilitating China's huge and extremely risky investment, for which success is entirely dependent on the continued US-led military occupation in Afghanistan, might be a cunning tactic as part of the engagement-containment strategy outlined in the US National Defense Strategy (Skinner 2008b). If this interpretation is accurate, it further complicates analysis of the Iranian-Afghan-Chinese railway-building strategy. Iranian state investments to build the trans-Afghan railway that will link to the Chinese rail project could become dependent on OEF-ISAF security forces, or these same forces could destroy the railways either directly or simply by allowing insurgents to do the dirty work. In this context, it is reasonable to question whether one achievement of OEF-ISAF operations is to have instituted the state of Afghanistan as a complex protection racket ultimately to benefit investors based in the US-led Empire of Capital.

To summarize, the privatization of Afghanistan's industries and resources, particularly its vast geological wealth, is one of many factors in the geopolitical and economic calculus of the 'global war on terror.' Afghanistan's undeveloped resource wealth is no secret to Afghans and is one of many sources of conflict among regional powers, multinational corporations, Afghan peasants, and the US and NATO occupying forces.

Conclusion

After a decade of fighting the 'global war on terror' it might be possible to claim misfortune or ineptitude as the cause of failure in Afghanistan. Nevertheless the 'global war on terror' demonstrates that the United States and its closest allies – the military enforcers of the Empire of Capital – will use retaliatory force regardless of international law or of the cost in lives and collective wealth. A closer examination of a range of geopolitical and economic objectives, of which only a few could be examined here, demonstrates the ways in which a few powerful states, investors, and transnational corporations profit from the 'global war on terror.' This suggests that greater scepticism and further evidence-based research is required. Accepting the notion that the 'global war on terror' is a 'necessary evil' has proven disastrous to date, and could prove cataclysmic should the war expand into a regional conflagration.

I have argued that expanding what Brzezinski called 'America's global primacy' in order to liberate capital is an objective far outweighing concerns for protecting the security of Canadians, let alone liberating Afghans. Fighting in Afghanistan provides an opportunity for the Canadian state to assert its position as a powerful ally within the Empire of Capital. The war has provided greater freedom for transnational firms to accumulate wealth, and has stimulated the military, security, and development industries as well as a broad range of other, peripherally related industries. Canadian-based corporations are at the head of the line to profit from developing Afghanistan's infrastructure and resources. All these factors synergistically combine as concrete reasons Canada is at war in Afghanistan and beyond.

Therefore, the political question is not whether Canadians should liberate Afghans. We cannot liberate Afghans; only they can liberate themselves and only by means they choose. There are many solidaristic means by which Canadians could act alongside Afghans towards their liberation, but instigating and perpetuating this war is not conducive to that end. Instead the question is: Should Canadians fight, whether in Afghanistan or elsewhere, in a war to secure global primacy for the United States and to globalize capitalist social relations? Is expanding the free reach of capital a just cause for which to kill, injure, displace, arbitrarily detain, torture, and generally humiliate Afghans, while sacrificing Canada's soldiers and collective resources? Canadians who thought they were sending soldiers to battle for self-defence and to liberate Afghans might not be as eager to send soldiers to battle in Afghanistan or any other battlefront of the 'global war on terror' for the purposes of securing US global primacy and liberalizing trade. Some investors and the states that make up the Empire of Capital might emerge as big winners in this latest inning of the Great Game. But it is evident that few Canadians and even fewer Afghans are winners in this global war – a war that has no foreseeable end, unless the people of the Empire of Capital refuse to support its perpetual expansion.

NOTES

1 The 'global war on terror,' capitalized and abbreviated as GWOT, was replaced in most US government documents by Overseas Contingency Operations (OCO) after March 2009. To avoid confusion, I use 'global war on terror' throughout, regardless of whether describing pre- or post-March 2009 events.

2 In the early nineteenth century, an officer of the East India Company, Arthur Conolly, coined the phrase 'The Great Game' to describe the inter-imperial rivalry between the British and Russian empires. The phrase was later popularized by Rudyard Kipling in his novel *Kim*, set after the Second Afghan War (1878–80) in northern India (now Pakistan] and Afghanistan. So many books have been written about the nineteenth- and twentieth-century British-Russian and US-Soviet inter-imperial wars in Afghanistan that it is impossible to list just a few definitive sources. For well-informed analyses of the late-twentieth-century US-Soviet proxy war and its consequences, see Rubin (1995); Rashid (2000); Maley (2002); and Coll (2004).

3 Ellen Meiksins Wood (2005) coined the phrase 'Empire of Capital' to describe the current US-led empire as one in which the United States dominates as the leader of a globalizing empire, in alliance with other powerful subdominant states, including Canada.

4 I am deeply indebted to Hamayon Rastgar for his research assistance, his intellectual debate, which contributes to my analysis, and his friendship. Without Hamayon, his extended family, and many friends in Afghanistan, my research would have been impossible.

5 A blog documenting our journey is maintained by Trade Unionists Against the War at http://tradeunionistsagainstthewar.blogspot.com/.

6 United Nations Security Council Resolution 1368 (2001) is often cited as the UN sanction of the OEF invasion of Afghanistan. The resolution is certainly a strongly worded condemnation of the 9/11 terrorist attacks and urges states to seek out and bring the perpetrators to justice, but it does not in any terms sanction the invasion of Afghanistan.

7 The recent case of military intervention in Libya demonstrates yet another variation of this strategy. The United Nations multilaterally sanctioned a multinational military intervention in Libya based on the argument that military action was necessary to protect Libyan civilians – an argument legitimized by the recent adoption of the 'responsibility to protect' doctrine. However, the multinational military forces of the multilaterally sanctioned mission unilaterally proceeded beyond the United Nations mandate of protecting civilians to participate in forceful regime change.

8 Substate/transnational actors include, but are not limited to, labour, peasant, indigenous, women's, environmental, religious, and political organizations, which may defend and/or promote their interests via a broad range of political, cultural, economic, and forceful means. Terrorism is a small subset of forceful means that substate/transnational actors might choose to employ. However, the threat of terrorism, blown out of all proportion, is used to rationalize suppression of any potentially subversive substate/transnational actors.

9 It is important to recognize the variety of anti-imperialist movements and organizations in Afghanistan – for example, the Communist (Maoist) Party of Afghanistan, the Afghanistan Socialist Association, *Paikar-e-Zan* (Women's Struggle), the Revolutionary Association of the Women of Afghanistan, Left Radical of Afghanistan, the Afghanistan Liberation Organization, *Sazman-I Azadibaksh-I Mardum-I Afghanistan* (Afghanistan People's Liberation Organization), the Afghanistan Revolutionary Organization, and the Afghanistan Revolutionary Radical Youth Organization.

10 This observation is based in part on conversations with security experts in Moscow 2009.

References

Afghanistan Geological Survey. 2008. 'Minerals in Afghanistan: The Hajigak iron Deposit.' Kabul: Afghanistan Geological Survey, British Geological Survey, Afghanistan Ministry of Mines. http://www.bgs.ac.uk/AfghanMinerals/docs/Hajigak_A4.pdf.

Afghanistan Investment Support Agency. 2010. 'Priority Sectors.' Kabul. http://www.aisa.org.af/pri-sectors.html.

Asian Development Bank. 2009. *Islamic Republic of Afghanistan: Railway Development Study*. Technical Assistance Report, Project 42533. Manila. http://www.adb.org/Documents/TARs/AFG/42533-AFG-TAR.pdf.

Bacevich, Andrew. 2002. *American Empire: The Realities and Consequences of U.S. Diplomacy*. Cambridge, MA: Harvard University Press.

Becker, Elizabeth. 2001. 'A nation challenged: the protest; marchers oppose waging war against terrorists.' *New York Times*, 1 October. http://query.nytimes.com/gst/fullpage.html?res=9C05E7DB153DF932A35753C1A9679C8B63.

Brice, David. 2008. 'Network Expansion in Full Swing.' *Railway Gazette International*, 24 December. http://www.railwaygazette.com/news/single-view/view/10/network-expansion-is-in-full-swing.html.

Brzezinski, Zbigniew. 1997a. 'A Geostrategy for Eurasia.' *Foreign Affairs* 76, no. 5: 50–64.

–. 1997b. *The Grand Chessboard: American Primacy and its Geostrategic Imperatives*. New York: Basic Books.

–. 2009. 'An Agenda for NATO: Toward a Global Security Web.' *Foreign Affairs* 88, no. 5: 2–20.

Bush, George W. 2001. 'Transcript of President Bush's Address to a Joint Session of Congress on Thursday Night, September 20, 2001.' *CNN.com*, 20 September. http://archives.cnn.com/2001/US/09/20/gen.bush.transcript.

–. 2007. 'President Bush Discusses the War Supplemental.' Washington DC: White House, 22 October. http://www.whitehouse.gov/news/releases/2007/10/20071022–8.html.

Bush, Laura. 2001. 'Radio Address by Mrs. Bush.' Washington, DC: White House, 17 October. http://georgewbush-whitehouse.archives.gov/news/releases/2001/11/20011117.html.

Canada. 2010. National Defence and the Canadian Forces. 'Our Mission in Afghanistan: Why Are We There?' Ottawa. http://www.cefcom.forces.gc.ca/pa-ap/ops/fs-fr/afg-eng.asp.

–. 2011. 'Canadian Investment Supports Post-Combat Development in Afghanistan.' Ottawa. 4 December. http://www.afghanistan.gc.ca/canada-afghanistan/news-nouvelles/2011/2011_12_04.aspx?lang=eng&view=d.

Canadian Labour Congress. 2008. 'Resolutions WD-30 to WD-39 and WD-61' [Resolution to withdraw troops].' *World Resolutions Committee Report*. Ottawa. http://www.canadianlabour.ca/sites/default/files/conventions/910compositeEn.pdf.

CBC News. 2009. 'All Afghan detainees likely tortured: diplomat.' 18 November. http://www.cbc.ca/news/canada/story/2009/11/18/diplomat-afghan-detainees.html.

Chrétien, Jean. 2001. 'Canadian PM: "We Will Be There": Remarks by the President and Prime Minister of Canada.' Washington, DC: White House, 24 September. http://www.whitehouse.gov/news/releases/2001/09/20010924–7.html.

Coll, Steve. 2004. *Ghost Wars: The Secret History of the CIA, Afghanistan and Bin Laden, from the Soviet Invasion to September 10, 2001*. Toronto: Penguin.

Dalton, Rex. 2007. 'Geology: Mine Games.' *Nature* 449, no. 7165: 968–71.

Democracy Now. 2001. 'Thousands take to the streets in San Francisco and Washington, D.C. to call for peace and justice.' 1 October. http://www.democracynow.org/shows/2001/10/1.

Duffy, Helen. 2005. *The 'War on Terror' and the Framework of International Law*. Cambridge: Cambridge University Press.

Eggleton, Art. 2001. 'Speaking Notes for the Honourable Art Eggleton, Minister of National Defence, Press Conference: Canadian Military Contributions, National Defence Headquarters, Ottawa, 8 October 2001.' Ottawa: Department of National Defence/Canadian Forces. http://www.forces.gc.ca/site/Newsroom/view_news_e.asp?id=518.

ECO (Economic Cooperation Organization). 2010. 'Regional Summit Meeting of Afghanistan and Neighbors, Istanbul, 26 January, 2010.' *Economic Cooperation Organization Secretariat*. Tehran. http://www.ecosecretariat.org/Sg%20Statement/SUM-AF.HTM.

English, Allan. 2005. 'The Operational Art: Theory, Practice, and Implications for the Future.' In *The Operational Art: Canadian Perspectives, Context, and Concepts*, ed. Allan English, Daniel Gosselin, Howard Coombs, and Laurence M. Hickey. Kingston, ON: Canadian Defence Academy Press.

Eunjang Cha, Ariana. 2009. 'China gains key assets in spate of purchases: oil, minerals are among acquisitions worldwide.' *Washington Post*, 17 March, A01.

Fars News Agency. 2009. 'ECO urged to invest in Iran-Afghanistan railway project.' 23 August. http://english.farsnews.com/newstext.php?nn=8806011324.

Featherstone, Liza. 2001. 'Operation Enduring Protest.' *Nation*, 18 October. http://www.thenation.com/doc/20011029/featherstone20011018.

Foster, John. 2008. 'A Pipeline through a Troubled Land: Afghanistan: Canada, and the New Great Energy Game.' Foreign Policy Series 3.1. Ottawa: Canadian Centre for Policy Alternatives.

Gallup International. 2001. 'Gallup International Poll on Terrorism in the U.S.' http://www.gallup-international.com/surveys.htm and http://www.peace.ca/galluppollonterrorism.htm.

Gilman, Benjamin. 1997. 'The Silk Road Strategy Act of 1997, H.R. 2867 (Extension of Remarks, November 8, 1997).' Washington, DC: US House of Representatives.

Guardian. 2001. '20,000 join anti-war protest.' 13 October. http://www.
guardian.co.uk/world/2001/oct/13/afghanistan.terrorism5.

Harvey, David. 2003. *The New Imperialism*. New York: Oxford University Press.

Huntington, Samuel. 1996. *The Clash of Civilizations and the Remaking of World Order*. New York: Simon & Schuster.

Hughes, Murray. 2008. 'Opening up Afghan trade route to Iran.' *Railway Gazette International*, 29 January. http://www.railwaygazette.com/news/single-view/view/10/opening-up-afghan-trade-route-to-iran.html.

Ignatieff, Michael. 2003. *Empire Lite: Nation-Building in Bosnia, Kosovo and Afghanistan*. Toronto: Penguin Canada.

Kantor, Paula. 2010. 'Improving Efforts to Achieve Equitable Growth and Reduce Poverty.' In *Speaking from the Evidence: Governance, Justice, and Development*. Kabul: Afghanistan Research and Evaluation Unit (AREU), 21 April.

Kaplan, Robert. 2009. 'Beijing's Afghan gamble.' *New York Times*, 7 October.

Katzman, Kenneth. 2010. 'Afghanistan: Post-Taliban Governance, Security, and US Policy.' *CRS Report for Congress*. Washington DC: Congressional Research Service, 21 June.

Keen, David. 2006. *Endless War? Hidden Functions of the 'War on Terror.'* Ann Arbor, MI: Pluto Press.

Khalilzad, Zalmay. 1995a. *From Containment to Global Leadership? America & the World after the Cold War*. Santa Monica: RAND.

–. 1995b. 'Losing the Moment? The United States and the World after the Cold War.' *Washington Quarterly* 18, no. 2: 85–107.

Klett, Timothy, et al. 2006. 'Afghan Resource Assessment Fed Positive Outlook for Exploration.' *Oil & Gas Journal* 104, no. 30: 33–8.

Landay, Jonathan. 2009. 'China's thirst for copper could hold key to Afghanistan's future.' *McClatchy Newspapers*, 8 March.

Lipshutz, Ronnie. 2002. 'The Clash of Governmentalities: The Fall of the UN Republic and America's Reach for Empire.' *Contemporary Security Policy* 23, no. 3: 214–31.

Maley, William. 2002. *The Afghanistan Wars*. New York: Palgrave Macmillan

Mandel, Michael. 2004. *How America Gets Away with Murder: Illegal Wars, Collateral Damage and Crimes against Humanity*. London: Pluto Press.

McCombs, Dave. 2009. 'Afghanistan's first railroad aims to undercut Taliban.' *Bloomberg*, 27 October.

Miller, David. 2002. 'Opinion Polls and the Misrepresentation of Public Opinion on the War with Afghanistan.' *Television & New Media* 3, no. 2: 153–61.

Mora, Alberto. 2006. 'Dan Rather Interviews Alberto J. Mora, Former U.S. Navy General Counsel.' *Carnegie Council for Ethics in International Affairs*, 2 November.

Najafizada, Eltaf, and James Rupert. 2010a. 'Afghan railway to draw Taliban fire as it boosts economy, NATO.' *Bloomberg*, 5 May.

–. 2010b. 'Afghanistan will invite new iron mine bids after issues over transparency.' *Bloomberg*, 3 February.

National Catholic Reporter. 2001. 'In New York, thousands march for peace – Nation – protesting Afghanistan bombing.' 19 October.

Noorzoy, Siddieq. 1990. 'Soviet Economic Interests and Policies in Afghanistan.' In *Afghanistan: The Great Game Revisited*, rev. ed., ed. Rosanne Klass. New York: Freedom House.

–. 2006. 'New Petroleum Discoveries, Past Lessons, Economic Development and Foreign Investment in Afghanistan.' *Afghan Research Society*, 12 August. http://www.afghanresearchsociety.org/New_Oil_and_Gas_Finds_ Foreign_Investment_and_the_Afghan_EconomyII.html.

Oil & Gas Journal. 2006. 'Afghanistan resource base larger, USGS says.' *Oil & Gas Journal* 104, no. 12: 34.

Obama, Barack. 2009. 'Remarks by the President at the Veterans of Foreign Wars Convention, Phoenix Arizona.' Washington, DC: White House, 17 August http://www.whitehouse.gov/the_press_office/ Remarks-by-the-President-at-the-Veterans-of-Foreign-Wars-convention/.

Page, Jeremy. 2008. 'Afghanistan copper deposits worth $88 billion attract Chinese investors.' *Times*, 15 May.

Partlow, Joshua. 2009. 'Afghan minister accused of taking bribe: $30 million payment alleged.' *Washington Post*, 18 November.

Rashid, Ahmed. 2000. *Taliban: Militant Islam, Oil and Fundamentalism in Central Asia*. New Haven, CT: Yale University Press.

Reuters. 2008. 'German military proposes new Afghan rail link.' *Radio Free Europe/Radio Liberty*, 30 August. http://www.rferl.org/content/German_ Military_Proposes_New_Afghan_Rail_Link/1195128.html.

–. 2009. 'Canadian firms step up search for rare-earth metals.' *New York Times*, 10 September.

Risen, James. 2010. 'U.S. identifies vast riches of minerals in Afghanistan.' *New York Times*, 14 June.

Rubin, Barnett. 1995. *The Search for Peace in Afghanistan: From Buffer State to Failed State*. New Haven, CT: Yale University Press.

Serjeant, Jill, and Bernard Woodall. 2008. 'West coast ports working after daytime strike.' *Reuters*, 1 May.

Seth, Shivom. 2011. 'Indian consortium bags Afghan's Hajigak iron ore deposits.' *Mineweb*, 28 November.

Shroder, John. 1981. 'Physical Resources and the Development of Afghanistan.' *Studies in Comparative International Development* 16, nos. 3–4: 36–63.

–. 2007. 'Afghanistan's Development and Functionality: Renewing a Collapsed State.' *Geojournal* 70: 91–107.

Skinner, Michael. 2008a. 'Canadian Workers Demand an Immediate End to War in Afghanistan.' *Bullet*, e-bulletin 113, 14 June. http://www.socialist project.ca/bullet/bullet113.html.

–. 2008b. 'Multi-billion Dollar Mining Boom: The Economics of War and Empire in Afghanistan.' *Dominion* 55 (Winter).

Stein, Janice Gross and Eugene Lang. 2007. *The Unexpected War: Canada in Kandahar.* Toronto: Viking.

Stock Exchange of Hong Kong. 2008. 'Jiangxi Copper Company Inc' [RNS Number: 8029X; Stock Code 0358 Disclosable Transaction]. 29 June. http:// www.infomine.com/index/pr/PA649088.pfd.

Synovitz, Ron. 2008. 'China: Afghan Investment Reveals Larger Strategy.' *Radio Free Europe*, 29 May. http://www.rferl.org/featuresarticle/2008/05/ fb001c04-dfc1–48b2–851c-928a0fad05ea.html.

Taguba, Antonio. 2008. 'Preface.' In *Broken Laws, Broken Lives: Medical Evidence of Torture by US Personnel and Its Impact*. Washington, DC: Physicians for Human Rights.

United Kingdom. 2001a. Department of Defence. 2001. 'DoD News Briefing.' London, 20 October. http://www.defenselink.mil/news.

–. 2001b. House of Commons Library. 'Research Paper 01/81, 31 Oct. 2001.' London: House of Commons Library, International Affairs & Defence Section. http://www.parliament.uk/commons/lib/research/rp2001/rp01–081.pdf.

United Nations. 2010. Office of the High Commissioner for Human Rights. *Human Rights Dimension of Poverty in Afghanistan*. Kabul: UN OHCHR, March. http://unama.unmissions.org/Portals/UNAMA/ human%20rights/Poverty%20Report%2030%20March%202010_ English.pdf.

United States. 1998. Congress. House of Representatives. Committee on International Relations. 'U.S. Interests in the Central Asian Republics: Hearing before the Subcommittee on Asia and Pacific.' Washington, D.C., 12 February. http://commdocs.house.gov/committees/intlrel/hfa48119.000/ hfa48119_0.htm.

–. 2002a. Department of Defense. 'Fact Sheet May 22, 2002: International Contributions to the War against Terrorism.' Washington, DC: Department of Defense, Office of Public Affairs, 22 May. http://www.defenselink.mil/ news/May2002/d20020523cu.pdf.

–. 2002b. *The National Security Strategy of the United States of America*. Washington, DC: White House.

–. 2004. Department of State. Bureau of Democracy, Human Rights, and Labor. *Afghanistan: International Religious Freedom Report*. Washington, DC, 15 September. http://www.state.gov/g/drl/rls/irf/2004/35513.htm.

–. 2007. Department of State. Bureau of Democracy, Human Rights, and Labor. *Afghanistan: Country Reports on Human Rights Practices 2006*. Washington, DC, 6 March. http://www.state.gov/g/drl/rls/hrrpt/2006/78868.htm.

–. 2008. Department of Defense. *US National Defense Strategy*. Washington, DC. http://www.defenselink.mil/news/2008%20national%20defense%20 strategy.pdf.

–. 2009. Congressional Research Service. 'The Cost of Iraq, Afghanistan, and Other Global War on Terror Operations since 9/11.' *CRS Report for Congress*. Washington, DC, 15 May. http://assets.opencrs.com/rpts/ RL33110_20090515.pdf.

–. 2010. Department of State. Bureau of Economic, Energy and Business Affairs. '2010 Investment Climate Statement – Afghanistan.' Washington, DC. http://www.state.gov/e/eeb/rls/othr/ics/2010/138776.htm.

–. 2011. Department of State. 'The United States' "New Silk Road" Strategy: What Is It? Where Is It Headed?' Washington DC. http://www.state.gov/e/ rls/rmk/2011/174800.htm.

Vance, Jonathan. 2005. 'Tactics without Strategy or Why the Canadian Forces Do Not Campaign.' In *Operational Art: Canadian Perspectives, Context, and Concepts*, ed. Allan English, Daniel Gosselin, Howard Coombs, and Laurence M. Hickey. Kingston, ON: Canadian Defence Academy Press.

Vulcan, Tom. 2009. 'China dominant: Why rare earth metals matter.' *Mineweb*, 18 May. http://www.mineweb.net/mineweb/view/mineweb/en/page 72102?oid=83419&sn=Detail.

Warnock, John. 2008. *Creating a Failed State: The US and Canada in Afghanistan*. Halifax, NS: Fernwood.

Whittington, Les. 2010. 'Canadian mining firms worst for environment, rights: Report.' *Toronto Star*, 19 October.

Wines, Michael. 2009. 'Uneasy engagement: China willing to spend big on Afghan commerce.' *New York Times*, 30 December.

Wood, Ellen Meiksins. 2003. *Empire of Capital*. London: Verso.

Wright, Ann. 2009. 'Anniversary of My Dissent: From Three Decades as a Colonel and Diplomat to Six Years as a Peace Activist.' *CommonDreams.org*, 19 March.

Yardley, William. 2008. 'Union's war protest shuts west coast ports.' *New York Times*, 2 May. http://www.nytimes.com/2008/05/02/us/02port.html?ex=1 210392000&en=df55d41129729fe1&ei=5070&emc=eta1.

5

Methods of Empire: State Building, Development, and War in Afghanistan

JEROME KLASSEN

In the wake of 9/11 the United States and its allies in the North Atlantic Treaty Organization (NATO) invaded Afghanistan under the rubric of the 'global war on terror.' After defeating the Taliban regime and destroying al-Qaeda training camps, the United States and NATO launched an ambitious project of state building and economic reconstruction. Through what came to be known as the Bonn Process the United States and NATO helped to build a new state under the leadership of President Hamid Karzai, his cabinet, and an elected parliament. They also backed a reconstruction and development agenda, supported by the international financial institutions and many non-governmental organizations (NGOs). To provide security for this project the United States and NATO waged a low-intensity war against any remaining 'anti-government forces.' Through this matrix of operations Afghanistan was promised a future of democracy, development, peace, and security.

A decade later, however, these goals have yet to be met. The security situation remains highly precarious, and the Taliban insurgency operates in four-fifths of the country. Aid and development programs have been scaled back, while the production and distribution of opium has emerged as a multi-billion-dollar industry. Systematic corruption is present in many aspects of public administration, and the Afghan government is highly dependent on outside finance and military protection. For such reasons many international relations specialists believe that the war has reached an impasse or even a terminal point of crisis – a crisis portending more instability and violence as the United States and NATO attempt to contain the Taliban insurgency on both sides of the Afghanistan-Pakistan border (Afghanistan Study Group 2010; Dorronsoro 2010; Ruttig 2010a).

In this context it is vital to assess the US-NATO mission to date and the reasons that violence, drugs, and corruption increasingly beset Afghanistan. In the international relations literature, the crisis in Afghanistan is often explained by *external factors*, including Taliban safe havens in Pakistan, arms shipments from Iran, and double-dealing strategies by Inter-Services Intelligence (ISI), Pakistan's military intelligence service (Rubin 2007; Rashid 2008).[1] A second explanation highlights *technical inefficiencies* within the nation-building project, such as an overemphasis on counterinsurgency as opposed to aid and reconstruction work or public sector reform (Azarbaijani-Moghaddam et al. 2008; Banerjee 2009). While the first explanation lends itself to a strategy of military escalation in Afghanistan and the region, the second seeks an operational rebalancing to win 'hearts and minds' through developmental or humanitarian methods.

In Canada the public debate tends to consist of a similar narrative, in which Canadian policy has been undermined by factors beyond our control, such as terrorism, or by technical mistakes in the organization of the mission, such as a lack of coordination between the Department of National Defence, the Department of Foreign Affairs, and the Canadian International Development Agency (CBC News 2007; Stein and Lang 2007; Canada 2008; Koring 2009; Alexander 2010). Given these parameters the current discussion tends to focus on whether or not Canada should remain engaged in the military conflict as part of the 'war on terror' or put greater emphasis on aid and reconstruction work in support of the Karzai government and the US military surge. What both perspectives ignore, however, is a critical evaluation of the military mission and the developmental project as twin aspects of a *neocolonial occupation*, which is fundamentally unstable given the political, economic, and military program imposed upon Afghanistan and the geopolitical interests of western powers in the region.

A careful examination of the current crisis, then, must look closely at the occupation itself as a primary source of instability and violence in Afghanistan. More specifically it must reconstruct the ways in which the US-NATO mission established a state apparatus in Afghanistan run by factional warlords and neoliberal technocrats, both of whom lack a social base of support and thus rely upon outside military actors for safety and legitimacy. In this context the war in Afghanistan must be understood as a *war for empire* – as a systematic imposition of violence for the purpose of expanding western military power and capitalist social relations. With this in mind, the current crisis stems from neither external shocks nor internal errors in the organization of the mission, but from the political, economic, and military methods of *neoliberal imperialism* – from the integrated strategy by which the United States and NATO imposed a free market warlord government through military occupation.

To present this argument the chapter is divided into four sections. The first examines the invasion of Afghanistan in 2001 and the military collaboration between the United States and the warlords of the United Islamic Front or 'Northern Alliance' (see Warnock, in this volume). The second section covers the Bonn Process, through which a formal structure was created in Afghanistan under the control of Hamid Karzai and various armed factions. The third section reviews the neoliberal development agenda for Afghanistan, while the fourth analyses the Taliban insurgency and the ongoing war. In looking at these issues, the chapter highlights the political logic by which the occupation has operated and the reasons the US-NATO mission is in crisis. It argues that the current debacle in Afghanistan is a product of the pro-warlord military strategy and the neoliberal economic strategy of the western occupation. It demonstrates how these 'methods of empire' have been deployed to the detriment of democracy, development, peace, and security for Afghans. In the process it sheds light on the model by which the United States and NATO might plan future interventions in other 'failed states.'

Befriending Warlords: The War on Terror Begins

The war in Afghanistan commenced on 7 October 2001, when the United States launched an air campaign to remove the Taliban regime and to destroy al-Qaeda bases. The air strikes were supported on the ground by US Special Forces and the militias of the Northern Alliance, which captured Kabul on 13 November. On 7 December the Taliban stronghold of Kandahar fell to a fighting force of Pashtun warlords and their US advisors. Although no clear statistics on civilian casualties have been produced, between October 2001 and January 2002 hundreds of civilians were killed directly by military strikes, while several thousand are thought to have died indirectly from hunger, starvation, displacement, and disease (Herold 2002; Steele 2002; Zucchino 2002; Rashid 2008, 98), casualty levels that had been predicted by United Nations aid workers and other humanitarian organizations (BBC News 2001; Ikram 2001; Nebehay 2001).

Nevertheless the war was fought, the Taliban were uprooted, and the Northern Alliance and other warlords filled the power vacuum across the country. International human rights groups criticized the western intervention for collaborating with the same warlords who destroyed Kabul and committed many atrocities during the pre-Taliban civil war period (1992–6). These warlords and their militias were previously guilty of 'widespread or systematic . . . crimes against humanity,' including 'killings, indiscriminate aerial bombardment and shelling, direct attacks on civilians, summary executions, rape, persecution on the basis of religion or ethnicity, the recruitment and use of children as soldiers, and the use of antipersonnel landmines' (Human Rights Watch 2001).

In the wake of the US-NATO intervention the same militias – especially those of the Northern Alliance – committed new human rights abuses. At the end of November 2001 the *Jombesh* militia of Uzbek general Abdul Rashid Dostum captured hundreds of Taliban fighters in Kunduz. These prisoners were packed into shipping containers for transfer to Shibarghan and for three days were starved of food and water, causing mass starvation and dehydration. Hundreds died en route, and those who survived were killed when Dostum's men fired rounds into the containers (Lasseter 2008). According to the *New York Times* the Bush administration ignored calls for an investigation 'because the [Northern Alliance] warlord, Gen. Abdul Rashid Dostum, was on the payroll of the CIA [Central Intelligence Agency] and his militia worked closely with United States Special Forces in 2001' (Risen 2009). In the same month the *Jombesh* militia, supported by US Special Forces, British commandos, and the CIA, also carried out a three-day bombing and mass execution of hundreds of Taliban prisoners at Dostum's prison fortress in Qala-i-Janghi (Perry 2001; Warnock 2008, 19). Furthermore, in the early months of the war, tens of thousands of ethnic Pashtuns in northern and western Afghanistan were made refugees by 'pogroms' carried out by Uzbek and Tajik warlords allied with the United States (Rashid 2008, 94). According to Physicians for Human Rights (2002), the Northern Alliance carried out 'shocking . . . attacks against ethnic Pashtuns in Afghanistan's western provinces,' including 'killings, beatings, looting, and sexual assault.' According to another study, '[t]he ethnic cleansing to which [the Pashtuns] have been subjected in the north . . . [was] tolerated or even connived at by the two principal backers of the [new] government, Jamiyat-i Islami and Jombesh,' two militias of the Northern Alliance (Dorronsoro 2005, 343).

Through such means the US-led war in Afghanistan was waged in 2001. Despite the warnings of human rights groups and aid workers, the Pentagon unleashed a massive air campaign against the Taliban regime, while at the same time financing and supporting various militias as surrogate forces on the ground. Thousands of civilians were killed, wounded, or displaced by the fighting, and the same warlords who destroyed the country after the Soviet withdrawal were rearmed and reconstituted as local authorities across the country. As the next section demonstrates, this early alliance between the US-led Operation Enduring Freedom (OEF) and the warlords of Afghanistan established the political logic for everything that followed in the name of nation building and reconstruction, especially as part of the Bonn Process.

Democracy under Occupation: The Bonn Process

The Bonn Agreement

The Bonn Agreement of 5 December 2001 was a political pact on democratization and political reconstruction among the United Nations, the United States, and various Afghan stakeholders. The agreement outlined a timetable for an Interim Authority, a Transitional Authority, a Constitutional Assembly, and presidential and parliamentary elections for Afghanistan. The stated objectives were to 'end the tragic conflict in Afghanistan and promote national reconciliation, lasting peace, stability and respect for human rights' ('Agreement on Provisional Arrangements' 2001). Despite these objectives the organization and political composition of the Bonn Process, as well as the agreed-upon text, gave clear cause for concern.

While the text recognized the 'independence, national sovereignty and territorial integrity of Afghanistan,' and the 'right of the people of Afghanistan to freely determine their own political future,' it said nothing about the invasion and occupation, the legal status of foreign forces, or the ongoing activities of OEF. It also failed to discuss the issue of political reconciliation or peace making with the Taliban and their social and ethnic base, the Pashtun people. In addition, the agreement ignored issues of retroactive justice and accountability, and went so far as to express 'appreciation to the mujahideen' of the Northern Alliance, whose recent efforts had made them 'both heroes of jihad and champions of peace, stability and reconstruction.' As a result it presented few principles by which to guide the nation-building process away from the influence of armed factions, which held real power on the ground and de facto power within the Bonn Process itself.

This power was evident in the organization of the Bonn meetings and in the decision-making process therein. Under the direction of the United States and United Nations, the Bonn Process excluded democratic parties, which were committed to a secular state in Afghanistan (Ruttig 2006; Warnock 2008). It also ignored or bypassed other political initiatives by Afghan parties and organizations, including the Peshawar Assembly of 25–26 October 2001, which advocated a national leadership council, a UN security force from Muslim countries, restrictions on warlords, and an end to US air strikes (Kolhatkar and Ingalls 2006, 89–90). Perhaps most dangerously the Bonn Agreement did not include the main counterparty to the conflict, the Taliban, and did not include representation of, or participation by, ethnic Pashtuns, who represent up to 50 per cent of the population (Warnock 2008, chap. 6). Instead the meetings were stacked by representatives of the Northern Alliance, who 'infiltrated and manipulated the process for selecting the meeting's delegates, and . . . [attended] the meeting in large numbers or through proxies,' according to Human Rights Watch (cited in Dorronsoro 2005, 330).

As a result the Northern Alliance was able to shape both the meetings and the outcomes of the Bonn accords. Hamid Karzai, the presidential candidate favoured by the United States, received no votes in the first round of selection, which overwhelmingly favoured Professor Abdul Sattar Sirat of the Rome Group of King Zahir Shah (Kolhatkar and Ingalls 2006, 124–6). However, after much delay and outside pressure, 'all the delegates understood that the Americans wanted Mr. Karzai . . . [s]o on Dec. 5, they finally chose him' (Onishi 2001). To build a government, Karzai, the Northern Alliance, and other warlords eventually struck a twofold compromise or tacit arrangement. First, in exchange for their support, Karzai granted the Northern Alliance the new ministries of defence, interior, national intelligence, and foreign affairs in the Interim Authority. Second, Karzai allowed warlords from across the country to establish themselves, alongside US forces, as the real source of power and authority in the provinces. Through this arrangement the warlords were integrated into the top echelon of the state and given free rein to work alongside OEF without oversight or regulation.

This compromise, which secured the presidency for Karzai, is aptly described by Antonio Giustozzi (2007, 16): 'At the end of 2001, as he set out to establish his provisional administration, with the blessing of his

American patrons, President Karzai opted to co-opt regional warlords and strongmen into the central government and the subnational administration.' As Human Rights Watch argued, this deal between the international community, the warlords of Afghanistan, and the faction around Karzai authorized the ongoing military occupation by US forces and contradicted the stated goals of the Bonn accords: 'The mandate of these troops is to combat the Taliban, not to provide security for Afghans. In fact . . . these troops freely engage and support local warlords and military commanders who ostensibly will fight the Taliban, with little or no regard for how the warlords treat the local citizenry' (Zia-Zarifi 2004, 4). In these ways, the Bonn Agreement institutionalized the power of warlords and militias both formally inside the state and informally at the local level. In other words it extended the 'warlord strategy' of the Pentagon as the primary means by which the United States constructed a state in Afghanistan and waged war against al-Qaeda and Taliban 'remnants' without regard for the security and welfare of Afghans (Rashid 2008, 129, 133).

The Emergency Assembly

Washington's 'warlord strategy' was maintained and strengthened throughout the Bonn Process. On 11 June 2002 the international community sponsored an Emergency Assembly to pick a transitional president and cabinet for two years. With the organizational help of the United Nations, the Assembly included a diverse representation of the Afghan population, including a number of women activists, and demonstrated broad notional unity around peace, security, development, education reform, and having former king Zahir Shah serve as president (Kolhatkar and Ingalls 2006, 131–2; Johnson and Leslie 2008, 183–4). At the same time the parties of the 'new democracy' movement, which had emerged in Afghanistan in the aftermath of the war, were not invited to participate, while armed factions were given presence through a host of provincial governors and Karzai appointments (Ruttig 2006, 35–6). Gilles Dorronsoro (2005, 330) captures the decision-making process that followed: 'There was inevitably some confusion, but the positions of the various delegates gravitated towards the exclusion of former "commanders" and to support for Zahir Shah. However, the crucial decisions, and in particular the choice of Hamid Karzai, had already been taken by the Americans, at whose request Zahir Shah was obliged to step aside. Actually, a majority of delegates appeared to be prepared to cast their votes for Zahir Shah, a development which would have blocked the election of the Americans' candidate.' In another account, 'democracy nearly broke out in Afghanistan on Monday [10 June 2002], but was blocked by backroom dealing to prevent former King Moham- med Zahir Shah from emerging as a challenger to Karzai' (Hess 2002). According to the *Washington Post*, '[r]ather than [addressing] the issue democratically, almost two days of the six-day loya jirga were wasted while a parade of high-level officials from the interim government, the United Nations, and the United States visited Zahir Shah and even- tually "persuaded" him to publicly renounce his political ambitions' (Zahkilwal 2002).

Through such manipulation the United States, NATO, and the United Nations managed to re-ensconce Karzai and the Northern Alliance as the principal leadership of the Transitional Authority. On 24 June 2002 the Assembly announced the new government, which gave the North- ern Alliance eighteen of thirty cabinet seats, including defence, foreign affairs, and national intelligence. Newly appointed President Karzai se- lected two prominent warlords, Muhammad Qasim Fahim and Karim Khalili, and a former World Bank technocrat, Hedayat Amin Arsala, as vice-presidents, and appointed at least twenty 'militia command- ers, warlords or strongmen' to provincial governorships and several smaller commanders to district governor positions (Dorronsoro 2005, 336; Giustozzi 2007, 16; Warnock 2008, 116). Only two women, Suhaila Seddiqi and Sima Samar, were granted seats in cabinet, and the latter was soon forced to resign after being charged with blasphemy for de- manding a secular state in Afghanistan (Warnock 2008, 145). Another limitation was that political parties with national or secular programs were not included in the Emergency Assembly, which thereby encour- aged the political tendencies towards sectarianism, regionalism, and fundamentalism. These developments were encouraged or ignored by the United States, which supported the Northern Alliance and other warlords across the country as proxy forces against any resistance to the occupation (Rashid 2008, 129, 33).

The Constitutional Assembly

The next stage in the Bonn Process was the Constitutional Assembly of December 2003 to January 2004. The Assembly was convened by 500 delegates (344 of whom were elected) and charged with the task of rati- fying a new constitution. Once again the nexus between Hamid Karzai and various warlords dictated the selection of delegates, the course of negotiations, and the constitutional outcomes. For example, the formal delegate elections were systematically compromised by 'vote-buying, death threats and naked power politics,' by the participation of 'war criminals,' and by the open mixing of international security forces with delegates at balloting sites (Sifton 2004). Furthermore the nine-person Constitutional Drafting Commission was highly divided, and produced two separate documents alongside a third written by a foreign advisor to President Karzai. On 26 April 2003 a new, thirty five-member commission was established, representing a broader spectrum of political perspectives. The new commission undertook a two-month consultation process with pre-selected groups, and issued a public questionnaire instead of holding wide-ranging deliberations. The final draft, which was submitted in late September 2003, was never made public. Over the next two months members of the Afghan cabinet and National Security Council rewrote key elements of the draft constitution (Thier 2006/07, 566–9). These alterations included the imposition of a centralized presidential system over a parliamentary and federal one (Johnson and Leslie 2008, 190), an amendment that proved highly contentious in the Constitutional Assembly, which was boycotted by roughly half the delegates (Kolhatkar and Ingalls 2006, 141; Ruttig 2006, 20; Warnock 2008, 119). According to the *New York Times* (Sifton 2004) the Assembly had 'an atmosphere of fear and corruption,' and 'sweet-talking, intimidating and even bribing delegates' was used to break the boycott. The end result was a 'scripted affair' in which the warlords, the United Nations, and President Karzai arranged a deal and rubber-stamped the constitution without amendments.

The new constitution was a contradictory document. It guaranteed popular sovereignty through elections, equal citizenship rights, language rights, and representation for women in the lower house, yet emphasized 'the holy religion of Islam' as the first principle of the state in matters of law, education, party organization, and constitutional reform. By establishing a highly centralized political system under the Office of the President, which holds power of appointment over the police, cabinet, courts, army, mayorships, and one-third of the upper house, the constitution also failed, according to the International Crisis Group, 'to provide meaningful democratic governance, including power-sharing, a system of checks and balances, or mechanisms for increasing the representation of ethnic, regional and other minority groups' (2003, 1). As aid experts Chris Johnson and Joylon Leslie

(2008, 190) argue, however, the constitution's flaws were not just *formal* in the sense of establishing institutional contradictions, but *substantive* in terms of failing to achieve political reconciliation, transitional justice, and legal accountability for atrocities committed over the previous two decades. In their assessment, the new constitution reproduced the political conditions through which Karzai gained power at the top of the system with internal support from the Northern Alliance and other warlords, and external support from NATO and the Pentagon (see also Their 2006/07).

Presidential and Parliamentary Elections

With a constitution in place Afghanistan prepared for presidential elections on 9 October 2004. The election was scheduled earlier than planned to assist the re-election campaign of George W. Bush in November of that year. The election in Afghanistan was clearly won by the incumbent Karzai, who received 55 per cent of the approximately eight million votes cast, representing three-quarters of registered voters. The common assessment of the election is that millions of people chose democracy over violence and that Karzai won as a well-known candidate who was unimplicated in the crimes of previous decades. While true in many respects, such an assessment tends to elide a number of factors, which complicate the story of democratic transition.

For example, during the election campaign, United States embassy officials pressured several candidates to withdraw in order to guarantee Karzai's victory (Watson 2004). Furthermore, during the election the voting process was compromised by the fact that only 12 per cent of balloting stations had international observers, of whom there were only 150 in total (Warnock 2008, 120–2). According to the US State Department, '[o]bservers stated that [the election] did not meet international standards and noted irregularities, including pervasive intimidation of voters and candidates, especially women' (United States 2008). Moreover, in the aftermath of the election, Karzai appointed, under the direction of US ambassador Zalmay Khalilzad, numerous warlords to cabinet posts and provincial governorships (Kazem 2005). While Karzai reduced the number of warlords in cabinet, key factional leaders such as Ismael Khan, Abdul Rashid Dostum, Abdul Rasul Sayyaf, Mohammad Qasim Fahim, Karim Khalili, and Gul Agha Sherzai – all of whom have been accused of war crimes or abuses by Human Rights Watch – were still given important posts in cabinet or as provincial governors

(Zia-Zarifi 2004, 7; Kolhatkar and Ingalls 2006, 156; Warnock 2008, 122). The presidential election thus ensconced a system of power in which Karzai managed a highly centralized political apparatus with the vital support of warlords and the western occupation.

The parliamentary elections of 18 September 2005 represented the final stage of the Bonn Process. Contrary to expectations there was no violence on election day, and 6.4 million voters cast ballots to elect representatives to the lower house of the National Assembly and to 34 provincial councils. Women accounted for 50 per cent of voters in some provinces and were themselves elected to sixty-eight seats in the lower house. Despite these achievements the parliamentary elections failed to represent what western states described as a full transition to democracy and, in fact, accentuated problems of warlordism and sectarianism and laid the foundation for the current crisis of governance. These problems were evident in the preparations for the election, in the electoral process itself, and in the parliamentary results.

The Political Parties Law of September 2003, for example, was designed to curtail the development of national parties with secular political programs. It stipulates that the 'political system . . . is based on the principles of democracy and pluralism,' but is qualified to exclude any parties whose 'objectives are opposed to the principles of the holy religion of Islam' (cited in Ruttig 2006, 18). Similarly the Electoral Law of May 2004 disallowed the use of party lists and adopted a single nontransferable voting system, both of which reinforced the personalization of politics in Afghanistan and the influence of regional warlords and ethnic voting blocs (Ruttig 2006, 42, 45). Despite numerous appeals by an alliance of thirty-four democratic and secular parties, Karzai refused to amend the electoral laws to encourage greater party formation, active citizen engagement, and internal party reform, all of which are needed for democracy to exist substantively, not just formally (Ruttig 2006, 42). By rejecting such proposals by the 'new democracy' movement in Afghanistan, Karzai organized a parliamentary election in which secular and democratic parties were barred from participation.

The limitations of the voting system were evident on election day. Only 50 per cent of registered voters turned out, with only one-third voting in Kabul and the southeastern provinces (Wilder 2005, 32; Human Rights Watch 2006). The Afghan Research and Evaluation Unit 'attributed the decline [in voter participation] to growing frustration and disillusionment with President Karzai and his government' (Wilder 2005, 32). It revealed that 'there is widespread perception among Afghans that the 2005 elections were marred by weak candidate vetting, fraud and intimidation' (35), echoing Human Rights Watch, which said that 'voters were put off by the complexity of the ballots, disenchantment with the performance of the government and international community, and the presence of too many candidates with records of serious human rights abuses' (2006, 3). According to Womankind Worldwide (2006, appendix 18) female participation was extremely low in provinces such as Uruzgan (9 per cent), Zabul (10 per cent), and Helmand (16 per cent). Infamous warlords such as Rabbani, Sayyaf, Qanooni, Almas, and Atef were elected despite their implication in 'war crimes and crimes against humanity that occurred during hostilities in Kabul in the early 1990s' (ibid., 4). According to the *New York Times* 50 per cent of elected parliamentarians were 'religious figures or former fighters' (Gall 2005). Two further assessments indicated that 60 per cent of parliamentarians were linked to atrocities in the past (Human Rights Watch 2006), while 'more than 80% of winning candidates in the provinces and more than 60% in the capital . . . [had] links to armed groups' (Afghan Independent Human Rights Commission, cited in Warnock 2008, 124).

According to Andrew Wilder (2005, 4) the elected parliament was 'a highly fragmented institution' resulting from 'the absence of strong and effective political parties, compounded by the decision to adopt a voting system that benefited independent candidates at the expense of . . . parties.' As Thomas Ruttig (2006, 44) specifies, the real demarcation in the new parliament ran between the 'new democrats' and the post–People's Democratic Party of Afghanistan left on the one hand, and the ethno-nationalists, Islamists, and *mujahideen* commanders on the other. Despite this clear division political pluralism has been stultified by 'the lack of a legal framework and of a safe political environment – in particular, by the failure to disarm the factional militias.' As a result 'alternative political forces live in constant fear of persecution and are only able to operate relatively freely in the largest cities and a few rural areas' (Ruttig 2006, 17–18).

Perhaps the best description of the new political process in Afghanistan was voiced by Daan Everts, head of NATO in Afghanistan, who blamed NATO for 'deliberately' sabotaging the political transition:

[In Afghanistan] politics and governance are extremely personalised. This has been encouraged by the electoral system of a single non-transferable vote . . . it reinforced individualized dynamics . . . [I]t would have been better to have allowed more organised structures, more political actors like parties. This has been done elsewhere with good results . . . [T]he result has been an extremely chaotic parliament. There are 248 talking heads with very little discipline and little organised deliberations that are meant to produce legislation which the country so badly needs. *We deliberately did this.* To reinforce presidential position and power you weaken the parliament – understandable from the US perspective who felt that the country, given its history and shattered state of economy, needed a strong hand. This approach is so personalised and very centred on one person to be in command. (Al Jazeera 2007; emphasis added)

The Policy Output

In this political context it was inevitable that Karzai would ally himself with two domestic power groups: the armed commanders and the religious fundamentalists in parliament. The result has been a socially conservative and politically regressive set of policy initiatives and legal decisions, many of which were altered or reversed after domestic and international protests. To cite a few examples, in 2003 the (former) chief justice, Fazl Hadi Shinwari, attempted to re-establish the Department for the Promotion of Virtue and Prevention of Vice, which had previously enforced a welter of laws on women's activities during the civil war and Taliban periods (Lamb 2006). In April 2008 the parliament drafted a new moral law that sought to disallow women from wearing make-up in public, prevent young men from wearing female clothing, enforce the hijab at work, and ban female dancing (Agence France Presse 2008). The Ministry of Information and Culture has banned Indian soap operas, just as the Taliban did in the 1990s (Sterling 2008). More recently the Karzai government approved a Shia Personal Status Law that allows husbands to rape (in the first draft) or starve (in the second draft) their wives if they refuse to have sex (Boone 2009; Human Rights Watch 2009; Starkey 2009). As Murray Brewster (2009) and Michelle Collins and Jeff Davis (2009) reveal, the first draft was made known to Canadian diplomats, who raised no concern about, and showed no interest in, the contents of the law, despite the concerns of other countries. Canadian lawyers may have also vetted the second draft, which legalized child marriage, the starvation of spouses, and the marrying of rapists to their victims. These policy initiatives are the result of the compromises and alliances that Karzai has struck with warlords and religious leaders both inside and outside parliament.

Equally problematic has been the silencing of dissident voices and independent media. Consider the following, reported by the US Department of State (United States 2008):

- In early 2006 the Office of the Attorney General detained and interrogated Dr. Khalil Narmgoi for ten days for publishing a critical article on President Karzai.
- In February 2006 Afghan citizen Abdul Rahman was arrested and sentenced to death for the crime of converting to Christianity. After international protests Rahman was released and sought asylum in Italy.
- In 2007 outspoken female MP Malalai Joya was suspended from parliament for speaking out against the role of warlords in Afghanistan.
- On 11 September 2008 a Kabul court sentenced Ahmed Ghous Zalmai and Mullah Qari Mushtaq each to twenty years in prison for translating the Qur'an into Dari.
- In January 2008 a three-judge panel sentenced twenty-three-year-old journalism student and newspaper reporter Sayed Pervez Kambaksh to death for distributing a pamphlet on the treatment of women in certain Islamic traditions. In August 2009 Kambaksh was granted amnesty by Karzai and subsequently fled Afghanistan.
- The new Afghan Media Law includes a number of content restrictions on information that is contrary to Islam, religion in general, humiliating to 'legal persons,' disruptive of the 'public's mind,' and threatening to the 'stability' and 'security' of the country.

All of these cases express what the Nai Center for Open Media in Afghanistan describes as a rising trend of harassment and censorship of new media, especially of those critical of the war and the Karzai government. According to one study by the Center, the 'Afghan government [itself was] responsible for at least 23 of 45 reported incidents of intimidation, violence, or arrest of journalists between May 2007 and May 2008' (see Gopal 2008). This censorship is another example of the contradiction in the Bonn Process between the rhetoric of democratization and the reality of warlordism, social conservatism, political centralization, and suppression of independent voices.

The Bonn Process: A Summary

The antidemocratic actions of the Karzai government are an expression of the unstable political system established by the Bonn Process. The promise of democratization and nation building was vitiated by the organization of the political process, by the formal mechanisms for establishing authority, and by the political coalition between Karzai, the military occupation, and various warlords. For these reasons Johnson and Leslie (2008, 178) argue that the Bonn Process was bound to set off a deadly dialectic of internal popular revolt and outside military intervention: 'In the post-Bonn period, the central state model offered the option only of an American puppet state or a [Northern Alliance] state. Both would provoke resistance. The Afghan state was from its creation a Pashtun state . . . A non-Pashtun state would, therefore, be impossible without a completely unacceptable level of coercion which would have to be aided by outside powers; and the more heavy-handed outsiders are in pursuit of a "strong" state, the more of a problem external intervention will become.' With this in mind, the next section demonstrates the limitations of the security sector reform and development project in Afghanistan, and the reasons the Taliban re-emerged as a resistance movement, forcing the Obama 'surge' of military conflict.

Security and Development in Occupied Afghanistan

In the aftermath of the war the international community launched an ambitious project of security sector reform, aid, and developmental reconstruction, all of which were designed to compliment the Bonn Process of rebuilding a state apparatus. The security sector reform project was designed to establish a new national army, police corps, and legal system in Afghanistan as well as to disarm militias and reduce opium production and distribution. The aid project was designed to accelerate the economic and social development of Afghanistan, which ranks as one of the poorest countries in the world (UNDP 2009). As the evidence demonstrates, this wide-ranging security and development project has not met stated goals; in fact it has contributed to, or exacerbated, the crisis tendencies of the military occupation and Bonn Process.

Security Sector Reform

Consider, first, the security sector reform project. In April 2002 the Geneva Agreements outlined an ambitious plan by which five countries assumed responsibility for each pillar of the project, including military reform (the United States), police reform (Germany), disarmament (Japan), counternarcotics (the United Kingdom), and judicial reform (Italy). Under US auspices, the Afghan National Army (ANA) was established in May 2002 and has since been a central focus of US state-building efforts in Afghanistan, accounting for billions of dollars of US aid. The ANA is conceived as a multi-ethnic, non-factional institution, and is commonly advertised as the most professional pillar of the Afghan state (International Crisis Group 2010a, 1).[2] In May 2009 it consisted of 90,000 active troops; by 2013 ANA numbers are set to reach 195,000.

Beyond these formal achievements, however, are substantive problems in the form and function of the ANA. First, it is widely known that Northern Alliance militias were incorporated into the ANA in 2002. As a result the ANA was not created as a neutral or autonomous party to the conflict in Afghanistan; rather, it is seen as the 'fief of [the Tajik] Panjshiris, who almost entirely made up the garrison in Kabul and for that reason were not able to present themselves as the credible nucleus of a national army' (Dorronsoro 2005, 337–8; see also International Crisis Group 2010a, 10).[3] Furthermore the ANA has been commanded by key leaders of the Northern Alliance, including Generals Dostum and Fahim, both of whom are implicated in past human rights abuses. While the current composition of the ANA roughly matches the ethnic divide in Afghanistan, the Pashtun contribution from the southern and eastern provinces, where the majority of fighting occurs, is largely non-existent. As the US Department of Defense puts it, '[r]ecruiting of southern Pashtuns remains a significant challenge. Although the majority of recruits from the southern provinces are Pashtun, *these provinces only produced 3 percent of this solar year's recruits* . . . Overall, the total number of Pashtuns in the ANA meets national ethnicity goals, however, southern Pashtuns are underrepresented' (United States 2010, 26; emphasis added).

The ANA demonstrates other 'intrinsic weaknesses,' including inappropriate training, coerced enrolment, low wages, hazing rituals, low re-enlistment, allegations of corruption, involvement in narcotics, dependence on foreign advisors and trainers, lack of equipment, taxing convoys and travellers, and executing prisoners (Giustozzi 2007, 181; Oxfam International 2011). According to the US Congressional Research Service, the ANA 'suffers from at least a 20% desertion rate. Many officers are illiterate or poorly motivated. Some accounts say that a typical ANA unit is only at about 50% of its authorized strength at any given time, and there are significant shortages in about 40% of equipment items' (Katzman 2010, 47).

As Justin Podur argues (in this volume), many of these problems stem from the misuse of the army as a tool of counterinsurgency against a domestic target. The relationship of dependence between the United States and the ANA is likely to grow, however, as 'the annual cost of building and maintaining the existing Afghan force is more than four times larger than the entire Afghan economy' (Youssef 2009). A more recent analysis by the *Wall Street Journal* reveals that coalition spending on Afghan security forces in 2012 will reach US$12.8 billion, or more than two-thirds of the projected estimate by the International Monetary Fund (IMF) of Afghanistan's gross domestic product (GDP) (Abi-Habib 2011). In these conditions the ANA has developed not as an independent institution but as an extension or a dependency of the western occupation.

The same is true of the Afghan National Police (ANP). In April 2002 Germany outlined a comprehensive plan to build a national police service with the secondary support of the United States and the UN Law and Order Trust Fund. The plan entailed a number of initiatives, including the creation of a central command in Kabul, professional training services, and the purchase of new equipment, the goals of which were to field a national squad of 50,000 officers and 12,000 border guards by 2005. At that time the United States assumed command of the police reform project, with supplementary support offered by European governments and Canada. As part of the Afghanistan Compact of 2006, ANP numbers were increased to 82,000 in order to fight the growing insurgency. Alongside the US 'surge,' ANP numbers were set to rise to 134,000 by November 2011.

The plans to build the ANP as another pillar of the security sector reform project, however, 'have been a failure' according to Hans-Christoph Ammon, the head of Germany's army commando unit (Deutsche Welle 2008). Likewise the US$860 million spent on police training by the United States between 2003 and 2005 was 'almost totally useless' according to Pakistani journalist Ahmed Rashid (2008, 205). The Afghan Research and Evaluation Unit argues that 'the overall . . . process has been slowed by a number of factors, including a lack of equipment[,] . . . crumbling infrastructure[,] poor pay[,] . . . and problems with recruitment' (Sedra 2004, 7).

Beyond this technical critique are more substantive problems in the organization and operation of the ANP, including corruption, smuggling, looting, drug use, desertion, high turnover, executions, torture, land theft, extortion, militiaties, and ethnic imbalances (Giustozzi 2007, 175–6; Wilder 2007, 52; Agence France Presse 2010; Oxfam International 2011). According to Wilder (2007, 52–3) there is 'grand corruption' linking the ANP and the Ministry of the Interior, 80 per cent of whose officials are linked to the drug trade. This assessment is shared by the World Bank and the UN Office on Drugs and Crime, which have accused the Ministry of the Interior of appointing police chiefs 'to protect and promote criminal interests' (Shaw 2006, 199–200). Further problems include the outsourcing of training to the private corporation, Dyncorp, and the heavy recruitment of officers 'from existing militia groups, linked to local political or tribal strongmen, and often to provincial governors' (Wilder 2007, vii–xii, 3, 14). In 2006, for example, Karzai enlisted an 11,000-strong Auxiliary Police tied to ex-*mujahideen* and criminal groups (Stein and Lang 2007, 222). In June of that year, after riots swept Kabul, Karzai also appointed commanders with established links to 'drugs smuggling, organized crime and illegal militias' (Walsh 2006).

According to Mark Sedra (2004, 1–2) these multiple problems in the organization and deployment of the ANP are not just the result of technical inefficiencies in training and funding, but also of political factors such as the misuse and misdirection of the ANP as a tool of counterinsurgency. In his assessment, '[i]n a country where, in the recent past, the basic rights of the citizenry have been transgressed so brazenly by statutory security forces, such an approach is irresponsible and imprudent.' Although the Taliban's methods of adjudicating justice are highly unpopular across the country (International Council on Security and Development 2011), Afghans in certain areas have turned against the ANP and once again welcomed or begrudgingly accepted the Taliban as a much-needed source of law and order (Graff 2009).

Similar problems exist in the other pillars of security sector reform. The judicial reform process that was launched under Italian supervision in 2002 made little progress, and collapsed in 2004. While a number of gains have been achieved through other means – including the 'redrafting of legal codes covering a number of subjects; the ratification of an Interim Criminal Procedure Code; the completion of law collection; the establishment of a training programme . . . and the launch of administrative reforms' – the 'acute lack of judges, prosecutors, defence counselors, legal clerks, etc. . . . has paralysed the process, leaving a legal vacuum across the country' (Sedra 2004, 13). According to the International Crisis Group,

Afghanistan's justice system is in a *catastrophic state of disrepair*. Despite repeated pledges over the last nine years, the majority of Afghans still have little or no access to judicial institutions. Lack of justice has destabilised the country and judicial institutions have withered to near non-existence. Many courts are inoperable and those that do function are understaffed. Insecurity, lack of proper training and low salaries have driven many judges and prosecutors from their jobs. Those who remain are highly susceptible to corruption. Indeed, there is very little that is systematic about the legal system, and there is little evidence that the Afghan government has the resources or political will to tackle the challenge. The public, consequently, has no confidence in the formal justice sector amid an atmosphere of impunity. A growing majority of Afghans have been forced to accept the rough justice of Taliban and criminal powerbrokers in areas of the country that lie beyond government control . . . *The strong presidential system adopted under the 2004 constitution has only exacerbated the weakness of judicial institutions . . . Extrajudicial actions by the U.S. and its coalition partners against Afghan citizens have also distorted the justice system and are fuelling the insurgency.* (2010b, i–ii; emphasis added)

For similar reasons the program for Disarmament, Demobilization, and Reintegration (DDR) organized by Japan and the United States in September 2003 made little progress and no longer exists today. While the DDR program claimed to have demobilized 6,230 combatants and 4,945 weapons, those 'disarmed were largely irregular . . . militiamen that had effectively demobilized after the fall of the Taliban regime and the bulk of the weapons submitted were of very low quality' (Sedra 2004, 15). Organized militias continue to operate across Afghanistan, and the country is still awash with weapons, as the current violence attests. Given the growing level of military conflict, there exist few incentives for demobilization; in any case the Pentagon still recruits armed tribes and militias for the purpose of counterinsurgency (see Sedra 2004, 15; Giustozzi 2007, 166–7; Johnson and Leslie 2008, 34–5; Rubin 2010; Rubin and Oppel 2010).

The issue of opium production is perhaps the greatest failure of the security sector reform project. The harvest of opium, which was largely banned by the Taliban, has exploded under the watch of the Karzai government and the military occupation, making Afghanistan the source of 90 per cent of the world's heroin. In 2007 Afghanistan exported an estimated 8,200 tonnes of heroin, up from 3,400 in 2002. The export value of the 2007 crop exceeded US$4 billion, accounting for more than half of Afghanistan's GDP (Yousafzai and Moreau 2008). The industry pays relatively high salaries for the 2.3 million farmers who grow opium, and employs approximately 14 per cent of the rural population (Rashid 2008, 235). There is overwhelming evidence that the Afghan state is linked to the drug trade and that Karzai maintains political connections to well-known drug dealers, many of whom are elected members of parliament or are provincial governors and senators appointed by Karzai himself (Gall 2008; Rashid 2008, 326–7, 329). Furthermore it is widely known that Karzai's late brother, Ahmed Wali – with whom Canada worked in Kandahar – operated one of the largest drug operations in Afghanistan (Gall 2008). While poppy cultivation decreased in 2008 and 2009 and held constant in 2010, the United Nations Office on Drugs and Crime (2010) estimates that poor weather conditions and market saturation, not increased security, were the primary causes of this reduction. While Canada has not engaged in poppy eradication, Canadian forces were instructed to combat drug traffickers and facilities 'linked to the terrorists' (CBC News 2009). In other words, Canadian forces targeted the drug infrastructure of their opponents, but turned a blind eye to the trafficking operations of their allies in the Karzai government.[4] For this reason the interests of the occupation have limited the counternarcotics project in Afghanistan.

To summarize, the evidence on security sector reform reveals how another aspect of nation building and reconstruction in Afghanistan has been subordinated to, or compromised by, the logic of occupation. While the United States and NATO have claimed to support democratic transition and local capacity building, the reality is that, in every pillar of security sector reform, the interests of the occupation have trumped or contradicted the idealistic claims of western forces in Afghanistan.

Neoliberalism as Development? Aid in the Service of Empire

The official aid and development project for Afghanistan has been equally problematic as a facet of occupation. This project began with the Tokyo Agreement of January 2002, which pledged US$4.4 billion in development and reconstruction funds. This agreement was prepared by the World Bank and the Asian Development Bank, even though neither institution had been involved in Afghanistan for years. Under such guidance 'private entrepreneurship' was 'strongly underscored . . . as an engine of growth.' Furthermore, despite the commitments of international donors, the total amount pledged amounted to only US$42 per annum per inhabitant for the period from 2002 to 2006, as opposed to much higher amounts allocated for other recent post-conflict situations

(Zia-Zarifi 2004, 2; Dorronsoro 2005, 334). Lastly, of the total amount committed by international parties to the Tokyo Agreement, only US$112 million had been delivered as of November 2003 (Johnson and Leslie 2008, xiii), a massive shortfall that delayed the reconstruction project in Afghanistan and was an early sign of western disinterest in rebuilding the country.

The Tokyo Agreement was complimented by the Interim Government's National Development Framework of April 2002, drafted by foreign experts committed to a neoliberal development strategy in which free trade, foreign investment, zero inflation, and privatization of state assets were offered as economic principles for the new state (Johnson and Leslie 2008, 117, 204; Shah 2009, 8–9). The influence of foreign experts was also evident in *Securing Afghanistan's Future* (2004), an Afghan government document written by the UN Development Programme (UNDP), the United Nations Assistance Mission to Afghanistan (UNAMA), the World Bank, and the Asian Development Bank (Shah 2009, 9).

These conditions of external control were reproduced in the establishment in 2002 of the Afghan Reconstruction Trust Fund (ARTF), a secretariat of the World Bank, the Asian Development Bank, the UNDP, the Islamic Development Bank, and the UNAMA to allocate funding for development projects. The ARTF was designed so that donors could bypass the Afghan state and direct their funding allocations from abroad (Roberts 2009, 6–7). As part of the ARTF the major international financial institutions demanded that Afghanistan repay US$45 million in loans from the pre-1979 period before new allocations would be dispensed (Johnson and Leslie 2008, 201–2).

To balance out this externally driven development agenda, the National Solidarity Project (NSP) was conceived in 2003 to support local development works, as determined by community development councils operating in four thousand communities in all 364 districts of Afghanistan. The NSP was designed to provide quick-impact, small-scale development projects through the distribution of microcredit for wells, bridges, schools, and clinics (Rashid 2008, 84–5). While the NSP notes the completion of tens of thousands of much-needed projects, some aid experts have criticized the microloan model for impeding state capacities and for generating new dependence on highly contingent funding sources (Johnson and Leslie 2008, 208). According to another study (Beath et al. 2010, vii), the NSP has created 'new village institutions for women' and produced 'tangible improvements in access to drinking water and electricity,' yet 'does not appear to have [had] any impact on the access of villagers to infrastructure or result[ed] in any changes in economic activity, levels of community trust, or the likelihood of a village suffering a dispute or an attack.'

Before 2006, then, the development and aid project for Afghanistan was beset by several limitations, including shortfalls in funding, external direction in the form of the ARTF, and a neoliberal development plan that restricted the capacity of the state. As the military conflict with the Taliban escalated in 2005, there emerged another round of nation-building plans, including the Afghan National Development Strategy (ANDS) of 2005 (updated 2008) and the Afghanistan Compact of 2006. These documents were written as post-Bonn agreements between Afghanistan and the international community. They constitute a systematic statement on the development needs of Afghanistan and the principles by which the government and international donors will direct funding. The ANDS, in particular, was written as a poverty reduction strategy paper in order for Afghanistan to qualify for debt relief under the Heavily Indebted Poor Country (HIPC) initiative of the IMF and the World Bank. The 2008 revised version of the ANDS was written by foreign experts and domestic technocrats who promote a neoliberal development strategy (see Afghanistan 2005, 2008). This strategy includes attracting foreign capital to build the mining, agricultural, communications, and energy industries – a process already under way through the Hydrocarbons Law, the Mining Law, and the Law on Foreign Private Investment; maintaining low inflation and 'prudent fiscal and monetary policies'; an export-led growth model; and privatization of state assets, including sixty-five state-owned enterprises (Paterson, Blewett, and Karimi 2006, 6; ANDS 2008, 18; Johnson and Leslie 2008, 204; Warnock 2008, 35; Shah 2009, 27).[5]

With the expansion of NATO across Afghanistan from 2003 to 2005 there emerged a further component of the neoliberal aid program: the Provincial Reconstruction Team (PRT). NATO's PRTs were modelled on the counterinsurgency strategy of the US Marines, who try to integrate the military, developmental, and diplomatic responsibilities of occupation in a single setting. As many experts predicted, the PRTs subordinated the delivery of aid to military and geopolitical objectives, were quickly targeted by the insurgency, and 'fell back on . . . local warlords for security and administration' (Rashid 2008, 199). For these reasons the PRTs have been condemned by many NGOs with a long history of working in Afghanistan, including InterAction (2003), Oxfam

International (Oxfam International et al. 2009), Act!on Aid, Care Afghanistan, Christian Aid, Afghanaid, Concern Worldwide, and Trocaire (Act!on Aid et al. 2010; see, also, Waldman 2006: 3). Senior UN officials have criticized the 'militarization of humanitarian aid' in Afghanistan and in 2010 blocked UN agencies from supporting the US-UK 'surge' in Helmand province.

The misuse and misdirection of aid and development funds is another major problem. Even though aid and development funding has accounted for only 10 per cent of western spending in Afghanistan since 2001, that amount has been misused and misallocated consistently. As the US Senate Foreign Relations Committee has revealed, '[m]ost US aid bypasses the Afghan Government in favor of international firms,' and is directed towards 'short-term stabilization programs instead of longer term development projects' (United States 2011, 2–3). Likewise, a major study by ninety-four aid organizations has described how the development program has been systematically compromised by the war against the Taliban; by the failure of major donors to meet even half of their commitments; by the misdirection of funds to urban centres; and by the perversion of aid through PRTs. For example, two-thirds of aid bypasses the Afghan government, while 50 per cent of operating costs typically are lost to corporate profits and consultants' salaries. Furthermore nearly 50 per cent of aid in Afghanistan is 'tied aid' and thus functions as an indirect means of recycling funds back to corporations in donor countries (Waldman 2008, 1–7; World Bank 2008). For all of these reasons Ahmed Rashid (2008, 171, 177) argues that the international aid program has created a 'donor bureaucracy' that competes with the state, misdirects funds towards private purposes, and engenders new forms of national dependency.

In sum, while the development agenda in Afghanistan has achieved a number of goals in terms of school construction, irrigation, immunization, road construction, and elementary school enrolment, there remain systematic weaknesses, which are linked to the economic, social, and military project of the western occupation. In other words, beyond the technical problems of donor coordination and finding the right balance between large- and small-scale projects is a political and economic context in which military occupation, neoliberal ideology, and external direction take precedent. The result has been a systematic failure of the 'aid juggernaut' to make real advances in economic development or quality of living for Afghan citizens (Loyn 2006). Instead, aid and development programs have been redirected to the ends of occupation and neoliberalism. With this in mind, the final section examines the neo-Taliban and the counterinsurgency war.

Descent into Chaos: The Taliban, Counterinsurgency, and Torture

The Taliban Insurgency

The Taliban redux from 2005 onwards must be understood in the context of an occupation in crisis. The failure of the Bonn Process to establish a democratic state, the failure of aid programs to improve economic and social conditions, the failure of security sector reform to disarm militias and to create an effective police corps and national army, and the widening occupation by NATO military forces – all have combined to give the Taliban the motivation and capacity to escalate its struggle against the Karzai government and the US-NATO presence. While the United States and NATO continue to frame the conflict in terms of the 'war on terror' against 'al-Qaeda,' the reality is that the Taliban are a complex indigenous movement motivated largely by local grievances and national sentiment against the occupation (Strick van Linschoten and Kuehn 2011).[6]

This conceptualization of the Taliban insurgency is confirmed by a number of major studies. As Anand Gopal (2010, 2) demonstrates, the Taliban's resurgence post-2001 'was not inevitable or preordained.' From 'senior leadership levels down to the rank and file [it] by and large surrendered to the new government' and offered multiple forms of accommodation. The Karzai government and its US patrons rejected these offers, however. In Gopal's account the Taliban re-emerged in response to several material factors, including the 'lack of a genuine, broad-based reconciliation process,' 'growing disillusionment in the countryside,' 'the dominance of one particular set of tribes [in Kandahar],' the 'weakness of the judiciary and police,' the 'heavy-handed tactics of U.S. forces,' and 'widespread torture and abuse at the hands of pro-government strongmen' (2010, 2–3). For such reasons, 'many Taliban did not take up arms simply as an exercise of the principle of jihad or the expulsion of foreigners . . . but rather because it was the only viable alternative for individuals and groups left without a place in the new state of affairs. In other words, initially it was not the existence of a new government per se that drove these former Taliban back, but the *behaviour* of that government. Likewise, initially it was not the presence of foreign troops as such that spawned opposition from these former Taliban, but the *behaviour* of those troops' (20). In this context the Taliban should be viewed not as a tribal or a transnational religious movement, but more properly as a 'nationalist Islamist insurgency that feeds on and manipulates tribal imbalances and rivalries to its own ends' (14).

According to another study (Giustozzi 2007, 12) the Taliban must be understood ideologically as a 'mix of the most conservative village Islam mixed with Deobandi doctrines' in the context of Pashtun culture and Afghan politics. The Taliban recruit from refugee camps, religious schools, and villages under attack by US-NATO forces, and offer protection, security, and law and order in the territories they control. The Taliban are more flexible on certain social issues and now make use of Internet and video technology as part of their organizational and propaganda efforts. Drugs 'remain a secondary source of revenue for the Taliban and . . . there is little evidence of [their] encouraging farmers to grow poppies [or] of their involvement in the trade' outside key southern provinces (Giustozzi 2007, 88). Instead the Taliban are waging a 'fourth generation' guerrilla war, in which political, economic, social, military, and cyber tactics are used to win a base of support and to undermine the occupation (111–16). While the Taliban draw resources from a pan-Islamic solidarity network in the region, and build cross-ethnic alliances within Afghanistan on the basis of religion (Ruttig 2010b), they do not advance or participate in a transnational religious war; in fact they have engaged the Karzai government in peace talks since 2002 (Gopal 2010). According to Giustozzi (2007, 136) a primary obstacle in these negotiations is the status of foreign troops, which the Taliban want removed as a *condition sine qua non* of any agreement.

This understanding of the Taliban insurgency is confirmed in a series, 'Talking to the Taliban' (G. Smith 2008), published in the *Globe and Mail* newspaper. From interviews with dozens of Taliban fighters Smith discovered that international terrorism plays no role in their perception of the conflict, that Taliban fighters are motivated by a nationalist agenda to expel foreign armies, that many of them joined the insurgency after friends and family members were killed by NATO operations, and that many favour a negotiated settlement and are not averse to joining the government (see also Weera and Santa Barbara 2008). As a result neither the Taliban nor the wider conflict can be understood through the paradigm of the 'war on terror' against 'al-Qaeda.'[7]

While the Taliban lack the military capacity and political support to overthrow the NATO-backed government, they have built an organizational network of insurgent groups, local tribes, family structures, and religious institutions, and are now present in four-fifths of the country (Synovitz 2008). To present themselves as a national liberation movement that can form alliances with non-Pashtun ethnic groups, the Taliban anchor the armed struggle in the political language of religion (Ruttig 2010b). In many provinces the Taliban operate a parallel administration of governance and law and order, which is sometimes welcomed as a positive alternative to the ANP and the warlords (Dreazen and Gorman 2008; Salahuddin 2009; Witte 2009). While the Taliban are xenophobic, misogynistic, conservative, fundamentalist, antidemocratic, and violently indiscriminate, they do express a quasi-popular movement against the Karzai government and western occupation, most notably in southeastern Afghanistan.[8]

Given this evidence one can draw three tentative conclusions: first, that the war and occupation cannot be understood through the framework of the 'war on terror'; second, that the Taliban are a 'nationalist Islamist insurgency'; and third, that the Taliban redux is largely an outcome of the US-NATO occupation, which is becoming increasingly violent, with deadly consequences for civilians.

Counterinsurgency, Civilian Casualties, and Torture

The expansion of NATO across Afghanistan between 2003 and 2005 was coterminous with the crisis of occupation discussed above and the re-emergence of the Taliban. The increase in NATO troop levels from 4,500 in 2001 to 50,000 in 2008 and the effort to establish PRTs in each of Afghanistan's thirty-four provinces quickly drew NATO into a fierce counterinsurgency. Since 2005 more than two thousand coalition personnel have been killed and thousands more wounded. At the same time NATO is using ever-greater levels of violence and intimidation just to manage the status quo.

Consider, first, the issue of house raids and detentions. According to Human Rights Watch (2006), 'U.S. and coalition forces . . . arbitrarily detain civilians and use excessive force during arrests of non-combatants. Ordinary civilians arrested in military operations are unable to challenge the legal basis for the detention or obtain hearings before an adjudicative body.' Elsewhere Human Rights Watch has accused NATO of using psychological tactics that are tantamount to 'collective punishment,' such as the use of radio broadcasts to threaten villages suspected of supporting the Taliban (North and Sarwary 2005). Likewise the Afghan Independent Human Rights Commission has condemned the practice of night raids: 'Afghan families [have] experienced their family members killed or injured, their houses or other property destroyed, or homes invaded at night without any perceived justification or legal authorization' (cited in Rennie 2008). A UN special rapporteur has also accused NATO of conducting secret raids and targeted killings outside the realm of both Afghan and international law (Associated Press 2008; Burch 2008). Beyond this, coalition forces deploy artillery, tank, mortar, and air fire in and around civilian centres on a regular basis. Furthermore, coalition forces are experimenting with new counterinsurgency weapons, including vacuum bombs, white phosphorous, laser technology, satellite terrain mapping, attack helicopters, unmanned aerial drones, microwave skin-burning technology, biometric surveillance, and light armoured vehicles (Pugliese 2007; M. Smith 2008; McLean 2009; Straziuso and Faiez 2009; Weinberger 2010).

Most dangerously NATO has conducted an aerial war strategy to compensate for the growing power of the Taliban on the ground. In 2007 NATO carried out 12,992 air strikes, dropped 1.2 million pounds of munitions, and killed at least 321 Afghan civilians in the process (Human Rights Watch 2008). According to a study by the Red Cross, US air strikes in April 2007 destroyed 173 houses and left 2,000 people homeless (Agence France Presse 2007). On 4 May 2009 US air strikes in Farah province killed up to 140 civilians (UPI 2009). Such tragedies are part of a growing trend, in which civilians are caught in the crossfire and displaced from their homes and villages. According to the United Nations civilian casualties reached 2,118 in 2008, a 40 per cent increase over 2007 (Straziuso 2009). Of this total the insurgency was responsible for 55 per cent and NATO for 39 per cent (or 829 in total). A study by Afghan Rights Monitor found that approximately 4,000 civilians were killed in 2008, including 1,100 by US and NATO forces and 520 by Afghan security personnel (Agence France Presse 2009). In 2009 civilian casualties increased by 14 per cent to 2,412, with pro-government forces responsible for at least 596 and antigovernment forces for at least 1,630 (UNAMA 2010). According to the United Nations civilian casualties also rose in 2010, with antigovernment forces responsible for three-quarters of deaths reported, though such findings are open to question.[9]

Moreover the Obama 'surge' served only to increase the violence. Between July and October 2010 the US air force carried out more than 2,600 sorties in which munitions were fired. On the ground the air campaign was complemented by counterinsurgency methods that detained

more than 2,400 alleged insurgents and killed approximately 1,400
(Starr 2010). By May 2011 the US Joint Special Operations Command
had killed or captured more than 12,000 suspected Taliban insurgents
as part of a program that Lieutenant Colonel John Nagl of the US Army
has described as an 'almost industrial-scale counterterrorism killing
machine' (PBS 2011). From April to July 2011 the same special operations machine captured a further 2,941 alleged insurgents and killed 834
more (Dozier 2011). The surge also employed large-scale razing tactics –
for example, the bulldozing and bombing of hundreds of homes and
farms in southern Afghanistan as part of Operation Dragon Strike (CBS
News 2010). The escalation of fighting has had a catastrophic impact on
civilians. According to the International Committee of the Red Cross
(Reuters 2010), approximately a thousand civilians were treated for war
wounds in the Mirwais Hospital in Kandahar in August and September 2010, a record high and double the number for the same period of
2009. According to Georgette Gagnon, UN director of human rights in
Afghanistan, '[t]he human cost of the Afghan conflict for Afghan civilians rose in the first six months of 2011. Afghan civilians experienced a
15 per cent increase in conflict-related civilian deaths over the past first
six months compared to the same period in 2010' (UNAMA 2011a).[10]
Reflecting on an earlier phase of the surge, General Stanley McChrystal, who commanded all US-NATO forces in Afghanistan in 2009–10,
revealed that '[w]e've shot an amazing number of people and killed
a number and, to my knowledge, none has proven to have been a real
threat to the force' (Oppel 2010). Beyond this the surge relied upon
funding and training a network of warlords and militias, which were
subsequently empowered to 'beat, rob and kill with impunity' in areas
cleared of Taliban fighters (Farmer 2011). According to Human Rights
Watch (2011) these warlords and militias formed the backbone of the
Afghan Local Police (established in July 2010), which have been guilty
of targeted killings, extortion, smuggling, and rape with impunity. In
these ways the surge has been premised on maximizing the level of
violence and repression in Afghanistan.[11]

The United States and its Afghan and NATO allies are also implicated in the torture and abuse of detainees. Since 2001 the United States
has turned Afghanistan into a test lab and staging ground for a regime
of torture, abuse, summary execution, disappearance, and rendition of
'terrorist suspects.' Between 2001 and 2008 the Afghan secret intelligence unit, the National Directorate of Security (NDS), was funded as a
'virtual subsidiary' of the CIA and oversaw the 'pervasive' torture and

abuse of prisoners (Sedra 2009; Walkom 2010). Ten years into the occupation the UNAMA found 'a compelling pattern and practice of torture and ill-treatment at a number NDS and ANP detention facilities'
(2011b, 49). At Bagram and Kandahar air bases, as well as at secret detention facilities across the country, detainees have been caged, beaten,
killed, frozen, deprived of sleep, humiliated, hooded, stripped, kicked,
electrocuted, executed, sexually assaulted, water boarded, threatened
with rape, and attacked with dogs. This pattern of torture and abuse
implicates not just the United States and the NDS, but also, to a lesser
extent, Australia, Canada, Germany, the Netherlands, and the United
Kingdom, as well as 'outsourcing' countries such as Azerbaijan, Egypt,
Jordan, Morocco, Pakistan, Qatar, Romania, Saudi Arabia, Syria, Thai-
land, and Uzbekistan, all of whom collaborate in a global system of torture and punishment (Rashid 2008, chap. 14; Andersson 2010). Within
this system Taliban and al-Qaeda suspects have been denied lawyers,
hearings, and the right to review their status under Afghan, US, and
international law (Amnesty International 2009). The torture of detainees has been a systematic component of the occupation, and serves as
a tool of repression, a form of intimidation, and a mechanism by which
occupation soldiers affirm their sense of racialized power and authority
over colonized (non-)subjects (Razack 2004).

In summary the Taliban-led insurgency re-emerged in 2005 after the
Bonn Process and the development agenda were used to impose a warlord government and a neoliberal aid package on Afghanistan. NATO
forces, deployed across the country, have functioned as a military protectorate for the Karzai regime and are perceived as reinforcing the
occupation. NATO has responded to the Taliban rebellion with night
raids, air strikes, targeted killings, heavy artillery, detentions, and torture, thereby fuelling both the insurgency and the growing disillusionment with the Karzai government and the occupation regime.

Conclusion: A Crisis of Occupation and Empire

Consensus is emerging among western governments and international
relations experts that the war in Afghanistan has reached an impasse,
or at least a moment of crisis. In the mainstream literature this crisis
typically is explained as an outcome of external shocks or internal mis-
calculations. As this chapter demonstrates, however, the crisis cannot
be pinned simply on outside factors or bureaucratic errors in the organization of the mission. Instead, to a large extent, the crisis is linked to

the project of occupation itself – in particular, to the western strategy
of building a warlord state, imposing a neoliberal development model,
and pacifying all resistance. Simply put the current crisis is best explained by the nature and logic of the occupation regime, which was
imposed and constructed by western imperialism. In the process the
occupation regime has made allies of – and thus legitimated – some
of the most antidemocratic, fundamentalist, corrupt, and violent actors
in the Afghan political economy, *against the wishes and interests of many
democratic and secular forces in the country*. Through such an understanding of the US-NATO mission, one can draw four conclusions about the
'methods of empire' in Afghanistan.

First, the state-building project is closely linked to the political, economic, and military interests of the western occupation. The Bonn
Process established a centralized presidential system through which
Hamid Karzai exercises power alongside that of the Northern Alliance
and other warlords. Democratic and secular parties were excluded
from shaping fundamental aspects of the Bonn Process, which is dominated by a coalition of warlords, militias, and religious fundamentalists. For these reasons the new politics in occupied Afghanistan do not
represent a positive example of democratic transition or political reconstruction. Instead they demonstrate the mechanisms of formal democracy through which western imperialism collaborates with local elites
to suppress or subvert popular sovereignty and national liberation.

Second, the development program for Afghanistan is dominated by
a neoliberal economic strategy devised by foreign and domestic technocrats who support a free market system. NGOs and international donors control the distribution of aid and development funds, which are
often used for private purposes and in support of the military occupation and counterinsurgency war. This neoliberal strategy weakens the
Afghan state and creates a new regime of dependence on transnational
capital, foreign service providers, and western military forces. The failure of this model, then, must be explained in terms of the occupation itself. The greater part of the official aid and development program is not
distant from the occupation, but central to it. It is the means by which
the western occupation attempts to pacify resistance and marketize the
Afghan economy to the ends of neoliberalism.

Third, the Taliban redux is a product of an occupation in crisis. The
Taliban re-emerged as a logical response to both the Bonn Process and
the neoliberal development project, both of which were designed as
instruments of foreign domination. The Taliban as a movement remain

violent, sectarian, undemocratic, and patriarchal, yet they represent a semi-popular opposition to the US-NATO occupation.[12] In this context the United States and NATO have launched a violent counterinsurgency that is guilty of bombing villages, collaborating with warlords and drug dealers, torturing prisoners, and bribing the population with aid and development works. With this in mind the Obama 'surge' must be understood as a war of occupation, rather than as a 'war on terror.'

Finally, as Canadians are aware, our country is deeply implicated in the Afghan crisis. Canada was an active participant in the 2001 war and played a key role in bringing NATO into Afghanistan. Canada supported the Bonn Process without concern for the role of warlords and voiced no opposition to the aid and development project, which was co-opted by geopolitical and military interests. Canada has been closely embedded within the Afghan state and has not opposed the reactionary social policies of Karzai, his cabinet, or the Afghan parliament. Moreover Canada has waged a violent war in Kandahar province and is guilty of killing civilians, destroying infrastructure, and transferring detainees to torture. In these and other ways Canada has been an ally to empire in Afghanistan.

NOTES

1 In summer 2009 Dennis Blair, US Director of National Intelligence, informed Congress that Iran was covertly shipping weapons to the Taliban insurgency. Canadian defence minister Peter MacKay had made the same assertion a few years earlier (see *CBC News* 2007). However, according to a US embassy cable dated 12 February 2010, US defense secretary Robert Gates 'noted that intelligence indicated there was little lethal material crossing the Afghanistan-Iran border.'

2 The ethnic breakdown of the ANA is roughly 42.6 per cent Pashtun, 40.98 per cent Tajik, 7.68 per cent Hazara, 4.05 per cent Uzbek, and 4.67 per cent others (International Crisis Group 2010a, 19).

3 According to the International Crisis Group (2010a, 11) the ANA is divided into four factions: Pashtuns allied with defence minister Abdul Rahim Wardak and the National Islamic Front party; Tajiks allied with General Bismillah Khan and the historic Shura-e Nazar; Uzbeks allied with General Hamayoun Fauzi; and Hazaras allied with General Baz Mohammad Jawhari.

4 At the same time, '[s]ince 2007, Canada has allocated $55-million to support the Afghan National Drug Control Strategy, including $52-million for the

UN Office on Drugs and Crime, which focuses on disruption of trafficking and seizures of opiates within Afghanistan, and $3-million for the Afghan government's Counter Narcotics Trust Fund, which pays for poppy eradication and other anti-drug work. Canada has allocated another $47-million since 2005 to programs, such as wheat-seed distribution, intended to boost legitimate farming and reduce reliance on poppy growing' (Baron 2010).

5 Other studies by the World Bank consistently demand neoliberal prescriptions such as 'fiscal discipline' and the 'containment of overall expenditures – notably for non-discretionary expenditures such as wage bills and pensions – in line with medium-term resource constraints,' 'ensuring that downstream expenditure liabilities created by public investments and other spending decisions are affordable.' It also recommends the delivery of public services by private actors, NGOs, and contractors instead of by the state. See World Bank (2005, vii–vii, x). The World Bank (2006) has also called for scrapping barriers to foreign direct investment and impediments to land ownership.

6 For reasons of brevity it is impossible to review the factional composition of the neo-Taliban. According to the US Department of Defense (United States 2010, 42) the neo-Taliban consists of three major sub-groups: the Shura Council of Mullah Omar, based in Quetta, Pakistan; the Hizb-e Islami organization of Gulbuddin Hekmatyar; and the father/son-led insurgent network of Jalaluddin and Sirajuddin Haqqani.

7 In June 2010 CIA director Leon Panetta estimated that only '50 to 100, maybe less' members of al-Qaeda were in Afghanistan. In his assessment, 'there's no question that the main location of Al Qaeda is in tribal areas of Pakistan.' See Sonmez (2010). A major study of the Taliban in Kandahar province by Anand Gopal (2010, 34) reveals that, 'in recent years, the importance and relevance of such fighters appears to have diminished greatly.'

8 Human Rights Watch (2010) documents the misogyny and sexism of the Taliban resistance – in particular, brutal attacks on women working for the government. According to a provincial survey in Kandahar by Glevum Associates (2010, 53) for NATO-ISAF, 94 per cent of the population believes the Afghan government should negotiate with the Taliban, 54 per cent 'strongly support,' and 37 per cent 'somewhat support' the Taliban. According to another survey, by Anthony Cordesman (2009, 32), a strong majority in Kandahar opposes the presence of foreign troops. At the same time the Taliban uses extreme violence against those suspected of working with the government and foreign forces, including 'arbitrary imprisonment, collective punishment, summary execution, beheadings, extortion, and kidnapping for ransom' (Gopal 2010, 37).

9 As a party to one side of the conflict the United Nations excludes alleged insurgents killed by US-NATO forces from the casualty figures. It is also unclear from the UN methodology how it determines who is a civilian and who is a Taliban fighter. Furthermore the UN research is limited to areas of the country to which it has access. Finally, UN statistics on civilian casualties surely underestimate the overall numbers and the responsibility of coalition forces. For example, the 'war logs' published by Wikileaks (July 2010) revealed nearly 150 incidents between January 2004 and December 2009 in which coalition forces killed or injured Afghan civilians, most of which were never reported.

10 The United Nations claims that the insurgency was responsible for 80 per cent of these civilian casualties, though these numbers are open to question, as the previous note suggests.

11 By spring 2011 the surge in Kandahar seemed to have disrupted Taliban command-and-control networks and weakened its hold on certain areas such as Arghandab. Several Taliban commanders were killed and many foot soldiers were forced to flee to Pakistan. The surge has not achieved any significant political gains, however, and the Taliban still dominates the Panjwayi-Zheray-Maiwand region.

12 The Taliban may be supported in some areas of Afghanistan as a popular resistance movement, but there is no evidence that the majority of the population wants a Taliban-run government, as in the 1990s. See the Introduction of this volume for a short discussion of opinion polls on the Taliban.

References

Abi-Habib, Maria. 2011. 'US and allies cut plans for funding Afghanistan's forces.' *Wall Street Journal*, 4 July.

Act!on Aid et al. 2010. 'Quick Impact, Quick Collapse: The Dangers of Militarized Aid in Afghanistan.' Oxford: Oxfam International. January.

Afghanistan. 2005. 'Afghanistan National Development Strategy.' Kabul.

–. 2008. 'Afghanistan National Development Strategy.' Kabul.

Afghanistan Study Group. 2010. 'A New Way Forward: Rethinking U.S. Strategy in Afghanistan.' http://www.afghanistanstudygroup.org/.

Agence France Presse. 2007. 'US raids made 2,000 Afghans homeless: Red Cross.' 19 May.

–. 2008. 'Afghan parliament committee drafts Taliban-style moral law.' 16 April.

–. 2009. 'Afghan unrest killed 4,000 civilians in 2008: report.' 21 January.

–. 2010. '70 percent of Afghan police recruits drop out: US trainer.' 2 March.

'Agreement on Provisional Arrangements in Afghanistan Pending the Re-Establishment of Permanent Government Institutions [Bonn Agreement].' 5 December 2001.

Alexander, Chris. 2010. 'The huge scale of Pakistan's complicity.' *Globe and Mail*, 30 July.

Al Jazeera. 2007. 'Afghanistan needs Muslim aid and effort: Interview with Daan Everts.' 31 December.

Amnesty International. 2009. 'USA: government opposes habeas corpus review for any Bagram detainees; reveals "enhanced" administrative review procedures.' London. 16 September. http://www.amnesty.org/en/news-and-updates/report/usa-must-grant-bagram-detainees-access-us-courts-20090916.

Andersson, Hilary. 2010. 'Afghans "abused at secret prison" at Bagram airbase.' BBC News, 15 April. http://news.bbc.co.uk/2/hi/8621973.stm.

Associated Press. 2008. 'Foreign agents behind spate of Afghan killings: UN.' 15 May.

Azarbaijani-Mohgaddam, Sippi, et al. 2008. *Afghan Hearts, Afghan Minds: Exploring Afghan Perceptions of Civil-Military Relations*. London: British & Irish Agencies Afghanistan Group.

Banerjee, Nipa. 2009. 'Afghanistan: No Security, No Governance.' *Policy Options* 30, no. 10: 66–71.

Baron, Ethan. 2010. 'Afghanistan opium harvest a dilemma for Canadian Forces.' *CanWest News Service*, 25 April.

BBC News. 2001. 'Millions at risk in Afghan crisis.' 14 October.

Beath, Andrew, et al. 2010. *Estimates of Interim Program Impact from First Follow-Up Survey*. National Solidarity Program. Randomized Impact Survey. http://www.nsp-ie.org.

Boone, Jon. 2009. ' "Worse than the Taliban" – new law roles back rights for Afghan women.' *Guardian*, 31 March.

Brewster, Murray. 2009. 'Canada knew about Afghan rape law in advance – NDP.' Canadian Press, 30 June.

Burch, Jonathon. 2008. 'U.N. Expert says more must be done to avoid Afghan deaths.' Reuters, 18 May.

Canada. 2008. *Independent Panel on Canada's Future Role in Afghanistan*. Ottawa: Government of Canada.

CBC News. 2007. 'MacKay says Iran giving weapons to Taliban.' 25 December.

–. 2009. 'Canadian soldiers to target drug trade linked to Taliban.' 6 February.

CBS News. 2010. 'U.S. Military bulldozes through Kandahar.' 10 November.

Collins, Michelle, and Jeff Davis. 2009. 'Afghan Law: "that this came out of nowhere was not true."' *Embassy Magazine*, 8 April.

Cordesman, Anthony. 2009. *Afghan Public Opinion and the Afghan War: Shifts by Region and Province*. Washington, DC: Center for Strategic and International Studies.

Deutsche Welle. 2008. 'Army general calls German campaign in Afghanistan a "failure."' 28 November.

Dorronsoro, Gilles. 2005. *Revolution Unending: Afghanistan 1979 to the Present*. New York: Columbia University Press.

–. 2010. *Afghanistan at the Breaking Point*. Washington, DC: Carnegie Endowment for International Peace.

Dozier, Kimberly. 2011. 'Headed for CIA, Petraeus leaves a revamped war zone.' Associated Press, 19 July.

Dreazen, Yochi J., and Siobhan Gorman. 2008. 'Taliban regains power, influence in Afghanistan.' *Wall Street Journal*, 20 November.

Farmer, Ben. 2011. 'US-funded Afghan militias "beat, rob and kill with impunity."' *Telegraph*, 13 July.

Gall, Carlotta. 2005. 'Islamists and mujahedeen secure victory in Afghan vote.' *New York Times*, 23 October.

–. 2008. 'Bush ex-official says corrupt Afghans and a hesitant military hinder drug fight.' *New York Times*, 24 July.

Giustozzi, Antonio. 2007. *Koran, Kalashnikov and Laptop: The Neo-Taliban Insurgency in Afghanistan*. London: Hurst & Company.

Glevum Associates. 2010. *Kandahar Province Survey Report: March 2010*. Burlington, MA.

Gopal, Anand. 2008. 'Afghan officials clamp down on the press.' *Christian Science Monitor*, 19 August.

–. 2010. *The Battle for Afghanistan: Militancy and Conflict in Kandahar*. Washington, DC: New America Foundation.

Graff, Peter. 2009. 'Afghans turn to Taliban in fear of own police.' Thomson Reuters, 12 July.

Herold, Marc. 2002. 'A Dossier on Civilian Victims of United States' Aerial Bombing of Afghanistan: A Comprehensive Accounting.' http://cursor.org/stories/civilian_deaths.htm.

Hess, Pamela. 2002. 'Afghan council postponed, king steps aside.' United Press International, 10 June.

Human Rights Watch. 2001. *Military Assistance to the Afghan Opposition*. New York.

–. 2006. *Afghanistan: Country Summary*. New York.

–. 2008. *Troops in Contact: Airstrikes and Civilian Deaths in Afghanistan.* New
    York.

–. 2009. *'We Have the Promises of the World': Women's Rights in Afghanistan.* New
    York.

–. 2010. *The 'Ten Dollar' Talib and Women's Rights.* New York.

–. 2011. *'Just Don't Call It a Militia': Impunity, Militias, and the 'Afghan Local Po-
    lice.'* New York.

Ikram, Tahir. 2001. 'One million Afghans face starvation – UN.' Reuters,
    20 September.

InterAction. 2003. 'Provincial Reconstruction Teams in Afghanistan: Position
    Paper.' 23 April.

International Council on Security and Development. 2011. *Afghanistan Transi-
    tion: The Death of Bin Laden and Local Dynamics.* Kabul.

International Crisis Group. 2003. 'Afghanistan: The Constitutional Loya Jirga.'
    Kabul; Brussels.

–. 2010a. 'A Force in Fragments: Reconstituting the Afghan National Army.'
    Kabul; Brussels.

–. 2010b. 'Reforming Afghanistan's Broken Judiciary.' Kabul; Brussels.

IRIN. 2006. 'Afghanistan: thousands displaced by fighting in Kandahar.'
    6 September.

Johnson, Chris, and Jolyon Leslie. 2008. *Afghanistan: The Mirage of Peace.* Lon-
    don: Zed Books.

Katzman, Kenneth. 2010. *Afghanistan: Post-Taliban Governance, Security, and
    U.S. Policy.* Washington, DC: Congressional Research Service.

Kazem, Halima. 2005. 'US ambassador, "Viceroy of Afghanistan," turns to
    Iraq.' *Los Angeles Times*, 21 June.

Kolhatkar, Sonali, and James Ingalls. 2006. *Bleeding Afghanistan: Washington,
    Warlords, and the Propaganda of Silence.* New York: Seven Stories Press.

Koring, Paul. 2009. '"Safe havens" in Pakistan fuel Afghan insurgency:
    MacKay.' *Globe and Mail*, 6 March.

Lamb, Christina. 2006. '"Ministry of vice" fills Afghan women with fear.'
    Sunday Times, 23 July.

Lasseter, Tom. 2008. 'As possible Afghan war-crimes evidence removed, US
    silent.' *McClatchy Newspapers*, 11 December.

Loyn, David. 2006. 'Western projects are bleeding Afghanistan dry, says minis-
    ter.' *Independent*, 18 May.

McLean, Archie. 2009. 'Canada's unmanned Afghan drones will carry bombs.'
    CanWest News Service, 5 March.

Nebehay, Stephanie. 2001. 'Millions face starvation in Afghanistan – UN.'
    Reuters, 8 June.

North, Andrew, and Bilal Sarwary. 2005. 'The "enemy central" province in Afghanistan.' BBC News, 8 December.

Onishi, Norimitsu. 2001. 'A nation challenged: war in south; G.I.'s had crucial role in battle for Kandahar.' *New York Times*, 15 December.

Oppel, Richard A. 2010. 'Tighter rules fail to stem deaths of innocent Afghans at checkpoints.' *New York Times*, 26 March.

Oxfam International. 2011. 'No Time to Lose: Promoting the Accountability of the Afghan National Security Forces.' Oxford. 10 May. http://www.oxfam.org/en/policy/no-time-to-lose.

Oxfam International et al. 2009. 'Caught in the Conflict: Civilians and the International Security Strategy in Afghanistan. Oxford. 3–4 April. http://www.oxfam.org.uk/resources/policy/conflict_disasters/bp_caught_in_conflict_afghanistan.html.

Paterson, Anna, and James Blewett, with Asif Karimi. 2006. 'Putting the Cart Before the Horse? Privatisation and Economic Reform in Afghanistan.' Briefing Paper Series. Kabul: Afghanistan Research and Evaluation Unit.

PBS. 2011. 'Kill/Capture.' *Frontline*, 10 May.

Perry, Alex. 2001. 'Inside the battle of Qala-i-Janghi.' *Time*, 1 December.

Physicians for Human Rights. 2002. 'New Survey Finds Persistent Attacks Against Ethnic Pashtuns in Western Afghanistan: Call for Protection.' Cambridge, MA. 9 May.

Pugliese, David. 2007. 'Military sets out plan to test high-tech weapons.' *National Post*, 24 December.

Rashid, Ahmed. 2008. *Descent into Chaos: The United States and the Failure of Nation Building in Pakistan, Afghanistan, and Central Asia.* London: Penguin.

Razack, Sherene H. 2004. *Dark Threats and White Knights: The Somalia Affair, Peacekeeping, and the New Imperialism.* Toronto: University of Toronto Press.

Rennie, Steve. 2008. 'Coalition forces slammed for "abusive" Afghan raids.' Canadian Press, 23 December.

Reuters. 2010. 'War casualties soar in south Afghanistan – Red Cross.' 12 October.

Risen, James. 2009. 'U.S. inaction seen after Taliban P.O.W.'s died.' *New York Times*, 11 July.

Roberts, Rebecca. 2009. 'Reflections on the Paris Declaration and Aid Effectiveness.' Kabul: Afghan Research and Evaluation Unit.

Rubin, Alissa J. 2010. 'Afghans to form local forces to fight Taliban.' *New York Times*, 14 July.

Rubin, Alissa J., and Richard A. Oppel. 2010. 'U.S. and Afghanistan debate more village forces.' *New York Times*, 12 July.

Rubin, Barnett. 2007. 'Saving Afghanistan.' *Foreign Affairs* 86, no. 1: 57–78.

Ruttig, Thomas. 2006. *Islamists, Leftists – and a Void in the Center: Afghanistan's Political Parties and Where They Come From (1902–2006)*. Berlin: Konrad Adenauer Foundation.

–. 2010a. 'The General in his Labyrinth.' Afghanistan Analysts Network. 23 June. http://aan-afghanistan.com/index.asp?id=845.

–. 2010b. 'How Tribal Are the Taleban? Afghanistan's Largest Insurgent Movement between Its Tribal Roots and Islamist Ideology.' Kabul: Afghanistan Analysts Network. June.

Salahuddin, Sayed. 2009. 'Taliban call for peace with Afghans.' Reuters, 26 February.

Sedra, Mark. 2004. 'Security Sector Reform in Afghanistan.' Working Paper 143. Geneva: Geneva Centre for the Democratic Control of Armed Forces.

–. 2009. 'Where cruel and unusual is the norm.' *Mark News*, 29 November. http://www.themarknews.com/articles/713-where-cruel-and-unusual-is-the-norm.

Shah, Sayed Mohammed. 2009. *Afghan National Development Strategy (ANDS) Formulation and Process: Influencing Factors and Challenges*. Kabul: Afghan Research and Evaluation Unit.

Shaw, Mark. 2006. 'Drug Trafficking and the Development of Organised Crime in Post-Taliban Afghanistan.' In *Afghanistan's Drug Industry: Structure, Functioning, Dynamics, and Implications for Counter-Narcotics Policy*, ed. Doris Buddenberg and William A. Byrd. New York: United Nations Office on Drugs and Crime and the World Bank.

Sifton, John. 2004. 'Afghanistan: flawed charter for a land ruled by fear.' *New York Times*, 7 January.

Smith, Graeme. 2008. 'Talking to the Taliban.' *Globe and Mail*, 22 March.

Smith, Michael. 2008. 'Britain admits to using "brutal" vacuum bomb against Taliban.' *Australian*, 23 June.

Sonmez, Felicia. 2010. 'Panetta: "Maybe 50 to 100" al Qaeda left in Afghanistan.' *Washington Post Online*, 27 June. http://voices.washingtonpost.com/44/2010/06/cia-chief-maybe-50-to-100-al-q.html.

Starkey, Jerome. 2009. 'Law will let Afghan husbands starve wives who withhold sex.' *Independent*, 10 July.

Starr, Barbara. 2010. 'Counterinsurgency the main focus of strategy in Afghanistan.' *CNN*, 30 October.

Steele, Jonathan. 2002. 'Forgotten victims.' *Guardian*, 20 May.

Stein, Janice Gross, and Eugene Lang. 2007. *The Unexpected War: Canada in Kandahar*. Toronto: Viking.

Sterling, Harry. 2008. 'Afghan ban on soap operas recalls bad old Taliban days.' *Toronto Star*, 2 May.

Straziuso, Jason. 2009. 'Afghan civilian deaths up 40 per cent: UN.' Associated Press, 17 February.

Straziuso, Jason, and Rahim Faiez. 2009. 'Chemical weapons suspected in Afghan battle.' Associated Press, 10 May.

Strick van Linschoten, Alex, and Felix Kuehn. 2011. *An Enemy We Created: The Myth of the Taliban/Al-Qaeda Merger in Afghanistan, 1970–2010.* London: C. Hurst.

Synovitz, Ron. 2008. 'Afghanistan: Taliban evolves into network of groups.' Radio Free Europe, 26 April.

Their, J. Alexander. 2006/07. 'The Making of a Constitution in Afghanistan.' *New York Law School Law Review* 51, no. 3: 558–79.

UNAMA (United Nations Assistance Mission in Afghanistan). 2010. *Annual Report on Protection of Civilians in Armed Conflict, 2009.* Kabul.

–. 2011a. Press Conference with Stafan de Mistura and Georgette Gagnon, Kabul, 14 July.

–. 2011b. *Treatment of Conflict Related Detainees in Afghan Custody.* Kabul: United Nations Office of the High Commissioner for Human Rights.

UNDP (United Nations Development Programme). 2009. *United Nations Development Report 2008/09.* New York: United Nations.

United Nations Office on Drugs and Crime. 2010. *Afghan Opium Survey 2010.* New York.

UPI (United Press International). 2009. 'Reparations paid for Afghan bombing.' 12 May.

United States. 2008. *Human Rights Report 2008.* Washington DC: US Department of State.

–. 2010. Department of Defense. *Report on Progress toward Security and Stability in Afghanistan.* Washington, DC.

–. 2011. Congress. Senate. Foreign Relations Committee. *Evaluating U.S. Foreign Assistance to Afghanistan.* Washington, DC.

Waldman, Mark. 2008. *Falling Short: Aid Effectiveness in Afghanistan.* Kabul: Agency Coordinating Body for Afghan Relief.

Walkom, Thomas. 2010. 'Wikileaks offer insights into Canada's detainee affair.' *Toronto Star*, 28 July.

Walsh, Declan. 2006. 'UN report accuses Afghan MPs of torture and massacres.' *Guardian,* 12 June.

Warnock, John W. 2008. *Creating a Failed State: The US and Canada in Afghanistan.* Halifax, NS: Fernwood.

Watson, Paul. 2004. 'US hand seen in Afghan election.' *Los Angeles Times*, 23 September.

Weera, Seddiz, and Joanna Santa Barbara. 2008. 'Talking to the Taliban: when and why.' *Globe and Mail*, 7 April.

Weinberger, Sharon. 2010. 'US may unleash microwave weapon in Afghanistan.' *AOL News*, 17 June.

Wilder, Andrew. 2005. *A House Divided? Analyzing the 2005 Afghan Elections.* Kabul: Afghan Research and Evaluation Unit.

–. 2007. *Cops or Robbers? The Struggle to Reform the Afghan National Police.* Kabul: Afghan Research and Evaluation Unit.

Witte, Griff. 2009. 'Taliban shadow officials offer concrete alternative.' *Washington Post*, 8 December.

Womankind Worldwide. 2006. *Taking Stock: Afghan Women and Girls Five Years On.* London.

World Bank. 2005. *Afghanistan: Managing Public Finances for Development.* Washington, DC.

–. 2006. 'The Investment Climate in Afghanistan: Exploiting Opportunities in an Uncertain Environment.' Washington, DC. 25 February.

–. 2008. 'World Bank urges effectiveness of development spending in Afghanistan.' Washington, DC. 3 June. http://www.worldbank.org.af/WBSITE/EXTERNAL/COUNTRIES/SOUTHASIAEXT/AFGHANISTANEXTN/0,,contentMDK:21788937~menuPK:306004~pagePK:2865066~piPK:2865079~theSitePK:305985,00.html.

Yousafzai, Sami, and Ron Moreau. 2008. 'The Opium Brides of Afghanistan.' *Newsweek*, 29 March.

Youssef, Nancy A. 2009. 'New U.S. Afghan strategy will cost billions, take years.' *McClatchy Newspapers*, 2 June.

Zahkilwal, Omar. 2002. 'Stifled in the Loya Jirga.' *Washington Post*, 16 June.

Zia-Zarifi, Sam. 2004. *Losing the Peace in Afghanistan.* New York: Human Rights Watch.

Zucchino, David. 2002. 'The Americans . . . they just drop their bombs and leave.' *Los Angeles Times*, 2 June.

PART II

The Political Economy of Canadian Foreign Policy

6

From the Avro Arrow to Afghanistan: The Political Economy of Canadian Militarism

We are a generation into a newly militaristic posture by the Canadian state. From the 1991 war in Iraq to the current NATO-led war in Afghanistan, the Canadian state has a now-established record of open military engagement. This flies in the face of the 'peacekeeping' ideology that continues to dominate much of the discourse about Canadian foreign policy. This chapter will argue that the transition from peacekeeping to open militarism is not accidental. Both the earlier peacekeeping moment and the current return to militarism reflect conjunctural trends in Canada's economy and its relationship to emerging and declining regions of the world market. The peacekeeping moment can be best understood not with the traditional view of Canada as a junior partner dependency, but with a political economy perspective that sees Canada as an independent 'military parasite.' Similarly the 'new militarism' of the twenty-first century is best understood not as a meek submission to US dictates, but one that has deep economic roots and that is expressive of the interests of the Canadian state and the class it represents.

As the hegemonic power the United States since the Second World War has sustained an extensive global empire, backed up by a massive military. The contention of the argument developed here is that an overdeveloped arms sector in the United States has progressively starved resources going towards, among other things, social and economic development. As an ally of the United States, Canadian capitalism has benefited from the markets kept open by US military power, but as an independent state it has been able to resist US pressures to 'carry the burden' of high levels of arms spending. Like other such military parasites (in particular, Japan and Germany), Canada has been able to devote resources to economic development, resources which in the United States were drained into the military. For two generations this created circumstances where it was economically beneficial for Canadian capitalism to do business in the US empire without paying the overhead. Today the picture is changing. There are powerful material incentives for Canada to emerge as a military power in its own right. The implications this holds for the strategy and tactics of the anti-war movement are extremely serious.

Towards a Political Economy of Capitalist Militarism

Liberalism and realism are the two dominant frameworks in the discipline of international relations. Both approach the issue of militarism quite differently. For liberalism, war and militarism are ethical issues, mistaken economically, dangerous politically – mistakes and dangers that can be addressed through the expansion of institutions of global governance. Liberals are the optimists who feel strongly that war can be 'read out' of the international system through appropriate policies and institutions. Their pessimistic friends in the realist tradition disagree. For realism, states are the key unit of the international system. States operate, in an anarchic international environment, to maximize their own power and position. The ultimate instrument of state policy in this competitive environment is the military. Realistic policy needs to be about preparing for war, not eliminating it.

The historical materialist literature develops a counter approach to international relations. For that wing of historical materialism which strives to 'bring the state in,' there is a view of states and militarism quite distinct from the liberal and realist discourses. A key first step in this process is to understand the relationship between state and capital (or government and the markets). The two are conceptually distinct, of course – but exist in a tight interrelationship and, in fact, cannot exist one without the other. It is a simplistic framework, to which some on both the left and the right subscribe, that reduces capitalism to the free market. From its inception state action has been central to the construction of the capitalist market – as in the state-supported pillaging of Latin America and the Caribbean during the mercantilist period, Lord Simcoe's use of state action to create an infrastructure for capitalist development in the early nineteenth century (in what is today southern Ontario), or John A. Macdonald's National Policy, which picked up the railway-building baton after it had been dropped by private capital.

Indeed our own free market neoliberalism is heavily dependent on state action to create the modern conditions for capital accumulation.

It is from Nikolai Bukharin, one of the least-studied twentieth century Marxist theoreticians, that historical materialism has acquired key tools with which to conceptualize the relationship between the state and capital, and on that basis build a political economy of war and militarism. Bukharin – in his classic *Imperialism and World Economy* ([1918] 1973), written during the horrors of the First World War – was thinking through how, in the early twentieth century, we had to see the 'state as capital,' to borrow a phrase from Colin Barker (1978). The concepts Bukharin deployed are still critical to theorizing these processes. Bukharin was confronted with the Great War, the centralization of capital in the form of monopoly corporations, and the large-scale intervention into the economy by Britain, Germany and the other belligerent powers.

> We have here the process of accelerated centralisation within the framework of a state capitalist trust, which has developed to the highest form, not of State Socialism, but of State Capitalism . . . To apply to such a state of affairs a terminology fit for post-capitalist relations, is not only very risky, but also highly absurd . . . The capitalist mode of production is based on a monopoly of the means of production in the hands of the class of capitalists within the framework of commodity exchange. There is no difference in principle whatsoever whether the state power is a direct expression of this monopoly or whether the monopoly is 'privately' organised. In either case there remains commodity economy (in the first place the world market) and, what is more important, the class relations between the proletariat and the bourgeoisie. ([1918] 1973, 157)

Bukharin argued for a reconceptualization of the relationship between state, capital, and world economy in order to come to grips with the causes of the war. If the 'state-as-capital' is his first point, his second – developing the notion of 'world economy' – is equally important.

> The 'national economic organisms' . . . have long ceased being a secluded whole, an 'isolated economy' . . . On the contrary, they are only parts of a much larger sphere, namely, *world economy.* Just as every individual enterprise is part of the 'national' economy, so every one of these 'national economies' is included in the system of world economy. This is why the

struggle between modern 'national economic bodies' must be regarded first of all as the struggle of various competing parts of world economy – just as we consider the struggle of individual enterprises to be one of the phenomena of socio-economic life. (17)

For Bukharin, the internationalization of capitalist relations in the world economy occurs simultaneously with a drive towards state capitalism in the internal economies of the world market's competing nations. Parallel to the process of the internationalization of economic life, a reverse tendency takes place 'towards the nationalisation of capitalist interests . . . the internationalisation of capitalist interests expresses only one side of the internationalisation of economic life . . . its other side [is] . . . that process which most strikingly expresses the anarchy of capitalist competition within the boundaries of world economy . . . the process of the nationalisation of capital' (61–2).

It is widely understood that capitalist competition is about comparing the social productivity of rival firms. Deploying Bukharin's categories allows us to extend this and to include within the rubric of capitalist competition state-to-state competition. In other words state-to-state competition is not reducible to diplomacy and war; it is also economic – a comparison between the social productivity of labour in rival states. With these two categories it is self-evident that trade in goods and direct price competition are not the only vehicles by which the social productivity of two national economies are brought into relation in the world system. The two most important alternative forms of competition – of comparing the social productivity of labour of two national economies – are military competition and debt financing. The issue of debt financing is not directly relevant to the argument being developed here. The issue of military competition, however, has real relevance. Bukharin's treatment of it is instructive. He began with an account of the rise of imperialism and the drive towards war that is an outgrowth of the increasing centralization and concentration of capital. The world internationalizes – there is the establishment of 'world economy' – but this internationalization occurs in a context of competing firms, and competing states. If the weapon in firm-to-firm competition is price, the ultimate weapon in state-to-state competition is war (a point with which realism would have no argument). There is, Bukharin argued, a growing pressure towards militarization of the economy: 'Every improvement in military technique entails a reorganization and reconstruction of the military mechanism; every innovation, every expansion of the military power of one state stimulates all the others' (126). This in itself is very much parallel to what was accepted as orthodoxy in the Third International in the 1920s. But his conclusion is completely original: 'of course, here, too, we have before us only a case of a general principle of competition, for the military power of the state capitalist trust is the weapon to be used in its economic struggle' (127).

Bukharin, like other theorists in the early Third International, saw state-to-state military competition as an extension of economic competition in the era of monopoly capitalism. But the key concern for most was the political one of identifying the roots of inter-imperialist war in order to develop a strategy against it. In the post–Second World War era, however, this aspect of the conceptualization of the state in the context of the world economy took on an additional economic dimension. In the context of the contest for empire between the United States and the Soviet Union there developed in these two economies, and in certain other advanced economies, the unprecedented phenomenon of very high – indeed, wartime – levels of military expenditure in an era of (relative) world peace, at least as it concerned military relations between the Great Powers. This was not a condition Bukharin analysed, because it was one that did not exist in his lifetime. The essential reason for the military establishments, on both sides of the Iron Curtain, was the maintenance of empire. For the Soviet Union its new spheres of influence in eastern Europe and Central Asia were indispensable to its accumulation project. For the United States a massive Pacific sphere of influence and a continuing highly profitable role in Latin America and the Caribbean became embedded in its own accumulation project. For both the Soviet Union and the United States Africa was an 'on-again, off-again' point of contestation. On this militarized foundation of 'empire maintenance,' the competition between the two blocs was built, and enormous levels of arms spending resulted.

In other words, using Bukharin's concepts of the 'state-as-capital' and 'world economy,' the Cold War era need not be reduced to the unsatisfying paradigm of capitalism versus socialism (unsatisfying because what passed for socialism in the Soviet Union was, to say the least, uninspiring) or to the equally unsatisfying paradigm of freedom versus totalitarianism (unsatisfying because the 'freedom' of the West was embedded in a network of risible dictatorships, from Marcos to Suharto to the shah of Iran). We can rather see the Cold War as embedded in the accumulation projects of two rival imperial blocs.

This framework was used, with varying degrees of success, to try to explain the post-war economic expansion. A liberal Military Keynesian school and a Marxist Permanent Arms Economy school both attempted to demonstrate the way in which high levels of arms spending were central to the economic expansion of the post-war era (Oakes 1944; Draper 1969; Kidron 1969; Melman 1974; Harman 1984; Treddenick 1988; Cliff 1999). Most insisted on locating the pressures for sustained arms spending solely in the competition between the United States and the USSR – neglecting the utility for both of maintaining massive military presences to control, contain, and exploit the informal empires that were central to their economies. All agreed that high levels of military spending were a permanent feature of capitalism in the post–Second World War period, and that this had important economic effects in stabilizing the world economy.

An additional aspect of this framework is being considered here. The permanent arms economy was sustained primarily by the two superpowers of the era – the Soviet Union and the United States. But high levels of arms spending were not the universal profile for all the major capitalist powers. Most important, Germany and Japan – the two powers vanquished in the Second World War – were prevented by treaty and/or internal political constraints from maintaining high levels of military spending. This introduced an important additional factor into the 'texture' of a peacetime economy. Arms spending seemed to be a factor – maybe a very important factor – in keeping the system stable. But the cost was born unequally. Roughly put, the United States and the USSR spent massively on arms; Japan and Germany did not. This is a key factor in explaining the remarkable way in which Japan and Germany managed to repair their economies and catch up with (and in some cases surpass) the victorious powers of the war.

Maintaining high levels of military spending – as both the United States and the Soviet Union did during the years of the Cold War – had long-run negative effects on the economic development of those countries compared with that of their competitors. The existence of a permanent government market for military products builds in an incentive for manufacturers to direct production towards that market, squeezing out the development of the civilian sector. If states can avoid these pressures and 'benefit' from the investment climate they create, they will prosper relative to the hegemon. Further, from the standpoint of government finances, pressures to sustain a military budget create pressures to squeeze what one might call the 'welfare budget' – spending on health, education, and welfare.

Canada, like Japan and Germany closely linked economically to the United States, 'benefited' from this hegemony without having to pay for it. The Caribbean and Latin America, for instance, were going to be kept open for business by the United States with or without help from Canada. Over time a pattern developed whereby Canadian corporations invested and profited from operations in areas such as Latin America and the Caribbean, but operated in a state that did not have to sustain a military on the scale of the United States. In economics and international relations the term for this is 'free rider' (Gompert and Kugler 1995). From the standpoint of the analysis being developed here, a more useful term is 'military parasitism.' This military parasitism not only benefited Canada's corporations; it also meant that in Canada greater portions of government spending could go towards the welfare state rather than the warfare state. In the long run the cost of sustaining empire was to drag down the US economy relative to its rivals – not as dramatically as in the Soviet Union, but inexorably nonetheless. But as a state with relatively low levels of military spending, Canada's situation was quite different.

The Push for NATO

A hypothesis has been put forward that relatively low levels of arms spending in Canada, relative to the United States, can be properly understood, within a historical materialist framework, through the lens of 'military parasitism.' Canadian capitalism invested in, and profited from, spheres of influence 'kept safe for capitalism' by Canada's closest ally – the highly militarized United States. With this as a frame, one can now examine the different phases of the Canadian state's relationship to militarism and to the United States, and see if such a framework is of some use. The first moment bearing examination is the push to create the world's biggest military alliance, the North Atlantic Treaty Organization (NATO). Was Canada a dependent junior partner, quietly following the lead of the United States? An examination of the 'NATO moment' between the end of the Second World War in 1945 and the creation of NATO in 1949 reveals something quite different. It portrays a Canadian state that was independent and, in the immediate post-war years, best characterized as a warfare, rather than a welfare, state.

Jon McLin argues that Canada's acceptance of a role as a supporter of US foreign policy and the establishment of the new configuration of post-war alliances (of which NATO was by far the most important) were more a case of the Canadian state's attempting to secure its independence than meekly following orders from Washington: 'Never before had Canada been a party to a formal alliance in peacetime. But in the late 1940's, apprehension concerning Soviet power and objectives in Europe caused all Western countries to reconsider their security policy . . . [D]istaste for alliances in general became less relevant for Canada than a calculation of what kind of alliance would be most favorable, or least unfavorable, for it. In particular, Canada needed a counter-weight to the US, if an alliance were not to mean unacceptable degrees of US control' (1967, 12). The picture McLin paints of Canadian state action as it concerned defence policy in the post-war era is not that of the junior partner reluctantly complying with the wishes of an imperialist giant, but that of a genuine player in the construction of Cold War policies.

Tom Axworthy (1979, 90) makes much of this. Canada, he argues 'was in the forefront of those nations seeking a North Atlantic Alliance.' Canadian politicians, in effect, became the advanced salesmen for the idea of a new Cold War alliance separate from the United Nations. As McLin notes, 'a series of official speeches, delivered in 1947–48 . . . broached ideas being considered at that time in many Western capitals. Most of these ideas were somewhat ahead of the time, at least as publicly expressed, elsewhere . . . In the actual negotiation of the North Atlantic Treaty, Canadian diplomats continued to play an active role' (1967, 13–14).

In fact the key role of Canadian diplomats in initiating the move towards NATO was quite in keeping with the role Canada played in the years previous. Between 1946 and 1949 the United States, Britain, and Canada were members of a secret tripartite defence planning group that was very much NATO's predecessor. This is definitely not the picture of a junior partner in the sense the term is usually employed. As Axworthy (1979, 93) points out, 'Canada was the first Western nation to publicly advocate the creation of the North Atlantic Alliance,' and this 'early and public advocacy of a North Atlantic Alliance may have helped influence United States opinion on the subject.'

Louis Saint-Laurent, then secretary of state for external affairs, embarked on a near-evangelical tour of Canada to promote the idea of an Atlantic 'collective defence' pact. The reaction of the United States to this is interesting: 'The US Secretary of Defense, visiting Ottawa during April 1948, was struck and even startled by what he described in his diary as "the curious fact" that his hosts were such fervid advocates of a North Atlantic treaty; no such advocacy then existed at comparable levels in Washington' (Eayrs 1967, 62). Saint-Laurent and his successor at External Affairs, Lester Pearson, were quite clear, however, as to the advantages of Canada's participation in a regional defence pact. The option, according to Pearson, was an over-reliance on the United States. A regional pact would lessen 'the difficulties arising in Canada from the fear of invasion of Canadian sovereignty by the United States.' So Europe could be used as a counterweight to the enormous power of the United States in arriving at military decisions. Moreover, argued Pearson, such a treaty 'would help to ensure that Canada was not pushed out ahead of the United States in the event of war. In the last two wars Canada has gone to war more than two years before the United States. A treaty commitment by the United States instead of a congressional resolution would lessen the danger that this might happen again' (cited in Eayrs 1967, 369). This account is supported by several policy observers. Robert Spencer (1959, 243) argued that 'never before had [Canada] taken a leading part in working out so binding and formal a document.' Marilyn Eustace (1976, 6) says that 'Canada's spokesmen were dominant in the creation of NATO in 1949 and were among the first to enunciate "the North Atlantic idea."'

Once again this is not the image of a dependent junior partner, but of a smaller, quite independent power attempting to situate itself in military terms to maximize its own national interest. It is a picture that is fully compatible with the analysis of military parasitism developed here. Canada and the United States have an identity of interests between them on matters of continental defence, and in many ways Canada shaped a key component of the foundation of this identity of interests – the formation of the NATO regional defence pact. Moreover, this arrangement – entered into voluntarily on terms partially shaped by the Canadian state – worked to the distinct advantage of the Canadian economy by providing Canada with its strategic military requirements without having to shoulder the cost.

With the framework of military parasitism, these accounts of the origins of NATO, as McLin, Axworthy, and others have developed, are quite in keeping with a picture of an independent Canadian state that is pursuing its own interests in foreign affairs. That these interests have coincided in the main with those of the United States is not in any way sufficient to prove 'dependency.' It is more plausible to reject the dependency view and to see these policy initiatives by Canada as evidence of rational calculations by an independent capitalist state based on perceived national self-interest.

The Avro Arrow and the Transition to Peacekeeping

Let us turn now to the moment when Canada began to evolve from a militarized state at the end of the Second World War to the 'peacekeeping' state of the 1960s, 1970s, and 1980s. While the United States was embroiled in wars in Indochina, proxy wars in Central America, and coups d'état in Asia – Canada more than any other country became associated with the 'blue helmets' of United Nations peacekeeping missions. As the veterans' association, the Blue Helmets, notes, '[d]uring the Suez Crisis of 1956, Secretary of State for External Affairs Lester B. Pearson . . . proposed that a multinational UN peacekeeping force be sent to the Suez to separate the warring parties.' From that initiative came the institution of UN peacekeeping: 'Tens of thousands of Canadians have served in more than 40 separate peacekeeping missions . . . In 1988, the Nobel Peace Prize was awarded collectively to UN peacekeepers in recognition of their historic efforts' (Blue Helmets 2010, 1).

This 'peacekeeping moment' is usually seen in ideological and ethical terms – the 'Canadian' approach to foreign policy as distinct from the militarism of the United States. This is misleading. The military parasitism framework, outlined above, illuminates the political economy rationale behind the 'peacekeeping moment' and, by contrast, the political economy rationale for the return to militarism. The Canadian transition to peacekeeping occurred in the 1950s and is usually associated with the role of Lester Pearson in defusing the Suez crisis, as in the fragment quoted above. From a political economy standpoint the cancellation of the Canadian-built Avro Arrow jet fighter by Progressive Conservative prime minister John Diefenbaker is more significant as a symbol of the dramatic change the new peacekeeping face meant for Canadian politics and economics.

Canada in the 1950s was a far more militarized society than many today realize. At the end of the Second World War Canada had more than a million people under arms; Canada's navy was the third largest in the world, behind only those of the United States and Britain (Canada 2008). In the years following, demobilization took place, but Canada still played

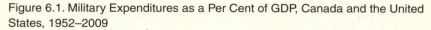

Figure 6.1. Military Expenditures as a Per Cent of GDP, Canada and the United States, 1952–2009

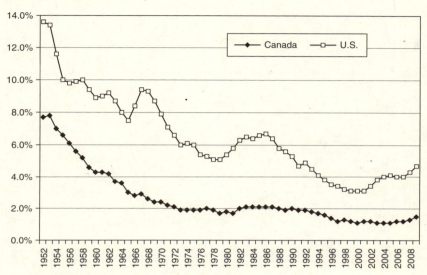

Sources: SIPRI 1973, 208–17; 1979, 34–46; 1988; 2011.

a major role in the Korean War, contributing 26,791 women and men, 516 of whom were killed (CBC News 2008). This military action abroad corresponded to high levels of military spending at home: in 1952 through 1954 it accounted for more than 7 per cent of Canada's gross domestic product (GDP); in contrast, since 1990, military spending in Canada has annually represented less than 2 per cent of GDP (see Figure 6.1). Perhaps more interesting is military spending as a percentage of overall federal government spending. In 2006 military spending represented just 7.1 per cent of all federal government spending; in 1961 that figure was almost three times as high, at 21.8 per cent, and in 1952 it was an astonishing 42.2 per cent. In other words, in 1952 more than 40 cents of every dollar of federal government spending went to the military (see Figure 6.2). As high as these numbers are for Canada in the 1950s, in the United States they were astonishing: in 1952, for example, military spending was the equivalent of 13.6 per cent of US GDP, and the military received 68.1 cents of every dollar spent by the US federal government (United States 2011, table 6.1).

Figure 6.2. Military Expenditures as a Per Cent of Total Federal Expenditures, Canada and the United States, 1945–2010

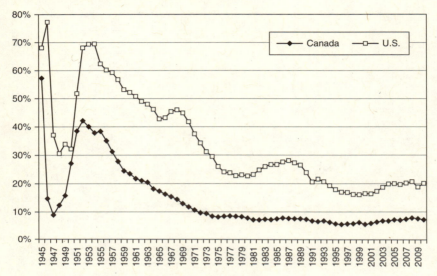

Sources: Bird 2008; Canada 2010, 2011a; United States 2011.

This provides essential context for the controversy over the Avro Arrow. The project reflected the continuation of the 'warfare state' created in the context of the Second World War and the Korean War, a warfare state now embedded in a military alliance, NATO, with whose origins the Canadian state was closely associated. Work on the Arrow, an 'all-Canadian' 'interceptor' designed to chase down and destroy incoming bombers and built in Canada (by a British branch plant), began in 1953. The plane was intended to be the successor to the Canadian-designed and -built CF-100. The details of the rise and demise of the Arrow have been told adequately elsewhere (McLin 1967, 61–84; Axworthy 1979; Shaw 1981; Campagna 2003). Despite the project's technological and scientific innovations, it was soon in difficulty. The fundamental dilemma was quite simple. The plane made economic sense only if markets outside Canada could be found. They could not: the United States was not interested in a military plane that it did not produce and there was no interest in Europe.[1] The Arrow would have to be built strictly for Canadian use. But given the relatively small Canadian market, its cost would have been extremely high – almost $8 million per plane, a very high sum in the 1950s. Further, with the advent of intercontinental missiles, the need for a plane that was designed to shoot down bombers was not clear. Finally, the federal government's fiscal room for manoeuvre was reduced by an economic downturn and growing demands for increases in health, education, and welfare spending.

Eventually, in 1959, in a ham-handed way, the decision was made to scrap the Arrow. The immediate impact of the cancellation of the project, which was caused by economic difficulties, was to increase those difficulties. Fourteen thousand people lost their jobs immediately and countless others were affected indirectly. Several of the laid-off workers committed suicide in the despair that followed (Keene 1989). To add insult to injury all thirty-seven prototypes of the aircraft, which some had called the best in the world, were scrapped. But the decision to cancel the Arrow must not be judged only by the benchmark of political ineptitude; it needs to be placed in a wider political and economic framework. That done, the killing of the Arrow does not appear in any way the disaster it has been portrayed in political mythology.

The end of the Arrow is usually seen as the death of Canada's independent manufacturing potential, although the plane was a machine to be put to military purposes. E.K. Shaw's book-length history of the Arrow makes absolutely fascinating reading in terms of a documentary history of bureaucratic bungling by Ottawa. His political economy is very much part of a 'dependency' orthodoxy: 'Our branch-plant economy spends only 0.35 percent of its [GDP] on research and development, and little of that is innovative or of high-technology content. Patents are registered in the name of the US parent, and are not available to Canada except at a high cost. But Avro by 1958 was accounting for 70 percent of all the research and development being done in Canada' (1981, 242). The implication is clear: the killing of the Arrow represented the intensification of Canada's branch-plant dependency. However, the destruction of the research and development work that had gone into the Arrow was only a temporary setback to the Canadian aerospace industry. By the late 1980s, John Treddenick could write: 'Since the demise of the Arrow in the late 1950s, the aircraft industry has had to turn to civilian and defence export markets for a substantial share of its sales. It has been remarkably successful in doing so. By the early 1980s, employment in the industry had regained the levels reached at the peak of the Arrow project and today, there are approximately twice as many firms in the industry as there were at that time'

(1988, 43). In the first part of the twenty-first century – even in the midst of significant job losses in automobile manufacturing in southern Ontario – the high-tech aerospace sector has held up quite well. In 2008 Michel Legault of Bell Helicopters was quoted as saying: 'It's a strange situation in the Montreal area. Aerospace is demanding more people than are actually available' (Deveau 2008, 1).

Military parasitism as a framework helps make sense of all of these policy twists and turns. The Arrow decision was the first in a series of ad hoc decisions by both Progressive Conservative and Liberal governments whose overall effect was to increase the gap between Canada and the United States in terms of each federal government's relationship to militarism and military spending. Interestingly, the Canadian government made these decisions despite considerable pressure from its principal ally, the United States, to go in the other direction – to be a warfare, not a welfare, state. But successive Canadian governments successively resisted this pressure. The long slide in Canadian military spending, then, is a sign not of dependence on the United States, but of independence. From the 1950s to the present, as a percentage of both GDP and overall federal government expenditures, military spending has declined continuously in both countries, but faster and to much lower levels in Canada than in the United States.

At the same time, in the late 1950s, expenditures on social security began to rise. As Tom Axworthy has noted, '[t]he percentage of the [federal] budget devoted to defence services began to decline as spending on social security received new impetus under the Diefenbaker government' (1979, 248). This increase was real. Spending on welfare and social services represented between 17 per cent and 19 per cent of federal government expenditures from fiscal years 1947/8 to 1956/7, but rose to 23 per cent by fiscal year 1962/3, at the end of Diefenbaker's tenure; it stayed at that level for ten years of Liberal rule, and then began to rise again (Axworthy 1979, tables 2–10).

This chapter is not concerned with the issue of political ineptness. Were it, the manner in which the federal government stumbled into the production of an interceptor aircraft and the way in which the Arrow was cancelled would certainly provide grist for the mill. It was probably a decision that could have been sold to the public had its implications been properly understood. The long-run impact of this decision was, economically, beneficial: it contributed to the pre-empting of the possibility of Canada's attempting to develop on the basis of an over-developed war economy as did the United States, the Soviet Union, and Britain, with quite negative consequences. It was perceived by many to be an inevitable decision in any case. Diefenbaker's Liberal predecessor, Louis Saint-Laurent, while he was prime minister, 'had decided on the same course, according to evidence given by General Foulkes in the House of Commons Defence Committee in 1964' (Van Dusen 1968, 37). Further, since it was accompanied by a steady rise in federal government spending on what Diefenbaker termed 'social justice,' it would not have been hard to portray the decision as one made with the public's best interest in mind. The fact that the Tories made the decision as ineptly as they did is, however, unimportant. What is important as far as this chapter is concerned is that the decision could be made at all. A choice was made to forgo the development of the Arrow, and this represented a watershed in the economically taxing exercise of sustaining an independent Canadian military economy. Given an economic downturn and the strain this represented on government finances, pressures exerted themselves to cut money somewhere, and the Arrow decision meant that the military and the warfare state would feel these pressures to a considerably greater extent than the welfare state.

Whether this was conscious government policy is not the point. The facts on the decline in arms spending are clear, the decline was accompanied by an increase in spending on the welfare state, and evidence is mounting that, in the long run, squeezing the warfare state to sustain the welfare state improves a country's economic standing. This is exactly military parasitism. The United States, faced with similar pressures, could not make a similar decision unless, of course, it abandoned its role as the world's policeman – something that, even after decades of relative decline in its position in the world economy, it has refused to do. The United States had no Great Power on which to rely parasitically for its military and strategic interests. Canada, however, did have such a power – the United States itself.

The Defence Production Sharing Agreement

The military parasitism argument revolves around two key points. The first is that it is economically detrimental over time to maintain high levels of arms spending, though a short chapter such as this can only assert that this is true. Anecdotally, think of the massive arms sector of the Soviet Union and the spectacular economic collapse of that country that eventually occurred in the late 1980s and early 1990s. In the contemporary period, think of the devastation that the severe recession of

2008–9 visited upon Michigan and California and the relative ease with which Canadian capitalism returned to growth. An important factor – perhaps an extremely important one – in the old story of the economic weakness of the USSR and the developing story of the economic weakness of the United States might be that both of them sustain bloated arms sectors.

The other key point has to do with the issue of dependence and independence. It is not difficult to see that Canada's economic fortunes are closely tied to those in the United States. But most analysts see this as accompanied by a greater or lesser degree of Canadian 'dependence' on the United States. What is interesting about the Avro Arrow decision and the following long years of decline in military spending – in the face of constant US demands that Canada increase its military spending – is that it highlights not the dependence of the Canadian state, but its relative independence. Several other key policy debates in the wake of the Arrow cancellation highlight this as well.

The cancellation of the Arrow project was followed immediately by a conscious integration of Canadian defence needs with those of the United States. In 1959 the two countries entered into a Defence Production Sharing Agreement (DPSA). As Middlemiss and Sokolsky explain, '[t]he arrangements involved a partial free-trade regime in defence products, giving Canadian industry access to a large defence market and the armed forces the benefit of lower prices . . . As a result of DPSA, and subsequent agreements covering development, Canada's defence industry abandoned the goal of producing a complete range of defence equipment for the armed forces and instead concentrated on producing specialized, internationally competitive products for export, mainly to the United States' (1989, 23). The DPSA signalled the conscious completion of the integration of the two countries' defence industrial base, a process that had begun much earlier.

Melissa Clark-Jones (1987) has provided a classic 'junior partner' analysis of this integration. She argues that it flowed from the dominance of a 'continentalist strategy of resource development' within the Canadian ruling class (211). She sees this strategy as leading to the 'over-development' of the resource sector of the Canadian economy and 'decreasing the emphasis on building domestic manufacturing' (20, 154). Further, she sees the role of the Canadian state in this process as 'largely reactive to outside initiatives' (211).

The evidence for one of her key premises – that of the overdevelopment of the resource sector in Canada and the underdevelopment of manufacturing – is questionable (Kellogg 2005, 2009). But what of the latter point, that the Canadian state, in the process of integrating its defence industries with those in the United States, was largely reactive and dependent? D.W. Middlemiss carefully researched the process by which the DPSA was created and how it developed over time, and he calls into question this junior partner view. Prior to the DPSA, the two countries exchanged a series of letters 'which together constituted the "United States-Canadian Industrial Security Agreement"' (1976, 154). Part of the intent of the agreement was to facilitate cooperative use of each nation's defence manufacturing potential despite protection-ist measures, particularly in the United States. The impact on the mili-tary balance of trade between the two countries was striking indeed. 'Canadian defence expenditures in the United States remained rela-tively constant at $130 million annually,' but 'United States expen-ditures in Canada rose from $27.7 million for the last nine months of 1951, to $103 million in 1952 and finally $127 million in 1953' (157). In other words, through the Korean War period, military trade between the two countries moved roughly into balance. Thus, the first initia-tives towards increased defence production integration worked clearly to Canada's economic benefit.

There remained considerable problems, however. Once the Korean War, with its increased demand for armaments of all sorts, was over, the Canadian defence industry found itself in the aggravating situation of having constantly, and on a case-by-case basis, to attempt to receive exemption from US protectionist measures. This was the spur for the DPSA initiative, and it is of the most interest to the paradigm of mili-tary parasitism. As we have seen in the case of NATO, the initial and strongest push for this arrangement came not from the United States, but from Canada. A similar pattern unfolded in the push for the DPSA. In July 1958, in meetings between Prime Minister Diefenbaker and President Eisenhower in Ottawa, Diefenbaker 'raised the issue of the possible integration of the productive capacities of the defence indus-tries of the two countries.' After these initial talks, a senior Canadian civil servant, Dave Mundy, 'sought to convince [Eisenhower's secre-tary of state John Foster] Dulles that it was in American interests to have some form of joint production sharing with Canada.' Indeed, through-out 1958, Canadian officials 'had been struggling to get the produc-tion sharing principle accepted by US procurement officers vis-à-vis specific US defence production programmes' (Middlemiss 1976, 219, 221). Thus it is simply not accurate to picture Canada as entering into an arrangement with the United States as a dependent follower. The initiative came, at least in part, from within the Canadian state, and had to overcome opposition, or at least indifference, in Washington; as Middlemiss notes, 'the US role was essentially the passive one of hearing out the various arguments offered by the Canadian representatives' (232).

It is also extremely interesting to examine the composition of the negotiating teams put together by each country when a fully fledged DPSA was finally on the agenda. According to Middlemiss (226), '[t]he US side of the discussions was handled exclusively by Department of Defense officials while Canadian representation in the discussions incorporated a broader spectrum of political, economic, as well as military officials. As a result, US perceptions of production sharing were mainly, but not exclusively, oriented to considerations of military strategy, whereas Canadian perceptions tended to derive mainly from economic considerations' (1976, 226). The United States, with its economic hegemony under no visible threat, paid little heed to the economic side of the DPSA; rather, of principal concern to its negotiating team were the military and strategic aspects of the DPSA and how they facilitated US strategic planning. 'The Canadians, on the other hand, were able to view the principle as the embodiment of a practical solution to the pressing problem of the continued economic viability of Canada's defence industry' (226). This is a profile completely in line with military parasitism. Indeed, as Robert Keohane has written,

[w]e should not assume that the leaders of secondary states are necessarily victims of false consciousness when they accept the hegemonic ideology, or that they constitute a small, parasitical elite that betrays the interests of the nation to its own selfish ends. It is useful to remind ourselves . . . that during the *Pax Britannica* and the *Pax Americana*, countries other than the hegemon prospered, and that indeed many of them grew faster than the hegemon itself. Under some conditions—not necessarily all – it may be not only in the self interest of peripheral elites, but conducive to the economic growth of their countries, for them to defer to the hegemon. (Cited in Resnick 1989, 286)

Thus the 'leaders of the secondary state,' Canada, accommodated themselves to the military preoccupations of the hegemon. But they did so in such a way as to advance Canada's economic interests at the expense of the hegemon. Indeed, much of the Canadian argument for the DPSA consisted of 'statistics which emphasized Canada's chronic defence trade imbalance with the United States . . . Canadian spokesmen argued that a viable Canadian defence industry would provide an important guaranteed alternate source for US procurement requirements' (Middlemiss 1976, 226–8).

The net impact of the DPSA was to consolidate the movement of trade that had begun in the 1950s, to reduce the traditional Canadian deficit in cross-border military trade, and to replace it over time with a Canadian surplus. Between 1951 and 1958 'the United States spent $586 million in Canada, and the Canadian government $690 million in the United States for military procurement' (Kirton 1972, 14), a net deficit for Canada of $104 million. Between 1959 and 1965 the balance of defence production sharing procurement teetered back and forth almost yearly between the two countries, but ended ultimately in a $177.2 million surplus in Canada's favour. With the escalation of the Vietnam War this balance in Canada's favour increased dramatically to $508.6 million over the twelve-year period from 1959 to the peak of the war in 1970 (30).

So, on all fronts, the DPSA that followed on the heels of the Arrow cancellation does not fit the profile of Canada as a dependent, reactive, junior partner. The push for the DPSA came in the first place from the Canadian, not the US, state. US officials were concerned primarily with the military aspect of the agreements and the Canadians with the economic. The net impact of the agreement in the 1960s was a reversal of Canada's traditional deficit with the United States in defence procurement and its replacement with a surplus. The Canadian state acted independently, with related but separate interests to those of the United States. By attaching itself to the US military project, Canada did so in such a way as to benefit economically. Military parasitism is again a better framework with which to understand these developments.

Afghanistan and the Return to Militarism

The story sketched above creates a framework that helps us to understand the peacekeeping moment of Canadian foreign policy. If military parasitism was beneficial to Canada economically, peacekeeping was its perfect ideological counterpart. From the end of the Korean War in 1953 until the Gulf War in 1991, Canada was not at war. Further, spurred by Pearson's role in the Suez Crisis of 1956, Canada came to be symbolized as the country best representing the new hope of international

peacekeeping. Probably more than any other nation, Canada was identified as the country of the peacekeepers. It meant that, for hitchhikers
after the 1960s, it was much better to have a maple leaf stitched to your
knapsack than the stars and stripes. That peacekeeping moment was
accompanied by a state much less burdened by the sustaining of an
arms economy than was its principal economic rival to the south. The
advantages were considerable – money not tied up in arms spending
was available for social welfare, infrastructure, and other investments
necessary to the development of the Canadian economy.

This Canadian peacekeeping moment is now over, as Steven Staples
has documented graphically. On 31 August 31 1991, 1,149 Canadian
military personnel (out of 10,801 of all nationalities) were participating in UN peacekeeping missions; by 31 August 2006, that number
had dropped to 56 (out of 66,786 of all nationalities) (Staples 2006, 1).
By June 2010 the Canadian figure was up slightly to 215, but the total
number from all countries had increased to 100,645 (United Nations
2010). Canada in the twenty-first century might have a self-image as a
peacekeeping nation, but this is not borne out by the country's current
contribution to UN peacekeeping efforts.

In fact, that same time frame – from 1991 to the present – has witnessed a parallel increase in Canadian military operations abroad. In
1991 Canada was a full participant in the Gulf War. Its 1993 intervention
in Somalia looked to Somalis more like occupation than peacekeeping
(Razack 2004). In 1999 Canada was one of the principal contributors to
NATO's bombing campaign against Yugoslavia. And from 2001 to 2011
it was a central actor in the war in Afghanistan. These twenty years of
warfare have been accompanied by initiatives from both Liberal and
Conservative governments to increase spending on the military. Most
recently, Prime Minister Stephen Harper's government announced a
plan for a significant expansion of Canada's military: 'Over the next
20 years, the Tories want to commit Ottawa to spending $30 billion
more on the military. Mr. Harper foresees an expansion of our Forces
to 100,000 soldiers, sailors and airmen. Troop strength will include
70,000 regular forces, up from 65,000 today, while the reserves will
expand from 24,000 to 30,000. Ageing warships will be replaced, and
new transport aircraft and armoured vehicles will be purchased. New
medium-lift helicopters will be bought immediately to ferry our troops
over and around roadside bombs and snipers in Afghanistan' (*National
Post* 2008). A report by the Canadian Centre for Policy Alternatives has
shown that, in real terms, military spending under the Harper Conservatives is at its highest level since 1952, during the Korean War

(Staples and Robinson 2007).[2] That expenditure is being used for purchases that are less and less useful for peacekeeping purposes and almost exclusively useful for engaging in offensive military operations. A good example is the Leopard 2 tank, in use in Afghanistan since 2007 (CBC News 2009). An even better example is the wildly unpopular announced intention to spend $18 billion to purchase 65 new F-35 fighter jets (Prontzos 2010).

One area where this new militarism is evident is not abroad but in the Arctic Ocean, much of which Canada claims as its own internal waterways. Throughout the entire period of the Cold War, naval presence in this ocean was left almost entirely to the United States, and by 1990 Canada 'had ceased all efforts to even send a token presence to the Canadian Arctic waters.' Since 2002, however, the Canadian navy 'has begun to take initial steps to commence new operations in those waters' (Huebert 2007, 9). The political intent to increase these efforts was made abundantly clear during a visit by Harper to the Arctic in August 2010. Travelling to Resolute Bay, Nunavut, to witness Canadian military exercises, Harper contended in a speech to the troops that their efforts were directed 'towards one non-negotiable priority . . . the protection and promotion of Canada's sovereignty over what is our north' (Campion-Smith 2010). The Arctic is coming increasingly into focus as an important site for economic development, and this realization is being accompanied by a new military focus on the region (Byers 2009).

Along with this remilitarization of Canadian foreign policy is a serious intensification of attempts to recruit young people into the military. In February 2006 then chief of the defence staff, General Rick Hillier, launched 'Operation Connection' whose goal was to enlist all the 86,000 uniformed personnel of the Canadian Forces into the recruitment effort, saying, 'I expect every sailor, soldier, airman and airwoman to recognize their role as a potential [Canadian Forces] recruiter, effectively spreading the load from the shoulders of recruiting centre personnel to the shoulders of all Regular and Reserve personnel' (Canada 2006), a goal that sparked a critique from the anti-war movement (see Penner 2006).

This twenty years of more open militarism by Canada clearly has been embedded in the architecture of a US-centred imperialism, with NATO as the principal military alliance. But while it might be tempting to see Canada's increasingly militarized foreign policy as happening at the behest of the United States and NATO, that would be misleading. A clear political economy approach is crucial here. The shift from peacekeeping to war making, from pacifism to militarism, is related to the transformation of the underlying economy since the days of the

Figure 6.3. Base Country of Top 500 Corporations, 1994–2010

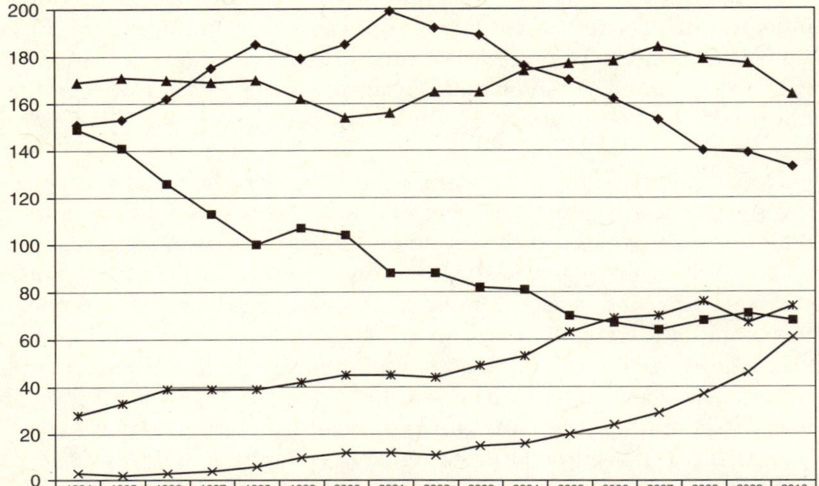

	1994	1995	1996	1997	1998	1999	2000	2001	2002	2003	2004	2005	2006	2007	2008	2009	2010
U.S.	151	153	162	175	185	179	185	199	192	189	176	170	162	153	140	139	133
Japan	149	141	126	113	100	107	104	88	88	82	81	70	67	64	68	71	68
Europe	169	171	170	169	170	162	154	156	165	165	174	177	178	184	179	177	164
China	3	2	3	4	6	10	12	12	11	15	16	20	24	29	37	46	61
Other	28	33	39	39	39	42	45	45	44	49	53	63	69	70	76	67	74

Source: *Fortune*, 1995–2011.

Avro Arrow. Central to the emergence of a more openly militarist stance by the Canadian state has been the long, slow erosion of US hegemony. There are many indicators of this decline, and it is beyond the scope of this chapter to demonstrate them fully. But one fragment from a longer analysis (Kellogg 2011) provides a good snapshot. Behind the constantly fluctuating trade and currency statistics and the ups and downs of succeeding booms and slumps, one useful way of conceiving of the world economy is as a constellation of corporations. A central aspect of capitalist power is embodied in the large corporations that dominate the world economy, and a key indicator of the relative strength of different zones of the world economy is the extent to which they are 'home' to these large corporations. Figure 6.3 documents the dramatic shift under way in this regard: the relative decline of the United States as a centre of corporate power, the return of Europe, and the beginnings of a remarkable rise by China and other parts of the world economy as centres of corporate power, as measured by the editors of the 'Global 500' in *Fortune* magazine. From a high point in 2001 when 199 of the world's top 500 corporations were based in the United States, by 2010 that figure had declined to 133. Since 2005 there have been consistently more top 500 corporations based in Europe than in the United States. And the number of top 500 corporations based in China grew from just 3 in 1994 to 61 in 2010. The world economy is less and less a US-centred one.

Two aspects of the changes under way need to be seen together. One is the long-term relative, though not absolute, decline of the United States. The other is the rise, both absolute and relative, of new economies of the Global South, particularly in Asia. Taken together, these developments are dramatically changing the contours of the world economy, including trade. As *The Economist* (2009) notes, '[i]n 2000, developing countries accounted for 37% of world output . . . Last year [2008] their share rose to 45%. The share of [Brazil, Russia, India, and China] leapt from 16% to 22%.' In Canada these changing contours of the world economy have been dramatically reflected in aspects of the country's trade profile. It has long been the case that the vast majority of Canadian exports are destined for the United States, but the percentage reached its peak in 2002 and has been declining every year since. Indeed, the pace of decline accelerated as the economic crisis started to bite in 2008 and 2009, and continued even into the recovery in 2010 and 2011 (see Figure 6.4). Of course, Canada remains tightly tied to the United States through cross-border production chains, investment flows, and exchange relations. But other centres of production and accumulation in the world economy are playing an increasingly prominent role.

A dramatic sign of Canada's changing position in the world economy is the reversal of a century-long trend of its importing more capital than it exports. Foreign direct investment (FDI) into Canada has long been seen as one of the principal mechanisms through which Canadian dependency, particularly on the United States, has been maintained. Through the 1980s and 1990s, however, direct investment from Canada was steadily growing faster than FDI into Canada, so that, since 1997, as Figure 6.5 shows, there has been, in every year, more Canadian direct investment abroad than there is FDI into Canada. This captures the increased weight of Canada as a centre of capital export – a statistical representation of, for instance, the aggressive expansion of Canadian banking and mining operations in Latin America and the Caribbean.

What has been broached here is clearly a very big discussion that takes us beyond the confines of one chapter. But these figures suggest that the relative weight of the United States in the world economy is

Figure 6.4. Canadian Exports to the United States as a Per Cent of All
Canadian Exports, 1986–2011

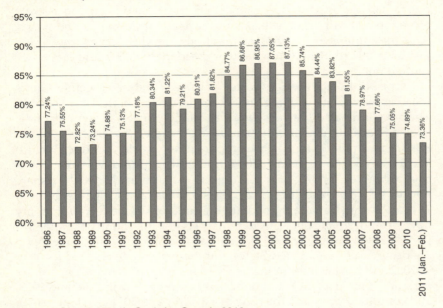

Sources: Canada 2011b; Statistics Canada 2010.

steadily declining, and with that relative decline Canada is tending to
loosen its connections to that country and being drawn towards other
emerging poles of accumulation. Canada's west and north are well
equipped to feed the economic expansion of the Global South and its
hunger for industrial commodities and, not surprisingly, the centre of
the Canadian economy has shifted west and north in the twenty-first
century. Less visible, but quite real, has been an increase in connection
between the economies of Canada and the European Union – one of
the big stories of 2009, which happened without much fanfare, was the
opening of free trade talks between the two (Field 2009). New 'gravita-
tional pulls,' then, are acting on the Canadian economy from sections
of the world system other than that centred on the United States. Moreover, independent economic activity in the world has been a constant
feature of advanced capitalist countries. Thus, along with Canada's
increasingly aggressive and independent direct investment expansion
and diversified economic presence abroad, there is increasing pressure
for an independent Canadian military presence abroad. In short, there

Figure 6.5. Net Foreign Direct Investment in Canada, 1926–2010

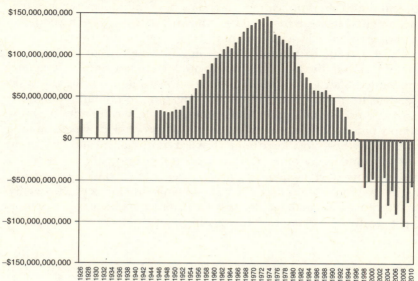

Sources: Statistics Canada 2011a,b.

is no reason to think that the independent actions of Canadian capital abroad would not be accompanied by its evil twin, independent Canadian militarism.

Canada is, however, at a very early stage in this transition, and there are no moments more difficult to analyse than those of transition. What I am arguing in this short chapter is, first, that military parasitism provides a political economy framework that can help to explain the peacekeeping moment in Canadian foreign policy. I offer this model as an alternative to the junior partner, dependent, 'weak Canada' model that has dominated most analysis of this period. Second, I argue that the peacekeeping moment is now clearly in the past – indeed, one can date the beginning of the end of the peacekeeping moment to 1991, the year of Canada's involvement in the first Gulf War. After more than twenty years, as Canada's involvement in Afghanistan stretches into 2012, a whole generation of Canadian young people has been recruited to serve and potentially to die in foreign wars. This transition to war-making from peacekeeping is the foreign policy accompaniment to a profound shift in both the Canadian and the world economy, related to the decline of US hegemony and the rise of the economies of the Global South. By implication, Canada's new militarism is more than just a policy; its deep material roots make it increasingly embedded as part of the political framework of the major political parties.

Third, I argue that this shift is profoundly significant for the shaping of tactics in the anti-war movement. We are not simply up against the United States: the Canadian state now has its own reasons, independent from the United States, for engaging in military adventures abroad. And in challenging that Canadian state, we are not up against simply bad policies, but against a state that is rooted in an economic architecture whose very logic points towards imperialism and militarism. The movements we build need to focus not just on policy change, but also on how to challenge the perverse geopolitical and geo-economic logics that make war and militarism an embedded part of the twenty-first century Canadian reality. Anti-war politics are incomplete without a perspective informed by anticapitalism.

NOTES

1 It is conceivable, of course, to argue that the lack of interest in the United States was a feature of Canadian dependence, with the United States insisting on self-reliance and being unwilling to cooperate in the development of an independent Canadian military potential, preferring to see Canada tied to and dependent on the US military. However, there is a strong case to be made that 'dependency' was not really a factor at all – Canada could not sell the Arrow to the United States because Canadian officials behaved in a somewhat incompetent manner. 'The Canadian government's belated attempts to interest the [US Air Force] in the [Arrow] could only be described as half-hearted, inept, and totally ineffectual. [Minister of National Defence George] Pearkes, who headed the Canadian sales delegation, was not an experienced weapons salesman and his zealous but simplistic sales pitch was no match for the high-pressure, counter-campaign waged by the Americans on behalf of their F-108 interceptor. Moreover, the available evidence suggests that the question of sales was not seriously considered until the staggering costs of development had become more fully appreciated in 1958' (Middlemiss 1976, 189).
2 It is important to remember that Figures 6.1 and 6.2 show relative, not absolute, numbers for arms spending. Representing military expenditures as a percentage of GDP or as a percentage of overall federal government

expenditures does provide an important window into the relative place of military expenditures in the economy and the priorities of the government. But just because relative figures decline over time, it does not automatically follow that absolute spending is declining, even when adjusted for inflation, given that both the economy and population have increased substantially since the 1950s.

References

Axworthy, Tom. 1979. 'Soldiers without Enemies: A Political Analysis of Canadian Defence Policy, 1945–1975.' PhD diss., Queen's University.

Barker, Colin. 1978. 'The State as Capital.' *International Socialism Journal* 2, no. 1: 16–42.

Bird, Richard M. 2008. 'Section H: Government Finance,' Series H19–34. In *Historical Statistics of Canada*, ed. F.H. Leacy. Ottawa: Statistics Canada. http://www.statcan.ca/english/freepub/11–516-XIE/sectiona/toc.htm.

Blue Helmets. 2010. 'National Peacekeeper's Day.' http://www.thebluehelmets.ca/documents/United%20Nations%20Missions.pdf.

Bukharin, Nikolai. [1918] 1973. *Imperialism and World Economy*. New York: Monthly Review Press.

Byers, Michael. 2009. *Who Owns the Arctic? Understanding Sovereignty Disputes in the North*. Vancouver: Douglas & McIntyre.

Campagna, Palmiro. 2003. *Requiem for a Giant: A.V. Roe Canada*. Toronto: Dundurn Press.

Campion-Smith, Bruce. 2010. 'Standing on guard in harsh north.' *Toronto Star*, 26 August.

Canada. 2006. Department of National Defence. 'Op CONNECTION: Reaching Out and Touching Canadians.' Ottawa. 9 March. http://www.army.gc.ca/lf/English/6_1_1.asp?id=941.

–. 2008. Department of National Defence. *Canada First Defence Strategy*. Ottawa.

–. 2010. Department of Finance. *Fiscal Reference Tables, October 2010*. Ottawa.

–. 2011a. Department of Finance. *The Fiscal Monitor: Highlights of Financial Results for February 2011*. Ottawa.

–. 2011b. Foreign Affairs and International Trade Canada. Office of the Chief Economist. 'Monthly Trade Report, February 2011.' Ottawa. http://www.international.gc.ca/economist-economiste/assets/pdfs/Monthly_Trade_Statistics.pdf.

CBC News. 2008. 'Canadian Forces in the 21st century.' 21 April. http://www.cbc.ca/news/background/cdnmilitary/.

–. 2009. 'Canada's equipment in Afghanistan.' 9 July. http://www.cbc.ca/crossroads-afghanistan/story/2009/07/08/f-canada-military-land-vehicles.html.

Clark-Jones, Melissa. 1987. *A Staple State: Canadian Industrial Resources in Cold War*. Toronto: University of Toronto Press.

Cliff, Tony. 1999. *Trotskyism after Trotsky*. London. Bookmarks.

Deveau, Scott. 2008. 'Choppers propelling growth.' *Financial Post*, 2 June.

Draper, Hal, ed. 1969. *The Permanent War Economy*. Berkeley, CA: Independent Socialist Press.

Eayrs, James. 1967. *In Defence of Canada: Appeasement and Rearmament*. Toronto: University of Toronto Press.

Economist. 2009. 'BRICs, emerging markets and the world economy: not just straw men.' 18 June.

Eustace, Marilyn D. 1976. 'Canada's Participation in Political NATO.' National Security Series 5. Kingston, ON: Queen's University, Centre for International Relations.

Field, Alan. 2009. 'EU, Canada Open Trade Talks.' *Journal of Commerce Online*, 11 June. http://www.joc.com/node/411835.

Fortune. 1995–2011. 'Global 500.' Various issues.

Gompert, David, and Richard Kugler. 1995. 'Free-Rider Redux: NATO Needs to Project Power (And Europe Can Help).' *Foreign Affairs* 74, no. 1: 7–12.

Harman, Chris. 1984. *Explaining the Crisis*. London: Bookmarks.

Huebert, Ron. 2007. 'Canadian Arctic Maritime Security: The Return to Canada's Third Ocean.' *Canadian Military Journal* (Summer): 9–16.

Keene, Tony. 1989. 'Canada's Forgotten Arrow.' *Air Classics*, January.

Kellogg, Paul. 2005. 'Kari Levitt and the Long Detour of Canadian Political Economy.' *Studies in Political Economy* 76 (Autumn): 31–60.

–. 2009. 'Of Nails and Needles: A Reconsideration of the Political Economy of Canadian Trade.' *Socialist Studies* 5, no. 1: 67–92.

–. 2011. 'NAFTA Unplugged? Free Trade with the EU and Its Implications for Canada's "Three Economies." ' In *Europe, Canada, and the Comprehensive Economic and Trade Agreement*, ed. Kurt Hübner. London: Routledge.

Kidron, Michael. 1969. *Western Capitalism since the War*. London: Penguin Books.

Kirton, John J. 1972. 'The Consequences of Integration: The Case of the Defence Production Sharing Agreements.' Occasional Paper 21. Ottawa: Carleton University, School of International Affairs.

McLin, Jon B. 1967. *Canada's Changing Defense Policy, 1957–1963: The Problems of a Middle Power in Alliance*. Baltimore: Johns Hopkins University Press.

Melman, Seymour. 1974. *The Permanent War Economy: American Capitalism in Decline*. New York: Simon & Schuster.

Middlemiss, Danford W. 1976. 'A Pattern of Co-operation: The Cases of the Canadian-American Defence Production and Development Sharing Arrangements, 1958–1963.' PhD diss., University of Toronto.

Middlemiss, Danford W., and Joel J. Sokolsky. 1989. *Canadian Defence: Decisions and Determinants*. Toronto: Harcourt Brace Jovanovich.

National Post. 2008. 'Bolstering our Forces.' 14 May.

Oakes, Walter J. 1944. 'Toward a Permanent War Economy.' *Politics* 1 (February): 11–17.

Penner, Dylan, ed. 2006. *War Free Schools: The Rise of the Counter-Recruitment Movement*. Toronto: Act for the Earth. http://operationobjection.org/war-free-schools/backgrounder.pdf.

Prontzos, Peter G. 2010. 'Harper's $18-billion fighter jet misadventure.' *rabble.ca*, 19 July. http://rabble.ca/news/2010/07/harpers-18-billion-fighter-jet-misadventure.

Razack, Sherene H. 2004. *Dark Threats and White Knights: The Somalia Affair, Peacekeeping, and the New Imperialism*. Toronto: University of Toronto Press.

Resnick, Phil. 1989. 'From Semiperiphery to Perimeter of the Core: Canada's Place in the Capitalist World-Economy.' *Review, A Journal of the Fernand Braudel Center* 12, no. 2: 263–97.

Shaw, E.K. 1981. *There Never Was an Arrow*. Ottawa: Steel Rail Educational Publishing.

SIPRI (Stockholm International Peace Research Institute). 1973. *Yearbook of World Armaments and Disarmament, 1974*. Cambridge, MA: MIT Press.

–. 1979. *World Armaments and Disarmament, SIPRI Yearbook, 1979*. New York: Crane, Russak.

–. 1988. *World Armaments and Disarmament, SIPRI Yearbook, 1988*. New York: Oxford University Press.

–. 2011. 'The SIPRI Military Expenditure Database.' http://milexdata.sipri.org/.

Spencer, Robert A. 1959. *Canada in World Affairs: From UN to NATO 1946–1949*. Toronto: Oxford University Press.

Staples, Steven. 2006. 'Marching Orders: How Canada Abandoned Peacekeeping – and Why the UN Needs Us Now More than Ever.' Ottawa: Council of Canadians. http://www.canadians.org/peace/documents/Marching_Orders_06.pdf.

Staples, Steven, and Bill Robinson. 2007. 'More than the Cold War: Canada's Military Spending 2007–08.' *Foreign Policy Series* (Canadian Centre for Policy Alternatives) 2, no. 3.

Statistics Canada. 2010. 'Merchandise Imports and Exports, by Major Groups and Principal Trading Areas for All Countries, Annually (Dollars).' CANSIM database, table 2280003.

–. 2011a. 'Consumer Price Index, 2005 basket, Monthly.' CANSIM database, table 3260020.

–. 2011b. 'International Investment Position, Annually (Dollars).' CANSIM database, table 3760037.

Treddenick, John. 1988. 'The Economic Significance of the Canadian Defence Industrial Base.' In *Canada's Defence Industrial Base*, ed. Dave Haglund. Kingston, ON: Ronald P. Frye.

United Nations. 2010. Department of Peacekeeping. 'Monthly Summary of Contributions.' New York. http://www.un.org/en/peacekeeping/contributors/2010/june10_1.pdf.

United States. 2011. Executive Office of the President. Office of Management and Budget. *Historical Tables, Budget of the United States Government, Fiscal Year 2009*. Washington, DC. http://www.whitehouse.gov/omb/budget/fy2009/pdf/hist.pdf.

Van Dusen, Thomas. 1968. *The Chief*. Toronto: McGraw-Hill.

7

Canada in the Third World: The Political Economy of Intervention

TODD GORDON

This chapter starts from a premise that may not seem obvious to many observers of Canada's role in Afghanistan: the Canadian intervention needs to be understood within the broader dynamics of Canada's political and economic relationship to the Third World. To be more precise, at a considerable human and ecological cost, Canadian capital is engaged in the systematic exploitation of the wealth and resources of Third World economies, and this relationship is actively facilitated by the diplomatic and security policies of the state. Canada is, in a word, an imperialist power. It is not a superpower, but that does not deny the relationship of domination and subordination it pursues with Third World nations.

Current scholarship on Canadian foreign policy leaves us ill equipped to make sense of Canada's role in either the Third World more generally or in Afghanistan in particular. For one thing, two of the more influential foreign policy frameworks, the Middle Power and dependency approaches, offer little in the way of systematic investigation of Canada's relations with the Third World. This gap in these bodies of literature is significant given how extensive Canada's economic interests in the Third World have become and, concomitantly, how important the Third World is to the Department of Foreign Affairs and International Trade (DFAIT) and the Department of National Defence (DND).

Perhaps historically the most influential in the study of Canadian foreign policy, the Middle Power framework includes several schools of thought, including realists who stress the anarchic context of international relations and the pursuit of power by self-interested states; liberal internationalists who focus on Canada's supposed efforts to mediate tensions between contending superpowers or between superpowers

and smaller powers; and global governance theorists who look at the
need for and efforts to develop international institutions and frameworks for a stable and transparent world order (for example, Cooper,
Higgott, and Nossal 1993; Cooper 1997; David and Roussel 1998; Clarke
2005; Bernard 2006). Yet the Middle Power perspective offers little in
the way of a political-economic analysis of Canada's position in the
world system. It tends to proceed methodologically from Canada's specific relations – diplomatic, political, and geostrategic – with the United
States and/or transnational institutions such as the United Nations or
the North Atlantic Treaty Organization (NATO), instead of from the
broader dynamics of global political economy. The dynamics of capital
accumulation on a global scale, and the systemic relations of power and
inequality between the First and Third Worlds, are rarely if ever analysed. Instead this framework tends to highlight the 'niche' diplomacy
of the Canadian state in, for example, peacekeeping, human rights, and
international cooperation and security. More recently writers in this tradition have focused on how Canada might meet these objectives in the
context of dwindling public resources and US unilateralism.

With little analysis of the global political economy and Canada's position within it, writers in this tradition often rely on the default assumption about Canada's Middle Power status. Canada's role as one of
the wealthiest nations in the world economy seldom rates any mention
at all. Moreover, for a writer like Hart (2008), the possibility of Canada's
playing an imperialist role in the global order is not fathomable. He la-
ments the 'depressing number of academics who seek inspiration from
the paranoia of people such as Noam Chomsky,' but happily notes that
'most of them no longer consider Canadian foreign policy to be central
to their interests' (2008, 49). Thus the logic of aid and security policies,
among others, is often misunderstood in the Middle Power literature,
while Canada's economic and military push into the Third World is
ignored.

The dependency approach is more attentive to dynamics of the
global political economy (Clarkson 2002; McQuaig 2007; Laxer 2008).
This perspective argues that Canadian foreign policy is an expression
of continental forms of economic dependence. However, it has not analysed Canada's penetration of Third World economies and the way in
which Canadian foreign policy reflects this intervention. Instead dependency writers tend to focus more narrowly on the continental relationship between Canada and the United States, and often argue that
US capital has stunted capitalist development in Canada. As a result

they underestimate the agency of the Canadian state, and often argue that Canadian foreign policy is a product of US economic domination. In other words they downplay the ability of the Canadian state to function and operate as a global power in its own right, reflecting the independent interests of Canadian capital.

The one framework that does situate Canada near the top of the hierarchy of nations and offers some analysis of Canada's role in the Third World is the Principal Power theory (Lyon and Ismael 1976; Lyon and Tomlin 1979; Dewitt and Kirton 1983). However, this perspective has never gained traction among students of Canadian foreign policy and has not framed a major study in more than two decades. While challenging the idea that Canada is a mere Middle Power, it too fails to theorize adequately Canada's role within the unequal power dynamics of the global political economy.

In recent years, however, a new body of critical research has emerged on Canada's role in Third World economies (North, Clarke, and Patroni 2006; Gordon and Webber 2008, 2011; Gordon 2010). This research focuses on the social, economic, political, and environmental impacts of Canadian corporate expansion into Third World countries. Most of this analysis, however, falls outside academic boundaries and has been conducted in non-governmental organizations such as Mining Watch, Rights Action, and the Halifax Initiative or in alternative media. It also does not typically account for Canada's asymmetrical relationship with the Third World as a whole.[1] In fact the analysis consists primarily of case studies of corporate malfeasance. As a result it expands our understanding of Canadian corporate activity in the Third World, but fails to raise the level of analysis beyond the actions of particular corporations.

As an alternative, the Marxist theory of international political economy begins with the recognition that global capitalism is shaped by *imperialist relations* through which countries of the First World – operating bilaterally and multilaterally – systematically drain the wealth and resources of the Third World via economic, political, and military means. The period of formal empire is long gone, but the capitalist world market still generates *uneven development* on a systematic basis between the North and the South (Harvey 2005). According to Ellen Meiksins Wood (2003) the period of neoliberalism has produced the most developed form of capitalist imperialism, as corporate interests based in the North, with support of their respective nation-states and transnational bodies such as the International Monetary Fund (IMF) and the World Bank, exploit the resources and labour supplies of Third World countries. In place of territorial conquest and direct colonization, then, is economic exploitation through 'free market' exchanges. As I argue below, a key expression of the new imperialism is the massive growth of foreign direct investment (FDI) in markets of the Global South and the corresponding transfer of wealth from Third World economies to First World capital (Harvey 2005; McNally 2006).

With a highly advanced economy, Canada operates within the core group of states in this new system of imperialism. Canadian capital, like US capital, participates in the competition for profits and market shares, and, in the past two decades, it has developed an extensive set of economic interests in the Third World and encouraged a more aggressive military and security policy from the state. The geographic expansion of Canadian capital into Third World markets and the militarization of Canadian foreign policy towards 'rogue' and 'failed' states in the Third Word are closely linked and set the structural context in which Canada is currently waging war in Afghanistan.

To present this argument, this chapter extends and contributes to the existing literature on imperialism and the Canadian state developed by Moore and Wells (1975), Carroll (1986), Burgess (2000), and Klassen (2009). In particular it maps the structure of economic relations between Canada and the Third World and the impact of this relationship on the foreign policies of the state. The fundamental argument is that Canadian capital and the Canadian state are linked in a process of imperialist exploitation, and that the war in Afghanistan must be viewed in this context. The first section maps the expansion of Canadian capital into the Third World during the period of neoliberalism. The second and third sections analyse the new foreign policy agenda vis-à-vis Third World countries. The fourth section considers a number of case studies, including recent policies towards Latin America. The final section then offers a reinterpretation of the war in Afghanistan as a further instance of Canada's new imperialism in the Third World.

The Expansion of Canadian Capital
into the Third World

It is important to grasp how significant the international expansion of Canadian capital has been over the past two decades. The neoliberal period, which began roughly in the late 1970s and early 1980s, has been witness to profound changes in Canadian capitalism. The goal of neoliberalism has been the restoration of capitalist profitability through the unleashing of free market forces and increasing the rights of corporations. It has entailed a reduction of working-class living standards, a criminalization of immigrants and tighter border controls, a rollback of labour rights, severe cuts to the welfare state, and integration with world markets. In the Canadian context neoliberalism is associated with new forms of continental convergence and with economic expansion into First Nations' territories, especially for the purpose of accessing resources (Gordon 2006). The net result has been a massive transfer of wealth from the bottom to the top of the economic pyramid (Jackson 2007).

But neoliberalism has not just transformed Canadian capital on the domestic front; key developments in the international sphere have given Canadian capital a new orientation. As foreign ownership in the Canadian economy decreased after the peak year of 1971, Canadian ownership of assets abroad increased. Canada is now one of the world's leading sources of FDI, which, as mentioned, is a driving force behind economic globalization. For McNally (2006, 37–42), it is FDI, not trade, that has increased most significantly over the past twenty years. For example, global FDI has increased more rapidly than the world economy as a whole, surpassing the trillion-dollar mark in the early 2000s. Because FDI confers some measure of managerial control, it is one of the principal ways by which capital from the North has gained economic power and influence in the Third World during the period of neoliberalism.

Canadian direct investment (CDI) abroad has increased sharply since the early 1990s – indeed, Canada has been a net exporter of direct investment since 1997 – and by 2007 the cumulative stock of CDI reached C$514.5 billion. Measured in annual investment flows Canada ranked eighth in the world in 2007, and has consistently ranked in the top ten in the past several years, with direct investments in 150 different countries, including thirty with at least $1 billion in CDI stock (Statistics Canada 2008; UNCTAD 2008, 76). Among the Group of Eight large industrial economies, Canada has the fourth-highest ratio of outward direct investment stock to gross domestic product (GDP) (UNCTAD, World Investment Directory On-line, 'Key Data,' table 23).

Perhaps the most interesting development here, however, is Canada's economic penetration of Third World markets. As the global debt crisis hit the Third World in the early 1980s, the advanced capitalist countries used the IMF and the World Bank to alter radically the political and economic landscape of the Third World. In return for much-needed loans, the IMF and World Bank imposed free market reforms on poor countries. Markets were opened to First World capital, public utilities and land privatized, social spending and subsidies cut, currencies devalued, and natural resources commodified, all of which sparked an investment wave in pursuit of natural resources, cheap labour supplies, and fire-sale assets.

Canadian corporations have since been among the most assertive in penetrating Third World markets. In the early 1950s the Third World received approximately 10 per cent of total CDI stock, but this has increased sharply since the early 1990s, reaching more than 27 per cent by 2007. The increase in CDI in developing economies corresponds to the decrease of CDI, as a proportion of the total, flowing to advanced capitalist countries. While the United States is still the biggest destination for CDI, its share of the total has declined considerably, from 60 per cent in 1990 to 44 per cent in 2007, even though Canadian assets in the United States tripled in absolute terms.[2] Among the Group of Seven (G7) countries, Canada had the second-highest flows of FDI to Third World countries as a proportion of GDP in 2007.[3] At the same time, income from direct investment in the Third World as a proportion of total investment income earned abroad has risen significantly, from just under 25 per cent for the years from 1973 to 1979 to more than 45 per cent for the 2000–7 period. Income from the Third World, then, has actually increased at a much faster pace than has direct investment in the region as a proportion of total CDI. Direct investment income from the Third World rose from C$1.1 billion in 1990 to $17.9 billion in 2007.[4] Total foreign investment income reached C$23.6 billion after tax by 2007, an increase of 535 per cent from 1980, which is greater than the increase in profits earned at home over the same period of time.[5]

Canadian investment in the Third World is led by the 'finance and insurance' and the 'energy and metallic minerals' sectors, which, in 2007, together accounted for just over 78 per cent of CDI stock in Third World countries (57.1 per cent and 21.1 per cent, or C$77.6 billion and C$28.7 billion, respectively), with 'services and retailing' accounting for 11.5 per cent and 'other' 7.4 per cent (Statistics Canada, CANSIM database, table 376–0053). However, the growing importance of the Third World as a destination for Canadian direct investment has occurred across most sectors.

Canadian banks and insurance companies have increasingly established themselves in Third World offshore financial centres (OFCs), which are a draw for Canadian investors because of their low taxation rates, limited regulations, and secrecy. From 1990 to 2003 Canadian assets in OFCs grew eightfold from C$11 billion to C$88 billion, and by 2003 accounted for a remarkable one-fifth of all CDI – double the share of thirteen years earlier. Since 1996 OFCs have been the most popular destination for CDI in the financial sector, accounting for two-thirds of this measure. Of the forty-two OFC jurisdictions identified by the IMF, Canadian corporations held assets in twenty-five of them in 2003. The largest growth of CDI in OFCs has been in Barbados, Bermuda, the Cayman Islands, and the Bahamas, with Singapore, Hong Kong, and Malaysia also being significant destinations (Lavoie 2005).[6]

While OFCs are key destinations for capital investment, banking sector liberalization has occurred across the South in the past two decades. These reforms have allowed for more foreign competition and fewer controls on credit, interest rates, and international transactions, leading to an increase in speculative inflows, unstable asset bubbles, and spectacular meltdowns. While banks based in the First World traditionally have invested in Third World financial markets to assist multinational corporations, since the 1990s these same banks have tried to access local credit markets and to purchase failed firms. From 1990 to 2003 there was a sharp increase in FDI to developing countries, the majority of which – US$46 billion – targeted Latin America. Over this period, Canadian firms were the fourth-largest financial sector investors in the region (BIS 2004, 6). For example, between 2003 and 2006 Scotiabank spent nearly C$2 billion in acquisitions in Latin America, including the purchase of thirty-nine branches in the Dominican Republic, adding to an existing twenty-branch network in the country; it has also acquired banks in Peru, Costa Rica, Chile, Uruguay, and the Cayman Islands in recent years, and in 2011 purchased Colombian Banco Colpatria for C$1 billion following the implementation of the Canada-Colombia Free Trade Agreement (*Globe and Mail* 2010; *Investment Executive* 2003; Waldie 2006; Silcoff 2007; Robertson 2011). Scotiabank is not the only bank expanding in the region, however. In 2007 the Canadian Imperial Bank of Commerce (CIBC) became the majority owner of FirstCaribbean International Bank, and in 2010 bought part of Bermuda's largest independent bank, N.T. Butterfield and Son (Willis 2007; Perkins 2010). Canadian banks control the three largest banks in the English-speaking Caribbean. Their C$42 billion in assets in this region is four times what the approximately forty locally owned banks control (*Economist* 2008). More broadly it is estimated that Canadian banks now earn approximately 40 per cent of their revenues abroad, especially from Latin America (Willis 2007). Given their strong balance sheets, the international expansion of Canadian banks, particularly in the Third World, is likely to continue. For example, Scotiabank has voiced its intention to increase acquisitions in Latin America and Asia. According to CIBC chief executive officer, Gerry McCaughey, his bank's purchase of FirstCaribbean is one step of an expansionary plan: 'From a First Caribbean viewpoint, we will continue to look at opportunities within the region, and we think growing within the region is of interest' (ibid.).

Canadian companies also have a strong presence in Third World oil and gas development, dam-building projects, and sweatshop manufacturing – Montreal's Gildan Activewear is a dominant player in the latter market. But Canada's greatest international presence is in mining. Canada's mining industry is the largest in the world, and the Toronto Stock Exchange is the most important market for raising investment capital in the mining sector. Canadian-based mining companies comprise 60 per cent of all mining companies (of a total of 1,138) in the world that spend more than C$133,000 on exploration, account for more than 40 per cent of all worldwide exploration activity, and conduct approximately 30 per cent of all mining investment worldwide (Canada 2004). Canadian mining companies are most active in Latin America, but there are many signs of expansion on a global scale. In 2009, the last year for which data are available, Canadian mining companies owned more than C$109 billion in assets in more than ninety foreign countries; $56.1 billion were held in Latin America, $20 billion in Africa, $6 billion in Asia, and $4.7 billion in Oceania. While the expansion of Canadian mining capital is broad and far reaching, it is also concentrated: in twenty-one countries, nine of them in Latin America, Canadian mining assets exceeded $1 billion (Canada 2011).

In terms of overall investment patterns, Latin America and the Caribbean are the destinations of the largest amounts of CDI in the Third World, accounting for more than 70 per cent of total CDI to Third World economies since 1996 and for more than 80 per cent in 2007 alone – the Caribbean, in particular, has received just under 50 per cent over that period (Statistics Canada, CANSIM database, tables 376–0051, 376–0053). The growth in these regions' share of total CDI in the Third World is related to the liberalization trend of the 1980s and 1990s, especially in the financial services and natural resources sectors, and has fostered a new ambition in Canada for greater political and economic influence there. Not surprisingly, then, nine of the ten fastest-growing CDI destinations from 1987 to 2007 were in this region and eight of the top ten Third World recipients of CDI stock in 2007 were in Latin America and the Caribbean (four in the Caribbean and four in Latin America).[7] By 2006 Canada had actually become the third-largest investor in the region. From 1996 to 2006 Canada was the largest investor in Ecuador, second in Honduras, third in Chile and the Dominican Republic, and fifth in Mexico, El Salvador, and Costa Rica; in 2007 Canada was the fourth-largest investor in Peru (ECLAC 2003, 2006).

Canadian investment in Africa, dominated by natural resources development, is small compared with that in other regions, but it increased from C$268 million in 1990 to C$4 billion in 2008 (Statistics Canada, CANSIM database, table 376–0051). While data for Africa are uneven, Canadian investments tend to be concentrated in a relatively small number of countries, including Ghana and Tanzania. In the Asia-Pacific region, the share of CDI growth declined over this period as investment to Latin America and the Caribbean took off, but in absolute terms it increased from C$4.1 billion in 1990 to C$19.3 billion in 2007. As a result Canadian companies have a not-insignificant presence in the Pacific: Canada was the tenth-largest foreign investor in Indonesia in 2006 (with more than C$2 billion by 2008) and in Malaysia in 2007 (with more than C$1 billion by 2008); and the eleventh-largest in the Philippines in 2007 (with C$671 million in 2008).[8]

The presence of Canadian capital in Central Asia is less clear, as there are gaps in Statistics Canada's records for several countries. For instance, despite Canada's diplomatic, military, and developmental role in Afghanistan, Statistics Canada has no publicly disclosed data for the presence of Canadian capital in the country. The government of Afghanistan offers no such information either. We know that Canada has made efforts to open up Afghanistan for business (Warnock 2007), and that the Karzai government is actively courting Canadian and other western investors with their market-friendly regulations and ample supply of cheap labour. The Afghanistan Investment Support Agency, a government office promoting foreign investment, declares that 'Afghanistan offers a pro-business minded environment with legislation favourable to private investments,' and that Afghanistan 'is rich in natural resources' and 'is keen on establishing a low-cost, labor-intensive manufacturing sector which absorbs the many unemployed Afghans.'[9] Afghan officials have tempted Canadian companies with their claim that only 5 per cent of the country's rich mineral deposits have been explored because of decades of war. Ibrahim Adel, Afghanistan's minister of mines, is a regular attendee at the annual gatherings of the Prospectors and Developers Association of Canada. He has been supported by DFAIT, which has set up roundtables between Adel and Canadian mining executives at the meetings. During his sojourns to Canada Adel has also enjoyed the hospitality of David Emerson and Gary Lunn, former ministers of international trade and natural resources, respectively, in the Harper government (Hoffman 2007; Chernos 2008, 16).

Canada's presence is certainly felt in the nearby former Soviet republics. In Kazakhstan Canada was the fifth-largest foreign investor in 2008, with US$945 million invested, most of it in mining (National Bank of Kazakhstan 2009; Canada 2007a). In Kyrgyzstan Canada was the sixth-largest investor in 2007, with US$500 million in assets, much of it also in mining (National Bank of the Kyrgyz Republic 2008). In Tajikistan, meanwhile, Canada ranked lower, as the tenth-largest foreign investor in 2007, with US$1.4 million invested (National Bank of Tajikistan 2009). Canadian oil and gas companies have also shown interest in the region. Buried Hill Energy won a licence to explore and develop a gas field in Turkmenistan in the winter of 2008. This was followed shortly after by the signing of formal agreements between the four participating countries in the Trans-Afghan Pipeline (TAP) project in April 2008. The 1,680-kilometre pipeline will start in the Turkmen city of Dauletabad and pass through the Afghan cities of Herat and Kandahar, where Canadian forces are heavily concentrated, before entering Pakistan and India (Foster 2008; McCarthy 2008; Pannier 2008).

In these ways Canadian capital has expanded throughout the Third World during the period of neoliberalism. It is strongest in Latin America and the Caribbean, but is quickly establishing global interests in Africa, the Asia-Pacific, and Central Asia. Canada has become one of the largest investors in Global South markets, and competes successfully with other rich nations for natural resources and cheap labour supplies.

Promoting Canadian Capital's Penetration of the Third World

The global expansion of Canadian capital has been made possible by new Canadian foreign policy strategies. Indeed, imposing liberalized market relations and exploiting the Third World are central goals of Canadian foreign policy planners. While support for the expansion of Canadian capital is certainly not new to either DFAIT officials or political leaders, it has nevertheless received significant attention since the 1990s. As Canadian capital has penetrated Third World markets, corporate leaders and the state have placed a new premium on free market policies. In this context the Canadian state has increasingly intervened in the international arena to protect the global interests of Canadian firms. These interventions have come in many forms, including trade and investment agreements and foreign aid policy.

Free trade deals and investment treaties have been critical for securing Canadian capital's access to the Third World. Trade and investment deals are designed to lock in market access for capital by establishing a strong investor rights regime, including most-favoured-nation and national treatment clauses, and dispute settlement mechanisms that allow non-parties (corporations) to sue governments. Such mechanisms first appeared in Chapter 11 of the North American Free Trade Agreement (NAFTA), and have since been included in all subsequent trade agreements and bilateral investment treaties Canada has pursued, most of which are with Third World governments. Governments weakened by either debt or trade deficits have been willing to abandon national tariffs, environmental protections, and reasonable royalty rates in order to access new loans and foreign investment.

Since the signing of NAFTA, Canada has actively pursued bilateral and multilateral treaties with Third World countries. Multilaterally Canada was a major proponent of the Free Trade Area of the Americas (FTAA) – perhaps more so than George Bush's administration after it lost fast-track negotiation authority – until negotiations stalled in the face of Brazilian opposition and the election of left-leaning governments in South America. Canada is currently a strong proponent of a World Trade Organization (WTO) investment treaty, which is modelled in part on NAFTA and has received lukewarm reception from many Third World countries (Canada 1999, 2005c, n.d.). While Canada may prefer to negotiate large multilateral agreements because of their broad scope, it recently turned its attention to smaller regional and bilateral agreements after the failure of the FTAA and the WTO investment agreement. As of summer 2011, Canada had signed ten trade agreements: NAFTA (with the United States and Mexico), the Canada-European Free Trade Association Agreement (involving Iceland, Liechtenstein, Norway, and Switzerland), and bilateral agreements with Israel, Chile, Costa Rica, Peru, Colombia, Panama, Honduras, and Jordan. At the time of writing, it has concluded, though not officially implemented, deals with Colombia and Panama. Canada also has twenty post-NAFTA foreign investment protection agreements in force and several others 'pending,' all with Third World countries.[10]

Aid policy represents another method by which the Canadian state facilitates economic expansion into developing countries. Both Conservative and Liberal governments highlight foreign aid contributions as a sign of Canada's progressive internationalism, but this perspective is short sighted (Morrison 1998). In reality the Canadian government commits a pitiful amount to aid, both absolutely and relatively in terms of the budget. Following drastic cuts to overseas development assistance (ODA) in the late 1980s and 1990s – 33 per cent in real terms – Canada's ratio of ODA to gross national income (GNI) fell to a mere 0.28 per cent in fiscal year 2007/8, ranking it fourteenth out of twenty-two Development Assistance Committee members. At its current rate of spending Canada will not come close to reaching the United Nations' Millennium Development Goal of 0.7 per cent of GNI by 2015 (Morrison 1998; Tomlinson 2000–1; Black 2005; CIDA 2009). Indeed, Canada spends more on agricultural subsidies – assisting its own producers against foreign competitors from Third World countries – than it does on international aid, while Canada's military budget is more than three times that of ODA. The total investment income earned by Canadian capital in the Third World is nearly six times what Canada offers in aid, and represents the primary means by which Canada *extracts value* from poor countries (Canada 2005a; *Economist* 2006). In short, Canada draws more wealth from Third World economies than it spends on aid and development assistance.

Troubling the matter further, Canada attaches 'structural adjustment conditionalities' to aid disbursements: in order for a country to receive aid, it must liberalize and restructure domestic markets in the interests of foreign capital. Structural adjustment has been a condition of Canadian aid policy since Marcel Massé's tenure as president of the Canadian International Development Agency (CIDA) in the 1980s (Pratt 1994). Opposition to structural adjustment policies – which have been widely critiqued for *worsening* Third World poverty in the 1980s and 1990s – led Canada and other wealthy nations to change the name of conditionality programs to Poverty Reduction Strategies (or Poverty Reduction Growth Facility). But the change of name has not altered the general thrust of policy. Canada still imposes neoliberal restructuring on poor countries (including Afghanistan), even if it now gives national governments the opportunity to devise their own restructuring strategy (known as the Poverty Reduction Strategy Paper process) (IMF 2004). As a result markets have been liberalized and the rights of foreign investors strengthened considerably.

Canadian governments also like to boast of their commitment to African development and Third World debt forgiveness. But here again these efforts are trumped by the globalizing agenda of capital. There are a number of ways in which the Canadian government is worsening an already tragic situation in Africa. Canada's role in the Heavily Indebted Poor Country (HIPC) Initiative, which is targeted primarily at African nations, is a good example. The IMF created the HIPC process as a debt-rescheduling strategy in 1996. The idea was for multilateral donor agencies such as the IMF and regional development banks to write off the debts of some of the world's poorest countries.[11] But in order to be eligible for the write-off, the heavily indebted country must first endure six years of structural adjustment to prove its commitment to neoliberal principles. Yet for most of the poor countries participating in the initiative, the debt written off is only a small portion of their total international debt and does not cover most of what they owe to private financial institutions. It is also debt they have actually stopped servicing, so creditor nations are only writing off debt they know will never be paid back (Canada 2005d; Bond 2006). At the end of 2005 Canada supported an IMF plan to delay a debt-relief package for six countries to which some G7 members initially had discussed granting non-conditional relief. IMF leaders, backed by Canada, opposed the G7 plan, delayed relief, and imposed new austerity measures as a precondition for any future debt forgiveness (Social Justice Committee 2005).

Much of Canadian aid money is focused, furthermore, on infrastructural development to support foreign investment, particularly in resources extraction. This is clearly the case with CIDA's 'enhanced' aid partnerships, as Campbell (2004, 104–6) points out with respect to Africa. Announced in 2002 and again in 2005, the enhanced aid partnerships were promoted as focused and more meaningful aid disbursements to smaller groups of countries. However, the program targeted countries with which Canadian companies have investment relations (typically in mining) or which are rich in natural resources. CIDA declares that it will focus on countries with 'good governance' potential, which entails a liberal climate for foreign investment. This program was replaced in 2009 with the new 'Countries of Focus' program, which concentrates 80 per cent of bilateral aid on twenty countries, seven of which are in Africa – though the program reflects the Harper government's increased interest in the Americas, with six countries (one is actually the Caribbean Regional Program) included from the region. Canada has concluded trade agreements with three of those countries (Colombia, Honduras, and Peru), is actively pursuing agreements with one other (the Caribbean region), and has supported coups in two (Haiti and Honduras).

A key determinant of Canadian foreign policy today, then, is the globalization of Canadian capital. Through trade, investment, and aid policies, the Canadian state is securing access for Canadian firms to exploit the wealth and resources of developing countries. Promoting liberalized markets and investor rights, while reinforcing debt bondage, has expanded the international footprint of Canadian capital. It has also led to increasing conflicts with local communities.

Political Resistance and Security Policy

Canada's asymmetrical relationship with the Third World has come at considerable cost to the region's workers, indigenous peoples, and peasants. The toll of global capitalism and market liberalization on the Third World over the past twenty-five years has been well documented: a staggering billion people have been dispossessed of their land, inequality between the richest and poorest countries has increased, and poverty has dramatically intensified, particularly in Africa (Bond 2006; Davis 2006; McNally 2006). If gains have been made for some of the poorest in Latin America in recent years (at least, before the 2008 economic meltdown), it is because of a commodities-boom driven by overheated economies in the First World and the redistribution policies of left-of-centre governments.

As a member of the G7, Canada bears its share of responsibility for this unjust state of affairs. At the same time Canadian investment itself is often directly based on extracting as much value as possible, regardless of the consequences of displacement, economic exploitation, and ecological degradation. As a result Canadian capital in the Third World is commonly met by popular resistance and sometimes by government opposition to neoliberal restructuring. Whether it is strikes in Colombo against Bata, community resistance to Barrick Gold in the Philippines, mass strikes and road blockades in Ecuador against EnCana, or the denial of mineral exploration permits by the Venezuelan and Honduran governments, Canadian companies face growing resistance in developing countries.

With opposition mounting to Canadian corporate activity, new developments in Canadian security strategy have emerged to protect investor interests. The war in Afghanistan is the most prominent example of this strategy, but it should be viewed as part of a wider approach to security and military intervention in the Third World.

For the past two decades military leaders, defence ministers, and DND policy documents have warned repeatedly of new dangers in the global system and of new threats emanating from the Third World (Hooey 1994; Couture 1998; Canada 2007b). As early as 1994 a DND White Paper argued that 'Cold War stability has given way to instability and uncertainty – the world is in many ways a more dangerous place than it has been for the past 40 years . . . If anything, we are in a more unstable and unpredictable international environment [than the] balance of terror that has hung over the world since 1950' (quoted in Hooey 1994, 469). Likewise Canada's 2005 International Policy Statement refers to the dangers of 'regional flashpoints' in the Third World (Canada 2005b, 5–6). It would be a mistake to ignore the links between Canadian security policies and the global expansion of Canadian capital. Indeed, it is telling that many of the speeches and documents prepared by the defence apparatus employ very similar language to those produced by DFAIT, dwelling as they do on the perceived lack of 'stability' and 'unpredictability' in Third World nations. In some cases military leaders make the link clearly between the global interests of Canadian capital and security policy. While chief of the defence staff, General Maurice Baril noted quite clearly that '[o]ur economic future depends on the global stability required to trade freely with other nations. As a major trading nation, we are therefore compelled by interest to protect and promote international peace and security' (Baril 1999).

The 'war on terror' and the current occupation of Afghanistan have allowed both Liberal and Conservative governments to ramp up military spending. Canada's military spending increased by C$31 billion from 2001 to 2010 alone (with incremental increases devoted to the Afghan war accounting for approximately half of that), and a total of approximately C$400 billion (in 2010 dollars) in spending is projected between 2008 and 2027 under the Conservative's Defence First plan, which does not include spending on future missions (Robinson 2011). This spending is on top of the $8 billion given recently to other security agencies, including the Canadian Security Intelligence Service, the Royal Canadian Mounted Police, and the Canada Border Services Agency (Bell 2004; Chase 2008). Canada ranked thirteenth among the world's top military spenders and the sixth-largest in NATO in 2009, and its rate of spending increase from 2000 to 2007 was the third-highest in NATO (Robinson 2011; SIPI 2008).

The occupation of Afghanistan is not Canada's only major foreign intervention of note – indeed, such interventions are increasingly commonplace, with the 2011 Libyan campaign being the most recent. In the process Canada is developing a flexible toolkit with which to advance its interests. The full spectrum of Canadian foreign policy tactics are not elaborated in security doctrines, but appear clearly enough in recent foreign policy engagements. Certainly both Liberal and Conservative governments have placed considerable stress on the promotion of democracy and human rights in their foreign policy initiatives of recent years, as the Harper government has made clear in its aid policy towards the Americas.[12] While such goals appear benign, they are often a cover for destabilizing left-leaning governments.[13] At the same time Canada has been at the forefront of efforts to rewrite international law by establishing more flexible justifications for military invasions of 'failed states.' Canada played a critical role (with Michael Ignatieff as co-author) in developing and promoting the 'responsibility to protect' (R2P) doctrine at the United Nations, which was used informally to justify the coup against Haitian president Jean-Bertrand Aristide (International Commission on Intervention and State Sovereignty 2006). Canada has also developed a new counterinsurgency manual for its military forces. Among other things, the manual distills lessons from the intervention in Haiti for pacifying civilian populations and possible insurgents, and is premised on the assumption that future counterinsurgency efforts against asymmetrical opponents in the Third World will be a focus of the military (Canada 2007b).

While the form of intervention changes from case to case, the imperialist goal of policy-makers is to 'open' and 'stabilize' poor countries for transnational capital. Canada's new security doctrine is imperialist in the way it constructs an image of the South as a dangerous zone in need of military intervention and neoliberal development. The road to stability, in the eyes of Canadian policy-makers, is economic advancement through liberalized markets with strong protections for corporate investors. If states fail to support this agenda, they face a real possibility of military intervention by Canada and its western allies.

The Coup in Haiti

The military intervention in Haiti in 2004 provides an early example of Canada's new security policy. In February that year the popular and democratically elected president, Jean-Bertrand Aristide, was overthrown in a coup and forcefully removed from the country. Aristide was a left-of-centre politician with a history of links to liberation theology, and had been previously removed from office in a coup in 1991. After his re-election in November 2000 Aristide raised the minimum wage, introduced literacy programs, built new health clinics and hospitals, increased taxes on the rich and subsidies on price-sensitive consumer goods, and publicly criticized the IMF, all of which failed to endear him to the country's wealthy elite or to the Canadian, US, or French states (Engler and Fenton 2005; Hallward 2008).

The coup was led by the country's business elite and paramilitary forces featuring ex-army officers and death squad members from previous dictatorships (Hallward 2008, 75ff). Canada, the US, and France supported these forces diplomatically and militarily. Prior to the coup Canada engaged in a destabilization campaign against the Aristide government. Along with France, the United States, and the World Bank, Canada cut off aid to the Haitian government following Aristide's election in 2000, precipitating a sharp drop in the GDP of what was already the poorest country in the hemisphere. CIDA directly funded many opposition groups with very poor human rights records as well as anti-Aristide media (Engler and Fenton 2005, 50ff). Canadian government officials also participated at least twice in high-level meetings with their French and US counterparts to develop a coordinated strategy to undermine Aristide's government. As early as 2000 then Liberal foreign affairs minister Lloyd Axworthy travelled to Washington for a 'Friends of Haiti' meeting. Fenton (2005–6, 18) argues that '[t]hese "friends" of Haiti feared that, unless Aristide's Lavalas Party was reined in, the neoliberal vision for that country was in dire jeopardy.' In 2003 Denis Paradis, who later became the Liberal government's secretary of state for Latin America and the Caribbean and minister responsible for La Francophonie, hosted a high-level meeting called the Ottawa Initiative on Haiti in the government's conference centre at Meech Lake, Quebec, with representatives from the United States and France. While the federal government has refused to disclose details of that meeting, Montreal-based newspaper *L'Actualite* reports that participants discussed – approximately one year before Aristide's ouster – the need to remove Aristide and place Haiti under the control of the United Nations (Engler and Fenton 2005, 41–3; Hallward 2008, 106).

In support of the actual coup members of Canada's Joint Task Force 2 reportedly secured the airport for Aristide's removal. Canadian Forces members then worked with their French and US allies and the Haitian

National Police (HNP) to violently pacify the slums where Aristide's support was strongest. Slum residents reported violent reprisals by the HNP and Canadian military, including the shooting of demonstrators. Upwards of a thousand Haitians were killed in the first few days following the coup, while as many as four thousand died during the reign of coup leader Gérard Latortue. Most of those killed were supporters of Aristide's Lavalas party (Fenton 2005–6, 18; Hallward 2008, 147, 249). The HNP, which was led by a Canadian, waged a campaign of repression through 2005. Through CIDA's Interim Cooperation Framework (CIDA 2006), Canada spent C$20 million on the establishment and training of the HNP. One hundred RCMP officers were also sent to Haiti to help train and integrate ex-soldiers into the new police force. The effort to train the HNP to make Haiti 'more secure' included working on patrols, crowd control, and intelligence. CIDA also spent $800,000 on the correctional system. With CIDA funding, a Port-au-Prince prison, built to hold five hundred people, held more than two thousand in squalid conditions by the spring of 2006, only eighty-one of whom had been convicted of a crime. This was all done under the watch of Haiti's CIDA-paid deputy minister of justice, Philippe Vixamar (Engler and Fenton 2005, 52–3; Hallward 2008, 253–4, 271). CIDA also helped the Latortue regime prepare its Poverty Reduction Strategy Paper. As a CIDA document stated at the time, the Haitian government 'has achieved the zero-deficit objectives of the International Monetary Fund' (CIDA 2006).

Canada cloaked its role in the Haitian coup in a humanitarian guise, with Paradis invoking the R2P doctrine to justify Canada's intervention (Engler and Fenton 2005, 41–3). But the use of R2P in the Haitian context only shows the shallow and ideological nature of such justifications. Aristide's government was democratically elected and had a relatively strong human rights record, particularly when compared to the slaughter that followed the coup. What Canada did accomplish, however, was the removal of a government that sought an independent development path, the rollback of workers' rights and regulations on mining and sweatshop manufacturing in Haiti's export-processing zones, and the projection of diplomatic and military power in a region in which it has long-standing economic interests.

Destabilizing Democracy in the Andes and Honduras

Canada also worked to destabilize the governments of Hugo Chávez in Venezuela and Manuel Zelaya in Honduras. In Venezuela CIDA funded groups, including Sumate A.C. and Fundación Justicia de

Paz Monagas, that participated in the 2002 attempted coup (Golinger 2007).[14] At the same time, DFAIT has funded the Justice and Development Consortium, another far-right organization, and brought Sumate's Maria Corina Machado to Ottawa, where she spoke with government officials and politicians about political rights in Venezuela (Fenton 2009).

Funding for these organizations is part of the Canadian state's agenda of 'democracy promotion' in the Andes, which the Harper government has declared a key component of Canadian foreign policy in the Americas. Canada's support for Colombia, a country with one of the worst human rights records in the world and whose former leader, Álvaro Uribe, had links to paramilitary death squads, should be seen in this light. While the country is rich in natural resources, the Colombian government also proudly aligns itself with imperial interests and maintains antagonistic relations with Chávez and the moderately left-wing president of Ecuador, Rafael Correa. Thus, Canada has sought to isolate Venezuela by branding it as authoritarian, while openly supporting Colombia through military exports. During his state visit to Colombia in summer 2007, Prime Minister Harper dismissed the country's human rights problems and instead made a point of distinguishing countries, such as Colombia, that pursue strong free markets from the 'economic nationalism, political authoritarianism and class warfare' taking hold in other parts of the Andes (quoted in Freeman 2007).

In Honduras, President Manuel Zelaya was overthrown in a military coup on 28 June 2009 and forced into exile. Zelaya had raised the minimum wage, announced a moratorium on new mining concessions, sought to nationalize energy generating plants and the telephone system, entered the Bolivarian Alternative for the Americas, and called a vote for 28 June on whether or not to hold a referendum in November on calling a constitutional assembly to discuss Honduras's constitution, which had been adopted in 1982 by a military dictatorship.

As the second-largest foreign investor in the country, Canada had cause for concern about Honduras's leftward tilt. Thus, when the first rumblings of a coup were heard two days before it eventually took place, Canada said nothing. In contrast, DFAIT had issued three press releases in a two-week span earlier in the month condemning the Iranian government's clampdown on protests following that country's presidential election.[15] The Organization of American States (OAS) did pass a resolution on 26 June calling for the maintenance of democracy and the rule of law. Yet in the special session of the OAS Permanent Council on the situation in Honduras held that same day, the Canadian representative remained silent (OAS 2009). Finally, very late in the evening of 28 June, more than twelve hours after the coup became known outside Honduras, Peter Kent, minister of state for the Americas, issued a press release. While Kent condemned the coup d'état, he called 'on all parties to show restraint and to seek a peaceful resolution' to the crisis, as if all parties, including Zelaya and his supporters, were responsible for the military coup or were equally unrestrained in their actions (Kent 2009a). This position was echoed in the Canadian representative's statement to the OAS Permanent Council following the coup. As the OAS president was planning a trip to Honduras to press for Zelaya's return, Kent argued that the international community had been too one-sided in its approach, and that '[t]he coup was certainly an affront to the region, but there is a context in which these events happened . . . There has to be an appreciation of the events that led up to the coup' (Lacey and Thompson 2009). Along with the United States, Canada worked against the imposition of OAS sanctions on Honduras and called instead for a weaker review of diplomatic relations (Markey and Rosenberg 2009).

When mediation talks between Zelaya and coup leader Roberto Michelleti broke down several weeks later, Kent abruptly declared that Zelaya should return only after a negotiated settlement had been achieved and when the risk of violence had passed (Kent 2009b). Kent failed to mention, however, that the violence that followed the coup had been perpetrated by the military, not by Zelaya's supporters. By making Zelaya's return conditional on a settlement, Canada lent credibility to an undemocratic government and put pressure on Zelaya to make major concessions to Michelleti. While Canada did not openly support the coup, it did little to challenge the military government and worked instead to undermine Zelaya's claim to power. Canada subsequently has become one of the biggest allies of the post-coup government of Porfirio Lobo, even though his election took place in a context of repression against anti-coup forces and the refusal of international election observers to participate.[16]

Afghanistan

Given the international interests of Canadian capital and the wider militarization of Canadian foreign policy, Canada's intervention in Afghanistan should be viewed in terms of *imperialism*, not *dependency* or *Middle Power internationalism*. The United States certainly exerts influence over policy-makers and political leaders in Canada, but other, more powerful structural features of Canadian capitalism shape and determine Canada's role in the Third World. As we have seen, these variables include the economic and political relations through which Canadian firms and the Canadian state exploit the periphery.

As Kolhatkar and Ingalls (2006) and Ali (2008) point out, the invasion and subsequent occupation of Afghanistan is not just a matter of US strategic interests; NATO has been centrally involved in the Afghanistan campaign from the beginning. The Afghan mission reflects an ongoing effort by the transatlantic alliance to recast itself as an organization with not only the ability but also the right to project collective military power in circumstances where common interests are threatened. It is also an attempt by the United States and NATO to secure a military foothold in a geopolitically important region. Developments in the region – notably the belligerence of Russia and the competitive rise of China – are viewed as security matters by the transatlantic alliance. As a long-time member of the G7 and NATO, the Canadian state has identified the occupation of Afghanistan as an important, if costly, endeavour.

The occupation of Afghanistan also gives hawkish elements among political leaders and policy-makers ammunition against the resonant, if mythical, claim that Canada is first and foremost a peacekeeping nation. The notion of Canada as a peacemaker is the basis for challenges to Canadian militarism by the New Democratic Party and the Council of Canadians, but the war in Afghanistan makes this form of antimilitarism difficult to sustain. As Colonel D. Craig Hilton (2007) argues, '[w]hile the clear articulation of military roles and missions defined in both the International Policy Statement 2005 and its Defence counterpart put a formal end to any suggestion of a peacekeeping *raison d'être* for Canada's military, it is the evolution of Canada's mission in Afghanistan . . . that has utterly shattered the widely-accepted myth of Canada as benign peacekeeper.'

It should be clear from the preceding discussion that Canada's intervention in Afghanistan is not an isolated endeavour, but part of a broader shift in Canadian foreign policy. Along with its allies, Canada supports a global system of imperialism that reproduces economic and political inequalities between the First and Third Worlds. As Canada's political and economic interests in poor countries have grown, the perceived dangers and insecurities of 'failed states,' 'rogue states,' and 'insurgencies' have become the ideological lenses through which policy-makers engage the world.

Canada, in this respect, is not qualitatively different from other imperialist countries. It seeks actively to subordinate the Third World politically and economically, and is not beyond employing state violence to achieve these goals. Outside its own borders Canada may be less experienced than some of its allies at the conquest, occupation, and re-engineering of economic and political structures of foreign nations. But its military interventions in Haiti and Afghanistan reflect Canada's increasing experience in the exercise of imperial domination. As Canada's political, military, and corporate elites have been insisting, Canada needs, in this regard, to be taken seriously on the international stage. Prime Minister Harper has asserted quite plainly that, unless Canada is willing to participate in military actions abroad, it will fail to earn international respect and leadership roles in global politics: 'Countries that cannot or will not make real contributions to global security are not regarded as serious players' (Clark 2008).

The war in Afghanistan needs to be understood in the context of Canada's changing economic relationship with the Third World, and not foremost as a war against terrorism or an attempt to foster liberal forces for human development. The war is a testing ground for the new Canadian imperialism, and is connected to the economic and geopolitical interests of Canadian capital abroad. For this reason, the anti-war movement must address the *capitalist* nature of Canadian foreign policy if it wants to end the current war of empire and prevent future ones.

NOTES

1 My book *Imperialist Canada* (2010) represents an attempt at such an analysis.
2 These figures on CDI to the Third World are from Canada (2003) and Statistics Canada, CANSIM database, tables 376–0051 (a country-specific breakdown of CDI) and 376–0053 (aggregated data for regions). Total CDI in the Third World is taken from the latter table; however, the category that most closely corresponds in the table to the Third World is 'all other foreign countries' – namely, all countries not in the European Union or the Organization for Economic Co-operation and Development (OECD) – and so it is an imperfect account of investment in the Third World. CANSIM table 376–0051 does have specific data for Mexico, which is a member of the OECD, so I added Mexican data to that of table 376–0053's 'all other foreign countries' to get the Third World totals.
3 Data on FDI stock to developing countries is from OECD, International Direct Investment Statistics, 'Direct Investment By Country,' using the 'Total

World, excluding-OECD' and 'Mexico' data sets. Data on GDP are from OECD, 'Stat Extracts,' http://stats.oecd.org/WBOS/index.aspx (accessed October 2008).

4 Third World data are from the 'all other countries' category in Statistics Canada, CANSIM database, table 376–0001, which excludes OECD and EU nations. The estimate of Third World investment income as a proportion of total foreign investment income is conservative, as Mexico, which is an OECD member and a major destination for CDI, is not included.

5 Third World profits are from Statistics Canada, CANSIM database, table 376–0001, 'investment income,' which includes direct, portfolio, and 'other' earnings for countries not in the OECD or European Union. Canadian-based profits are from CANSIM table 187–0001, operating profits, 'total all industries, after tax.' Third World earnings are after tax as well. The comparison is imperfect, as the operating profit methodology includes some writedowns, such as for inventory, while the foreign investment profits, collected on a GDP basis, do not. Canadian-based profits collected on a GDP basis are not after tax.

6 It should be noted that many of these countries have seen significant improvements in national income (if not always a corresponding decline in inequality), and the financial flows to these centres do not simply constitute a drain of wealth from the Third World. For some of these destinations, however, financial capital is then reinvested in other economic developments (such as mining) within the local region.

7 The ten fastest-growing destinations over the period from 1987 to 2007 were, in order, China, Peru, Chile, the Cayman Islands, Barbados, the Bahamas, Colombia, Costa Rica, Mexico, and Argentina.

8 Central Bank of Malaysia, http://www.bnm.gov.my/index.php?ch=109&pg=249&mth=8&yr=2008 (accessed 30 October 2008); Central Bank of the Philippines, http://www.bsp.gov.ph/statistics/spei_new/tab22.htm (accessed October 2008); and Indonesian Central Bank, http://www.bi.go.id/biweb/html/sekiTxt/T3x805.txt (accessed 15 October 2008).

9 See the website of the Afghanistan Investment Support Agency, http://www.aisa.org.af.

10 The list of free trade and foreign investment protection agreements is available on the DFAIT website, http://www.international.gc.ca/trade-agreements-accords-commerciaux/agr-acc/neg_country-pays_region.aspx?lang=eng&view=d.

11 Countries qualify for HIPC relief as a result of arbitrary determinations by the IMF and World Bank of whether or not their debt is 'sustainable.' A country's debt is sustainable if the net present value of the debt is less than

twice as large as the country's export earnings or if annual debt-service payments are less than 20 per cent of export earnings.

12 See the Americas section of CIDA's website, http://www.acdi-cida.gc.ca. Democracy and human rights support also provided the basis for Harper's criticism of Chávez during his trip to Colombia in the summer of 2007 (Freeman 2007).

13 Robinson (2006) dissects the move towards 'democracy promotion' in US foreign policy.

14 See also CIDA, Access to Information, file number A-2007–00124, received 23 November 2007.

15 DFAIT press releases can be found in the 'Media Room' of its website, http://www.international.gc.ca/media/index.aspx?view=d.

16 For a full exploration of Canada's orientation to the Honduran coup forces, see Gordon and Webber (2011).

References

Ali, Tariq. 2008. 'Afghanistan: Mirage of the Good War.' *New Left Review* 50 (March–April): 5–22.

Baril, Maurice. 1999. 'About the Canadian Forces.' Speech to the Huron College History Club, London, ON, 14 October. http://www.forces.gc.ca/site/newsroom/view_news_e.asp?id=452.

Bell, Stewart. 2004. 'Canada is a terrorist haven: CSIS.' *National Post*, 1 March.

Bernard Jr., Prosper. 2006. 'Canada and Human Security: From the Axworthy Doctrine to Middle Power Internationalism.' *American Review of Canadian Studies* 36, no. 2: 233–61.

BIS (Bank for International Settlements). 2004. Committee on the Global Financial System. *Foreign Direct Investment in the Financial Sector of Emerging Market Economies*. Basel, Switzerland: Bank for International Settlements.

Black, David. 2005. 'From Kananaskis to Gleneagles: Assessing Canadian "Leadership" on Africa.' *Behind the Headlines* 62, no. 3: 1–17.

Bond, Patrick. 2006. *Looting Africa: The Economics of Exploitation*. London: Zed Books.

Burgess, Bill. 2000. 'Foreign Direct Investment: Facts and Perceptions about Canada.' *Canadian Geographer* 44, no. 2: 98–113.

Campbell, Bonnie. 2004. 'Peace and Security in Africa and the Role of Canadian Mining Interests: New Challenges for Canadian Foreign Policy.' *Labour, Capital and Society* 37, nos. 1–2: 98–129.

Canada. 1999. Department of Foreign Affairs and International Trade. *Canada and the Future of the WTO*. Ottawa.

–. 2003. Industry Canada. *Trade and Investment Monitor*. Ottawa: Minister of
    Public Works and Government Services.
–. 2004. Natural Resources Canada. *Canadian Mineral Yearbook, 2004*.
    Ottawa.
–. 2005a. Department of National Defence. http://www.forces.gc.ca/site/
    Reports/budget05/back05_e.asp (accessed 1 June 2007).
–. 2005b. 'Canada's International Policy Statement – Defence.' Ottawa: Minis-
    ter of Supply and Services.
–. 2005c. Parliament. House of Commons. Standing Committee on Foreign
    Affairs and International Trade. *Elements of an Emerging Market Strategy for
    Canada*. Ottawa.
–. 2005d. Department of Finance. 'Helping the Poorest: An Update on
    Canada's Debt Relief Efforts.' Ottawa. http://www.fin.gc.ca/toc/2005/
    cdre0105_-eng.asp.
–. 2007a. Natural Resources Canada. *Canadian Mineral Yearbook, 2007*. Ottawa.
–. 2007b. Department of National Defence. *Counter-Insurgency Manual*.
    Ottawa.
–. 2011. Natural Resources Canada. 'Canadian Mining Assets Abroad.' http://
    http://www.nrcan.gc.ca/minerals-metals/publications-reports/3086
    (accessed 23 March 2012).
–. n.d. Department of Foreign Affairs and International Trade. 'Investment:
    Canadian Government Positions and Other Policies, WTO.' http://www.
    international.gc.ca/tna-nac/other/invest-en.asp (accessed 5 September
    2006).
Carroll, William K. 1986. *Corporate Power and Canadian Capitalism*. Vancouver:
    UBC Press.
Chase, Steve. 2008. 'Defence plan to cost $50-billion over 20 years.' *Globe and
    Mail*, 15 May.
Chernos, Saul. 2008. 'One gem of a mission.' *Now*, 20–26 March, 16.
CIDA (Canadian International Development Agency). 2006. 'Canada-Haiti
    Cooperation – Interim Cooperation Framework – Result Summary.'
    Ottawa. http://www.acdi-cida.gc.ca/CIDAWEB/acdicida.nsf?En/
    JUD-61414295-PP8?OpenDocument.
–. 2009. *Statistical Report on ODA, Fiscal Year 2006–2007*. Ottawa. http://www.
    acdi-cida.gc.ca.
Clark, Campbell. 2008. 'Compromise on Afghanistan muffles election drum-
    beat.' *Globe and Mail*, 22 February.
Clarke, John. 2005. 'Bridging the Political and Global Governance Gap: A
    Two-Step Approach to Canadian Foreign Policy.' *Canadian Foreign Policy* 12,
    no. 2: 47–64.

Clarkson, Stephen. 2002. *Uncle Sam and Us: Globalization, Neoconservatism, and the Canadian State*. Toronto: University of Toronto Press.

Cooper, Andrew. 1997. *Canadian Foreign Policy: Old Habits and New Directions*. Scarborough, ON: Prentice Hall, Allyn and Bacon Canada.

Cooper, Andrew, Richard Higgott, and Kim Nossal. 1993. *Relocating Middle Powers: Australia and Canada in a Changing World Order*. Vancouver: UBC Press.

Couture, C. 1998. Speech to the Canadian Defence Association Institute. 14 November. http://www.forces.gc.ca/site/news-nouvelles/news-nou velles-eng.asp?id=444.

David, Charles-Philippe, and Stéphane Roussel. 1998. ' "Middle Power Blues": Canadian Policy and International Security after the Cold War.' *American Review of Canadian Studies* 28, no. 1: 131–56.

Davis, Mike. 2006. *Planet of the Slums*. London: Verso.

Dewitt, David, and John Kirton. 1983. *Canada as a Principal Power: A Study in Foreign Policy and International Relations*. Toronto: John Wiley.

ECLAC (Economic Commission for Latin America and the Caribbean). 2003. *Canada's Trade and Investment with Latin America and the Caribbean*. Santiago, Chile: ECLAC.

–. 2006. *Foreign Investment in Latin America and the Caribbean, 2006*. Santiago, Chile: ECLAC.

Economist. 2006. 'Agricultural Subsidies.' 1 July.

–. 2008. 'The Canadian Connection.' 27 March.

Engler, Yves, and Anthony Fenton. 2005. *Canada in Haiti: Waging War on the Poor Majority*. Halifax, NS: Fernwood.

Fenton, Anthony. 2005–6. ' "Legalized Imperialism": "Responsibility to Protect" and the Dubious Case of Haiti.' *Briarpatch* (December–January). http://briarpatchmagazine.com/articles/view/legalized-imperialism-responsibility-to-protect-and-the-dubious-case-of-hai/.

–. 2009. 'The Revolution Will Not Be Destabilized.' *Dominion*, 3 April. http://www.dominionpaper.ca/articles/2557.

Foster, John. 2008. 'Countries vie for access to Turkmenistan's huge gas deposits.' *Monitor* (Canadian Centre for Policy Alternatives) (June).

Freeman, Alan. 2007. 'PM sells Canada as third market option.' *Globe and Mail*, 18 July.

Globe and Mail. 2010. 'Scotiabank makes move into Uruguay.' 6 December. http://www.theglobeandmail.com/globe-investor/scotiabank-makes-move-into-uruguay/article1826313/ (accessed 8 December 2010).

Golinger, Eva. 2007. *The Chávez Code: Cracking US Intervention in Venezuela.* London: Pluto Press.

Gordon, Todd. 2006. 'Canada, Empire and Indigenous People in the Americas.' *Socialist Studies* 2, no. 1: 47–76.

–. 2010. *Imperialist Canada*. Winnipeg: Arbeiter Ring.

Gordon, Todd, and Jeffery R. Webber. 2008. 'Imperialism and Resistance: Canadian Mining Companies in Latin America.' *Third World Quarterly* 29, no. 1: 63–88.

–. 2011. 'Canada and the Honduran Coup.' *Bulletin of Latin American Research* 30, no. 3: 328–43.

Hallward, Peter. 2008. *Damming the Flood: Haiti, Aristide, and the Politics of Containment*. London: Verso.

Hart, Michael. 2008. *From Pride to Influence: Towards a New Canadian Foreign Policy*. Vancouver: UBC Press.

Harvey, David. 2005. *The New Imperialism*. London: Oxford.

Hilton, D. Craig. 2007. 'Shaping Commitment: Resolving Canada's Strategy Gap in Afghanistan and Beyond.' Carlisle, PA: US Army War College, Strategic Studies Institute. July.

Hoffman, Andy. 2007.'Afghan copper lode a key to renewal?' *Globe and Mail*, 9 March.

Hooey, David. 1998. 'The South as a "Threat"? [Re]Assessing North-South Dimensions of National Security.' *Canadian Journal of Development Studies* 19, no. 3: 461–89.

IMF (International Monetary Fund). 2004. *Evaluation of the IMF's Role in Poverty Reduction Strategy Papers and Poverty Reduction Growth Facility*. Washington, DC.

International Commission on Intervention and State Sovereignty. 2001. *The Responsibility to Protect*. Ottawa: International Development Research Centre.

Investment Executive. 2003. 'Scotiabank signs final Dominican Republic agreement.' 19 September.

Jackson, Andrew. 2007. 'From Leaps of Faith to Hard Landings: Fifteen years of "Free Trade." ' In *Whose Canada? Continental Integration, Fortress North America, and the Corporate Agenda*, ed. R. Grinspun and Y. Shamsie. Montreal; Kingston, ON: McGill-Queen's University Press.

Kent, Peter. 2009a. Statement by Minister Kent on the Situation in Honduras, Ottawa, 28 June.

–. 2009b. Statement by Minister Kent on the Situation in Honduras, Ottawa, 19 July.

Klassen, Jerome. 2009. 'Canada and the New Imperialism: The Economics of a Secondary Power.' *Studies in Political Economy* 83: 163–90.

Kolhatkar, Sonali, and James Ingalls. 2006. *Bleeding Afghanistan: Washington, Warlords, and the Propaganda of Silence*. New York: Seven Stories.

Lacey, Marc, and Ginger Thompson. 2009. 'Envoy prepares to visit Honduras, warning of obstacles.' *New York Times*, 3 July.

Lavoie, François. 2005. 'Canadian Direct Investment in "Offshore Financial Centers."' Analysis in Brief. Cat. 11–621-MIE2005021. Ottawa: Statistics Canada.

Laxer, James. 2008. *Mission of Folly: Canada and Afghanistan*. Toronto: Between the Lines.

Lyon, Peyton, and Tareq Ismael. 1976. *Canada and the Third World*. Toronto: Macmillan of Canada.

Lyon, Peyton, and Brian Tomlin. 1979. *Canada as an International Actor*. Toronto: Macmillan of Canada.

Markey, Patrick, and Mica Rosenberg. 2009. 'Honduran airport bars president's flight home after deadly day of riots.' *Globe and Mail*, 6 July.

McCarthy, Shawn. 2008. 'Would help protect pipeline, Canada says.' *Globe and Mail*, 20 June.

McNally, David. 2006. *Another World Is Possible: Globalization and Anti-Capitalism*. Winnipeg: Arbeiter Ring.

McQuaig, Linda. 2007. *Holding the Bully's Coat: Canada and the US Empire*. Toronto: Doubleday Canada.

Moore, Steve, and Debi Wells. 1975. *Imperialism and the National Question in Canada*. Toronto: Better Read Typesetting.

Morrison, David. 1998. *Aid and Ebb Tide: A History of CIDA and Canadian Development Assistance*. Waterloo, ON: Wilfrid Laurier Press.

National Bank of Kazakhstan. 2009. 'Statistics.' Almaty. http://www.national-bank.kz.

National Bank of the Kyrgyz Republic. 2008. 'Balance of Payments.' Bishkek. http://www.nbkr.kg/balans/Bal_3q_2008_E.pdf.

National Bank of Tajikistan. 2009. 'Report on Private Non-guaranteed External Debt and Foreign Investment of the Republic of Tajikistan for 2008.' Dushanbe. http://www.nbt.tj/en/files/docs/pl_balans/vnesh_dolg_en.pdf.

North, Liisa, Timothy David Clark, and Viviana Patroni, eds. 2006. *Community Rights and Corporate Responsibility: Canadian Mining and Oil Companies in Latin America*. Toronto: Between the Lines.

OAS (Organization of American States). 2009. Special Meeting of the Permanent Council to receive information from the Permanent Mission of

Honduras regarding the risk to the democratic institutional political process and/or the legitimate exercise of political power in the Republic of Honduras, Washington, DC, 26 June. http://www.oas.org/OASpage/videosonde mand/show/video.asp?nCode=09–0168&nCodeDet=2 (accessed 28 June 2009).

Pannier, Bruce. 2008. 'Trans-Afghan Pipeline Discussions Open in Islamabad.' Radio Free Europe/Radio Liberty, 23 April. http://www.rferl.org/content/ article/1109618.html.

Perkins, Tara. 2010. 'CIBC buys stake in Bermuda's Butterfield.' *Globe and Mail*, 3 March.

Pratt, Cranford. 1994. 'Humane Internationalism and Canadian Development Assistance Policies.' In *Canadian International Development Assistance Policies: An Appraisal*, ed. Cranford Pratt. Montreal; Kingston, ON: McGill-Queen's University Press.

Robertson, Grant. 2011. 'Scotiabank buys Banco Colpatria.' *Globe and Mail*, 20 October. http://www.theglobeandmail.com/globe-investor/scotiabank-buys-banco-colpatria/article2207597/ (accessed 20 October 2011).

Robinson, Bill. 2011. 'Canadian Military Spending 2010–11.' Ottawa: Canadian Centre for Policy Alternatives. March.

Robinson, William. 2006. 'Promoting Polyarchy in Latin America: The Oxymoron of "Market Democracy."' In *Latin America after Neoliberalism: Turning the Tide in the 21st Century*, ed. Eric Hershberg and Fred Rosen. New York: New Press.

Silcoff, Sean. 2007. 'Quietly, Scotia builds an empire.' *National Post*, 3 August.

SIPI (Stockholm International Peace Research Institute). 2008. 'The 15 Major Spender Countries in 2007.' Stockholm. http://www.sipri.org (accessed 11 July 2008).

Social Justice Committee. 2005. 'Canada's representatives at the IMF agree to suspend G7 debt relief plan for six.' Montreal. http://www.s-j-c.net/ English/news/IMFsuspendsdebtplan.html (accessed 1 December 2006).

Statistics Canada. 2008. *Canada's International Investment Position*. Ottawa. http://www.40.statcan.ca/l01/cst01/econ08.htm.

Tomlinson, Brian. 2000–1. 'Tracking Changes in Canadian ODA: New Directions for Poverty Reduction? Canadian NGO Reflections.' *International Journal* 56, no. 1: 54–72.

UNCTAD (United Nations Conference on Trade and Development). 2008. *World Investment Report 2008*. New York: United Nations.

Waldie, Paul. 2006. 'Scotiabank in an acquisitive mood.' *Globe and Mail*, 30 August.

Warnock, John. 2007. *Creating a Failed State: The US and Canada in Afghanistan.*
    Halifax, NS: Fernwood.
Willis, Andrew. 2007. 'No mergers here, banks look abroad.' *Globe and Mail,*
    18 January.
Wood, Ellen Meiksins. 2003. *The Empire of Capital.* London: Verso.

8

Fewer Illusions: Canadian
Foreign Policy since 2001

GREG ALBO

It is now more than a decade since Canada first deployed troops to Afghanistan under the Liberal government of Jean Chrétien. The mobilization of the Canadian Forces and, indeed, the remaking of security and defence policies since 9/11 have generated intense public and academic debate about Canada's foreign policy. The coming to power of the Conservative government of Stephen Harper in January 2006, with an agenda of deepening ties with the United States, has crystallized the dissension. Across a phalanx of foreign policy fronts the Canadian state appears to be setting a radical new course: embracing deeper integration with the United States; shifting from multilateralism to bilateralism; neglecting traditional zones of interest in Europe and Africa in favour of a focus on Latin America; openly buttressing US policies on Palestine and the Middle East, in contrast to the so-called policy of balance; and departing from developmentalism and peacekeeping to take up militarism and imperialism (Grinspun and Shamsie 2007; Bow and Lennox 2008; Hampson and Heinbecker 2010).

For Conservatives these policies have brought a 'new realism' to Canadian statecraft after years of drift and misguided adventures. Liberals, in contrast, lament what they see as a break from the internationalism of the Pearson-Trudeau-Chrétien regimes. Indeed, the Liberal leadership, from Paul Martin and Stéphane Dion to Michael Ignatieff and Bob Rae, has defended a policy of 'balance' – sending troops to Afghanistan and the navy into the Persian Gulf, but not joining the 'coalition of the willing' in Iraq or adopting ballistic missile defence. For its part the New Democratic Party (NDP) has criticized the drift away from peacekeeping and multilateralism in support of US policies to remake the global order. Although the NDP initially backed the dispatching of troops to

Afghanistan, it has since taken a calibrated opposition to the mission, largely on the technocratic concern that developmental and diplomatic objectives have been superseded by military ones.

The differences between parliamentary forces have had their correlates in academic discussions. The conventional narrative is one in which Canadian foreign policy is either dependent on a world power such as the United States or sufficiently independent to support a more regulated – even 'ethical' – world order as a 'non-imperialist' power. For 'realists' the new foreign policy is simply a matter of defending the nation from new threats such as terrorism, rogue states, and weapons of mass destruction.

These debates have roots in the historical evolution of Canadian foreign policy and in the strategies by which Canada has navigated the politics of empire. From Confederation to the 1930s, the key struggle for Canadian statecraft was simply to gain recognition of an 'independent interest' via 'functional representation' in matters of global importance (Eayrs 1975; Nossal 1997, 53–4). Having achieved such independence in 1931, Canada was then forced to engage the new structure of power emerging from the Second World War. That war altered the system of relations between states and the means by which the Great Powers exercised hegemony. At the end of the war, Canada developed a 'Middle Power' strategy of mediating conflicts and supporting multilateralism in the Cold War system (Gordon 1966; Neufeld and Whitworth 1997). At the same time the Middle Power project institutionalized a set of relations with Washington. In particular, it consisted of formalizing the economic and military interdependence of the continent, collaborating with the United States in building a liberalized international trading system, defending North American capitalism from real or imagined Soviet threats and internal socialist movements, prioritizing détente and 'systemic peace' in the Cold War system, cultivating a 'quiet diplomacy' around points of difference with the United States, and contributing to multilateral institutions where Cold War tactics could be debated and compromises achieved (Neufeld 1995).

Since the early 1980s, however, the Middle Power terminology has fallen to the wayside. This is partly due to the popular notion that globalization has 'levelled' the capitalist world economy and empowered new state and non-state actors, and partly as a consequence of calculations – proven to be misplaced – of a decline in US power and a rise in the foreign policy capacities of Europe and Japan. The Middle Power terminology has also declined in recognition that Canada confronts two primary limitations – namely, its deep linkages to the US economy and the 'superintendent' power of Washington over the capitalist world system (Panitch and Gindin 2005; Stein and Lang 2007, chap. 3).

For 'realists' it has become of little importance whether Canada is defined as a 'Middle' or 'Principal' power. The calculus is still the trade-off between the 'economic security' gained through 'deep integration' with the United States versus the 'autonomy' lost through the disciplines of free trade agreements. In this perspective, the 'rule of law' applies equally to both states, just as the 'law of value' applies with equanimity in the market. In practice, however, the disciplines of integration fall asymmetrically on Canada as the lesser power (although realists like to argue that 'national sovereignty' is enhanced through the increased prosperity of cross-border trade) (Campbell and Finn 2006; McDougall 2006). Nevertheless realists endorse and welcome the incorporation of US security and defence strategies into Canadian foreign policy as a buttress of the 'national interest' (Kirton 2006; Rempel 2006; Granatstein 2007).

'Liberal internationalists' in Canada have always accommodated the same trade-off between economic security and US hegemony. They have done so, for example, through the bilateralism of the North American Aerospace Defense Command (NORAD) and the Auto Pact, and through the multilateralism of the UN system. They insist, however, that Canadian foreign policy go beyond the interests of economic security. Today the imperatives of economic integration need to be 'balanced' by 'human security' fostered through multilateral institutions. In this perspective an arsenal of 'soft power' doctrines must be integrated into the foreign policies of 'agenda-setting' powers. These doctrines include democracy promotion, peace-building, the 'responsibility to protect,' rebuilding failed states, enhancing civil society, and so on – in other words a foreign policy program that places development and diplomacy alongside defence in building 'human security' globally. States with a history of Middle Power diplomacy are typically said to be well placed to advance such an agenda (Axworthy 2003; Welsh 2004).

For those in the social democratic tradition, Canadian foreign policy must distance itself from the unilateralism of Washington and create new institutions to offset the many 'failures' of the market. In this perspective, globalization reflects a permanent shift in the distribution of power outside the 'container' of states and towards a 'global civil society.' Capitalist market relations, moreover, now exist in a network of flows between different nodes and scales in the world market, with non-state actors permeating state boundaries. As a result foreign policy doctrines need to be embedded in a project of 'global governance' or 'cosmopolitan democracy.' For social democrats multilateral institution-building is fundamental to closing the 'democratic deficit' in the world order and to advancing redistributional politics. In falling more deeply into economic dependence on the United States and supporting its practice of pre-emptive warfare, Canada is said to have lost its capacity to engage the new social forces and agendas necessary to stabilize global order (Byers 2007; Beier and Wylie 2010).

The transformations in Canadian foreign policy over the past decade – what some have described as a 'revolution in military affairs' or a 'revolution in foreign policy' (Moens 2008; Sloan 2010) – has challenged these traditional formulations. In the process popular illusions about Canada's role in the world have been shattered. The most enduring mythology has typically invoked an image of the Canadian state as a peacekeeper that mediates conflicts and secures justice in the world order. In this mythology it is often claimed that Canada enhances its own sovereignty and leverage through bilateral arrangements with the United States, while at the same time using that leverage to coax the United States into multilateral and continental forms of cooperation. The illusion of this strategy is that the US-Canada alliance is one of equality, with positive consequences for the world system and the 'nation.' Behind this illusion, however, is the reality of US preeminence and of Canadian foreign policy as a secondary form of imperialism, linked to US primacy strategies and to 'dominant class interests' at home (Pratt 1983; Gowan 1999).

With this in mind, this chapter develops a critical perspective on Canadian foreign policy since 2001. It begins by recognizing the unchallenged pre-eminence of the United States in the world market and geopolitical system, which has allowed it to pursue a strategy of 'global primacy.' Canada, however, occupies a secondary position in the North American bloc and the wider world system (Klassen 2009). In this context Canadian foreign policy practices have adopted a dualtrack strategy of 'stratified multilateralism': on the one hand, using a degree of policy autonomy in pursuit of diplomatic initiatives and extra-market state assistance for the internationalization of Canadian capital and, on the other, facilitating and buttressing US and western hegemony over the world order.

Since 9/11 the reassertion of US primacy has encouraged a radical realignment of Canadian foreign policy. This shift is often described in terms of 'Canadian dependence' or 'continentalism.' These notions, however, are blind to the formal sovereignty of the Canadian state, the institutional autonomy of the foreign policy apparatus, and the specific features of Canadian militarism and imperialism. As a result the restructuring of Canadian foreign policy is better understood as a strategy of 'cooperative specialization,' following from Canada's location as a secondary power in the US-led 'Empire of Capital' (Wood 2005). The Canadian intervention in Afghanistan – with its '3D' matrix of defence, development, and diplomacy – has been a key terrain for refashioning foreign policy practices in the form of a 'disciplinary militarism.' Indeed, the war in Afghanistan has been the principle means by which Canada has realigned the foreign policy apparatus for military interventions in developing countries. This remaking of the Canadian state as an ally to empire has, however, been strongly contested by social movements, which advance an internationalist and anti-imperialist agenda. In addressing these issues this chapter charts the political-economic development of Canadian foreign policy since 2001.

US Geopolitical Strategies

International relations cannot be examined apart from the world market. Economic exchanges and political relations between states are formally carried out between equals – under the 'law of value' and the 'rule of law' – in the interstate system (Albo 2004; Wood 2005). The world market, however, is characterized by 'uneven and combined development,' and the world order is constituted by a hierarchy of states. The study of international relations, then, is the study of how imperialism – the structure of political and economic domination in the world system – operates between formally sovereign entities. For this reason foreign policy analysis must focus on the ways in which states navigate the economic and geopolitical contradictions of the capitalist world system. In particular it must study the way in which states and capitalist classes interact with global patterns of accumulation and trade and of military and diplomatic conflict (Cox 1987; van der Pijl 2007).

This point of departure highlights a central contradiction in the capitalist world system – that between the internationalization of capital and the political stratification of states. A core issue of international relations is the means by which the circuits of capital penetrate other states in a multiplicity of money forms, including loans, direct investments, currency holdings, and so forth. This poses a contradiction: the law of value regulating market competition and exchanges is international, while state sovereignty and institutions are national – international state institutions either being a specific functional allocation of state capacities or forums for negotiation between states. The foreign policy practices of capitalist states, therefore, are preoccupied with the legal protection of private property rights internationally, the extra-market institutions – including the coercive powers of the state – that protect and advance the internationalization of capital, and military-diplomatic capacities to navigate the coercive and consensual alliances of the interstate system through which capitalist competition takes place.

If the globalization of capital incorporates states into a common mode of production, it distributes the profits unequally among them. The world market thus turns around a central contradiction: that between the economic integration of states through the cross-penetration of capital and the geopolitical rivalries through which economic inequalities are expressed. Paradoxically, as capital internalizes, its dependence on the political and institutional capacities of the territorial state increases, pushing interstate relations into a more prominent place in the array of state apparatuses.

Because of this contradiction the capitalist world market has always depended on the exercise of hegemony – on a situation in which 'a dominant state leads the system of states in a desired direction and, in so doing, is widely perceived as pursuing a general interest' (Arrighi and Silver 1999, 27). For example, the appeal of US hegemony rests not merely on economic and military preponderance in the world order, but also on the understanding by the US state that, as capitalism becomes universalized as a regulator of socio-economic relations and the interstate system, a 'rules-based' system can provide a 'public good' for all capitalist states and enhance US primacy. Today this primacy is evident in the US-led management of international economic regulations, in the creation of US-centred security alliances and protectorates, and in its claims for special rights and privileges as the global hegemon (Gowan 2004). As a result primacy does not mean dispensing with multilateralism. On the contrary, other states accept US leadership, and the United States depends on other states to provide support through a network of military posts and ideological alliances. This has formed the basis for the 'stratified multilateralism' under US hegemony to which Canada has adhered.

US hegemony over the capitalist world market was firmly established by 1945. It was achieved by the overwhelming power of US capitalism globally and by the domination of US capitalists over the state apparatus at home (Kolko and Kolko 1972). This internal balance of class power underpinned and motivated the Cold War division of international relations between the Soviet Union and the United States. In fact, it was the logic of capital that impelled the external agenda of US foreign policy (Williams [1959] 2009). The primary goal was the extension of capitalist social relations in a rules-based international framework guided by the precepts of US finance and production. This agenda was formalized in the Bretton Woods institutions of the International Monetary Fund (IMF) and the World Bank and in many other economic and geopolitical bodies.

The internationalization of capital was also supported by the building of multiple security zones. US foreign policy strategies were designed to support the free trade of resources and the global expansion of capitalism. This meant acceptance of Washington-led initiatives to defend and expand the economic space of capitalism diplomatically and militarily, affirmation of the US nuclear deterrent with its first- and final-strike capacity, and, within the confines of formal state sovereignty, allowing the US government territorial access to pursue these objectives via a string of military bases. The Pax Americana system of alliances was anchored in western Europe and East Asia, but was built on the hemispheric foundation of the Monroe Doctrine and on the Open Door policy towards China. At the same time the number of countries claiming a 'special relationship' with the United States multiplied as security alliances spread. In each case the United States gained access and sway over other capitalist states, whose geopolitical and security policies in effect internalized US interests. These allies varied not according to their democratic credentials (for the United States was just as fond of dictators), but in terms of their opposition to socialism and their degree of integration with the Empire of Capital. These arrangements carried the illusion of collective security pacts among equals, but the real balance of power allowed the United States to exercise unipolar capacities. In fact the multilateral system was stratified by regional zones: European integration through NATO and a West German hub; East Asian integration via Japanese subcontracting and US military bases; an equilibrium of dependence in the Middle East formed around Saudi Arabia, Iran, and Israel; and North American integration of capital and commodity markets (Clark-Jones 1987). This multilateral system provided the framework for what Harry Magdoff (1978) called 'imperialism without colonies' – a series of protectorates incorporating US interests via the law of value and the rule of law. In this new structure of empire geopolitical competition was contained, while economic competition was enabled.

The post-war American empire had a structural weakness, however, which was fully exposed in the early 1970s. The world market depended upon a steady supply of US dollars – through capital exports or current account deficits – to maintain growth and liquidity. These capital flows led to a growing interdependence of the Triad zones of Europe, North America, and Japan, but they also increased the competitiveness of firms in Europe and Japan, and, by 1971, they had eroded the international monetary system based on the US-dollar-exchange standard. The post-war system of international economic regulation therefore entered a period of turbulence that destabilized the rate of growth globally and the capacity for US power projection. In this context the United States confronted various forms of political and military contestation – notably in Vietnam, Central America, and Iran, and calls from the Non-Aligned Movement for a 'new international economic order' – that threatened the old hierarchy and alignments of the Cold War (Heller 2006).

Since the turmoil of the 1970s the geopolitical context of the world market has been radically transformed. Although this period can now be seen as the formative years of neoliberal globalization under a new US hegemony, it was marked by different phases, contradictions, and rivalries in world order. In a sense the United States turned the crisis into an advantage (Gowan 1999; Grandin 2006). For example, in the 1970s, the United States imposed the dollar as the international fiat currency anchored by the depth of the US Treasury bill as a 'risk-free' haven in which to hold reserves. This, in turn, allowed the United States to play a decisive role in setting the rules of the 'Washington Consensus' between the Treasury, the IMF, and the World Bank. In the early 1980s, the United States initiated a military build-up against the Soviet Union, reinforcing the dependence of other capitalist centres on US security pacts. The emergence of neoliberalism was thus a means to reassert US hegemony and to address questions of US competitiveness, foremost by strengthening the global position of Wall Street (Gowan 1999). These tactics undermined the 'Third Option' efforts of some European and

Canadian governments to pursue more independent economic policies and to form an alternate approach to collective security.

The Cold War system was shredded at the end of the 1980s with the collapse of the Soviet bloc and the explicit turn towards capitalism in China. The construction of new regional alliances and international trade agreements – notably the European Union, the North American Free Trade Agreement (NAFTA), and the World Trade Organization (WTO) – gained momentum through the 1990s. These economic and political alliances both responded to and fostered the internationalization of capital. In this context the US strategy was to maintain primacy and to manage the globalization of capitalist production. As Simon Bromley argues with respect to oil markets, 'the United States has used its military power to fashion a geopolitical order that provides the political underpinnings for its preferred model of the world economy . . . The power of the US state is deployed, not just to protect the particular interests of the United States' consumption needs and US firms, but rather to create the general preconditions for a world oil market' (2005, 254). Beyond this, the US strategy was to expand global capitalism and reinforce the 'Washington Consensus' on financial liberalization (Helleiner 1994).

It is a striking fact that the end of the Cold War did not lead the United States to dismantle its military empire and regional alliances – suggesting that these had less to do with the 'Soviet threat' and more to do with US power and the projection of capitalism. Indeed, the 'strategy of enlargement' under the Bush I and Clinton administrations extended US military deployments. It even became common across the political spectrum to speak of a 'new American empire.' Interstate relations were again defined, in the first instance, by particular relations to Washington. In this context the Pentagon increasingly dominated the making and administration of US foreign policy. This dominance was symbolized by the development of five command structures spread across the world, combining military and political roles and organizing literally hundreds of overseas bases (Johnson 2004).

In short, a new American empire emerged out of the debris of the Cold War system. This empire was not a flashback to the British system of colonies, but a particular 'Empire of Capital' operating through the law of value in the world market and (ostensibly) the rule of law in the nation-state system. At the same time the absence of any check on US power, such as that offered previously by the Soviet Union, meant that US governments were more able to use 'disciplinary militarism' to expand primacy and to enforce property rights (Ali 2004; Bennis 2006). In the 1990s such a strategy was evident in Panama, Iraq, Afghanistan, the former Yugoslavia, Colombia, Haiti, Somalia, and Sudan. In each of these cases the United States deployed a new set of pretexts – from 'antiterrorism' and 'counternarcotics' to 'human rights' and 'democracy' – for waging war or intervening in developing countries.

With this in mind it is important to recognize that 9/11 radicalized, rather than transformed, US efforts at re-establishing primacy. The attacks on New York and Washington provided an opportunity for the United States to place the strategy of primacy in a new set of security doctrines. The attacks also paved the way for the further extension of US military capabilities, most importantly over the oil supplies of the Middle East and Central Asia. The new US agenda was enshrined in the 2002 'National Security Strategy,' which articulated the 'Bush Doctrine' of preventative warfare. This strategy statement warned that US 'forces will be strong enough to dissuade any potential adversaries from pursuing a military build-up in hope of surpassing, or equalling, the power of the United States . . . In exercising our leadership . . . we will be prepared to act apart when our interests and unique responsibilities require' (United States 2002, 30–1). In other words it claimed a permanent right of primacy and a rationale for the United States to act without sanction – a form of American exceptionalism – from multilateral institutions, particularly the UN Security Council.

The remaking of US foreign policy in terms of a globally assertive national interest meant an even greater willingness to act unilaterally than had been the case in the past, when Cold War politics compelled nominal consultation with key allies. The dedication to primacy motivated the wars in Afghanistan and Iraq, both of which were fought without the sanction of the UN Security Council. At the same time the United States became more aggressive in the governance of the world market, as in the scuttling of the Doha Round of WTO negotiations and the pursuit of bilateral trade agreements. In this arena the United States has been willing to adjust neoliberal doctrines in pursuit of its own trade and currency interests (Callinicos 2009, chap. 5).

Neither the Democratic victory in the congressional elections of 2006 nor the presidential election of Barack Obama in 2008 meant a turn away from US primacy objectives. In fact, between 2006 and 2010, the Democratic majority in Congress funded and expanded the wars in Iraq and Afghanistan. For his part President Obama endorsed the

Pentagon's plan for a 'surge' in Afghanistan, and expanded the 'war on terror' into Pakistan, Somalia, and Yemen. Part of this strategy was articulated by the Iraq Study Group, whose 2006 bipartisan report called for a repositioning of US forces in the Middle East, for negotiation with a wider set of internal Iraqi forces, and for tactical deployments of special forces to stabilize the Iraqi government. This logic is currently present in the US troop surge in Afghanistan and in recent discussions with the Taliban under the Obama administration (Green 2010; Dombey 2011). In both cases US strategy has been reworked to accommodate certain factors and powerbrokers in the region, but in no way has it abandoned the goals of primacy and hegemony.

It needs to be underlined that the so-called rogue states of the region – from Iraq and Afghanistan to Iran and Syria – want to normalize their relations with the global capitalist order. The ruling classes in these states would be quite happy to have greater freedom to pursue neoliberal strategies with the support of the international economic agencies. US policy, however, is to incorporate these states into global capitalism on US terms, or in ways that expand and support US dominance in the region. As it is, a heightening of chaos in Iraq or a messy withdrawal from Afghanistan would signal only a localized defeat for US strategy. The US position in the Middle East and Eurasia would still be far ahead of where it was in 1991 in terms of military alliances and bases.

In any case it would be a mistake to see any such defeats as entailing a fundamental recasting of the US primacy strategy and its operational modalities. With the US state pushing ahead on other fronts and with both US political parties in favour of militarism and imperialism, there is no alternate strategy forthcoming inside the United States. Moreover the European Union has neither the will nor the capacity to offer any alternate world order. A parallel point can be made with respect to the regulation of the world market. Since the financial crisis erupted in 2008, the United States and other capitalist centres have stabilized the banking system, shifted the credit crisis into the public sector, and sustained neoliberal policy orientations. It is not self-evident that neoliberalism still offers a framework for global accumulation or a vehicle for integrating the different zones of the capitalist world market. But it remains clear that, even with the rise of China and other East Asian economies, the United States remains the preponderant power and the only one able to act globally. The ruling blocs in the central zones of capitalism remain quite interdependent with the United States, even

if they are competitive rivals for market shares and have no model
for remaking the world economy. It would be ludicrous to rule out an
evolution to a multipolar world, but in this phase of capitalism it is still
the strategy of US primacy that sets the agenda of interstate relations
and the strictures of foreign policy in allied states.

Canada and World Order

The US strategy for remaking interstate relations over the period of
neoliberal globalization has had serious implications for Canada's role
in world order. The new strategies by which Canada operates internationally must be understood not simply in terms of shifts in policy or
personnel within the state, but also in terms of Canada's shifting position in global structures of power. For this reason the study of Canadian
foreign policy must begin with the patterns of 'uneven interdependence' in the world economy and nation-state system. By examining
the forms of 'stratified multilateralism' through which Canada works
globally, we can better understand the transformation of Canadian
foreign policy since 2001.

To begin it is important to recognize how economic contradictions
across the world market have heightened the importance of multilateral institutions such as the IMF, the WTO, and NATO. Such institutions have been critical for the management of economic imbalances
and geopolitical rivalries, as well as for the exercise of US primacy. In
the case of Canada the 'uneven interdependence' of the world market
is experienced first and foremost on a regional scale. Structural imbalances between the United States and Canada have reinforced regional
institutions such as NAFTA and NORAD. These institutions subordinate Canada to the aims of US foreign policy, but they also advance or
secure an independent set of economic and political interests. In fact it
is through this system of 'stratified multilateralism' that the Canadian
state maintains a secondary position in the American empire.

The neoliberal agenda has also produced an interpenetration of
capital between states – in particular, new forms of trade, finance, investment, and profit repatriation. At the global scale the internationalization of capital has occurred through a particular structure of flows,
which are concentrated in and between the Triad blocs and anchored
by Wall Street and the US Treasury. Canada's integration into this
global structure of flows has been through the North American bloc.
The preferential trading arrangements of NAFTA, for example, have

supported the internationalization of Canadian capital. Through new forms of cross-border trade, investment, and production, the Canadian corporate elite have found a material interest in 'deep integration' of the continent. Despite NAFTA's many failures the Canadian state has defended the project of regional integration as the framework through which Canadian capital expands globally (Clarkson 2002; Campbell and Finn 2006; Klassen 2009).

The same dynamics are evident in the reorganization of state apparatuses. The period of neoliberalism has witnessed an increase in the relative power of military and security structures inside states, since the globalization of capital depends upon a military and security infrastructure for the protection and projection of transnational property rights. In Canada this combination of economic and geopolitical interests has produced an internal realignment of the state, with military and security structures absorbing new funds and resources. For a secondary power such as Canada, this military and security agenda takes the form of a 'cooperative specialization' with US imperialism. The material foundation for this new policy or strategy is the internationalization of capital through NAFTA. The 'economic security' of NAFTA for the Canadian capitalist class has become directly connected to 'North American security' and thus 'imperial security' (McQuaig 2007; Hart 2008, chap. 5). This fusion of economic and geopolitical interests has made untenable the independent space for Canadian foreign policy that once existed during the Cold War. In the present there is little room for Canada to specialize in peacekeeping or cooperate in conflict mediation, or to carve particular Canadian positions in relation to independent states in the Third World, as Canada once claimed, for example, towards China, Cuba, and some African states.

In the 1990s the Liberal minister of foreign affairs, Lloyd Axworthy, attempted to reinvent the 'cooperative specialization' between Canada and the United States through 'soft power' methods such as the 'human security' agenda. This attempt to reposition Canadian foreign policy was, however, still-born. The logic of neoliberalism and US primacy closed off any attempts at embedding norms in international relations and at finding 'autonomy' in foreign policy decision-making. At the same time the liberal internationalist doctrines that Canada sponsored – in particular, the 'responsibility to protect' – became little more than vehicles for US-led interventions and policies, which themselves violated international laws and any semblance of 'human security.' Indeed the arbitrariness of their invocation (at the behest of the United States and the West itself) gave resonance to the critique that these doctrines formed little more than a pretext for a 'human rights imperialism' (Bartholomew and Breakspear 2004).

For all of these reasons Canada swiftly adapted to the US strategy of primacy after 2001. In line with historical patterns the United States exercised primacy in establishing the basic orientation of Canadian foreign policy, with Canada adjusting its state apparatuses and national security doctrines to US norms. Within these parameters Canada offered particular foreign policy specializations, including legal and policy supports for neoliberal trade agreements, Arctic sovereignty and circumpolar relations, diplomatic and development supports for military interventions, police and security sector training for counter-insurgency wars, and special forces deployments in Afghanistan and other 'failed states.'

The key point is that Canadian foreign policy reacted to the global structures of power linked to US primacy objectives and the asymmetries of the world market. As a secondary power tightly integrated with US capitalism, the Canadian state was impelled to internalize the military and security doctrines of Washington. This realignment linked Canada more closely to the US strategy of primacy in the Middle East, Afghanistan, and beyond.

Recasting Canadian Foreign Policy

Before 2001 the international branches of the Canadian state already incorporated neoliberal norms and US primacy strategies into their organizational structures. However, with the United States' revamping of security measures after 9/11, a further reorganization of the Canadian state took place, linking national security to continental integration and a forward military force projection. This structural transformation was organized and directed by the central agencies of the state without public mandate through election manifestos or extensive parliamentary debate. The core decision was to incorporate 'imperial security' norms directly into the Canadian state, and thus to pattern Canada's administrative and policy response after Washington's. The new framework of US foreign policy – the nascent 'war on terror' – quickly informed the international strategies of the Department of National Defence (DND), the Department of Foreign Affairs and International Trade (DFAIT), the intelligence and security services, and the Prime Minister's Office (PMO) (Lennox 2007).

For Canada the 'war on terror' meant first accepting US 'threat assessments' of world order. The key operable threat to Canada, however, was not the risk of external violence or internal subversion, but
the fear of US border controls inhibiting the bidirectional flow of trade.
Such controls might disrupt the internationalization of Canadian capital and the interpenetration of the two states. In this context the Canadian state recognized the continental relationship as the means by
which it preserves a secondary position in the world order and, therefore, the necessity of following US dictates and doctrines in matters
of foreign policy. In fact in recasting its foreign policy after 9/11, the
Canadian state had the support of a wide range of economic interests –
notably the Canadian Council of Chief Executives and the C.D. Howe
Institute (Gabriel and MacDonald 2006, 94). The Canadian corporate
elite were particularly concerned about export markets, but they also
identified an opportunity to accelerate the project of 'deep integration'
of the continent. As a consequence there was broad support among corporate and political elites for reshaping the foreign policy strategy of
'cooperative specialization' with US imperialism. To this end Canadian
governments sought to increase the operational capacity of the military,
to subordinate other international activities to concerns of national and
continental security, and to reorganize the administrative apparatus of
the state accordingly. It is difficult to catalogue the full array of changes
in Canadian state structures and foreign policy doctrines that followed,
but one can identify several key features here.

First, in the immediate aftermath of 9/11, security and military services were positioned at the apex of the state and given central prominence in both the PMO and the Privy Council Office. In organizational
terms this meant implementing a new security agenda that kept pace
with US developments, while warding off any disruptions to North
American economic integration. To this end Canada coordinated a response to the terrorist attacks by establishing an Ad Hoc Cabinet Committee on Public Security and Anti-Terrorism, an Anti-Terrorism Plan,
and the mobilization of CF-18 fighter jets to patrol shared airspace
with the United States. An astonishing set of administrative and policy
changes quickly followed. At the core of the state an unprecedented
emphasis was given to security: a new National Security Committee was formed in cabinet; budgetary increases were granted for all
agencies involved in policing, antiterrorism, and security work; border
administration and security were thoroughly overhauled; and nearly
$8 billion was allocated for Canada's 'war on terror.' Furthermore, in

2001, a new Anti-terrorism Act altered ten different statutes and ratified two UN conventions on terrorism. The act widened the definition
of terrorism, the scope for police investigation, and the basis for issu-
ing security certificates for detaining and deporting foreign nationals.
It also supported a range of measures to increase surveillance of Canadian residents and allowed for the 'preventative detention' of terrorist
suspects and Canadian citizens and for an extension of the Official Se-
crets Act (Roach 2002; Lennox 2007, 1024).

Similarly the Smart Border Declaration and Action Plan, introduced
in coordination with the United States in 2001, increased funds and
powers for policing borders and airports. The new border security
agenda included special screening measures such as the NEXUS program; the introduction of new technologies to manage border security,
including biometric identifiers; coordination with the United States on
immigration and refugee processing, including third-country exemptions; special security screening procedures for commercial traffic (the
FAST program); joint US-Canada customs teams at key ports of entry;
the upgrading of port and border infrastructure; increased numbers of
border patrol agents; the right of aircraft operators to share passenger
information with foreign states; increased policing and detention capacities at ports and border crossings; and the creation of a new air
security agency (Canada 2003; Drache 2004, chap. 1).

Alongside these changes Canada at once deployed troops to Afghanistan and made available Canadian frigates in the Persian Gulf as
a direct contribution to the US-led 'war on terror.' As well there was
an immediate increase in the military budget, particularly for the JTF2
Special Forces engaged in rapid deployment operations. These measures were the initial steps in wider negotiations between Canada and
the United States to extend continental security into a de facto 'Fortress
North America' through joint military strategies, the coordination of
intelligence, and the synchronization of border management. To support these changes a special federal budget in December 2001 allocated
$7.7 billion to 'fighting terrorism.'

Second, the architecture of the Canadian state was redesigned significantly to give institutional prominence, permanency, and additional
organizational breadth to the new security measures and foreign policy
stance. National security and defence issues, for example, were given
particular prominence in the political and bureaucratic centres of the
state. This was done by strengthening the security and defence committees and secretariats in the PMO and Privy Council Office, by raising the

profile of Canada-US relations in Parliament, and by giving the Canadian ambassador in Washington access to the US cabinet. The upshot of these developments was a new standing for the Canadian Forces and DND relative to DFAIT and the Canadian International Development Agency (CIDA) in setting out Canadian foreign policy positions (Regehr and Whelan 2004; Daudelin and Schwanen 2008).

Furthermore, under the Public Safety Act, a new Department of Public Safety and Emergency Preparedness was established in 2003 in parallel with the US Department of Homeland Security. The mandate of the new department was to integrate national policing, security, border issues, prisons, and emergency measures, and to ensure appropriate coordination with matching US agencies. The institutional changes were sweeping. A new security apparatus was created, including an Integrated Threat Assessment Centre under the Canadian Security Intelligence Service (CSIS); Integrated Border Enforcement Teams and Integrated National Security Teams, linking Canadian policing and border agencies to their US counterparts; new coordination between CSIS and the US Central Intelligence Agency; new capacities for border integration via shared databases, coordination of refugee processing, and plans for biometric screening; the creation of marine security operations centres; and extensive cross-border cooperation among all departments having either a security or a borders dimension in their mandates. In effect, Public Safety Canada became a 'central agency' responsible for reviewing and addressing government security operations, US security concerns, and a wide range of new operational practices to embed day-to-day surveillance mechanisms across the state and Canadian society (Sokolsky 2004).

Third, a new framework for foreign policy was hammered out to guide strategic thinking, administrative reorganization, and military and diplomatic relations. The Chrétien government's *Securing an Open Society: Canada's National Security Policy* (Canada 2004) moved away from Axworthy's 'human security' agenda, yet also distanced itself from certain elements of the Bush Doctrine in defence of multilateral consultations. At the same time it affirmed US security concerns and positions, and committed Canada to meeting the new US security requirements. *Canada's International Policy Statement* (Canada 2005a) released by the Martin government and the *Waco Declaration on a Security and Prosperity Partnership of North America* (Canada 2005c) further aligned Canada with US security and economic concerns.

The Harper government has largely left these documents fall by the wayside, but it would be a mistake to dismiss them as irrelevant to understanding Canadian foreign policy over the rest of this period. The Liberal foreign policy documents have provided a reference point for mediating foreign policy debates across the minority Parliaments of 2005 to 2010. The Harper government has also maintained the administrative changes undertaken by the Liberal governments of Chrétien and Martin; the Conservatives have mainly consolidated the trend towards executive control by making the PMO the fulcrum for security and foreign policy decision-making. The Harper government has primarily sought to convey that Canadian foreign policy should be aligned more directly with US security concerns and imperial agendas, and it has done so across several key policy areas, from adopting US positions on Palestine and Lebanon to opposing 'left' reform governments in Latin America. The Harper government also has pushed ahead with the Fortress North America agenda, notably placing Arctic sovereignty and security within this framework, albeit through a 'Canada First' discourse (Coates et al. 2008; Hampson and Heinbecker 2010).

The Canadian military has also been systematically renovated in its organization and operational capabilities. Although Canada did not participate directly in the war on Iraq, by many tallies it was the third-largest contributor after the United States and the United Kingdom. While the Chrétien government had already begun to expand military budgets, the Martin government pledged in 2005 a $13 billion increase over five years. The first Harper budget of 2006 pledged an additional $5 billion, and real expenditure increases followed the next year as well. The 2008 budget went further and raised defence spending for fiscal year 2008/9 to $18.8 billion, including an automatic annual defence spending escalator of 2 per cent. Currently the Harper government is relatively insulating military expenditures from the austerity plans being proposed for Canadian budgets over the next five years. Additional spending in the order of $12 billion remains anticipated for defence spending over the next twenty years. With these allocations Canadian military expenditures have reached their highest levels since the Second World War (Staples and MacDonald 2009).

The Canadian arms race is important in itself as a register of the shift in foreign policy priorities and of the 'hardening of the state' under the new military agenda. The expenditures have doubled the size of the Canadian military to 75,000 soldiers and 35,000 reservists. They have also expanded field operations, and assisted in the renovation of military capabilities under the new Canada Command (CANCOM) in Ottawa. These transformations are matched by the most significant rethinking of Canadian military doctrines since the 1960s. In contrast to a focus on continental defence, the European theatre, and peacekeeping, the new strategy shifts the focus towards 'networked joint capabilities' and 'interoperability' with allied militaries as part of 'multiforce, multicountry' operations. This new doctrine, pushed by General Rick Hillier while chief of the defence staff, was released as the DND's contribution to *Canada's International Policy Statement* (Canada 2005b). This doctrine demands an improved capacity to support military operations in pursuit of US primacy and NATO ambitions. The increasing role of the Canadian military in southern Afghanistan is the foremost symbol of this shift. Under the Harper government, the new military agenda appears in the *Canada First Defence Strategy* (Canada 2008a), which links the sovereignty of the nation to an expansion of military capacities. This strategy builds upon and extends the military policies put forward by the Liberals. But it also proposes an augmentation of naval, airlift, and operational capacities, particularly linked to Arctic security but expanding in general Canada's ability to deploy troops globally. In the process the linkage between 'security at home,' 'security abroad,' and the 'national interest' has been directly integrated into the basic concepts of Canadian defence and foreign policy (Sloan 2006; Middlemiss and Stairs 2008; Canada 2010).

Finally, it is important to recognize how peacekeeping and development programs have been thoroughly devalorized or instrumentalized in Canadian foreign policy. Peacekeeping, for example, traditionally functioned as a multilateral contribution to western foreign policy practices. Over the past decade, however, Canada has all but abandoned peacekeeping and has no significant peacekeeping missions under way. A similar withdrawal has occurred in terms of arms control and disarmament, which would run against the more active role of NATO in expanding global military operations. In contrast Canada's multilateralism is now focused on coercive modes of intervention. For example, Canada is now using its diplomatic offices and overseas funding to support destabilization efforts of governments identified as insufficiently 'market oriented.' This role has been evident in Venezuela, Bolivia, Honduras, and Ecuador. Haiti, however, has been the archetype case. In 2004 Canada participated in both the destabilization campaign led by France and the United States and in the subsequent coup, which was supported by Canadian forces (Engler and Fenton 2005; Hallward

2007). The Canadian government's response to the 2009 earthquake in Haiti saw a similar mobilization of Canadian troops, while other relief supports were either absent or minimal. The transformation of Canadian foreign policy as a tool of coercion is further reflected in the instrumentalization of development policy. In the 3D (defence, diplomacy, development) strategy of the Martin Liberals – and in the 'whole-of-government' approach of the Harper Conservatives – the function of CIDA has been transformed to support of counterinsurgency and stabilization efforts, anchored by a strategy of pacification determined by the Canadian Forces (Lennox 2009, chap. 6).

We can see, then, that the 'war on terror' has provided a framework through which the Canadian state has been reorganized around the security and military institutions of the state, commanded by a highly centralized and strengthened executive authority. The new security and foreign policy agenda reflects the global and regional interests of Canadian capital and the stratified ways through which Canada articulates itself to the United States and the wider world system. As the next section demonstrates, the recent conflicts in the Middle East and Afghanistan have provided the catalyst for this revolution in Canadian foreign policy.

Canada, the Middle East, and Afghanistan

The 'single war' being waged from the Middle East to Afghanistan has been the battleground upon which Canada's new foreign policy is being tested (see Hanieh, in this volume). The same war has spurred and reorganized the international form and functions of the state. These transformations can be illustrated, on the one hand, by the modifications in a series of diplomatic positions on the Middle East, and, on the other, by the war in Afghanistan.

In terms of Middle East policy, Canada has long adhered to British and US positions. Notably, as part of the majority opinion of the 1947 United Nations Special Committee on Palestine, Canada played a major role in arguing for partition. Canada also helped broker differences among Britain, France, and the United States during the Suez Crisis of 1956 and proposed a UN peacekeeping force. At the same time Canada has only begrudgingly recognized the right of Palestinians to self-determination. Even after supporting UN Security Council Resolution 242 after the 1967 war (during which Israel occupied the West Bank, the Gaza Strip, East Jerusalem, and the Golan Heights), Canada avoided reference of a Palestinian state, preferring to speak only of a Palestinian 'entity' or 'homeland.' Canada also refused to demand a full implementation of UN Resolution 194 (Article 11) on the 'right of return' of Palestinian refugees. However, the first intifada compelled Canada to acknowledge the Palestinian right to self-determination, and, with the Oslo Accords, to recognize that a Palestinian state might result from negotiations. It was only with UN Security Council Resolution 1397 in 2002 outlining a 'two-state solution' that Canada came to recognize, albeit in the most abbreviated form, Palestinian statehood. At the same time Canada supports Israel as an ethnic-religious Jewish state and thus ignores the 'civic' understanding of democracy and state formation used in Canadian diplomacy elsewhere.

The qualified recognition of Palestinian rights has been defended by various Canadian governments as a policy of 'balance.' But with the post-2001 recasting of foreign policy, Liberal governments, particularly under Paul Martin, started to tie Canada closer to US policies in the region and thus to Israel. The Martin government, for example, began shifting Canada's UN General Assembly votes to side with Israel, the United States, and a few other US protectorate states. With these new allies Canada voted against or distanced itself from the vast majority of world opinion on Israel's failure to recognize UN resolutions on Palestine and other human rights issues. The most important vote was Canada's July 2004 abstention on a General Assembly resolution calling for Israel to abide by the International Court of Justice ruling on the 'Wall' in the West Bank, despite Canada's many previous stances, especially in the 1990s, on the necessity of international legal norms. The Harper government has more consistently allied Canada's votes on Palestinian rights with those of the United States and other minor dissenters. Under Harper's leadership Canada has abstained on UN resolutions on the Palestinian right to self-determination, on Israel's lack of assent to the Nuclear Non-Proliferation Treaty, and on Israeli exploitation of natural resources in the Occupied Territories. The Harper government has also abandoned the diplomatic language of Palestinian statehood, preferring now to speak only of Palestinian 'aspirations' within the region (Heinbecker and Momani 2007).

These diplomatic shifts in themselves have meant little in the way of resource commitments. But they are a significant – even strident – acknowledgment of the guiding precepts of Canada's Middle East policy. While Canada has couched its 'relative autonomy' in foreign policy in the language of multilateralism, this shift in stance is a major

concession to the United States (and Israeli) exercise of unilateral warfare and of separate treatment in international law. Canada's new foreign policy position on the Middle East effectively endorses the right of
the United States and Israel to invoke extraterritorial sovereignty in the
name of security, while other states can exercise sovereign rights only
at the discretion of Washington.

Apart from the diplomatic weight Canada has given to US positions,
the policy shift also has had material impacts on the Palestinian Authority and on other conflicts in the region. In 2006 the Conservative government made Canada the first to place sanctions on the newly elected
Hamas government. This included ending direct aid to the Palestinian Authority, reviewing all partnership projects, and limiting contact
of Canadian officials with Palestinian counterparts. Canadian aid to
Palestine was relatively marginal, but the sanctions added to the pressures leading to hostilities in Gaza and to the Israeli embargo. Canada
subsequently worked closely with the United States, Britain, and Israel
to isolate Hamas in Gaza, while attempting to work with the Fatah
government and the 'Dayton army' in the West Bank, thus effectively
splitting the Palestinian Authority. As part of this strategy Canada has
restored its assistance to the West Bank regime and accepted the Israeli
siege of Gaza.

Similarly, Canada's response to the war on Lebanon in 2006 indicated
an openly partisan embrace of US and Israeli positions. Israel's intervention in Lebanon clearly violated international law in the 'collective
punishment' and wholesale destruction of civilian life and infrastructure. Israel's actions faced the condemnation of world opinion and of
the vast majority of states of the world. But the Harper government
lined up Canada with the United States at the July 2006 Group-of-Eight
meetings in defence of the Israeli bombardment. Indeed, Harper became – and has remained – the most vociferous defender of the 'proportionality' of the Israeli attacks, terming them a 'measured response.'
Even after the Israeli Defence Forces killed Canadian civilians, Harper
refused to condemn Israel for the large number of civilian casualties
and continued to defend its use of force, including blanket aerial and
cluster bomb attacks. Indeed, at the September 2006 Francophonie
meetings, Harper vetoed a resolution deploring the impact of the war
on Lebanese civilians. The Harper government took the same stance
with respect to the war on Gaza in late 2008 and to the war crimes cited
by UN authorities (Engler 2010). Even with President Obama pushing
for new peace talks in light of the Arab Uprising in spring 2011, Harper,

with a newly minted majority government in hand, stood beside Israel and the belligerent stance of its leadership against even modest concessions (Walkom 2011).

The unflinching support for Israel as a western proxy in the Middle East has been a critical marker of Canadian diplomacy, binding it more tightly to US policies in the region. The intervention in Afghanistan, however, has been the principal spur to the remaking of Canadian state capacities to operate abroad. The war has been a key catalyst for the reorganization of the foreign policy apparatus, the revamp of defence strategy, and the upgrade of military infrastructure.

The escalation of Canada's role in Afghanistan demonstrates these transformations. Immediately in 2001 Canada offered operational support for the 'war on terror' in Afghanistan, deploying the JTF2 commando unit and several hundred other troops, and a third of its naval fleet to the Persian Gulf. This was followed by an additional two-thousand troop commitment in 2002 to assist in the stabilization of air and transport routes and to engage in combat operations in southern Afghanistan. From 2003 to 2005, Canada deployed two thousand troops to Kabul, eventually taking charge of the NATO-led International Security Assistance Force, with particular responsibility for protecting and aiding the new Karzai government. But with the insurgency growing across Afghanistan and with pressure building for Canada to take a larger role in the aftermath of Iraq, the Martin and then Harper governments accepted a more prominent position in the counterinsurgency effort. As a result, in 2005, a new Canadian mission reported to Kandahar. Consisting of two thousand five hundred battle troops and a Provincial Reconstruction Team (PRT) of more than three hundred officials from the Canadian Forces, CIDA, DFAIT, the Royal Canadian Mounted Police, and other branches of the state, this mission confronted the Taliban insurgency head on. Although the mission was designed as a two-year deployment, this plan was troubled by the Taliban resistance. As a result the Harper government immediately extended the mission for another two years, and then in 2008 put forward another resolution in the House of Commons to extend the pullout from Kandahar to 2011. The latter extension followed on the heels of the report of the Independent Panel on Canada's Future in Afghanistan (Canada 2008b), led by a former Liberal cabinet minister and various political and business elites, who warned of 'chaos' and the loss of NATO credibility without further military support for regime stabilization (Lennox 2009, 93–113). Despite the many failures of the mission, the Conservative government and the Liberal opposition endorsed, in the fall of 2010, a three-year reassignment to Kabul, leaving approximately a thousand troops and numerous other officials to assist in further training Afghan security forces until at least 2014 (Clark 2010).

The massive organizational effort of the Canadian state to deploy this number of troops over a decade – the longest period of military conflict in Canadian history – alone signals the transformation in its international form and functions. It means, for instance, a clear break with Canada's 'specialization' in peacekeeping. Instead, Canada is now developing its military capacities to engage in counterinsurgency wars. This means putting into practice new forms of tactical combat, including airlift, rapid deployment, and rotational capacities; 'three block' warfare linked to air strike capabilities; specialized treatment of detainees in 'atypical' contexts; and military directives over diplomatic and developmental ones. This rupture in the theory and practice of Canadian military strategy has required, of course, a major overhaul of military hardware, including the equipping of naval vessels, airlift and helicopter capacities, tanks with long-range firing capability, small arms and protective gear for troops, and so forth. In fact a significant portion of the billions spent on the Afghan War by the Canadian government has been for retooling the military (Warnock 2008, chap. 8).

The new policy of 'disciplinary militarism' also requires a capacity to engage in multiple terrains of conflict in liaison with allied militaries. The intervention in Afghanistan has tested this proficiency of the Canadian Forces. This occurred directly with the sending of troops to Haiti in both 2004 and 2009 as part of 'stabilization' missions, and indirectly through Canada's contribution to the 'coalition of the willing' in Iraq, which – although Canada did not participate formally in that war – was significant in terms of naval support, army exchange programs, and diplomatic recognition of, and support for, the occupation regime (Engler 2009, 43–7; Lennox 2009, 105–9). These deployments were a positive test of Canada's new capacity for 'multiforce, multicountry' operations.

The Afghan War has effected other transformations in Canadian foreign policy. *Canada's International Policy Statement* (Canada 2005a) laid out a 3D approach to building state and market structures in conjunction with counterinsurgency warfare. From the outset of the Afghan War the Canadian state mobilized diplomatic and other state facilities to support the creation of a new Afghan government. Indeed the war has encouraged the development of diplomatic 'specializations' in the realm of state or nation building. This has occurred in terms of supporting elections and training police, corrections, intelligence, and other officials in the fledgling Afghan state. A Strategic Advisory Team comprised of Canadian military and civilian personnel became a key variable of this strategy, with the function of providing advice to cabinet ministers in the Karzai government.

In similar terms the establishment of the Kandahar PRT symbolizes the realignment of development policy to the ends of 'pacification' and 'regime stability' in counterinsurgency conflicts. For example, the 'model village' strategy in southern Afghanistan deploys aid officials to 'stabilize' villages after the Taliban have been defeated by military forces. The various members of the PRT then attempt to establish governance, security, and development projects. The new modes of administration, however, are dominated by neoliberal precepts that give priority to the building of markets and providing opportunities for capital investment (Law 2009; Lennox 2009, 108–9). Thus, Canadian private security firms, consulting companies, suppliers, and non-governmental organizations have been integrated into both the PRT and the infrastructure necessary to support development work. Canadian aid to the Afghan state has also facilitated long-term investors, such as major Canadian mining companies, which are bidding on licences and future projects (Gordon 2010, 364–5). It is clear, though, that military objectives dominate the PRT, that development is subordinated to military strategy, and that both are designed to stabilize capitalist development in Afghanistan.

It is difficult, therefore, to underestimate the Middle East and Afghanistan as terrains for the remaking of Canadian foreign policy. This vast zone of imperial conflict has allowed Canada to practise new forms of 'cooperative specialization' with US foreign policy, to develop new forms of 'disciplinary militarism', and to build an infrastructure for capitalist development and regime stabilization. In the process Canada has transformed the organizational hierarchy of its foreign policy apparatus and secured the internationalization of Canadian capital in North America and beyond.

Conclusion: Empire and Its Discontents

Canada has supported in multiple ways the US effort at reasserting primacy through the 'war on terror' since 2001. This new alignment, however, has triggered an unexpected consequence: widespread dissent and public unease with the direction of Canadian foreign policy. This

opposition is plainly evident in attitudes towards the military intervention in Afghanistan and US foreign policy in the Middle East, and is
often expressed as a popular desire for an 'independent foreign policy,'
as opposed to the corporate strategy of alliance with US imperialism.
While this debate is often centred in policy circles around the question of whether Canada should employ a 'continental' or 'independent'
strategy, the widespread discontent with Canada's international policies has given impetus to a far more critical perspective. It begins from
the recognition that Canadian foreign policy is embedded in the economic and political agenda of a domestic capitalist class that advances
a particular set of interests through an alliance with US imperialism.

This critical perspective has called for troop withdrawal from Afghanistan and for international solidarity and the democratization of
Canadian foreign policy. This perspective has a social base in sections of
the union, environmental, indigenous, and global justice movements. It
is linked historically to the anti-war movements of the 1960s and 1970s
and to some of the campaigns for an 'independent foreign policy' in
those decades as well (Clarkson 1968; Warnock 1970). In the 1980s the
dissent fused into a 'counterconsensus' on the 'Middle Power project' in
favour of a more egalitarian and less US-centric multilateralism (Pratt
1983; Neufeld 1999). Since the beginning of the new century, however,
the imperialistic posture of the Canadian state has fostered more radical
movements against globalization, war, and environmental destruction
(Panitch and Leys 2004; McNally 2006). These movements link opposition to the current world order to a politics of radical transformation
at both global and local levels. Through these struggles social movements in Canada have defined an internationalist and anti-imperialist
agenda. The key positions of these movements can be summarized as
follows.

1 *Withdrawal of troops from Afghanistan.* The US-NATO intervention
   follows from a series of western alignments with warlords and
   Islamist commanders since the late 1970s. The western mission is in
   disarray and increasingly at odds with Afghan 'national interests.'
   The US 'surge' is prolonging the war, and will not avoid a peace
   summit of regional states and multiple constituents in Afghanistan,
   including the Taliban and the Afghan left (Ali 2008, 21–2; Warnock
   2008, 176–7). Troop withdrawal needs to be followed by a plan for
   reparations and reconstruction paid for by western governments,

a point made forcefully by the Canadian Peace Alliance (Lacombe 2007).

2 *Remaking Canada's role in the Middle East, beginning by reordering ties with Israel and Palestine.* From historical and geopolitical perspectives, it is difficult to avoid the observation that the United States and its western allies have engaged in a 'single war' spanning the Middle East and Afghanistan for several decades. This unified endeavour is to guarantee US and western control over critical oil supplies. As part of this strategy the United States and Canada support the expansionist policies of Israel and undemocratic governments in Saudi Arabia, Jordan, and Egypt. As a result there is a direct connection between the Israeli occupation of Arab territories and the western strategy for the wider Middle East. Beyond the war in Afghanistan, support for Israel is Canada's second key orientation in the region. For this reason the anti-war movement strongly opposes Israel's territorial occupations and apartheid policies (Davis 2003; White 2009). Although there is much debate within the movement on the nature of this conflict, there is growing support for the Boycott, Divestment, and Sanctions campaign against Israel, and for a one-state, democratic future in Israel/Palestine.

3 *Playing a central role in supporting multipolarity in the world order and the democratic sovereignty of states to choose alternate development paths.* A new agenda of international solidarity must begin with a radical reconstruction of the present UN system – in particular, by democratizing or abolishing the Security Council (Amin 2006). This is necessary to achieve peace, disarmament, environmental protections, the rights of indigenous peoples, reparations for colonialism and slavery, and economic and social development. To these ends Canada must also support new regional alliances such as the Bolivarian Alliance for the Americas.

4 *Pulling out of international military alliances, and redeploying troops within Canadian borders.* NORAD and NATO are legacies of the Cold War that have little to do with national defence and everything to do with protecting and advancing western capitalism and US primacy (Warnock 1970). With the end of the Cold War this agenda has been laid bare with the illegal wars in the Balkans, Afghanistan, and Iraq. NATO and NORAD are now directed at disciplining Third World countries while building a parallel 'Fortress North America' (Denholm-Crosby 2010). These alliances are

also being used to ratchet up the arms race with China and Russia
and to impede other advances in 'multipolarity.' Canada has the
democratic right and obligation to redeploy troops for its own self-
defence and sovereignty. The financial savings from such a move
could then be allocated for reparations, aid, and social spending
at home.

5 *Reviewing international trade institutions and policies, and formulating
a plan for trade regulation and controls on capital movements.* In light of
the global financial crisis it is clear that the neoliberal development
model has fundamental flaws. The potential steps are lengthy: abandoning the Security and Prosperity Partnership with the United
States; reviewing all ongoing security and trade relations with the
United States; and a moratorium on hydrocarbon energy and water
development until concerns of sovereignty, greenhouse gas emis-
sions, and aboriginal rights are addressed. A review of neoliberal
development policies would also mean reopening NAFTA and fundamentally recasting international trade regulations and the Bretton
Woods institutions.

These positions constitute a minimal platform for remaking Canadian foreign policy. This platform would reinforce democratic sovereignty and advance the struggle for an equalizing world order. It stands
opposed to the neoliberal system built around the internationalization
of capital and the disciplinary militarism of Canadian and western imperialism. To put forward such a democratic and egalitarian agenda in
the current world order means confronting US hegemony and, more
directly, the domestic political and social relations that underpin Canadian imperialism. Avoiding the need for radical social transformation
in the hope of returning to a more UN-centred multilateralism is to fall
prey to the fictions of a liberal world order.

Indeed the belief that Canadian foreign policy has been – or can be –
a force for a more just or balanced world has been one of the most crip-
pling illusions of political life in Canada, particularly in progressive
circles. This illusion has shielded from scrutiny the reality of Canada as
an imperialist power and its particular role as an ally of the US project
of asserting primacy and expanding capitalism globally. The restructuring of Canadian foreign policy over the past decade, and in particular
the Canadian intervention in Afghanistan, has played no small part in
revealing these illusions for what they are. They make clear the need
for more radical departures in Canadian politics and the reclaiming of a

vision of a democratic socialism, if a more just, peaceful, and egalitarian foreign policy is to be found.

References

Albo, Greg. 2004. 'The Old and New Economics of Imperialism.' In *Socialist Register 2004: The New Imperial Challenge*, ed. Leo Panitch and Colin Leys. London: Merlin Press.

Ali, Tariq. 2004. *Bush in Babylon: The Recolonisation of Iraq*. London: Verso.

–. 2008. 'Afghanistan: Mirage of the Good War.' *New Left Review* 50 (March–April): 5–22.

Amin, Samir. 2006. 'Whither the United Nations?' In *Empire's Law: The American Imperial Project and the 'War to Remake the World,'* ed. Amy Bartholomew. Toronto: Between the Lines.

Arrighi, Giovanni, and Beverly Silver. 1999. *Chaos and Governance in the Modern World System*. Minneapolis: University of Minnesota Press.

Axworthy, Lloyd. 2003. *Navigating a New World: Canada's Global Future*. Toronto: Knopf.

Bartholomew, Amy, and Jennifer Breakspear. 2004. 'Human Rights as Swords of Empire.' In *Socialist Register 2004: The New Imperial Challenge*, ed. Leo Panitch and Colin Leys. London: Merlin Press.

Beier, Marshall, and Lana Wylie, eds. 2010. *Canadian Foreign Policy in Critical Perspective*. Toronto: Oxford University Press.

Bennis, Phyllis. 2006. *Challenging Empire: How People, Governments and the UN Defy US Power*. Northampton, UK: Olive Branch Press.

Bow, Brian, and Patrick Lennox, eds. 2008. *An Independent Foreign Policy for Canada? Challenges and Choices for the Future*. Toronto: University of Toronto Press.

Bromley, Simon. 2005. 'The United States and the Control of World Oil.' *Government and Opposition* 40, no. 2: 225–55.

Byers, Michael. 2007. *Intent for a Nation: What Is Canada For?* Vancouver: Douglas and McIntyre.

Callinicos, Alex. 2009. *Imperialism and the Global Political Economy*. Oxford: Polity.

Campbell, Bruce, and Ed Finn, eds. 2006. *Living with Uncle: Canada-US Relations in an Age of Empire*. Toronto: James Lorimer.

Canada. 2003. *Canada's Actions against Terrorism since September 11*. Backgrounder. Ottawa: Department of Foreign Affairs and International Trade. http://www.dfait-maeci.gc.ca/anti-terrorism/canadaactions-en.asp.

–. 2004. *Securing an Open Society: Canada's National Security Policy*. Ottawa: Department of Public Safety and Emergency Preparedness.

–. 2005a. *Canada's International Policy Statement: A Role of Pride and Influence in the World – Overview*. Ottawa: Department of Foreign Affairs and International Trade.

–. 2005b. *Canada's International Policy Statement: A Role of Pride and Influence in the World – Defence*. Ottawa: Department of National Defence.

–. 2005c. *Security and Prosperity Partnership of North America*. Ottawa: Privy Council Office.

–. 2008a. *Canada First Defence Strategy*. Ottawa: Department of National Defence.

–. 2008b. *Independent Panel on Canada's Future Role in Afghanistan*. Ottawa: Government of Canada.

–. 2010. *The Future Security Environment, 2008–2030*. Ottawa: Department of National Defence.

Clark, Campbell. 2010. 'After Afghanistan, the world will need Canada more than ever.' *Globe and Mail*, 23 October.

Clark-Jones, Melissa. 1987. *A Staple State: Canadian Industrial Resources in Cold War*. Toronto: University of Toronto Press.

Clarkson, Stephen, ed. 1968. *An Independent Foreign Policy for Canada?* Toronto: McClelland and Stewart.

–. 2002. *Uncle Sam and Us: Globalization, Neoconservatism, and the Canadian State*. Toronto: University of Toronto Press.

Coates, Ken, et al. 2008. *Arctic Front: Defending Canada in the Far North*. Toronto: Thomas Allen.

Cox, Robert. 1987. *Production, Power, and World Order*. New York: Columbia University Press.

Daudelin, Jean, and Daniel Schwanen, eds. 2008. *Canada among Nations 2007: What Room for Manoeuvre?* Montreal; Kingston, ON: McGill-Queen's University Press.

Davis, Uri. 2003. *Apartheid Israel: Possibilities for Struggle Within*. London: Zed Books.

Denholm-Crosby, Ann. 2010. 'Canada-US Defence Relations.' In *Canadian Foreign Policy in Critical Perspective*, ed. Marshall Beier and Lana Wylie. Toronto: Oxford University Press.

Dombey, Daniel. 2011. 'Obama presses for Afghan-Taliban talks.' *Financial Times*. 22 May.

Drache, Daniel. 2004. *Borders Matter: Homeland Security and the Search for North America*. Halifax, NS: Fernwood.

Eayrs, James. 1975. 'Defining a New Place for Canada in the Hierarchy of World Powers.' *International Perspectives* (May–June): 15–24.

Engler, Yves. 2009. *The Black Book on Canadian Foreign Policy*. Halifax, NS: Fernwood.

–. 2010. *Building Apartheid: Canada and Israel*. Halifax, NS: Fernwood.

Engler, Yves, and Anthony Fenton. 2005. *Canada in Haiti: Waging War on the Poor Majority*. Black Point, NS: Fernwood.

Gabriel, Christina, and Laura Macdonald. 2006. 'Chrétien and North America: Between Integration and Autonomy.' In *The Chrétien Legacy: Politics and Public Policy in Canada*, ed. Lois Harder and Steve Patten. Montreal; Kingston, ON: McGill-Queen's University Press.

Gordon, J. King, ed. 1966. *Canada's Role as a Middle Power*. Toronto: Canadian Institute of International Affairs.

Gordon, Todd. 2010. *Imperialist Canada*. Winnipeg: Arbeiter Ring.

Gowan, Peter. 1999. *The Global Gamble: Washington's Faustian Bid for World Dominance*. London: Verso.

–. 2004. 'Triumphing toward International Disaster: The Impasse in American Grand Strategy.' *Critical Asian Studies* 36, no. 1: 3–33.

Granatstein, Jack. 2007. *Whose War Is It? How Canada Can Survive in the Post-9/11 World*. Toronto: HarperCollins.

Grandin, Greg. 2006. *Empire's Workshop: Latin America, the United States, and the Rise of the New Imperialism*. New York: Metropolitan Books.

Green, Mathew. 2010. 'US welcomes approaches to Taliban.' *Financial Times*, 22 October.

Grinspun, Ricardo, and Yasmine Shamsie, eds. 2007. *Whose Canada? Continental Integration, Fortress North America, and the Corporate Agenda*. Montreal; Kingston, ON: McGill-Queen's University Press.

Hallward, Peter. 2007. *Damming the Flood: Haiti, Aristide, and the Politics of Containment*. London: Verso.

Hampson, Fen, and Paul Heinbecker, eds. 2010. *Canada among Nations 2009–2010: As Others See Us*. Montreal; Kingston, ON: McGill-Queen's University Press.

Hart, Michael. 2008. *From Pride to Influence: Towards a New Canadian Foreign Policy*. Vancouver: UBC Press.

Heinbecker, Paul, and Bessma Momani, eds. 2007. *Canada and the Middle East: In Theory and Practice*. Waterloo, ON: Wilfrid Laurier Press.

Helleiner, Eric. 1994. *States and the Reemergence of Global Finance: From Bretton Woods to the 1990s*. Ithaca, NY: Cornell University Press.

Heller, Henry. 2006. *The Cold War and the New Imperialism*. New York: Monthly Review Press.

Johnson, Chalmers. 2004. *The Sorrows of Empire: Militarism, Secrecy, and the End of the Republic*. New York: Metropolitan Books.

Kirton, John. 2006. 'Harper's "Made in Canada" Global Leadership.' In *Canada among Nations 2006: Minorities and Priorities*, ed. Andrew F. Cooper and Dane Rowlands. Montreal; Kingston, ON: McGill-Queen's University Press.

Klassen, Jerome. 2009. 'Canada and the New Imperialism: The Economics of a Secondary Power.' *Studies in Political Economy* 83 (Spring): 163–90.

Kolko, Joyce, and Gabriel Kolko. 1972. *The Limits of Power: The World and United States Foreign Policy, 1945–1954*. New York: Harper and Row.

Lacombe, Sid. 2007. 'Bring the Troops Home Now: Why a Military Mission Will Not Bring Peace to Afghanistan.' Toronto: Canadian Peace Alliance.

Law, David. 2009. 'Security Sector Reform in Afghanistan: The Canadian Approach.' In *The Afghanistan Challenge: Hard Realities and Strategic Choices*, ed. Hans-Georg Ehrhart and Charles Pentland. Montreal; Kingston, ON: McGill-Queen's University Press.

Lennox, Patrick. 2007. 'From Golden Straitjacket to Kevlar Vest: Canada's Transformation to a Security State.' *Canadian Journal of Political Science* 40, no. 4: 1017–38.

–. 2009. *At Home and Abroad: The Canada-US Relationship and Canada's Place in the World*. Vancouver: UBC Press.

Magdoff, Harry. 1978. *Imperialism: From the Colonial Age to the Present*. New York: Monthly Review Press.

McDougall, John. 2006. *Drifting Together: The Political Economy of Canada-US Integration*. Peterborough, ON: Broadview Press.

McNally, David. 2006. *Another World Is Possible: Globalization and Anti-Capitalism*. Winnipeg: Arbeiter Ring.

McQuaig, Linda. 2007. *Holding the Bully's Coat: Canada and the US Empire*. Toronto: Doubleday.

Middlemiss, Dan, and Denis Stairs. 2008. 'Is the Defence Establishment Driving Canada's Foreign Policy?' In *Canada among Nations 2007: What Room for Manoeuvre?*, ed. Jean Daudelin and Daniel Schwanen. Montreal; Kingston, ON: McGill-Queen's University Press.

Moens, Alexander. 2008. 'Afghanistan and the Revolution in Canadian Foreign Policy.' *International Journal* 63, no. 3: 569–86.

Neufeld, Mark. 1995. 'Hegemony and Foreign Policy Analysis: The Case of Canada as a Middle Power.' *Studies in Political Economy* 48 (Autumn): 7–29.

–. 1999. 'Democratization in/of Canadian Foreign Policy.' *Studies in Political Economy* 58 (Spring): 97–119.

Neufeld, Mark, and Sandra Whitworth, 'Imagining Canadian Foreign Policy.' In *Understanding Canada: Building on the New Canadian Political Economy*, ed. Wallace Clement. Montreal; Kingston, ON: McGill-Queen's University Press.

Nossal, Kim. 1997. *The Politics of Canadian Foreign Policy*, 3rd ed. Scarborough, ON: Prentice Hall.

Panitch, Leo, and Sam Gindin. 2005. 'Superintending Global Capital.' *New Left Review* 35 (September–October): 101–23.

Panitch, Leo, and Colin Leys, eds. 2004. *Socialist Register 2004: The New Imperial Challenge*. London: Merlin.

Pratt, Cranford. 1983. 'Dominant Class Theory and Canadian Foreign Policy: The Case of the Counter-Consensus.' *International Journal* 39 (Winter): 99–135.

Regehr, Ernie, and Peter Whelan. 2004. *Reshaping the Security Envelope: Defence Policy in a Human Security Context*. Waterloo, ON: Project Ploughshares.

Rempel, Roy. 2006. *Dreamland: How Canada's Pretend Foreign Policy Has Undermined Sovereignty*. Montreal; Kingston, ON: McGill-Queen's University Press.

Roach, Kent. 2002. 'Did September 11th Change Everything? Struggling to Preserve Canadian Values in the Face of Terrorism.' *McGill Law Journal* 47: 894–947.

Sloan, Elinor. 2006. 'Canada's International Security Policy under a Conservative Government.' In *Canada among Nations 2006: Minorities and Priorities*, ed. Andrew F. Cooper and Dane Rowlands. Montreal; Kingston, ON: McGill-Queen's University Press.

–. 2010. *Security and Defence in the Terrorist Era: Canada and the United States Homeland*. Montreal; Kingston, ON: McGill-Queen's University Press.

Sokolsky, Joel. 2004. 'Northern Exposure? American Homeland Security and Canada.' *International Journal* 60, no. 1: 35–52.

Staples, Steven, and David MacDonald. 2009. 'How Much Is This War Costing Canadians?' In *Afghanistan and Canada: Is There an Alternative to War?*, ed. Lucia Kowaluk and Steven Staples. Montreal: Black Rose Books.

Stein, Janice Gross, and Eugene Lang. 2007. *The Unexpected War: Canada in Kandahar*. Toronto: Viking.

United States. 2002. *The National Security Strategy of the United States of America*. Washington, DC: White House.

van der Pijl, Kees. 2007. *Nomads, Empires, States: Modes of Foreign Relations and Political Economy*. London: Pluto Press.

Walkom, Thomas. 2011. 'Canada and Obama's not-so-new Israel policy.' *Toronto Star*, 21 May.

Warnock, John. 1970. *Partner to Behemoth: The Military Policy of Satellite Canada*.
    Toronto: New Press.

–. 2008. *Creating a Failed State: The US and Canada in Afghanistan*. Halifax, NS:
    Fernwood.

Welsh, Jennifer. 2004. *At Home in the World: Canada's Global Vision for the 21st
    Century*. Toronto: Harper.

White, Ben. 2009. *Israeli Apartheid: A Beginner's Guide*. London: Pluto Press.

Williams, William Appleman. [1959] 2009. *The Tragedy of American Diplomacy*.
    New York: W.W. Norton.

Wood, Ellen Meiksins. 2005. *Empire of Capital*. London: Verso.

PART III

Canada's War in Afghanistan

9

Failed States and Canada's 3D Policy in Afghanistan

ANGELA JOYA

In the aftermath of 9/11 the United States and its western allies declared Afghanistan to be a 'failed state.' The Taliban government, they exhorted, was guilty of collaborating with al-Qaeda and therefore of violating the political and legal responsibilities of states to the international community. In this context the US-led invasion of Afghanistan was justified as a necessary response to a condition of state failure. The war was also advertised as a state-building project that would thwart future terrorist attacks against the West. On 2 December 2009 US President Barack Obama emphasized this two-track agenda of intervening in and building up failed states as part of his justification for a troop surge in Afghanistan.

The same agenda has guided Canada's involvement in Afghanistan since 2001. Canada's mission has taken the form of a '3D' strategy that combines defence, diplomacy, and development projects in pursuit of nation building in Afghanistan. Through this framework the Canadian government aims to build up the Afghan state's political and military capacities through various development and reconstruction projects. After eleven years of involvement, however, Canadian policy seems to be faltering.

This chapter examines Canada's role in the Afghan state-building project through the 3D approach, and highlights the strategic shifts whereby development has been subordinated to military and security goals. The first section reviews the literature on failed states and the way in which Afghanistan was classified as such by various international actors and by the Canadian government. The second section focuses on Canada's involvement in Afghanistan and the accompanying changes that Canada's mission has undergone in the course of eleven years. The third section points out the contradictions of the western state-building strategy in Afghanistan. The final section provides a critique of Canada's state-building efforts, and argues that building a democratic society through meaningful long-term development cannot occur under military occupation. More specifically this chapter argues that the state-building project in Afghanistan has been unsuccessful because it relies upon the doctrine of failed states. This doctrine assumes that state failure results solely from internal factors instead of external ones, including imperialism, underdevelopment, and military occupation. In the current context the perceived solutions to this impasse – such as an increase in development aid or military personnel – also fail to break with the mistaken presumptions of the failed state doctrine and thus are unlikely to succeed.

The Failed State Doctrine

The failed state doctrine broadly refers to states that exist on the world map but that lack the central authority to enforce law and order or to respond to the needs of citizens, and thus pose a threat to the international community of liberal democracies (Thürer 1999). The failed state doctrine is rooted in a functionalist and Weberian notion of the modern state, which is defined as 'the political authority in which the monopoly of physical force or violence is legitimately vested within a given territory' (Weber 1946, 78). While remaining nominally sovereign, failed states can no longer maintain themselves as viable political or economic units and lack the capacity for providing law and order or basic infrastructure. More important, a state becomes failed or fragile when power becomes dispersed in the hands of warlords or criminals who exert de facto sovereign power through private armies or militias. It is under such conditions that failed states are seen as a threat, as they become hiding grounds for terrorists or criminal organizations, as well as a source of unregulated migration across borders (Mallaby 2002; Rotberg 2002; Ghani and Lockhart 2008).

According to former United Nations secretary general Boutros Boutros Ghali, the main problem arising from failed state situations is the problem of governance and human rights. In his view, '[a] feature of such conflicts is the collapse of state institutions, especially the police and judiciary, with resulting paralysis of governance, a breakdown of law and order, and general banditry and chaos. Not only are the functions of government suspended, but [state] assets are destroyed or looted and experienced officials are killed or [forced to] flee the country'

(1995, 9). Under such circumstances, he argues, the international community must intervene to establish an effective government or build a viable state in order to preserve international peace and security. Early cases of state failure include Cambodia, Haiti, Rwanda, and Sierra Leone. More recently the Fund for Peace (2011), a US-based think tank, provided a list of 177 countries that have experienced, or are currently experiencing, different degrees of state failure or fragility.

Scholars have pointed out that, over the course of the 1990s, with the collapse of the Soviet Union and the Eastern Bloc, the forces of globalization and free market capitalism led to state instability and, in some cases, to state collapse (R. Kaplan 1994; Zartman 1995; Ghani and Lockhart 2008; Griffiths, O'Callaghan, and Roach 2008, 108–10; S. Kaplan 2008). Non-state actors such as corporations, workers, criminal gangs, and immigrants increasingly crossed borders, albeit for different reasons. The resulting anarchy was seen as destabilizing to the West and its prosperity and security.

While the failed states doctrine has descriptive value in certain cases, it is problematic as a more general theory of international relations, for several reasons. First, the concept remains too broad and unclear, especially given the lengthy list of countries at some stage of state failure. Second, the discourse typically focuses on domestic factors alone, and thus fails to examine the global and historical context that might have contributed to the condition. The failed state doctrine also has been used as a justification for military intervention by western countries with geopolitical and economic interests in the Third World. For instance the UN Security Council has characterized, at various points, Iraq, Haiti, and Somalia as 'failed states,' and supported military interventions in these countries by western powers with motivations beyond humanitarianism (Thürer 1999; Chomsky 2006, 108–9). Finally, based on past practice, it is difficult to foresee a situation in which failed states can be rehabilitated by military interventions, which often spur national liberation movements against foreign occupation and thus prolong conditions of instability and violence. Under such circumstances actors such as warlords and criminals often emerge as powerful decision-makers in government and politics, as Afghanistan and Iraq bear witness today (Nawa 2006; Klein 2008; Engler 2009, 146; Kahler 2009, 289–90, 293; Roston 2009; Bannerman 2010). In this context democratic development is typically stunted and exploitative relations reinforced.

A more historically accurate investigation of state failure must indicate, first, that, in many cases, a colonial heritage and decolonization have left a political vacuum and a paucity of institutional structures.

Second, after decolonization most Third World countries were caught in the rivalry between the United States and the Soviet Union and relied on external aid disbursements as opposed to building an effective democratic state and, at the end of the Cold War, many of these states simply collapsed. Third, in many cases, structural adjustment policies imposed by the International Monetary Fund (IMF) and the World Bank have undermined the economic basis for national self-subsistence and generated new stratifications of wealth and income, while protests against neoliberal policies have destabilized weak states and attracted religious fundamentalist groups such as al-Qaeda (Moghadam 2003). In short state failure occurs as a result of multiple factors, both external and internal – the legacy of colonialism, the unequal structure of the world economy, the geopolitics of the Cold War, and the turn to neoliberalism since the 1980s – and not simply for endogenous reasons (Kahler 2009, 288–9).

The discourse of state failure also meshes with new imperatives of capital accumulation. The world economy demands new forms of 'security' for capital to flow seamlessly and to reproduce itself on a global scale. This is not easy to achieve, as the reproduction of capital depends on relations of exploitation in multiple states around the world. Failed states, however, cannot provide such guarantees. As a result the United States and its allies have argued that failed states must respect and adopt the values of the West – namely, liberal democracy, free markets and privately owned media – or risk invasion. In the aftermath of 9/11 it was this conception of world order that the United States and its allies began dictating to other states, especially Afghanistan.

Afghanistan: Rebuilding a Failed State

The invasion of Afghanistan occurred on the pretext of its being a failed state, although it was not so much violations of human rights that prompted the invasion, but the threat that Afghanistan was deemed to pose to the West. After the events of 11 September 2001 US leaders and their global allies argued that failed states provide safe heavens for terrorist groups. In the words of British foreign secretary Jack Straw (2002), '[t]he best way to counter the many threats posed by a failed state is to do precisely what we are beginning to do in Afghanistan: helping to build a successful state.' Straw emphasized that failed states pose a direct threat to the security of the West: 'It is clearer than ever since September 11 that our domestic security and prosperity depend on our willingness to assume our share of responsibility for global security and global prosperity. Our challenge today is to stave off the Afghanistans of the future.' Thus, in order to prevent future attacks on the West, it was important to rehabilitate failed states. This rehabilitation meant, on the one hand, destroying al-Qaeda and related groups in Afghanistan (and later on in Pakistan as well). On the other, it meant rebuilding a new state that could be trusted by the international community to respect international law and order.

This new project of western imperialism (Ignatieff 2003) must be considered in relation to the history of state building in Afghanistan (see Warnock, in this volume). The modern state in Afghanistan was a short-lived phenomenon in the context of the Cold War. As a terrain of conflict between the United States and the Soviet Union, the Afghan state collapsed after just a few decades of moderately successful development. The state's authority, in any case, was limited to major cities, while the provinces were largely out of reach. The civil war of the 1990s and the subsequent rule of the Taliban completely shattered any remnants of the modern state (Rubin 2002, 7–10). While Afghanistan fit the definition of a failed state throughout the 1990s, it attracted the attention of the West only after 11 September 2001.

The main goal of the western mission to date has been identified as building the Afghan state in order to prevent another terrorist attack. On 2 December 2009 President Obama justified the war in terms of fighting al-Qaeda and providing collective security to the world:

[I]t's important to recall why America and our allies were compelled to fight a war in Afghanistan in the first place. We did not ask for this fight. On September 11, 2001, 19 men hijacked four airplanes and used them to murder nearly 3,000 people . . . If I did not think that the security of the United States and the safety of the American people were at stake in Afghanistan, I would gladly order every single one of our troops home tomorrow . . . I am convinced that our security is at stake in Afghanistan and Pakistan. This is the epicenter of violent extremism practiced by al Qaeda. It is from here that we were attacked on 9/11, and it is from here that new attacks are being plotted as I speak. This is no idle danger; no hypothetical threat. In the last few months alone, we have apprehended extremists within our borders who were sent here from the border region of Afghanistan and Pakistan to commit new acts of terror. And this danger will only grow if the region slides backwards, and al Qaeda can operate with impunity. We must keep the pressure on al Qaeda, and to do that, we must

increase the stability and capacity of our partners in the region . . . And
we must strengthen the capacity of Afghanistan's security forces and
government so that they can take lead responsibility for Afghanistan's
future . . . For what's at stake is not simply a test of NATO's credibility –
what's at stake is the security of our allies, and the common security of the
world. (Obama 2009)

Similarly, the North Atlantic Treaty Organization (NATO) seeks to rebuild a state in Afghanistan to ensure future security for the 'International Community.' According to NATO's 2009 report on Afghanistan,
'[t]he International Community, including NATO, is helping the Afghan Government enhance security, improve governance and step up
reconstruction and development. Progress in all three areas is essential
in helping Afghanistan establish itself as a secure, stable country that
poses no threat to itself or the International Community' (NATO 2009, 4).
To this end western states have tried to create institutional structures
in Afghanistan to provide public services, to impose law and order,
and to neutralize other political forces in the country. Concretely the
state-building project in Afghanistan has entailed building institutions
of popular governance, training law and order authorities and personnel, and building an infrastructure through which various parts of the
country can be incorporated under central government control.

Before addressing these issues, consider the weakness of failed state
doctrine in the case of Afghanistan. Both Rubin (2002) and Gannon
(2005) argue that Afghanistan became a case of state failure not simply
because of internal dynamics and conflicts, but also because of outside
intervention by two superpowers. Between 1978 and 1989 the United
States provided billions of dollars to the *mujahideen* factions, which were
fighting the Soviet-backed government in Kabul. It was in this context of
external intervention and domestic class conflict that warlords became
a permanent feature of the Afghan political economy. In the early 1990s,
after the Soviet withdrawal, the *mujahideen* fought a violent civil war
that destroyed the Afghan state, precipitated a new flight of refugees,
and fragmented the country into rival warlord territories. The Taliban
emerged in southern Afghanistan and in the refugee camps of Pakistan
in response to the breakdown of law and order during the civil war
(Rashid 2002, 18; Rubin 2002; Gannon 2005; Rubin 2006). The Taliban
were supported financially, militarily, and diplomatically by Pakistan,
Saudi Arabia, and the United States, and were viewed at first by many
Afghans as a much-needed source of political stability. None of these
developments can be ignored if we want to understand the current

conflict in Afghanistan. Within policy circles and academic debates, however, there was little discussion as to why Afghanistan became a failed state; instead, the discourse focused on how the Taliban were a force of 'evil' that threatened not only Afghan women, but also the West. The Taliban had been in power since 1996, yet there was little condemnation of their brutal use of force until after 9/11. It is for this reason, as Regehr (2007) points out, that many Afghans perceived the US-led invasion as an act of revenge rather than a humanitarian mission.

To reiterate, characterizing Afghanistan as a failed state tends to locate the roots of failure in the country's internal dynamics, ignoring the international context of state formation. Such a characterization is efficacious to those supporting or seeking to legitimate foreign military intervention and occupation (see Paris and Sisk 2009). This characterization also tends to overlook examples of domestic stability and progress in Afghanistan – most important, the period of peace and development between the 1950s and the early 1980s, when Afghan women took a more active part in politics and public life and real progress was made in achieving higher living standards and the building of modern state institutions. According to Amin Saikal (2006, 123–6), a program of land reform was launched in the 1950s to reduce the exploitation of peasants and to encourage economic development in all parts of Afghanistan. All of this was achieved with the financial, technological, and expert aid of the Soviet Union, which fully funded the First Five Year Plan (1956–61) and the Second Five Year Plan (1962–7) (Saikal 2006, 121–6, 130–2). As a result, the real trajectory towards state failure began in the late 1970s, when the United States began funding the *mujahideen* under the auspices of the Cold War (Rubin 1995, 2000). The *mujahideen* not only destroyed the state institutions of Kabul, but also brought development projects to a halt and displaced millions of Afghans. The reactionary politics of the Taliban and the enduring problem of warlordism thus are legacies of the US intervention in Afghanistan in its bid to bring down the Soviet Union.

This history is important for a number of reasons. First, it suggests the possibility that tribal conflicts in Afghanistan can be overcome through political solutions and negotiations. Second, it reveals a domestic interest in democratization and development outside of the direction of western states. Third, it indicates that democracy and development are unlikely under military occupation and conditions of warlordism.

In short western powers have used the failed state doctrine to launch a project of state building in Afghanistan, but characterizing Afghanistan as a failed state relies on a number of false assumptions about the people and history of the country, and covers up the experience of progressive state building and policy development between the 1950s and early 1980s. As such, the failed state doctrine tends to serve as an ideological tool for military intervention.

Canada and the Failed State of Afghanistan

Canada has been deeply engaged in the Afghan war since 2001. Canadian politicians have offered many reasons for this commitment, but rebuilding a failed state has been cited as the central goal (Canada 2003). To this end successive Liberal and Conservative governments have attempted to restore peace and democratic institutions in Afghanistan (Canada 2004, 2005a). According to then defence minister Bill Graham, '[o]ur role in Afghanistan is quintessentially Canadian: we are helping rebuild a troubled country and we are giving hope for the future to a long suffering people. This is a clear expression of our Canadian values at work' (Graham 2005). In a speech to the Canadian Forces in summer 2005, Graham stated that 'Afghanistan was a fragile state that needed expertise, development assistance, and military help to stabilize the region of Kandahar, and the Afghan government asked Canada to undertake this mission' (quoted in Stein and Lang 2008, 198–9).

For the Conservative government of Stephen Harper the war in Afghanistan has been closely linked to security and defence issues. During the debate to extend the mission in Afghanistan beyond 2007, Prime Minister Harper referred to 9/11, stating that 'Canada is not safe from such attacks. We will never be safe so long as we are a society that defends freedom, democracy and human rights' (2006). According to the Conservative government the war is a necessary fight against terrorism and keeps Canada safe by bringing stability to Afghanistan (CIDA 2007, v).

While the failed state doctrine has been used to bolster support for the war, there are a number of other reasons for Canada's mission. According to Stein and Lang (2008, 290), Canada has been fighting in Kandahar to prevent the Taliban from retaking the province, from which they might launch a war against the Karzai government in Kabul. The US-Canadian relationship is another factor in the conflict. As Greg Albo has argued, closer economic integration with the United States has resulted in a parallel security sector integration, which has meant a radical shift in Canadian foreign policy. He explains that 'the defence of the general economic interests of Canadian capital, which necessarily

includes . . . American capital invested in Canada and Canadian investments in the US, has recast the entire foreign policy apparatus of the
Canadian state' (2006, 4). Confirming these ties, former deputy prime
minister John Manley stated that '[e]very Canadian prime minister . . .
has two overriding priorities. The first is national unity. The second
is managing Canada's relationship with the United States. The two
economies and the two societies are so intermingled that it would be
surprising if Ottawa did not consider – and consider carefully – what
Washington wanted' (quoted in Stein and Lang 2008, 262).

Canada's role in Afghanistan is very much a direct reflection of this
continental relationship. Indeed Stein and Lang argue that Canada is
in Afghanistan solely due to Canadian military leaders' concern for US
interests. In their view, 'Afghanistan was never the subject but only the
object, the terrain in which the Canadian Forces operated as they struggled with an assertive Bush administration. Afghanistan could have
been anywhere. It was no more than a spot on the map' (2008, 262).

According to these perspectives, therefore, Canadian policy towards
Afghanistan has been guided by several interrelated motives, including
security and defence imperatives, continental relations, and development
objectives under the failed states theory.

Canada's 3D or Whole-of-Government Approach in Afghanistan

Canadian foreign policy in Afghanistan has evolved through three
stages since 2001, corresponding to each prime minister's tenure in
office. In the first phase (2001–3) Liberal prime minster Jean Chrétien
provided military support to the US-led invasion (Hassan-Yari 2006).
Under Operation Apollo Canada dispatched up to twenty naval ships,
six aircraft, and more than two thousand soldiers, including JTF2 commandos. Despite this new type of military engagement the Chrétien
government did not articulate a new foreign policy strategy. In the
second phase (December 2003–February 2006) the Liberal government
of Paul Martin developed a '3D' approach by which Canada would advance development, diplomacy, and defence in Afghanistan and other
failed states. In the third stage (February 2006–present) Prime Minister Stephen Harper has mobilized a 'whole-of-government' approach
to the war in Afghanistan and made the counterinsurgency mission in
Kandahar the primary engagement of Canadian policy abroad.

The 3D, or whole-of-government approach, was first articulated in
the Paul Martin Liberal government's International Policy Statement

(Canada 2005b). Through this approach the foreign policy apparatus, including the Department of National Defence (DND), the Department of Foreign Affairs and International Trade (DFAIT), and the Canadian International Development Agency (CIDA), would work together to achieve common goals in Afghanistan and other failed states (Hassan-Yari 2006, 4–5; Stein and Lang 2008, 259–60). In theory the work of each department was to reinforce and support the work of the others: diplomacy, development and defence operations were to be integrated as part of the same counterinsurgency strategy. In the Afghan theatre, however, the new Canadian foreign policy has been largely dominated by the military, with only secondary influence or direction from the Privy Council Office, DFAIT, and CIDA.

Defence

Canada's intervention in Afghanistan was from the very beginning one of fighting a war. During the first phase of military conflict, between October 2001 and August 2003, Canada sent 2,800 troops initially to Kandahar and then to Kabul. In fall 2001 and winter 2002 Operation Apollo and Operation Harpoon were formed as part of the US-led Operation Enduring Freedom. These deployments were designed as short-term combat missions and were supposed to end in 2003 (Travers and Owen 2007, 19).

In the second phase, between September 2003 and August 2005, Canadian troops under the command of General Rick Hillier conducted Operation Athena, operating as part of the UN-mandated International Security Assistance Force in what government officials called a short-term mission aimed at stabilizing Kabul to facilitate the 2004 presidential elections and the 2005 provincial elections.

In the third phase, which has been ongoing since August 2005, Task Force Afghanistan, consisting of 2,500 Canadian solders and a 220-person Provincial Reconstruction Team has operated in Kandahar province. In 2007 Canada's soldiers were placed under NATO command. This final phase clearly became a war-fighting phase against the Taliban, with no clear end in sight. The rising number of Canadian casualties would characterize this period as the bloodiest phase of Canada's war in Afghanistan – in 2006 alone thirty-four soldiers died in Kandahar, the largest number since the Korean War (Hassan-Yari 2006, 7; Stein and Lang 2008, 244–5).

As chief of the defence staff, General Hillier used the war in Afghanistan as a catalyst for instigating wider changes in DND. In his view the Canadian Forces had to be reorganized and retrained to face an emerging global threat – that of failed and failing states. He argued that, to deal with such states, the Canadian Forces had to prepare for what the US Marine Corps describes as a 'Three Block War' – a new form of urban combat in which the military fights in one city block, provides humanitarian aid in another block, and supports diplomacy in a third. Hillier argued that peacekeeping was an artefact of the Cold War and that the Canadian Forces needed to prepare for complex urban counterinsurgency missions (Stein and Lang 2008, 147). As Stein and Lang state, 'Hillier's appointment would fundamentally change the philosophy, the strategy, the organization, and the culture of the Canadian Forces' (2008, 151). More important, Hillier saw Afghanistan as a key testing ground for the implementation of the 3D or whole-of-government approach. Under his guidance and influence Afghanistan became a laboratory for a new international policy agenda, centred around the DND and a war-making strategy for failed or failing states, in alliance with US foreign policy objectives.

Diplomacy

Since 2001 a close relationship has developed among Canadian diplomats, military officials, and the Afghan government of Hamid Karzai. The main features of Canada's diplomacy in Afghanistan are worth mentioning here. First, in opening an embassy in Kabul in January 2002, Canada expressed support for Karzai's Transitional Government and for the Bonn Process (see Klassen, in this volume). During the same period Canada supported policy development within Karzai's cabinet, as well as public sector training. Additionally Canadian diplomats played an important role in providing legal education through the Afghan Ministry of Justice and Kabul University's Faculty of Law. These efforts were important for the Afghan Peace, Justice and Reconciliation Plan.[1] Canada also provided $4 million for the Human Rights Monitoring and Reporting System, while emphasizing gender equality (Samar 2008, 59).

Canadian diplomats have also tried to strengthen the institutional and political capacities of the Afghan state. To this end they have supported disarmament, elections, and democratic governance. In 2005,

through the initiative of General Hillier, Canada launched a Strategic
Advisory Team (SAT), consisting of fifteen military officers and one
CIDA official, to work directly with Afghan government officials on
program development, 'including administrative reform, gender equity policy, and rural rehabilitation' (Schmitz and Phillips 2008, 2–3; see
also Cox 2007; Stein and Lang 2008, 299). Given the dominance of the
military in the SAT, it is clear that Canadian diplomacy has undergone
a radical change within the 3D approach. As the SAT in Afghanistan
demonstrates, the 3D strategy has given the Canadian military a larger
and more important role in shaping and affecting state policies around
the world.

Canadian diplomats have also been assigned the task of making the
3D strategy work more effectively. Their main role has been one of
mediation between DND and CIDA, coordinating their work so that
military and development projects are complementary. In addition,
Canadian diplomats have worked with international organizations
such as the United Nations and the World Bank through, for example, the Afghanistan Reconstruction Trust Fund (Schmitz and Phillips
2008, 3). As well, Canadian diplomats have bolstered international
support for Afghanistan's reconstruction, as evidenced by the role former Canadian ambassador Christopher Alexander played in drafting
the Afghanistan Compact (see Afghanistan Compact 2006).

In 2007 the Harper government mandated DFAIT to recalibrate the
relationship between DND and CIDA in Afghanistan, as part of which
the Afghanistan Task Force was created, under the direction of David
Mulroney, to enhance the performance of the 3D strategy (Mulroney
2007; Schmitz and Phillips 2008, 4). At the same time, experienced diplomat Arif Lalani was appointed as Canada's ambassador to Afghanistan. In the next section I explore further the role of DFAIT in making
the 3Ds more effective by recommending changes to CIDA.

Development

Canada's development aid for Afghanistan has been part of an international effort to rebuild the state under the Bonn Agreement of
December 2001 and the Afghanistan Compact of 2006. Prior to 2005
CIDA's role in Afghanistan focused on the long-term development of
the Afghan state through building institutions and supporting social
and economic development policies that would extend the authority of
government across the country. At the time CIDA's projects did not bear

a Canadian flag and were not intended to win 'hearts and minds' as part of a counterinsurgency effort (Stein and Lang 2008, 270). With the resurgence of the Taliban in southern Afghanistan, however, DND and DFAIT officials began questioning CIDA's role in achieving Canada's foreign policy goals. They argued that long-term development was not going to win the war – that, instead, short-term projects were needed to win over Afghan civilians and defeat the Taliban. This concern laid the groundwork for transforming CIDA's role through a Provincial Reconstruction Team in Kandahar, thus fundamentally shifting the balance among government departments by marginalizing CIDA vis-à-vis DND and DFAIT.

CIDA's Approach to State Building

Before the shift to Kandahar, most of CIDA's funds were invested in state-building projects linked to Afghanistan's National Development Strategy, with funds directed to the Afghanistan Reconstruction Trust Fund (to pay the salaries of civil servants), the National Solidarity Program, the Micro Finance Investment Support Facility, the National Area Based Development Program, and the Mine Action Project (Mychajlyszyn 2007, 4–7; Stein and Lang 2008, 270). Similarly, between January 2002 and July 2003 CIDA contributed $15 million to support the operational budget of the Afghan Transitional Government and $1.2 million to security-related projects (Canada 2005a).

After General Hillier assumed the post of chief of the defence staff, CIDA became the subject of criticism by DND and DFAIT for not helping in reconstruction projects that could immediately impact residents of Kandahar and thus contribute to military success in the region (Stein and Lang 2008, 271). CIDA's long-term state-building objectives appeared irrelevant to the Canadian military, which sought quick results in its military campaign against the Taliban. In this context CIDA was characterized as an aid agency trapped in the past century. According to Hillier, 'CIDA only delivers at the long-term end of the spectrum. And it is the military that is picking up the slack. CIDA has to move into the twenty first century!' (quoted in Stein and Lang 2008, 272). Indeed, blaming CIDA for not contributing to military objectives in Kandahar, Hillier stated that 'there is a Three D policy and the military does all three of the Ds' (quoted in Stein and Lang 2008, 277). In his view CIDA had to adapt to military imperatives in Kandahar if it wanted to make an effective contribution to the 3D strategy.

DFAIT has also critiqued the work of CIDA. In 2005, for example, DFAIT chaired a committee to identify ways of making the 3D strategy more coherent. The committee concluded that CIDA was not contributing to the 3D effort in Afghanistan in 'any meaningful way.' It further added that 'CIDA was hopeless in bringing to the table what they were accomplishing on the ground' and that 'CIDA either be drastically changed or abolished and that its staff and authority be transferred to Foreign Affairs' (quoted in Stein and Lang 2008, 278–9). Indeed, since 2006, DFAIT has taken charge of Canada's 3D policy and made every effort to make this an effective framework for achieving Canada's foreign policy goals (OECD 2006 48–9; see also Canada 2006).

After first resisting demands to shift its focus towards quick-impact projects, CIDA complied and reassessed its role in Afghanistan. As a result, since 2005, Canadian funds for development have been directed mostly towards short-term projects in Kandahar province within the framework of the PRT, with priority given to security, basic services, humanitarian aid, border control, national institutions, and reconciliation, as well as to three signature projects: education, polio eradication, and the Dhala Dam and Irrigation System – the Dhala Dam project later exposed as a failure (Watson 2012). The latter, known as the Arghandab Irrigation Rehabilitation Project, has absorbed more than $50 million, disbursed through the PRT (NATO 2009, 36). CIDA also paid $5.1 million to run a 'rapid village development plan,' although nearly 40 per cent of the contract was earmarked for professional fees (Engler 2009, 150). In fiscal year 2006/7, more than $39 million – approximately 50 per cent of CIDA's funding in Afghanistan – was geared towards projects in Kandahar province (CIDA 2007). In these ways CIDA's operations have been redirected towards the political and military ends of DFAIT and DND.

The Provincial Reconstruction Team

Since 2006 the PRT in Kandahar has been the institutional and political vehicle through which Canadian development and counterinsurgency efforts have been advanced (Capstick 2007). The PRT consists of 330 people, including 'a civilian advisor or political director from DFAIT, four [Royal Canadian Mounted Police] officers, an officer from the Charlottetown City police, development aid specialists from CIDA, and military personnel.' The PRT's objective is to 'enhance security in Kandahar, enhance links between the provincial, district and central authorities, improve the lives of the residents and build confidence among them about the international presence. In this way, the PRT intends to diminish the population's vulnerability to insurgent activities, thereby improving stability in the region as well as the implementation of development and reconstruction efforts' (Mychajlyszyn 2007). The specific projects undertaken by the PRT include police training, supporting health and education programs while also helping in enhancing governance structures, offering landmine awareness programs, and 'carrying out patrols in remote regions to enhance the presence of a security force and build confidence and trust among the population' (ibid.).

The PRT is supposed to reflect a closely coordinated effort among DND, DFAIT, and CIDA. As opposed to the development work and state building projects that CIDA carried out prior to 2005, PRT funds are redirected towards short-term projects recommended by DND and DFAIT (Stein and Lang 2008, 276–7). PRT funds bypass the Afghan government and instead are handed out by the Canadian military to local actors for local projects. The PRT's structure and function in Kandahar thus reflects the changing nature of the 3Ds and the new balance among Canadian government departments. The dominance of the military in the PRT reflects the strength of DND and its role in shaping development goals. As such, CIDA's role has been marginal within the overall structure and mode of operation of the PRT. Regardless, there are many reasons to doubt whether the Canadian military can win 'hearts and minds' in Kandahar as the Taliban gain ever more strength.

The Limits of State Building under Occupation

An assessment of the current situation in Afghanistan indicates that state building through war and military occupation has not reduced the Taliban threat or provided security for the Afghan people. The Afghan state continues to be limited in terms of its capacity and authority, with warlords remaining powerful both outside and inside the government, and thus it remains a failing state. But what accounts for this crisis? Barfield (2008, 416) and Ottaway and Lieven (2001) argue that the reasons can be found in the 2001 plans for state building. Through the Bonn Process the United States and its allies have attempted to build a highly centralized state in a society where all governing institutions had collapsed after 1992 and warlords exercised power autonomously. The

United States has also worked with these warlords as part of the counterinsurgency war against the Taliban and supported them as politicians in the Karzai government (see Klassen, in this volume)

Alongside the US-led effort to build a centralized security state under Karzai has been a corresponding attempt by the major international financial institutions – namely, the IMF and the World Bank – to keep the state's role in the economy and in the rebuilding of Afghanistan to a minimum (World Bank 2005a,b, 2007; Hilary 2008). According to this neoliberal model, funds for state building were to be distributed by civil society actors, including non-governmental organizations and UN agencies; for instance, in 2008, only 20 per cent of international aid went to the Afghan state, leaving the government with very few resources to build a public sector or provide services (Hilary 2008). Yet, for Afghanistan, with its fragile infrastructure, weak economy, and non-existent public programs, such neoliberal prescriptions have contributed only to a further *delegitimization* of the state. As Hilary (2008) argues, the free market model has failed to strengthen the Afghan state and instead has reinforced Afghanistan's dependence on foreign aid (see also Suhrke 2009, 232–3).

For these reasons the state-building project in Afghanistan has failed to achieve both security and development goals. The security situation has deteriorated rapidly since 2005, and civilian deaths continue to fuel public anger over foreign military activities (Barfield 2008, 414–15; *Economist* 2009, 21; Suhrke 2009, 229; Oppel and Sahak 2010; Oppel and Wafa 2010; Starkey 2010). Between 2005 and 2006, suicide bombings increased by 400 per cent (from 27 to 139), while the use of improvised explosive devices more than doubled (from 783 to 1,677) (Barfield 2008, 415).[2] In the early months of 2010 the insurgency was able to attack the Karzai government and NATO forces in Kabul through complex bombings and military manoeuvres (Patience 2010). By spring 2010 insurgent violence reached an all-time high, resulting in major losses for NATO forces and a higher civilian casualty rate.

We can see, then, that military occupation does not offer the best circumstances in which to engineer state-building projects; instead, it often precipitates insurgent violence, which makes political reconstruction and development impossible. In this context a military occupation tends to make common cause with local powerbrokers, including warlords, drug syndicates, and black market criminals. Consequently, attempts to build a state under military occupation often result in prolonged conflict, billions of dollars wasted, civilian casualties, and corrupt modes of governance. Political and financial resources are concentrated in the hands of those who have military power and weapons, and exploitation is reproduced. In recent history these dynamics have materialized in both Iraq and Afghanistan – the two main sites of western intervention since 2001 (Abbott, Rogers, and Sloboda 2006; Dobbins 2008, 163–8; Klein 2008, 407–60; Roston 2009).

Despite NATO and US claims of progress in Afghanistan, independent reports highlight dire circumstances (Tyson 2008; United Nations 2009). Lacking any viable economic development program, unemployment remains high among the largely young population. Linked to economic deprivation is a radical and persistent decline in living standards. According to Barnett Rubin (2006, 31), '[b]asic indicators of human welfare place Afghans among a handful of the world's most hungry, destitute, illiterate, and short-lived people. The country ranks approximately 173 out of 178 countries in the basic index of human development, effectively putting it in a tie for last place with a few African countries' (see also Stein and Lang 2008, 269). By 2009, according to the United Nations (2009), the number of internally displaced persons had reached 275,945, while chronic malnutrition rates across the country remained at 50 per cent. The Asia Foundation (2008) reports that Afghans suffer from high levels of unemployment and lack access to clean drinking water and health care. Mass refugee camps are spreading in the southern provinces, with large numbers of people living without access to food, shelter, medical aid, or security (Human Rights Watch 2003, 2007; Senlis Council 2007b;). According to the Senlis Council, the western preoccupation with the military dimension of the conflict has contributed to this social and economic impasse, noting that, in fact, 'military expenditure outpaces development and reconstruction spending by 900%' (2007a, 66). Thus, from 2002 to 2006, $82.5 billion was spent on military and security as opposed to $7.3 billion on development and reconstruction.

As a result the war in southern Afghanistan has left the population disillusioned, impoverished, bereft of security, and sympathetic to the Taliban. As Engler (2009, 46) points out, 'when the *Globe and Mail* interviewed 43 Taliban foot soldiers in Kandahar on why they joined the insurgency, 12 said their family members were killed in airstrikes and 21 said their poppy fields were targeted for destruction by anti-drug teams.' In this context the Taliban have begun protecting the people, and thus have gained a modicum of support among the population (Glevum Associates 2010). According to US general Stanley McChrystal

the Taliban function as the de facto government in much of the south
and east, taxing the population, running courts, and addressing popular complaints (see Walkom 2009a). It is not surprising, then, that the
Taliban have made a strong return after years of heavy fighting in the
south (Senlis Council 2006a). The Taliban have not been defeated; instead they have been transformed into a relatively popular guerrilla
army, rooted in the south, yet spreading to other parts of the country
(Ali 2009, 61; see also Senlis Council 2006c, 2007b; Burke 2007; Walkom
2007).

To summarize, the ongoing military occupation since 2001 has failed
to provide security, development, or good governance to Afghanistan.
The commonly proposed solution of increasing troop levels reflects a
failure to grasp the complexity – indeed, the impossibility – of delivering
development, reconstruction, and peace under military occupation.

The Failures of Canadian Policy in Afghanistan

The Canadian strategy of state building in Afghanistan, which is coordinated with those of the United States and other NATO allies, has
failed to produce either a strong state or a democratic society in which
human rights are respected. The militaristic approach of Canadian foreign policy has undermined the developmental role of CIDA and subordinated the provision of aid to short-term military calculations. The
Canadian military has failed to bring long-lasting peace or security to
the population of Kandahar. Instead counterinsurgency methods have
alienated the population, which increasingly supports the insurgency
or opposes the presence of foreign troops. The combination of these
factors and links between local warlords and the Canadian military
have undermined not only the credibility of DND and the Canadian
government more generally, but also that of the international effort in
Afghanistan.

The war in Afghanistan is now the longest in Canadian history, yet it
lacks strong support among the Canadian public (Angus Reid Global
Monitor 2008; Angus Reid 2010; Taber 2010). Given these realities it is
important to assess Canada's role in the Afghan crisis. The political and
organizational divide between DND and CIDA is the most commonly
cited reason for the failure of the 3D strategy in Kandahar (Travers and
Owen 2007; Stein and Lang 2008, 259). As Stein and Lang point out,
'Afghanistan was the first real test of the Three D policy, and officials
from all three departments do not think that Canada has done as well

as it could. The Three Ds are not working well together and some .are not working well alone. In Ottawa, words like *dysfunctional, debilitated* and *broken* are common descriptions of the institutions at the centre of Canadian foreign policy' (2008, 260, emphasis in original). The reason for this discord among various government departments has been traced to CIDA's inability to work with the military. CIDA's commitment to long-term development and state-building projects came into direct conflict with the military's short-term goal of winning 'hearts and minds' through immediate projects that carried the flag (Schmitz and Phillips 2008, 5). This counterinsurgency method succeeded in forcing CIDA to change its ways of undertaking development in Afghanistan. CIDA's autonomy, in effect, was undermined as military objectives were prioritized over poverty reduction and development (Brown 2008). Under the Conservative government of Stephen Harper, security interests increasingly have determined CIDA's priorities, leading to the militarization of aid while undermining CIDA officials' expertise and power of decision-making (Brown 2008, 1–3; see also Shah and Gall 2010).

This shift in Canada's development strategy has manifested itself through the PRT in Kandahar province and the replacement of long-term development plans with short-term reconstruction projects. For example, the PRT has developed a new program of building 'model villages' that are first secured from the Taliban and then offered aid and reconstruction funds and projects (Woods 2009). As Senator Colin Kenny (2009) has argued, however, the strategy of building model villages likely will remain more of a dream than a reality due to reasons of conflict between CIDA and DND, not to mention the growing strength of the insurgency and rising public anger against foreign forces in Kandahar (see also Senlis Council 2006b, 2006d, 2007b). The limited impact of supporting just a few model villages across the province also undermines the efficacy of such a strategy.

Furthermore, from the beginning, the Canadian government has prioritized military over development spending in Afghanistan by a factor of ten (Canada 2003; Gilmore 2003; CBC News 2006, 2009; Stein and Lang 2008, 187). The total cost of the war was estimated to reach $18.1 billion by 2011 (CBC News 2008); however, according to Parliament's independent budget watchdog, Kevin Page, the costs could exceed $14 billion (cited in Chase 2012).[3] Despite such discrepancy in funding, CIDA has sponsored a number of key projects in Afghanistan. While some of these projects have been successful, including efforts at de-mining and disarmament, others have been much less so, including efforts at rebuilding education programs, communications infrastructure, and water supply services (CIDA 2007, ix). Moreover, the Canadian PRT in Kandahar very rarely ventures outside security compounds and only under heavy military guard (Potter 2006; Druzin 2012). In January 2006 Canada's first PRT political director, Glyn Berry, was killed by a car bomb one kilometre outside the compound in Kandahar, reinforcing the focus on security and the controlled movement of PRT officials.

The dominant role of the military in the Canadian PRT (in terms of personnel numbers and decision-making powers) has rendered the operation incapable of reaching out to the Afghan population or engaging in actual development work. As the Manley Report (Canada 2008) revealed, the PRT is largely dominated by its military personnel, of whom there are 250, rather than by its 47 civilian development experts; as Barnett Rubin has observed, military officers are not the best development partners for local administration (2006, 18).[4]

At the same time, DND's military strategy has brought neither peace nor security to Kandahar, but instead has helped to further instigate the insurgency. According to the Senlis Council, '[s]ome locals stated that they see the Canadian troops as overly aggressive, indifferent, militaristic and lacking communication skills' (2006b,18), while, as Laxer (2007) notes, the Canadian government has failed to recognize that '[i]nsurgencies are for the most part deeply rooted in grievance and a sense of exclusion, not in a detached or apolitical fanaticism.' From accounts of soldiers, it is obvious that the Canadian Forces know very little about the local population and tend to paint everyone as a possible insurgent, which contributes to public anger against the presence of foreign troops in Kandahar (Potter 2006). For such reasons it is the Taliban, not the Canadian Forces, that have won 'hearts and minds,' or at least political influence, in southern Afghanistan (Senlis Council 2006d).

Furthermore the reputation of the Canadian government and military has been tainted due to partnerships and alliances formed with local warlords and militias. For instance, the Canadian government has partnered with figures linked to human rights abuses and violent crimes against civilians during Afghanistan's recent civil war. Thus, '[b]etween January 2006 and March 2007 . . . the Canadian military gave $1.14 million in contracts to a company bearing the same name as Gul Agha Sherzai, a former warlord who fought against the Taliban and who served as Kandahar's governor until 2005' (Engler 2009, 146). As well, since 2006, the Canadian military has relied on local militias to provide security for reconstruction projects. According to Engler (2009, 150), DND has disbursed at least $42 million to private contractors in Afghanistan. In fact,

> [i]n 2006–2007 Foreign Affairs spent at least $15 million on private security contractors in the country. Saladin Security protected the Canadian embassy in Kabul, visiting dignitaries, as well as forward operating bases in Kandahar province . . . Canadian Brigadier General Denis Thompson explained that 'without private security firms it would be impossible to achieve anything here. There are many aspects of the mission here in Afghanistan, many security aspects that are performed by private security firms that which, if they were turned over to the military, would make our task impossible.' (Engler 2009, 148–9)

The implication of the Canadian Forces in the illegal transfer of detainees to Afghan authorities, with full awareness that these prisoners would likely face torture, has further tarnished the reputation of the Canadian government and military (Walkom 2009b). Yet despite demands by opposition parties for legal accountability and a public inquiry, the Harper government and the Canadian military have made every attempt to obfuscate their role in and knowledge of the torture of transferred prisoners.[5]

In short, Canada's policy in Afghanistan has followed that of the United States and NATO in ostensibly seeking to rehabilitate a failed state and establishing a democratic structure of governance, to which end Canada has deployed a 3D strategy for achieving peace, development, and security. But this strategy has had little success given the dominance of the military and its commitment to short-term development goals. Canada's political and financial ties to warlords in Kandahar have further complicated the mission and contradicted the goals of disarmament and humanitarian reconstruction. The unlawful transfer of detainees to torture represents, perhaps, the final failure of the mission.

Conclusion

Under the failed state doctrine Canada intervened in Afghanistan with the aim of rebuilding the administrative capacity, territorial reach, and military power of the Afghan state. As the evidence demonstrates, however, Canada's 3D strategy has failed to resuscitate the state or provide security for the Afghan people. Despite the recent 'surge' of US and NATO forces, Afghanistan remains a conundrum for the western alliance.[6] A democratic state has not been produced by the war and occupation; instead the war has entrenched the power of local commanders and religious fundamentalists, while failing to open up space for democratic politics.

The situation in Afghanistan, in terms of both security and economic development, continues to grow grimmer by the day. The Taliban have managed to tap into grievances of the local population and, as counter-insurgency expert David Kilcullen warns, '[a] government that is losing to a counter-insurgency isn't being outfought, it is being out-governed. And that's what's happening in Afghanistan' (quoted in Tran 2009). In the eyes of many Afghans, it is the Taliban that have made a difference in their lives by providing justice and law and order, while the Karzai government is seen as dependent, corrupt, and linked to warlords (Hess 2008).

It is a striking fact that Canadian foreign policy in Afghanistan has reproduced the broader problems of the western intervention. The current 3D approach lacks an understanding of the political prerequisites for establishing peace in a country like Afghanistan. The 'war on terror' was supposed to end the threat of terrorism at home and abroad, but the misguided and ideological nature of this war is merely increasing the threat of terrorism as the real grievances of an occupied people continue to escalate. For this reason Canada and the United States urgently need to rethink their strategy. Building a democratic Afghanistan will require concerted efforts to find a political solution. As Regher (2007, 3) points out, for this goal to be achieved, there is a need for international support that 'lends legitimacy and authority to the process.' And this is where Canada could adopt a meaningful but very different role from the one it now plays. Instead of being empire's ally, Canada could help steer Afghanistan towards a more sustainable and equitable economy and society with the active participation of Afghan citizens. A genuine reassessment of Canada's foreign policy would only boost the country's standing on the world stage as a power that seeks to help those in need, rather than one that pursues its own self-interest or the geopolitical ends of Washington. Canadians must acknowledge that Afghans do not need democracy exported to them; they simply need a chance to participate fully in building an egalitarian society free of violence and outside intervention. A militaristic policy will not bear these results, but will continue to impede meaningful development in the country. In such circumstances the current trajectory of Canadian foreign policy will simply recreate conditions of state failure to the detriment of democracy, development, and peace in Afghanistan.

NOTES

1 The Peace, Reconciliation and Justice Conference was held in The Hague on 6–7 June 2005. Given the recent history of violence and civil war in Afghanistan, the implementation of transitional justice has been identified as crucial to building peace and stability. For more on the Peace, Reconciliation and Justice framework, see http://www.aihrc.org.af/actionplan_af.htm.

2 According to Barfield, Afghanistan received the lowest level of post-conflict reconstruction aid, which reflected the political will of the United States and its allies in rebuilding the Afghan state and society: 'In 2003, per capita aid in Afghanistan was $50 per person. It had risen to $66 by 2005. This fell short of post-conflict aid packages elsewhere at the same time, such as Mozambique ($111 per capita) or Serbia and Montenegro ($237 per capita).' Despite the low levels of aid, a large portion of it (40 per cent) has found its way back to the donor countries through corporate profits and salaries (Barfield 2008, 413).

3 The total cost of the Afghan war remains unknown; as recently as April 2012 CBC journalist Brian Stewart highlighted the high level of secrecy that keeps the total costs of war hidden from Canadian citizens (Stewart 2012).

4 The Canadian PRT was handed over to the United States at the beginning of 2011 (Rennie 2011).

5 Canada became a signatory to the United Nations Convention Against Torture twenty-two years ago. Yet the actions of the Conservative government and its masking of the torture file is a clear violation of that Convention under Section 269.1.

6 Rubin argues that state building in Afghanistan will not succeed unless more resources are committed to Afghanistan. However, he fails to acknowledge that military occupation cannot achieve sustainable and democratic development. He writes, '[u]nless the shaky Afghan government receives both the resources and the leadership required to deliver tangible benefits in areas cleared of insurgents, the international presence in Afghanistan will come to resemble a foreign occupation – an occupation

that Afghans ultimately reject . . . Washington and its international partners must rethink their strategy and significantly increase both the resources they devote to Afghanistan and the effectiveness of those resources' use' (2007, 57).

References

Abbott, Chris, Paul Rogers, and John Sloboda. 2006. 'Global Responses to Global Threats: Sustainable Security for the 21st Century.' Briefing Paper. London: Oxford Research Group. June.

Afghanistan Compact. 2006. 'Building on Success: The London Conference on Afghanistan.' London, 31 January–1 February.

Albo, Greg. 2006. 'Empire's Ally: Canadian Foreign Policy.' *Canadian Dimension* 40, no. 6: 54–6.

Angus Reid Global Monitor. 2008. 'Canadians Reject Extending Afghan Mission.' 11 February.

Angus Reid Public Opinion Poll. 2010. 'Support for the Afghanistan Mission Falls Markedly in Canada.' 21 April.

Asia Foundation. 2008. 'Afghanistan in 2008: A Survey of the Afghan People.' San Francisco.

Bannerman, Mark. 2010. 'The Warlord's Tune: Afghanistan's War on Children.' *ABC News*, 22 February.

Barfield, Thomas. 2008. 'The Roots of Failure in Afghanistan.' *Current History* 107, no. 713: 410–17.

Boutros Ghali, Boutros. 1995. 'Concluding Statements.' United Nations Congress on Public International Law: Towards the Twenty-First Century: International Law as a Language for International Relations, New York, 13–17 March.

Brown, Stephen. 2008. 'CIDA Under the Gun: Reduced Autonomy and the Securitization of Development in Canada.' Paper presented at the 49th Annual International Studies Association Convention, San Francisco, CA, 26–29 March.

Burke, Jason. 2007. 'The New Taliban.' *Observer*, 14 October.

Canada. 2003. 'A Dialogue on Foreign Policy: Report to Canadians.' Ottawa: Department of Foreign Affairs and International Trade.

–. 2004. *Securing an Open Society: Canada's National Security Policy*. Ottawa: Privy Council Office.

–. 2005a. 'Canada in Afghanistan: The International Policy Statement in Action.' http://www.canada-afghanistan.gc.ca/IPS-in-action-en.asp?Print=1.

–. 2005b. 'Canada's International Policy Statement: A Role of Pride and Influence in the World.' Ottawa: Department of Foreign Affairs and International Trade.

–. 2006. Parliament. Senate. Standing Committee on National Security and Defence. 'Managing Turmoil: The Need to Upgrade Canadian Foreign Aid and Military Strength to Deal with Massive Change,' Interim Report. Ottawa: Department of National Defence.

–. 2008. *Independent Panel on Canada's Future Role in Afghanistan*. Ottawa: Government of Canada.

Capstick, Mike. 2007. 'The Civil-Military Effort in Afghanistan: A Strategic Perspective.' *Journal of Military and Strategic Studies* 10, no. 1: 1–27.

CBC News. 2006. 'In depth: Afghanistan.' 21 March.

–. 2008. 'Canada's Afghan mission could cost $18.1 B.' 9 October.

–. 2009. 'In depth: Canada in Afghanistan.' 10 February.

Chase, Steven. 2012. 'PM to "examine all options" on 2014 withdrawal from Afghanistan.' *Globe and Mail*, 25 April.

Chomsky, Noam. 2006. *Failed States: The Abuse of Power and the Assault on Democracy*. New York: Metropolitan Books.

CIDA (Canadian International Development Agency). 2007. 'Review of the Afghanistan Program, Final Version.' Ottawa: CIDA, Evaluation Division, Performance and Knowledge Management Branch. May.

Cox, Jim. 2007. 'Afghanistan: The Canadian Military Mission.' Ottawa: Library of Parliament.

Dobbins, James F. 2008. *After the Taliban: Nation Building in Afghanistan*. Washington, DC: Potomac Books.

Druzin, Heath. 2010. 'Running out of time, US and Canadian troops rush to pacify Kandahar.' *Stars and Stripes*, 18 January. http://www.stripes.com/news/running-out-of-time-u-s-and-canadian-troops-rush-to-pacify-kandahar-1.98073 (accessed 20 April 2011).

Economist. 2009. 'Afghanistan: From Insurgency to Insurrection.' 22 August.

Engler, Yves. 2009. *The Black Book of Canadian Foreign Policy*. Halifax, NS: Fernwood.

Fund for Peace. 2011. 'The Failed States Index.' Washington, DC. http://www.fundforpeace.org/global/?q=fsi-grid2009.

Gannon, Kathy. 2005. *I Is for Infidel: From Holy War to Holy Terror in Afghanistan*. New York: Perseus Books.

Ghani, Ashraf, and Clare Lockhart. 2008. *Fixing Failed States: A Framework for Rebuilding a Fractured World*. Oxford: Oxford University Press.

Gilmore, Scott. 2003. 'Canadian Foreign Policy and Afghanistan.' Presentation to the 11th Annual CANCAPS Conference, Calgary, 6 December.

Glevum Associates. 2010. *Kandahar Province Survey Report: March 2010.* Burlington, MA.

Graham, Bill. 2005. 'The Canadian Forces' Mission in Afghanistan: Canadian Policy and Values in Action.' 9 November. http://www.forces. gc.ca/site/mobil/news-nouvelles-eng.asp?id=1805 (accessed 20 April 2008).

Griffiths, Martin, Terry O'Callaghan, and Steven C. Roach. 2008. *International Relations: The Key Concepts*, 2nd ed. New York: Routledge.

Harper, Stephen. 2006. 'Canada's Commitment in Afghanistan.' House of Commons Debates, Ottawa, 17 May.

Hassan-Yari, Houchang. 2006. 'Canada in Afghanistan: Continuity and Clarity.' *Journal of Military and Strategic Studies* 9, no. 1: 1–14.

Hess, Pamela. 2008. 'Karzai only controls 1/3 of Afghanistan.' Associated Press, 28 February.

Hilary, John. 2008. 'Donor dogma is threatening the prospects of reconstruction in Afghanistan and other countries alike.' *Guardian*, 14 February.

Human Rights Watch. 2003. 'Afghanistan Report.' 15.5(c). New York. July.

–. 2007. 'World Report 2007: Afghanistan.' New York. 11 January.

Ignatieff, Michael. 2003. 'The American Empire: The Burden.' *New York Times Magazine*, 5 January.

Kahler, Miles. 2009. 'State Building after Afghanistan and Iraq.' In *The Dilemmas of Statebuilding: Confronting the Contradictions of Postwar Peace Operations*, ed. Roland Paris and Timothy D. Sisk. New York: Routledge.

Kaplan, Robert D. 1994. 'The Coming Anarchy.' *Atlantic* 273, no. 2: 44–76.

Kaplan, Seth D. 2008. *Fixing Fragile States: A New Paradigm for Development.* Santa Barbara, CA: Praeger Security International.

Kenny, Colin. 2009. 'Setback for "Canadian approach" in Afghanistan.' *Toronto Star*, 24 November.

Klein, Naomi. 2008. *The Shock Doctrine: The Rise of Disaster Capitalism.* New York: Metropolitan Books.

Laxer, James. 2007. 'Afghan Mission Folly.' February. http://www.jameslaxer. com (accessed September 2008).

Mallaby, Sebastian. 2002. 'The Reluctant Imperialist: Terrorism, Failed States, and the Case for American Empire.' *Foreign Affairs* 81, no. 2: 2–7.

Moghadam, Valentine. 2003. 'Nationalism, Globalization, and Fundamentalism: Some Reflections on Islamic Fundamentalism in the Middle East.' Illinois State University. Unpublished.

Mulroney, David. 2007. 'Canada in Afghanistan: From Collaboration to Integration.' 9 May. http://www.igloo.org/ciia/download/Branches/national/afghanis/davidmul (accessed 23 January 2010).

Mychajlyszyn, Natalie. 2007. 'Afghanistan: Reconstruction and Development.' Ottawa: Parliament of Canada. November.

NATO (North Atlantic Treaty Organization). 2009. 'Afghanistan Report 2009.' Brussels. http://www.nato.int/nato_static/assets/pdf/pdf_2009_03/20090 331_090331_afghanistan_report_2009.pdf.

Nawa, Fariba. 2006. 'Afghanistan, Inc.' *CorpWatch Online.* http://www.corp watch.org/article.php?id=13518 (accessed 15 January 2009).

Obama, Barack. 2009. 'Speech on Troops' Surge in Afghanistan.' *New York Times,* 2 December.

OECD (Organisation for Economic Co-operation and Development). 2006. *Governance, Peace and Security: Whole of Government Approaches to Fragile States.* Paris: OECD.

Oppel Jr., Richard A., and Sharifullah Sahak. 2010. 'Dispute flares after NATO convoy kills 4 in Afghanistan.' *New York Times,* 20 April.

Oppel Jr., Richard A., and Abdul Waheed Wafa. 2010. 'Afghan investigators say U.S. troops tried to cover up evidence in botched raid.' *New York Times,* 5 April.

Ottaway, Marina, and Anatol Lieven. 2001. 'Rebuilding Afghanistan: Fantasy versus Reality.' Washington, DC: Carnegie Endowment for International Peace. 12 January.

Paris, Roland, and Timothy D. Sisk, eds. 2009. *The Dilemmas of Statebuilding: Confronting the Contradictions of Postwar Peace Operations.* New York: Routledge.

Patience, Martin. 2010. 'Suicide attack on Afghan capital.' BBC News, 26 February.

Potter, Mitch. 2006. 'War, Canadian style: bringing the war home.' *Toronto Star,* 12 March.

Rashid, Ahmed. 2002. *Taliban: Militant Islam, Oil and Fundamentalism in Central Asia,* 2nd ed. London: I.B. Tauris.

Regehr, Ernie. 2007. 'Failed States and the Limits to Force: The Challenge of Afghanistan.' *Ploughshares Monitor* 28, no. 4.

Rennie, Steve. 2011. 'Canada hands over Kandahar PRT to US.' MSN News, 12 January. http://news.ca.msn.com/canada/cp-article.aspx?cp-documen tid=27217138 (accessed 26 April 2012).

Roston, Aram. 2009. 'How the US Army protects its trucks – by paying the Taliban.' *Guardian,* 13 November.

Rotberg, Robert I. 2002. 'Failed States in a World of Terror.' *Foreign Affairs* 81, no. 4: 127–40.

Rubin, Barnett R. 1995. *The Search for Peace in Afghanistan: From Buffer State to Failed State.* New Haven, CT: Yale University Press.

–. 2000. 'The Political Economy of War and Peace in Afghanistan.' *World Development* 28, no. 10: 1789–1803.

–. 2002. *The Fragmentation of Afghanistan: State Formation and Collapse in the International System*. New Haven, CT: Yale University Press.

–. 2006. 'Afghanistan's Uncertain Transition: From Turmoil to Normalcy.' New York: Council on Foreign Relations.

–. 2007. 'Saving Afghanistan.' *Foreign Affairs* 86, no. 1: 57–78.

Rubin, Elizabeth. 2006. 'In the Land of the Taliban.' *New York Times Magazine*, 22 October.

Saikal, Amin. 2006. *Modern Afghanistan: A History of Struggle and Survival*. London: I.B. Tauris.

Samar, Sima. 2008. 'Annual Report 2008.' Kabul: Independent Afghan Human Rights Commission.

Schmitz, Gerald, and Karin Phillips. 2008. 'Afghanistan: Canadian Diplomatic Engagement.' Ottawa: Library of Parliament. 4 February.

Senlis Council. 2006a. 'Afghanistan Five Years Later: The Return of the Taliban.' Executive Summary. London. September.

–. 2006b. 'Canada in Kandahar: No Peace to Keep, a Case Study of the Military Coalitions in Southern Afghanistan.' London. June.

–. 2006c. 'Helmand at War: The Changing Nature of Insurgency in Southern Afghanistan and Its Effects on the Future of the Country.' London. June.

–. 2006d. 'Losing Hearts and Minds in Afghanistan: Canada's Leadership to Break the Cycle of Violence in Southern Afghanistan.' London. October.

–. 2007a. 'The Canadian International Development Agency in Kandahar: Unanswered Questions.' London. August.

–. 2007b. 'Taliban Politics and Afghan Legitimate Grievances.' London. June.

Shah, Taimoor, and Carlotta Gall. 2010. 'American aid official visits Kandahar after attacks on contractors.' *New York Times*, 18 April.

Starkey, Jerome. 2010. 'US special forces "tried to cover up" botched Khataba raid in Kabul.' *Times* (UK), 5 April.

Stein, Janice Gross, and Eugene Lang. 2008. *The Unexpected War: Canada in Kandahar*. Toronto: Penguin Canada.

Stewart, Brian. 2012. 'The F-35 Fiasco and Ottawa's Culture of Secrecy.' CBC News, 4 April.

Straw, Jack. 2002. 'Re-Ordering the World.' *Guardian*, 25 March.

Suhrke, Astri. 2009. 'The Dangers of a Tight Embrace: Externally Assisted State Building in Afghanistan.' In *The Dilemmas of Statebuilding: Confronting the Contradictions of Post-war Peace Operations*, ed. Roland Paris and Timothy D. Sisk. New York: Routledge.

Taber, Jane. 2010. 'Support for Afghan mission slipping, poll finds.' *Globe and Mail*, 21 April.

Thürer, Daniel. 1999. 'The "Failed State" and International Law.' *International Review of the Red Cross* 836: 731–61.

Tran, Mark. 2009. 'Afghanistan strategy must change, US commander McChrystal says.' *Guardian*, 31 August.

Travers, Patrick, and Taylor Owen. 2007. 'Peacebuilding while Peacemaking: The Merits of a 3D Approach in Afghanistan.' *Walrus* (July–August).

Tyson, Ann Scott. 2008. 'NATO's not winning in Afghanistan, report says.' *Washington Post*, 31 January.

United Nations. 2009. 'Afghanistan Humanitarian Action Plan, 2010.' Executive Summary. New York. 30 November.

Walkom, Thomas. 2007. 'Afghan poll not as clear as it seems: do ordinary Afghans want Canada to stay in Kandahar until the Taliban is defeated?' *Toronto Star*, 21 October.

–. 2009a. 'Afghanistan sacrifices may have been in vain.' *Toronto Star*, 31 October.

–. 2009b. 'Only the losers need to fear war-crime laws.' *Toronto Star*, 21 November.

Watson, Paul. 2012. 'Canada's Afghan legacy: Failure at Dahla Dam.' *Toronto Star*, 14 July.

Weber, Max. 1946. *From Max Weber: Essays in Sociology.* New York: Oxford University Press.

Woods, Allen. 2009. 'Trouble in the "model village": CIDA slow in awarding contracts for projects, senator, Afghans say.' *Toronto Star*, 24 November.

World Bank. 2005a. *Afghanistan – State Building, Sustaining Growth, and Reducing Poverty.* Country Study 31673. Washington, DC.

–. 2005b. *The Investment Climate in Afghanistan: Exploiting Opportunities in an Uncertain Environment.* Washington, DC.

–. 2007. 'Afghanistan: Supporting State-building and Development.' Washington, DC.

Zartman, I. William. 1995. *Collapsed States: The Disintegration and Restoration of Legitimate Authority.* London: Lynne Reiner.

10

Building an Expeditionary Force for Democracy Promotion

ANTHONY FENTON AND JON ELMER

Since the United States emerged as an imperial power in the early twentieth century, successive administrations have premised the projection of power on the claim that they are making the world 'safe for democracy' (Smith 1994, 84). More recently, post–Cold War imperialism has been premised on the claim that western powers are exporting democracy to non-western countries. The crucial difference in contemporary imperialism as compared to colonial occupations like those in the Philippines, Haiti, and the Dominican Republic in the early twentieth century is that it 'involves the imposition of a Western (neo) liberal procedural form of democracy on imperialised peoples,' rather than a reliance on direct occupation (Ayers 2009, 1). Today, as Gendzier (1998, 57–8) notes, 'the objectives of promoting democracy and increasing participation . . . [are] rhetorical props for policies supported by elites fearful of both.' From aid conditionalities to destabilization, regime change and de facto trusteeships, the instruments of political, economic, and/or military power employed in non-western countries have become more subtle and less overtly objectionable than the 'boots on the ground' that dominated a century ago.

Acting in virtual lockstep with other western powers, Canada has been a key player in the promotion of democracy in recent decades, with a hands-on role in the re-engineering of 'a plan for world order' (Straus 1987, 243). As one of the leading western states to undertake a policy shift towards neoliberalism since the 1970s (Dobbin 1998), Canada has reoriented its foreign policy to facilitate the export of neoliberal economics. Globally Canada has influenced policies in this direction through its membership in all of the key supranational institutions, particularly, the World Bank, the International Monetary Fund, the

Organisation for Economic Co-operation and Development, and the North Atlantic Treaty Organization (NATO), among others (Carty and Smith 1981; Albo 2006).

The erosion of state sovereignty via the 'human security' and 'responsibility to protect' (R2P) doctrines are the crucial apparatuses through which Canada has helped engineer justifications for twenty-first-century interventionism in the form of 'democracy promotion,' which is the subject of this chapter. In the span of twenty years democracy has evolved from a taboo to an openly proclaimed priority for Canada. The most intense period of institutionalizing democracy promotion as a core priority of Canadian foreign policy has coincided with the transformation of the Canadian military into an expeditionary force, in addition to Canada's unprecedented 'whole-of-government' commitment to the counterinsurgency war in Afghanistan.

Both the western model of democracy and that which is exported to non-western countries are properly termed *polyarchy*, following the usage of Dahl (1972), as acknowledged by its proponents[1] as well as its critics,[2] both of whom note the elitist roots of this view of democracy. Canadian political theorist C.B. Macpherson noted that these conceptions of democracy were preoccupied with protecting 'the minority of the opulent against the majority' (1977, 15–16, n. 6). This view was echoed by earlier US proponents of democracy promotion, who saw it as requiring the 'leadership of the new institutions by the modernized elite' (Douglas 1972, 139).[3] Critics have argued that polyarchy 'promot[es] a limited form of democracy as part of the effort to replace coercive means of social control in the South with consensual ones' (Neufeld 1999, 108). Thus, polyarchy promotion can be seen as part and parcel of the western pursuit of hegemony in the world order (Robinson 1996, 72). As Bates (1975, 352) writes, '[t]he concept of hegemony is really a very simple one. It means political leadership based on the consent of the led, a consent which is secured by the diffusion and popularization of the world view of the ruling class.' Critics provide a useful framework for discussing the post-9/11 period of democracy promotion as polyarchy promotion – although, for the sake of consistency, we use the term 'democracy' in this chapter.

The chapter is divided into four sections. The first provides a brief overview of the development of democracy promotion as a tool of Canadian foreign policy. Because the US empire has used democracy promotion as a tool of destabilization, subjugation, and the maintenance of social and economic inequalities globally, it is important to examine the extent to which Canadian democracy promotion is integrated with the US apparatus – a subject that tends to be ignored in mainstream discourse. This section concludes at the turn of the twenty-first century, on the eve of Canada's shift towards democracy promotion as a central focus of foreign policy, and describes how Canada began to lay the groundwork for expeditionary democracy promotion as an integral part of future military campaigns.

The second section traces the ascension of democracy promotion in Canadian foreign policy following 9/11 up to 2009, with an emphasis on the increasing interoperability of Canada's democracy promotion policies and practitioners with those of the United States. This integration is a subset of a broader transformational trend that Jean Daudelin tags as 'the profound, and radically asymmetric, interdependence that has developed with the United States' (2005, 120), as well as with emerging regional and global democracy networks.

The third section is the first of two that examine the specific case of Afghanistan, covering the evolution of Canada's democracy promotion during the core of its involvement in Afghanistan from 2001 to 2009. The latter half of this period (mid-2005 to 2009) overlaps with an overwhelming intellectual and policy-centred consensus-building effort that argues that Canada should (and can) promote democracy while waging counterinsurgency. The final section looks at the Strategic Advisory Team-Afghanistan as a concrete manifestation of Canada's increasing turn to 'expeditionary democracy promotion.' Overall, we demonstrate that, as a foreign policy tool, democracy promotion is essential to maintaining Canada's place among the 'new imperialist' states of the twenty-first century. Only by understanding modes of power and the exercise of hegemony can we hope to counter them; in a small way, we hope this chapter contributes to such an understanding.

Democracy Promotion in Canadian Foreign Policy before 2001

Canada's first foray into democracy promotion followed President Ronald Reagan's 1982 address to the British Parliament in which he pledged to foster 'the establishment of conditions of freedom and democracy as rapidly as possible in all countries' (Reagan 1982). This commitment grew out of Cold War national security imperatives and debates that began in the early 1970s (Douglas 1972, 130–1). In order to counter Soviet influence, the United States saw a need to develop a more sophisticated approach to statecraft to complement traditional foreign policy tools – diplomacy, economy, military, and propaganda (ibid., 132). Such capabilities that this would entail creating 'would thus be a stabilizing factor in world power politics' (ibid., 137), meaning the preservation of US hegemony and access to raw materials, the fostering of environments conducive to US capital, and the like. Bringing into the open activities that were once the purview of covert agencies such as the Central Intelligence Agency (CIA) would resolve the 'ethical considerations' surrounding such operations and the potential for political fallout, as seen in CIA-related scandals in the period (Chile, Iran-Contra, and so on) (ibid., 150).[4] From the earliest planning stages the US government envisioned a role for western countries such as Canada in the conduct of 'political warfare' (Codevilla 1989; Fenton 2010) towards 'a long-range strategy for the spread and stabilization of democracy . . . among existing democracies' (Straus 1987, 242).

Following Reagan's speech and an extensive 'non-partisan' study, the United States established a set of private, arm's-length foundations with the express purpose of fostering democracy promotion in conjunction with other foreign policy tools. The core organization established for this purpose was (and remains) the congressionally funded National Endowment for Democracy (NED). While covert operations did not cease the NED brought 'a more specialized, sophisticated entity with a focus on political operations, a long-term vision, and a strategic agenda' (Robinson 1996, 87–8).[5]

In Canada a formal process initiated in 1987 by the Progressive Conservative government resulted in the issuance of a report titled *International Cooperation for the Development of Human Rights and Democratic Institutions*, which recommended that Canada institutionalize its own democracy promotion apparatus (Côté-Harper and Courtney 1987). Based on this report, in a move seen as indicating that 'the first step had been taken' towards embracing democracy promotion as a foreign policy objective (Miller 2005, 1), the Canadian government established the International Centre for Human Rights and Democratic Development (ICHRDD, later renamed Rights and Democracy) in 1988. The ICHRDD was meant to be an arm's-length organization to complement existing Canadian institutions with mandates that included democracy promotion – in particular, Elections Canada, the International Development Research Centre (IDRC), and the Canadian International Development Agency (CIDA). Other Canadian non-governmental organizations (NGOs) and arm's-length bodies were created to fill the gap throughout the 1990s, albeit somewhat disparately.[6]

In addition to following the US lead on the democracy-promotion shift, broader geopolitical developments helped pave the way for Canada's ascendency. After the Cold War Canada worked alongside the United States to help 'build a stable world order based on democracy and market economies,' beginning in the former Soviet Union (Laux 1994; Wedel 1998). Officials described Canadian efforts in the region as supporting 'an irrepressible push towards democracy and private enterprise' (Laux 1994, 185; Chandler 1995, 237). The Department of Foreign Affairs and International Trade (DFAIT) explained that the Canadian state has 'a direct stake in ensuring the success of democratic and economic reforms in Central and Eastern Europe' (Laux 1994, 187). Successive Liberal governments supported neoliberal globalization and gradually entrenched democracy promotion as a prominent 'source and . . . objective of Canadian foreign policy' during the 1990s (Neufeld 1999, 98).

Canada's growing support for democracy promotion developed alongside the 'human security agenda' (Hubert and Bonser 2001, 119–20). As an indication of the cross-partisan nature of the human security paradigm, its origins can be found in statements such as those made by Progressive Conservative prime minister Brian Mulroney in 1991 at Stanford University: 'the world looks to the United States for leadership on the integration of the newly emerging democracies into the global economy.' In turn it was Canada's role to share the 'burden' of democracy promotion with the United States: 'I tell you today, Canada will fulfill every single one of its obligations,' Mulroney promised (Stanford University News Service 1991). Assistance to developing countries would be conditioned on their ability to democratize according to western standards while opening up their economies to free market capitalism. As Tony Smith has pointed out, such sentiments eventually brought together both neoconservatives and neoliberals in support of 'a new standard of sovereignty, one to be enforced where necessary by military means,' as part of a broader project that he terms 'liberal imperialism' (2007, 175).

The first person to call explicitly for the creation of a Canadian equivalent to the NED was former diplomat Christopher Cooter, whose conception of democracy promotion shared the same tenets as those of US planners: 'democracy-building normally will be a long-term project . . . As such, it is worth re-examining if the existing instruments available to Canada are sufficient for this complex aspect of the "new diplomacy"' (2000, 101).

At nearly the same time that Cooter presented his case, Prime Minister Jean Chrétien, at the behest of United Nations Secretary-General Kofi Annan, launched the Special Commission on Humanitarian Intervention and Sovereignty (McRae and Hubert 2001, 273). Later renamed the International Commission on Intervention and State Sovereignty (ICISS),[7] the commission produced the R2P doctrine, pushing the envelope of humanitarian justifications for imperialism even further.

Although the imperatives of the 'global war on terror' and opposition from the Non-Aligned Movement thwarted the implementation of Cooter's proposal and the advance of the R2P doctrine, the ideas remained on the table. Indeed 'Canada stood "almost alone" in trying to persuade states to commit to R2P' (Bellamy 2009, 70). Leading up to the UN World Summit in 2005, Canada went to considerable lengths to see to it that R2P was adopted by member states in the Summit Outcome document. This, combined with some 'diplomatic sleight of hand' (ibid., 89), found R2P nominally, if conditionally, endorsed by the UN General Assembly.

Several countries had reservations about R2P beyond its symbolic adoption in 2005. As Smith (2007, 173) points out, the ICISS report 'justified liberal imperialism.' Drawing an important link between R2P and democracy promotion, Smith writes how, as a consequence of the report, the ICISS 'asserted not simply the right . . . to intervene but *the responsibility* of the international community – ultimately defined as the UN Security Council – [was] in effect to put a state into receivership, and to put its people in what another time would have been called a trusteeship, until such a time as a more responsible government, defined as being a democracy, could be created.'

The Canadian Organic Intellectuals of Polyarchy

Since democracy promotion has been adopted as a component of Canadian foreign policy, a number of prominent advocates of 'expeditionary democracy' have emerged, many forging links to US institutions. They assume the characteristics of Gramsci's organic intellectuals in that they act 'as "experts in legitimization" who do the political and theoretical thinking of the dominant groups. But organic intellectuals also . . . theorize on the conditions of existence of a social order as a whole, suggest policies and their justifications, and even participate in their application' (Robinson 1996, 42). Many of Canada's democracy promoters have accrued critical experience by working directly with

counterparts in the US national security milieu. And, as David Donovan, one of the key theorists of democracy promotion in Canadian foreign policy, has pointed out, hundreds of Canadians have worked for
'other organizations and other countries' aid and foreign policy objectives' (2008, 24).

Several of Canada's key democracy promotion boosters have been
informed by direct experience in Afghanistan and Iraq. Grant Kippen,
for example, is a colleague of democracy-promotion advocates Leslie
Campbell and Thomas Axworthy at Queen's University's Centre for
the Study of Democracy (CSD) and is both a practitioner and key theorist of democracy promotion in Afghanistan. In 2003 Kippen was in
Afghanistan with the National Democratic Institute (NDI), a US non-
governmental organization, supporting the Afghan election process.
From there he became the chair of the UN-backed Electoral Complaints
Commission for both the 2004 and 2009 Afghan presidential elections,
playing an integral role in determining the outcome and perceived legitimacy of the process (Verma 2009).[8] Kippen has been a central voice
in numerous consensus-building events with Canadian foreign policy
stakeholders, arguing that 'the Canadian government has the opportunity to assume a lead role, if it so chooses . . . to develop a long-term
democratic development process' (Kippen 2006, 34).

Another important theorist-practitioner is Ben Rowswell, Canada's
first diplomat in post-war Iraq from 2003 to 2005, where he assisted in
the oversight of Iraq's elections (Canada 2006). Rowswell also worked
for NDI in the Kurdistan region of Iraq (Bouillon, Malone, and Rowswell 2008, 110). Differing from his NDI colleagues who advocated
democracy promotion largely *outside* government, Rowswell returned
to Canada to help spearhead the policy from inside the state. In 2007
the Conservative government of Stephen Harper created the Democracy Unit within DFAIT, with Rowswell appointed its first manager.
Reflecting the fusion of democracy promotion and counterinsurgency
with the Afghanistan war, Rowswell became deputy head of mission
for the Canadian Embassy in Kabul. In September 2009 he was named
Canada's top diplomat in southern Afghanistan as the representative of
Canada in Kandahar, a position that requires intimate knowledge of democracy promotion in the midst of counterinsurgency and, specifically,
the US approach. As Rowswell remarked to an embedded journalist
about the joint Canada-US approach, '[w]e work at full integration . . .
We are cheek by jowl . . . The best way to integrate is to integrate completely' (Fisher 2009).

The interchangeability between Canadian and US democracy promotion exists at both the institutional and state levels. Increasing numbers of academic institutions are involved in theorizing, policy framing, activism, and/or democracy-promotion implementation, the most prominent of which are located at Queen's University, Carleton University, the University of British Columbia, and the University of Toronto. Beginning in 2004, for instance, the NED and the Munk School of Global Affairs at the University of Toronto began a collaboration when they inaugurated the Seymour Martin Lipset Lecture on Democracy in the World.[9] Described as a 'catalyst for further cooperation,' the initial lecture, delivered by former Brazilian president Fernando Henrique Cardoso, took place at the Canadian Embassy in Washington (Cardoso 2005). In February 2008 the NED's long-time president Carl Gershman participated in a CSD conference entitled 'Creating Democratic Value: Evaluating Efforts to Promote Democracy Abroad.' In turn the NED invited representatives of the CSD to the Fifth Assembly of the NED-sponsored World Movement for Democracy (WMD), alongside other Canadian NGOs who have collaborated with the NED network, formally or otherwise.[10] DFAIT has also helped build this network in providing funds for democracy-promotion programs for the Council for a Community of Democracies, the International Foundation for Electoral Systems, NDI, NED, and WMD. Canadian organizations and prominent individuals have enjoyed particularly close relations with the WMD, specifically on initiatives that have helped foster a consensus on the Afghanistan war.[11]

Canada has made the most significant bureaucratic strides towards democracy promotion under the Harper government, which has established a number of key institutions. First among them is the Office for Democratic Governance in CIDA, designed to act as a 'home to coordinate and synthesize Canada's role in advancing democratic governance' (Canada 2007b). Also of note are the Democracy Unit in DFAIT and the arm's-length 'Governance Village' collaboration with the Centre for International Governance Innovation, which aims 'to create a knowledge exchange gateway for all stakeholders involved in democratic governance' (ibid.). While the Conservatives have expanded these policies these trends are a continuation of, and have their origins in, the policies and practices of the Liberal governments of Jean Chrétien and Paul Martin, both of which were committed to building state capacity for democracy promotion. In 2003, only a few years after Cooter's initial proposal, the Institute for Research on Public Policy

(IRPP) initiated a democracy-promotion program. The Martin government further moved to formalize democracy promotion in foreign policy institutions, especially after tabling its International Policy Statement in 2005 (Canada 2005a). This was followed by the establishment of the Canada Corps initiative (soon folded into the Office for Democratic Governance) (Smilie 2007), and, more important, the creation of the Democracy Council, fulfilling a recommendation going back to the 1987 report by Côté-Harper and Courtney.[12] In addition to working as a consultative committee, the Democracy Council promotes 'a better understanding of what Canadians, in and out of government, are doing with respect to democracy promotion – not least in failed and failing states' (O'Neill 2006).[13] Minutes of one of its meetings indicate that the Democracy Council perceives itself as a twenty-first-century 'incarnation of earlier models such as NDI and NED in the United States.'[14]

The rapid advance of democracy promotion in the Ottawa bureaucracy compelled the House of Commons Standing Committee on Foreign Affairs and International Development (FAAE) to conduct an extensive review. Some fifty meetings involving more than fifty witnesses took place between September 2006 and March 2007, leading to the tabling of a 224-page report, *Advancing Canada's Role in International Support for Democratic Development*, in July 2007.[15] The chief recommendation called for the creation of a Canadian democracy foundation 'to carry out our nation's democratic development efforts' (Canada 2007a, 1).

Although none of those consulted for the study was overly critical of democracy promotion as a foreign policy priority, the New Democratic Party (NDP) and the Bloc Québécois submitted 'dissenting opinions' that reflected some of the criticism found elsewhere. The Bloc said the report 'contains a number of inconsistencies that have us wonder[ing] about the real objectives behind the creation of such a [democracy] foundation' (ibid., 191–2). Implicitly referring to the *organic intellectuals* who have led the campaign for the foundation's creation, the Bloc wrote that 'it is risky, if not dangerous, that the majority of the Committee accepted the idea put forward by a few promoters of a foundation oriented toward providing assistance to political parties' (ibid., 192). Democracy promotion's 'difficulty,' the Bloc added, 'should not be underestimated, despite the enthusiasm generated . . . among a few intellectuals at Queen's University's Centre for the Study of Democracy' (ibid., 194). The Bloc was also concerned that 'Canada could use democratic development assistance as a foreign-policy tool and decide to influence certain political groups or forces rather than others,' and that certain recommendations 'allow for the possibility of a more interventionist foreign policy' (ibid., 201).

The NDP, in contrast, accepted the premise of exporting democracy, conceding it as an 'important yet sensitive domain' (ibid., 205). While expressing some concern for the 'politicization of the report' by the Conservatives, the NDP only cautioned that ' "[d]emocracy" promotion can be [sic], and has frequently undermined indigenous democratic processes around the world, when abused for the partisan foreign policy purposes of an external state' (ibid., 209, 210–11).[16]

In the Harper government's response to the FAAE report, democracy promotion as a foreign policy imperative was made clear: 'Supporting freedom and democracy is a key priority of the Government of Canada' (Canada 2007c, 2). The minister of state for democratic reform was mandated to study the FAAE's recommendations further and, in mid-2009, the minister created an Advisory Panel on the Creation of a Canadian Democracy Promotion Agency, consisting of key organic intellectuals of democracy promotion: Thomas Axworthy of the CSD and NDI's Leslie Campbell, co-authors of the blueprint for a 'democracy Canada institute' published as part of IRPP's democracy promotion series (Axworthy, Campbell, and Donovan 2005); Éric Duhaime, a long-time advisor to right-wing political figures in Quebec and the Conservative party and the current deputy country director for NDI's Political Parties Program in Iraq; and Pamela Wallin, a former Canadian broadcaster, diplomat, Conservative senator and, notably, a member of the 'blue ribbon' Independent Panel on Canada's Future Role in Afghanistan.

In November 2009 the advisory panel recommended that the government create a Canadian Centre for Advancing Democracy, with a proposed budget of between $150 million and $350 million for five years (Canada 2009). The panel's report reflected the evolution of Canada's foreign policy approach, and especially the influence of the war in Afghanistan, recommending that the new democracy foundation open field offices in 'high conflict states' such as Afghanistan and Haiti. The panel's recommendations reflected well the 'diffusion and popularization' of the worldview and foreign policy prescriptions of the Canadian state and ruling elites in building hegemony for democracy promotion for the early twenty-first century.

Countering Insurgency and Promoting Democracy:
The Case of Afghanistan

During the FAAE's democracy promotion hearings, CIDA president
Robert Greenhill called Afghanistan 'a great example of where democracy and development go hand in hand' (Greenhill 2007). This
perspective is shared by many supporters of the Canadian war and occupation effort, leading to a frequent conflation of democracy building
and the counterinsurgency war. In 2006, for example, Douglas Bland,
of Queen's University's School of Policy Studies and a former soldier,
told the House of Commons Standing Committee on National Defence
that '[w]e need to make the Taliban and these other people afraid of
a liberal democracy that's upset . . . There's nothing more fearsome
than a liberal democracy that's working together against these kinds
of people' (Bland 2006).

   In assessing democracy-promotion efforts, it is both what Canada
does *in Afghanistan* as part of western foreign policy interests and
the Afghanistan-related programs, conferences, and debates that
occur *in Canada* that merit attention. Both play a critical function in
the legitimacy-building process for military intervention, in stifling
dissent, and in the battle for 'hearts and minds' in both Canada and
Afghanistan.

   From the perspective of Canadian policy-makers, the more Canadian
NGOs that can be mobilized to contribute to the war effort, the more
difficult it will be to foment a movement in opposition to the war. As
Paul LaRose-Edwards, the head of CANADEM, one of these organizations, said, '[t]he fact that we're not part of government makes us valu-
able to government. We're a tool they can use' (LaRose-Edwards 2006).
As he explained, the Canadian state encouraged the creation of such
NGOs in the first place, since outsourcing some of the higher-risk aspects of its foreign policy 'allows a certain arm's-length relationship for
Foreign Affairs and CIDA . . . [I]f it goes wrong, it's our fault all the way'
(ibid). Among a variety of tasks in support of the counterinsurgency effort, CANADEM has recruited a multitude of Afghan Canadians for
the Canadian military. Through its recruitment roster, CANADEM also
helps place other Canadian democracy promoters in places such as
Afghanistan.[17]

   Closely involved in the creation of the R2P doctrine, the IDRC,
since 9/11, has deepened its focus on democracy promotion. A Crown

corporation, the IDRC functions as an arm's-length foreign policy tool of the Canadian state. With the coming to power of the Harper Conservatives, the IDRC added a commitment to 'a whole new field of endeavour: helping to rebuild democratic institutions in Afghanistan' (IDRC 2007a, 28).[18] Some of its many programs are carried out solely by the IDRC, while others are undertaken in conjunction with agencies such as the Parliamentary Centre (IDRC 2007b, 1). As a well-respected, non-partisan Canadian institution, the IDRC has also played an important legitimacy- and consensus-building role for the Afghanistan war domestically.

In 2008 the CSD published a DFAIT-funded series of case studies, carried out in close consultation with NED and its affiliates. The chapter on Afghanistan was written by Patricia DeGennaro of the United States Agency for International Development (USAID), who discussed the pervasiveness in that country of US democracy promoters NDI and the International Republican Institute, described as democracy's 'mentors' (Axworthy 2008). CSD has openly played an elite consensus-building role, helping to lay the groundwork for Canada's shift to more intensive counterinsurgency efforts in southern Afghanistan. As an earlier CSD report on Afghanistan notes, '[t]he consensus of the [November 2004] meeting of academic experts, NGOs, and senior government officials was that Canada should assume responsibility for a Provincial and Reconstruction Team (PRT) in Kandahar' (Axworthy 2006, 2–3). This was part of a consistent pattern of seeking, and co-opting, civil society support for Canada's campaign in Afghanistan. These developments were tracked closely by high-level planners: 'At the annual DFA/NGO human rights consultations in February 2004, it was clear that Canadian non-governmental organizations are strong supporters of Canada's role in Afghanistan and would encourage continued defence, development and diplomatic activity . . . Canadians, in general, are strongly supportive of Canadian efforts in Afghanistan to date.'[19]

In addition to the consensus-building – and dissent-stifling – work of democracy promoters within Canada, there are several examples of Canadian organizations that have undertaken such programs inside Afghanistan, almost without exception in concert with USAID and/or NED-linked organizations, as well as with Afghan organizations that are part of the NED funding network.[20] Of the huge number of Canadian democracy efforts in Afghanistan, a couple of examples will illustrate the general practices.

In the first example, at least two Canadian democracy promoters, IMPACS and Rights and Democracy, collaborated with a prominent USAID 'media democracy' NGO, Internews, to support 'the development of free media in Afghanistan' (Paterson 2005). Part of an extensive program, IMPACS received some $2.7 million to set up four radio stations in relatively peaceful parts of the country, out of a total of twenty-nine radio stations under the program that reach an estimated 43 per cent of the population. These stations are part of a broader program linked to the US-led effort to achieve 'information dominance' in occupied countries (Barker 2008, 113). According to an official evaluation, however, the IMPACS program largely failed to achieve any of the benchmarks set out for it, and in 2007 IMPACS declared bankruptcy, though CIDA's audit of its activities was largely ignored by the media. The program nevertheless might be deemed 'successful' to the extent that it closed off space for the expression of democratic, anti-occupation forms of media.

As Canada shifted to the heart of the counterinsurgency in southern Afghanistan in mid-2005, its media democracy programs took on a different orientation. Instead of continuing to fund a Canadian media NGO,[21] DFAIT turned to funding the Afghanistan National Participation Association, a long-time NED grantee whose programs have included efforts to 'raise public awareness of democratic values, human rights, women's rights, and political decision making' (NED 2006). Direct Canadian media efforts were also largely taken over by the Canadian Forces' Psychological Operations (PSYOPS) Branch, which was created under the command of then-Army head General Rick Hillier in November 2003 (Fontaine 2004).

Reflecting the 'information warfare' side of counterinsurgency operations in Afghanistan, the Canadian deputy commander of the PSYOPS Branch articulated that 'a conflict is a fight which happens not only on the battlefield, but also in the human spirit' (Davis 2005). A subset of information operations, PSYOPS is inherently used in Afghanistan in the promotion of democracy. Discussing PSYOPS and Information Operations, a former commander of Canada's PRT, Colonel Steve Bowes, said, '[t]his whole mission is based around the concept of information operations . . . We have to extend the authority of the Afghan government, because we want to avoid a relapse into a failed state' (Smith 2005). To supplement the brochures and fliers that the PSYOPS teams distribute on the ground (and from the air), the Canadian Forces began creating 'soldier-journalists' through a program that would 'train [soldiers] to become "journalists" to help win the hearts and minds of populations during military operations abroad.' An expert was hired to 'teach soldiers how to become effective news broadcasters to get the military's messages out to locals in Afghanistan and elsewhere' (Beeby 2006). At the same time a contract was tendered by the military for an operation that would broadcast radio into Afghanistan from the Canadian Forces base in Kingston, Ontario. By early 2007 RANA-FM was broadcasting from Kingston 'mixing music with a pro-NATO, anti-Taliban message aimed at young people in Kandahar, Afghanistan.' The station manager insisted that, 'when you talk about military and radio, the first word is the P word, propaganda, you know. And we're anything but' (CBC News 2007).

A second example of how Canadian democracy-promotion efforts are enmeshed within complementary US programs is the Peace Dividend Trust (PDT). The PDT is 'a unique non-profit organization dedicated to making peace and humanitarian operations more effective, efficient and equitable so that they deliver cheaper, faster, smarter missions – resulting in a stronger peace and a larger peace dividend.'[22] Run by a former DFAIT official, Scott Gilmore, who oversaw the development of Canada's 3D policies from 2002 to 2004, PDT's Afghan operations are funded by CIDA, the United Kingdom's Department for International Development, and USAID; other partners include the World Bank, and the NED arm, the Center for International Private Enterprise. Through its Afghan programs, PDT claims to have 'helped facilitate over $350 million into the Afghan economy since 2006.' Helping to facilitate this is the Building Markets program, 'an online resource for Buyers and Suppliers operating in Afghanistan,' which is 'primarily funded by [USAID].' This program helps companies 'win contracts,' including those tendered by the 'procurement arm of the U.S. military,' the United Nations, the European Union, and Afghan ministries. Entering the realm of assisting the counterinsurgency effort, PDT also conducts research into 'increas[ing] the local impact of development spending.' In December 2009, recognizing PDT's contribution to the counterinsurgency effort, General Stanley McChrystal and US Ambassador Karl Eikenberry directed US agencies to use PDT's services in the issuance of their 'Afghan First Policy.' In addition to advancing the neoliberal model, by implication, PDT equates counterinsurgency and foreign occupation with the pursuit of 'peace' in Afghanistan.

Operational Counterinsurgency

If counterinsurgency is as much political as military warfare, how the intervening force places its political personnel is a crucial operational

calculation. In his seminal book, *Low Intensity Operations*, considered
a 'classic' by the United States Marine Corps counterinsurgency field
manual, the British counterinsurgency theorist Frank Kitson writes:
'The ally should be in a position to co-ordinate all its aid in such a
way that one individual person can represent it on the host nation's
supreme council thereby ensuring that the ally takes a proper part in
formulating the overall policy for the prosecution of the campaign . . .
[while at the same time] the ally should be represented at every level on
the host country's committee of staffs according to the system in force,
but always in a subordinate or advisory capacity' (1971, 59). Canada's
Strategic Advisory Team-Afghanistan (SAT-A) program followed this
strategic mandate, and provided an important initial operating model
for the type of expeditionary democracy promotion that Canada has
been developing.

Created in July 2005 under the guidance of the chief of the defence
staff, General Hillier, SAT-A was a unit of fifteen Canadian Forces personnel that would provide 'core planning experts who will be used to
develop strategic level advice for the [government of Afghanistan]'
(Canada 2005b, 2; see also Davis 2008b).[23] These 'strategic military
planners,' according to the Department of National Defence, were embedded within the highest offices of the ministries of Hamid Karzai's
government in order to 'develop key national strategies, and mechanisms for the effective implementation of those strategies' (Canada
2008a, 87). While almost all of Canada's contribution in Afghanistan
falls under the auspices of the International Security Assistance Force
(ISAF), the SAT-A agreement was bilateral and functioned as an independent military operation – code-named Operation Argus – answer-
able to the chief of the defence staff (Cox 2007).[24] The strategic advisory
concept was borne out of General Hillier's term as head of ISAF in 2003
and 2004, during which he provided President Karzai, in a more ad hoc
manner, several officers to advise him. In winter 2005, shortly after taking over as chief of the defence staff, Hillier met with Karzai in Kabul.
According to an account by SAT-A's first commander, Colonel Mike
Capstick, it was at this first meeting that Karzai asked if Hillier would
'provide those guys again' (Capstick 2007).[25]

The SAT-A unit was composed of civilian and military members, and
'reflect[ed] the changing nature of diplomacy. Although diplomats have
traditionally taken the role of establishing relationships with foreign
governments, intervention in failed states has increasingly involved the
military, who forge diplomatic ties while they lend their expertise to the

implementation of civilian projects' (Phillips 2008, 2–3).[26] Indeed, the military staffing was seen as a key asset of SAT-A; as Lieutenant-Colonel John Malevich, a veteran of the program, described, '[t]hat was the advantage of the [SAT-A]. Because we were military . . . there was a certain amount of risk you could take with us. You could give me a 9mm and a truck and I could go all over Kabul and do whatever I wanted, work in the ministries, travel with the minister to different parts of Afghanistan.'[27] Canadian Forces officers, embedded in the top ministries and national agencies of the Afghan government, worked side by side with the ministers responsible for writing and implementing key policy, most notably the Afghanistan National Development Strategy (ANDS) (Mulroney 2007), the key program responsible for the more than $32 billion spent on aid in Afghanistan (*Economist* 2009). Andy Tamas, the CIDA representative on the first SAT-A rotation and author of *Warriors and Nation Builders*, believes the high-level embedding was 'instrumental' to the ratification of the ANDS and the Afghanistan Compact, the key UN-sanctioned operational umbrella for the international intervention (2009, 44).

The SAT-A operation sought to harmonize Afghanistan's national policy with the interests of the counterinsurgency strategy. According to Tamas, following the ratification, the SAT-A team helped 'Afghan officials bring this framework to the attention of ISAF, the US's Enduring Freedom leadership and the PRTs.' Indeed, 'these government planning documents subsequently began to act as an organizing framework for the efforts of most major military and development agencies in the country' (ibid., 41). This type of influence was appreciated by the leadership and did not go unnoticed. The head of Canada's Expeditionary Force Command at the time of the SAT-A program, Lieutenant-General Michel Gauthier, boasted to a parliamentary committee that the small team of officers had an impact out of 'all proportion' to its size (Gauthier 2006). Colonel Capstick goes further: 'The level of influence, respect and access that Canada had in Kabul in 05–06 is directionally proportional to the reputations of the Canadians that senior Afghans know: you can't talk to a senior Afghan without Gen Hiller, Gen Andrew Leslie, [top diplomat] Chris Alexander or [CIDA head] Nipa Banerjee being mentioned. Those people working together built Canada a superb reputation and gave us a lot of [political] capital' (Capstick 2007).[28] As Department of National Defence soldier-historian Sean Maloney told a parliamentary committee, the nuances of intervention have to be appreciated to assess the whole: '[H]aving SAT-A's influence in the course of Kabul was dependent on the blood of our guys on the ground. It all works together. We wouldn't have that influence if we didn't have guys on the ground down south, or people in the provincial reconstruction team, or special operations forces, whatever. The package gives us the influence to do that' (Maloney 2006). That influence is both a key pillar of counterinsurgency and a source of considerable influence for Canada on the world stage.

One of the principle goals of the SAT-A operation was to build and extend the life of the Karzai government. It has been necessary, therefore, for there to be what General Hillier has called the 'Afghan face' on strategic planning. To this end SAT-A officer Lieutenant-Colonel Malevich said, 'I know that Lawrence of Arabia says it's better if they do it with their hands then you do it with your own, but sometimes you just have to do some of it with your own hands to kind of get the ball rolling, and that's what the [SAT-A] was able to do, was able to do stuff with our hands, and then kind of, you know, pass it on to the Afghans, sort of learn by demonstration and then hand it over for them to do.'[29]

The proximity of SAT-A members to the highest offices in Karzai's administration was remarkable. Malevich, now program director of Course Development Planning and Irregular Warfare for the Canadian Forces, has described the unit's resonance within the broader alliance in Afghanistan: 'My colleagues here [at Fort Leavenworth] that were in Kabul at the same time I was there call the [SAT-A] the "no fingerprint gang." They were pretty envious of it and I think what was excellent about the [SAT-A] is the fact that unlike a lot of people who walk around Kabul and call themselves advisors, you know a lot of them are guys that are actually working at ISAF headquarters ... whereas the [SAT-A] was actually embedded in the Afghan government.'[30] Malevich also describes how SAT-A's advisors were one level below the ministers – for example, working on the ANDS for the senior economic advisor to the president or as security and operations advisors to the chief electoral officer of the Independent Electoral Commission,[31] thus meeting Kitson's criteria nearly perfectly of placing officers in the highest offices, and giving the intervening nation – in this case, Canada – a significant influence without the immediately obvious optics of a military government.

The Canadianization of US Policy

Canada, as well as its NATO allies, has placed a great deal of importance on the type of bureaucratic counterinsurgency efforts focused on 'capacity building' and 'good governance.' The SAT-A unit, operating, as we have seen, at the highest levels of the government of Afghanistan, was among the most important examples of this whole-of-government approach to the counterinsurgency war.[32] The bilateral SAT-A agreement between Canada and Afghanistan has been judged a highly strategic asset in the war effort by several key members of team, including its first commander, Colonel Mike Capstick, and CIDA's point-person on the unit, Andy Tamas. Writing in *Vanguard* magazine, Capstick observed that 'the minute Afghans learned that – that [SAT-A] wasn't part of either of those two military headquarters in Kabul – doors opened that I'm sure would not have otherwise opened. We were not perceived as acting in NATO or US interests' (2007). Tamas similarly has written that 'many recipients of international aid see most donor agencies such as USAID, [the United Nations Development Programme] and the [World Bank] as neo-colonial agents of a new form of imperialism and they are regarded with some suspicion by host country officials who depend on their support. Apparently Canada has not been tarred with that same brush' (2009, 46).

SAT-A thus has served as a key reference for democracy-promotion efforts for NATO forces as the Afghanistan war has dragged on. Speaking at the annual meeting of the Conference of Defence Associations in Ottawa, General James Mattis, then-NATO supreme allied commander transformation and one of the lead authors of the counterinsurgency field manual for the US military, described Canada's effort as a 'comprehensive approach' that is a model counterinsurgency strategy for the alliance: 'Canada's long-term plan, your strategy here, is very consistent with where NATO needs to go. I would even go so far as to say that your plan, your strategy . . . makes you the role model for what the rest of NATO's got to follow.' As General Mattis articulated, '[t]here are very few issues today in which a purely military approach is sufficient to avert the situation . . . It's going to have to be a whole-of-government, a comprehensive approach, one that brings what we call in the American forces, the interagency, in.' Mattis added, 'a second aspect that comes out loud and clear is the need for expeditionary forces and I hardly need to carry that message to Canada when you look at your expeditionary forces' (Mattis 2009).

The SAT-A program appears to fit in many ways with what could be called the Canadianization of US intervention. Since the second term of George W. Bush, US defense secretary Robert Gates has been at the forefront of the repositioning of US intervention away from the 'shock and awe' bombardment that began the Afghanistan war and into the realm of more classical counterinsurgency. Gates has often described the need to increase the tools of intervention to deal with the twenty-first-century environment: 'We can expect that asymmetric warfare will be the mainstay of the contemporary battlefield for some time. These conflicts will be fundamentally political in nature and require the application of all elements of national power. Success will be less a matter of imposing one's will and more a function of shaping behaviour – of friends, adversaries, and most importantly, the people in between' (2008, 6).

The SAT-A project also provides an important example of the workings of the counterinsurgency information strategy. According to Tamas, this was one of the primary tasks of the first SAT-A rotation. The unit immediately identified the lack of an effective communications strategy: 'The strategic importance of good public communications in a counterinsurgency [campaign] was evident to all major actors and it was also a concern that the insurgents seemed to be making better use of this "weapon" than the government or the international community . . . SAT's strategic communications specialist began addressing this challenge at the outset of the mission' (2009, 47). In establishing the case for democracy promotion, the goal was not simply Kandahar, but also a Canadian audience that had to be persuaded to support the efforts by visits from Afghan officials (ibid., 48).

The implications of this information strategy were on full view to the Canadian public during a visit to this country in September 2006 by President Karzai. According to documents obtained through Access to Information, Karzai's speech was apparently penned in large measure by his SAT-A communications team, members of which accompanied him on his trip to Ottawa and Washington. According to the internal document, '[w]orking closely with [the Minister of] Rural Rehabilitation and Development . . . [the] team prepared [an] initial draft of [the] president's address to parliament 22 Sep. It was noted that key statistics, messages and themes, as well as overall structure, were adopted by the president in his remarks to joint session.'[33] The document added that the Afghan minister's exposure to the Canadian political and media landscape 'bode well' for his speaking tour across Canada. According to the document, the SAT-organized communications campaign was clear: 'The aim of the tour is to capitalize on the recent president's visit and address to parliament by emphasizing the development work in Canada and drawing attention away from persistent media reporting of the security situation.'[34]

While the existence of the SAT-A document and the influence of the military staffers within Karzai's government made news and entered the debate in Question Period in the House of Commons, the depth of the program has seen very little exposure. At the same time as the discussion about Karzai's speech, Colonel Capstick, SAT-A's first commander and most outspoken member, immediately embarked on a lecture tour and media junket after the end of his rotation in 2006 to extol the virtues of Canada's comprehensive fight against the insurgency. Tellingly, Capstick's 2006 tour was pegged to a talk entitled 'Strengthening the Weak' (Capstick 2006b), which he delivered at universities and other venues across Canada. Significantly, the SAT-A communications model found its way into the Canadian Forces counterinsurgency training manual, which cited it as particularly successful, and pointed specifically to the SAT-A commander's lecture tour and media appearances:

> The longer-term influence aspects of the military's engagement, particularly in conjunction with other agencies, that lead to enduring solutions of the crisis must be highlighted to both indigenous and domestic audiences [. . .] efforts must be made to advertise the use of strategic-level advisory teams and other means used to build lasting capacity within a developing nation. Such was the case with the former Canadian commander of the Afghanistan Strategic Advisory Team engaging a wide variety of audiences upon his return from theatre. Such publicity, locally and domestic, may help protect two strategic centres of gravity. (Canada 2008b)

Although it has been predicted that the Canadian Forces 'will use similar mechanisms [to those of SAT-A] to deliver strategically placed governance assistance' (Gilmore and Mosazai 2007, 158), the project was transferred in 2008 to CIDA, which, in turn, changed its name to the Canadian Governance Support Office, staffed by consultants provided by CANADEM with additional support from DFAIT. Canada's ambassador to Afghanistan called the transition a 'natural evolution' of the program. An unnamed official added, '[t]his is a natural transition and reflects that we are balancing away from a largely military to more of a civilian mission' (quoted in Davis 2008a), suggesting that, from a public relations perspective, the model might be only temporarily sustainable.

Although the exact reasons for the transition from a military to a civilian-led project have not yet been disclosed, it seems that the

Canadian government heeded the advice of CANADEM's Paul
LaRose-Edwards, who told the Standing Senate Committee on
National Security and Defence in December 2007:

> I would suggest that sometimes the Canadian government does not al-
> ways recruit the right people. I must admit I am slightly critical of the
> Canadian Forces Strategic Advisory Team in Afghanistan. Sending a lot
> of military personnel to do civil service reform was perhaps not the best
> option; perhaps they were not our strongest candidates to undertake that
> kind of activity. I can reassure you that we have over 2,000 governance
> experts, many of whom have worked in developing countries and know
> how to bring along an Afghan government in those early stages of devel-
> oping a coherent government structure that works in Afghanistan, as op-
> posed to in Canada. We have them. (LaRose-Edwards 2007)

The shift of SAT-A to the Canadian Governance Support Office fits
the increasing push to civilianize the democracy-promotion apparatus in Afghanistan where possible. What will be maintained, in any
case, is democracy promotion's functional importance to counterinsurgency operations. Already, in the case of Afghanistan, one estimate is
that nearly 69 per cent of CIDA's operating budget is devoted to de-
mocracy-related programs (Gilmore and Mosazai 2007, 154). Indeed
the allied forces' counterinsurgency doctrine suggests that promoting
democracy is an essential part of fighting insurgencies. As such, the
Canadian Forces, operationally, will continue to play a critical role as
expeditionary democracy promoters.

Expeditionary Democracy Promotion versus Democracy

The 'surge' of US occupation forces in Afghanistan in early 2010 was
accompanied by a downgrading of expectations where the prospects
for democracy are concerned. In the face of a resilient resistance to the
foreign occupation, US rhetoric has shifted from nation building and
democracy promotion to stabilization in the interests of preventing
the establishment of a safe haven for terror. Yet, as US forces (alongside their NATO and Canadian counterparts) set about to undertake
the largest and longest counterinsurgency offensive in the nine-year
history of the war, the top US general, Stanley McChrystal, also proclaimed that troops would be undertaking population-centric counterinsurgency. After taking it to the Taliban and clearing the area of

insurgents, the occupiers will roll-out a 'government-in-a-box' (Bacevich 2010).

As revolutionary and counterrevolutionary warfare theorist Eqbal
Ahmad has described, counterinsurgents 'progressively give up on
winning the hearts and concentrate on conquering the minds ("its the
minds that matter")' (2006, 60). Contrast this with the frank procla-
mation of General McChrystal – whose surge, launched as Operation
Mushtarak in Helmand province in February 2010, was designed to
'convince the American public that they deserve more time to demonstrate that extra troops and new tactics can yield better results on the
battlefield' (Porter 2010) – stated flatly that '[t]his is all a war of perceptions . . . This is not a physical war in terms of how many people you
kill or how much ground you capture, how many bridges you blow up.
This is all in the minds of the participants' (quoted in ibid.).

Such 'mind games,' as Ahmad stresses, cannot help but function to
'erode . . . the democratic processes and institutions of metropolitan
countries' (2006, 62) that are waging counterinsurgency, just as they will
erode the democratic processes, such as they exist, in the occupied country. Ahmad warns of how counterinsurgency 'politicizes the military'
(ibid., 63) in a way that undermines democracy, a development that has
had profound effects on Canada owing to its corollary militarization
of Canadian culture (Dobbin 2007) and the concerted public relations
campaign to sell the Canadian Forces to the Canadian public. Likewise
Canadians have only begun to see the corrosive effects of waging counterinsurgency in the parliamentary context; the detainee scandal and
the arbitrary prorogation of Parliament by the government of the day
offers perhaps a chilling prelude to the means by which the counterin-
surgent democracy eludes accountability to public institutions.

What is undertaken operationally 'in theatre' cannot be distinguished from its political underpinnings in the intervening states,
what was earlier referred to as polyarchy. Adequate theorizing of the
functions of democracy promotion in Afghanistan necessitates examining it in the context of managing expectations and outcomes, both
at home and abroad. In her essay, 'Democracy as Ideology of Empire'
(2006, 1), Ellen Meiksins Wood explains how the new imperialism is
opposed to real democracy and the reconfiguration of class power.
This is true in the context of Afghanistan, and the flip side of this
has its domestic roots: in its origins western democracy has been premised on the notion that 'the power of the majority had to be disarmed
by fragmenting and diluting the majority as much as possible, to

prevent its coalescence into an overwhelming force' (ibid., 18). As Wood elaborates, the resulting 'democracy,' akin to the polyarchic def-inition introduced earlier, 'was to depoliticize the citizenry and turn democracy into rule by propertied classes over a passive citizen body, and also to confine democracy to a limited, formal political sphere' (ibid., 17). It is only by understanding the collective internalization of this process of domestic depoliticization that we can address the problem of how democratic principles, in turn, are *used* to justify war and the new imperialism.

Canada's role in countering insurgency and promoting democracy in Afghanistan is the culmination of years of structural change of the Canadian political economy and the reconfiguration of the Canadian state and the operational forms of foreign policy. As part of the 'new imperialists' who are 'the core group of powers that dominate the world system' (Klassen 2009, 163), it is only natural that Canada should develop the interventionist capabilities that have been central to the international apparatuses of these states. In this sense, as the Canadian military itself has told us, Afghanistan is a model for the future of Ca-nadian foreign policy efforts. As such, barring the development of a truly participatory culture of democracy within Canada, one can an-ticipate that the Canadian state will find it in its interests to continue to wage interventions that attempt to make the world 'safe' for liberal democracy and global capitalism. Such a polyarchic spirit, we argue, precludes genuine democratic gains and counters popular aspirations both where democracy is being promoted and in its own national con-text. It is what Wood (2006, 20) refers to as 'obstructing democracy in the name of democracy.'

NOTES

1 See, for example, Shmitz and Gillies (1992, 3–8, 22); Perlin (2006); Donovan (2007); Unsworth (2007, 21); Welsh and Woods (2007, xii); Axworthy (2008).
2 See, for example, Robinson (1994, 1996); Graf (1996); Neufeld (1999); Roelofs (2003); Barker (2008).
3 As Robinson (1996, 50) argues, '[t]he concept of polyarchy is an outgrowth of . . . elite theories developed by Italian social scientists Gaetano Mosca and Vilfredo Pareto.' On this basis, Robinson says, 'polyarchy [is] a distinct form of elite rule [that] performs the function of legitimating existing inequalities, and does so more effectively than authoritarianism' (51).

4 As *Washington Post* correspondent David Ignatius (1991) would report
   nearly two decades later, '[p]reparing the ground for last month's triumph
   of overt action was a network of overt operatives who during the last
   10 years have quietly been changing the rules of international politics.
   They have been doing in public what the CIA used to do in private – providing money and moral support for pro-democracy groups, training resistance fighters, working to subvert communist rule.'

5 'This new entity would not only play the role of skilful political surgeon,
   but it would overcome the taint associated with the covert political operations that the CIA had been carrying out abroad' (Robinson 1996, 88). On
   the CIA's operations, see Blum (2004).

6 Among the Canadian organizations that were created or changed their
   mandates to allow for global democracy promotion throughout the 1990s
   were the Forum of Federations, the Canadian Foundation for the Americas
   (FOCAL), the Parliamentary Centre, the Canadian Association of Former
   Parliamentarians, the Institute of Public Administration of Canada, and
   Elections Canada.

7 'Humanitarian' was removed from the title due to controversy surrounding the term. When the ICISS brought out its first report, entitled 'Responsibility to Protect,' later dubbed the R2P doctrine, its proponents went to
   great lengths to distinguish between R2P and humanitarian intervention.

8 As Robinson (1996, 111) notes, '[t]he objective of political intervention is
   not to organize or impose free and fair elections on a nation . . . but rather,
   to organize an elite and to impose it on the intervened country through
   controlled electoral processes.'

9 A US political scientist associated with the anti-communist left, Lipset
   taught at the University of Toronto and is considered one of the key early
   democracy-promotion theorists. Guilhot (2005, 113) writes of Lipset, '[i]n
   tune with a whole elitist tradition within American political science . . . the
   masses were thought to be better off when kept in political apathy based
   on relative material welfare. In this elitist view, the intellectual classes bear
   the "responsibility to keep democracy representative and free" [quoting
   Lipset].'

10 These organizations include the Canadian Association of Former Parliamentarians, CANADEM, FOCAL, Rights and Democracy, the Forum of
   Federations, and the Parliamentary Centre.

11 Including representatives of DFAIT's Democracy Unit, Rights and Democracy, the Forum of Federations, and former prime minister Kim Campbell,
   who is the chair of the WMD's 'Eminent Person's Group' for the 'Defending Civil Society' project, which is funded in part by DFAIT. Rights and

Democracy provided funding for democracy activists to participate in the WMD's 4th Assembly in Istanbul in 2006, which gave it the privilege of co-organizing a workshop entitled 'Beyond Failed States: Civil Societies in Transition,' with the NED-funded Afghans for Civil Society.

12 The Democracy Council consists of representatives from DFAIT, CIDA, Rights and Democracy, IDRC, the Forum of Federations, Elections Canada, and the National Judicial Institute.

13 Failed states, according to the IDRC's Maureen O'Neill (2006) are 'a menace that must be addressed across the whole of international policy' – sentiments that were reflected in the 3D approach formally introduced in the Martin government's International Policy Statement.

14 Democracy Council lunch discussion with co-chairs V. Peter Harder and Robert Greenhill, Ottawa, 30 June 2006. Access to Information document A-2008–00489/TR, 483.

15 The committee also travelled to New York to meet with academics, UN officials, the Council on Foreign Relations, and Canadian diplomats. In Washington they met with representatives from the NED, NDI, the International Republican Institute, officials from the Department of State, USAID, and the Carnegie Endowment for Peace. They also travelled extensively overseas, conducting democracy-promotion meetings in Denmark, Finland, London, Sweden, and Norway. Each of these countries, to differing degrees, also has made democracy promotion a foreign policy priority.

16 The most extensive studies into the potentially nefarious effects of democracy promotion are Robinson (1992, 1996); Ciment and Ness (1999); Blum (2004); Ayers (2006); and Chomsky (2006, esp. 102–65).

17 The Canadian Association of Former Parliamentarians (CAFP) is a key conduit for Canadian democracy-promotion operations. In 2005 CAFP signed democracy-promotion-related Memorandums of Understanding with CANADEM, the Parliamentary Centre, and NDI (CAFP 2005, 4). CANADEM maintains a roster of CAFP members 'wishing to do democracy work abroad,' as advertised in CAFP's quarterly bulletin, Beyond the Hill (CAFP 2006, 4).

18 Of twenty-five Afghan or Afghan-related projects initiated between 2001 and 2009, eighteen were initiated by the Conservatives; see the IDRC website, http://www.idrc.ca.

19 Cabinet Document, 'Stakeholder Positions,' Privy Council Office, Access to Information document A-2005–0479/HD, 000070.

20 The main democracy-promoting NGOs and Crown corporations active in Afghanistan are Rights and Democracy, IMPACS, Alternatives, Elections

Canada, CANADEM, the Parliamentary Centre, and the IDRC. Other democracy-oriented organizations, such as CAFP, feed democracy promoters to sister organizations in Afghanistan.

21 Rights and Democracy used to produce an array of radio shows all over Afghanistan.

22 See Peace Dividend Trust, 'Peace Dividend Trust: Our Mission,' http://www.pdtglobal.org/index.php?sv=andcategory=31. All quoted material in this paragraph is from the PDT website.

23 Writes Davis, '[a]ccording to a DND spokesman, the SAT had a total of 14 Canadian soldiers on its staff when it closed. Of these, three were at the SAT's head office in Kabul while 11 were posted within Afghan ministries. The SAT's budget was $1.33 million in fiscal year 2006–07, and $1.5 in 2007–08' (2008b).

24 As Cox's summary for the Library of Parliament makes clear, '[t]he SAT-A is a Canadian, not NATO, organization. It includes 15 CF members augmented by a CIDA officer to advise on development issues. Although the SAT-A is a military unit on an independent operation and is therefore legally responsible to the Chief of the Defence Staff, the team works in consultation with Canadian Ambassador Arif Lalani, the Canadian Head of Aid and a senior representative of the Afghan government. [Canadian Forces] planners work under Afghan leadership within their partner Afghan government ministries and agencies' (2007, 3).

25 The e-mail was sent to Capstick in June 2005; the team was assembled in July and deployed by late August.

26 Likewise, Gilmore and Mosazi (2007, 158) described SAT-A as 'a remarkable deviation from normal practices.'

27 Interview with authors, 5 June 2009.

28 Capstick also commented to the House of Commons Standing Committee on National Defence that '[m]y guys had Government of Afghanistan e-mail addresses' (Capstick 2006a).

29 Interview with authors; Lawrence's actual words were '[d]o not try to do too much with your own hands. Better the Arabs do it tolerably than that you do it perfectly. It is their war, and you are to help them, not to win it for them' (1917, art. 15).

30 Interview with authors; indeed, Malevich cites his SAT-A experience as qualifying him for the Counterinsurgency Center post: 'I had Afghanistan experience working at Operation Enduring Freedom and I also went back for a second tour where I was seconded to the Afghan government as part of the Strategic Advisory Team, so I had a scholarly background and I also

had actual counterinsurgency experience in that I was working for the Afghans as an advisor, working on that whole of government, good governance approach.'

31 Interview with authors.

32 As Gilmore and Mosazi (2007) make clear in their extensive discussion of SAT-A. Gilmore was one of the key Canadian diplomats who, as deputy director for South Asia, 'focused on the development of Canada's diplomatic, defence, and development operations in Afghanistan' from 2002 to 2004.

33 'Strat Comms: Communications advisor accompanied Afghan presidential delegation on visits to New York and Ottawa 18–22 Sep.' Access to Information document, 6.A.2., 1.

34 'Team A Activities.' Access to Information document, 6.A.3, 2.

References

Ahmad, Eqbal. 2006. *The Selected Writings of Eqbal Ahmad*. New York: Columbia University Press.

Albo, Greg. 2006. 'Empire's Ally: Canadian Foreign Policy.' *Canadian Dimension* (November–December).

Axworthy, Thomas S. 2006. 'Foreword.' In *Transitions to Democracy – Afghanistan*. Kingston, ON: Queen's University, Centre for the Study of Democracy.

–, ed. 2008. *Creating Democratic Value: Evaluating Efforts to Promote Democracy Abroad*. Kingston, ON: Queen's University, Centre for the Study of Democracy.

Axworthy, Thomas S., Leslie Campbell, and David Donovan. 2005. 'The Democracy Canada Institute: A Blueprint.' IRPP Working Paper 2005–02e. Montreal: Institute for Research on Public Policy.

Ayers, Allison J. 2006. 'Demystifying Democratisation: The Global Constitution of (Neo)liberal Polities in Africa.' *Third World Quarterly* 27, no. 2: 321–38.

–. 2009. 'Imperial Liberties: Democratisation and Governance in the "New" Imperial Order.' *Political Studies* 57, no. 3: 1–27.

Bacevic, Andrew J. 2010. ' "Government in a box" in Marja.' *Los Angeles Times*, 17 February.

Barker, Michael J. 2008. 'Democracy or Polyarchy? US-funded Media Developments in Afghanistan and Iraq Post 9/11.' *Media, Culture, and Society* 30, no. 1: 109–30.

Bates, Thomas R. 1975. 'Gramsci and the Theory of Hegemony.' *Journal of the History of Ideas* 36, no. 2: 351–6.

Beeby, Dean. 2006. 'Military wants to turn soldiers into "journalists" to win minds overseas.' Canadian Press, 22 September.

Bellamy, Alex J. 2009. *Responsibility to Protect*. Cambridge, UK: Polity Press.

Bland, Douglas. 2006. Evidence before the House of Commons Standing Committee on National Defence, 39th Parliament, 1st Session, Ottawa, 23 October.

Blum, W. 2004. *Killing Hope: U.S. Military and C.I.A. Interventions since World War II*. Monroe, ME: Common Courage Press.

Bouillon, Markus E., David M. Malone, and Ben Rowswell, eds. 2008. *Iraq: Preventing a New Generation of Conflict*. Boulder, CO: Lynne Rienner.

CAFP (Canadian Association of Former Parliamentarians). 2005. *Beyond the Hill*, Winter.

–. 2006. *Beyond the Hill*, Winter.

Canada. 2005a. 'Canada's International Policy Statement: A Role of Pride and Influence in the World.' Ottawa: Department of Foreign Affairs and International Trade.

–. 2005b. National Defence Headquarters. Chief of the Defence Staff. 'CDS Initiating Directive: Deployment of a Strategic Advisory Team (SAT) to Kabul, Afghanistan.' 3350–165/A38 (J3 Intl 2–1). Ottawa. 18 July.

–. 2006. Department of Foreign Affairs and International Trade. *Canada World View* 29 (Spring).

–. 2007a. Parliament. House of Commons. Standing Committee on Foreign Affairs and International Trade. *Advancing Canada's Role in International Support for Democratic Development*. Ottawa. July.

–. 2007b. Parliament. House of Commons. Standing Committee on Foreign Affairs and International Development, 39th Parliament, 1st Session. *Evidence*. Ottawa. 1 March.

–. 2007c. 'A New Focus on Democracy Support: Government Response to the Eighth Report of the Standing Committee on Foreign Affairs and International Development.' Ottawa. November.

–. 2008a. Parliament. House of Commons. Standing Committee on Foreign Affairs and International Development. *Canada in Afghanistan*. Ottawa. July.

–. 2008b. Department of National Defence. Land Force. *Counter-Insurgency Operations*. B-GL-323–004/FP-003. Ottawa. 13 December.

–. 2009. Privy Council Office. 'Advisory Panel Report on the Creation of a Canadian Democracy Promotion Agency.' Ottawa. November.

Capstick, Mike. 2006a. Evidence before the House of Commons Standing Committee on National Defence, 39th Parliament, 1st Session, 23 October.

–. 2006b. 'Strengthening the Weak: The Canadian Forces in Afghanistan.' Occasional Paper 3.5. Toronto: Canadian Institute of International Affairs.

–. 2007. 'A Military Solution to Fostering Civil Service Capacity.' *Vanguard*, May–June. http://www.vanguardcanada.com/CivilServiceCapacity Capstick.

Cardoso, Fernando Henrique. 2005. 'Scholarship and Statesmanship.' *Journal of Democracy* 16, no. 2: 5–12.

Carty, Robert, and Virginia Smith. 1981. *Perpetuating Poverty: The Political Economy of Canadian Foreign Aid*. Toronto: Between the Lines.

CBC News. 2007. 'Canada's Radio Kandahar goes to air.' 6 January.

Chandler, Andrea. 1995. 'Democracy and the Problem of Government in Russia.' In *Canada Among Nations 1995: Democracy and Foreign Policy*, ed. Maxwell A. Cameron and Maureen Appel Molot. Ottawa: Carleton University Press.

Chomsky, Noam. 2006. *Failed States: The Abuse of Power and the Assault on Democracy*. New York: Owl Books.

Ciment, J., and I. Ness. 1999. 'NED and the Empire's New Clothes.' *Covert Action Quarterly* 67 (Spring–Summer): 65–8.

Codevilla, Angelo M. 1989. 'Political Warfare.' In *Political Warfare and Psychological Operations: Rethinking the US Approach*, ed. Carnes Lord and Frank R. Barnett. Washington, DC: National Defense University Press.

Cooter, Christopher. 2000. 'A Canadian Foundation: Promoting Democratic Civil Society by New Means.' *Canadian Foreign Policy* 7, no. 3: 99–113.

Côté-Harper, Gisele, and John Courtney. 1987. 'International Cooperation for the Development of Human Rights and Democratic Institutions.' Ottawa. 30 June.

Cox, Jim. 2007. 'Afghanistan: The Canadian Military Mission.' Publication PRB 07–19E. Ottawa: Parliamentary Information and Research Service. 6 November.

Dahl, Robert A. 1971. *Polyarchy: Participation and Opposition*. New Haven, CT: Yale University Press.

Daudelin, Jean. 2005. 'Bobbling Up, Trickling Down, Seeping Out: The Transformation of Canadian Foreign Policy.' In *Canada Among Nations 2004: Getting Priorities Straight*, ed. David Carment, Fen Osler Hampson, and Norman Hillmer. Montreal; Kingston, ON: McGill-Queen's University Press.

Davis, Jeff. 2008a. 'Afghan SAT Successor to Have Fewer Staff.' *Embassy Magazine*, 20 August.

–. 2008b. 'Military's Afghan Strategic Advisory Team to Be Replaced by CIDA, Consultants.' *Embassy Magazine*, 13 August.

Davis, Kristina. 2005. 'Psychological Operations: The Battlefield's Human Dimension.' *Maple Leaf*, 24 August.

Dobbin, Murray. 1998. *The Myth of the Good Corporate Citizen: Democracy under the Rule of Big Business*. Toronto: Stoddart.

–. 2007. 'The Militarization of Canadian Culture.' *Hill Times*, April 9.

Donovan, David. 2007. Evidence before the House of Commons Standing Committee on Foreign Affairs and International Development, 39th Parliament, 1st Session, Ottawa, 13 February.

–. 2008. 'From Here to Real Action Worldwide.' *Diplomat and International Canada* (March–April): 21, 24.

Douglas, William A. 1972. *Developing Democracy*. Washington, DC: Heldref Publications.

Economist. 2009. 'Briefing: From Insurgency to Insurrection.' 20 August.

Fenton, Anthony. 2010. 'Foundation for "political warfare" takes cue from US strategy.' Inter Press Service, 9 February.

Fisher, Matthew. 2009. 'Afghan-Canadian strategy aims to defeat Taliban town by town.' *National Post*, 15 April.

Fontaine, Cynthia. 2004. 'Psychological operations plays with soldiers' minds.' *Canadian Army News*, 7 September.

Gates, Robert M. 2008. 'Beyond Guns and Steel: Reviving the Nonmilitary Instruments of American Power: Remarks as delivered verbatim by Secretary of Defense Robert M. Gates, Manhattan, Kansas, 26 November 2007.' *Military Review* (January–February): 2–9.

Gauthier, Michel. 2006. Evidence before the Standing Senate Committee on National Security and Defence, Issue 2, Ottawa, 29 May.

Gendzier, Irene L. 1998. 'Play It Again Sam: The Practice and Apology of Development.' In *Universities and Empire: Money and Politics in the Social Sciences during the Cold War*, ed. Christopher Simpson. New York: New Press.

Gilmore, Scott, and Janan Mosazai. 2007. 'Defence, Development, and Diplomacy: The Case of Afghanistan, 2001–2005.' In *Exporting Good Governance: Temptations and Challenges in Canada's Aid Program*, ed. Jennifer Welsh and Ngaire Woods. Waterloo, ON: Wilfrid Laurier University Press and the Centre for International Governance Innovation.

Graf, W. 1996. 'Democratization "for" the Third World: Critique of a Hegemonic Project.' *Canadian Journal of Development Studies*, Special Issue: 37–56.

Greenhill, Robert. 2007. Evidence before the House of Commons Standing Committee on Foreign Affairs and International Development, 39th Parliament, 1st Session, Ottawa, 1 March.

Guilhot, Nicolas. 2005. *The Democracy Makers: Human Rights and the Politics of Global Order*. New York: Columbia University Press.

Hubert, Don, and Michael Bonser. 2001. 'Humanitarian Military Intervention.' In *Human Security and the New Diplomacy: Protecting People, Promoting Peace*, ed. Rob McRae and Don Hubert. Montreal; Kingston, ON: McGill-Queen's University Press.

IDRC (International Development Research Centre). 2007a. *IDRC Annual Report 2006–2007*. Ottawa.

–. 2007b. 'IDRC on Just Societies and Healthy Democracies: Afghanistan.' Ottawa.

Ignatius, David. 1991. 'Innocence abroad: the new world of spyless coups.' *Washington Post*, 22 September.

Kippen, Grant. 2006. 'The 2004 Presidential Election: On the Road to Democracy in Afghanistan.' In *Transitions to Democracy – Afghanistan*. Kingston, ON: Queen's University, Centre for the Study of Democracy.

Kitson, Frank. 1971. *Low Intensity Operations: Subversion, Insurgency, Peacekeeping*. London: Faber and Faber.

Klassen, Jerome. 2009. 'Canada and the New Imperialism: The Economics of a Secondary Power.' *Studies in Political Economy* 83 (Spring): 163–90.

LaRose-Edwards, Paul. 2006. Evidence before the House of Commons Standing Committee on Foreign Affairs and International Trade, 39th Parliament, 1st Session, Ottawa, 24 October.

–. 2007. Evidence before the Standing Senate Committee on National Security and Defence, Ottawa, 3 December.

Laux, Jeanne Kirk. 1994. 'From South to East? Financing the Transition in Central and Eastern Europe.' In *Canada Among Nations 1994: A Part of the Peace*, ed. Maureen Appel Molot and Harald von Riekhoff. Ottawa: Carleton University Press.

Lawrence, T.E. 1917. 'Twenty-seven articles.' *Arab Bulletin*, 20 August.

Macpherson, C.B. 1977. *The Life and Times of Liberal Democracy*. Oxford: Oxford University Press.

Maloney, Sean. 2006. Evidence before the House of Commons Standing Committee on National Defence, 39th Parliament, 1st Session, Ottawa, 20 September.

Mattis, James. 2009. Special Address to the Conference of Defence Associations 72nd Annual General Meeting, Ottawa, 27 February.

McRae, Rob, and Don Hubert, eds. 2001. *Human Security and the New Diplomacy: Protecting People, Promoting Peace*. Montreal; Kingston, ON: McGill-Queen's University Press.

Miller, Robert. 2005. 'The Role of NGO's in International Democratic Development: Canada's Support for International Political Development, the Case of Legislative Development.' IRPP International Democratic Development Series. Montreal: Institute for Research on Public Policy.

Mulroney, David. 2007. 'Canada in Afghanistan: From Collaboration to Integration.' Keynote Speech, Canadian Institute of International Affairs, Toronto, 9 May.

NED (National Endowment for Democracy). 2006. 'Grants Program – 2006: Afghanistan.' Washington, DC.

Neufeld, Mark. 1999. 'Democratization in/of Canadian Foreign Policy: Critical Reflections.' *Studies in Political Economy* 58 (Spring): 97–119.

O'Neill, Maureen. 2006. 'Remarks on Canada's Engagement with the Developing World: Priorities for the Next Ten Years.' Canadian Institute of International Affairs Foreign Policy Conference, Vancouver, 10 March.

Paterson, I. 2005. 'Support to the Development of Free Media in Afghanistan Project: Final Evaluation Report, Project A-3218933.' File No. AI-2006–00005. Ottawa: Canadian International Development Agency. September.

Perlin, George. 2006. Evidence before the House of Commons Standing Committee on Foreign Affairs and International Trade, 39th Parliament, 1st Session. Ottawa, 4 October.

Phillips, Karin. 2008. 'Afghanistan: Canadian Diplomatic Engagement.' Publication PRB 07–38E. Ottawa: Parliamentary Information and Research Service. 4 February. http://www.parl.gc.ca/content/LOP/Research Publications/prb0738-e.htm.

Porter, Gareth. 2010. 'Afghanistan: Marja offensive aimed to shape U.S. opinion on war.' Inter Press Service, 23 February.

Reagan, Ronald. 1982. 'Promoting Peace and Democracy.' Address before the British Parliament, London, 8 June, 1982.

Robinson, William I. 1992. *A Faustian Bargain: U.S. Intervention in the Nicaraguan Elections and American Foreign Policy in the Post-Cold War Era*. Boulder, CO: Westview Press.

–. 1994. 'Low Intensity Democracy: The New Face of Global Domination.' *Covert Action Quarterly* 50 (Fall): 40–7.

–. 1996. *Promoting Polyarchy: Globalization, US Intervention, and Hegemony*. New York: Cambridge University Press.

Roelofs, Joan. 2003. *Foundations and Public Policy: The Mask of Pluralism*. Albany: State University of New York Press.

Schmitz, G.J., and D. Gillies. 1992. The Challenge of Democratic Government: Sustaining Democratization in Developing Societies. Ottawa: North-South Institute.

Smilie, Ian. 2007. 'Boy Scouts and Fearful Angels: The Evolution of Canada's International Good Governance Agenda.' In *Exporting Good Governance: Temptations and Challenges in Canada's Aid Program*, ed. Jennifer Welsh and Ngaire Woods. Waterloo, ON: Wilfrid Laurier University Press and the Centre for International Governance Innovation.

Smith Graeme. 2005. 'Colonel predicts shorter Afghan stay; extremist militias could be defeated within three years, Canadian says.' *Globe and Mail*, 26 September.

Smith, Tony. 1994. *America's Mission: The United States and the Worldwide Struggle for Democracy in the Twentieth Century*. Princeton, NJ: Princeton University Press.

–. 2007. *A Pact with the Devil: Washington's Bid for World Supremacy and the Betrayal of the American Promise*. New York: Routledge.

Stanford University News Service. 1991. 'Mulroney on Canadian, U.S. roles in new world order.' 29 September.

Straus, Ira. 1987. 'Organizing the Democracies to Promote Democracy.' In *Promoting Democracy: Opportunities and Issues*, ed. Ralph M. Goldman and William A. Douglas. New York: Praeger.

Tamas, Andy. 2009. *Warriors and Nation Builders: Development and the Military in Afghanistan*. Kingston, ON: Canadian Defence Academy Press.

Unsworth, Sue. 2007. 'Focusing Aid on Good Governance: Can It Work?' In *Exporting Good Governance: Temptations and Challenges in Canada's Aid Program*, ed. Jennifer Welsh and Ngaire Woods. Waterloo, ON: Wilfrid Laurier University Press and the Centre for International Governance Innovation.

Verma, Sonja. 2009. 'Canadian made the call that left Afghans in limbo.' *Globe and Mail*, 10 September.

Wedel, Janine R. 1998. *Collision and Collusion: The Strange Case of Western Aid to Eastern Europe 1989–1998*. New York: St Martin's Press.

Welsh, Jennifer and Ngaire Woods, eds. 2007. *Exporting Good Governance: Temptations and Challenges in Canada's Aid Program*. Waterloo, ON: Wilfrid Laurier University Press and the Centre for International Governance Innovation.

Wood, Ellen Meiksins. 2006. 'Democracy as Ideology of Empire.' In *The New Imperialists: Ideologies of Empire*, ed. Colin Mooers. Oxford: Oneworld Publications.

11

Incompatible Objectives: Counterinsurgency and Development in Afghanistan

JUSTIN PODUR

With a per capita gross domestic product (GDP) of only US$457 per year, Afghanistan is one of the world's poorest countries. From 2007 to 2009 the number of Afghans telling pollsters they could not afford food increased from 54 to 63 per cent (Isby 2010, 22). Some 90 per cent of Afghanistan's government budget comes from external aid, and the country has 'one of the lowest domestic revenue-to-GDP ratios in the world, around seven percent,' giving donors decisive control over the country's economic fate and development trajectory (ibid., 336).

In contrast the expense of US combat operations in the country was estimated to be US$93.8 billion in 2010, and higher than $100 billion in 2011, according to analysis by the Congressional Research Service (Belasco 2011, 3). Indeed the greater share of expenditure by the North Atlantic Treaty Organization (NATO) in Afghanistan goes to combat operations, with US$227 billion expended through summer 2009, only $16 billion of which was on foreign aid and diplomacy (ibid., 376). The US-NATO mission is centred around a counterinsurgency strategy to suppress the Taliban through a combination of military tactics and development projects. Afghans themselves 'identify unemployment and the lack of a way to legally prosper as the most important single threat to national security' (ibid., 359). As a result economic development is a central, if underappreciated, problem in Afghanistan. It is a critical factor in the political evolution of the country over the past three decades and a key lever through which the US-NATO mission is attempting to fortify a national state apparatus.

In a work intended to advise donor countries, Paul Collier (2007) analyses the world's poorest economies in terms of 'traps.' Afghanistan falls into several of these traps, including being landlocked by, and having uneasy relations with, its neighbours. Following on this point, David Isby (2010, 23) writes:

> Since 2001, no effective Afghan national economy has emerged to tie (its) diverse and disparate regions together. As a landlocked country, the importance of the port of Karachi as Afghanistan's most important link to the world has meant that the relationship with Pakistan is critical to the economy and future of Afghanistan . . . The failure to have an effective national economy post-2001 and the continuing economic reliance on Pakistan reflects . . . that Afghanistan lacks infrastructure and established relationships with other countries that would provide an alternative path to markets. Afghanistan has no railroads. The limited road system has, as a result, taken on a great deal of importance.

Another one of Collier's 'traps' that Afghanistan has fallen into – at least since the 1970s – is the 'conflict trap.' For more than thirty years Afghanistan has experienced internal social, ethnic, religious, and tribal struggles, exacerbated by external forms of military intervention. Since October 2001 many of these internal conflicts have been compounded by the US-NATO occupation – in particular, the political marginalization of ethnic Pashtuns relative to ethnic Tajiks and Uzbeks, and the subordination of domestic working-class interests to global market imperatives (Kolhatkar and Ingalls 2006). For Collier, escaping the conflict trap implies peace, development, and sovereignty for Afghanistan. But, as this chapter argues, the priority of the US-NATO intervention is a counterinsurgency war aimed at pacifying the Pashtun-led Taliban resistance and keeping Afghanistan in the western sphere of influence.

Instead of counterinsurgency war, Afghanistan requires 'human development' in the sense of meeting basic human needs and developing political, economic, and administrative capacities for endogenous growth. The United Nations Human Development Report (2010) defines development as being 'about creating an environment in which people can develop their full potential and lead productive, creative lives in accord with their needs and interests,' and 'expanding the choices people have to lead lives that they value.' According to Canadian economist Michael Lebowitz, 'a precondition for . . . development is sufficient food, good health, education, and the opportunity to make decisions for [oneself]' (2009).

By way of contrast 'distorted development' can be defined as a structural failure to address poverty and human needs, overdependence on a few cash crops for export with few linkages to industrial and services sector activities, and the lack of coherent government and state structures. Before 2001 Afghanistan's economy was characterized by fragmentation, scarcity, and disorganization. Since 2001 new forms of dependency and distorted development have evolved. In 2007 Afghanistan ranked 174th out of 178 countries on the United Nations Human Development Index. As NATO's strategy is not to seek development on its own terms, but rather to use development as part of a counterinsurgency effort, it is unable to help Afghanistan recover from decades of distorted development, and is instead exacerbating its worst features.

Canada has been an important part of the US-NATO mission in Afghanistan. The mission is presented to the Canadian public as having two main goals: to help Afghanistan out of a self-inflicted cycle of misery and destruction, and to help Canada's ally, the United States, in the 'war on terror.' The first goal presents the war as a development project, implemented through the '3D' or 'whole-of-government' approach described in other chapters of this volume. The limitation of this approach is that authentic development depends, as Collier demonstrates, on sovereignty and peace: war and occupation are as harmful to development in Afghanistan as they are elsewhere. The open-ended 'war on terror,' now often called the 'long war' by US strategists, guarantees the extension and expansion of conflict, and contradicts any developmental objectives. The stated goals of Canada's mission are impossible on their own terms, and incompatible with one another.

In addressing this contradiction at the heart of Canada's effort in Afghanistan, this chapter argues the following: (1) modern counterinsurgency wars attempt to incorporate development as an operational arm to 'pacify' the local population by incorporating it within western economic and political structures; (2) development in this context is subordinated to the counterinsurgency war and thus remains distorted, limited, and incoherent; (3) the US-NATO war in Afghanistan exemplifies the application and failure of this kind of development agenda; (4) Canadian military and development policies in Afghanistan are consistent with the NATO counterinsurgency strategy and exhibit parallel failures; and (5) the counterinsurgency war has reinforced – rather than transcended or even begun to transform – the main historical blockages to development in Afghanistan: fragmentation, continued overdependence on the 'poppy economy,' and the lack of sovereignty resulting from external military occupation, a dependent state structure, and regional destabilization.

Perspectives on the War

There are four common interpretations of the war in Afghanistan, each of which has an element of truth. These perspectives view the war as: (1) a political struggle against an enemy with a political, or religious, agenda; (2) an expanding counterinsurgency against a devastated society with an ethnic, national character (Pashtuns) that is destabilizing the region; (3) a struggle to help a society develop, the failure of which has led to dangers that eventually threaten NATO countries at home; and (4) a geopolitical struggle for hegemony in Afghanistan, Central Asia, and the wider Middle East. Let us examine these perspectives in turn.

Political Struggle with the Taliban

Some very astute analysts, including Pakistani writer Pervez Hoodbhoy (2009), interpret the war in Afghanistan and Pakistan primarily as a struggle of rationality against Islamist fanaticism, and Canada's mission as one against such fanaticism. Rationality ultimately will prevail, in this view, because 'the forces of irrationality will surely cancel themselves out because they act in random directions, whereas reason pulls in only one' (Hoodbhoy 2009).

In this view Islamism has advanced to a position of great strength in Afghanistan, and the Taliban are now threatening Pakistan as well. According to this perspective the Taliban are irrational and therefore antidevelopment. Showing the Afghan population development gains will help, therefore, to isolate the Taliban, which will likely to try to undermine development efforts to better control an impoverished and hostage population.

While this view acknowledges the structural economic problems in Afghanistan and Pakistan and the influence of political Islam in these countries' political parties and governing institutions, it neglects the specifically Pashtun character of the insurgency. The most intense fighting is occurring in the Pashtun areas of Afghanistan. The Taliban are predominantly a Pashtun force. The Pakistani Taliban operate in the Pashtun areas of that country (the Northwest Frontier Province and the Federally Administered Tribal Areas). US political scientist Abdulkader Sinno has analysed the success of the Taliban in terms of their ability to co-opt, defeat, and win over their Pashtun rivals. In a hard-headed realist view that rejects worries of development, Sinno suggests directly that NATO forces should have attempted to defeat the Taliban by emulating their success:

> Instead of focusing on creating the image of a state, the United States and
> its clients should have done what the Taliban did before them: dismantle
> rival power structures. Of course, the Taliban's knowledge of the complex
> Pashtun tapestry of power, the preferences of warlords and their follow-
> ers, and their credible promise to bring back Pashtun greatness, allowed
> them to fine-tune their image, message, and strategies in a way that is im-
> possible for the alien US military and its minority of emigre clients to do.
> In fact, this window of opportunity closed a long time ago. The tools left
> at US disposal are the use of *brute force* and *patronage*, both of which have
> proven to be self-defeating in the past. (2008, 88; emphasis added)

For this reason, framing the war in Afghanistan and Pakistan as a conflict against irrational forces fails to understand the motives and methods of insurgent forces and makes it more difficult to bring the war to
a just conclusion.

An Expanding Counterinsurgency

Another view is that Canadian and NATO forces are involved in a counterinsurgency war against an ethnic group that spans two countries. In
such a war the tools at disposal are 'brute force' and 'patronage.' Brute
force is generally referred to as 'security' or 'defence,' while patronage
takes the form of 'humanitarian aid' or 'development assistance' in the
counterinsurgency literature.

While the United States and NATO attempt to use development as
a tool, the Afghan insurgency attacks the symbols of western development support. Isby (2010, 160) presents the following figures: 'The Taliban burned down 1,089 schools in Afghanistan in 2005–7 alone. In the
same period, over 40 health workers were killed or kidnapped while
delivering services; and at least 36 health facilities were shut down in
the east and south due to insecurity. Some 5,000 schools have closed in
Pushtun areas. As a result of the insurgency being concentrated in the
south and east, only 44 percent of Pushtuns have access to girls' schools
while the figures for other groups are over 70 percent.'

Development projects have thus become sites of struggle and negotiation between NATO, the Taliban, and the Afghan population. The Taliban will sometimes negotiate with non-governmental organizations

(NGOs) to allow health or other projects, if they are popular and not supported by the West (Isby 2010, 161). In this perspective of the war, development projects are strategic areas of conflict between the insurgency and the counterinsurgency, as well as tools of a 'hearts and minds' military campaign. Development policy remains a specific – and subordinate – instrument of war-making.

As this chapter will argue in more detail, the methods and requirements of counterinsurgency are incompatible with the methods and requirements of development. The latter presupposes sovereignty and peace, rather than occupation and warfare. As a consequence genuine development cannot be a tool of counterinsurgency, nor can it even take place in the context of a military conflict. For this reason the war should not be framed as a counterinsurgency, with its operational modes partly located in developmental or humanitarian assistance.

A Struggle for Development

The combination of security ('brute force') and development ('patronage') gives rise to a third understanding of the war in Afghanistan and Canada's participation. In this view NATO forces are fighting a struggle to help a devastated society recover and develop, a struggle which has several components. Canada's intervention in Afghanistan, for example, is based on a 3D approach: defence, development, and diplomacy. This approach is based on the idea that Afghanistan lacks capacity in each of these areas. Without security there can be no development, and without development there is political division and insecurity (see Stein and Lang 2007).

However, while humanitarianism and development are offered as justifications for the intervention, NATO is not in Afghanistan to develop it. The dilemma was put succinctly by Suhrke, Harpviken, and Strand (2004, 89): '[NATO forces'] very presence influences the transition – including important security issues – but its main function is to pursue the war against al-Qaida and its supporters, and this will determine its future deployment. The consequent disjunction between the logic of the war and its more incidental effects on the peace-building process creates considerable uncertainty in the transition.' In other words the 'disjunction' between the 'logic of the war' and the 'peace-building process' comes about because development, or 'peace-building,' is subordinated to the means and ends of war. Had development been the objective, the pattern of expenditure would be reversed, with the majority of money going to development rather than to combat operations. For this reason framing the conflict in Afghanistan as a struggle for development neglects the basic facts of NATO, US, and Canadian deployments in the country.

A Struggle for Hegemony

Part of NATO's presence in Afghanistan is certainly to 'pursue the war against al-Qaeda and its supporters,' but there are other overriding reasons, which inform the fourth perspective on the NATO occupation of Afghanistan and Canada's role there. They relate to control of the region, the positioning of military bases, the economic integration of the region on US-friendly terms (ensuring that pipelines for Central Asian oil and gas do not pass through Iran), and the restoration of 'credibility' through a demonstration of force after the 9/11 attack (Kolhatkar and Ingalls 2006, chap. 7).

Regional control as a reason for the war is less invoked than humanitarian goals or the need to keep NATO populations safe from terrorism. But this view of the war provides a better platform for understanding why development has taken the form it has in Afghanistan under NATO occupation and why so little progress has been made. Indeed NATO's stated humanitarian and development goals are incompatible with its counterinsurgency and regional strategy. The logic of the 'war on terror' virtually guarantees protracted, unsuccessful, and destructive warfare against civilian populations in the region. Whether the agenda of regional control pursued by the United States and NATO succeeds or fails, it is inimical to any agenda of genuine development, and is bound to extend Afghanistan's long trajectory of distorted growth and fragmented state power.

As Tariq Ali (2008) argues, the best alternative is to end the war against the Taliban; facilitate a power-sharing agreement among the Afghan government, the Taliban, and democratic parties; end the western military occupation in concert with a peace agreement among regional powers; and offer new grants for reconstruction and development as determined by the Afghan state and grassroots institutions in the country. This logic of peace, democracy, and self-determination offers a more likely path to human development than the current one premised on distorted development through counterinsurgency warfare.

Counterinsurgency and Development

US and NATO Strategies

It is important to understand how development is conceptualized as a facet of counterinsurgency by US and NATO planners. In fact development aid and humanitarian assistance play a central role in new counterinsurgency doctrines. In the post–Cold War security context of 'failed states,' 'terrorism,' and 'peace-building' operations, US and NATO forces are expected to fight a 'three-block war' of delivering aid, fighting insurgents, and facilitating diplomacy. As General Charles C. Krulak of the US Marines puts it, '[i]n one moment in time, our service members will be feeding and clothing displaced refugees, providing humanitarian assistance. In the next moment, they will be holding two warring tribes apart – conducting peacekeeping operations – and finally they will be fighting a highly lethal mid-intensity battle – all on the same day, all within three city blocks (cited in Capstick 2008, 265).' Canadian army colonel M.D. Capstick continues that, 'in the absence of direct military threats to the survival of Western states, most future conflicts [will] be "wars of choice" and the enemy [will] have to adopt "asymmetrical" strategies and tactics in the face of the "overwhelming force" represented by American military power' (ibid.). In this vision of warfare, humanitarianism and diplomacy are instruments of military victory. Instead of pursuing political, diplomatic, or humanitarian goals through military tactics, warfare is the end for which humanitarianism and diplomacy are means.

Aid institutions such as the World Bank and the Asian Development Bank, both of which are involved in reconstruction and humanitarian efforts in Afghanistan, do not share this vision. To these institutions, security is one component of a comprehensive peace-building effort. This leads to a paradoxical result. In a single anthology on the Afghanistan war (Hayes and Sedra 2008), Capstick (2008) argues that humanitarianism and diplomacy are tools of counterinsurgency, while Patel (2008, 162) suggests that economic factors underpin the insurgency, as '[y]oung men are joining the fighting ranks of the Taliban-led insurgency, criminal gangs, or local militias to earn cash, undermining progress made on the battlefield by national and international armed forces.'

The discussion of 'progress' on the battlefield in a context where foreign forces are fighting an indigenous insurgency is a complex one. If development workers and military commanders differ in their opinions on the primacy of military or developmental goals, it is the vision of the commanders that generally predominates. A leaked NATO training document for its International Security Assistance Force (ISAF) Media Operations Center from 2008 describes the 'messaging' for the media: 'Progress in security is sustainable only with progress in all three fields of the Afghan National Development Strategy. Good governance, including the rule of law and human rights, together with economical and social development require the coordinated effort of the International Community with ever increasing Afghan ownership' (NATO 2008, 2).

The document describes the humanitarian elements of NATO's effort. A 'Post Operational Humanitarian Relief Fund' of several million euros will 'finance rapid humanitarian assistance to the population directly affected by a military operation.' The document cautions that this assistance is not compensation: 'The term "compensation" is inappropriate and should not be used because it brings with it legal implications that do not apply. ISAF makes every effort to minimise the risk of any damage, injury or loss of life to civilians in the course of its operations in Afghanistan. NATO/ISAF deeply regrets the death or injury of any innocent civilian as a result of its operations' (ibid., 21). The document concludes with a list of ISAF achievements that NATO's press relations are to emphasize in reconstruction and development: economic growth (in double digits each year since 2002), greatly expanded cell phone service (4.5 million new subscribers), health centres, immunization programs, teacher training colleges, schools built, students enrolled, and highways improved. These achievements are presented to bolster the conflict as a struggle for development, but elsewhere the document states that the foremost engagement is an 'asymmetric war,' to which development goals are inevitably subordinate: 'NATO fully recognises that threats to our security are no longer limited to opposing state armies or marked by geographic boundaries. NATO will meet all security challenges with determination' (ibid., 25).

Despite the evident contradictions, aid is seen as an indispensable part of counterinsurgency warfare. Infusions of monetary aid are credited with the success of the 'surge' in Iraq and are considered by US counterinsurgency experts as indispensable in Afghanistan as well. A November 2008 RAND Corporation study states the case clearly: 'Aid, short term or longer in aim, is a part of most [counterinsurgency] efforts. The value of being able to immediately affect a local population has been repeatedly touted in Afghanistan and Iraq. The work by the

military, [the] United States Agency for International Development
(USAID), and other U.S. and coalition organizations, NGOs, and [in-
tergovernmental organizations] has deservedly received widespread
praise' (RAND 2008, 68).

In the humanitarian literature, however, there is a debate about the
role of aid in peace-building operations. In the case of Afghanistan Jonathan Goodhand (2004, 40) delineates ethical and pragmatic reasons
that aid must be disassociated from counterinsurgency: 'Rather than
being coherent with wider political objectives, humanitarian aid should
be kept separate and distinct from them – both for ethical (humanitarian mandates) and pragmatic reasons – aid does not have the leverage
to get to grips with the fundamentally political dynamics of contemporary conflicts. It might be argued that donor governments, in expecting aid instruments to support peace building processes in Afghanistan
are expecting a child to do the job of an adult.' In making this argument Goodhand points to the fundamental contradiction between the
instrumentalization of aid for counterinsurgency, which is accepted in
military doctrine, and the use of aid for development purposes, which
humanitarians understand is incompatible with military and political
imperatives. Since aid cannot be used for both, it will be used for one
or the other – in the case of Afghanistan, for counterinsurgency first. As
the next section demonstrates, Canada's war in Afghanistan has been
guided by the same precept of counterinsurgency warfare – namely, the
subordination of aid to political and military exigencies.

Canadian Strategies

While humanitarians debate with military strategists about whether
aid should be politicized or neutral, Canadian soldiers in Afghanistan
understand aid to be both politicized and militarized. In *Dancing with
the Dushman* (2008), Lieutenant-Colonel Ian Hope presents a diagram
of the battle for the 'Center of Gravity,' which is the 'Confidence & Support of Afghans' that is being contested by ISAF on the one side and
the Taliban on the other. ISAF tries to win the 'Confidence and Support
of Afghans' through 'Governance, Security, and Reconstruction.' The
Taliban try to win through 'Coercion & Preaching,' 'Attacks Against
[ISAF],' and 'Destruction (clinics and schools).'

According to Hope, '[ISAF] and the TALIBAN share the same [Cen-
ter of Gravity] and are fighting to win the confidence and support of
the people and to reduce their support to the enemy' (ibid., 49). From

his experience Hope understood Canada's 'tactical actions in terms of ultimate purposes – the winning and maintenance of local confidence, and measured our effectiveness against this litmus test' (ibid., 50). He reports that development, political, and military goals were completely integrated: 'All of our efforts would focus upon creation and development of an Afghan Development Zone . . . that incorporated the triangular area around Kandahar City and foresaw massive coordinated initiatives for enhanced security, governance, and development in this small area to create a "shining example" of political, economic and social success that other districts would quickly want to emulate by evicting Taliban forces and transforming from poppy crop to legitimate crop economies' (ibid., 51).

This understanding of the conflict flows from the logic of Canada's International Policy Statement (Canada 2005) – in particular, the chapter on defence written by General Rick Hillier (Stein and Lang 2007). The statement describes a new rationale for the Canadian Forces to engage in counterinsurgency conflicts in 'failed states,' and develops the concept of 'three-block warfare' in relation to the '3D' strategy of Canadian foreign policy. Viewed in this context the Canadian mission in Kandahar has been a concrete application of that counterinsurgency strategy – a strategy in which aid and development are used as tools of warfare in Third World conflict zones, especially in 'failed states.'

This approach to the Afghanistan war is shared by leading planners in the Canadian International Development Agency (CIDA). Nipa Banerjee (2008), for example, suggests that strengthening the Afghan National Army has been more successful than strengthening the Afghan National Police (about which, Banerjee reports, the US State Department has found 'serious failures'). In this context Banerjee (2008, 245) writes that, 'army training must be accelerated and the troop numbers expanded to help the Kabul government establish its presence and legitimacy across the country and provide security against insurgents.' Banerjee, as a developmental practitioner, is principally concerned with development, not military, issues. But it is a sign of the full-scale transformation of the Canadian foreign policy apparatus that CIDA has been enlisted in a counterinsurgency effort, deploying funds to support the military ends of Washington and NATO. Elsewhere Banerjee (2009, 71) accepts the paradigm of the 'war on terror' for explaining the conflict in Afghanistan, supports the counterinsurgency against the 'jihadist Taliban movement,' and offers methods by which a 'human security' agenda can be grafted onto the military strategy of the Canadian Forces.

The leading planners of both the military and the development wings of the Canadian foreign policy apparatus are therefore united around a counterinsurgency strategy for Afghanistan. This strategy makes principal use of development funds for winning the war against the Taliban resistance to the Karzai government and the western occupation. In this respect the development project is a component of the weapons systems deployed in Afghanistan.

It is important to highlight how the development project as a weapons system is targeted not just at Afghan civilians but also at Canadian citizens back home – in other words, how the Canadian population is a second target of the counterinsurgency strategy in Afghanistan. Several Canadian military writers on the Afghanistan war explicitly state that the North American public is a 'target' of the military's psychological messages. For example, Sean Maloney (2007, 48) of the Royal Military College in Kingston, Ontario, describes maintaining the public's will to fight as a central objective of psychological operations. Lieutenant-Colonel Hope does as well: 'This was a counter-insurgency operation, not a war of attrition against a military organization, and not simply a counter-terrorist conflict. At stake, every day and in every action, was the confidence of the people. Our military efforts to find, fix, and finish (physically and morally) Taliban groups, were all aimed at increasing local confidence and the *more strategic "public will" at home'* (2008, 144, emphasis added).

In these ways Canada's methods of counterinsurgency in Afghanistan parallel those of the United States and NATO. The primary objective is to pacify the Taliban-led insurgency through a combination of lethal and non-lethal methods, ranging from outright military operations to developmental and state-building efforts. The key point is that such development efforts have been instrumentalized as part of a wider strategy of geopolitical and military control. Furthermore, in emphasizing this strategy, the Canadian state attempts to inculcate sympathy for the war and occupation among citizens back home. In particular it tries to 'message' the war, just as NATO does, as one for developmental or humanitarian purposes. However, as I argue next, the very practice of counterinsurgency denies Afghanistan a legitimate government that could begin a course of independent development and correct the many historical distortions in the Afghan economy. In fact the war has relied increasingly on military methods that impede the realization of democracy, development, and security for Afghans. In the process it has turned the contradictions in counterinsurgency theory into material contradictions in the Afghan reality.

Distorted Development in Afghanistan

Historical and Structural Factors

The Afghan economy has long suffered from distorted development, and after ten years of NATO occupation little has changed. Geographical and historical constraints, and especially decades of war, meant that Afghanistan was a devastated economy prior to 2001 (Jalalzai 2003). Afghanistan is a dry, landlocked country with a relatively small amount of cultivable land, no railroads, and a limited road system, and its rural majority lives at a subsistence level while regional and national elites (warlords or mafias) struggle to extract sufficient surplus – through legal and illegal taxes, businesses, and foreign sponsors – to generate resources to rule.

The Soviet intervention and war produced what William Maley (2009, 127) calls 'a multilayered destructuring of politics, economy, and society.' The agricultural economy suffered tremendously: 'By 1987, output was only a third of what it had been in 1978 – a result of the loss of land for cultivation, 50 per cent falls in yields from land which could be cultivated, and the deaths of draught oxen. Much of this damage was a product of deliberate attacks designed to deny the resistance access to food in sensitive areas' (ibid., 129).

Antonio Giustozzi (2009) describes the political economy of 'warlordism' in Afghanistan, emphasizing the period between the Soviet withdrawal in 1989 and the NATO invasion of 2001. He argues that warlords, whom he describes as regional armed actors who exercise patrimonial control over territory in the absence of central authority, engage in a kind of primitive accumulation of power, which might lead to the formation of a state. The regime of warlordism, however, has had severe effects on economic development. In the pre-2001 period, warlords captured important revenue streams and used the money for their own, generally non-developmental purposes. For example, Rashid Dostum, an Uzbek warlord and current general in the Afghan National Army, controls gas, electricity, oil, customs revenue, a fertilizer factory, and road taxes worth millions of dollars annually (Giustozzi 2009, 134). Ismail Khan, a much wealthier warlord in the Herat border region with Iran, controls customs revenues that have totalled 'well over [US]$100 million, based on a traffic of 300–350 imported vehicles a day and on an estimated average duty of $1,000 per vehicle, plus about 100 trucks loaded with goods' (ibid., 234).

Since the 2001 NATO occupation revenue streams controlled by warlords in some cases have reverted to the Afghan state; in other cases they have ended up in the hands of Taliban insurgents; and in still others new illegal capitalist actors have captured these resources. The experience of Dostum is again illustrative, as he was forced to pass many of his resources on to the central government: 'During 2004 the total internal revenue of [Dostum's] Junbesh [militia] was estimated at US$7 million a year, of which each vassal ("division commander") pocketed $240,000–600,000. Even by 2007 most of this much reduced revenue base had gone, with the customs, Khod-i-Barq and Dawlatabad salt mines now under the control of the central government' (Giustozzi 2009, 134). Ismail Khan succumbed to similar pressures to pass revenues on to the central government after 2001: 'By early 2003 he had passed on some $8–10 million, or around 10% of his estimated revenue' (ibid., 234). In 2003 Afghanistan's finance minister, Ashraf Ghani, visited Herat and reclaimed the revenue from the Islam Qala border crossing: 'He managed to return to Kabul with $20 million in cash and the hope that revenue would start flowing regularly from Herat. That did happen, but it took almost a year and the reorganization of Islam Qala customs. By the summer of 2004, Herat was sending cash to Kabul to the tune of $8 million a month. As a result, Ismail Khan's revenue must have been dramatically reduced' (ibid.).

A 2005 report by the Center for Strategic and International Studies, a US-based think tank, interviewed Afghans on a number of issues relating to post-conflict reconstruction (Courtney et al. 2005). A majority of Afghans interviewed supported the presence of international troops, did not support the Taliban, and wanted improved economic opportunities and social services. Standing out among these conclusions was a finding that 'Afghans fear intimidation by commanders more than the violence of insurgents.' In fact 'a poll in 2003 indicated that 65 percent of Afghans believed that commanders were the main source of insecurity in Afghanistan . . . The US military's employment of commanders to fight Taliban and al-Qaeda elements has armed and financed "friendly" militias. [Disarmament, Demobilization, and Reintegration] has brought a number of commanders into the police. Most problematically, President Karzai has dealt with troublesome governors – including former commanders – by moving them around, sometimes into cabinet positions, rather than removing them from power' (ibid., 39).

For their part the Taliban insurgents collect donations and tax revenues, including on narcotics trade: 'In 2009, the US government estimated the Afghan insurgents' donation income in the past 12 months at about 106 million dollars, compared to 70–400 million dollars from narcotics in differing estimates' (Isby 2010, 168). Donations come principally from Saudi Arabia and the Persian Gulf. Besides narcotics, insurgents raise funds from clear-cutting forests, kidnapping, extortion, and gem mining and trafficking (ibid.). These exactions occur with limited developmental benefit beyond the raw income earned by the warlords.

Even where the government has seized control of financial resources from warlords, the funds are inadequate to meet Afghanistan's development needs. Revenues are collected in a way that exacerbates regional differences and resentments: because tax collectors would be a target for insurgents in Pashtun areas, tax revenues are directed from non-Pashtun to Pashtun territories, 'in effect penalizing [the former] for maintaining order and a civil society' (ibid., 212).

Such revenues as the Afghan government collects are thus not well channelled towards development needs, particularly with the lack of sovereign control of the country's territory. That western aid is not fully controlled by the Afghan government, but is directed from abroad and subordinated to the counterinsurgency, only complicates the project of building a responsible and effective developmental state.

Compounding Distortion: Western Development Strategy in Afghanistan

Even if it were not subordinated to counterinsurgency the western development effort in Afghanistan would be hindered by several other limitations. First, only a fraction of the aid dollars pledged are spent in Afghanistan. Isby (2010, 339) contends that '[s]ome 40 percent of aid never leaves the donor country, as it is turned into corporate profits and consultant salaries; when in-kind transfers of aid to Afghanistan are counted, the percentage of many aid-for Afghanistan programs that end up going to the donor country is nearly double.' To get a sense of the incremental losses from pledge to expenditure, data cited by Maley (2009, 237) are instructive: 'Figures compiled by the Center on

International Cooperation at New York University showed that while a total of US$5.2 billion had been pledged for Afghanistan in January 2002, the total funds committed by May 2003 came to only US$2.6 billion, reconstruction disbursements came to only US$1.6 billion, and the value of projects actually completed was only US$192 million.'

Second, the simple amount pledged is nowhere near adequate to restore Afghanistan's infrastructure to its pre-war state. A 2006 assessment by the Afghan government shows the inadequacy of donor pledges: 'Over five years, Afghanistan would require US$18.865 billion to cover development needs; but domestic revenue was anticipated to amount to US$4.489 billion, not enough even to cover non-development recurrent costs of US$5.453 billion. Therefore US$19.829 billion, or just under US$4 billion per year over five years, would be required in the form of assistance from the wider world' (Maley 2009, 244). In the face of these needs, nothing like this was pledged: 'Future donor commitments made at the London conference in 2006 totalled a mere US$10.5 billion, barely half the figure Afghanistan needed. This arguably has left Afghanistan in the worst of both worlds: under-funded but dependent' (ibid.). The situation had not changed by 2008: 'As of March 2008, only 15 billion dollars of the 39 billion originally pledged in aid to Afghanistan has been spent . . . In May 2008, the Kabul government estimated the total cost of reconstruction at 30 billion dollars, with a further 50 billion being required for a five-year development program aimed at creating effective governance, a functioning state, and a national economy' (Isby 2010, 340). It is clear, then, that insufficient funds have been pledged, that pledged funds have not been delivered, and that Afghanistan lacks the resources to begin a national development program.

A third limitation is the primacy that western donors have given to the private sector in development, even in instances when developing the public sector would be much more efficient. Economic historian Ha-Joon Chang (2002, 2007) shows how developed countries achieved economic growth through a combination of active industrial and banking policies, protectionism, and public sector development. Two key points in Chang's work that are particularly relevant for Afghanistan are that developmental capacities typically are linked to the ability of states to exercise sovereignty and that the neoliberal, private sector–driven model is inadequate to build developmental capacities in poor countries.

The western countries now in charge of Afghanistan's economy, however, have focused on a commitment to private sector–based development in the absence of sovereignty and effective state capacities. The Word Bank's 2005 country study reflects this orientation: 'A dynamic private sector will be essential for Afghanistan to achieve the robust, sustained economic growth that is necessary for national poverty reduction, state building, and other reconstruction objectives' (2005, 69). Wholly dependent upon the West for support, Afghanistan's government has, of course, endorsed this approach. Hedayat Amin Arsala, advisor to President Karzai, describes the government's plan for the Afghan economy as follows: 'From the outset there has been fundamental agreement that Afghanistan would have a free market economy, with the private sector responsible for making the key commercial decisions regarding production and investment. Most of the rest of the world has seen that this model is essentially the only workable solution. Afghanistan has had the opportunity to learn this lesson itself' (Amin Arsala 2007, 152).

That donors and the Afghan state have followed a neoliberal agenda cannot be denied. This has included, in opposition to the developmental state model put forward by Chang, the privatization of state enterprises and the delivery of services by NGOs, with very mixed results. One of the more important reviews of development progress has concluded that donors followed 'a neoliberal agenda, which challenged the leadership role of the state, not just its inhibiting bureaucratic culture, and promoted privatisation and the shrinking of state institutions' (Barakat and Chard 2004, 24–5). By replacing state leadership with market forces, government institutions that could organize development have been starved out of the picture: '[i]nstitutional "reform", consisting mainly of reducing government personnel and privatising all but core activities, went hand in hand with economic "reform" to replace state leadership with "market forces"' (ibid.). This kind of hollowing-out of the state would be detrimental enough in a well-developed economy; in a poor country the situation becomes even worse 'since the overwhelming majority of public employees in poor countries work in the public services such as education and health, which (in the light of the general poverty of the population) are not capable of yielding profits or even any significant "cost recovery"' (ibid.).

For this new problem donors chose a solution that made the situation still worse: 'to promote social provisions by non-governmental organisations to which funds were channelled on a project by project basis . . . This gave further encouragement to ignore the lessons of integration and building on existing institutions, with predictably unsustainable results' (ibid.).

Furthermore foreign aid-based economic activity often excludes the rural population and can contribute to additional fragmentation. According to Isby (2010, 159), '[b]y 2008–10, in much of Afghanistan, perceptions of aid were that it does not prevent, but rather contributes to, instability, with insurgents being paid protection money by donor-funded contractors.' By circumventing local leaders and leadership structures, donors can weaken the informal networks and social basis for an economy, damaging these leaders' legitimacy and contributing to further social and political conflicts.

The 'poppy economy' is a major consideration in virtually all of the Afghan development literature produced in the West, and it is a fourth limitation of the development strategy (see, for example, Barakat 2004; Montgomery and Rondinelli 2004; Courtney et al. 2005; World Bank 2005; Rotberg 2007; Hayes and Sedra 2008). Afghanistan has become a central node in the global drug market and in 2008 and 2009 produced approximately 98 per cent of the world's illegal opium (Isby 2010, 170). With this volume of trade and production, poppy cultivation is important to the local economy, especially in southern Afghanistan. In fact, '[t]he UN estimated that the 2007–08 growing season produced some 8,200 tons of raw opium. Poppy cultivation in 2007–08 increased in overall yield even while the area cultivated declined 19 percent' (ibid., 171).

Local drops in cultivation and price, furthermore, lead only to stock-piling, not to crop substitution: 'In 2009, when opium prices reached a ten-year low and more was being seized, poppy cultivation dropped by 22 percent and opium production by ten percent. Faced with falling world prices, in 2009 it was estimated that the Afghan insurgents have a stockpile of some 10,000 tons of raw opium that they are holding to manipulate market prices' (ibid.). For this reason opium is structured into the Afghan economy much more so than emphasized by the UN Office on Drugs and Crime (2010).

While the opium economy has a long history in Afghanistan, its importance grew dramatically during the Soviet occupation because of the destruction of irrigation infrastructure. Opium is now 'easily irrigated from melting snows. In the Soviet attacks on the traditional irrigation systems of rural Afghanistan, notably the ingenious karez network of interconnected tunnels, lay the foundations of the illicit economy of the mid-to-late 1990s' (Maley 2009, 130). According to sociologist David Macdonald the poppy economy supplies 60 per cent of Afghanistan's GDP and employs 10 per cent of its labour force (2007, 96). He also estimates that up to 60 per cent of elected parliamentarians are linked to warlords and drug trafficking in some way (ibid., 95). Similar percentages probably apply to the Afghan National Police, given the control of local areas by warlords. In this context the governor of Helmand province suggested in 2006 that those in the drug business should be encouraged to invest their profits in Afghanistan (in construction companies and industries) rather than take the money out to tax havens (ibid., 97).

A suggestion in 2005 by the Senlis Council, a European think tank, to license Afghanistan to produce opium legally, was dismissed by the donor community and the Afghan government. But licit opium is produced by Turkey, India, France, Australia, Hungary, Spain, and a few other countries (Macdonald 2007, 34). This kind of licencing would drastically lower the price available to farmers, who would probably then require some form of price support (which could also be applied to other crops). Without such support, and so long as an illegal market exists, smuggling will continue.

In any case neither licit medicinal opium nor the idea of a legal market for non-medicinal opium has been seriously entertained by the West, which remains caught in a 'war on drugs' that compounds other problems, especially in Afghanistan. Indeed the pursuit of the 'war on drugs' is counterproductive for development; according to Isby (2010, 171), '[m]any of the tactics aimed to defeat narcotics have the potential to help spread the insurgency. By effectively chasing opium production into those provinces where the insurgency is strong, the insurgents secured a powerful revenue stream to support their operations.'

In short the western development plan for Afghanistan has been limited by an overemphasis on counterinsurgency, a misuse and misdirection of aid funds for corporate profits, an explosion of poppy cultivation linked to warlords and the Karzai government, and a neoliberal orientation that is incompatible with genuine development. In fact the new 'poppy economy,' which avoids legitimate channels of taxation and generates profits for corruption and narco-cartels, is much more compatible with insurgency and counterinsurgency than with social and economic development. Indeed, Alfred McCoy (2003) argues that illicit industry – specifically, the drug trade – thrives in situations of counterinsurgency. By sponsoring warlords, neoliberalism, and counterinsurgency, US and NATO policies have impeded human development in Afghanistan.

The Limitations of Canadian policy

Given the convergence between US-NATO and Canadian strategies in Afghanistan, it is not surprising that Canadian development policy has suffered from similar troubles and contradictions as those described above. First, although Canada's military and development planners share interpretations of how to proceed strategically in Afghanistan, it is the military effort that has largely taken precedence. In fact Canada's diplomacy and development efforts have been secondary to its use of force, accounting for only 10 per cent of Canadian spending in Afghanistan since 2001 (Stein and Lang 2007, 187). The primacy of military considerations is further demonstrated by the rehabilitation of warlords, sometimes referred to as 'commanders' by NATO forces, against the will of Afghan civilians. For its part Canada has worked directly with local commanders or warlords in Kandahar, including Rahmatullah Raufi, Asadullah Khalid, Ahmed Wali Karzai, and others (York 2006; Smith 2008).

The militarization of Canadian foreign policy in recent years is one structural reason Canada is unable to focus on diplomacy and development in Afghanistan. A guiding focus on interoperability with the United States and on Canada's military as a fighting, as opposed to a peacekeeping, force – as per General Hillier's famous quote: 'We're the Canadian Forces and our job is to be able to kill people' – has contributed to the subordination of diplomacy and development to military objectives. In Kandahar this subordination has resulted in civilian casualties, anti-Canadian protests, and the transfer of suspected insurgents (including children) over to Afghan security forces for torture and detention (CBC News 2007; *Globe and Mail* 2010; Smith 2010).

Second, Canada's development project in Afghanistan has been run at times without any objective benchmarks or even transparent reporting on the development effort. According to University of Ottawa professor Amir Attaran (2006), CIDA distributes money in a secretive and unreported manner, and often takes months to respond to freedom of information requests. In August 2007, the Senlis Council (2007) released a document of 'Unanswered Questions' for CIDA in Kandahar, finding no real food distribution program, minimal infrastructure development, no evidence of improvements at the hospital, and no program for civilian casualties of war. Although CIDA has financed a number of positive initiatives, including polio eradication and de-mining programs, it has done so under intense pressure from the Canadian government and military to provide 'quick-impact' projects that might serve Canada's political and military purposes in Kandahar, instead of long-term, nation-building objectives for the Afghan state (see Joya, in this volume). Furthermore, while Canada has funded national drug eradication programs in Afghanistan, it has consciously ignored, for political and military exigencies, the production and harvest of poppies in Kandahar, including by allies of the Canadian mission. Moreover tens of millions of dollars have been circulated in Kandahar through a network of local 'contractors,' seemingly run by warlords or commanders allied to the Canadian military (Blanchfield and Mayedo 2007). The outcome is that Canada's development strategy has made little impact on the standard of living and security situation in Kandahar.

In fact, by 2010, Canada's effort left a situation in which the United Nations was forced to cut staff over security concerns (Brewster 2010), the local government was unable to fill posts because of a Taliban assassination campaign (Partlow and DeYoung 2010), and a majority in Kandahar opposed foreign forces (Cordesman 2009). After six years of fighting, Canada's 3D strategy also failed to diminish the depth and breath of the insurgency, which inflicted major casualties on the Canadian Forces and operated a de facto state in the province, including checkpoints, military operations, and popular courts in Kandahar City. In these and other ways the failures of Canada's mission parallel those of the United States and NATO in Afghanistan.

Sovereignty, Development, and Peace

Many of the measures needed for genuine development require a sovereign state that can collect revenues, build infrastructure, and organize economic activity. The Afghan state has been unable to do so for much of its recent history, and none of the policies implemented after 2001 suggests a developmental state capacity is forming – indeed the absence of a functioning public sector has exacerbated unemployment and contributed to the fragmentation of the country (Isby 2010, 160).

Afghanistan also suffers chronically from outside interference, so much so that without outside agreement peace is impossible. An analogy for this regional interference is provided by the late political scientist Eqbal Ahmad, who describes attending a game of *buzkashi*, or 'goat grabbing,' in Afghanistan with friends. *Buzkashi* has some similarities to US football, where the goal is to grab the 'ball' (in this case a headless calf weighing 50 to 100 pounds) and carry it to a goal, though it is played on horseback and depends more on the skill of the individual riders and their horses than on teamwork:

> The game reflects a culture that places enormous value on physical courage and individual enterprise, allows untrammelled competition, and assumes that order will emerge from anarchy. 'But there is more to it,' one of our Afghan friends said. 'It is not possible to play this game without sponsors. It involves great expense, prizes, payments to the *chapandazan* [horsemen], horses above all, good horses, which very few people have. It is a game that only the rich can afford to sponsor: no sponsor, no game. It is a game of dependency. That is how this war is. We are being torn to pieces by teams sponsored by outsiders.' (2004, 154–5)

Today's game features, on the one hand, the United States and NATO, as well as India and Iran, supporting the Afghan government. Pakistan, on the other hand, continues to stand accused of supporting the insurgency, and is expected by the United States to prove otherwise by attacking the Taliban with ever-greater violence. Instead it attempts to negotiate with the Taliban while US drones bomb Pashtun villages and suspected al-Qaeda safe houses on the Pakistan side of the border. Insurgents have attacked Indian targets in Afghanistan, such as the Indian Embassy in Kabul. They have also attacked many targets in Pakistan.

Given this complex matrix of activity, the urgent need is for a regional solution – involving Iran, India, Pakistan, and China – that would disarm the warlords and focus on agricultural development. Greater regional economic integration, and especially détente between India and Pakistan, is an important component of any lasting solution for Afghanistan.

According to Tariq Ali (2008, 247), peace and stability in Afghanistan require '[a] withdrawal of all NATO forces either preceded or followed by a regional pact to ensure Afghan stability for the next ten years. Pakistan, Iran, India, Russia, and possibly China could guarantee and support a functioning national government pledged to preserving the ethnic and religious diversity of Afghanistan. A serious social and economic plan to rebuild the country and provide the basic necessities for its people would become a necessary prerequisite for stability.' Ali proposes the gradual restoration of Afghan sovereignty through a negotiated settlement by the actors in the proxy war in which Afghans have been implicated. These actors include every one of Afghanistan's neighbours: Russia, Pakistan, India, and Iran, as well as, on a different basis, China. Such proposals for multilateral negotiations have a better chance of success than NATO's prevailing ideas of escalating the war and encroaching further on Pakistan's sovereignty. NATO's agenda of regional control is also incompatible with lasting peace for Afghanistan and the wider region. A similar proposal has also been made by British military analyst Anatol Lieven (2011), who argues for a complete US withdrawal, a core strategy of 'handing responsibility for guaranteeing Afghanistan's security to the major regional states,' and a dispensation of 'Taliban control of the south of the country, continued development aid to this region and some participation in central government in return for the exclusion of al-Qaeda, a crackdown on the heroin trade and recognition of the Afghan national government.' Lieven cautions that, in the absence of such an arrangement, the collapse of Pakistan remains a possibility. Such a collapse 'is the really terrible threat to America and its allies from this part of the Muslim world.'

Yet neither the United States nor Canada has understood this. Instead they continue to try to fit development and humanitarian goals into the incompatible framework of counterinsurgency and free market economics, both geared towards projecting western power into Central Asia. NATO's intervention is, in fact, increasing popular anger and regional resistance to the occupation, creating an ever-widening scope of conflict. US drone attacks in Pakistan, for example, killed 14 al-Qaeda members and 687 civilians in two years, according to a Pakistani report (Mir 2009). A report in the *Washington Post* (Miller 2011) gives a figure of 581 'militants' killed in 2010, a maximum of 13 of whom were 'high-value targets,' the rest 'mere foot soldiers.' The Pakistani government's deals with the Taliban and NATO's relationships to warlords are hugely unpopular, as are the legal and constitutional concessions to these warlords. The recent Afghan family law giving men the right to have sex with their wives every fourth day and forbidding women to leave the home alone is an example of such a concession. It was condemned by Afghan women and was eventually revised because of western pressure (CBC News 2009). The family law, however, is far from unique – the constitution of 2004, which was ratified by many warlords and

supported by NATO, states that political parties must accept the principles of Islam (Warnock 2008).

Such concessions to warlords, made of military necessity, give trouble
to NATO's claim that it is interested in development or social progress
when, as frequently occurs, these goals clash with those of counterinsurgency and regional control. Step by step, and under NATO's supervision, Afghanistan is returning to the pre-2001 dispensation: warlords,
the Taliban, an anti-secular government, civil war, and regional rivalries and interference. NATO's recent posture has been to threaten to
extend this conflict into Pakistan.

The rebellion against NATO is now based in the Pashtun areas both
Afghanistan and Pakistan. Pashtuns on both sides of the border do not
recognize the Durand Line that divides their national homeland. From
their perspective the United States made war on them starting in 2001
and wants Pakistan to make war on them as well. Frightening scenarios
of wider regional instability arise: as Pakistan starts to deploy more
military operations in the area, the country could unravel. If Pakistan
unravels, so will South Asia. India is increasingly and dangerously
isolated, having sided with the United States on the nuclear deal, the
invasion of Afghanistan, and various conflicts in the Middle East. In
exchange the United States has dropped its support for Pakistan in the
conflict over Kashmir, leaving the Pakistani establishment feeling increasingly isolated and prone to reacting unpredictably (Ali 2008). The
risks are considerable and go well beyond Afghanistan.

For its part Canada entered this conflict to play its traditional role of
assisting US foreign policy aims. But by entering with a military and
counterinsurgency agenda, it has discredited its developmental and
humanitarian alibis. It has also added danger and suffering to an already precarious and miserable situation. As these dangers mature, the
alibis will ring increasingly hollow.

Conclusion

Modern counterinsurgency wars attempt to instrumentalize development and subordinate it to military objectives, but the US-NATO war
in Afghanistan exemplifies the application and failure of this kind of
development agenda. Canada's policies in Afghanistan are consistent
with the US-NATO strategy and thus exhibit parallel failures. As a result all of the blockages to development in Afghanistan, including fragmentation, overdependence on opium, and the lack of a sovereign state

able to guide the development process, remain in place or have been exacerbated by NATO's, and Canada's, intervention.

To achieve genuine development Afghanistan needs a sovereign state that is free of outside intervention and has the capacity to build infrastructure and meet human development needs. Western efforts have proven practically and ideologically unable to create such conditions, even when focused on them. Because NATO's and Canada's development efforts are subordinated to counterinsurgency, the possibility that they will lead to genuine human development is slight at best. Instead NATO and Canadian policies are creating new kinds of distortions in Afghanistan's economic structure. For this reason western countries must rethink and radically change their policies in Afghanistan. Given the failures of the past decade, and the growing risks of the present one, it is vitally important to end the counterinsurgency war against the Taliban, restore sovereignty to the Afghan state, give support to a regional peace agreement, and decouple aid and development from the instrumental ends of war and occupation. The logic of regional control and western hegemony must give way to peace, independence, and self-determination on the path of human development. Only then will Afghanistan achieve what NATO and Canadian leaders profess to offer under the aegis of counterinsurgency.

References

Ahmad, Eqbal. 2004. 'Bloody Games.' In *Eqbal Ahmad: Between Past and Future: Selected Essays on South Asia*, ed. D. Ahmad, I. Ahmad, and Z. Mian. Oxford: Oxford University Press.

Ali, Tariq. 2008. *The Duel: Pakistan on the Flight Path of American Power*. New York: Scribner.

Amin Arsala, Hedayat. 2007. 'Revitalizing Afghanistan's Economy: The Government's Plan.' In *Building a New Afghanistan*, ed. R.I. Rotberg. Cambridge, UK: World Peace Foundation.

Attaran, Amir. 2006. 'CIDA silent on Afghan projects.' *Toronto Star*, 6 October.

Banerjee, Nipa. 2008. 'Peace Building and Development in the Fragile State of Afghanistan: A Practitioner's Perspective.' In *Afghanistan: Transition under Threat*, ed. G. Hayes and M. Sedra. Waterloo, ON: Wilfrid Laurier University Press.

–. 2009. 'Afghanistan: No Security, No Development.' *Policy Options* 30, no. 10: 66–71.

Barakat, Sultan, ed. 2004. *Reconstructing War-Torn Societies: Afghanistan*. New York: Palgrave-Macmillan.

Barakat, Sultan, and Margaret Chard. 2004. 'Theories, Rhetoric and Practice: Recovering the Capacities of War-torn Societies.' In *Reconstructing War-Torn Societies: Afghanistan*, ed. S. Barakat. New York: Palgrave-Macmillan.

Belasco, Amy. 2011. 'The Cost of Iraq, Afghanistan, and Other Global War on Terror Operations since 9/11.' RL 33110. 7–5700. Washington, DC: Congressional Research Service. http://www.fas.org/sgp/crs/natsec/RL33110.pdf.

Blanchfield, Mike, and Andrew Mayedo. 2007. 'The Business of War.' *CanWest News Service*, 19 November.

Brewster, Murray. 2010. 'UN cuts Kandahar staff over security concerns.' *Canadian Press*, 21 May.

Canada. 2005. 'Canada's International Policy Statement: A Role of Pride and Influence in the World – Overview.' Ottawa: Department of Foreign Affairs and International Trade.

Capstick, Mike. 2008. 'Establishing Security in Afghanistan: Strategic and Operational Perspectives.' In *Afghanistan: Transition under Threat*, ed. G. Hayes and M. Sedra. Waterloo, ON: Wilfrid Laurier University Press.

CBC News. 2007. '"Death to Canada," some Afghan protesters chant,' 26 September. http://www.cbc.ca/world/story/2007/09/26/afghan-protest.html.

–. 2009. 'Controversial family law halted: minister,' 5 April. http://www.cbc.ca/world/story/2009/04/05/afghanistan-family-law.html.

Chang, Ha-Joon. 2002. *Kicking Away the Ladder: Development Strategy in Historical Perspective*. London: Anthem Press.

–. 2007. *Bad Samaritans: The Myth of Free Trade and the Secret History of Capitalism*. London: Bloomsbury Press.

Collier, Paul. 2007. *The Bottom Billion: Why the Poorest Countries Are Failing and What Can Be Done about It*. Oxford: Oxford University Press.

Cordesman, Anthony. 2009. *Afghan Public Opinion and the Afghan War: Shifts by Region and Province*. Washington, DC: Center for Strategic and International Studies.

Courtney, Morgan L., et al. 2005. *In the Balance: Measuring Progress in Afghanistan*. Washington DC: CSIS Press.

Giustozzi, Antonio. 2009. *Empires of Mud: Wars and Warlords in Afghanistan*. New York: Columbia University Press.

Globe and Mail. 2010. 'Canadians handed children over to notorious Afghan security unit: Reports,' 28 November.

Goodhand, Jonathan. 2004. 'Aiding Violence or Building Peace? The Role of International Aid in Afghanistan.' In *Reconstructing War-Torn Societies: Afghanistan*, ed. S. Barakat. New York: Palgrave-Macmillan.

Hayes, Geoffrey, and Mark Sedra, eds. 2008. *Afghanistan: Transition under Threat*. Waterloo, ON: Wilfrid Laurier University Press.

Hoodbhoy, Pervez. 2009. 'The Saudi-isation of Pakistan.' *Newsline Pakistan*, 2 January. http://www.newsline.com.pk/NewsJan2009/cover2jan2009.htm.

Hope, Ian. 2008. *Dancing with the Dushman: Command Imperatives for the Counter-Insurgency Fight in Afghanistan*. Kingston, ON: Canadian Defence Academy Press.

Isby, David. 2010. *Afghanistan, Graveyard of Empires: A New History of the Borderland*. New York: Pegasus Books.

Jalalzai, Musa Khan. 2003. *The Political Economy of Afghanistan*. Lahore, Pakistan: Sang-E-Meel Publications.

Kolhatkar, Sonali, and James Ingalls. 2006. *Bleeding Afghanistan: Washington, Warlords, and the Propaganda of Silence*. New York: Seven Stories.

Lebowitz, Michael. 2009. 'The Path to Human Development: Capitalism or Socialism?' *Monthly Review* (February). http://www.monthlyreview. org/090223lebowitz.php.

Lieven, Anatol. 2011. 'A Mutiny Grows in Punjab.' *National Interest* 112 (March–April): 15–23. http://nationalinterest.org/article/mutiny-grows-punjab-4889.

Macdonald, David. 2007. *Drugs in Afghanistan: Opium, Outlaws and Scorpion Tales*. London: Pluto Press.

Maley, William. 2009. *The Afghanistan Wars*, 2nd. ed. New York: Palgrave-Macmillan.

Maloney, Sean. 2007. *Enduring the Freedom: A Rogue Historian in Afghanistan*. Dulles, VA: Potomac Books.

McCoy, Alfred. 2003. *The Politics of Heroin*. Chicago: Lawrence Hill Books.

Miller, Greg. 2011. 'Increased U.S. drone strikes in Pakistan killing few high-value militants.' *Washington Post,* February 21. http://www.washingtonpost.com/wp-dyn/content/article/2011/02/20/AR2011022002975.html.

Mir, Amir. 2009. '60 drone hits kill 14 al-Qaeda men, 687 civilians.' *The News, Pakistan*, 10 April. http://www.thenews.com.pk/top_story_detail.asp?Id=21440.

Montgomery, John D., and Dennis A. Rondinelli. 2004. *Beyond Reconstruction in Afghanistan*. New York: Palgrave-Macmillan.

NATO (North Atlantic Treaty Organization). 2008. Media Operations Centre. 'NATO in Afghanistan: Master Narrative as at 6 October 2008.' http://www.wikileaks.org/leak/nato-master-narrative-2008.pdf (accessed 5 April 2009).

Partlow, Joshua, and DeYoung, Karen. 2010. 'Afghan government falls short in Kandahar.' *Washington Post*, 2 November.

Patel, Seema. 2008. 'Laying Economic Foundations for a New Afghanistan.' In *Afghanistan: Transition under Threat*, ed. G. Hayes and M. Sedra. Waterloo, ON: Wilfrid Laurier University Press.

RAND Corporation. 2008. *Intelligence Operations and Metrics in Iraq and Afghanistan*. http://wikileaks.org/wiki/Major_RAND_study_with_300_interviews:_Intelligence_Operations_and_Metrics_in_Iraq_and_Afghanistan,_Nov_2008 (accessed 5 April 2009).

Rotberg, Robert I., ed. 2007. *Building a New Afghanistan*. Cambridge, UK: World Peace Foundation.

Senlis Council. 2007. 'The Canadian International Development Agency in Kandahar: Unanswered Questions.' Ottawa.

Sinno, Abdulkader. 2008. 'Explaining the Taliban's Ability to Mobilize the Pashtuns.' In *The Taliban and the Crisis of Afghanistan*, ed. R. Crews, D. Robert, and A. Tarzi. Cambridge, MA: Harvard University Press.

Smith, Graeme. 2008. 'Tribal animosity drawing Taliban recruits; according to The Globe's survey, the majority of insurgents in the south do not come from tribes well-represented in local government.' *Globe and Mail*, 25 March.

–. 2010. 'House of pain: Canada's connection with Kandahar's ruthless palace guard.' *Globe and Mail*, 10 April.

Stein, Janice Gross, and Eugene Lang. 2007. *The Unexpected War: Canada in Kandahar*. Toronto: Viking.

Suhrke, Astri, Kristian Harpviken, and Arne Strand. 2004. 'After Bonn: Conflictual Peace Building.' In *Reconstructing War-Torn Societies: Afghanistan*, ed. S. Barakat. New York: Palgrave-Macmillan.

United Nations. 2010. *Human Development Report 2010*. New York: United Nations.

United Nations Office on Drugs and Crime. 2010. *Afghanistan Opium Survey 2010*. New York: United Nations.

Warnock, John W. 2008. *Creating a Failed State: The US and Canada in Afghanistan*. Halifax, NS: Fernwood.

World Bank. 2005. *Afghanistan – State Building, Sustaining Growth, and Reducing Poverty: A World Bank Country Study*. Washington, DC.

York, Geoffrey. 2006. 'Grenade attack killed soldier; shrapnel from RPG hit female officer standing in hatch of armoured vehicle, military sources say.' *Globe and Mail*, 19 May.

12

From the Somalia Affair to Canada's Afghan Detainee Torture Scandal: How Stories of Torture Define the Nation

SHERENE H. RAZACK[1]

On 23 April 2007 the *Globe and Mail* reported that thirty face-to-face interviews with Afghan prisoners detained by Canadian soldiers and then sent to Kandahar jails run by Afghanistan's National Directorate of Security revealed that torture was rampant and that the Canadian Forces were unlikely to be ignorant of it. Reporter Graeme Smith related the men's stories of being whipped with electric cables to the point of unconsciousness, stripped naked and forced to stand in freezing cold cells, hung by the ankles for eight days of beating, and deprived of sleep and food (Smith 2007). Challenged in Parliament about the treatment meted out to Afghan detainees, the Canadian government protested that it did not know that transferred prisoners were being tortured, but it nevertheless zealously blocked investigations into the matter, going so far in 2009 as to shut down Parliament and to refuse to provide information to the House of Commons. In April 2010, compelled by the speaker of the House to produce the documents relating to Afghan detainees, either to the public or to a multiparty parliamentary committee, or face the contempt of Parliament, the government finally agreed at the eleventh hour to the second option. It remains to be seen what story of torture will emerge from these deliberations, but a memo among the documents released to the multiparty parliamentary committee revealed that the Judge Advocate General had warned senior military officials as early as 2007 that they would be liable if they ignored warnings of prisoner abuse. Critics allege that this warning reveals that the government should have known it was violating international law when it transferred detainees to Afghan authorities knowing that there was a chance they would be tortured (Brennan 2010a).

As it unfolds, Canada's Afghan detainee scandal may well reveal that social, legal, and political support for torture is rising. The Conservatives, led by Stephen Harper, won a majority in the May 2011 federal election notwithstanding its actions on the Afghan detainee issue and its efforts in the Federal Court to exclude evidence from a report prepared by the Military Police Complaints Commission about the military leadership's knowledge of the transfer of detainees into Afghan custody, where they faced the risk of torture (Smith 2011). The Federal Court has ruled that the Canadian Charter of Rights and Freedoms does not apply to troops outside the country, and it has refused to hear the challenge by Amnesty International and the British Columbia Civil Liberties Association to the Canadian military's policy of transferring detainees in Afghanistan (Amnesty International 2008, 2009). Perhaps most troubling of all is the low level of interest that Canadians display in the possibility that their government has been complicit in the torture of Afghans. The news in 2007 and again in 2009 that professors Michael Byers and William Schabas have asked Luis Moreno-Ocampo, the prosecutor of the International Criminal Court, to investigate Canada's role in the torture of Afghan detainees and the prosecutor's response (captured in a documentary film in 2010) that, if Canada fails to investigate itself adequately it could find itself charged with war crimes, have caused little stir in Canadian society (Byers and Schabas 2007, 2009; Stevens 2010).

If, as several legal observers have alleged with respect to Afghanistan, the idea of a military accountable to the rule of law and to civilian government has been seriously eroded in Canada (Scott 2010), and if the investigation into allegations of complicity in torture continues to be blocked by the Canadian government, apparently with political impunity, then are we in an age when torture – and specifically the torture of Arabs and Muslims – has gained social approval? If this is the case, then an urgent question that confronts us is how, at this historical moment, Canadians (among others) have come to accept that Arabs and Muslims who are suspected of involvement in terrorism, or resistance to occupation, should be deprived of fundamental legal rights and thus tortured with impunity?

In this chapter I approach this question through a consideration of how torture operates to produce nations and national subjects as dominant, a topic I first pursued in an exploration of prisoner abuse of Somalis by Canadian peacekeepers in 1993 (Razack 2004). In drawing connections between peacekeepers who tortured Somalis and the possible willingness, if not a more active desire, on the part of the Canadian military in Afghanistan to hand over detainees to Afghan authorities when they knew the detainees would be tortured, I rely on the idea that torture itself is a narrative. Torture writes the story of power on the body. During torture, Elaine Scarry (1985, 57) writes, the torturer becomes voice but no body; the tortured becomes body but no voice. In this way the torturer is civilization – he or she transcends the body; while the tortured becomes reduced to body, to the guttural sounds of pain. Torture is 'the undoing of civilization' (ibid., 38). Significantly, torture is also a narrative of power written on the *social body*. The nation, and the fraternity of nations on whose behalf torture is conducted, establishes its power through torture. As Michael Taussig (1987) points out about torture and terror in colonial regimes, most of us are neither tortured nor torturers, and we come to know about torture and its role in making the nation or colony only through the mediation of narrative. Democratic regimes as well as totalitarian ones each can come to depend on torture to tell the story of their power. Because torture is a narrative, and does its work in sustaining regimes of power as narrative, there is little difference between the torturer and those who have made his or her work possible. Each contributes to the same story of power.

The way we act towards others and our capacity to approve of torture are shaped both by how we imagine others *and* how we legally treat them (Scarry 1999). Social and political support for torture thrives in a moral environment where there is an increasing expulsion of groups – in this case, Muslims – from the human and political community. As I have written elsewhere, the post-9/11 period has brought an increasing emphasis in the United States and other western democracies, including Canada, on the eviction of Muslims and other racialized groups from the rule of law on the basis that those suspected of involvement in terrorism are not entitled to full legal rights (Razack 2008). For example, the right to *habeas corpus* has been denied to those suspected of involvement in terrorism. Race becomes an integral part of who is included and who is excluded from the political community when we believe that certain groups are not entitled to the rule of law by virtue of their innate characteristics (a propensity to violence, a fanatical devotion to religion, and so on). We declare ourselves to be both morally and racially superior through evicting groups with what we perceive as undesirable innate characteristics from the protection of the law.

Torture, either doing it or facilitating it, as in the rendition of detainees post-9/11 to places where they will be tortured, provides western states such as Canada with membership in the fraternity of 'white nations,' led by the United States, that are waging a 'war on terror.' As several analysts – notably Phillipe Sands (2008) – have pointed out, President George W. Bush was in direct contact with the room in which the torture of Mohammed al-Qahtani took place, and Secretary of State Donald Rumsfeld personally authorized torture techniques. Torture has thus been central to the 'war on terror.' Importantly, as Elaine Scarry (2010) has argued, since there is an absolute prohibition on torture in international law, the Bush administration's authorizing of torture (discussed as coercive interrogation techniques, rather than torture) announced its contempt for the rule of law and marked legally authorized lawlessness as the key feature of the 'war on terror.' When the Canadian state acquiesces to torture, Canadians declare themselves to be a part of this political community and simultaneously expel Afghans (among others) from it. That is to say, Canada is participating in a growing project involving the West's domination of the Global South. Through torture Canadians establish themselves on the right side of the colour line, where Europeans stand on one side and Arabs and Muslims, imagined as barbaric and undeserving of the protection of the law, stand on the other. As both a nation and as individuals the interpellation into 'empire' and 'whiteness' is hard to resist. In emphasizing the racial underpinnings of torture narratives, I suggest *how* we are seduced into accepting the torture of Afghans in our name. We are seduced, I suggest, into a racial global order, and thus into racial superiority, plain and simple.

The story we tell about torture is as significant as the story torture writes on bodies. We stop torture from penetrating our consciousness when we believe in its instrumentality (Scarry 1985). That is, if torture is something we do only to extract information from a terrorist or a fanatical, misogynist Taliban prisoner, it is not torture but self-defence. As we have seen with the classification of prisoners as enemy combatants (and thus incarcerated as detainees, not prisoners of war) and techniques such as water boarding as an interrogation method, it is possible to legally authorize torture by calling it something else. The word torture is often replaced by the word abuse in North American newspaper headlines about the treatment of detainees in Iraq, Afghanistan, or Guantánamo. In one study only 19 per cent of US press articles on Abu Ghraib referred to torture compared with 81.8 per cent of such articles in the European press; in the Canadian press articles on Abu Ghraib referred to torture 41 per cent of the time (Jones and Sheets 2009). When 'torture' is replaced by 'abuse,' torture easily becomes a story about an overzealous or incompetent administration or, alternatively, about an especially savage enemy who requires extra 'coercion.' Abuse stories rarely focus on how one human being deliberately inflicts pain on another on behalf of the state. Torture as abuse, or torture as an interrogation method, even one that has gone too far, shields us from confronting what is involved when one human being tortures another and what is accomplished by annihilating the personhood of another.

In what follows I read Canadian responses to the torture of Afghan detainees through the 1993 incidents of torture in Somalia and argue that the tracks have long been laid for Canadians to understand our participation in the 'New World Order' as a western nation and a member of the fraternity of white nations, obliged to discipline and keep in line a chaotic Third World. Violence, of which torture is one manifestation, has a central role to play in this narrative about an apocryphal encounter between the civilized and the uncivilized. When we examine national responses to torture we can see torture as a narrative producing a racial state. The involvement of the Canadian government in the rendition of Canadian citizen Maher Arar to Syria, where he was tortured, its support of the detention of then-fifteen-year-old Canadian Omar Khadr at Guantánamo (where he alleges that he has been tortured), and its indifference to, if not active participation in, the torture of Canadian citizens Abdullah Almalki, Ahmad El Maati, and Muayyed Nureddin in Egypt and Syria suggest that an even stronger case can be made for growing national support of the torture of racialized peoples than could have been made in 1993 (Canada 2006; Iacobucci 2008). The torture of Afghan detainees, then, might simply be a part of how Canadians have come to understand their place in the world. If this is true we will both ignore and depend on it.

The Afghan Detainee Scandal: A Government Committed to Torture?

In a timeline of events constructed by the *Globe and Mail* and the opposition Liberal Party of Canada and the New Democratic Party (NDP), the events of the Afghan detainee issue are not in dispute (see *Globe and Mail* 2010; Liberal Party 2010; New Democratic Party 2010). The Conservative government of Stephen Harper appears to have been aware at least of the possibility of Afghan detainees' being tortured for some time. In 2002, when Canada first confronted the issue of what to do with captured Afghans, the source of concern for Parliament was whether prisoners turned over to the United States would have the protection of international law. Specifically, would the United States respect the Geneva Convention? Under President George W. Bush al-Qaeda prisoners were classified as enemy combatants and not as prisoners of war as defined by the Geneva Convention. The Liberal government of Jean Chrétien agreed to these terms.

In 2005, when Canadian troops took on a leading fighting role in Kandahar province and began working with the UN-led International Security Assistance Force and the Afghan government, rather than with the US-led coalition, Canada signed an agreement that detainees would be handed over to Afghan custody, where they would be treated according to the Geneva Convention. By March 2006 the US State Department had already begun reporting that torture and abuse of detainees were rampant among Afghan authorities. Canada's Louise Arbour, then UN High Commissioner for Human Rights, reporting on the activities of the Afghan National Security Directorate, noted complaints of serious human rights violations, including arbitrary arrest, illegal detention, and torture. Arbour also noted the absence of transparent and public investigations and of due process (United Nations 2006). One month later Canadian diplomat Richard Colvin arrived in Afghanistan and also began expressing concern about the treatment of detainees by Afghan authorities. In April 2006 NDP defence critic Dawn Black raised the issue of the prisoner transfer agreement and pressed the Harper government to renegotiate it in view of allegations of torture in Afghan-run prisons. In response Minister of National Defence Gordon O'Connor explained that Canada would be informed by the Red Cross if there was abuse or torture, a position he maintained even after the Afghan Independent Human Rights Commission announced in June 2006 that one-third of the prisoners handed over by Canadians to Afghan authorities were abused and tortured. For the rest of 2006 reports by Richard Colvin continued to warn of abuse and torture and the Red Cross formally complained that Canada was not informing it of detainee transfers in a timely manner.

In early February 2007 University of Ottawa law professor Amir Attaran produced documents he had obtained through an Access to Information request that revealed that three prisoners handed over by Canadians to Afghan authorities showed evidence of torture, possibly by Canadian and/or Afghan soldiers. The Military Police Complaints Commission (MPCC) began an investigation into the three cases and into the detainee handover agreement, and soon discovered that the three detainees could not be found. It is not known whether they died in custody, were transported to another prison, or were released and returned to their communities. In the same month Amnesty International and the British Columbia Civil Liberties Association sought a judicial review in Federal Court of the military's detainee handover policy and an injunction to stop detainee transfers. The Harper government took the position that the Charter of Rights and Freedoms did not apply and that no individual detainee had been identified as having been tortured. On 19 March 2007 the government informed Parliament that the Red Cross was never required to share information with Canadian authorities. Subsequently the minister of national defence apologized to the House of Commons for having misled it on this matter. On 3 May 2007, in a bid to stop the injunction to halt detainee transfers, the government announced a new detainee agreement that would enable Canadians to monitor Afghan jails, while continuing to insist that it had not received information about one single incident of torture. Nonetheless, in August 2007, the *Globe and Mail* reported that the government had hired a British legal scholar to submit an opinion to the Federal Court that Canada had no obligation to accord Afghan detainees full legal rights (Cheadle 2007). Towards the end of 2007 detainee transfers were halted due to concerns about torture, although the Canadian public did not learn of this until late January 2008.

The story that unfolded in Federal Court revealed that some government officials did not consider the human rights of Afghan detainees to be their concern. The MPCC, for example, informed the government that some officials were refusing to provide it with information. The government itself applied to Federal Court to delay the MPCC hearings, but the application was denied. Through 2009 the government continued to attempt to block witnesses from testifying at the MPCC and failed to produce the requested documents, even as Colvin testified before the House of Commons Special Committee on Afghanistan about Canada's implication in torture. Government officials vehemently insisted that Colvin had been duped by the Taliban into believing their stories of torture; as former defence minister Peter Mackay asked, how can you believe men who 'who throw acid in the face of schoolgirls?' (*CBC News* 2009).

In an unprecedented move Prime Minister Harper prorogued Parliament on 30 December 2009, shutting down the Special Committee on Afghanistan until late March. In March 2010 the justice minister asked former Supreme Court of Canada justice Frank Iacobucci to review the documents relating to Afghan detainees in order to determine what documents could be released without damaging national security, a measure opposition parties insisted simply delayed the issue (Brennan 2010b). As military sources began reversing their earlier positions and acknowledging that that they had known of torture, the government released 2,500 pages of heavily censored documents. Most shocking of all, when Parliament resumed and the government continued to refuse to provide uncensored documents, the speaker of the House, Peter Milliken, ruled on 27 April 2010 that, by doing so, the government had breached parliamentary privilege. He also ruled that the government would be in contempt of Parliament if it failed to hand over documents or to arrive at an all-party agreement on how to examine the documents. The government accepted the latter suggestion.

Colvin's Testimony

Richard Colvin's testimony to the House of Commons Special Committee on Afghanistan offers the clearest account of Canada's role in the torture of detainees. Colvin, currently first secretary in the Canadian embassy in Washington, is a senior diplomat who had previously served in Sri Lanka, Russia, and the Occupied Palestinian Territories and also served for seventeen months in Afghanistan with the Department of Foreign Affairs and International Trade as a representative of the Provincial Reconstruction Team and as acting ambassador, in both Kandahar and Kabul. His responsibilities were wide ranging and included detainee transfers. Colvin told the Special Committee that Canada transferred six times as many detainees to the Afghan authorities as did the British and twenty times as many as the Dutch. Unlike these governments, however, Canada did not monitor detainees after their transfer; instead the Canadian transfer system relied on the Afghanistan Independent Human Rights Commission, which had such limited resources that Colvin characterized them as 'useless' (quoted in Wherry 2009). The Canadian government also relied on the Red Cross, which, however, could only inform Afghan, not Canadian, authorities about prisoner abuse. In any event, again unlike the British and the Dutch, Canada was slow to inform the Red Cross about the prisoners it transferred to the Afghan authorities, using a six-step process that took weeks and months as opposed to the twenty-four hours it took the British and the Dutch to do so.

Colvin testified that he was certain that virtually all detainees handed over were tortured. Citing US State Department and UN reports that clearly spelled out that Afghan torture and abuse 'consisted of pulling out fingernails and toenails, burning with hot oil, sexual abuse and sodomy,' among other practices, Colvin testified that detainees handed over by Canadians to Afghan forces showed physical evidence of torture (scars and missing toenails). Detainees told Canadian officials of electroshocks and beatings with cables (Colvin 2009b). Canada had extremely poor record keeping, and it was virtually impossible to track what happened to detainees, some of whom simply disappeared. Finally, Colvin revealed that Canada 'cloaked our detainee practices in extreme secrecy,' again in contrast to the practice of other nations (quoted in Wherry 2009); both the British and Dutch, for instance, informed their governments when a detainee had been detained and transferred. In contrast the Canadian Forces refused to reveal even the number of detainees they had transferred to Afghan authorities. Once those in the field, such as Colvin, became aware of the scope and severity of the problem, they began to inform Ottawa. Here Colvin documented his own efforts, showing that reports were not only ignored but actively resisted. Ultimately he was told to stop writing reports altogether and to raise detainee issues on the phone only. When Ottawa did sign a new detainee policy with the Afghan government in 2007 giving Canadians the right to monitor the treatment of transferees, for the first five months monitoring was undertaken by officers who, in Colvin's view, were not able to obtain information easily in their short-term visits. When a dedicated monitor finally arrived, however, he soon found evidence of torture. Yet, for a year and a half, though Ottawa knew that torture was being committed, the Canadian Forces continued to hand over prisoners to Afghan authorities.

Colvin, meanwhile, believed he was being punished for his efforts. He was denied legal counsel and access to his own reports, and was threatened with prison if he revealed anything either to the MPCC or to the Special Committee. Ending his testimony by reminding the committee that most of the Afghans captured were 'completely innocent' ordinary people who were not members of the Taliban (with which the Afghan Human Rights Commission also agreed), Colvin concluded that Canada was indeed heavily implicated in torture (quoted in Wherry 2009). Colvin's affidavit to the MPCC shows in exhaustive detail the communications between himself and Ottawa about torture in Afghan jails

(Colvin 2009a). Confronting a government that insisted that it had not been told anything about torture, on 16 December 2009 Colvin itemized his efforts to do so in further evidence he offered to the Special Committee, citing six written reports and a number of meetings with embassy officials (Colvin 2009b). He reminded the committee that, alongside his reports, a number of key allies and international organizations also had reported on the substantial risk of torture in Afghan prisons. Yet, when confronted with evidence of torture, Colvin declared, Ottawa often stalled. Detainees were not the highly trained al-Qaeda operatives claimed by the government but instead were illiterate, poorly educated Afghan villagers. Describing in substantial detail his interviews with detainees that had been reported to the government, Colvin rejected the government's claim that the first credible account of torture had not been received until November 2007. Furthermore Colvin clarified that his sources revealing torture were highly credible. In his reports he suggested options the government could have taken to avoid handing over detainees. In sum, Colvin demolished government arguments that the reporting of torture was not reliable or that Ottawa encouraged reporting rather than punish it. Canadian generals did have direct information about torture, Colvin insisted, but simply refused to act on it (2009b). From Colvin's testimony it is difficult not to conclude that Canada knew a great deal about the torture of prisoners it handed over to Afghan authorities and did very little to stop it.

Déjà vu: From Somalia and Back Again

Why would Ottawa remain indifferent to the torture of Afghan prisoners, or worse, actively enable it? Analysts disagree on the answer to this question. *Toronto Star* columnist James Travers, for instance, offers this explanation. Remembering Somalia (when both the military and the government were called to account), Guantanamo, and, presumably, Abu Ghraib, Canadian politicians did not want to be tarnished with allegations of prisoner abuse and torture. As Travers put it, '[s]ometime between Somalia and Kandahar, the military concluded that the best way to manage [prisoners of war] was to wash Canada's hands of them as quickly as possible' (2010). Although it suggests that torture has now become something we expect to happen, Travers' explanation is kinder to the military than that of law professor Amir Attaran, who proposes that the military *wanted* prisoners transferred to the Afghan authorities to be tortured – a Canadian version of rendition to torture where the destination is not Syria, as it was with Maher Arar, but Afghan authorities. Attaran believes that, when the Afghan detainee documents are released, they will reveal that, far from merely ignoring torture, the government partnered deliberately with Afghan torturers (*CBC News* 2010).

Political science professor Janice Gross Stein and policy analyst Eugene Lang, seeking to explain the origin of Canada's decision in 2005 to sign a detainee agreement that did not include ongoing monitoring of. what happened to detainees once they were transferred, advance the less plausible argument that the military leadership did not feel it had the capacity or the skills to monitor for torture. Stein and Lang even propose that the military's argument about its lack of skills was compelling to the government at the time because Canadian diplomats had failed to recognize that both Arar (rendered to Syria by the United States with Canadian complicity) and William Sampson (imprisoned in Saudi Arabia) were tortured (Stein and Lang 2007, 248). As the inquiry into Arar's rendition to Syria (Canada 2006) and the Iacobucci report (2008) on the torture of Almalki, El Maati, and Nureddin in Egypt and Syria revealed, however, the government did not lack the skills to recognize torture but rather the will to ensure that Canadian citizens of Arab and Muslim origin were not being tortured.

The timeline of events and Colvin's testimony leave little room for doubt that the Canadian state was remarkably steadfast in its indifference to the torture of Afghan prisoners. Ignoring reports of torture, both from its own diplomats and from its allies, and leaving in place systems such as poor records keeping and delayed information to the Red Cross, Canada appears not only indifferent but actively desirous, as Attaran alleges, of the torture of Afghan prisoners. In either case, however, the question remains how a democratic nation, one that has long mythologized its peacekeeping role, remained indifferent to, or actively sought, the torture of Afghan prisoners. Although unlike Somalia, where Canadian soldiers were the torturers, Canadian complicity in the torture of Afghan detainees is nonetheless a heavy one and clearly a violation of international law. Transferring prisoners to jails where it is known or ought to have been known that they will be tortured is considered a war crime. Indifference is as morally culpable as direct complicity, and lacking the 'skills' to detect torture cannot stand up as an excuse. When we consider the work that torture as narrative and narratives about torture do, it is imperative to ask what it is that torture can provide to a democratic nation that has mythologized itself as a peacekeeping nation.

Drawing on my study of the Somalia Affair I suggest that, just as torture enables the torturer to impose his meaning on the body of the tortured, thus evicting the tortured from the category of the human, torture offers the nation a chance to install the story of a civilized West and a savage non-West, the very same story that underpins peacekeeping. Torture, as Scarry so powerfully argues, is a story of power – one person's physical pain becomes another person's power: 'The torturer's questions – asked, shouted, insisted upon, pleaded for – objectify the fact that he has a world, announce in their feigned urgency the critical importance of that world, a world whose asserted magnitude is confirmed by the cruelty it is able to motivate and justify' (1985, 36). Torture magnifies one world and destroys another. We must therefore ask a disturbing question: does a national mythology that depends on a cast of characters of civilized white men and savage racial others *require* racial violence, a violence that can include torture and its systematized offspring, terror? Put another way, what are the material and symbolic practices that enable nations to tell a story of civilization, the story of *their* world, a story that ignores history and context and insists only on apocryphal encounters between good and evil?

In 1993, ten years earlier than Abu Ghraib, Canadian peacekeepers tortured and abused Somalis whom they had come to protect. The Somalia Affair, as the incidents became known in Canada, can shed some light on the troubling question of why the Canadian government remained indifferent to, or facilitated, the torture of Afghan detainees. As the Canadian peacekeeping mission in Somalia demonstrated, the West understands peacekeeping and humanitarian interventions as an encounter in which 'civilized' nations confront the savagery of cultures and peoples that have yet to enter modernity. The peacekeeper in this imaginary, entrusted with the task of sorting out the tribalisms and the warlords, inevitably finds himself (and perhaps herself) in an apocryphal encounter between good and evil. A civilized West called upon to take up the white man's burden is a storyline that necessarily ignores the histories that have brought the mostly white men of the West to Africa, Asia, and the Middle East. It is a storyline in which non-European peoples have no personhood.

Middle Powers have a particular stake in the western story of peacekeeping as the white man's burden. Peacekeeping provides an opportunity to participate internationally – to grow up, as it were, on the world stage – simultaneously supporting the United States, but not bearing the risk of being seen as an aggressor or colonizer. Invested nationally in the mythology of the good younger brother of the United States, or 'the hero's friend' as Canadian novelist Robertson Davies once put it, Canada, like all Middle Powers, nevertheless runs the risk of being confined to the sidelines and to a lesser, distinctly unheroic role. Middle Power anxiety was manifest at the start of the 1990s when Canadians began lobbying the United States for a prominent role in Somalia. Soldiers, as much as military leaders and politicians, were anxious to 'show the world what we are made of,' something that was difficult to do then since the United States largely ignored Canada (Razack 2004, 67–8).

Importantly the colonial story of peacekeeping is one in which violence plays an indispensible role. Canadian soldiers imagined themselves as disciplining and keeping in line, through practices of violence, uncivilized Somalis whose resentment and anger at western peacekeepers who had come to save them they did not comprehend. More than eighty soldiers watched or heard Canadian soldiers torture Shidane Arone, a Somali teenager being held as a prisoner, and did not think it wrong or try to stop it. No peacekeeping venture involving western peacekeepers has been without such violence directed at the local population. Far from being connected to actual problems encountered in theatre (problems, for example of petty thievery of items in the well-stocked peacekeepers' camps), peacekeeping violence has often been sexualized, openly and collectively performed against vulnerable groups such as children and women and recorded in photos and diaries as important acts – characteristics that provide an indication of its role in making men anxious to establish their own power and superiority. Through violence, soldiers gained an embodied sense of the colour line of the New World Order.

The nation's responses echo the soldiers' responses. The violence of Canadian soldiers and the racism demonstrated in the videos of soldiers yelling racial epithets were hard to ignore, and the Canadian public struggled valiantly with the unsettling idea that Canadians, far from being mythologized peacekeepers to the world, were in fact torturers and racists. The struggle to reclaim national innocence was not a long one. A national inquiry established that the soldiers suffered from bad leadership. Rudderless, they could not easily cope with the heat, the dust, and the ungrateful natives. Indeed, as the inquiry speculated, it was perhaps the nation's own legendary niceness that so ill equipped its soldiers to endure the trials and tribulations of an encounter in Africa (Razack 2004). The story of ill-prepared and rudderless soldiers secured in this way the innocence of Canadians, impeding them from probing further into how it came to be that ordinary Canadian soldiers engaged in torture.

What the Somalia Affair has to teach us is the strength of the colonial narrative and its capacity not only to produce soldiers who torture and military leaders who condone or ignore it, but also a nation that ultimately remembers the torture as a moment of its own kindness and superiority. Relying on mythology, Canadians ultimately stopped the torture of Somalis from penetrating the national consciousness. Few Canadians remember the Somalia Affair as Canada's Abu Ghraib. At the end of my study of the Somalia Affair I came to two conclusions. First, we are seduced through racism into the colonial storyline of civilized nations disciplining, keeping in line, and saving uncivilized nations. Second, in this moral universe of intrepid white men and those aspiring to be like them, saving countries from warlords and chaos, whole categories of people are declared superfluous, people whom we evict from the political community and people at whom violence may be directed with impunity. Has this happened again in Afghanistan?

'What the Afghans Need Is Colonizing'

Unlike in Somalia, where Canadian soldiers themselves were the torturers, in Afghanistan it is the Afghan authorities who tortured the transferred prisoners. However, by failing to monitor detainees even when the evidence mounted that they were tortured, Canadians became part of the military, political, and social project that torture sustains. In this way Canadians chose the torturer's world – the one that is magnified through the annihilation of the world of the tortured. Applied to Afghanistan the salutary lessons of the Somalia Affair require us to consider, first, the colonial nature of the Afghan encounter that produced Afghans as a community outside the rule of law and outside humanity. Second, we can consider whether torture itself, and stories of torture, sustained this colonial divide by producing and sustaining Canadians as colonizers and Afghans as a subject race. Finally, as in the Somalia Affair, will torture and the stories about it ultimately confirm that Canada is a grown-up member of the family of civilized nations, a state that is able to assist 'failed states' into maturity and into civilization? Is this the world that torture protects?

Columnist Mark Steyn, an advocate of the far right, was neither the first nor the only Canadian to believe in 2001 that 'what the Afghans need is colonizing' (Steyn 2001). Indeed the venture in Afghanistan bears all the hallmarks of a colonial venture. Canada, burdened by its Middle Power aspirations, actively sought a leading role in the 'war on terror,' including in Afghanistan. Stein and Lang (2007) attribute this desire more to the Canadian military than to the Canadian government, although the latter was clearly concerned to show that, while it could not support the invasion in Iraq, to which Canadians were massively opposed, it would support the United States in Afghanistan (ibid., 18). David Jefferess (2009, 709) argues that, when Canada participated in the US invasion and occupation of Afghanistan in late 2001 and 2002, it did so with a 'nostalgic hunger for national distinction.' Jefferess shows that, while the terms of the Afghan mission changed in 2005 and began to be expressed as 'a job of killing detestable murderers and scumbags,' in the words of the chief of the defence staff, General Rick Hillier (quoted in ibid., 710), Canadian journalists, scholars, and politicians nevertheless clung to the idea of Canada as uniquely suited to, and engaged in, peacekeeping in Afghanistan, albeit the muscular version. The idea of a more aggressive Canada engaging in war was simply explained as something the country did because it was bullied by the United States or, as Stein and Lang suggest, because Canada was simply beholden to its friend and ally. The words of defence minister Gordon O'Connor in 2007 that Canada was in Afghanistan for 'retribution' for the 9/11 attacks suggests how far the 'friendship' might go (quoted in Stein and Lang 2007, 239).

Ideas about the ties of friendship, indeed *kinship*, with the United States and the political pressure to participate in the invasion and occupation of Afghanistan, or ideas that the Canadian military overly influenced the decision to send troops to Afghanistan, all install the notion that, absent these factors, Canada would not participate in invasion and occupation. National mythology sustains a profound historical disavowal of Canadian participation in military offensive operations and its support for various imperial ventures. Jefferess reminds us, however, that, in Afghanistan, Canada's national mythology entirely elides the political interests that underpin such missions, masking imperial agendas and practices. If Canada is in Afghanistan to help the

Afghans – help that requires killing 'scumbags' – then it cannot also be guilty of invasion and occupation.

Where does torture enter this picture? The story begins, I suggest, as it did in Somalia, with the idea that Canadians represent a higher level of civilization present in Afghanistan to assist the Afghans by bringing peace and order to an intrinsically chaotic world. Jefferess describes this mentality as manifest in the political memoirs of former Liberal cabinet minister Lloyd Axworthy, whose narrative of Canada as helper and the keeper of peace and order depends fundamentally on the Afghans having no voice, desire, or history. The helper, constructed as the intervener in a conflict, does not consider his or her own ideological assumptions and implication in what has happened in Afghanistan. Instead of asking why some states are in this position and why others are positioned as helpers, Canadians can only wonder at the chaos that has come so inexplicably to Afghanistan (Jefferess 2009, 722). What else can this chaos be but a chaos born of the Afghan people themselves? The task for peacekeepers, then, is to separate the good Afghans from the bad Afghans, and to do so resolutely in the conviction that it is Canadians who are the knowers and the Afghans who are to be known. If Canadians find themselves in a long-drawn-out insurgency, and ultimately in a situation where they are complicit in torture, it can only be because Afghanistan presents an intractable problem that few can solve in other ways.

We can see the colonial line of argument, with its cast of benevolent Canadians and uncivilized Afghans in Stein's and Lang's book on Canada's involvement in Afghanistan. Pressured either by the military or by the United States, Canadians agreed to be a part of bringing democracy and stability to Afghanistan. Instability, however, arises because of warring tribes. Described as a fanatical people so intent on defending the faith that they only once manage to transcend their tribalism in order to unite against the infidel Soviet Union, Afghan tribes are said to have become particularly enraged when the Soviets killed women and children. Such acts 'offends their honour' (Stein and Lang 2007, 25–6). Afghan resistance to foreign occupation and to the killing of their own people is understood here as a quaint and pre-modern response largely related to the nature of tribal society. It is from this starting position of a cultural and civilizational divide between Afghans and the West that Stein and Lang understand what Canadians are doing in Afghanistan.

A similar analysis underpins virtually all mainstream scholarly and political responses to Canada's role in Afghanistan, as Jefferess shows.

Of course I cannot draw a straight line from imperial entitlement and assumptions of superiority to torture, even though violence demonstrably accompanies such imperial beginnings, as indeed they have in every peacekeeping mission thus far. Colonial attitudes, however, go a long way towards explaining why it might not alarm Canadians unduly that Afghan detainees were being tortured. How easy is it to ignore torture or to understand it as something that is necessary if one imagines the Afghans as a pre-modern people, a people with terrorist elements from which the West must protect itself by resorting to violence and torture if necessary? Is this what lies behind the facts revealed by Richard Colvin that show a Canadian government indifferent to the fate of the Afghan detainees it handed over? The assumptions that records keeping and monitoring were unnecessary, that evidence of torture was best ignored, and that dissenting voices had to be suppressed suggest that, for Canadians, the Afghans are not the same kind of human as they. Going further, these facts betray a deep Canadian conviction that lesser humans should be handled no other way. Paradoxically, when Canadians do acknowledge that Afghan detainees were tortured, it is also easy for them to claim that the fault lies with the Afghans, whose very barbarism makes it difficult for Canadians to stop torture. As former defence minister Peter Mackay told reporters, Canada 'is trying to change the culture in Afghanistan' (quoted in Holloway 2009).

Conclusion: The Moral Climate of Torture

To understand the moral climate in which torture becomes acceptable, and to see its racial underpinnings, it is useful to return to what torture *is*, and how torture narratives work in the New World Order. In an article on the film *Salò* by Pier Paolo Pasolini, a film that 'specifically narrates the practices of sexual violation, torture and execution carried out by fascist European states during the wars of the 1940s,' Eduardo Subirats (2007, 177–8) begins, as many do, by reminding us not to reduce torture to a pure technological problem (whose purpose is to extract information) or to an issue of corrupt administrations. Rather, torture is 'one among many expressions of human dominance' and 'the most privileged spiritual expression of this power' (ibid., 174). Torture reveals 'the sub-structures of the moral, epistemological, and political systems that put torture into practice'; it is 'the calculated expression, at once rational and necessary, that defines modernity, the global capitalist system, or Western civilization as such' (ibid., 175). Put another way, torture reveals who is excluded from the human and political community, and it is the exclusion or exception that constitutes the legal and moral order. Importantly, Subirats observes that, to do its work, torture 'must hide its primitive, bloody, and sacrificial brutality from society, while, at the same time, making sure to exhibit itself as a public demonstration of a power that is as absolute as it is arbitrary' (ibid., 177).

Following Subirats, and thinking about torture as a public demonstration of power, we can ask: what is gained through the torture of Afghan prisoners? Torture institutes a political system in which Afghans are excluded from the law. Simultaneously it installs a morality in which the excluded are marked as less than human (a lower race), whom it is legitimate to exclude from law. Finally the torture of Afghans depends on an epistemology in which we can know who is of a lesser race, and therefore who is to be expelled from law, through their external and intrinsic characteristics. Marnia Lazreg, reflecting on the use of torture by the French during the Algerian War of Independence, reminds us that torture works as a source of social integration, uniting the government and the military and turning the state into a militaristic institution (2008, 121). In the same way torture unites the North against the South, turning the globe into a militarized zone. In joining the United States as a nation that tortures or that is able to render others to be tortured, Canada's entry into the club of white nations can be secured.

Torture, Todorov (2009, 60) writes, 'leaves an indelible mark – not only on the victim but also on the torturer.' When torture is institutionalized, these effects are even greater. Democracies become willing to adopt totalitarian attitudes (ibid., 61). Todorov's warning is an ominous one for Canada. While the Conservative government of Prime Minister Stephen Harper might be denounced in the press for its undemocratic impulses in denying Parliament access to information, it is possible to be critical of democratic process and still not substantially disturb the idea that some groups must be tortured for the sake of all humanity. Torture is a narrative of power. Torture can still tell its story within a narrative of disapproval of government secrecy. As I have argued, torture narratives provide the warm glow that comes from a nationalism that is premised on a colour line. When Canadians read in their daily newspapers, or see on the nightly news, that Canada has participated deliberately or indirectly in the torture of Afghans, what do we gain? We secure a sense of racial superiority, marking ourselves as different from 'those who throw acid in the face of schoolgirls.' Simultaneously we prove that we are a nation grown up enough to take our place among the family of western nations that know how to make the world safe for democracy.

We cannot be in a post-torture or post-terror world until we are in a post-colonial or post-empire world, since torture is a key mechanism in establishing racial/colonial relations. Torture, it must be remembered, annihilates one world in order to magnify another. The world that remains is the world of the torturer and those who acquiesce in or enable torture. We must, then, critically interrogate torture narratives, carefully examining the work they do in installing colour lines and undoing civilization.

NOTE

1 The author thanks Corey Balsam and Nashwa Salem for research assistance, Jerome Klassen for sharing his media files, and Leslie Thielen Wilson and Larry Brookwell for their invaluable comments.

References

Amnesty International. 2008. *Canada v. Canada*, 2008 FC 336, 4 F.C.R. 546.

–. 2009. *Canada v. Canada*, 2009 FCA 401, 4 F.C.R. 149.

Brennan, Richard J. 2010a. 'Military told to heed abuse claims.' *Toronto Star*, 25 February.

–. 2010b. 'Torture review a stall, critics say.' *Toronto Star*, 6 March.

Byers, Michael, and William Schabas. 2007. 'Re War Crimes and the Transfer of Detainees from Canadian Custody in Afghanistan.' Letter to the International Criminal Court, 25 April. http://nathanson.osgoode.yorku.ca/// wp-content/uploads/2010/09/A13-Byers-Schabas-2007-Letter-to-ICC-Prosecutor.pdf (accessed 16 May 2011).

–. 2009. 'Re War Crimes and the Transfer of Detainees from Canadian Custody in Afghanistan.' Letter to the International Criminal Court, 3 December. http://nathanson.osgoode.yorku.ca/wp-content/uploads/2010/09/A14-Byers-Schabas-Dec-3–2009-Letter-to-ICC-Prosecutor.pdf (accessed 16 May 2011).

Canada. 2006. Commission of Inquiry into the Actions of Canadian Officials in Relation to Maher Arar. *Report of the Events Relating to Maher Arar: Factual Background, Volumes 1 & 11*. Ottawa: Public Works and Government Services Canada.

CBC News. 2009. 'Tories reject call for Afghan torture inquiry.' 19 November. http://license.icopyright.net/user/viewFreeUse.act?fuid=ODQxMTMw Nw%3D%3D (accessed 18 May 2010).

–. 2010. 'Canada wanted Afghan prisoners tortured: lawyer.' 5 March. http:// www.cbc.ca/canada/story/2010/03/05/afghan-attaran005.html (accessed 6 March 2010).

Cheadle, Bruce. 2007. 'Academic hired to argue detainees' rights case.' *Globe and Mail*, 31 August.

Colvin, Richard. 2009a. 'Affidavit in the matter of a hearing before the Military Police Complaints Commission.' 5 October. http://www3.thestar.com/static/PDF/Colvin_Affidavit.pdf (accessed 9 June 2010).

–. 2009b. 'Further Evidence of Richard Colvin to the Special Committee on Afghanistan.' Ottawa: Military Police Complaints Commission. 16 December. http://www3.thestar.com/static/PDF/FurtherEvidencetoSpecialCommittee.pdf (accessed 9 June 2010).

Globe and Mail. 2010. 'The Canadian government's practices regarding prisoners detained in Afghanistan have sparked controversy since troops entered the war in 2001.' http://v1.theglobeandmail.com/servlet/story/RTGAM.20070423.wxdetaineehistory23/BNStory/Afghanistan (accessed 13 February 2010).

Holloway, Tessa. 2009. 'Building human rights in Afghanistan takes time.' *Prince Albert Daily Herald*, 5 December.

Iacobucci, Frank. 2008. *Internal Inquiry into the Actions of Canadian Officials in Relation to Abdullah Almalki. Ahmad Abou-Elmaati and Muayyed Nureddin.* Ottawa: Public Works and Government Services Canada.

Jefferess, David. 2009. 'Responsibility, Nostalgia, and the Mythology of Canada as a Peacekeeper.' *University of Toronto Quarterly* 78, no. 2: 709–27.

Jones, Timothy M., and Penelope Sheets. 2009. 'Torture in the Eye of the Beholder: Social Identity, News Coverage, and Abu Ghraib.' *Political Communication* 26, no. 3: 278–95.

Lazreg, Marnia. 2008. *Torture and the Twilight of Empire: From Algiers to Baghdad.* Princeton, NJ: Princeton University Press.

Liberal Party of Canada. 2010. 'Timeline of Detainees in Afghanistan.' Ottawa. http://www.liberal.ca/en/newsroom/media-releases/17440_just-the-facts-updated-timeline-of-events-surrounding-canadas-handling-of-detainees-in-afghanistan (accessed 19 May 2010).

New Democratic Party of Canada. 2010. 'Timeline of New Democratic Party Leadership on Treatment of Afghan Detainees.' Ottawa. http://www.ndp.ca/press/timeline-new-democrat-leadership-on-treatment-afghan-prisoners (accessed 19 May 2010).

Razack, Sherene. 2004. *Dark Threats and White Knights: The Somalia Affair, Peace-keeping, and the New Imperialism.* Toronto: University of Toronto Press.

–. 2008. *Casting Out: The Eviction of Muslims from Western Law and Politics.* Toronto: University of Toronto Press.

Sands, Phillippe. 2008. *Torture Team: Rumsfeld's Memo and the Betrayal of American Values.* New York: Palgrave Macmillan.

Scarry, Elaine. 1985. *The Body in Pain: The Making and Unmaking of the World.* New York: Oxford University Press.

–. 1999. 'The Difficulty of Imagining Other Persons.' In *Human Rights in Political Transitions: Gettysburg to Bosnia,* ed. Carla Hesse and Robert Post. Cambridge, MA: MIT Press.

–. 2010. *Rule of Law, Misrule of Men.* Cambridge, MA: MIT Press.

Scott, Craig. 2010. 'Moral and Legal Responsibility with Respect to Alleged Mistreatment of Transferred Detainees in Afghanistan: Presentation to the (Prorogued) House of Commons Special Committee on the Canadian Mission in Afghanistan.' 10 February. Ottawa: Parliament of Canada.

Smith, Graeme. 2007. 'From Canadian custody into cruel hands.' *Globe and Mail,* 23 April.

Smith, Joanna. 2011. 'Torture probe "coverup" alleged; Conservatives quietly seek ruling to limit findings of report on Afghan detainees.' *Toronto Star,* 5 April.

Subirats, Eduardo. 2007. 'Totalitarian Lust: From Salò to Abu Ghraib.' *South Central Review* 24, no. 1: 174–82.

Stein, Janice Gross, and Eugene Lang. 2007. *The Unexpected War: Canada in Kandahar.* Toronto: Viking Canada.

Stevens, Barry, dir. 2010. *Prosecutor.* Ottawa: National Film Board of Canada.

Steyn, Mark, 2001. 'What the Afghans need is colonizing.' *National Post,* 9 October.

Taussig, Michael. 1987. *Shamanism, Colonialism, and the Wild Man: A Study in Terror and Healing.* Chicago: University of Chicago Press.

Todorov, Tzvetan. 2009. *Torture and the War on Terror.* London: Seagull Books.

Travers, James. 2010. 'Abu Ghraib shaped our detainee policy.' *Toronto Star,* 8 May.

United Nations. 2006. Human Rights Council. Sixteenth Session, Agenda Items 2 and 10. *Annual Report of the United Nations High Commissioner for Human Rights and Reports of the Office of the High Commissioner and the Secretary-General.* New York. http://daccess-dds-ny.un.org/doc/UNDOC/GEN/G11/103/31/PDF/G1110331.pdf?OpenElement.

Wherry, Aaron. 2009. 'I will do my best to shed light within the limits imposed by my professional obligations.' *Maclean's.ca,* 19 November.

PART IV

The Anti-war Movement in Canada

13

Québec Solidaire and the
Anti-war Movement

BENOIT RENAUD AND JESSICA SQUIRES

The anti-war movement has played a significant role in shaping politics in Quebec over the past decade of neoliberal globalization and the 'war on terror.' The main impact of the anti-war movement has been felt in the new political formations that have emerged on the left, first with the Union des forces progressistes (active from 2002 to 2006) and then Québec solidaire (since February 2006). At the same time the crucible of Quebec debates on 'accommodation' and secularism has clarified the anti-war stance of Québec solidaire and others on the left, as recognition of the connection between Islamophobia and imperialism has become more apparent. In this chapter we draw from our own involvement in Québec solidaire and the anti-war movement to illustrate that point. We highlight the importance of anti-war and antiracist organizing to the left in Quebec today, and analyse a number of key issues at the heart of building a mass movement against the war in Afghanistan. In the process we shed light on new political currents in Quebec society and the debates through which Québec solidaire has emerged as a new party of the anti-war movement.

Quebec and Imperialism: A Brief History

Quebec has a long tradition of opposition to imperialist wars, from the Boer War at the turn of the twentieth century to mass movements against conscription during the First and Second World Wars. This legacy of anti-imperialism has always been tied up with resistance to oppression, both national and linguistic. In fact the evolution of anti-war sentiment in Quebec in many ways has set the pace for the independence or sovereignty movement.[1] For example, during the First

World War, the division between English and French Canadians over conscription was so sharp that a member of Quebec's Legislative Assembly argued for separation as a solution. Former prime minister Wilfrid Laurier, running against conscription in the 1917 election, privately feared that it would increase national sentiment in Quebec.

In 1917, at a time when anti-Catholic sentiment was still strong across the country, Regulation 17 limited French-language education in Ontario, and French Canadians generally did not enter military service, the government of Prime Minister Robert Borden enacted conscription, making the federal election of that year about conscription and Quebec's place in Canada. Borden won the election, in part by denying voting rights to conscientious objectors. In 1918, after conscription was put into force, a demonstration in Quebec City was attacked by Canadian soldiers, leaving five dead and many injured. At first conscription allowed for numerous exemptions, but after these exemptions were eliminated opposition to conscription grew beyond the French-speaking population.

In 1944 a similar crisis over conscription centred more clearly around language. Sharp divisions affected the electoral fates of many politicians, and a small group of anticonscription Liberals absconded in protest to form their own political party. Among them was Michel Chartrand, a prominent historic figure of the Quebec left. The party won a federal by-election and four seats in a Quebec election, but ceased to exist by 1949.

The war in Vietnam saw opposition across Canada, and Quebec was no exception. But the anti-war movement was arguably a much broader *anti-imperialist* movement, especially in Quebec, where sentiment for independence was expressing itself more clearly after the Quiet Revolution. More recently, there was a strong movement against the Gulf War of 1991 and the preceding military build-up, including a large demonstration in the streets of Montreal in summer 1990. Out of that movement emerged a campaign against sanctions, which rallied many organizations, including Objection de conscience (Voices of Conscience). This group was principally involved in raising awareness and organizing protest against the sanctions program, which led to the premature deaths of approximately one million Iraqis between 1990 and 2003.

The mass mobilizations against the recent wars in Afghanistan and Iraq emerged from this history, especially from the movement against sanctions and war in Iraq, as well as from the antiglobalization or global justice movement. In Montreal Objection de conscience transformed itself from an antisanctions movement to an anti-war movement, taking the lead in forming a coalition against the war on Iraq.

Before Iraq

One cannot discuss the recent anti-war movement without referring to its predecessor, the global justice or *altermondialiste* mobilizations that shook the neoliberal consensus from Seattle in 1999 to Genoa in July 2001. Hundreds of thousands of people converged on a series of meetings held by powerful international bodies such as the World Trade Organization, the Group of Eight major industrial countries, and the International Monetary Fund to denounce policies aimed at increasing the profits of multinational corporations to the detriment of human rights, living standards, and the environment. In Quebec and Canada the high point of this movement was the Summit of the Americas in April 2001. Approximately one hundred thousand people converged on Quebec City to demonstrate against this gathering of political leaders and to oppose the plan for a Free Trade Area of the Americas (FTAA).

The protests had a major impact on the ideological debate in Quebec. Before 2001 polls showed that two-thirds of *Québécois* viewed 'free trade' in a positive light; after the summit about half expressed a negative view of trade deals, though by 2008 support was back up to 55 per cent.[2] For nearly a year Quebec's social movement organizations mobilized against the FTAA through various coalitions, sometimes following different strategies and tactics. This organizing made it possible to reverse the effects of two decades of one-sided advocacy in favour of 'free trade' from mainstream politicians, chief among them Bernard Landry of the Parti Québécois (PQ), a pioneer on that front and premier of Quebec at the time of the 2001 summit.

On 9 April 2001, two weeks before the summit, a by-election was held in the riding of Mercier in the heart of Montreal, a riding very favourable to the left, with many artists, students, and young workers. At the time several groups on the left were in the middle of negotiations towards forming a united party, and an ad hoc coalition was put together to support the candidacy of Paul Cliche, a retired union activist. Given the favourable elements of the riding's demographics and the momentum of the FTAA mobilization, the PQ riding association went into a major internal crisis. As a result Cliche received 24 per cent of the vote. About a year later the Union des forces progressistes (UFP) was formed, many of whose founding members were involved in the global justice movement and the emerging anti-war movement on Afghanistan. The UFP represented a significant step towards regroupment by the left in Quebec, and tried to position itself as a party 'of the ballot box and the street.'

Multiple political currents coexisted more or less harmoniously within the global justice movement. Some groups, including unions and many non-governmental organizations, advocated a more regulated and controlled form of capitalism, with the inclusion of labour and environmental standards in trade agreements. A significant minority, itself including many currents, put forward anticapitalist perspectives. During the Quebec City protests differences arose over tactical questions, with anticapitalists arguing in favour of demonstrating 'at the fence,' as close as possible to the actual Summit, while the main unions decided to march away from the security perimeter. But all these groups would find themselves together against the Iraq war, just as they were against the FTAA.

A few days after 11 September 2001 delegates from several coalitions involved in organizing the protests against the Summit of the Americas came together in Hull, Quebec, to assess the mobilization and to chart a way forward. This gathering included members of two Montreal-based coalitions (CLAC and Le Groupe opposé à la mondialisation des marchés) as well as the OQP 2001 coalition from Quebec City, MobGlob from Halifax, Mob4Glob from Toronto, and the host coalition in the Outaouais region. All participants agreed to shift their focus immediately to an anti-war mobilization, since it was obvious the US government was planning a new military offensive with the support of Canada and the North Atlantic Treaty Organization (NATO). In fall 2001 Françoise David, then president of the Fédération des femmes du Québec (FFQ, Quebec Women's Federation), published an editorial arguing for a United Nations-led intervention with limited goals (David 2001). This approach to the Afghanistan War was to come back five years later in the Québec solidaire debate on the issue.

Organizing against the war was a challenge in fall 2001. Elements from the anticapitalist movement, combined with new layers of activists, were having a hard time finding a clear direction and base of support for anti-war organizing. The public was generally indifferent to or supportive of the invasion. As a result demonstrations were small and there was no organizational stability.[3]

The UFP Period: 2002–6

The political situation changed in fall 2002 as mass organizations joined the campaign against a war in Iraq. Together with Objection de conscience, the Fédération interprofessionelle de la santé du Québec (Quebec's largest nurses union) played a key role in founding Échec à la guerre, the primary anti-war coalition in Montreal.

The first general election campaign for the UFP, in March and April 2003, coincided with the highpoint of protest against the war in Iraq. There were demonstrations in all major cities in Quebec, including two marches of at least two hundred thousand people in Montreal, on February 15 and March 15. The union movement put its whole weight behind those mobilizations. For example, a demonstration on the issue of pay equity, planned several months earlier, was converted into the anti-war march on February 15.

What made these mobilizations so large, apart from the obvious impact of union organizing, was that many other social movements made it a priority, including the women's movement, elements of the student movement, and remnants of the global justice movement. Support for the demonstrations was so broad that mainstream news channels made it part of their advanced coverage to announce where and when the marches would start. This very broad consensus on opposing the war was rooted, of course, in the long history of anti-imperialism in Quebec, going back at least a century. It was also amplified by the international nature of the mobilization.

The UFP decided to merge its election campaign with anti-war organizing. This decision came with political risk, as all politicians in Quebec – including Jean Charest, then leader of the Official Opposition in the National Assembly – at the time wore white ribbons in opposition to the war. But the commitment of the UFP went beyond such symbolism. For example, the offices of the party were used as placard-making spaces and storage facilities for Échec à la guerre, the umbrella organization planning the demonstrations. The UFP, with candidates in 74 of 125 ridings, received just 1 per cent of the total vote, but this result was better than the 0.6 per cent received by the 96 candidates fielded five years earlier by the Parti de la démocratie socialiste – the former Quebec wing of the New Democratic Party (NDP) and one of the founding groups of the UFP. The relationship between the UFP and the rest of the anti-war movement was cordial, but since Échec à la guerre was a non-partisan organization, UFP candidates were not invited to speak at demonstrations.[4]

The election in April 2003 brought in a Liberal majority government under Jean Charest. During its first session the Charest government passed several bills undermining union rights and social services. Charest's attempt to advance neoliberalism in Quebec generated massive protests by unions and social movement organizations, and gave new impetus to efforts at regrouping the left. At this point, a group of activists from D'abord solidaires – a non-partisan political movement formed in 2002 to oppose the right-wing Action démocratique de Québec (ADQ) – left the organization and called for the founding of a new party. It was joined in this endeavour by a number of key social movement organizations, including Option citoyenne, which brought together feminist and antipoverty activists, including Françoise David, former president of the FFQ. David, as we saw earlier, had spoken out against the US-led invasion of Afghanistan in 2001, in line with a long tradition of pacifism in the women's movement. Amir Khadir, the most well-known figure in the UFP, was also involved in this new project to form a party, and had been to Afghanistan and Iraq as part of medical and humanitarian solidarity operations.

Québec solidaire

More than a year of negotiations between Option citoyenne and the UFP led to the founding of Québec solidaire on the weekend of 4–6 February 2006 at the Université de Montréal. Considering the history of both groups and the massive mobilizations of recent years, it was no surprise that the issue of peace was present in the founding policy document. One of the seven sections of the *Declaration de principes* (Declaration of Principles) was entitled 'Nous sommes altermondialistes.' The fourth and last paragraph under that heading stated: 'We are also pacifists. We reject wars used to subjugate peoples in order to loot their resources. We think that no tradition, religion, ideology or economic or political system justifies discrimination or violence against individuals and nations. Justice is a necessary precondition to peace, as are openness and dialogue' (Québec solidaire 2006a; this and all other translations in the text are by Benoit Renaud). This general statement was appropriate for the time. The question of how to apply these principles was posed sharply and quickly with the deployment of Canadian troops to Kandahar in 2006.

The principles were also tested in July and August 2006, when Israel launched a thirty-three-day war on Lebanon, precipitating large protests in Montreal and other cities in Quebec. On 6 August tens of thousands of protestors took to the streets of Montreal, denouncing the war and Canada's one-sided support for Israel. Several prominent political figures spoke at the rally, including the leaders of the PQ and Bloc Québécois, and Denis Coderre, a prominent federal Liberal. A coalition of sixty organizations, including the three largest union federations, condemned the attack in very clear language and mobilized their members. If there were many Lebanese flags and many members of the Arab community present, it was also a very diverse event and echoed the movement against the war in Iraq: 'according to Amir Khadir, Québec solidaire spokesperson, there is no doubt that all of Quebec was mobilised to carry a message of peace. "This rallied Quebec, there is no doubt," he said. "In 2003, there was a consensus, including all politicians, that this war was pointless. The people who took to the streets were right to do so. Today, we are taking to the streets again for the same reasons"' (Gervais 2006).

In this context of growing protest, newspaper columnist Barbara Kay (2006) coined the term 'Quebecistan,' and accused the anti-war movement of anti-Semitism. One should also remember that Prime Minister Stephen Harper described the Israeli attack, which left 1,200 dead in Lebanon, as a 'measured response,' confirming once again his unflinching support for Israel. Québec solidaire joined the mass demonstrations against the war and, in the process, developed its understanding of the link between war and Islamophobia. In doing so the party also built a new critique of the war in Afghanistan, which became a key point of contention in Quebec politics that fall. Indeed, at a national convention in Quebec City in September 2006, the NDP adopted an anti-war motion, calling for the withdrawal of troops from Afghanistan. In response, Québec solidaire's National Council adopted the following motion on October 1:

Be it resolved that:
1 Québec solidaire takes a position for the withdrawal of the Canadian military from Afghanistan.
2 Québec solidaire participates in the pan-Canadian mobilisation on 28 October, bringing together a coalition of civil society organisations demanding the withdrawal of Canadian troops from Afghanistan.

3 Québec solidaire calls for a Canadian and international mobilisation demanding that the UN – which shares the responsibility for the failure of the current intervention, having supported it, and whose goals have been betrayed – to lead a new multilateral initiative enabling the people of Afghanistan to overcome the crisis by supporting democratic forces and through massive support for social and economic development.

4 Québec solidaire calls on the governments of Quebec and Canada to give special support to women and feminist organisations in Afghanistan in their struggle for full recognition of their rights through legislation, programs and infrastructure aimed at creating real equality for women.

5 Québec solidaire supports Canadian participation in this multilateral initiative – which should be led by civilians and not be controlled by any military apparatus – but which could include a peacekeeping force supervising the disarmament of all parties in the conflict and the maintenance of peace. (Québec solidaire 2006c)

The complexity of this motion illustrates how difficult it was in Quebec at the time, even on the left, to argue for troop withdrawal from Afghanistan. The fifth paragraph, evoking a possible peacekeeping operation, was voted on separately and with significant opposition. The motion as a whole was trying to answer the question of what would happen if NATO troops withdrew and what alternatives existed to the current occupation. But overall, especially with the clarity of the first two paragraphs (with their message of withdrawing the troops and supporting the anti-war movement), one can say that Québec solidaire took a principled position against the war. This position is more remarkable if one considers that Québec solidaire is a provincial party and that, in contrast to their opposition to the war in Iraq, no other party in the National Assembly at the time pronounced its opposition to the war in Afghanistan or has done so since then.

The need for a credible and consistent anti-war voice in Quebec was highlighted by the positioning of the Bloc Québécois throughout this period. In a vote in Parliament on 17 May 2006 the Bloc voted against extending the mission to 2009, mainly because of the cost of the war and the lack of information. The basic assumption that troops were in Afghanistan to help civilians through reconstruction efforts was not questioned. In September 2007 the Bloc issued an ultimatum demanding an end to the mission by February 2009. A few weeks later, however, the party reaffirmed its support for the mission, and has steadily distanced itself from the position of the NDP, which has called for immediate withdrawal. In short, on this issue, the Bloc has usually followed the Liberal Party, until recently its main rival in Quebec, and has positioned itself opportunistically with that of mainstream media. In this context, and in the complete absence of any position whatsoever on the part of the PQ, the position of Québec solidaire, however initially contradictory, was at least principled, and has improved ever since.

The issue of Afghanistan became even more crucial for Québec solidaire and the anti-war movement when the Royal 22nd Regiment, the historic French-speaking infantry group in Quebec, was sent to Kandahar in summer 2007. The entire anti-war movement in Quebec saw this deployment as a challenge and an opportunity, and engaged in a series of actions, including a sit-in at the sending-off parade in Quebec City. That summer, a poll conducted by Léger Marketing found that 70 per cent of *Québécois* opposed sending soldiers from Quebec, 69 per cent would try to convince their children not to go if they were already in the military, 62 per cent thought Canadian troops should withdraw before the planned deadline of 2009, and 64 per cent approved the idea of demonstrating against the war in Quebec City on June 22, to coincide with the sending-off parade (Léger Marketing 2007).

In the following years Québec solidaire would participate in mobilizations against the war in Gaza, oppose Security Certificates in Canada, and protest the US prison camp in Guantánamo Bay, Cuba. Issues of peace and human rights remained constant areas of work, if not central ones. One notable exception was the lack of an international section in the party's first election platform (February–March 2007), due mostly to the large number of motions debated as part of the platform discussion and the decision to emphasize issues of provincial jurisdiction Québec solidaire (2006b).[5] In addition a guideline was adopted in June 2007 to set out a process for considering proposals for international solidarity work (Québec solidaire 2007c). The second election platform (November–December 2008) included a section on international solidarity and self-determination for First Nations in Canada (Québec solidaire 2008a). On issues of peace, the new election platform included the following three commitments:

8.3.1 Table a motion at the National Assembly opposing any Canadian imperialist intervention in Afghanistan.

8.3.2 Support the conversion of military industries, and ban publicity and recruitment activities by the Armed Forces in educational institutions.

8.3.3 Express Quebec's pacifist commitment by refusing to participate directly or indirectly in wars of aggression and imperialist occupations as well as in the rise of neo-conservatism and fundamentalism. Emphasize the fact that wars are especially harmful to women and that they lead to inhuman activities including the drafting of child soldiers.

The platform expanded on and clarified the positions taken in the *Declaration de principes* (February 2006) and in the Afghanistan motion (October 2006). Language choices such as 'imperialist Canadian intervention' and demands including banning the military from campuses are indicative of that evolution. This shift, visible from 2006 through 2008, came about in part because of other events taking place in Quebec at the time – namely, the evolving debate over 'reasonable accommodation.'

Québec solidaire, Islamophobia, and Human Rights

It is no coincidence that the debate on 'reasonable accommodation' started precisely when thousands of soldiers from Quebec were stationed in Afghanistan. The people at the forefront of the attack on accommodation were also those who supported the war and the federal Conservative government. Starting late in 2006 a few isolated incidents of minor conflict having to do with religious diversity were hyped by the media and turned into a national political crisis by ADQ leader Mario Dumont and right-wing talk radio hosts. Dumont considered the informal concessions made to religious minorities as infringements on Quebec's collective values and principles. The first response of Premier Jean Charest and PQ leader André Boisclair was to urge calm. But after a few months of non-stop media madness, Charest called for a special commission of inquiry to look into the issue, headed by prominent academics Gérard Bouchard and Charles Taylor. Hearings were held in the summer and fall of 2007, and the report, with its recommendations in favour of 'open secularism' and fairness for all religions, was presented to the National Assembly in May 2008. The Liberals, PQ, and ADQ were unanimous, however, in shelving the report and in passing a motion against removing the crucifix lording over the president's chair in the National Assembly.

Québec solidaire was thus engaged, along with many others, in a debate on religion, secularism, immigration, and cultural diversity. In those discussions positions ranged from complete acceptance of the practices of religious minorities, including the wearing of religious symbols by public servants, to 'French-style' secularism, including banning the *hijab*, the Muslim head scarf, from schools and hospitals. Younger members of Québec solidaire and most members in Montreal tended to favour the more tolerant and pluralist approach, while older members were more reluctant to accept nurses and teachers in *hijab*. In the end the position taken by the party in its presentation to the commission (in September 2007) included restrictions only for a short list of public positions deemed more symbolically sensitive, such as judges and the police. But the emphasis was to counter the anti-immigrant sentiment being generated through the thinly veiled pretext of 'secularism.' For example, in response to the creation of the Bouchard-Taylor commission, Québec solidaire issued a press release that stated, '[w]e should end the distinction between "us" and "them." This debate should not be about Quebecers whose origins go further back and other Quebecers of more recent origins. What we need is an inclusive debate taking into account recent questions and expressions of uneasiness. We want a sober and constructive debate.' Québec solidaire also took the opportunity to criticize the position taken by Mario Dumont: 'We will not be the accomplices of the creators of political spectacles who pit cities against regions, recent immigrants and the society that welcomes them. This spectacle is not what Quebec is about. Xenophobic ignorance is not Quebec. And demagogues who look for votes are mistaken in exacerbating tensions' (Québec solidaire 2007a).

Québec solidaire was strongly criticized by many commentators for supporting the Bouchard-Taylor commission's recommendations, especially those concerning *interculturalisme* and integration. At this point the party supported the idea that certain 'agents of the state' ought not to wear religious symbols. This position was based on a combination of historic fear of organized religion in Quebec, a legacy of years of Catholic domination, and the influence of French politics, which led some to believe that state officials such as judges and police officers should not be visibly religious. This position would later shift again in favour of individual freedom, as we will see. For the time being, however, the party also took a very clear stance in favour of the perspective that to regulate the attire of all public servants would exacerbate an already serious problem – namely, the high level of unemployment among immigrants. Accordingly, Québec solidaire made recommendations on other measures for advancing social and economic integration: 'Together with the commission, Québec solidaire is proposing to the government that they increase funding to employment and French programs for immigrants, while paying special attention to immigrant women' (Québec solidaire 2008b).

A year later the FFQ issued its own report on the topic of the Muslim headscarf. The report clearly recognized the need to avoid any additional limitations placed on women's employment. Québec solidaire supported this report and its *ni obligation, ni interdiction* ('neither obligation, nor a ban') position unequivocally: 'The ban on religious symbols: Let us not add another veil! . . . Québec solidaire supports the position of the Quebec Women's Federation on the wearing of religious symbols for public servants: neither obligation, nor interdiction. This position is generating passionate and sometimes intolerant comments. Québec solidaire is therefore calling for calm and respect' (Québec solidaire 2009).

Afghanistan Is Still the Issue

A theme throughout the debate over the headscarf and 'reasonable accommodation' revolved around a view of Muslim women that cast them in the role of victims, as people in need of rescue from an oppressive practice. It was not lost on many that, increasingly between 2006 and 2009, the same logic was used to justify the war in Afghanistan.

During the same period the public positioning of Québec solidaire became more strongly centred on challenging that logic. Here is an excerpt from a Québec Solidaire press release from August 2007, following the death of a female soldier from Quebec, which focuses on the need for a 'real' assistance mission led by the United Nations: 'Together with the majority of Quebecers, Québec solidaire demands the immediate withdrawal of Canadian troops. Instead, we suggest a significant support for the rebuilding of the country and Canadian participation in a UN led peacekeeping mission, if that is what the people of Afghanistan want. We are grieving. But we continue to put forward proposals for peace, justice and equality' (Québec solidaire 2007b).

A year and a half later the analysis shifted significantly. Now Québec solidaire focused on the underlying falsehood of women's rights as a motive for war:

> Since 2001, we have been repeatedly told that we are in Afghanistan to work towards the development of the country in a manner respectful of human rights. We should be most concerned with women's rights. Our work is supposed to be humanitarian as much as military. Yet, President Hamid Karzai, in order to convince the Shiite minority in the country to vote for him, brings down a heavy oppression on Shiite women: they are not allowed to attend school, cannot go out without a male relative, and on top of that, their husband will be allowed to rape them as he wishes with impunity . . . The Harper government must demand of Hamid Karzai that he respect the Afghan Constitution of 2004, which affirms equality between men and women. Otherwise, we will have even more reasons to ask: all this for that? (*Le Soleil* 2009)

Québec solidaire has also advanced an anti-war position in other ways. Amir Khadir, the party's first Member of the National Assembly (MNA), dedicated one of his first interventions to the war in Afghanistan, thus breaking with the consensus of uncritical support for the Royal 22nd Regiment. Beyond the Assembly, Khadir's first public gesture after being elected in December 2008 was to throw a shoe at a picture of George W. Bush. In some ways Khadir's election and his opposition to the war is a culmination of the process by which Québec solidaire has taken bold stances against racism, Islamophobia, and imperialism.

The Québec solidaire Convention of November 2009 and Its Aftermath

In 2008 Québec solidaire developed the first of a five-part political program. The sections on democracy, citizenship, and sovereignty (referred to as *Enjeu 1*) involved a great deal of internal debate about integration and, in particular, the Muslim practice of wearing headscarves of various kinds. The text proposed by the party's Commission politique included formulations on 'religious symbols' in the public service that were in continuity with the position taken by the party around the Bouchard-Taylor commission. But instead of advocating exceptions for certain positions, it stated that such symbols should be allowed on the condition that they were not used for proselytizing and did not interfere with a public servant's impartiality.

The Verdun riding association proposed a different formulation for exceptions, stating that symbolic clothing or accessories should be restricted only if they prevented public servants from performing their duties or infringed on health and safety standards. Several local associations, based in the suburbs of Montreal and in Quebec City, requested amendments banning all 'religious signs' for public sector jobs. The party association in Hull argued that no restrictions be made and that public sector workers who wore such symbols were no less impartial and fair in their jobs.

In the document submitted to the convention, the restrictions proposed by the Commission politique were merged with those from Verdun to create an intermediate motion between the complete ban proposed by some and the Hull position against any restrictions. After long discussions in workshops and on the plenary floor, the 'intermediate' motion passed with approximately 60 per cent of the votes. The motion to ban all religious signs was supported by roughly a third of delegates and the Hull motion by only a few. These votes showed that the debate on 'accommodation,' Islamophobia, and the rights of workers from religious minorities was far from over inside the party.

It should be noted that, before the motions were voted on, a unanimous motion was passed in support of the Boycott, Divestment, and Sanctions (BDS) campaign in solidarity with Palestinians living under Israeli occupation.[6] The fact that many delegates could enthusiastically support BDS while forbidding Muslim nurses and teachers from wearing the *hijab* is a perfect example of what Antonio Gramsci called 'contradictory consciousness.' Islamophobia has been used and abused in all conceivable ways by apologists for imperialism since 2001, and has even entered debates among the Quebec left on 'accommodation' and 'secularism.' At the same time the deep tradition of peace and international solidarity in Quebec offers a strong foundation for arguing against Islamophobic policies.

Following the convention several members of Québec solidaire expressed deep dissatisfaction with the result and/or the process. One member issued a public letter of resignation, which was circulated on PQ websites. A rejoinder by one of this chapter's authors, Benoit Renaud, general secretary of Québec solidaire, was published in *Le Devoir* on 6 January 2009 (Renaud 2009). In it, Renaud argued that a fanatical interpretation of secularism was leading parts of the Quebec left to align itself with right-wing anti-immigrant and pro-imperialist forces. Subsequently several members of Québec solidaire who had sided with the ban of religious symbols at the convention expressed anger at being called racist by association. The collective leadership of the party responded to the small controversy with an article published in *Le Devoir* on 18 January 2009. That text, while calling for a constructive and open debate on these issues, explained further the position taken at the convention.

This whole episode shows how the question of Islamophobia and its relationship with war and imperialism is not an easy one for many on the left in Quebec, including those in Québec solidaire. Therefore the work of those who are committed to the fight against both Islamophobia and war is far from over. In order for this debate to move forward and for the position of Québec solidaire to be strengthened, the union movement will have to adopt the same position as the FFQ and oppose the ability of employers to limit the rights of workers.

Lessons of Bill 94

The most recent political controversy about issues of war and Islamophobia took place around the question of the *niqab*, or Muslim face veil, a garment worn by very few women in Quebec. The controversy erupted when a recent female immigrant from Egypt was expelled from a French-language class for refusing to remove her *niqab*. This expulsion took place as the governments of France and Belgium were discussing bills banning any face covering in public (the 'anti-*burka*' laws). The Charest government quickly expressed its support for the public servants who had expelled the student, and proceeded to introduce Bill 94, which would make it mandatory for the public and those providing public services to show their faces at all times. Some exceptions were granted, but the criteria were spelled out in such broad terms as to give arbitrary power to public service administrators.

The lack of opposition to Bill 94 – apart from that of several immigrant rights groups, human rights activists (notably la Ligue des droits et libertés), Muslim organizations, and elements of the left – shows the limits of what has been accomplished in Quebec on the issue of Islamophobia. The fact that both Québec solidaire and the FFQ expressed very mild criticism of the bill and supported its general principles is especially saddening. Why was that the case? One could blame it on a type of fatigue in the bitter struggle against the aggressive campaign for hardline secularism, which gathers the support of many feminists and leftists. This reasoning was in fact that of the Charest government, which had been accused of doing nothing against *'unreasonable* accommodation' and was ostensibly trying to give the impression of a 'balanced approach' to issues raised since the accommodation crisis of 2007.

Thus, arguments to the effect that Muslim fundamentalism is a threat to the left and to women's rights have made inroads in Quebec, and women wearing the *niqab* or *burka* are often perceived, without any evidence or investigation, as supporters of radical fundamentalism.

Perspectives for the Movement

How can we build the anti-war movement in Quebec, ten years after 9/11? What are the challenges faced by the left and how can they be overcome? There are two main challenges that are closely linked: the impact of Islamophobia on public perceptions and the lack of a mass movement against the war in Afghanistan.

A strong campaign against Islamophobia, including intellectual challenges to commonly held ideas about political Islam and secularism, is a necessity. Without such a campaign, the anti-Muslim crusade led by proponents of right-wing identity politics as well as liberal feminism and left anti-clericalism will gain ground and push governments and civil society alike towards intolerance. This in turn will make it much more difficult to oppose imperialist operations in the Muslim world, notably in Afghanistan, where armed resistance to the occupation is organized in the name of Islam. The fight against Islamophobia needs to be taken to mass organizations, especially to unions, where the narrow and intolerant version of secularism has led some unions to allow restrictions on the rights of their own members (to show religious affiliation in the workplace).

In order to bring back mass mobilization, there is also a need to continue to link anti-war demands with economic questions, bringing together resistance to the economic crisis and imperialism. Why should anyone accept cuts to education, health care, welfare, or pensions when billions of dollars are spent on the military and on a one-sided notion of 'security' that serves corporate and state interests?

The growing campaign in Canada and around the world for the BDS campaign against Israel should also be supported, and could in fact show one possible way forward to unifying progressive forces and ideas in Quebec. The refusal of Israel and western governments to negotiate with Hamas, which won the Palestinian elections of 2006, is the latest excuse for collective punishment of Palestinians and the ongoing abuses of human rights and international law (United Nations 2009; Human Rights Watch 2010). Solidarity with Palestine, which has deep roots in the Quebec left, is a spearhead issue that can counter Islamophobia and western imperialism. On that issue Amir Khadir has sponsored a petition to the National Assembly calling for the suspension of Quebec's Cooperation Accord with Israel. The Centrale des syndicats du Québec (Quebec's second-largest public sector union), the FFQ, and Québec solidaire have all supported the BDS campaign, and the list of endorsers is growing quickly. The issue has created a predictable backlash: accusations of anti-Semitism have been launched at Amir Khadir for his open support of the BDS campaign, with some even alleging he has a hidden Islamist agenda – a ludicrous allegation to anyone who knows even a little of his background.

There are other opportunities for strengthening unity. In November 2010, a People's Summit against War and Militarism was hosted by Échec à la guerre, the coalition that led the historic mobilization against the Iraq war in 2003 and has continued its work of public education and campaigning ever since. This event represented a key moment to discuss strategy and perspectives for the movement in Quebec and elsewhere. It was a moderate success, but more work is needed.[7]

In all these efforts Québec solidaire has been an effective and reliable partner for the anti-war movement. It is not without flaws, but the success of bringing together thousands of activists and of staking out clear political positions on vital questions should make us optimistic as to the potential for the party and the anti-war movement to strengthen each other. The party can also act as an icebreaker to bring other social forces to the left and to grapple with enduring problems of Islamophobia and war.

Conclusion

Ideas and actions intersect in ways that are sometimes unexpected. The debate about 'reasonable accommodation,' a domestic debate taking place in various countries and in various forms, and taking a specific form in Quebec, has had a major impact on the left's capacity to take a clear position on the war in Afghanistan. Since 2001 the anti-war

movement has greatly influenced first the UFP and then Québec solidaire. As these parties learned from the anti-war movement, so the
movement grew in numbers and strength. For example, Québec solidaire's position on 'reasonable accommodation' was partially hardened
by the war; its position on the war was then hardened by opposition to
Islamophobia.

The result has been the development of a mass party of the left in
Quebec – a vital asset for campaigns around human rights, peace, ecol-
ogy, and international solidarity. At the same time the movement more
broadly has benefited from an analysis that recognizes the role of Islamophobia in justifying current wars and occupations in the Middle
East and Central Asia. Members of Québec solidaire are active in all of
these campaigns, and so the importance of debate and discussion about
these ideas within the party cannot be overstated.

Islamophobic attacks on Amir Khadir continue to this day. They flare
up each time Québec solidaire voices support for the rights of Muslims,
especially the right of women to wear the headscarf at work. Khadir's
gesture against the image of George W. Bush remains a symbol of defi-
ance, and cartoonists often portray him as missing a shoe. The very fact
that the first Québec solidaire MNA was born in Iran and converses flu-
ently with Afghan peers such as Malalai Joya demonstrates how Québec solidaire does not define the nation as descendents of New France.
While the PQ remains the first party among francophones in general,
Québec solidaire is becoming the party of younger generations, especially in Montreal, from diverse ethnic backgrounds.

The fight against imperialist war in Afghanistan is far from over. Rebuilding a capacity for mass mobilization on this issue will not be easy,
even in a place like Quebec, where anti-war sentiments have deep historical roots. In order to do so, the anti-war movement will have to re-
gain the active support of mass organizations, especially trade unions,
and this support will materialize more quickly if such organizations
turn their backs on Islamophobia and clarify an *anti-imperialist, antiracist* orientation. In that work the existence of a political party such as
Québec solidaire, with members in all regions including many union
activists, will be a vital asset.

NOTES

1 For an overview of pacifism in Quebec since the Second World War, see
   Babin (1981, 1984); Babin and Vaillancourt (1984a,b, 1986, 1987); Poole and

Bourret (1989); Langlois 1992; Vallaincourt (1992); Monet-Chartrand (1993); and issues of the Quebec peace journal, *Option Paix*, from 1982 to April 1998.

2 A 2001 poll published in *L'Actualité* (April 2001, 15) showed 67 per cent support, while a May 2001 Environics poll showed 48 per cent support (http://www.globescan.com/news_archives/eflash_Globalization.pdf). A 2008 poll reported in *Le Devoir* (23 April 2008, A9) indicated 55 per cent support.

3 Authors' interview with Matt Jones, Montreal-based anti-war activist, February 2010.

4 Authors' interview with Raymond Legault, spokesperson for Échec à la guerre, March 2010.

5 However, this aspect of the program will be elaborated as part of the party's program development, expected to be completed by 2014.

6 The BDS campaign generates much debate in the political mainstream and in the Palestinian solidarity movement. For more information on the politics and methods of the BDS movement, which is supported by a strong majority of Palestinian civil society organizations, see http://bdsmovement.net/.

7 Québec solidaire has also decided to join the ongoing efforts to challenge the Israeli naval blockade of Gaza. See for instance, http://canadaboatgaza.org/cms/sites/cbg/en/statements.aspx (accessed 25 April 2011).

References

Babin, Ronald. 1981. 'La lutte anti-nucléaire au Canada.' *Sociologie et sociétés* 13, no. 1: 131–45.

–. 1984. *L'option nucléaire: développement et contestation de l'énergie nucléaire au Canada et au Québec*. Montreal: Boréal Press.

Babin, Ronald, and Jean-Guy Vaillancourt. 1984a. 'Le mouvement anti-guerre Québécois prend forme.' *Peace Calendar* (February).

–. 1984b. 'Le mouvement pour le désarmement et la paix: le néopacifisme Québécois.' *Revue internationale d'action communautaire* 12, no. 52: 27–34.

–. 1986. 'The New Quebec Peace Movement.' In *Old Passions, New Visions: Social Movements and Political Activism in Quebec*, ed. M. Raboy. Toronto: Between the Lines.

–. 1987. 'La régionalisation du mouvement pour la paix au Québec.' In *Construction/destruction sociale des idées: alternances, récurrences, nouveautés*. Montreal: Association canadienne-française pour l'avancement des sciences.

David, Françoise. 2001. 'Bombardements américains en Afghanistan: ça suffit!' *Le Devoir*, 19 October.

Gervais, Lisa-Marie. 2006. 'Grand cri de colère.' *Le Devoir*, 7 August.

Human Rights Watch. 2010. *Israel/West Bank: Separate and Unequal*. New York.

Kay, Barbara. 2006. 'The rise of Quebecistan.' *National Post*, 9 August.

Langlois, Simon. 1992. *Recent Social Trends in Quebec, 1960–1990.* Montreal; Kingston, ON: McGill-Queen's University Press.

Léger Marketing. 2007. 'Les Québécois et la guerre en Afghanistan.' 18 June.

Le Soleil. 2009. 'Carrefour des lecteurs.' 5 April.

Monet-Chartrand, Simonne. 1993. *Les Québécoises et le mouvement pacifiste, 1939–1967.* Montreal: Éditions Écosociété.

Poole, Erik, and Annie Bourret. 1989. *Guerre, paix et désarmement: bibliographie thématique en langue française.* Quebec: Presses de l'Université Laval.

Québec solidaire. 2006a. *Déclaration de Principes.* Montreal, 6 February.

–. 2006b. Minutes of the Second National Convention, Montreal, 24–6 November.

–. 2006c. Minutes of the Second National Council, Montreal, 30 September–1 October.

–. 2007a. 'Accommodements raisonnables: nous sommes tous et toutes Québécois!' Press release, 10 February.

–. 2007b. 'Afghanistan: pourquoi meurent nos enfants, nos frères et nos sœurs?' Press release, 23 August.

–. 2007c. Minutes of the Third National Council, document CN-2007-D10, Montreal, 15–17 June.

–. 2008a. 'Engagement électoraux 2008.' Montreal.

–. 2008b. 'Québec solidaire salue la modernité et la sagesse des commissaires Bouchard et Taylor.' Press release, 22 May.

–. 2009. 'Interdiction de port de signes religieux: n'ajoutons pas un voile supplémentaire au voile!' Press release, 13 May.

Renaud, Benoit. 2009. 'Port de signes religieux – Québec solidaire ose aller à contre-courant.' *Le Devoir*, 6 January.

United Nations. 2009. Human Rights Council. *Human Rights in Palestine and Other Occupied Arab Territories: Report of the United Nations Fact Finding Mission on the Gaza Conflict.* New York.

Vaillancourt, Jean-Guy. 1992. 'Deux mouvements sociaux québécois: le mouvement pour la paix et le mouvement vert.' In *Le Québec en jeu: comprends les grands défis*, ed. G. Daigle. Montreal: Presses de l'Université de Montréal.

14

Bringing Ottawa's Warmakers to Heel: The Anti-war Movement in Canada

DERRICK O'KEEFE

In late July 2010 a remarkable anti-war meeting took place at Conway Hall in London, England. At a public forum hosted by the United Kingdom Stop the War Coalition, British soldier Joe Glenton spoke proudly of the months he spent in jail for refusing to fight in Afghanistan: 'In the current climate, I regard it as a badge of honour to have served a prison sentence.' Glenton explained to the crowd that his objection to the war had led him to an important understanding. 'I've come to the conclusion that the real enemy is not the man in front who is facing your rifle, but the man directly behind and above you telling you to pull the trigger.' In his speech Glenton recounted the warm reception he got from his fellow soldiers, the inmates he served time with in prison, and the general public. At one point he was receiving up to two hundred letters of encouragement a day. His speech at Conway Hall was, in part, a confident call to action: 'I really do believe that today the conditions exist for us to bring the government to heel: the wheels have truly fallen off the pro-war bandwagon' (Glenton 2010).[1]

Glenton's optimism is backed up by public opinion polls, with close to 80 per cent in the United Kingdom in favour of bringing the troops home from Afghanistan. The wheels have indeed long ago come off the ever-shifting pro-war arguments; the truth has seeped out and into the public's consciousness, both through Wikileaks and by way of torture and other scandals that even the mainstream media cannot avoid.

Yet despite all this the United Kingdom's participation in the war continues, and the issue remains completely off the radar of all the established political parties. On this most important of issues, a veritable 'conspiracy of silence' reigns (Brady 2010). The UK anti-war movement, along with a handful of outspoken Members of Parliament, has continued to work to break this silence and to mobilize opposition. But it remains a real challenge to draw big numbers into the streets for Afghanistan, even as opinion shifts more and more against the war.

In all of this the situation in the United Kingdom is not unlike that in Canada: the war is as unpopular as ever, the media and political establishments are locked in silence, and a beleaguered anti-war movement is doing what it can, with broad but largely passive support. So it is that – through inertia and lack of organized resistance – the war in Afghanistan rolls on, long after the wheels have come off its bandwagon. But Joe Glenton is neither a naïf nor a fool. In fact he is perfectly correct in saying that the conditions exist to bring our governments to heel. What follows are some basic ideas about the peace movement's struggle in Canada, given the country's political dynamics and the state of the anti-war and related social movements.

Ignatieff and Empire

A month before Glenton's rousing speech in London a less inspiring meeting took place at Toronto's historic Royal York Hotel at 100 Front Street West, less than a block from Bay Street, the centre of corporate Canada. Once the tallest building in the British Empire, today the old chateau-style building remains a favourite stomping ground of the Canadian establishment. In fact it is still the residence of choice for Queen Elizabeth and family, for that matter, whenever the royals visit.

On 15 June 2010, just days before the G20 meetings at the Toronto Convention Centre, then Liberal leader Michael Ignatieff took to the podium in the hotel's ornate Canadian Room. A year and a half into his disappointing stint as Liberal leader, on this day he was standing on familiar, comfortable ground. Ignatieff was at the Royal York to address a gathering of the 'National Forum,' a joint effort of the Canadian Club and the Empire Club, two century-old speakers' forums that boast members from among the 'most influential leaders from the professions, business, labour, education and government.' Michael's father, George Ignatieff, a top Canadian diplomat, addressed the Empire Club in 1969; his grandfather, Count Nicholas Ignatieff, a Czarist minister who brought the family to Canada (via Britain) following the Bolshevik Revolution, spoke at 100 Front Street back in 1938.

George Ignatieff's memoir was entitled *The Making of a Peacemonger* (1985). In 1969 his speech's topic was 'Canada's Stake in Arms Control and Disarmament.' Michael Ignatieff, however, has enjoyed a long, high-profile career as a public intellectual advocating for war in the Balkans, Iraq, and Afghanistan. He was at the Royal York to talk war. The author of *Empire Lite* (2003) – a manifesto for US warmaking under the rubric of humanitarianism and nation building – was here to explain to the Empire Club why Canada should continue its commitment to the occupation of Afghanistan by the North Atlantic Treaty Organization (NATO). More than that, he reaffirmed his core belief in liberal internationalism, which Ignatieff asserted was one of the three 'simple things' foundational to the Liberal Party.

The Liberal Party has certainly played a foundational role in establishing Canada's role in the world – the projection of Canadian diplomatic and military power in pursuit of the elite's geostrategic aims. Ignatieff's speech was a significant moment for him as a Canadian political leader. It simultaneously put the Liberal Party firmly out ahead of the Conservative government of Stephen Harper in pushing for a continued military or security role in Afghanistan, and re-established Ignatieff himself as the worldly advocate of a liberal interventionism once seemingly tarnished by the Iraq debacle.[2]

The speech was framed by an anecdote about his father George and Lester B. Pearson standing atop Canada House in London in 1940 watching the city burn after a Nazi bombing raid. Ignatieff's remarks on Afghanistan are quoted here in full. In them one can sense a hint of awareness that the mission has been a failure and that the public is weary of war. And yet, Ignatieff concludes, the Canadian-NATO intervention must continue, albeit more emphasis now must be put on framing it as an effort in diplomacy and development.

> Let's . . . remember what our goal in Afghanistan is. However strange as it may seem to say it our goal in Afghanistan is peace too. This is a country I know well. I began to visit it first in 1997. I've seen it ravaged by civil war. I've seen the ethnic hatreds, the hatreds that have left millions dead. It's a tormented country. It became a haven for terror. We went in for good reason, to protect the national security of Canada. 147 brave Canadians didn't come home. This is on our conscience, this is on our hearts.
>
> Mr. Harper behaves as if the Afghan mission never happened. It happened on his watch. He's walking away from it as if it never occurred. There's something about this that doesn't seem right to Canadians. We have to have an honest national discussion about where we go from here. We came in with an alliance, we came in to help an Afghan government. Canadians are serious people, if you ask us to do something serious and

difficult we'll do it, provided Canadians can be convinced as to what it is
we're trying to achieve. And the problem in my view has not been casualties, the problem has been futility, the sense of 'what are we achieving,
what progress are we making?' I'm very concerned that once the combat
mission ends, and I believe the combat mission should end, and should
end completely in 2011, we will walk away with the job undone. And we
will look back and ask, 'What was that about? Did we let ourselves down?
Did we let our allies down? Did we let Afghanistan down?

I think there is a place for Canada to commit to a training role, to train
the military, to train the police. What were we there for in the beginning?
It was to enable the Afghans to defend themselves. It's not our country,
it's their country. The whole purpose of our engagement in that country
was to enable that country to stand on its own feet and be self-sufficient.
We're not yet there. Are Canadians content to walk away with the job half
done? I think not. However difficult it may be to say so, I think there is
more work to be done. A training mission focused on raising the capability of the officer cadre in Afghanistan is a mission we can do. It does not
involve combat, but it involves building capacity. Remember peace, order
and good government. We've got to build the capacity of this people so
that they can defend themselves and so that we can come home with honour, with a sense Canadians always want to have, of a job well done, a
difficult job well done.

And so we are open as a party to a national discussion about this: a serious, thoughtful, to the roots national discussion about what we can do.
This is what parliament should do; this is what Canadians should do. You
can't have a foreign policy unless it's based on a national conversation.
Mr. Harper wants to stop that conversation, I want to start it. (Ignatieff
2010)

There is much to analyse and deconstruct in Ignatieff's speech. To
begin, beneath the assurances of working for peace, there is a strong
undertone that the real problem has been Stephen Harper's lack of
resolve and commitment to the war effort. In effect Ignatieff is accus-
ing the Conservative government of pretending to wind down the war
when it knows full well that Canada's establishment remains committed to helping the counterinsurgency and to maintaining the occupation through 'training' security forces in Afghanistan. Among other
things Ignatieff's words are an accusation of opportunism cast from the
all-glass Liberal house. The 'conversation' Ignatieff really has in mind
here is all about extending Canada's involvement in the occupation –

carrying its weight in the counterinsurgency even after the Kandahar battle group comes home – and avoiding any conclusions that the war has been futile, immoral, and wasteful. As Ignatieff is fully aware the growing opposition to the conflict in both Canada and Afghanistan is a challenge to the strategy of interventionist warfare against 'rogue' or 'failed' states advanced by Canada's political and economic elite over the past decade. To pre-empt this kind of political setback Ignatieff offers new justifications for entrenching the war: training Afghan security forces, aiding neoliberalism through 'development,' supporting 'our allies' in NATO, and helping 'Afghans to defend themselves.' While the latter justification is for public consumption, the first three represent the strategy by which a Liberal government would relabel and reorganize the mission in line with the broader agenda of western states in Afghanistan. Without contemplating the suffering of Afghans under the current military occupation, Ignatieff articulates a new set of rationales for maintaining Canada's role in the conflict post-2011. In doing so he sets the agenda for yet another Liberal-Conservative agreement on the Afghanistan file.

All Quiet on Parliament Hill

Despite the failures of the war to date Ignatieff's argument for a re-tooled Canadian mission has gained an audience on Parliament Hill. Liberal MP Bob Rae asserted this position even more strongly in June 2010, upon returning to Canada from an MPs' delegation to Afghanistan. Calling for 'intense discussions' on the war, Rae said: 'We have an obligation to see this thing through. The door is open to serious discussion in Canada – and between Canada and NATO – about what the future looks like' (CBC News 2010).

In the days and weeks following this hawkish Liberal shot across the bow of the Conservative government, the leadership of the New Democratic Party (NDP) remained utterly silent on the question of Afghanistan. For NDP leader Jack Layton this was true to his form over the past couple of years. As the war in Afghanistan expanded, the social democratic opposition became more muted. Save for the occasional *de rigueur* mention of the party's official policy calling for troop withdrawal, after late 2008 the now-deceased Layton rarely criticized the war.[3] In the early years of the Afghanistan War the NDP position on Canada's role in the occupation wavered. Leading party spokespeople, such as then foreign affairs critic Alexa McDonough, supported the military intervention, but tended to call for a different role for Canadian troops and a more humane waging of the war – 'a better war is possible.' In September 2006, however, at the party's federal convention in Quebec City, the membership overwhelmingly passed a resolution calling for troop withdrawal. A pro-war writer, lamenting this grassroots anti-war vote, accurately summed up the NDP position on Afghanistan from 2001 to 2006: 'The NDP's position has evolved from supporting the mission, to questioning its strategy, to calling for immediate withdrawal' (Ferrie 2007). However, while some of the party's MPs have been outspoken and consistent opponents of the war, the NDP as a whole has never followed through on its convention resolution by carrying out an energetic campaign on the issue. Following US president Barack Obama's election in November 2008 and the brief effort at a coalition with the Liberals in December 2008 – an agreement that would have seen the NDP as part of the government waging the war – the party's tepid and inconsistent anti-war pronouncements ground to an almost complete stop. From October 2008 to August 2009, for instance, not a single news release from the NDP called for the troops to be brought home.[4]

A testament to the utter lack of parliamentary opposition to the war, it was left to a Liberal senator to fire back at Rae's and Ignatieff's comments. While Rae and Ignatieff seem determined to be the tip of the spear for prolonging Canada's intervention in Afghanistan, an unexpected voice of Liberal opposition was raised by Senator Colin Kenny. The senator published an opinion piece in the *Ottawa Citizen* that was substantially more hard hitting than anything Jack Layton said about the war. Given his prior support for the war, and the character of his current opposition, it is worth quoting Senator Kenny at length:

> When it comes to military missions, the tough guys' mantra is that we Canadians don't cut and run. When the going gets difficult, Canadians keep fighting against the odds in order to create a better world wherever our troops are representing us.
>
> And if our military is completely burned out – as it is now after several years of engagement in Afghanistan – and we can no longer confront the enemy on the front lines, we at least leave enough people in the field to train local fighters to take our place. Oh, and one more thing: We'll keep shunting big aid dollars to Afghanistan to help ordinary Afghans whose lives have been made hell by the war that we have been fighting on their behalf.

That's the gist of a feel-good escape plan emerging in some circles – a scenario invented to make Canadians hug themselves while retreating from a bloody combat that Canada got suckered into on false pretences. My position is that getting burned once should be more than enough. We shouldn't be making plans to get burned twice . . .

Parliament has made the right decision. We can wallow around Afghanistan for another three years trying to save face. Or we can be adults and not get burned twice. Let us face a harsh truth: for all the efforts of our courageous troops, and the courageous troops of our allies, nation-building doesn't make sense in a nation that doesn't want to get built. Let's quit pretending. (Kenny 2010)

Kenny's discourse, including the implication that Afghans are to blame for their own misery, is not the same as the anti-war movement's argument against the war and occupation. The noteworthy thing is that it was left to a Liberal senator to challenge his own party leader's pro-war position. It reflects the sad state of affairs in Ottawa, where no party has taken a principled stand against western imperialism in Afghanistan and the wider Middle East.

A Decade at War

Before we take up the invitation to a serious discussion of Canada's role in Afghanistan, it is worth setting this intervention in the context of recent history. The war in Afghanistan – named Operation Athena, after the Greek goddess of heroic endeavour, though it is really more Sisyphean in character – has defined Canada's foreign policy for the past decade (Moens 2008). Although there have been visible tensions within the establishment about the scale and aggression of Canadian militarism, the Afghan mission is very much in continuity with Canada's historic position within the imperialist system.

For decades Canada has had an almost entirely undeserved reputation as a neutral arbiter in world affairs – a consummate 'peacekeeping' nation, committed to multilateralism and to the framework of international cooperation as organized through the United Nations. This is the 'foundational' narrative of Canadian foreign policy, which finds its highest expression in the myth of Lester Pearson as an eminent man of peace (Neufeld 2010).[5]

The post–Second World War reality is that Canada has always been a key player in the NATO alliance and a loyal upholder of the interests of the capitalist world system and its military enforcement (Warnock 1970; Engler 2009). Even when particular Canadian governments appear to poke the US empire in the eye by not going along with a particular military venture, they work hard to provide support by other means. During the Vietnam era Canada never sent troops to bolster that unpopular war, but was a key supplier of weapons to the United States and never voiced a principled opposition to the slaughter.[6] Chemical weapons such as napalm and Agent Orange, which the United States used across Indochina, were in fact developed and tested in Canada.

In this sense the debates and policy decisions around the war in Iraq in 2003 fit squarely within the historical pattern. Then Liberal prime minister Jean Chrétien, seeing crowds of hundreds of thousands on the streets in Quebec and across the rest of Canada in January and February of that year, made the popular announcement that Canada would not join the invasion. Only a short time later, however, Chrétien announced a new beefing up of Canadian forces in Afghanistan, a measure that many correctly noted freed up more US forces for Iraq – a sort of de facto endorsement of the invasion. According to Janice Gross Stein and Eugene Lang (2007), US and Canadian officials explicitly agreed upon this trade-off: Canada would not commit troops to Iraq but would take ownership of a NATO mission in Kabul as the United States redeployed to the Gulf. Furthermore the Canadian government wished US forces a speedy victory in Iraq and found myriad other ways to provide concrete support to the illegal war effort (Engler 2009, 43–8).

Likewise, a year later, in February 2004, Canada worked hand-in-hand with the governments of France and the United States to back a *coup d'état* that drove elected President Jean-Bertrand Aristide from Haiti and resulted in years of severe repression in that country (Engler and Fenton 2005; Hallward 2008). Canada's participation in this example of regime change was not marginal, with Special Forces playing a role in securing the airport on the night that Aristide was spirited out of the country by US Marines. Bill Graham, Liberal foreign affairs minister at the time of the coup, told me in 2005 that Canadian troops had been dispatched because '[Colin] Powell called me and said Aristide requested a flight out [of Haiti].' Given Powell's obviously bogus testimony to the United Nations in 2003 on weapons of mass destruction in Iraq, Graham's apparent credulity demonstrates just how integrated

Canada is in the US-led imperial system. Long before the actual kidnapping and removal of Aristide, the Liberal government had played an important role in planning the coup. Key to this process was Quebec MP Denis Paradis, who made a 'personal goal' out of 'the problem of Haiti' back in 2000, when he was parliamentary secretary to then foreign affairs minister Lloyd Axworthy.[7] Canada's role in subverting and overthrowing Haitian democracy has been a key second front of Canadian foreign policy, after Afghanistan, over the past decade, and likely will increase in the future as part of Canada's new 'Strategy for the Americas.'

Thus, in the decade since the 'war on terror' began following the 9/11 attacks, Canadian elites have worked to transform this country's foreign policy in a more explicitly imperial direction (Byers 2007). Although the peacekeeping label was massively oversold, it was a national self-perception of sorts that coincided with the preferences of a majority of the Canadian public. Hawks in Canada saw 9/11 and, in particular, the war in Afghanistan as the impetus to push the idea of a 'warrior' nation, finally abandoning what they saw as the emasculated posture of peacekeeping and working through the United Nations. The Gulf War of 1991 and the NATO bombing of Serbia in 1998 had already provided opportunities for Canada to assert its 'manliness' on the world stage, and Afghanistan offered a golden opportunity to ramp up this effort. Rick Hillier, then head of the Canadian Forces, took the 2005 redeployment to Kandahar to push this agenda (Stein and Lang 2007). His infamous statements – calling the Afghan resistance 'murderers and scumbags' and boasting that the Forces' job 'is to be able to kill people' – were designed not just to soften up the Canadian public for casualties in the war, but also to change the public's perception of the military and its purpose in society.

Hillier's approach to world order and defence policy has been warmly embraced by hawkish elements. In the words of Michael Ross, a leading neoconservative in the country and a former member of the Israeli Mossad (see Ross 2007),

Canada's biggest mistake is more than a social-policy blunder or constitutional miscalculation. I believe our biggest mistake has been the systematic emasculation of our military since Lester B. Pearson accepted the Nobel Peace Prize in 1957. In Canada, we like to see ourselves as 'peacekeepers' who insert themselves into other nation's conflicts, and 'honest

brokers' in the realm of international relations. This conceit may have
inflated our self-image, but it has weakened our position on the world
stage. And – notwithstanding recent advances highlighted by our outgo-
ing Chief of Defence Staff, Gen. Rick Hillier – it has reduced our military
might. (Ross 2008)

Since 9/11 successive Canadian governments have followed the advice
of those such as Hillier and Ross and pursued a more 'muscular' foreign policy closely aligned with Washington. Both Liberal and Conservative governments have pushed through extensions of Canada's
military mission in Afghanistan. But both traditional governing parties have been careful to avoid allowing the war to become an election
issue. Prime Minister Harper repeatedly stated that Canada's military
mission in Afghanistan would end in 2011. Hawks and doves alike
agree that the Canadian military is at the limit of its fighting capacity,
its battle-ready forces overextended after years in Kandahar province,
a site of consistent insurgent activity.

The government, however, left itself some wiggle room to keep hundreds of 'trainers' in Kabul or elsewhere. And, indeed, in fall 2010 the
Conservatives did announce a 'training' mission of up to one thousand
Canadian Forces troops and staff, extending Canada's military presence in Afghanistan until at least 2014. The game now for the government is to continue to give as much political and military support to the
occupation as possible without arousing too much popular opposition,
especially in traditionally anti-war Quebec. In this game the Liberal
Party was willing to play 'bad cop' in the good cop/bad cop Liberal-
Conservative foreign policy coalition, once again providing 'cover' for
another stage of Canada's war in Afghanistan. Given Canada's role historically as a sub-imperial power it is vital to understand the reasons
the Canadian political establishment is united around a strategy of endless occupation.

Blood for Treasure

Canadian foreign policy has always been carried out with the interests
of Canadian corporations in mind, and the war in Afghanistan has been
no exception (Pratt 1983; Engler 2009). In 2007 then foreign affairs minister Peter MacKay made exactly this point at an event hosted by the
Vancouver Board of Trade and sponsored by Canadian mining firms

Teck-Cominco and Hunter Dickinson. In his presentation MacKay admitted that 'Canada's overall foreign policy, including the country's involvement in Afghanistan, is designed to help promote security, good governance, and economic and social development, all of which dovetail with the interests of Canadian business' (quoted in Grimes 2007). Hunter Dickinson, in fact, was a runner-up in the bidding for the right to exploit Afghanistan's massive copper deposits in Aynak – the largest private investment in the history of Afghanistan. China's state-owned Metallurgical Group eventually won the contract. In 2009, however, it was alleged that the Afghan minister of mining had accepted a bribe of at least US$20 million from the heads of the Chinese bid. The Aynak decision certainly irked the United States and other NATO powers, not least of all Canada, and one could speculate that it has contributed to the increasing tensions between the Karzai regime and its western backers. Now it turns out that Aynak was far from the only mining prize in Afghanistan (Risen 2010). One hundred thousand NATO troops will help ensure that China does not gobble up the rest of the $1 trillion treasure. The western powers are sure to assert more forcefully now that 'to the belligerents go the spoils.'

The other noteworthy treasure in Central Asia is the region's oil and natural gas deposits. These are economically important in themselves, but also strategically important given the competition for these resources with Russia and China. Today's 'Great Game' in this pivotal region revolves primarily around energy resources (Foster 2010). The proposed route of the long-planned TAPI (Turkmenistan-Afghanistan-Pakistan-India) pipeline runs right through the heart of Kandahar province, where Canadian troops have been part of the counterinsurgency war. This fact was noted, in uncharacteristically direct fashion, by the Canadian citizen, Tooryalai Wesa, appointed governor of Kandahar in December 2008. Returning after decades abroad, including thirteen years living in the suburbs of Vancouver, Wesa explained his role: 'I will try to get to the people and try to explain what the Canadian Forces want in Afghanistan, especially in Kandahar . . . to restore peace, to restore security and implement the development projects the Canadian government has in the pipeline.'

At the time, Wesa's comments were an unfortunate admission of the geopolitical and geo-economic interests driving the occupation. By late 2008, however, the pipeline project was an open secret. In fact, CTV News (2008) reported the following:

Afghanistan and three other countries agreed in April to build a US$7.6-billion natural gas pipeline starting in 2010 that would deliver gas from energy-rich Turkmenistan to energy-hungry Pakistan and India.

The . . . TAPI . . . pipeline is strongly supported by the U.S. because it would block a competing pipeline from Iran that would bring oil to India and Pakistan. It would also reduce Russia's dominance of the energy sector in Central Asia.

A U.S-backed pipeline – more than 500 kilometres of it – in Afghanistan would be an inviting target for Taliban and al Qaeda operatives there. It would be very difficult to defend.

But Ottawa and the military have been quiet about what could be one of the biggest changes to the operational paradigm in Kandahar, despite plans for such a pipeline going back a decade.

The pipeline plan is only one example of the fusion of corporate and state interests in the region. Looking beyond Afghanistan, Canada has economic interests throughout Central Asia. Former Liberal prime minister Jean Chrétien, for instance, has made repeated trips to Turkmenistan on behalf of Canadian energy interests. In September 2004 Chrétien, as part of an Omani-Canadian delegation, 'met in Turkmenistan to negotiate a deal between Edmonton based Buried Hill Energy and the government of Turkmenistan to develop the Serdar block in the Caspian area.'[8] As Todd Gordon documents in this volume, Canadian firms in a number of sectors – especially mining and energy – have expanded investments across Central Asia over the past decade.

In sum the new revelations about Afghanistan's massive mineral wealth mean that the interests of Canadian business and Canadian warmaking now dovetail more than ever in Afghanistan and the wider region. It is all the more reason to expect Ottawa to find new ways to prolong Canada's military involvement in the occupation, and to place a stake in Afghanistan's underground riches.

The Truth about the War in Afghanistan

A truly 'serious' discussion of the war in Afghanistan would involve a lot fewer Second World War analogies, a lot less moralizing in general – both about the heroism of Canadian soldiers and about the perfidy of those fighting against them – and a lot more in-depth analysis of the complex political realities of Afghanistan today. Very little is understood about the reality of the Afghan state that the United States and NATO have installed and propped up. The dominant story – the narrative pushed by warmakers – is that the western military presence is acting as a block against the return of the medieval, misogynist Taliban regime, the main source of women's oppression in Afghanistan. In this version of the story the cause of the plight of Afghan women is grossly oversimplified and the plagues of warlordism, drug trafficking, and fundamentalist extremism built into the current Afghan state and government are completely ignored (see Kolhatkar and Ingalls 2006; Warnock 2008; and Klassen, in this volume).

Since 2001 the anti-war movement has tried to explain who these warlords are, the ways in which they dominate the current Afghan regime, and their records of massive human rights violations, embezzlement, and murder. We should focus on explaining some of their specific stories.

Warlords, Corruption, and Narcopolitics

We can begin in Kandahar, where the true nature of the western intervention has been laid bare. In October 2009 the *New York Times* reported that Ahmed Wali Karzai – the president's younger brother who, until his assassination in 2011, was the most powerful man in Kandahar province – had for years received payments from the US Central Intelligence Agency (CIA). In this southeastern corner of Afghanistan the lives of more than 155 Canadians have been sacrificed to the cause of protecting a toxic brew of nepotism, opium trafficking, and graft – all of it personified by this 'Al Capone of Kandahar' (Filkins, Mazzetti, and Risen 2009).

The revelation of CIA payouts was just one of a number of bombshells that the world's most influential newspaper saw fit to print. Not only do more sources corroborate allegations of Ahmed Wali Karzai's role as a drug kingpin, they even reveal that US taxpayers' money has been paying him rent: 'Mr. Karzai is also paid for allowing the C.I.A. and American Special Operations troops to rent a large compound outside the city – the former home of Mullah Mohammed Omar, the Taliban's founder. The same compound is also the base of the Kandahar Strike Force. "He's our landlord," a senior American official said, speaking on condition of anonymity' (Filkins, Mazzetti, and Risen 2009). There are figures similar to Karzai in provinces throughout Afghanistan. In fact the United States and its NATO allies have consciously pursued a strategy of paying off warlords. In June 2010 a US congressional report pointed out that millions of dollars were ending up indirectly funding the Taliban and other insurgents. According to *Reuters*:

> 'This arrangement has fueled a vast protection racket run by a shadowy network of warlords, strongmen, commanders, corrupt Afghan officials, and perhaps others,' Representative John Tierney, chairman of a House of Representatives national security subcommittee, said in a statement.
>
> Tierney, a Democrat, said the system 'runs afoul' of the Defense Department's own rules and may be undermining the US strategic effort in Afghanistan.
>
> The report by the subcommittee's Democratic staff called protection payments 'a significant potential source of funding for the Taliban,' citing numerous documents, incidents reports and emails that refer to attempts at Taliban extortion along the road. (Allen 2010)

As it happens I was in New York in October 2009 with leading Afghan dissident, women's rights leader, and suspended parliamentarian Malalai Joya for the launch of her new autobiography, *A Woman Among Warlords* (Joya 2009). On our way to one of her media appearances, we discussed the news of Ahmed Wali Karzai.

'This is a very important revelation,' I offered earnestly. 'Given that he is the most powerful man in Kandahar province, the allegations about Wali Karzai should be on the front pages of newspapers across Canada.'

'But this is not news for the Afghan people, everyone knows this man as a drug lord and a puppet,' Joya responded. She spoke again: 'I am not happy how much [events] have proven me right about this occupation.' She talked about the various massacres reported at the time – in both Afghanistan and Pakistan. 'Sometimes I wish that what I have been saying had been proven wrong, and that somehow things would have improved. I would have had to apologize for my mistake, but at least the situation would not be this disaster.'

It has now been more than eight years since Malalai Joya made headlines at the December 2003 post-invasion *loya jirga* where Afghanistan's new constitution was debated and the process of legitimizing the US-installed Karzai government was pushed forward. Since then she has survived numerous assassination attempts and lived an underground life to continue to air key grievances of the Afghan people. While Afghanistan has suffered, too many progressive forces in the

West have fiddled. It is no secret that the anti-war movement, especially in the United States but also in the United Kingdom and Canada, has thus far failed to mobilize adequately around the issue, with much of it either balkanizing to the point of irrelevance or folding up shop in deference to the Obama administration (especially in the United States).

But perhaps even those actively engaged throughout in opposing the Afghanistan War have failed to articulate fully the scandal of this intervention, which has been put forward in such clear terms by people like Joya. When she said years ago, for instance, that the Karzai regime was the 'most corrupt government in the world,' this was not hyperbole. When she warned that the West had 'turned Afghanistan back into the centre of the opium trade,' the peace movement has been slow to articulate fully just how much NATO soldiers and governments have been propping up a narco-state.

Against the Demonization of the Afghan People

Among the dissenters to Canada's Afghan policy are those who dismiss outright the potential of the people of Afghanistan, asserting that Canadian blood and treasure are not worth expending on such an irredeemable basket case.[9] Senator Kenny's objections to the war, in places, hit on this note. This *sauve qui peut* version of an anti-war argument – in this case every country for itself instead of every man for himself – emerges from the same political milieu as does the kind of stereotyping that sometimes slips into pro-war writing.[10]

It is important to highlight the work of the many analysts from across the political spectrum who argue that the war is now unwinnable. There is a clear consensus emerging that the war has reached an impasse, and that the time is ripe to organize a united front of anti-war forces against both the US 'surge' and the decision by the Canadian government to extend the mission. But however pragmatic we should be in uniting all people who oppose this war, we must do more.

The anti-war movement in Canada, led by the Canadian Peace Alliance, aims to build a culture of *internationalism* and *solidarity*. In making arguments against the war, it seeks to humanize Afghans, who are so often caricatured or dismissed – even by some opponents of the Canadian mission. To this end there is a need to develop a greater understanding of the culture and history of Afghanistan (see Warnock, in this volume) and to foster real links of solidarity, including providing material aid to organizations working for progressive social change

and self-determination in Afghanistan. The voice of Afghan dissidents,
like the examples of Malalai Joya and the heroic underground activists
of the Revolutionary Association of Afghan Women, should be given
special emphasis.[11]

Highlighting examples of Afghan women asserting their own rights
is essential, especially given the constant war propaganda invoking
women's oppression. In late July 2010 *Time* magazine ran a sensational-
ist cover story, 'What happens if we leave Afghanistan,' with a photo of
a young woman who had been brutally disfigured for the crime of leaving her abusive in-laws (Stengel 2010). Among those who responded to
the piece, the US-based South Asian Solidarity Initiative (2010) stood
out, making the salient points of rebuttal:

> For the last decade, the occupying forces of the US and its NATO allies
> have nourished warlords and supported a corrupt government, leading
> many to join the Taliban and increasing their influence across Afghani-
> stan. Increased civilian deaths, a fundamentalist resurgence, and deadly
> bombing raids have led to a devastated country and a Taliban stronger
> than ever before. *Time*'s claim to 'illuminate what is actually happening on
> the ground' falsely equates the last decade of occupation with progress.
> The occupation has not and will not bring democracy to Afghanistan, nor
> will it bring liberation to Afghan women. Instead, it has exacerbated deep-
> seated corruption in the government, the widespread abuse of women's
> rights and human rights by fundamentalists, including Karzai's allies,
> and stymied critical infrastructure development in the country. The ques-
> tion should not be 'what happens if we leave Afghanistan,' the question
> should be 'what happened when we invaded Afghanistan' and 'what hap-
> pens if we stay in Afghanistan.'

As anti-war activists we insist that the Afghan people are capable of
creating their own democratic future. Progressive groups and democratic parties in Afghanistan are fighting to reconstruct the peace and
safety of their country, and more often than not are forced underground
for fear of their safety. Despite repression by the US-backed Karzai government, thousands of brave students and women have come out onto
the streets of Kabul to protest the bombings and the continued war. It is
from these forces that a larger progressive movement will emerge that
could play a role in bringing real democracy to Afghanistan. As the
United States and NATO continue the occupation, however, the space
for progressive forces becomes increasingly limited.

With ramped up public relations from the warmongers who seek by any means necessary to shore up widespread disillusionment with the war, there are several specific things that the anti-war movement in Canada needs to do better. In some cases efforts are already under way and merely need to be developed; on other fronts there is a need to experiment or rediscover tools of resistance that are not currently being put to use at all.

Fundraising

The anti-war movement should work to become more systematic in raising funds and providing assistance and solidarity to grassroots organizations and groups in Afghanistan. This is an undeveloped but important aspect of our work, because we are dealing with a vast, bloated non-governmental organization (NGO) sector, much of which is explicitly pro-occupation. In fact many of the NGOs, including Canadian 'Women 4 Women' in Afghanistan, refuse to criticize any aspect of the war. This is a disaster for the whole concept of humanitarian aid, but its prevalence is suggestive of the steady 'NGO convergence' with the military occupation as part of the developmental agenda of Canada's 3D strategy and its 'peace-building' facet. As in Haiti, Afghanistan is overrun with NGOs and their western staffs, leading Malalai Joya among others to refer to 'NGO-lords' as one of the causes of the failure to build independent capacities of Afghan organizations.

A lot can be accomplished, however, with even the most modest of sums when the money raised is sent directly to legitimate projects on the ground run by Afghans themselves, rather than highly paid westerners and their now ubiquitous security personnel. For example, in 2007, events featuring Joya in Canada and Europe were able to raise approximately $40,000 after costs. This money was donated to local organizations in Joya's home province of Farah. A meeting of community leaders decided that the money could best be spent to build a new waiting room for the Hamoon Medical Clinic, a considerable expansion of this vital centre that provides free medical services for the poor of Farah and the surrounding areas.

Fundraising for these types of efforts should be built in to everything we do as an anti-war movement. In addition to the money raised this will add an important and dynamic educational aspect to our work, and lend credibility to our important criticisms of mainstream NGOs.

Confronting Growing Militarism

The tasks of the anti-war movement are much bigger than just explaining the realities in Afghanistan. We also have to confront head on the increasing militarism of Canadian society. Under General Rick Hillier, in particular, the Canadian Forces aggressively pursued recruitment campaigns targeting minority communities and generally worked to raise its public profile. The military is increasingly visible at summer festivals and sporting and cultural events throughout the country. 'Support Our Troops' bumper stickers, decals, and magnets have been added to police and emergency vehicles in major cities across the country. Even the CBC's *Hockey Night in Canada*, the public broadcaster's most-watched program, has become saturated with thinly veiled military propaganda.

These manifestations of a growing militarism may feel inevitable and unstoppable. But they can be contested. For example, well-thought-out interventions by anti-war activists can turn a recruiting or public relations exercise into an opportunity for popular education. In Vancouver, each summer activists from the Stop War Coalition have challenged the military's public outreach at events, including the annual Gay Pride Parade, the Pacific National Exhibition, and the Dragon Boat Festival. The actions run the gamut from full-on protests or pickets to simply handing out information in front of or nearby military personnel and equipment. In making these demonstrations the anti-war movement is not opposing the armed forces per se, but the militarization of Canadian society and the undermining of democracy by military attempts to foster blind support for wars abroad.

The Lost Art of Civil Disobedience

The euphoria of the unprecedented mass worldwide anti-war mobilizations in 2002–3 quickly faded when the invasion of Iraq was launched. The anti-war movement quickly refocused on opposing the occupation of Afghanistan, but it has never approached the same type of numbers at protests. Demoralization on this point can tend to obscure the very real accomplishments of the anti-war movement in Canada over the past decade, which include:

• helping force the Chrétien Liberals' decision not to openly and fully participate in the Iraq War;

- integrating Palestine into actions against the wars in Afghanistan and Iraq, ending the past practice of remaining silent on the Middle East in the name of 'unity' or avoiding 'controversy';[12]
- taking Islamophobia head on, and giving time and attention to issues of torture, secret trials, and rendition, since both these encroachments on civil liberties and the war in Afghanistan have been facilitated by the growth of distrust, suspicion, and outright hostility towards Muslims and those perceived to be Muslims in Canada; and
- leading the work of demanding sanctuary for war resisters from the United States, primarily those young men and women who have refused to fight in the illegal war in Iraq.

Recognizing its positive achievements, there is no denying a lack of dynamism in the anti-war movement, particularly when it comes to Afghanistan, a central and inescapable political issue in Canada. Since 2006 pan-Canadian 'Days of Action,' which typically have been organized in October, have tended to stagnate or decline in terms of numbers mobilized. With few exceptions, such as Malalai Joya's cross-Canada tour in 2009, numbers at public forums on the war have been very modest. Likewise, politicians' events and campaign stops are only rarely confronted or disrupted by anti-war activists.

This is not, primarily, the fault of the existing anti-war organizations and networks. Rather it reflects the failure of the Canadian left more broadly and the weakness of social and labour movements generally. One other explanation for the dwindling numbers at anti-war protests is the feeling, often expressed, that protests will not change anything, that the 'same old' demonstrations will not move politicians in Ottawa to act. Given this situation there is a need to find new and imaginative ways to raise both public awareness and the morale of those opposed to the war, and to raise the social costs of the war for the government. In short, the anti-war movement needs to rediscover *civil disobedience*.

It is possible, for example, for the anti-war movement to adopt the social movement tactic of the occupation of the offices of MPs, particularly those of the governing party. Other tools in the social movement toolbox might also be deployed. Recent examples include daring banner drops by anti-tar sands activists and the brilliant spoof pulled off by activists to draw attention to France's debt to Haiti.[13] These types of actions should be used to complement the work of broad coalitions and networks that have been the backbone of the Canadian anti-war movement and that are already trying to educate and mobilize against the war.

Linking Struggles

The building of an effective anti-war movement also requires the linking of political struggles against capitalism, imperialism, and climate change. For example, the Canadian anti-war movement was part of the mobilizations against the G20 in Toronto in June 2010, organizing around the theme 'Disarm the G20.' Protests and forums were held that linked the struggles against occupation in Iraq, Palestine, and Afghanistan with the struggle against austerity and state repression in Canada, the United States, and other G20 countries. Indeed, coming out of the Toronto summit, G20 governments, including Canada, began announcing austerity cuts across the board – except where the military and other security agencies were concerned. After police forces experimented with an array of new technologies against protesters on the streets of Toronto – and made the largest mass arrest in Canadian history – the Harper government announced a $16 billion purchase of new F-35 fighter jets (which we now know are actually estimated to cost $30 billion or more).

The blatant contradiction of cutting funding for social needs while boosting funding for the military required a response from the anti-war movement. In Vancouver, for example, the Stop War Coalition held a day of action against the F-35 purchase. It distributed flyers explaining the misplaced priorities and noting what public goods could have been purchased with the $16 billion: 'As Parliament resumes this month, MPs will debate the priorities for Canada, including choices between military hardware or urgent social and economic priorities. We urge readers to send their MPs a message: the Harper government's plan to spend $16 billion on F-35 fighter jets should be scrapped, in favour of public transit, social housing, clean drinking water, access to education, and humanitarian assistance.' The flyer went on to detail exactly what alternative goods could have been purchased: 5,000 buses, tuition for 50,000 students, 30,000 new homes, or clean drinking water for countless remote indigenous communities.

This type of campaigning is essential if the anti-war movement is to remain relevant in these times of economic crisis and social austerity. In Canada it is also imperative that the anti-war movement connect with and support indigenous struggles to defend land and territory, especially as Ottawa's military and police forces are routinely mobilized to suppress these struggles. The link between the corporate colonization of indigenous territories and the international expansion of Canadian capital more broadly is a direct one that must be highlighted and opposed.

One other important link for the anti-war movement is with the climate justice movement, a growing force worldwide that includes a strong youth component. The effort to prevent runaway climate change and transition to a low-carbon society will be a non-starter if wars of aggression and plunder remain the norm. It is impossible to imagine a successful movement to confront global warming without a total reworking of international relations – without putting an end to the imperialist world system based on domination and inequality. 'No War, No Warming' will become an increasingly important slogan in the years ahead.

The Canadian Peace Alliance: Against the Occupation

Since 2001 the Canadian Peace Alliance (CPA) has undertaken the task of linking these struggles and of organizing a movement against the war in Afghanistan. The CPA was founded in 1985 and now operates as the country's largest network of anti-war groups, providing a strong, coordinated voice for peace and social justice at the national level. The CPA's goals include redirecting funds from military spending to human needs; working towards global nuclear disarmament; making Canada a consistent leader for world peace; strengthening world institutions for the peaceful resolution of conflict; and protecting the rights of all people to work for peace, and social and economic justice.

Over the past decade the CPA has been the main coordinating body for mobilizations against the war in Afghanistan. Prior to 2003 the CPA played an important role in linking up the massive rallies against the war in Iraq. Its member groups and coalitions, including unions, church groups, and student organizations, have also been centrally involved in the fight to let US war resisters stay in Canada.

On Afghanistan the CPA has consistently called for an immediate withdrawal of Canadian troops, organizing many days of action. Since 2006 the CPA has organized under the slogan 'End It, Don't Extend It,' highlighting in particular the complicity of the Liberal Party in voting with the Conservatives to extend the mission in Kandahar on two occasions. The CPA has sponsored three speaking tours by

Malalai Joya, and has worked to raise awareness and funds for her cause. The CPA will continue organizing against the Canadian state's efforts to maintain the occupation of Afghanistan through counterinsurgency training. The CPA argues that NATO and US troops must end the military occupation of Afghanistan in order for democratic, secular, and progressive movements to present a real alternative to the Taliban, the Karzai government, and the Northern Alliance. To this end the CPA demands a withdrawal of foreign forces as part of peace negotiations and a regional settlement that does not exclude or sideline the feminist, democratic, and progressive movements of Afghanistan. Through years of active solidarity and political organizing, the CPA insists that ending the war and occupation is a necessary first step towards building peace, democracy, and development in Afghanistan.

Conclusion: Reasons for Optimism

Two developments in 2010 improved the organizing terrain and the 'optimism of the will' for the anti-war movement in Canada. As part of the G20 protests in Toronto in June, the mother of a Canadian soldier then deployed in Kandahar spoke out against the war. This has been an all-too-rare occurrence. Here is what military mom, Josie Forcadilla, told an anti-war rally that was part of the G20 protests: 'Considering the number of deaths, not to mention the injured and those who suffered from post-traumatic stress disorder, it is time for the Harper government to withdraw unconditionally all Canadian Forces personnel in Afghanistan. The expansionist and integrationist policy of the Canadian Forces has failed as evidenced by the mounting casualties in the rank and file – 148 fallen soldiers to date – and the toll the Afghan civilian population is taking.'[14] As well, in August a national public opinion poll suggested the extent to which Canada has an anti-war majority. As the *Vancouver Sun* reported, ' "[a]lmost 80 per cent of Canadians [wanted] to end the mission in Afghanistan in 2011, a new Ipsos Reid poll conducted exclusively for canada.com showed . . . These numbers are very indicative of a public that is now, in their minds, out of Afghanistan. They've made a conscious decision as a nation that we are exiting," John Wright, senior vice-president of the polling firm, said Wednesday' (Chai 2010).

The Canadian public may want Canada out of Afghanistan, but a great collective effort and mobilization is still needed to ensure this occurs. And an even greater effort is required to break the hold on the public mind of the mythologies of benevolent Canadian interventionism. It is going to require great tactical creativity, strategic vision, and determination. There is still a long way to go to extricate Canada from the occupation of Afghanistan, and further still to finally break Canada out of the club of empire once and for all. To this end the CPA, with its decades of experience in opposing militarism and linking together international solidarity movements in Canada and around the world, will be an invaluable asset.

NOTES

1 Joe Glenton's speech is worth watching in full: http://www.youtube.com/watch?v=3YKj3vH4YQY&feature=search.
2 Ignatieff's infamous and vocal support of the Iraq War arguably cost him his first attempt to gain the Liberal Party leadership, which he lost to Stéphane Dion.
3 A rare instance of the NDP leader's calling for troop withdrawal occurred at the August 2009 federal NDP convention in Halifax. In his speech to party members Layton said 'from day one, we said this conflict cannot, and will not, be settled militarily. That's why we say again today: support our troops and bring them home' (Layton 2009).
4 A Vancouver activist (Cariou 2009) scoured Layton's and the NDP's statements over the year, and concluded: 'The further I go through Layton's statements and speeches over the past year, the more it becomes clear that he is distancing himself from the activist core of the anti-war movement. He remains good on such issues as the war resisters, the cost of the war, the need for negotiations rather than endless war. But in his major statements, during and after the election last fall, Afghanistan has been simply absent.'
5 The myth predates Pearson, however. Even Louis Riel, for a time, trusted that an expedition of federal Canadian troops following the first Red River Rebellion (1870) would be an 'errand of peace.' Riel turned down Gabriel Dumont's offer to ambush the so-called Wolseley expedition with guerilla warfare tactics. As the Canadian troops approached the Red River settlement, Riel and other leaders fled for their lives.
6 Four million people are estimated to have died in the Vietnam War. It is telling that Ignatieff (2003) completely ignores this case of mass murder by the US government in his attempt to offer a liberal defence of empire; see Young (1991).

7 'For those seeking to understand the roots of Canada's latest intervention in Haiti, there appears to be no better place to begin than the central figure of the emerging Canada-Haiti controversy, Quebec MP Denis Paradis. (Fenton 2004).

8 See Canadian Peace Alliance, 'Canada, Kandahar and the Caspian,' http://www.acp-cpa.ca/ (accessed 28 September 2010).

9 The notion that Afghanistan has always been an ungovernable 'basket case' is ahistorical, ignoring the many decades in the twentieth century during which social movements and a vibrant left pushed Afghanistan's monarchy to implement a modicum of democratic institutions and social reforms, including in the area of women's rights. It is precisely the past three decades of massive foreign military intervention that has driven Afghanistan into social and political disaster, including the vicious subjugation of women.

10 *National Post* blogger and pro-war author Terry Glavin has referred to Taliban insurgents as 'unemployable hillbillies' on at least a couple of occasions. For examples, see his blog: http://transmontanus.blogspot.com/2009/02/toronto-rally-against-taliban.html. Glavin, speaking on CBC Radio's *Cross Canada Check-Up* in December 2009, lamented the attention given to the Afghan torture scandal, since it was just a matter of 'some of these drooling brigands that are apprehended by the Afghan National Army [getting] their ears boxed a little bit from time to time.'

11 See http://www.rawa.org.

12 The current imperial project covers the vast Middle East and Central Asian region, and Palestine has always been a central point of struggle. The uprising in Kashmir against Indian occupation is also important, given the involvement of both India and Pakistan in Afghanistan. Palestine is particularly vital for the Canadian anti-war movement to tackle, given the Canadian government's unstinting support for Israeli occupation and apartheid (Davis 2003).

13 On Bastille Day, 14 July 2010, a press release and video statement was issued by the French foreign ministry announcing that, in the wake of the earthquake disaster in Haiti, France would finally pay back more than US$21 billion dollars extorted from Haiti as indemnity for its liberation from slavery. The announcement, it turned out, was an elaborate hoax carried out by activists to bring attention to France's historic debt to Haiti. The issue remained in the headlines in August when a number of prominent writers and academics issued an open letter (available at http://links.org.au/node/1845) supporting the case for French restitution payments to Haiti.

14 Forcadilla's speech against the war was barely reported in the media amidst the wall-to-wall G20 coverage of mass arrests and burning cop cars in the streets of Toronto. One outlet that did report the story was Democracy Now! Amy Goodman's interview with Forcadilla is included as part of a larger segment on the G20, available at http://www.democracynow.org/2010/6/28/naomi_klein_the_real_crime_scene.

References

Allen, JoAnne. 2010. 'US indirectly funding Afghan warlords: House report.' *Reuters*, 22 June. http://www.reuters.com/article/idUSTRE65L0SK20100622.

Brady, Brian. 2010. 'Afghanistan: a conspiracy of silence.' *Independent*, 18 April. http://www.independent.co.uk/news/uk/politics/afghanistan-a-conspiracy-of-silence-1947857.html.

Byers, Michael. 2007. *Intent for a Nation: What Is Canada For?* Toronto: Douglas and McIntyre.

Cariou, Kimball. 2009. 'Where is Layton's NDP on the war in Afghanistan?' *rabble.ca*, 11 August. http://www.rabble.ca/news/2009/08/where-laytons-ndp-war-afghanistan.

CBC News. 2010. 'Afghan deployment past 2011 possible: MPs.' 3 June. http://www.cbc.ca/politics/story/2010/06/03/mps-afghanistan-military-2011.html.

Chai, Carmen. 2010. 'Canadians want to end Afghan mission by 2011, poll shows.' *Vancouver Sun*, 5 August. http://www.vancouversun.com/news/Canadians+want+Afghan+mission+2011+poll+shows/3360532/story.html#ixzz0xJkZJKmN.

CTV News. 2008. 'Canadians could be defending Afghan gas pipeline.' 21 June. http://www.ctv.ca/CTVNews/Specials/20080619/afghan_pipeline_080619/.

Davis, Uri. 2003. *Apartheid Israel: Possibilities for the Struggle Within*. London: Zed Books.

Engler, Yves. 2009. *The Black Book of Canadian Foreign Policy*. Halifax, NS: Fernwood.

Engler, Yves, and Anthony Fenton. 2005. *Canada in Haiti: Waging War on the Poor Majority*. Halifax, NS: Fernwood.

Fenton, Anthony. 2004. 'Engineering the Overthrow of Democracy.' *Znet*, 26 August. http://www.zcommunications.org/engineering-the-overthrow-of-democracy-by-anthony-fenton.

Ferrie, Jared. 2007. 'Staying the Course: Why Canada Shouldn't Pull Its Troops Out of Afghanistan.' *This Magazine*, March–April. http://www.thismaga zine.ca/issues/2007/03/stayingthecourse.php.

Filkins, Dexter, Mark Mazzetti, and James Risen. 2009. 'Brother of Afghan leader said to be paid by C.I.A.' *New York Times*, 27 October.

Foster, John. 2009. 'Afghanistan and the new Great Game.' *Toronto Star*, 12 August. http://www.thestar.com/article/679670.

Glenton, Joe. 2010. Speech at Stop the War Coalition forum, Conway Hall, London, 27 July. http://www.youtube.com/watch?v=3YKj3vH4YQY&featu re=search.

Grimes, Anna. 2007. 'The "best is yet to come" in Asia, foreign affairs minister says.' Vancouver Board of Trade, 11 April. http://www.boardoftrade.com/ vbot_speech.asp?pageID=1390&speechID=1090&offset=370&speechfind= (accessed 22 August 2010).

Hallward, Peter. 2008. *Damning the Flood: Haiti, Aristide and the Politics of Containment.* London: Verso.

Ignatieff, George. 1985. *The Making of a Peacemonger: The Memoirs of George Ignatieff.* Toronto: University of Toronto Press.

Ignatieff, Michael. 2003. *Empire Lite: Nation-Building in Bosnia, Kosovo and Afghanistan.* Toronto: Penguin Books.

–. 2010. 'Canada in the World.' Speech to The Empire Club of Canada and The Canadian Club, Toronto, 15 June.

Joya, Malalai. 2009. *A Women among Warlords: The Extraordinary Story of an Afghan Who Dared to Raise Her Voice.* Toronto: Simon & Schuster.

Kenney, Colin. 2010. 'Yes let's "cut and run."' *Ottawa Citizen*, 3 August.

Kolhatkar, Sonali, and James Ingalls. 2006. *Bleeding Afghanistan: Washington, Warlords, and the Propaganda of Silence.* New York: Seven Stories Press.

Layton, Jack. 2009. Address to the New Democrat National Convention, Halifax, NS, 19 August. http://www.ndp.ca/press/jack-laytons-address-to-new-democrat-national-convention (accessed 15 September 2010).

Moens, Alexander. 2008. 'Afghanistan and the Revolution in Canadian Foreign Policy.' *International Journal* 63, no. 3: 569–86.

Neufeld, Mark. 2010. '"Happy Is the Land That Needs No Hero": The Pearsonian Tradition and the Canadian Intervention into Afghanistan.' In *Canadian Foreign Policy in Critical Perspective*, ed. J. Marshall Beier and Lana Wylie. Don Mills, ON: Oxford University Press.

O'Keefe, Derrick. 2011. *Michael Ignatieff: The Lesser Evil?* New York: Verso.

Pratt, Cranford. 1983. 'Dominant Class Theory and Canadian Foreign Policy: The Case of the Counter-Consensus.' *International Journal* 39, no. 4: 99–135.

Ross, Michael. 2007. *The Volunteer: The Incredible True Story of an Israeli Spy on the Trail of International Terrorists*. New York: Skyhorse Publishing.

–. 2008. 'Canada's biggest mistake: the neglect of our armed forces.' *National Post*, 17 April.

Risen, James. 2010. 'U.S. identifies vast mineral riches in Afghanistan.' *New York Times*, 13 June.

South Asian Solidarity Network (US). 2010. ' "What Happens if We Stay in Afghanistan": A Response to *Time Magazine*.' http://www.southasiainitiative.org/content/what-happens-if-we-stay-a-0.

Stein, Janice Gross, and Eugene Lang. 2007. *The Unexpected War: Canada in Kandahar*. Toronto: Viking.

Stengel, Richard. 'What Happens if We Leave Afghanistan.' *Time*, 29 July. http://www.time.com/time/world/article/0,8599,2007269,00.html.

Warnock, John W. 1970. *Partner to Behemoth: The Military Policy of a Satellite Canada*. Toronto: New Press.

–. 2008. *Creating a Failed State: The US and Canada in Afghanistan*. Halifax, NS: Fernwood.

Young, Marilyn B. 1991. *The Vietnam Wars: 1945–1990*. New York: HarperCollins.

Contributors

Greg Albo is professor of Political Science at York University. He is an editor of *The Socialist Register* and a co-author of *In and Out of Crisis: The Global Financial Meltdown and the Left* (PM Press, 2010) and *A Different Kind of State: Popular Power and Democratic Administration* (Oxford, 1993). He is also an editor of *Studies in Political Economy*; *Capitalism, Nature, Socialism*; *Canadian Dimension*; and *Historical Materialism*.

Jon Elmer is a Canadian journalist based in the Middle East and a regular contributor to *Al Jazeera English* and *Inter Press Service* news agency. His work has appeared in scholarly and political journals, including *Journal of Palestine Studies*, *Canadian Dimension*, and *Z Magazine*, and he has a chapter in *The Plight of the Palestinians* (Palgrave Macmillan, 2010). He lives in the West Bank (http://jonelmer.ca).

Anthony Fenton is an independent author and journalist specializing in Canadian and US foreign policy. He has written for *Inter Press Service* and *Foreign Policy in Focus*, and is the co-author of *Canada in Haiti: Waging War on the Poor Majority* (Fernwood, 2005). He is currently pursuing a PhD in Political Science at York University.

Todd Gordon (PhD) teaches Political Science at York University. He is the author of *Imperial Canada* (Arbeiter Ring Publishing, 2010), and is currently working on a book on Canadian foreign policy in Latin America and the Caribbean. His academic publications have appeared in *Studies in Political Economy* and *Third World Quarterly*.

Adam Hanieh is assistant professor of Development Studies in the School of Oriental and African Studies, University of London. His publications have appeared in *Studies in Political Economy*, *Socialist Register*, *Monthly Review*, and *Journal of Palestine Studies*. He is the co-author of *Stolen Youth: The Politics of Israel's Detention of Palestinian Children* (Pluto, 2004) and author of *Capitalism and Class in the Gulf Cooperation Council* (Palgrave Macmillan, 2011).

Angela Joya is a doctoral candidate in Political Science at York University and recently taught Politics at the University of Ulster and at Durham University. Her research focuses on the political economy of development and state building in Afghanistan and the Middle East. Her publications have appeared in *Research in Political Economy, Canadian Foreign Policy*, and *Development Forum*.

Paul Kellogg is an assistant professor with the Athabasca University Master of Arts Integrated Studies Program. His articles have appeared in a variety of scholarly journals, including *Canadian Journal of Political Science, Contemporary Politics (U.K.), International Journal of Žižek Studies, New Political Science, and Political Studies.*

Jerome Klassen is a Social Sciences and Humanities Research Council of Canada postdoctoral fellow at the Center for International Studies at the Massachusetts Institute of Technology. His publications have appeared in *Studies in Political Economy, Canadian Journal of Sociology, Journal of World-Systems Research, Journal of Socialist Studies*, and *Labour/Le Travail*. He is working on a monograph entitled *Joining Empire: Political Economy, Class Formation, and the Canadian State.*

Derrick O'Keefe is co-chair of the Canadian Peace Alliance, the country's largest network of anti-war groups. He is co-author of Afghan MP Malalai Joya's political memoir, *A Woman Among Warlords: The Extraordinary Story of an Afghan Who Dared to Raise Her Voice* (2009). He is also author of *Michael Ignatieff: The Lesser Evil?* (Verso, 2011).

Justin Podur is an assistant professor in the Faculty of Environmental Studies, York University. Beyond publishing in academic science journals, he has written on foreign policy issues for *Z Magazine, Frontline* (India), and *New Left Review*, and reported from conflict zones including the Democratic Republic of Congo, Pakistan, Haiti, Israel/Palestine, and Colombia.

Sherene H. Razack is professor of Sociology and Equity Studies in Education at the Ontario Institute for Studies in Education, University of Toronto. Her most recent book is *Casting Out: The Eviction of Muslims from Western Law and Politics* (University of Toronto Press, 2008).

Benoit Renaud is a teacher in Adult Education in Gatineau, Quebec. He was general secretary of Québec solidaire from March 2008 to June 2010 and a candidate for that party in two elections. His involvement in the anti-war movement goes back to the Gulf War of 1991 and includes active participation in the Halifax Peace Coalition and Rassemblement Outaouais contre la guerre (ROCG). He has published several articles on peace, international, and human rights issues in *À Bâbord!*, the main magazine of the Quebec left.

Michael Skinner is a researcher at the York Centre for International and Security Studies and a doctoral candidate in Political Science at York University. In 2007 he and an Afghan-Canadian research partner, Hamayon Rastgar, travelled throughout Afghanistan to conduct field research on the international intervention. In the same year he also authored the 'Submission on behalf of the Afghanistan Canada Research Group to the Manley Inquiry.' His most recent fieldwork in Afghanistan took place in early 2011.

Jessica Squires (PhD Carleton) works at Library and Archives Canada. Her dissertation, 'A Refuge from Militarism? The Canadian Movement to Support Vietnam Era American War Resisters, and Government Responses, 1965–1973,' is being published by University of British Columbia Press (2012). She is a member of Québec solidaire, and is active in the anti-war and social justice movements in the Ottawa-Outaouais region.

John W. Warnock is a retired professor of Sociology and Political Economy at the University of Regina. He has authored seven books in the field, including *Creating a Failed State: The US and Canada in Afghanistan* (Fernwood, 2008).

Index